COUNTRY LIV
MAG

Guide to Rural England

THE WEST COUNTRY

Cornwall, Devon, Dorset and Somerset

By David Gerrard

© Travel Publishing Ltd

Published by:
Travel Publishing Ltd
7a Apollo House, Calleva Park
Aldermaston, Berkshire RG7 8TN
ISBN13   9781904434740
© Travel Publishing Ltd
Country Living is a registered trademark of The National
Magazine Company Limited.

First Published: 2001
Second Edition: 2004
Third Edition: 2006
Fourth Edition: 2008

COUNTRY LIVING GUIDES:

East Anglia	Scotland
Heart of England	The South of England
Ireland	The South East of England
The North East of England	The West Country
The North West of England	Wales

PLEASE NOTE:

All advertisements in this publication have been accepted in good faith by Travel Publishing and they have not necessarily been endorsed by *Country Living* Magazine.

All information is included by the publishers in good faith and is believed to be correct at the time of going to press. No responsibility can be accepted for errors.

Editor:	David Gerrard
Printing by:	Ashford Colour Press, Gosport
Location Maps:	© Maps in Minutes ™ (2008) © Collins Bartholomews 2008 All rights reserved.
Walks:	Walks have been reproduced with kind permission of the internet walking site: www.walkingworld.com
Walk Maps:	Reproduced from Ordnance Survey mapping on behalf of the Controller of Her Majesty's Stationery Office, © Crown Copyright. Licence Number MC 100035812
Cover Design:	Lines & Words, Aldermaston
Cover Photo:	Wheal Coates, St Agnes, Cornwall © fotolibra
Text Photos:	Text photos have been kindly supplied by the Pictures of Britain photo library © www.picturesofbritain.co.uk and © Bob Brooks, Weston-super-Mare

Foreword

From a bracing walk across the hills and tarns of The Lake District to a relaxing weekend spent discovering the unspoilt hamlets of East Anglia, nothing quite matches getting off the beaten track and exploring Britain's areas of outstanding beauty.

Each month, *Country Living Magazine* celebrates the richness and diversity of our countryside with features on rural Britain and the traditions that have their roots there. So it is with great pleasure that I introduce you to the *Country Living Magazine Guide to Rural England* series. Packed with information about unusual and unique aspects of our countryside, the guides will point both fair-weather and intrepid travellers in the right direction.

Each chapter provides a fascinating tour of the West Country area, with insights into local heritage and history and easy-to-read facts on a wealth of places to visit, stay, eat, drink and shop.

I hope that this guide will help make your visit a rewarding and stimulating experience and that you will return inspired, refreshed and ready to head off on your next countryside adventure.

Susy Smith

Susy Smith
Editor, Country Living magazine

PS To subscribe to *Country Living Magazine* each month, call 01858 438844

Introduction

This is the fourth edition of *The Country Living Guide to Rural England – the West Country* and we are sure that it will be as popular as its predecessors. The guide provides readers with interesting and useful information on places, people and activities in an area of England which definitely deserves the description "rural". In the introduction to each village or town we have also summarized and categorized the main attractions to be found there which makes it easy for readers to plan their visit. David Gerrard, a very experienced travel writer has, of course, completely updated the contents of the guide and ensured that it is packed with vivid descriptions, historical stories, amusing anecdotes and interesting facts on hundreds of places in Cornwall, Devon, Dorset and Somerset.

The advertising panels within each chapter provide further information on places to see, stay, eat, drink, shop and even exercise! We have also selected a number of walks from walkingworld.com (full details of this website may be found to the rear of the guide) which we highly recommend if you wish to appreciate fully the beauty and charm of the varied rural landscapes and coastlines of the West Country.

The guide however is not simply an "armchair tour". Its prime aim is to encourage the reader to visit the places described and discover much more about the wonderful towns, villages and countryside of Cornwall, Devon, Dorset and Somerset. In this respect we would like to thank all the Tourist Information Centres who helped us to provide you with up-to-date information. Whether you decide to explore this region by wheeled transport or on foot we are sure you will find it a very uplifting experience.

We are always interested in receiving comments on places covered (or not covered) in our guides so please do not hesitate to use the reader reaction forms provided at the rear of this guide to give us your considered comments. This will help us refine the content of the next edition. We also welcome any general comments which will help improve the overall presentation of the guides themselves.

For more information on other titles in the *Country Living Rural Guide* series and the full range of travel guides published by Travel Publishing please refer to the order form at the rear of this guide or log on to our website (see below).

Travel Publishing

Did you know that you can also search our website for details of thousands of places to see, stay, eat or drink throughout Britain and Ireland? Our site has become increasingly popular and now receives monthly over 160,000 visits. Try it!

website: www.travelpublishing.co.uk

Contents

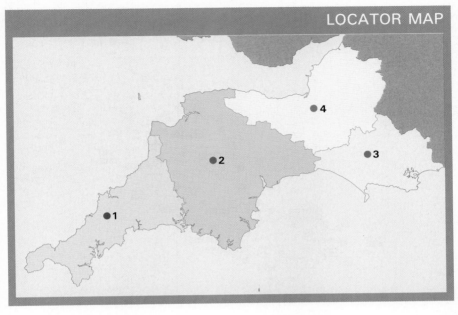

LOCATOR MAP

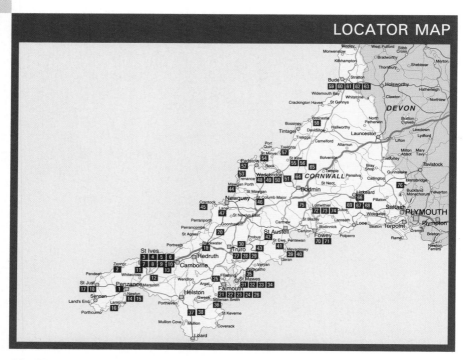

ADVERTISERS AND PLACES OF INTEREST

🏚 historic building　🏛 museum and heritage　🏛 historic site　🏵 scenic attraction　🌿 flora and fauna

1| Cornwall

"I like Cornwall very much. It is not England," wrote DH Lawrence. That was more than 80 years ago but the ancient Duchy of Cornwall remains stubbornly distinct from the rest of England, not just in its dramatic and spectacular scenery, but in its strong Celtic heritage. The landscape is dotted with ancient monuments, crosses and holy wells, and ancient legends – especially those relating to King Arthur and the Knights of the Round Table – appear to have been hot-wired into the Cornish psyche.

Cornish people have been recognised as a separate identity by the Commission for Racial Equality and they have their own distinctive and attractive dialect. According to the Cornish Language Board, around 2,600 people still speak Kernuack, the original language of

stories and anecdotes 🦜 famous people 🎨 art and craft 🎭 entertainment and sport 🏃 walks the peninsula. A firm in Helston occasionally publishes books in the ancient language and Kernuack has been recognised as a living language by the European Commission. Elements of Kernuack still survive in the names of Cornish places and people – as Sir Walter Scott put it: *By Tre-, Pol- and Pen- , You shall know all true Cornishmen.*

One simple fact about the county helps to explain its distinct character. Wherever you are in Cornwall, you are never more than 20 miles from the sea. Maritime trade started early here – in the days of King Solomon, the Cornish people were already trading tin with the Phoenicians. Cornish eyes, it seems, were always turned seawards rather than inland, and the people's cultural affinity was with the Celtic diaspora of Ireland and Brittany rather than their mainland neighbours.

Added to this cultural separation was the county's physical distance from major centres of population. Even today, Cornwall's population of around 500,000 is less than that of the city of Bristol. There's not a single mile of motorway within its boundaries and long stretches of the main through route, the A30 from Penzance to London, are still single carriageway.

St Mawes Harbour

It was this isolation – and the luminous light of the area – that attracted major artists to the little seaside resort of St Ives which now boasts a world-class art gallery in the Tate St Ives. More recently, an abandoned china clay pit has been transformed into what has been described as the Eighth Wonder of the World, the inspired – and phenomenally successful – Eden Project whose enormous bio-spheres celebrate the complex relationship between plants, people and resources.

Elsewhere, the county boasts the third largest natural harbour in the world, Falmouth; acres of glorious gardens such as the Lost Gardens of Heligan; King Arthur's legendary fortress at Tintagel, and other medieval castles at St Mawes, Falmouth and St Michael's Mount; the wonderful Elizabethan mansion of Prideaux Place at Padstow; and, of course, Land's End where the granite bulwark overlooks the Atlantic waters beneath which lies the legendary Land of Lyonesse.

Trevaunance Cove

Penzance

🏛 Maritime Museum   🏛 Lighthouse Centre

🎨 Penlee House Art Gallery   🏛 Egyptian House

🏛 Market House   🌿 Trengwainton Gardens

🏛 Cornwall Geological Museum

Penzance's famous promenade, the longest in Cornwall, runs from the open air art deco-style Jubilee Swimming Pool around the broad curve of Mount's Bay. Just along from the Jubilee Pool are the harbour and docks, still busy with fishing and pleasure boats. The town's main street is Market Jew Street, a busy shopping area that leads gently uphill to the handsome classical building of the **Market House** (1836) which now serves as a bank. In front of this domed granite structure stands a statue to Penzance's most famous son, Sir Humphry Davy, the scientist best remembered for inventing the miners' safety lamp. Born in a nearby street, Davy was one of the foremost chemists of the 19th century and, along with his contribution to miners' safety, he also founded both the Athenaeum Club and London Zoo.

Leading downhill from the Market House is the town's most interesting area, Chapel Street. Along this thoroughfare stands the exotic **Egyptian House**, created from two cottages in the 1830s by John Lavin, to entice customers into his shop. Although the designer of the magnificent façade is unknown, it is believed to have been inspired by the Egyptian Hall in Piccadilly, London. The house is now a National Trust shop.

Opposite this splendid building stands the Union Hotel, whose Georgian façade hides an impressive Elizabethan interior. From the Minstrel's Gallery in the sumptuous dining room was made the first announcement in mainland England of the victory of Trafalgar and the death of Lord Nelson. Chapel Street was also the childhood home of Marie Branwell, the mother of the Brontë sisters.

For centuries, a remote market town that made its living from fishing, mining and smuggling, Penzance today is popular with holidaymakers as well as being the ferry port for the Isles of Scilly. Along with its near neighbours, Newlyn and Mousehole, Penzance was sacked by the Spanish in 1595. Having supported the Royalist cause during the Civil War, it suffered the same fate again less than 60 years later. A major port in the 19th century for the export of tin, the fortunes of Penzance were transformed by the railway's arrival in 1859. Not only could the direct despatch of early flowers, vegetables and locally caught fish to the rest of Britain be undertaken but the influx of holidaymakers boosted the town's fledgling tourist industry.

Penzance celebrates its long-standing links with the sea at the **Maritime Museum** which houses a fascinating collection of artefacts

Trinity House Lighthouse Centre

🎭 stories and anecdotes   🍴 famous people   🎨 art and craft   🎟 entertainment and sport   🚶 walks

HARBOUR CRYSTALS

69 Causewayhead, Penzance, Cornwall TR18 2SR
Tel: 01736 874455(shop) or 01736 369356(Salon)
e-mail: helen@harbourcrystals.com
website: www.harbourcrystals.com

The founder of **Harbour Crystals**, Helen Stone, is an experienced practitioner in several complementary therapies. Discovering many years ago that she was a natural healer, Helen became proficient in Reflexology, Crystal Healing, Hopi Ear Candling and is also a Reiki Master.

Helen is one of 10 professional practitioners that work in the Complementary Therapy Centre which provides an extensive range of beauty and holistic treatments. The aim of the Therapy Centre is to restore harmony and balance in people's lives and also strive to get to the cause of their illness and not just treat the symptoms. All treatments are carried out in a peaceful environment with calming music to enhance the relaxing atmosphere.

Stress relief is one of today's main health concerns, so why not come along and try Chakra Balancing, Colour Therapy, Massage, Natural Nutrition, Othro-Bionomy, Shefa Healing, Shiatsu or have a Tarot Reading. You may prefer one of the many beauty treatments like a facial or body wrap which are holistic in their approach by using organic and natural products. As Helen says, "These therapies are gentle but powerful," and adds, "we like to create an environment that provides an optimum situation for the body to heal itself."

The shop offers an extensive collection of crystals, both natural and polished. The crystals are carefully handpicked by Helen herself from specialist suppliers from around the world. Helen says "Crystals are alive and vibrate just like ourselves and our environment and can therefore help us to establish harmony and balance in our own lives."

Harbour Crystals also sells a wide range of Silver and Gemstone Jewellery which is high quality with very unusual and beautiful gemstones. Some of the jewellery is made on the premises by Helen and her staff and they are happy to take orders for bespoke items. The shop tries to buy Fair Trade items whenever possible and stock an extensive range of gifts including lamps, clocks, vases, candle holders, carvings, aromatherapy products, candles, cards, music CDs and much more. Many of the items found in the shop can also be bought online through the Harbour Crystals website.

A recent addition to Harbour Crystals is a new hair salon called Isis Hair Design. The stylists are qualified professionals and offer all types of hair styling for both female and male clients, which completes the top to toe experience offered.

Harbour Crystals also holds courses, therapy awareness days and workshops throughout the year – full details are available from the shop or the website.

that illustrate the ferocity of the waters along this stretch of coast. The museum's interior re-creates an 18th century four-deck man-of-war, complete with creaking floorboards and contains displays of pieces of eight and other artefacts recovered from wrecks off the Isles of Scilly.

Down at the harbour, at the **Trinity House Lighthouse Centre**, the story of lighthouse keeping is told. Opened by Prince Andrew in 1991, the centre has assembled what is the probably the largest and finest collection of lighthouse equipment in the world. Visitors can operate the 100-year-old equipment, blast off a foghorn or just sit back and watch a video about the history of the lighthouse.

Elsewhere in Penzance, local history and the work of the Newlyn School of artists can be seen at the recently refurbished **Penlee House Art Gallery and Museum**. The county's long association with the mining industry is highlighted at the **Cornwall Geological Museum** which has some intriguing fossil displays and surveys 400 million years of Cornwall's past. Just to the northwest of the town, and close to the village

of Madron, lie **Trengwainton Gardens**, the National Trust-owned woodland gardens that are known for their spring flowering shrubs, their exotic trees and the walled garden that contains plants that cannot be grown in the open anywhere else in the country. The walled garden was built in the early 19th century by the then owner Sir Rose Price, the son of a wealthy Jamaican sugar planter.

Two miles west of Penzance, **Trewidden Gardens** is one of the finest informal gardens in Cornwall and contains one of the best collections of camellias in the country.

Around Penzance

ZENNOR
5½ miles N of Penzance on the B3306

🏛 Wayside Folk Museum

🏛 Chysauster Ancient Village

This delightful ancient village, situated between moorland and coastal cliffs, shows evidence of Bronze Age settlers. It also has a 12th century church, famous for its carved bench end depicting a mermaid holding a

Wayside Folk Museum

Zennor, nr St Ives, Cornwall TR26 3DA
Tel: 01736 796945

In the 1930s Colonel 'Freddie' Hirst started a collection of relics peculiar to Zennor. That collection was the basis of the **Wayside Folk Museum**, a privately owned museum which portrays the lives of ordinary people in the area through its displays of

artefacts, stories and photographs. Inside, 16 display areas contain more than 5,000 items including blacksmith's and wheelwright's equipment, a cobbler's shop, an 18th century kitchen, relics of local mining and quarrying and early agricultural implements. In the grounds are two waterwheels from the mining industry and a unique collection of corn grinding querns and stone tools dating back as far as 3000 BC. Bridge House Gift & Book Shop specialises in things Cornish as well as providing light refreshments.

🎨 stories and anecdotes 🐦 famous people 🎨 art and craft 🚶 entertainment and sport 🚶 walks

Bosullow

Distance: *4.0 miles (6.4 kilometres)*

Typical time: *180 mins*

Height gain: *70 metres*

Map: *Explorer 102*

Walk: *www.walkingworld.com ID:1052*

Contributor: *Dennis Blackford*

ACCESS INFORMATION:

From Penzance take the B3311 road to Madron and continue towards Trevowhan. 2½ miles along this road look for the 'Men-an-Tol' studio on your left and park in the parking area on the opposite side of the road. On this road you will pass the ancient healing well just outside Madron and Lanyon Quoit a bit over one mile further on.

From the St Just to St Ives road - turn at Trevowhan (approximately five miles from St Just) onto the Madron road. Approx one mile along this road look for the 'Men-an-Tol' studio on your right.

DESCRIPTION:

This walk takes you up onto Ding Dong Moor and visits ancient stone monuments. The first is The Men-an-Tol which is an ancient healing site about 6,000 years old and where sick or infertile people were passed through the holed stone. Secondly we visit Men Scyfa. This is an inscribed stone marking the grave of a warrior killed near this spot around 500AD. Next we pass the group of stones known as the 'Nine Maidens', which would have been used for various religious rites throughout the year. The age of this stone circle is unknown but is thought to have been redundant by 1250BC. The more modern building of Ding Dong Mine is next, although there has been a mine

here for over 2,000 years and legend has it that the young Jesus was brought here by his uncle Joseph of Arimathea. Finally we visit Lanyon Quoit, a classical monument whose massive stones were erected over 6,000 years ago. Those who are interested can also visit the ancient healing well just outside Madron, where even today hundreds of people tie tokens on the branches (please use biodegradable ones, plastics do not work!)

ADDITIONAL INFORMATION

This walk is on open moor so be sure to take 'moor care' and wear stout walking shoes and take an extra layer of clothing; a thin waterproof cagoule is most useful to keep out wind or rain. There are many old mine shafts and cave-ins in this area, so keep to the paths and be careful with children and dogs.

FEATURES:

Hills or fells, wildlife, birds, flowers, great views, butterflies, industrial archaeology, moor, ancient monument.

WALK DIRECTIONS:

1 | From the car park go through the gate leading to a farm track.

2 | About 1 kilometre up the track, go over the small stone bridge and steps signed 'The Men-an-Tol'. After visiting the Men-an-Tol return to the farm track and continue on up the track. The Men-an-Tol is an ancient healing site about 6,000 years old where sick or infertile people were passed through the holed stone.

3 | About another ½km up the track there is a stone stile to the left of a metal gate; this leads to Men Scyfa. This is an inscribed stone marking the grave of a warrior killed near this spot around 500AD. This 1.8-metre stone is

the same height as the warrior, although part is now underground. Return to the track and continue on up.

4|The track now curves to the left, but you should take the path leading straight on past a ruined building on the left and up to a metal gate. Pass through the gate and follow the path straight on up and over the moor.

5|The track is well-worn so is easy to follow. Remember that there are many old mine shafts and cave-ins in this area, so keep to the paths and be careful with children and dogs.

6|The path leads to the ring of standing stones known as the "Nine Maidens". Pass through the circle and follow the path to your right. This will lead past a fenced off mine shaft and go to Ding Dong mine engine house.

7|Having reached the engine house of Ding Dong Mine and looked around, there are three ways back. The shortest and best route is to walk to the end of the spoil heap in front of the mine and find the well-worn path to the NW of it (right-hand side when facing the heap from the engine house). This path meanders back to the Men-an-Tol, which, although out of sight for most of the way, is in line with the farm on the valley wall roughly midway between the farm on the horizon left and the tor on the right. From the Men-an-Tol, retrace your steps back to the car park. To visit Lanyon Quoit drive towards Madron, where you can also visit the Holy Well and Celtic Chapel.

8|The second route is very rough going especially in late summer and autumn, due to bracken and brambles. Take the smaller track past the engine house entrance and pass under the wooden pole onto a grassy path. Pass through the gate at the end and follow the field boundary on your left, down to the bottom of the hill and then another field boundary wall on your right as you ascend the hill to Lanyon Quoit. After visiting the Quoit go over the stone stile to the road and turn right to follow the road back to the car park (approx 1 kilometre).

9|The third route is the longest and has a lot of road walking. Follow the wide farm track past the mine and onto the metalled farm road down to the main road from Madron (approx 1.5 kilometres).

10|Turn right and follow the road back to the car park (approx 2.5 kilometres), passing Lanyon Quoit on your right about halfway along.

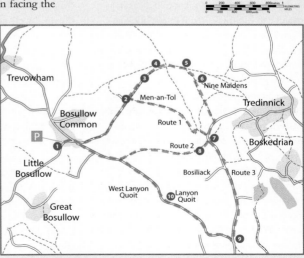

comb and mirror. A local legend tells of a mysterious young maiden who was drawn to the church by the beautiful singing of a chorister, the churchwarden's son Matthew Trewhella. An enchanting singer herself, the maiden lured Matthew down to nearby Pendour Cove where he disappeared. On warm summer evenings, it is said that their voices can be heard rising from the waves.

Zennor Quoit

By the porch in the church is a memorial to John Davey, who died in 1891, stating that he was the last person to have any great knowledge of the native Cornish language Kernuack. It is said that he remained familiar with the language by speaking it to his cat. There has recently been a revival of interest in Kernuack, and visitors to Cornwall who chance upon a Kernuack speaker might impress him by asking, "Plema'n diwotti?" and with any luck being directed to the nearest pub. Another useful entry in the Cornish phrasebook is, "Fatell yu an pastyon yn gwerthji ma? A wrons I ri dhymn drog goans?", which means, "What are the pasties like in this shop? Will they give me indigestion?"

For an insight into the history of Zennor and the surrounding area, the **Wayside Folk Museum** (see panel on page 7) is a unique private museum, founded in 1935, that covers every aspect of life in Zennor and district from 3000BC to the 1930s. On display are waterwheels, a millhouse, a wheelwright's and blacksmith's premises, a miller's cottage with kitchen and parlour, and exhibits on tin mining. The collection has more than 5,000 items in 16 display areas and includes an extensive collection of photographs and information on people who have lived in the area.

Tin mining is also referred to in the name of the local inn, The Tinners. DH Lawrence spent many hours at this pub while living in the village with his wife Frieda during World War I. It was during his stay here, under police surveillance, that Lawrence wrote *Women in Love*. However, his pacifist tendencies and Frieda's German heritage (her cousin was the flying ace the Red Baron von Richthofen) caused them to be 'moved on' in October 1917. Lawrence refers to the episode in his semi-autobiographical novel *Kangaroo* (1923).

To the southeast of the village are the dilapidated remains of the Neolithic chamber tomb, Zennor Quoit. One of many ancient monuments in the area, the tomb has a huge capstone that was once supported on five broad uprights.

A couple of miles to the south of Zennor, on a windy hillside, stands **Chysauster Ancient Village** (English Heritage), a Romano-Cornish village, built around 2,000 years ago, which has one of the oldest identifiable streets in the country. The site was only discovered during archaeological excavations in the 1860s. The villagers here were farmers, as cattle sheds have been unearthed. They also worked tin beside the nearby stream. Their housing consisted of stone-walled homesteads, each with an open central courtyard surrounded by several circular living rooms topped with thatch or turf.

ST IVES

7 miles NE of Penzance on the A3074

✍ Tate St Ives Gallery	🏛 St Ives Museum	
✍ Barbara Hepworth Sculpture Garden		
🏊 Carbis Bay	🏯 Knill Steeple	

This lovely old fishing town with its maze of narrow streets and picturesque harbour, has been showered with various awards in the last couple of years. It won the Gold Award in the international Entente Florale, has made off with more Britain in Bloom top prizes than any other UK town, and a recent University of Surrey survey, using a complex formula to decide which were the best beach destinations globally, placed St Ives at the top of its UK list, and 4th in the world. An organisation called "The Most Beautiful Bays in the World" has declared St Ives Bay one of its select few, on a par with Caribbean, Asian and American beauty spots. Another two of St Ives' five sandy beaches have also qualified for a Blue Flag award.

Culturally, the town is famous worldwide as an artists' colony. They were drawn by the special quality of the light – ultra-violet radiation is greater here than anywhere else in the country. JMW Turner was the first major artist to arrive, in 1811, to be followed in later

THE WILLS LANE GALLERY

Wills Lane, St. Ives, Cornwall TR26 1AF
Tel: 01736 795 723
e-mail: info@willslanegallery.co.uk
website: www.willslanegallery.co.uk

The recently refurbished **Wills Lane Gallery** provides a showcase for fine and applied art by both nationally known and up and coming artists, and exhibits paintings, drawings, ceramics, glass, furniture, weaving, photographs, original etchings and jewellery. Nationally known artists include Maggi Hambling, Michael Porter, Susan Derges and Sutton Taylor. Recent graduates include jewellers Melanie Georgacopoulos and Nutre Arayavanish, and ceramicist Danielle Spelman. Tavs Jørgensen's glass nominated for 2008 Bombay Sapphire Design Discovery Award - and Drummond Masterton's metalwork - selected for the Jerwood Contemporary Makers 2008 touring exhibition - is also showcased.

The gallery is run by Petronilla Silver, former director of the Contemporary Art Society, London. For years an influential figure in the London art world and a respected expert on collecting, she advised museums and major corporations on their acquisition policy, and is now available for the first time to advise private individuals on art collecting. Petronilla offers tailor-made advice on starting a collection: conservation, care, framing, hanging and maintenance of artworks.

The gallery is open from 10.30am to 5.30pm, Wednesday-Saturday; and from 11am to 4pm on Sunday, and at other times by appointment.

JAN JANSEN

Fish Street, St Ives, Cornwall TR26 1LT
Tel: 01736 799918
e-mail: annie@janjansen-stives.co.uk
website: www.janjansen-stives.co.uk

"Jan Jansen - who wouldn't want to be in his shoes?" goes the slogan for this stylish designer shoe shop. Jan Jansen was born in 1941 in Nijmegen, Netherlands, and designed and made his first pair of women's boots for Tonny Polman at the tender age of 18, followed by a pair for himself a couple of years later.

From these humble beginnings followed a career in shoe design that now spans more than 40 years in the limelight of the fashion industry - setting trends and keeping abreast with new movements every step of the way. Featuring regularly in Dutch fashion journals from as early as 1965, international acclaim followed swiftly through coverage in the French fashion magazines and an exhibition in the Museum of Contemporary Craft in New York called 'Bodycovering'. Jan's creations combine elements of architecture and sculpture, while simultaneously providing ergonomic quality that guarantees comfort.

In 1996 he received the Dutch fashion prize and was bestowed the title "Grand Seigneur" for his contribution to the national and international fashion scene. A Jan Jansen shoe is not your everyday footwear, but a creation of artistic merit.

TRELYON GALLERY

Fore Street, St Ives, Cornwall, TR26 1HE
Tel: 01736 797955
e-mail: trelyongallery@btconnect.com
website: www.trelyongallery.co.uk

Lucy Kemp, the owner of the **Trelyon Gallery,** has always loved making jewellery. As a young girl she would take apart her own jewellery and then re-assemble it. A big change in her career gave her the chance to train in the making of jewellery. Each of her pieces is hand-made using fine silver and sterling silver, and splashes of colour are added with the use of semi-precious beads or freshwater pearls. She finds inspiration for her pieces in Cornwall's moody landscapes and, because of the way she creates each piece, each one is unique.

Lucy established her gallery in 1991 in premises located half way along the historic cobbled Fore Street in St Ives, The gallery is a dedicated showcase for leading British contemporary designer jewellers. The atmosphere is informative and friendly and customers can view and buy exquisite pieces of jewellery from more than 40 jewellers showing their latest collections. Jewellery for every occasion is featured here. Gemstone necklaces, 18ct gold and stunning sterling silver. Many pieces are unique to Trelyon Gallery. The gallery is open from 10am to 6pm in summer; 10am to 5pm during the winter.

🏛 historic building   🏛 museum and heritage   🏛 historic site   🌿 scenic attraction   🐦 flora and fauna

decades by Whistler, Sickert, McNeill, Munnings, Ben Nicholson, the sculptor Barbara Hepworth and the potter Bernard Leach. Art still dominates and, along with the numerous private galleries, there is the **Tate St Ives Gallery** (see panel below), where the work of 20th century painters and sculptors is permanently on display in a rather austere three-storey building backing directly into the cliff face. Opened in 1993, the gallery offers a unique introduction to contemporary and modern art, and many works can be viewed in the surroundings that inspired them.

The Tate also manages the **Barbara Hepworth Sculpture Garden and Museum** at Trewyn Studio, where she both lived and worked until her tragic death in a fire in 1975. Sculptures in bronze, stone and wood are on display in the Museum and Garden, along with paintings, drawings and archive material. Many of her other works are exhibited in the Tate St Ives Gallery; still more are dotted around the town.

The original settlement at St Ives takes its name from the 6th century missionary St Ia, who is said to have landed here from Ireland

Tate St Ives

Porthmeor Beach, St Ives, Cornwall TR26 1TG
Tel: 01736 796226
website: www.tate.org.uk

St Ives has attracted artists of renown for well over a century, and among early visitors were Turner, Whistler and Sickert. That tradition continues in **Tate St Ives**, housed in a superb modern three-storey building backing directly into the cliff face. The gallery offers a unique introduction to contemporary and modern art, and many works can be viewed in the surroundings that inspired them. Apart from the permanent and changing exhibitions, Tate St Ives stages regular special events and talks. It also manages the town's Barbara Hepworth Museum and Sculpture Garden.

JULIA CICCONE

Studio 7, Harbour Galleries, Wharf Road,
St Ives, Cornwall TR26 1LP
Tel: 07813 555754 Home: 01736 368036
e-mail: juliaciccone@hotmail.co.uk

Julia Ciccone has lived in St Ives for some 35 years and previously owned an art gallery on Fish Street. Julia trained at Wimbledon Art College and later tutored at Leeds on history of art and portrait painting. She has been on TV and her work is exhibited and in collections both nationally and internationally. She specialises in portrait paintings of people and animals, mostly in oil but sometimes in pencil. Julia works through the day so visitors to her studio can see her working on commissions. She has also been Artist in Residence at Debenham's store in Guildford over a 4-5 year period. In addition to Julia's own works on display at Studio 7, there also the works of Ann Cummings, who specialises in sea and landscape paintings and shows mainly in London.

GAUGE GALLERY

26 Fore Street, St Ives, Cornwall TR26 1HE
Tel: 01736 795107
e-mail: info@gaugegallery.co.uk
website: www.gaugegallery.co.uk

The **Gauge Gallery** is located in the picturesque coastal town of St Ives, famous for its colony of craftsmen and artists. The gallery exhibits world-renowned jewellers and showcases original work rarely seen outside the prestigious galleries in the capitals of the world. Artists at the Gauge have exhibited at the Victoria & Albert, the British, Tokyo and New York museums, to name just a few. The Gauge's ethos is also to promote existing local and international talent. Amongst the artists exhibiting at the gallery are Fred Rich, Paul Spurgeon, Stacey Whale, Ndidi Ekubia, Alistair McCallum and many others, all producing uniquely crafted traditional and contemporary items that define the silversmith's art - individual creations in a mass-produced world.

Visitors to the gallery can choose from the range of classic and innovative pieces on display but Gauge also provides the rare opportunity to be fully involved in the creative design process, with complete access to the gallery's in-house silversmith/jewellers Tim Lukes and Ed Wilson. They are always on hand to discuss options and make suggestions to ensure that a perfect piece of jewellery is achieved. Bottom image: Five Gold Rings by Tim Lukes and Ed Wilson. Top Image: Life sized pheasants by Tim Lukes.

PENHAVEN GALLERY

4 St Peter's Street, St Ives, Cornwall TR26 1NN
Tel: 01736 798147
e-mail: beer@penhavengallery.co.uk
website: www.penhavengallery.co.uk

Located in the 'Downalong' area of the town, the **Penhaven Gallery** was opened in 1994 by the popular St. Ives artist David Beer, and now exhibits the works of 23 distinctive painters and potters, the majority of whom live and work in the Penwith area of West Cornwall. David himself paints seascapes and landscapes in oils using a palette knife, and makes life studies using pastel and acrylics. His work is exhibited in various galleries around the UK and also at Thomas Henry Fine Art in Nantucket, USA.

The Penhaven Gallery prides itself on showing work of real quality, spanning a range from the purely abstract through to more representational figurative works. The gallery maintains and displays a selection of works by each of its artists throughout the year, but also presents a seasonal programme of themed, one-person and mixed exhibitions. The gallery's website is updated weekly and allows those interested to view complete exhibitions and the gallery's entire stock online. Visitors are most welcome to the gallery throughout the year, where they can view pictures with or without the help of the informed gallery staff.

🏛 historic building   🏛 museum and heritage   🏛 historic site   ⌘ scenic attraction   🌱 flora and fauna

Barbara Hepworth Sculpture Garden

on an ivy leaf. The 15th century parish church bears her name along with those of the two fishermen Apostles, St Peter and St Andrew.

One of the most important pilchard fishing centres in Cornwall until the early 20th century, St Ives holds a record dating back to 1868 for the greatest number of fish caught in a single seine net. Known locally as The Island, St Ives Head is home to a Huer's Hut, from where a lookout would scan the sea looking for shoals of pilchards. A local speciality, heavy or *hevva* cake, was traditionally made for the seiners on their return from fishing. As well as providing shelter for the fishing fleet, the harbour was also developed for exporting locally mined ores and minerals. The town's two industries led the labyrinthine narrow streets to become divided into two

---

SERENDIPITY - FAIR TRADE

60 Fore Street, St Ives, Cornwall TR26 1HW
Tel: 01736 796235
e-mail: serendipitystive@aol.com   website: www.serendipitystives.co.uk

Opened in 2007, **Serendipity** is a new venture which aims to offer quality gifts from around the world. It deals only in goods which have been **fairly traded**. The gallery sells products from many countries in Africa, Asia and South America, including clothes, jewellery, lighting, mirrors, carvings, musical instruments and religious artifacts. Wherever possible the owners purchase items, which are produced sustainably. Most of the wood items are made from sustainable or re-used wood. The gallery also stocks some great recylced aluminium and tin products.

Serendipity is owned and run by Grant and Caroline Curnow who started the company following their visits to developing countries around the world. They say, "Our philosophy is to ensure our products are both bought at a fair price and sold to our customers at a fair price. This means we have a bigger turnover and, in return, can support more crafts people in the developing world." On a recent

visit to Uganda with A.C.E. (Aid through Conservation Education), they saw how local communities were struggling to pay for their children's education. Yet in this same region, the local communities were creating wonderful basket work, carvings and textiles. Unfortunately Kisoro is a very isolated region in Uganda so there is a very limited market for these crafts. "We hope to be able to provide an outlet for these crafts and will encourage the communities to use the profits to send their children to school."

🎬 stories and anecdotes 🦜 famous people 🎨 art and craft 🎵 entertainment and sport 🚶 walks

communities: *Downalong* where the fishing families lived and *Upalong*, the home of the mining families.

Housed in a building that once belonged to a mine, **St Ives Museum** displays a range of artefacts chronicling the natural, industrial and maritime history of the area. There is also a display dedicated to John Knill, mayor of the town in the 18th century. A customs officer by profession, he was also rumoured to be an energetic smuggler. Certainly one of the town's most memorable citizens, he built the **Knill Steeple** monument to the south of the town to be his mausoleum, but it also served to guide ships carrying contraband safely to the shore. Knill left a bequest to the town so that every five years, a ceremony would be held at the Steeple when 10 girls and two widows would first sing the 100th Psalm and then dance around the monument for 15

minutes to the tune of a fiddler. For performing this strange ceremony the participants received 10 shillings (50p). The custom is still maintained - the next will take place on July 25th, 2011.

It is not only artists who have been inspired by the beautiful surroundings of St Ives: Virginia Woolf recaptures the happy mood of her childhood holiday here in her novel *To the Lighthouse*, and Rosamunde Pilcher, famous for her books set in Cornwall, was born near the town in 1924.

Just to the southeast of the town, easy to reach on foot and a great favourite with families, lies the sheltered beach of **Carbis Bay**, where various water sports are also available. To the west of St Ives is a wonderful and remote coastline of coves, cliffs and headland that provides a wealth of wildlife and archaeological interest. Following the

THE COUNTRYMAN HOTEL

Old Coach Road, St Ives, Cornwall TR26 3JQ
Tel: 01736 797571
e-mail: the_countryman_hotel@yahoo.co.uk

Set in two acres of landscaped gardens, the **Countryman Hotel** at Trink is just a five-minute drive from the quaint fishing village of St Ives. Family-run by the Saunders family, this welcoming small hotel has been renovated to meet the needs of the modern visitor. All rooms have an en suite shower and toilet, radio, colour TV, hospitality tray and either a country or a garden view.

Good food is a priority at the Countryman Hotel. Guests can enjoy a candlelit dinner in the elegant restaurant. All meals are freshly cooked using fresh local produce and include steaks, local game and seafood, all supported by a sensibly priced wine list. Gather in the spacious lounge for your pre-dinner aperitif, and relax after dinner with coffee and liqueurs. There are roaring log fires and all rooms are heated in the winter. In the summer the conservatory is ideal with its stunning views of Trink Hill.

The hotel is located equi-distant from the beautiful beaches of Carbis Bay and St Ives, and there is a wealth of things to see and do - horse riding, coastal walks, golf and the major attractions of the Tate Gallery in St Ives and St Michael's Mount are all within easy reach.

🏛 historic building 🏛 museum and heritage 🏛 historic site 🝙 scenic attraction 🌱 flora and fauna

network of footpaths from St Ives to Pendeen, walkers can discover small wooded valleys, rich bogs, old industrial remains and prehistoric features such as the cliff castles at Gurnard's Head and Bosigran.

HAYLE
7½ miles NE of Penzance on the B3301

🐦 Paradise Park

Established in the 18th century as an industrial village, Hayle was also a seaport with a harbour in the natural shelter of the Hayle estuary. It was here, in the early 1800s, that the Cornish inventor Richard Trevithick built an early version of the steam locomotive. A short time later, one of the first railways in the world was constructed here to carry tin and copper from Redruth down to the port. With its industrial past, Hayle is not a place

naturally associated with cosmetics, but it was Hayle-born Florence Nightingale Graham who set up her own beauty parlour on New York's Fifth Avenue under the name Elizabeth Arden.

The Hayle estuary and sands around the town are an ornithologist's delight. Some of the world's rarest and most beautiful birds can be seen at **Paradise Park**, a leading conservation zoo located on the southern outskirts of the town. As well as providing a sanctuary for tropical birds and exotic animals, the park also has a huge indoor play centre and a special toddlers area.

Across the estuary lies **Lelant,** a thriving seaport in the Middle Ages that lost its traffic as the estuary silted up. Now a popular holiday village, with a golf course, Lelant is particularly loved by birders, who come to

WILDLIFE WOODCARVER

Steppy Downs Studio, 13 St Erth Hill,
St Erth, Hayle, Cornwall TR27 6EX
Tel: 01736 753342 Mobile: 07855 602183
e-mail: andy@wildlifewoodcarver.co.uk
website: www.wildlifewoodcarver.co.uk

Andrew Hewson learned his carving skills from his father Roy Hewson, who started his wildlife woodcarving business 21 years ago. After leaving college with a Diploma in Technical Illustration, Andy, also a musician and songwriter, pursued a successful career in the music industry whilst still keeping his wildlife woodcarving interests going.

For the past two years Andy has specialised in his woodcarving and pyrography skills full time, producing work of a very high standard and accepting many commissions for carvings, pyrography artwork and mobile birds.

Andy enjoys working from the studio at St Erth, built in 1914, which has extensive views over the Hayle estuary to the north and across sweeping countryside to St Michaels Mount in the south west.

A friendly welcome awaits you when you visit the studio, where you will see a wide variety of the work displayed in the gallery.

TREVASKIS FARM

12 Gwinear Road, Connor Down, Hayle,
Cornwall TR27 5JQ
Tel: 01209 713 931 Fax: 01209 714010
e-mail: hello@trevaskisfarm.co.uk
website: www.trevaskisfarm.co.uk

Trevaskis Farm was established in 1979, and nearly 30 years on, they are returning farm shopping to its roots with a shopping experience that is convenient, affordable and enables the customer to meet all their grocery needs without compromising quality and the authenticity of the food on offer. Trevaskis Farm grows over 90 varieties of crop including fruit and vegetables in addition to rearing their own Pork, Lamb and Poultry. These products are available to be purchased from the farm shop and the 'Pick your Own' fields.

The farm shop is divided into departments to ensure every aspect of the shopping experience is covered. The butchery sells the farm reared pork, their own and locally sourced lamb, local 'South Devon Breed' beef and a number of free range West Country poultry products. The experienced fishmonger stocks a variety of fish & seafood landed at Newlyn daily and the Dairy counter has many Cornish and world cheeses alongside local milks, creams, yoghurts and fruit juices. 'Baker Tom', based a few minutes from the farm, provides freshly baked breads from the finest organic flours.

Traditional wholemeal and white loaves are stocked together with flavoured breads such as Parmesan and red onion. The Deli counter is a feast of salads, olives and sun-dried tomatoes to enjoy with the chorizos, salami's and home-cured meats and hams. There is also a selection of wines available to compliment all the foods and as with all the produce at Trevaskis farm, customers are welcome to try before they buy.

To truly experience the quality of the foods on offer, it is essential to visit the Restaurant, which has been refurbished and extended to accommodate around 90 people. The menu consists of tempting meals made from the farms own ingredients and those from local suppliers. There are seasonal specials on offer and all the sweets are homemade. Open all day, customers can begin their day out at Trevaskis Farm with breakfast, and end it with an evening meal and a glass of wine from the licensed bar. The Restaurant can also cater for large parties.

The Organic Kitchen Garden completes the farm experience with some education about growing techniques, crop history, nutritional values and recipe ideas. Here you can see exotic and everyday plants growing and enjoy the picnic area surrounded by wild flowers and apple trees.

Trevaskis Farm is open from 8am to 8pm daily

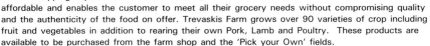

🏛 historic building 🏚 museum and heritage 🏛 historic site ♨ scenic attraction �'] flora and fauna

watch the wide variety of wildfowl and waders on the mud and salt flats. Lelant was the birthplace of Rosamunde Pilcher who celebrated her native county in enormously popular novels such as *The Shell Seekers*.

MARAZION
3 miles E of Penzance off the A394

🐦 Marazion Marsh 🦢 St Michael's Mount

🏰 St Michael's Mount Castle

Cornwall's oldest charter town (dating from 1257), Marazion was for many centuries the most important settlement around Mount's Bay. The legacy of this harbour town is its fine old inns and residential houses overlooking the sandy beach. The town is now a windsurfing and sailing centre, but to the northwest is **Marazion Marsh & RSPB Reserve**, an extensive area of wetland and reed beds behind Marazion Beach on the Penzance road. More than 450 plant species have been recorded here, and the reserve is

St Michael's Mount

home to many nesting and roosting birds, including herons, reed and sedge warblers and Cetti's warbler.

Situated a third of a mile offshore, **St Michael's Mount** rises dramatically out of the waters of Mount's Bay. It is connected to Marazion by a cobbled causeway that is exposed at low tide. Inhabited since prehistoric times, this granite rock is named after the Archangel St Michael who, according to legend, appeared to a party of fishermen in a vision in the 5th century. In the 11th century, Edward the Confessor founded a priory on the mount in tribute to the famous Benedictine Mont St Michel in Normandy. The remains of these buildings are incorporated into the marvellous **St Michael's Mount Castle** owned by the St Aubyn family from 1660 until 1954, when it was donated to the National Trust. The St Aubyn family remain in residence however, with a 999-year lease. Along with the impressive medieval remains, the castle incorporates architectural styles from the 17th to the 19th century. A fine plaster frieze of 1641 depicting scenes of bear and deer hunting, and some elegant Chippendale furniture are amongst the heritage treasures; a model of the castle made out of discarded champagne corks by the St Aubyns butler, Henry Lee, is amongst the quirkier attractions.

When the present St Aubyn resident, the 4th Lord St Levan, was asked what had been his most significant contribution to the family home, he replied, "The 10 tons of manure I had brought to the island." They were used to fertilise the extraordinary maritime garden created in terraces just above the sea. Sub-tropical plants flourish here in abundance and even in winter fuchsias and hydrangeas are still in bloom.

BADCOCKS GALLERY

Badcocks Block, The Strand, Newlyn,
Penzance, Cornwall TR18 5HW
Tel: 01736 366159
e-mail: badcocks@madasafish.com
website: www.badcocksgallery.com

Opened in 2000, Badcocks Gallery provides a showcase for the very best in Cornish art. The only commercial fine art gallery located in the historic fishing port of Newlyn in Cornwall, it began as a one-room gallery and jewellery workshop and then expanded to become a respected centre for contemporary Cornish art on both a local and national level. It has acquired a reputation for showing quirky and unusual work in a friendly and relaxed atmosphere.

The three rooms of open white light provide a beautiful setting to exhibit work sourced not only from the rich seam of local talent, but nationally and internationally as well. Alongside the varied painting and sculpture exhibitions, Badcocks showcases particular collections of studio ceramics, jewellery and glass.

Their comprehensive website can keep you updated with the gallery's monthly, changing exhibition schedule.

Artists for 2008/9 include Marilyn Browning and Hannah Davies (see images) Beth Carter and Emma Cameron's mythological and mischievous sculptures and paintings, Alice Mumford's more traditional, yet delicate still life paintings. The increasingly popular Simeon Stafford will exhibit his quirky Lowry-esque beach scenes, Scandinavian Kristin Vestgård's dream-like, beguiling figurative works and many more of the gallery's most popular artists such as Jessica Cooper and ceramicists Paul Jackson and Sandy Brown, will also be exhibiting.

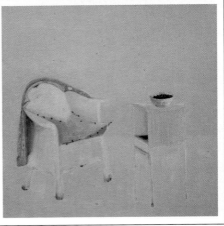

The gallery also holds a varied stock of artists' work, and can arrange for you to view work either in person or via e-mail.

Opening hours: 10.30am - 5.30pm Mon - Sat

GODOLPHIN CROSS

9 miles E of Penzance off the B3302

🏠 Godolphin House 🏚 Wheal Prosper Mine

To the northwest of the village stands **Godolphin House**, an exceptional part-Tudor, part-Stuart house that still retains its original Elizabethan stables. The former home of the Earls of Godolphin, the house has many splendid features. However the family members, who made their fortune in mining, are more interesting; Sidney, the poet, was killed during the Civil War fighting for the king; Sidney, the 1st earl, was a Lord High Treasurer to both William III and Queen Anne; the 2nd earl imported the famous Godolphin Arabian, one of three stallions from which all British thoroughbreds are descended. While the house remains in private ownership, the Godolphin estate is owned by the National Trust and this historic landscape includes more than 400 recorded archaeological features.

To the south of Godolphin lies the hamlet of **Rinsey** where evidence of tin mining can be seen in the restored 19th century engine house of **Wheal Prosper** and the ruins of the copper mine, **Wheal Trewavas**. Just to the west of Rinsey two headlands enclose the mile long crescent of **Praa Sands**, one of the finest family beaches in Cornwall. Further west again is **Prussia Cove**, a clifftop settlement named after a notorious 18th century smuggler, John Carter, who modelled himself on Frederick the Great of Prussia.

NEWLYN

1 mile S of Penzance on the B3315

🎨 Newlyn Art Gallery

The largest fish-landing port in England and Wales, Newlyn has a long association with

---

HELEN FEILER GALLERY

36 The Strand, Newlyn, Penzance, Cornwall TR18 5HW
Tel: 01736 330796
e-mail: helenfeiler@btinternet.com
website: www.helenfeilergallery.com

A painter and print-maker, Helen Feiler trained as a silversmith in a traditional jeweller's workshop but learned the lost-wax techniques her jewellery exploits with bravura in a sculptor's studio. Her exquisite creations can be seen in the **Helen Feiler Gallery** in Newlyn, located opposite the fish market and behind the Star Inn. The youngest in a large family of painters, Helen made and sold her first wax picture at the age of 10.

Today, her dynamic necklaces have been described as "pure sculpture for the body". Helen's attitude to her materials - crystals, fossils, stones, silver and bronze - is inspired by a "truth to materials" approach used by many sculptors, in particular Barbara Hepworth whose work Helen is familiar with. Her jewels have an affinity with the past, often suggesting ancient medieval baubles as well as the weighty pendants of the Elizabethan era. As the author and biographer Hilary Spurling noted: "Helen's experiments with size, scale, weight, texture and volume grow bolder all the time. She sees her jewels as microcosms of the natural world and her most recent pieces bear that out."

🎬 stories and anecdotes 🦅 famous people 🎨 art and craft 🎭 entertainment and sport 🥾 walks

fishing. Its massive jetties, built in the 1880s, embrace not only the existing 15th century harbour but also 40 acres of Mount's Bay. The arrival of the railway in 1859 allowed the swift transportation of fresh fish and seafood to London and beyond. Newlyn is still a base for around 200 vessels. Cornish sardines are landed in the early hours each morning, ready for processing and canning the same day.

However, it was not fish but the exceptionally clear natural light that drew Stanhope Forbes to Newlyn in the 1880s. He was soon joined by other artists, keen to experience the joys of painting outside. The **Newlyn School** of art was founded with the help of other artists such as Lamorna Birsh, Alfred Munnings and Norman Garstin, but to see their work you have to visit the Penlee

House Gallery in Penzance. The **Newlyn Art Gallery** exhibits a wide variety of work with special emphasis on the work of local artists, past and present.

MOUSEHOLE
2 miles S of Penzance off the B3315

Mousehole (pronounced 'Mowzel') was described by Dylan Thomas, who honeymooned here in 1937, as "the loveliest village in England". Still largely unspoilt, it fulfils the popular image of what a Cornish fishing village should look like, complete with a picturesque harbour where a small number of fishing boats off-load their daily catch. At the southern end of the quay, rising from the water, is Merlin's Rock. Here the great wizard is supposed to have prophesied:

LAMORNA POTTERY

Lamorna, Penzance, Cornwall TR19 6NY
Tel: 01736 810330
e-mail: mail@lamornapottery.plus.com
website: www.lamornapottery.co.uk

The **Lamorna Pottery** was established in 1948 by Chris Ludlow and Derick Wilshaw in a former milk factory in the Lamorna valley. In their early years they were greatly helped by the famous potter Bernard Leach of the Leach Pottery in St Ives. Today the pottery is well known for its range of colourful glazed pottery in the colours which reflect the surrounding landscape - blues, browns and a hint of green. The pieces are all hand-made on site by resident potters Arthur Walford and his daughter Emma Baldwin and are on display in the pottery shop which also stocks a range of unique gifts.

The present owner of the Pottery, Bermudian-born Ozzie Rego and his partner Andrea Bennetts have developed the Garden Restaurant where you can enjoy specialities such as Bermuda Fish Chowder or award-winning Cream Teas. You can relax in the garden surrounded by woodland or in the large conservatory.

The Pottery also offers charming and peaceful bed and breakfast accommodation comprising a large family room with a sitting area and patio, two twin rooms; two double rooms and an attic twin room. All rooms have tea and coffee making facilities, and vegetarian diets can be catered for. Lamorna is surrounded by wonderful scenery with abundant and wildlife and is close to the Merry Maidens stone circle, Minack Theatre, St Michael's Mount and Land's End.

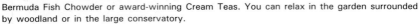

🏚 historic building   🏛 museum and heritage   🏛 historic site   🌳 scenic attraction   🌱 flora and fauna

There shall land on the Rock of Merlin
Those who shall burn Paul, Penzance and Newlyn.

In July 1595, four Spanish galleys fulfilled his prophecy. Every house in the village except one was destroyed - the sole survivor can still be seen.

Dolly Pentreath, reputedly the last person to speak only the Cornish language, lived in Mousehole. She died in the early 1800s and there is a memorial to her in the churchyard at Paul, a small village just above Mousehole.

In winter, the entrance to Mousehole harbour is closed by sturdy wooden beams to keep the force of the sea at bay. In past times, the village has suffered ferocious winter storms and one of these events is commemorated annually shortly before Christmas on "Tom Bawcock's Eve" when a huge fish pie is baked and consumed by the patrons of the Inn on the quayside. This event, which becomes a major village party, attracts visitors from both the surrounding district and from all over the world.

ST BURYAN
5 miles SW of Penzance on the B3283

🏛 Boscawen-Un Stone Circle

The landscape around this village is dominated by the 14th century tower of one of the finest churches in Cornwall. It also provides a day mark for shipping around Land's End. To the north of St Buryan is the isolated **Boscawen-Un Stone Circle**, whose central standing stone is an attractive leaning pillar of sparkling quartz.

To the southwest and sheltered in a shallow valley is the unspoilt hamlet of Treen. A short walk away is the spectacularly sited Iron Age coastal fort, Tretyn Dinas. Also on

this headland lies the famous Logan Rock, a massive 60-ton granite boulder that was once so finely balanced that it could be rocked by hand.

PORTHCURNO
7½ miles SW of Penzance off the B3315

🏛 Porthcurno Telegraph Museum

🎭 Minack Theatre

A recent survey by the *Sunday Times* listed the beach at Porthcurno as one of the Top Ten Best Beaches in the World. It praised its "secret coves, craggy cliffs, soft sand and proper rock pools".

It was from this dramatic cove, protected by Gwennap Head and Cribba Head, that the first telegraph cable was laid in 1870 linking Britain with the rest of the world. The **Porthcurno Telegraph Museum**, housed in a secret underground wartime communications centre, explains the technology that has been developed from Victorian times to the present.

This interesting village is also home to the **Minack Theatre.** This open-air amphitheatre cut into the cliffside looks as if it might have been created by the Romans but in fact it was

Porthcurno Telegraph Museum

founded by a very determined lady, Rowena Cade, in the 1930s. Appropriately, with the sea providing a not always serene backdrop, the first play produced here, in 1931, was Shakespeare's *The Tempest*. Since then the Bard's plays have provided the central focus for each season's performances, along with other classics, avant-garde plays and the perennially popular *Pirates of Penzance*. Daytime visitors can explore the **Rowena Cade Exhibition Centre** which tells the story of how Rowena spent decades developing the 750-seat theatre.

LAND'S END
9 miles SW of Penzance on the A30

Mainland England's most westerly point, Land's End, was once a mystical place. Somewhere beyond its craggy cliffs lay the Lost Land of Lyonesse and the stark, treeless surroundings often draped in sea mist spoke eloquently of elemental, hostile forces. Then in 1982, a London businessman, Peter de Savary, outbid the National Trust to buy the 120-acre site. At the same time he bought

John o'Groats, 874 miles away near the northern tip of Scotland. "Cornwall is a goldmine," he declared and proceeded to make Land's End into a kind of theme park with a huge hotel, amusements complex and car parks. The evocative name still draws many thousands here each year

Notable among the attractions here are an exhibition telling the story of the men of the RNLI and state-of-the-art displays of local tales and legends and the lives of the Cornish farmers and craftsmen. From this headland can be seen Longships Lighthouse, just off shore, and Wolf Rock Lighthouse, seven miles away.

SANCREED
3½ miles W of Penzance off the A30

🏛 Carn Euny   🌿 Bartinney Downs

The best example of an ancient Celtic Cross in Cornwall stands nine feet high in the churchyard of 15th century **St Credan's Church**. In the surrounding area are two Bronze Age monuments, the Blind Fiddler and the Two Sisters. Like many Cornish menhirs, they are said to represent humans turned to stone for committing irreligious acts on the Sabbath.

To the southwest of the village is **Carn Euny**, a fascinating Iron Age courtyard farming settlement that was founded around 200BC. By far the most impressive building here is the Fogou which was first discovered by miners

Carn Euny, nr Sancreed

in the 19th century and takes its name from the Cornish for 'cave'. This underground chamber was constructed in three separate stages, and the 65ft room was entered by a low 'creep' passage at one end.

Immediately west of Carn Euny is **Bartinney Downs**, a large area of heathland where programmes are in place to preserve both wildlife habitats and archaeological sites and historic features, including old china clay works, abandoned quarries and the ruins of Bartinney Castle.

ST JUST

7 miles W of Penzance on the A3071

🚶 The Tinners' Way

The westernmost town in mainland Britain, St Just was a copper and tin mining centre and the surrounding area is littered with industrial remains. A narrow road leads from this rather sombre town westwards to Cape Cornwall, the only cape in England, passing the last remnant of Cape Cornwall mine – its tall chimney. On the southern side of this headland lies Priest's Cove, a quiet boulder-strewn beach while, further along, the South West Coast Path follows the cliff tops. The coastal road from St Just to St Ives, the B3306, is regarded by many as the most spectacular coastal route in England.

St Just marks the start (or the end) of **The Tinners' Way**, an ancient track way between the town and St Ives. The track follows ancient moorland paths that were certainly used more than 2,000 years ago and may originally have been part of a network of paths dating back to Neolithic times.

To the northeast of the town lies Botallack,

NANCHERROW STUDIO

St Just, Penzance TR19 7LA
Tel: 01736 788552
e-mail: christinefeiler@virgin.net
website: www.theartangle.co.uk

Nancherrow Studio is the workplace and gallery of husband and wife Paul Mount and June Miles, two distinguished artists with a considerable body of outstanding work to their credit. Paul attended the Royal College of Art in 1940 and then saw wartime service as an ambulance driver with the 2nd French Armoured Division. From 1948 to 1955 he lectured at Winchester School of Art then taught in Lagos, Nigeria where he formed the Art Department and became its Director. He returned to Cornwall in 1962 and set up a working studio in Nancherrow near St Just with wife. Here he developed his sculptural techniques, for example learning welding from a local blacksmith. He became well known for his public sculptures - a good example can be seen on the exterior of the Co-Op in Falmouth. Rather than carving or modelling in plaster to be cast into metal, Paul has worked in stainless steel on intricate and linear welded constructions which are light and airy and which are often mobiles.

June Miles studied at The Slade from 1941 to 1943 (and drew maps during the war in an

Admiralty drawing office), followed by two more years at Art School in Bristol, at the then West of England College of Art.

June began teaching at the West of England College in 1966, where she remained as a member of the Faculty staff until 1976.

In 1968 June was a medallist in the Women's International Exhibition in Paris. She is a member of the Royal West of England Academy, the Newlyn Society of Artists and the Penwith Society of Artists.

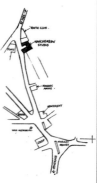

🏠 historic building 🏛 museum and heritage 🏛 historic site 🍃 scenic attraction 🌿 flora and fauna

Redruth

Three Crowns Mines, Botallack

Redruth was once the capital of the largest and richest metal mining area in Britain. The deep mining of copper after the 1730s brought prosperity to the town – at the peak of production in the 1850s, two-thirds of the world's copper came from Cornwall. Some pockets of Victorian, Georgian and earlier buildings bear witness to those days of comparative affluence for some. The miners themselves endured dreadful conditions. Children started work as young as eight and fatal accidents were frequent. The average life span of a miner was less than 40 years. The only memorials they have are the ruined mine buildings and chimney stacks dotted across the countryside around Redruth.

On a more cheerful note, Redruth was also the home of the Scottish inventor William Murdock, who is famous for such innovations as coal-gas lighting and vacuum powered tubes. His home was the first private house to have gas lighting installed, in 1792.

Immediately south of the town rises dramatic **Carn Brea**, a granite hill that reaches some 738 feet above sea level and is crowned by a 90-foot monument to Francis Basset, a local, benevolent mine and land owner. Once the site of an early Neolithic settlement, Carn Brea is also home to a small, part-medieval

where the remains of Three Crowns Mine stand on the dramatic clifftop. Here, tunnels were cut over half a mile out to sea, under the seabed, to extract rich copper lode.

PENDEEN
8 miles NW of Penzance on the B3306

🏚 Geevor Tin Mine   🏚 Levant Steam Engine

Tin has been mined at Pendeen since prehistoric times. At the Geevor Mine tin was still being extracted until 1985 when the international crash in tin prices sounded its death knell. The mine closed in 1990 but has been preserved as the **Geevor Tin Mine and Heritage Centre**. It not only preserves the mine but offers visitors the chance to experience the claustrophobic conditions of miners underground.

Close by, housed in a tiny building perched high on the cliff, is the National Trust-owned **Levant Steam Engine**, once again producing power. Further to the north, on the slate promontory of Pendeen Watch, stands Pendeen Lighthouse, which has been guiding ships for nearly a century.

BLACKWATER PINE ANTIQUES

Blackwater, Truro, Cornwall TR4 8ET
Tel: 01872 560919

It is easy to pass by the village of Blackwater, between Truro and St Agnes, but the short detour from the A30 is worth the time if you love the warm glow of polished pine furniture - so comfortable to live with, especially in an older house or cottage.

At Blackwater Pine Antiques, Peter and Linda search out good quality pieces of Victorian and Edwardian pine furniture, often in a sad and neglected state, and carefully restore them to fine condition, ready to provide service and pleasure for many decades to come. The spacious, welcoming showroom, scented with beeswax polish, offers a constantly changing selection of practical and decorative country furniture.

Visitors are welcome to browse, seek inspiration or discuss their ideas, free from pressure to buy; anyone travelling some distance, looking for something specific, would be advised to telephone first.

castle and it is still the site of the pagan ritual of the Midsummer Bonfire ceremony.

To the north, along the coast, lie the two thriving holiday centres of Porthtowan and Portreath. Although they developed as a copper mining village and ore exporting port respectively, they are now both the preserve of surfers and families during the summer season.

Just to the southeast of Redruth is the mysterious **Gwennap Pit**, a round, grass-covered amphitheatre, thought to have been created by the collapse of a subterranean mine shaft. Once used as a pit for the staging of cock fights, this curious theatre is sometimes known as the 'Methodist Cathedral' as John Wesley preached here on many occasions. Methodists from all around the world still gather here on Spring Bank Holiday.

Around Redruth

ST AGNES
7 miles NE of Redruth on the B3285

🏛 Stippy-Stappy   🏛 Blue Hills Tin Streams

🏛 St Agnes Parish Museum   🏛 Wheal Coates

Once known as the source of the finest tin in Cornwall, this old village still retains many of its original miners' cottages and grander mine owners' houses. Of particular interest is the steeply terraced row of 18th century cottages known as **Stippy-Stappy**. Surrounding the village are the ruins of old mine workings including the clifftop buildings of one of Cornwall's best known mines – **Wheal Coates** (National Trust). The mine operated between 1860 and 1890 and its derelict Engine House is one of the more exceptional landmarks along this stretch of coast. Walkers should watch out for the mass of abandoned mine shafts that litter the area but the walk to the remains of Wheal Kitty provides panoramic views over this once industrial area.

Visitors coming to this now popular seaside resort can learn more about the village's heritage through the displays on mining, seafaring and local natural history at the **St Agnes Parish Museum**. Those with an interest in learning about the tin production processes should take one of the guided tours around **Blue Hills Tin Streams** at nearby Trevellas where production still continues on a small scale.

Renowned as the birthplace of the Georgian society painter, John Opie, St Agnes was also introduced to thousands through the *Poldark* novels of Winston Graham in which the village appeared as 'St Ann'. From the village a footpath takes walkers out to St Agnes Head and St Agnes Beacon from whose summit may be seen 30 parish churches, both Cornish coasts, part of Devon and, at night, the lights of 12 lighthouses. There are also spectacular views over the old mine workings and also of remains from both the Bronze and Iron Ages. Now the home of some rare and localised plants and a wide variety of bird life, this area is criss-crossed by footpaths and is owned by the National Trust.

PENHALLOW
8 miles NE of Redruth on the A3075

 Cornish Cyder Farm

Acclaimed by the English Tourist Board as 'The Nation's Favourite Farm Visit', the **Cornish Cyder Farm** just south of Penhallow offers a fully guided tour of the site and orchards. Visitors can sample some of the 40 different fruit products made here, including jams, country wines, cider and traditional Cornish Scrumpy. The **Cyder Museum** tells the history of cider making through displays of old equipment and artefacts, and the Mowhay Restaurant serves Cornish cream teas and home-made food.

PERRANPORTH
10 miles NE of Redruth on the B3285

 Lowender Peran Festival St Piran's Oratory

This pleasant holiday resort, with its three-mile stretch of golden sand, was at one time a pilchard fishing and mining village that also harboured smuggling gangs. Though little has survived from those days, the small town's Celtic heritage is still remembered during the annual **Lowender Peran Festival** in mid-October which brings all the Celtic nations together through music and dance.

St Piran's Cross, Penhale Sands

High up in the dunes overlooking Penhale Sands, **St Piran's Oratory**, a ruined 6th or 7th century building constructed on the site of St Piran's grave, lay beneath the sand until it was uncovered in 1835. It's the oldest known church in the south-west but the shifting sands have once again claimed the remains. A simple plaque now marks the burial place of the saint who is said to have travelled from Ireland to the Cornish coast on a millstone.

ST ALLEN
9½ miles NE of Redruth off the A30

🌱 Chyverton Garden

As with many parts of the country with a Celtic tradition, Cornwall has its own 'little people' – the *piskies*. One legend tells of a boy from St Allen who failed to return home after going out to pick flowers in a nearby wood. His frantic mother began a search and eventually he was found, three days later, dazed but unharmed. All the boy could remember was being led deep into the forest, to a fantastic cave filled with jewels, and being fed the purest honey by the piskies.

Just to the north of St Allen, at the village of Zelah, is **Chyverton Garden** (see panel below) which is centred around the grand Georgian house built by a wealthy local mine owner. The landscaped garden is renowned for its rhododendrons, the first of which were planted in 1890, and for its magnolias, camellias and conifers. Admission to the garden is by appointment only.

POOL
2 miles SW of Redruth on the A3047

🏛 Industrial Discovery Centre   🌱 Shire Horse Farm

Now subsumed into the Camborne and Redruth conurbation, this village was very

Chyverton Garden

Zelah, Nr Truro, Cornwall TR4 9HD
Tel: 01872 540324 Fax: 01872 540648

The core of the house at Chyverton was built in 1730 and in 1770 two wings were added by John Thomas, a wealthy mine owner. Over the next 55 years he created a Georgian landscape garden on the property: he dammed a small stream to form a lake, built a bridge and a walled garden and planted 94 acres of woodland.

The first rhododendrons, for which **Chyverton Garden** is renowned, were planted in 1890; most of them are the old hybrid Cornish Red and many are of an immense size, perhaps the largest in cultivation in Europe. The garden also has notable magnolias and camellias and a fine collection of conifers. In 1924 the estate changed hands for the first time and became the home of Treve and Muriel Holman, keen gardeners who added many exotic plants brought back from plant hunting trips to the Far East and who created a woodland garden.

The whole garden is looked after by their son Nigel, who has encouraged the wild and natural appearance that is such a feature. Some of the plants are named after Treve Holman and Nigel's late wife Elisabeth, and in the memorial garden is a wooden bridge designed by Nigel that commemorates the death of Treve in 1959.

🏠 historic building 🏛 museum and heritage 🏛 historic site 🌿 scenic attraction 🌱 flora and fauna

much at the heart of Cornwall's mining industry. The **Cornish Mines and Engines**, owned by the National Trust, shows the two huge engines that were used to pump water from the mines. At the **Industrial Discovery Centre**, the secrets of the county's dramatic heritage are revealed.

Before the days of steam, heavy work was carried out by horses, and the **Shire Horse Farm and Carriage Museum**, at nearby Treskillard, pays a living tribute to these gentle giants. The museum has an interesting collection of private carriages and horse-drawn commercial vehicles, (including the largest collection of horse-drawn omnibuses in the country), farming implements and hand tools from days gone by. There are wheelwright and blacksmith shops, and wagon rides are available.

CAMBORNE
3 miles SW of Redruth on the A3047

🏛 Geological Museum

Once the capital of Cornwall's tin and copper mining area, in the 19th century the land around Camborne was the most intensely mined in the world. In the 1850s, more than 300 mines were producing some two thirds of the world's copper. However, the discovery of extensive mineral deposits in the Americas, South Africa and Australia led to the industry's decline in Cornwall in the early 1900s when it became no longer economically viable. Before the industry took off in the 18th century, Camborne was a small place and the traces of rapid expansion can still be seen in the numerous terraces of 18th and 19th century miners' houses.

As the town's livelihood has depended on mining for several hundred years, it is not surprising that Camborne is home to the world famous School of Mines. Its **Geological Museum** displays rocks and minerals from all over the world. Outside the town's library is a statue to Richard Trevithick, a talented amateur wrestler known as the Cornish Giant, who was responsible for developing the high pressure steam engine, the screw propeller and an early locomotive that predated Stephenson's Rocket by 12 years. His achievements are celebrated in Camborne on Trevithick Day, towards the end of April,

To the northwest of Camborne is **Godrevy Point** whose low cliffs mark the northern edge of St Ives Bay. It's a popular beauty spot from where seals can be sighted offshore. Just off the point lies **Godrevy Island** with the lighthouse that featured in Virginia Woolf's novel *To the Lighthouse*. Much of the coastline from Godrevy eastwards to Navax Point is owned by the National Trust and the clifftops support some of the botanically richest maritime heath in Europe.

Falmouth

🏰 Pendennis Castle   🌱 Fox Rosehill Gardens

🏛 National Maritime Museum Cornwall

Falmouth has grown up around a spectacular deep-water anchorage that is the world's third largest natural harbour – only Sydney and Rio de Janeiro are more extensive. Falmouth lies in Britain's Western Approaches and guards the entrance into Carrick Roads. First settled centuries ago, it was not until the 17th century that the port was properly developed, although Henry VIII, 100 years earlier, sought to defend the harbour from invasion. Standing on a 200ft promontory overlooking the entrance to Carrick Roads, Henry's **Pendennis Castle** (English Heritage) is one of Cornwall's great fortresses. Along with St

THE CORNISH STORE

11 Arwenack Street, Falmouth, Cornwall TR11 3JA
Tel/Fax: 01326 315514
e-mail: sales@thecornishstore.com
website: www.thecornishstore.com

The Cornish Store is a small family run business whose aim is to provide customers with some of the very best merchandise Cornwall has to offer. Wherever possible the products stocked are made by the many talented artisans living in this fascinating and beautiful part of the British Isles. Owners Keven and Anne Ayres are consummate retail professionals with more than 40 years combined experience. They are certain that if you are seeking that little Cornish something you will surely find it in their store.

The selection of top quality gifts, crafts and souvenirs from Cornwall ranges from luxury chocolates and Cornish pewter to traditional rugby shirts and distinctive tartan gifts. The range of Cornish clothing includes quality embroidered t-shirts, polo shirts, caps and hats, jackets and sweaters. For children there are Pasty Peeps toys, books, T-shirts. children's traditional Cornish Rugby shirts and Newlyn Fisherman's smocks. Or you could brush up your Cornish with a Cornish language dictionary, An Testament Nowydh, or books on Serpentine, The Falmouth Packet ships and *Oall rite me ansum!* The Cornish Store is a member of the Falmouth Shopper scheme by which holders of the Falmouth Shopper card receives substantial discounts at participating shops.

WILD IDEAS

40 Arwenack Street, Falmouth TR11 3JG
Tel: 01326 319517
e-mail: littleted@macace.net
website: www.wildideasfalmouth.co.uk

Occupying a prime location overlooking the Carrick Roads, Wild Ideas was established in 1999 by Kirsty Hedderly. "My main source of inspiration for the shop was our beautiful surroundings, and the talented people who live locally and make good quality gifts and jewellery. We aim to encourage creativity, she says "as we sell a large variety of loose beads as well as locally-made beaded jewellery, so people can either have a go at making their own or buying one already crafted!"

There is a great range of silver earrings and fun surf style jewellery along with sea inspired gifts such as locally sourced and made driftwood mirrors and clocks.

"We really are a one-stop shop for gifts and individual items for your home. We stock a sumptious range of soft furnishings - cushions in beautiful fabrics, throws and curtains all compliment the individuality and overall feel of the shop. Exquisite gift wrap and cards are available to complete your gift shopping experience."

Pendennis Castle

the Civil War. It remained in use until the end of World War II. Now, through a variety of displays and exhibitions, the 450-year history of the fortress is explained.

During its heyday in the early 19th century, Falmouth was the home of almost 40 packet ships, which carried passengers, cargo and mail to every corner of the globe. The introduction of steam-powered vessels put paid to Falmouth's days as a major port and, by the 1850s, the packet service had moved to Southampton. A charming legacy of the packet ships' prosperous days is **Fox**

Mawes Castle on the opposite bank, it served as a powerful deterrent against enemy attack. Strengthened further during the threat of a second Spanish Armada, Pendennis was one of the last Royalist strongholds to fall during

A-DEPT LIFESTYLE

4 High Street, Falmouth, Cornwall TR11 2AB
Tel: 01326 211109
e-mail: nickdobson@talktalkbusiness.net
website: www.a-dept.co.uk

a-dept is a family owned and run store whose two owners Nick and Vicki, both have qualifications in fashion/textiles and product design. This helps them select cutting edge, quality made and value for money lifestyle products for their customers.

Their eclectic mix includes a phone department stocking a range of some of the most iconic phone designs from the 20th century; a kitchen department with brands 'Joseph Joseph', 'Bodum', LSA Glassware & more. 'Made in Cornwall' Green Glass recycled glassware and 'Birdball' feeders and nest boxes are examples of local high quality products which sit comfortably with other internationally sourced items. V&A William Morris printed feminine garden and D.I.Y. tools, 'Pantone' bone china mugs and espresso sets in many colours, together with clocks and photo frames - a designer's dream aesthetic.

You'll also find departments devoted to well-designed and innovative gadgets and gizmos; a quirky range of greetings cards and wrap; traditional and modern toys for young and old - all this and more at a-dept and most things you won't find anywhere else in Falmouth.

BESIDE THE WAVE

10 Arwenack Street, Falmouth, Cornwall TR11 3JA
Tel: 01326 211 132 Fax:: 01326 212212
e-mail: gallery@beside-the-wave.co.uk
website: www.beside-the-wave.co.uk

Located on Falmouth's main street, overlooking the harbour,
Beside The Wave is one of Cornwall's best-known galleries and
has been hosting exhibitions for leading West Country artists
since 1989. Housed in a Regency building, the gallery provides
the perfect venue to show the work of leading contemporary
artists. Several of Cornwall's most well known artists exhibit at
the gallery including Emma Dunbar, Ted Dyer, Mike Hindle,
Amanda Hoskin, Robert Jones, Paul Lewin, Neil Pinkett, Andrew
Tozer, Richard Tuff, Andrew Waddington and Benjamin Warner.

Impressions of Cornwall through these artists works have
drawn customers from far and wide to the gallery. It offers a
lively and constantly changing display with up to 14exhibitions
a year at the gallery and in London featuring the work of
individual artists.

In addition to the paintings, the gallery also sells limited edition prints, a wide range of
ceramics, and a striking range of stylish jewellery. Various publications relating to the gallery's
featured artists are also on sale, together with a selection of art cards.

INTERIOR DYNAMICS

15 Church Road, Penryn, Cornwall TR10 8DA
Tel: 01326 373831 e-mail: shop@interiordynamics.co.uk
Fax: 01326 373831 website: interiordynamics.co.uk

Interior Dynamics was established in 1999 by Debbie McNally as
a small soft furnishings shop. Debbie's 25 years experience in
interiors has since transformed the business into one of the
leading interior design companies in Cornwall. Interior Dynamics
provides a full range of interior design services from Spatial Planning using
CAD Software for individual room designs to larger hotels, restaurants and
offices. Whether you are looking for your living room to be revamped with
sumptuous flair or a cushion to add a touch of comfort, Debbie and her
creative and professional team are ready to help your ideas flow, however
simple or extravagant they may be.

The showroom is bursting with vibrant colours, luxurious fabrics and
tempting textures in the shape of the extensive and impressive range of
designer pattern a wallpaper books from the leading companies including
Designers Guild, Colefax & Fowler, Romo and Osborne & Little to name just a
few. There is also stunning ranges of contemporary furniture, flooring and
lighting. Hand-made cushions, brightly coloured glass-ware, interesting pictures and unique ornaments
all add to the overwhelming inspiration that envelopes as you browse though the beautiful products
available. Interior Dynamics also offer a complete in-house curtain making, hanging and fitting service
and they can re-upholster any age or style of sofa or chair in the range of amazing fabrics available.
The in-house workroom is open to customers watching their bespoke furniture or soft furnishings being
made by the highly skilled staff, so you can always be assured of the quality of the workmanship.

Whatever your interior design need is, **Interior Dynamics** is the kind of business that has the
potential to change your place in the world for the better.

🏛 historic building 🏛 museum and heritage 🏛 historic site 𝒬 scenic attraction 🌱 flora and fauna

National Maritime Museum Cornwall

past is revealed at the **National Maritime Museum Cornwall** where the wealth of displays explain the rise in popularity of the town due to the packet ships. The museum's collection includes 120 historic British and international boats as well as contemporary vessels, prototypes and future designs. A great way to arrive at the museum is to use the Park & Float service, located on the A39 at the northern end of the town, and sail to the museum on a classic ferry.

Pirates and smugglers were also drawn to Falmouth. On **Custom House Quay**, stands an early 19th century brick-built incinerator known as the Queen's Pipe. It was here that contraband tobacco seized by Falmouth's customs men was burnt. Another unusual memorial can be found on Fish Strand Quay,

Rosehill Gardens which is stocked with many exotic plants from around the world brought back by various ships' captains, including one named Fox. Blessed by the mild Cornish climate, banana, eucalyptus, bamboos, agaves and a wide variety of palms flourish here – and in many private gardens.

Although the docks continue to be used by merchant shipping, the town's traditional activities are being overtaken by yachting and tourism. Falmouth's nautical and notorious

---

JUST LIKE THIS

37 High Street, Falmouth, Cornwall TR11 2AF
Tel/Fax: 01326 212895

Located on the old High Street of Falmouth, **Just Like This** was opened in the autumn of 2006 by Jane Thomas. After working for other people for some 25 years, Jane decided that there was a gap in the market for something different in Falmouth. So she has gathered together an eclectic mix of designer clothes and accessories. You'll find Irregular Choice and Tuk shoes, Peter Werth men's wear, Desigual women's wear, Vendula bags and purses, Fulton brollies and an interesting selection of jewellery. A great place to browse, where you may well find exactly what you are looking for.

🎭 stories and anecdotes 🦅 famous people ✐ art and craft ✐ entertainment and sport 🚶 walks

Trelissick Gardens

Distance: *4.4 miles (7.0 kilometres)*

Typical time: *180 mins*

Height gain: *50 metres*

Map: *Explorer 105*

Walk: *www.walkingworld.com ID:1513*

Contributor: *Jim Grindle*

ACCESS INFORMATION:

Trelissick is four miles south of Truro on the B3289. Buses T7 and 89B run from Truro where there is a railway station.

DESCRIPTION:

Trelissick House is in an enviable position with rivers on three sides, and this walk will enable you to see all of them - Lamouth Creek to the north; the Fal to the east; and Carrick Roads to the south, all three part of the complex Fal estuary. You begin by entering the park and dropping to the river which is followed through woods to King Harry Ferry. Further woodland paths are succeeded by open views of the estuary before a gentle climb back through the park to the starting point.

ADDITIONAL INFORMATION

The first house was built here in about 1750 and went through many hands with much development of the gardens before they were acquired by the National Trust in 1955. Among the notable restoration work by the Trust has been the re-planting of the once famous orchards with many old Cornish varieties of apple. The best place for seeing birds is between Waymarks 6 and 7. Between 7 and 8 is a sizeable Iron Age promontary fort, while at 8 is Roundwood Quay. This was built in the 18th century to ship tin and copper, and in past days there were buildings for smelting and refining and many wharves. Since 1888 the King Harry Steam Ferry Company has operated a ferry which pulls itself across the Fal by chains but the motive power is now diesel. Between Waymarks 10 and 11 watch for large sea-going vessels at anchor; some are waiting repair, others are more permanently anchored for economic reasons or because they have been impounded by customs for drug smuggling for instance, or are the subject of litigation.

FEATURES:

River, toilets, stately home, National/NTS Trust, wildlife, birds, flowers, great views, butterflies, café, gift shop, food shop, good for kids, industrial archaeology, nature trail, restaurant, tea shop, woodland, ancient monument.

WALK DIRECTIONS:

1 | The kiosk is where you pay for car parking. Take the tarmac path next to it - it is signposted 'Woodland Walks.' Go through a gate next to a cattle-grid (Waymark 12) and follow the tarred path to a junction.

2 | Turn right and stay on this driveway until at the edge of a wood you reach another cattle-grid.

3 | Go through the gate at the left of the grid and then turn to the right on a path going uphill. This will bring you to one of the lodge-gates on the estate.

4 | Pass the lodge and go through the green gate. Cross the road and go through the matching gate on the other side. Follow a gravel track which zig-zags downhill, passing a bench on one corner. When it straightens out there is a stream on the left, with pools made for the cultivation of water-cress. In a few metres you meet another track at right-angles.

At this point is a low notice in cast metal with directions - for people going the other way.

5|Turn left and you will see a footbridge over the stream that you have been following. Cross it, and on the other side the track forks again.

6|Take the right fork which follows Lamouth Creek which is below you on your right. (When the tide is out this is a good spot for waders and where we saw the egret more than once.) The woods become no more than a strip of trees with a field visible on the left, until you reach the next wood. There is an entrance of kinds here formed from two low stone banks.

7|There are several unmapped paths here. The simplest way is to take the right fork beyond the entrance. The path goes over the ditch and then straight through the rampart of the Iron Age fort before joining the other track where you turn right. Just before the quay you go down a few steps and emerge into the open.

8|This is a magical spot and you could spend some time here looking for the remains of the old industries. When you have had enough, retrace your steps over the bridge back to Waymark 5.

9|Now continue with the river on your left for 1.5km. You will reach a steep flight of steps leading down to the road you crossed earlier. The ferry is just to your left, and opposite is a white house with a flight of steps going up on its right.

10|This is Bosanko's Cottage. The track that you have been on continues on the far side.

Only one track branches off to the right away from the river and your way is signposted. This is the section where you might see the anchored boats; in fact you are quite likely to hear their auxiliary engines first. The track clears the woods to give beautiful views of the river, much of it used for rehearsing the D-Day landings of 1944. 1.5km from the ferry you leave the woods by a kissing gate.

11|This is where you re-enter the parkland. Go up the hill with the iron fence on your right and at the top cross the drive which enters Trelissick House. In a few moments you will reach the exit from the car park, recognised by the cattle grid.

12|Go through the gate on the right to complete the walk.

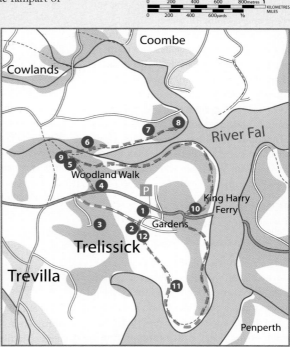

The tall granite obelisk here was erected in 1852 as a memorial to the men of the Post Office Packet Service which delivered mail all over the world in 'packet boats'.

From Falmouth's busy harbour, ferries and cruise boats ply the local waters to St Mawes, Flushing, Truro and other enticing destinations, including whale and dolphin spotting trips.

Around Falmouth

MYLOR
2 miles N of Falmouth off the A39

🏛 Celtic Cross

The two attractive waterside villages of Mylor Churchtown and Mylor Bridge have now blended into one another as a yachting and water sports centre. It was at Mylor Churchtown that the packet ships called and in the village's ancient churchyard lie the graves of many sea captains. Also in the churchyard, by the south porch, stands a 10-foot **Celtic Cross** which is one of the tallest in Cornwall. A further seven feet of the cross extends underground. Just to the southwest lies another popular yachting centre, Flushing, which was given its distinctive look by Dutch settlers from Vlissingen who arrived here in the 17th century.

FEOCK
4 miles N of Falmouth off the B3289

🏛 Smugglers Cottage   🏛 Trelissick

This is one of the prettiest small villages in Cornwall, and there is a pleasant creek-side walk to the west. This follows the course of an old tramway, which dates from the time when this area was a bustling port. To the south of the village is **Restronguet Point** and

the 17th century Pandora Inn, named after the ship sent out to capture the mutineers from the *Bounty*.

From Tolverne, just north of Feock, Allied troops left for the Normandy coast during the D-day landings. On the shingle beach the remains of the concrete honeycombed mattresses can still be seen. While in the area, General Eisenhower stayed at **Smugglers Cottage**, a lovely Grade II listed thatched cottage which is now a tearoom. Its owners have amassed a fascinating collection of memorabilia relating to that period.

Close by lies the estate of **Trelissick** (see walk on page 36), a privately owned 18th century house, surrounded by marvellous gardens and parkland with wonderful views over Carrick Roads. While the house is not open to the public, the estate, which is owned by the National Trust, offers visitors tranquil gardens of exotic plants and the chance to walk the miles of paths through its extensive park and woodland. Various outbuildings have been converted into restaurants, an art and craft gallery and a gift shop.

Feock can boast of sustaining one of only five remaining chain ferries operating in England. The King Harry Ferry has an all year round service and can take up to 28 cars per trip. It travels between Feock and Philleigh on the Roseland and cuts the journey time from Truro to the Roseland by up to 25-30 miles on a round trip.

TRURO
14 miles N of Falmouth on the A39

🏛 Truro Cathedral   🏛 Lemon Street

🏛 Royal Cornwall Museum

This elegant small city at the confluence of three rivers – 'Tri-veru' in Cornish – is the administrative and ecclesiastical centre of

---

🏛 historic building 🏛 museum and heritage 🏛 historic site 🍃 scenic attraction 🌿 flora and fauna

Cornwall. The city expanded from its ancient roots in medieval times following the prosperity originating from local mineral extractions. It was one of the first towns to be granted the rights of stannary, and several small medieval alleyways act as a reminder of those busy times before the silting up of the river saw Truro decline as a port and be overtaken by Falmouth. It was a fashionable place to rival Bath in the 18th century, and the short-lived recovery in mineral prices at that time saw the creation of the gracious Georgian streets and houses that are still so attractive today – **Lemon Street** in particular is regarded as one of the finest surviving Georgian streets in the country. Overlooking Lemon Street is a lofty memorial column to the African explorer Richard Lander who was born in Truro and in the 1830s discovered the source of the River Niger.

Nearby is one of the city's most recent developments, **Lemon Quay.** It occupies the site of the original quay which was covered over in 1923 and still remains beneath the surface. Above it, the pedestrianised piazza is busy with bars, restaurants and cafés, and hosts various events such as the regular French Markets and the popular Made in Cornwall Fairs.

The arrival of the railway in 1859 confirmed Truro's status as a regional capital. In 1877, it became a city in its own right when the diocese of Exeter was divided and Cornwall was granted its own bishop. The foundation stone of **Truro Cathedral** was laid by the future Edward VII in 1880. This

THE COTTON MILLS

Peoples Palace, Pydar Street, Truro, Cornwall TR1 2AZ
Tel: 01872 278545
website: www.cottonmills.co.uk

The Cotton Mills has the largest range of curtain fabrics in the county. There is a curtain measuring and making-up service from cushions to Roman Blinds to interlined curtains and the fabrics start from £5.99 a metre.

The Cotton Mills are located in one of the original parts of Truro. The building is over a hundred years old and has been used as a public house to a cinema to a Badminton Hall over the past century. The warehouse is over 5 metres tall with an abundance of natural light which makes selecting fabrics easy.

Ali, Joanne, Maureen and Andrew have been working in interiors for over four decades between them and have a wealth of knowledge to help you put the right scheme together. They also work with a

team of experienced fitters who can see the work through from concept to completion.

There is a great website where you will find a selection of the stock available and posting your order nationally or internationally would be no problem. Pop in or give them a call, they would look forward to seeing you!

SHOOZZE

2 Little Castle Street, Truro, Cornwall TR1 3DL
Tel: *01872 277200*
e-mail: *janet@shoozze.wanadoo.co.uk*   website: *www.shoozze.co.uk*

Located in the heart of Truro, **Shoozze** offers an enticing range of designer shoes that will quicken the heart of anyone who loves to be elegantly shod. Owner Jan Rees has put together a wonderful selection of beautifully crafted shoes and boots, both formal and casual, with sizes ranging from 3 to 6, together with a range of stylish bags. So put your best foot forward and make your way to Little Castle Street!

THE TRAIDING POST

1 Church Walk, Truro TR1 1JH
Tel: *01872 225235*
website: *www.thetraidingpost.co.uk*

The Traiding Post is a voluntary, Fair Trade shop, stocking products from around the world, including cards, paper, crafts, jewellery, linens, accessories and foods. Everything on sale in the shop is sourced from Fair Trade suppliers such as Traidcraft, Upavim, Pachamama and Wonderworld. The Fair Trade principle means that the people who produce these goods get a fair price for them and also a bit extra that must be invested in their local community. All the costs of production are covered and the workers get a living wage.

The Traiding Post stocks a range of Fair Trade jewellery from a variety of developing countries such as Thailand, Peru, Kenya and India. The shop also offers baskets from Thailand; glassware from Bolivia; tablecloths, placemats and aprons from India; cushion covers from Peru and Zambia; hammocks from Bangladesh; mugs from Vietnam; wooden toys from Sri Lanka; wooden stools from Indonesia; wall hangings from Kenya; juggling balls from Guatemala and more.

Also on sale is a range of multicultural children's books that help young people explore and understand the great variety and richness of the lives of people all over the world.

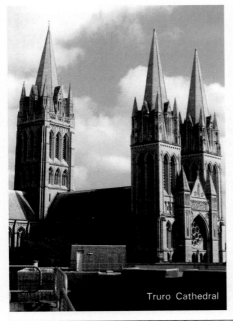

Truro Cathedral

splendid Early English style building, with its celebrated Victorian stained glass window, was finally completed in 1910. Its three spires soar high above a city in which high-rise buildings are still very much the exception.

Housed in one of Truro's fine Georgian buildings, the **Royal Cornwall Museum & Art Gallery** covers the history of the county from the Stone Age to the present day. Amongst its treasures are some early Bronze Age collars of beaten gold and the coffin of Ast Tayef Nakht dating from around 675BC, complete with unwrapped mummy. The Art Gallery, one of 10 scattered around the city, displays fine art from the Newlyn School to the present day.

The city has two major parks. The larger, Boscawen Park, sits beside the Truro River; Victoria Gardens, originally created to commemorate Queen Victoria's Diamond Jubilee, is filled with exotic trees, shrubs and

MANOR COTTAGE

Tresillian, Truro, Cornwall TR2 4BN
Tel: 01872 520212
e-mail: manorcottage@live.co.uk
website: www.manorcottage.com

Manor Cottage is a pretty Regency house built around 1820 which has been tastefully converted into a quality 4 star bed and breakfast. The guest house and its rooms are comfortable, warm and friendly and the family go out of their way to make visitors feel at home.

There are 5 letting rooms - 2 doubles, one en suite and one with a private shower; 1 twin; 1 single and 1 en suite family room. All the rooms are attractively furnished and decorated, and equipped with a television, a fully stocked refreshment tray, magazines for you to browse through, fluffy bath towels and toiletries. As well as serving superb breakfasts, a 3 course evening meal menu is also available for guests at pre-booked tables. Manor Cottage is licensed so wine, beer and cider are available. And why not order a delicious Cornish Cream Tea to be waiting for you on your arrival? Alternatively, you may want to order a 'beach box' of packed lunch goodies.

Owners Lyn Westcott and Mike Geary recently introduced their first watercolour long weekend, hosted by professional artist Peter Cronin. The fee for the 5-day course includes full board.

🏠 stories and anecdotes 🐿 famous people 🎨 art and craft 🎭 entertainment and sport 🚶 walks

THE SQUARE GALLERY

5 The Arcade, St Mawes, Nr Truro, Cornwall TR2 5DT
Tel: 01326 270720
e-mail: squaregallery@mac.com   website: www.thesquaregallery.co.uk

The Square Gallery with its beautiful harbour front location is much more than a place to hang paintings. Every inch of the cosy interior is occupied with an eclectic mix of individually selected arts and crafts, the majority of which are from Cornish artists. Painted silk scarves drape alongside collages and abstracts, hand-crafted jewellery twinkles next to boldly painted local scenes, ceramics and figurines line the walls beneath oil paintings and watercolours. There truly is a treasure for everyone and all can feel comfortable to browse for that unique piece of art. The Square Gallery is open from 10.30am to 5pm daily.

PHILIP MARTIN ESTATE AGENTS

3 The Arcade, St Mawes, Truro, Cornwall, TR2 5DT
Tel: 01326 270008   Fax: 01872 264007
e-mail: sales@philip-martin.co.uk   website: www.philip-martin.co.uk

Opening the doors to their St Mawes office in 2007 Philip Martin is the only independent qualified Estate Agent in St Mawes. Coupled with the successful office in Truro which was established in 1986 the partners Philip Martin, Steven Jenkin and James Harvey along with their professional dedicated team offer advice and proactive marketing on all matters relating to property sales and purchases as well as advice on letting, auctions, valuations, planning, development and legal matters. With all partners having a strong Cornish background and over 70 years combined experience in the local property market the firm offers a high quality professional and personal service that is backed by the Royal Institution of Chartered Surveyors.

LOOK AGAIN ANTIQUES & COUNTRY FURNITURE

4 The Arcade, St Mawes, Truro, Cornwall TR2 5DT
Tel: 01326 270988 Fax: 01326 270792

For over four years Ken Walkers' harbour front shop has been brimming over with a wide range of beautiful furniture from many a different era. Inside the shop is a treasure trove of collectable curiosities and small antique items nestled alongside larger pieces such as chairs, tables and dressers. All tastes and periods are catered for amongst the vast range which frequently spills out of the front of shop creating a pavement display of furniture history. So whether you are looking for that vital piece to finish a special room or a unique gift for a loved one, a trip to **Look Again Antiques & Country Furniture** is not to be missed.

DELI-CIOUS OF ST MAWES

1/2 The Arcade, St Mawes, Truro, Cornwall, TR2 5DT
Tel: 01326 270045   e-mail: deli@stmawes.co.uk

Roach and Claire bought **Deli-cious** 12 months ago with the aim of supplying only the best of West Country foods. Their local cheeses, shellfish and meats are truly delicious. To enhance this produce they also supply a range of chutneys and pickles along with quality, speciality Italian olive oils and flavoured stuffed olives. To complete your fantastic culinary experience, a range of fine wines and local chocolates are also available. They also make superb, handcut, made-to-order sandwiches. Deli-cious offer a hamper service for Christmas, birthdays and other special occasions.

🏫 historic building   🏛 museum and heritage   🏛 historic site   ♨ scenic attraction   ♣ flora and fauna

SPINDRIFT GALLERY

8 The Quay, Portscatho, Truro TR2 5HF
Tel: 01872 580155
e-mail: sdrift@hotmail.co.uk
website: www.spindrift-gallery.co.uk

Overlooking the sea in Portscatho, the light and airy **Spindrift Gallery** was opened by Cynthia Greenslade as a showcase for not only her own work but that of a range of Cornish artists and craftspeople. Paintings predominantly of the Roseland reflect the stunning countryside and coastline. This theme is echoed through the selection of ceramics, jewellery and glassware to be found in the gallery. There's also a range of hand-painted furniture, decorative items and cards that are exclusive to Spindrift. Regular exhibitors include Anne Preston, Adele Stanbridge (Hastha Kala), Chris Prindl, Frank Phillips, Jane Adams, Jo Wojtowycz, Kerry Raymond, Laetitia Miles, Livvy Wiegand, Lucy Kemp, Murray Tyers, Nick Orsler, Sue Gregor and Penny Gray.

Portscatho itself is an unspoilt fishing village whose picturesque appearance was made good use of in the BBC TV drama, *The Camomile Lawn*. Back in the 18th century, the village was popular with smugglers as the two headlands on either side of the bay provided excellent lookouts for any approach of the Revenue men.

---

flowers. On Sunday afternoons in the summer, concerts are held here. The park's peaceful atmosphere is occasionally disturbed by a train rumbling over the majestic granite viaduct nearby. Originally built by Isambard Kingdom Brunel but replaced in 1904, the viaduct carries the main line from Paddington to Penzance.

Truro combines a pleasant modern city with an attractive shopping centre with living historic traditions. During Advent, wassailers continue the age-old custom of circulating through the streets, drinking from a decorated wassail bowl and collecting money for charity.

PORTSCATHO
4½ miles NE of Falmouth off the A3078

This pleasant, unspoilt fishing village, with its sandy beach on Gerrans Bay, may appear familiar to anyone who watched the TV drama, *The Camomile Lawn*, for which it provided a scenic location. To the west, at St Just in Roseland, stands an exquisite 13th century church, surrounded by gardens containing many subtropical trees and shrubs first planted by the botanist John Treseder at the end of the 19th century.

ST MAWES
2 miles E of Falmouth by ferry,
on the A3078

🏰 St Mawes Castle

🏰 St Anthony's Lighthouse

This charming town, a popular and exclusive sailing centre in the shelter of Carrick Roads, is dominated by its artillery fort, **St Mawes Castle**. Built in the 1540s as part of Henry VIII's coastal defences, it is a fine example of Tudor military architecture. The castle's cloverleaf, or trefoil, design ensured that,

---

St Mawes Castle

contains many fine trees and exotic plants, and children will enjoy the famous Heade Maze, created in 1833 from laurels, as well as the Giant's Stride – a maypole.

To the southeast, the tower of the 15th century church at Mawnan has been a local landmark for sailors for centuries. An excellent place from which to take in the sweeping coastline, the tower was also used as a lookout post during times of war.

whatever the direction of an attack, the castle could defend itself. However, a shot was never fired from here in anger. Today visitors can look around the Tudor interiors which are in remarkably good condition.

From the town, ferries take passengers across the river to Falmouth and, during the summer, a boat also takes passengers down the river to the remote and unspoilt area of Roseland around St Anthony. From St Anthony Head, the southernmost tip of the Roseland peninsula, there are wonderful views across Carrick Roads. At the foot of the headland lies **St Anthony's Lighthouse**, built in 1834 to warn sailors off the notorious Manacles rocks. An excellent starting point for a number of coastal walks, St Anthony Head, owned by the National Trust, also provides a scenic setting for the remains of a military battery in use right up until the 1950s.

MAWNAN SMITH
3 miles S of Falmouth off the A39

🌿 Glendurgan Garden   🌿 Trebah Garden

Just to the west of this pretty village lies **Glendurgan Garden**, created in the 1820s in a wonderful wooded valley that drops down to the shores of the Helford estuary. The garden

Further up Helford Passage is the tiny fishing hamlet of Durgan along with the sub-tropical **Trebah Garden** (see panel opposite) that has often been dubbed the 'garden of dreams'. On a 25-acre site that falls down to a private beach on the Helford Estuary, the owner at the time, Charles Fox, set out to create a garden of rare and exotic plants and trees collected from around the world. Reaching maturity in the early 1930s and regarded at the time as one of the most beautiful in England, the garden was sold in 1939. Then began over 40 years of neglect before a massive restoration programme in the 1980s returned it to its original impressive state.

HELFORD
5½ miles SW of Falmouth off the B3293

🚶 Helford River Walk

A picture-postcard village standing on the secluded tree-lined southern banks of the Helford estuary, Helford must have one of the most attractive settings in the whole of the county. Once the haunt of smugglers who took advantage of the estuary's many isolated creeks and inlets, this is now a popular sailing centre. During the summer, it is linked to **Helford Passage**, on the northern bank, by a ferry that has been in existence since the

Trebah Gardens

Mawnan Smith, Cornwall, TR11 5JZ
Tel: 01326 252200
e-mail: mail@trebah-garden.co.uk
website: www.trebahgarden.co.uk

Trebah is a uniquely beautiful, 26-acre Cornish ravine garden - the wild and magical result of 160 years of inspired and dedicated creation. Glades of sub-tropical ferns and palms mingle with a forest of trees and shrubs in ever-changing colours and scents, contained beneath a canopy of century-old rhododendrons and magnolias. A steeply wooded ravine descends 200 feet down to a private secluded beach on the historic Helford River. A stream cascades over waterfalls and meanders through ponds of giant koi carp and exotic water plants before winding through two acres of blue and white hydrangeas and spilling onto the beach.

Trebah was first planted in the 1840s by Charles Fox, a Quaker landowner and inspired gardener. The rarest and most exotic trees and plants were imported from all over the world to create this lovely garden, and Fox ensured that every last sapling was painstakingly placed for maximum effect - even though he knew he'd never see the garden in its mature splendour. Subsequent occupants continued his work until WWII, when the house was sold, the estate split up and parts of the garden slowly reverted to nature under a succession of owners. Then, in 1981, Trebah was bought by the Hibbert family, who began a massive programme to restore the gardens to their Victorian heyday. Trebah opened to the public in 1987 and three years later the family donated the house and garden to the Trebah Garden Trust, a registered charity, to ensure that the garden is preserved for the pleasure of all future generations.

Middle Ages. The deep tidal creeks in the area have given rise to rumours that this is the home of Morgawr, the legendary Helford monster. The first recorded sighting of Morgawr was in 1926 and ever since then there have been numerous people who claim to have seen this 'hideous, hump-backed creature with stumpy horns'.

From the village, the five-mile **Helford River Walk** takes in several isolated hamlets and a 200-year-old fig tree in the churchyard at Manaccan before returning to the tea rooms and pubs of Helford. The rich mud of the Helford River, revealed at low tide, is a wonderful feeding ground for many birds including heron, cormorant and curlew, while the ancient natural woodlands along the shores support a wealth of plants and wildlife.

ST KEVERNE
7 miles SW of Falmouth off the B3293

Something of a focal point on this part of the Lizard Peninsula, the pleasant village of St Keverne is rare in Cornwall in that it has a handsome village square. Its elevated position has led to its church spire being used as a landmark for ships attempting to negotiate the treacherous rocks, **The Manacles**, which lie offshore. In the churchyard, there are some 400 graves of those who have fallen victim to this dangerous reef.

Just outside the village a statue

🎭 stories and anecdotes 🐟 famous people 🎨 art and craft 🎵 entertainment and sport 🚶 walks commemorates the 500th anniversary of the **Cornish Rebellion** of 1497, one of whose leaders was a blacksmith from St Keverne, while the church has a plaque in memory of the executed rebel leaders. Although St Keverne has been dominated by the sea for centuries, its agricultural heritage is continued in the ancient custom of 'Crying the Neck'. It was believed that the corn spirit resided in the last wheat sheaf cut, so this was plaited and hung over the fireplace until spring.

GWEEK

8 miles SW of Falmouth off the A394

🐾 National Seal Sanctuary

Set at the head of the Helford River, the picturesque village of Gweek developed as an important commercial port in the 13th century after Helston harbour became silted up. The same fate befell Gweek years later although it retains its links with its maritime past and the old harbour is very much alive with craft shops and small boatyards. Just a short distance from the centre of the village along the north side of the creek, is the **National Seal Sanctuary**, the country's leading marine rescue centre established over 40 years ago. The sanctuary cares for sick, injured and orphaned seals. Visitors can

National Seal Sanctuary, Gweek

witness the joyful antics of the seals at feeding time and explore the Woodland Nature Quest around an ancient coppiced wood.

HELSTON

10 miles SW of Falmouth on the A394

🏠 Blue Anchor Inn	🏛 Helston Folk Museum
🐾 Trevarno Estate	🎭 Lady of the Lake
🏛 National Museum of Gardening	🌿 Flambards

Dating back to Roman times when it was developed as a port, Helston is the westernmost of Cornwall's five medieval stannary towns. During the Middle Ages, tin was brought here for assaying and taxing before being shipped. However, in the 13th century a shingle bar formed across the mouth of the River Cober, cutting off the port's access to the sea. Helston's long history has left it with a legacy of interesting buildings. **The Blue Anchor Inn** was a hostel for monks before becoming an inn during the 15th century. It has its own private brewery, believed to be the oldest in the country. It's at the rear of the inn, next to the old skittle alley, and its beer, 'Spingo', comes in three strengths.

Another hostelry, the 16th century **Angel Hotel**, was originally the town house of the Godolphin family but was converted into a hotel in the mid-1700s. Around that time, the Earl of Godolphin provided funds for the parish church to be rebuilt after the previous structure had been struck by lightning and had to be demolished. In the churchyard lies a memorial to Henry Trengrouse, the Helston man who invented the rocket-propelled safety line that has saved so many lives around the British coast. Elsewhere, there are a surprising number of Georgian, Regency and Victorian buildings, which all help to give Helston a quaint and genteel air. Housed in one of the

---

🏠 historic building   🏛 museum and heritage   🏛 historic site   🏞 scenic attraction   🐾 flora and fauna

town's old market halls, close to the classical 19th century **Guildhall**, is the **Helston Folk Museum** which covers many aspects of the town's and the local area's history. The displays range from archaeological finds and mineral specimens to the reconstruction of a blacksmith's shop, an 18th century cider mill and a farm wagon from 1901.

Still very much a market town serving much of the Lizard Peninsula, Helston has managed to escape from the mass tourism that has affected many other Cornish towns. However, the famous **Festival of the Furry**, or Flora Dance, a colourful festival of music and dance, does bring people here in droves. The origins of the name are unknown but it is clear that the festival has connections with ancient pagan spring celebrations as it is held on May 8th. The climax of the celebration is the midday dance when invited participants wearing top hat, tails and dress gowns, weave in and out of shops, houses and gardens.

Just to the northwest of the town lies **Trevarno Estate and Gardens** – "the best excuse anyone could possibly want to go to Cornwall" according to *The Times*. This beautiful estate stocked with many rare shrubs and trees has a long history stretching back to 1296 when Randolphus de Trevarno first gave the land its name. Over the intervening centuries the gardens and grounds have been developed and extended so that, today, Trevarno is known as one of the finest gardens in a county with a great gardening tradition. The estate's **National Museum of Gardening** complements the grounds and highlights the ingenuity of gardeners down the ages by the range of gardening implements exhibited. Other attractions here include Soap and Skincare Workshops; a Vintage Soap Museum; the Colin Gregory Toy Museum; an adventure play area; a conservatory serving refreshments and a shop.

Trevano Estate and Gardens

To the east of the town lies another interesting and award-winning family attraction, **Flambards.** Based around a faithful recreation of a lamp-lit Victorian street, complete with more than 50 shops, it has numerous attractions for all the family. Exhibits include an undercover life-size re-creation of a World War II blitzed street, an Anderson Shelter and a wartime pub. Wedding Fashions Down the Years features a romantic assembly of changing styles with a collection of wedding dresses and wedding cakes from 1870 to 1970. Rides and slides keep the

stories and anecdotes 🐚 famous people 🖈 art and craft 🖋 entertainment and sport 🚶 walks

TREGADDRA FARM

Cury Cross Lanes, Helston, Cornwall TR12 7BB
Tel/Fax: 01326 240235
e-mail: june@tregaddra.co.uk
website: www.tregaddra.co.uk

Located in a peaceful Area of Outstanding Natural Beauty in the centre of the Lizard Peninsula. **Tregaddra Farm** offers home-from-home bed & breakfast accommodation in a quiet and peaceful setting with magnificent views. Tregaddra is a working farm that has owned by the Lugg family since 1864.

The present incumbents, Jonathan and June are the 5th generation of the family. The main enterprises of their 220-acre traditional family farm are the beef suckler herd and winter cauliflower, with a small acreage of cereals grown for their own cattle (the straw for their bedding in the winter months and the grain for feed). Jonathan's great-great-grandfather came to Tregaddra in 1864 as a tenant and then bought the farm in 1884. Incidentally, the name Lugg means 'cattle herder' or 'calf rearer' in the native Cornish language.

The house itself is set in a quiet, well-kept garden with fantastic views of open rolling countryside with distant sea. The interior is decorated with calm comfort in mind, a place to unwind whatever the time of year. Guests can enjoy the crackling log fires in the lounge's huge inglenook that dates back to 1717, catch the morning sun in the sun lounge before a hearty Aga-cooked farmhouse breakfast in the dining room with its individual tables.

The cosy and luxurious en suite bedrooms (two of which have balconies with magnificent views overlooking open fields and the distant sea) are beautifully decorated and equipped with colour TV, heaters, magazines and hospitality tray. Each room has been individually furnished with quality and comfort, and they include a four-poster room, family, twin or double room.

Guests at Tregaddra can relax in the beautifully maintained and peaceful garden, enjoy a game of tennis on the all-weather court, and splash about in the covered swimming pool (open seasonally). Tregaddra is open all year round and there's ample off road parking.

With its convenient location in the centre of the scenic Lizard Peninsula, Tregaddra Farm is an ideal base for exploring Cornwall. It is only 45 minutes from the Eden Project and Lands End, five minutes from the coastal path and beaches, and art galleries, horse riding, an 18-hole golf course, fishing villages and beautiful Helford village are all within easy reach.

🏭 historic building 🏛 museum and heritage 🏚 historic site 🌄 scenic attraction 🌿 flora and fauna

youngsters happy and for older children and adults the figure-of-eight karting circuit provides the opportunity to put driving skills to the test.

Close by is the Royal Navy's land and sea rescue headquarters at **Culdrose**, the largest and busiest helicopter base in Europe. Since the base was established here in 1947 as *HMS Seahawk*, it has carried out a great many successful search and rescue operations. There are guided tours and a special viewing area from which the comings and goings of the helicopters can be observed. In early August each year the base hosts Cornwall's largest one-day annual event, the Culdrose Air Day which includes a five-hour flying display and attracts aircraft from around 20 countries.

In the 13th century when the shingle bar formed to the west of Helston and dammed the River Cober, it created the largest freshwater lake in Cornwall, **Loe Pool**. This is now owned by the National Trust and is a haven for sea birds as well as waterfowl such as mallard, mute swan, coot, teal and red-necked grebe. A Cornish folk tale links Loe Pool with the Arthurian legend of the **Lady of the Lake** – Tennyson himself favoured

this site. As at Bodmin Moor's Dozmary Pool, a hand is said to have risen from the depths of the water to catch the dying King Arthur's sword. Another local story connects Loe Bar with the legendary rogue, Jan Tregeagle, who was set the task of weaving a rope from its sand as a punishment.

MULLION
12 miles SW of Falmouth on the B3296

Mullion Cove   Guglielmo Marconi

Future World @ Goonhilly

The largest settlement on the peninsula, Mullion has a 15th century church and a 16th century inn and is an ideal base from which to explore this remarkable part of Cornwall. A mile to the east lies the pretty, weather-worn harbour of **Mullion Cove** (National Trust), and just up the coast is the popular sandy beach of **Poldhu Cove**. It was from the clifftops above the beach in 1901 that the radio pioneer, **Guglielmo Marconi**, transmitted the first wireless message across the Atlantic. His Morse signal, the letter 's' repeated three times, was received in St John's, Newfoundland, quelling the doubts of the many who said that radio waves could not

Goonhilly Satellite Earth Station
Goonhilly Downs, Helston, Cornwall TR12 6LQ
Tel: 0800 679593
website: www.theroyaloakhawkeridge.co.uk

Goonhilly has over 60 dishes on site and is the largest satellite earth station in the world. With the ability to transmit to every corner of the globe via space, and through undersea fibre optic cables, Goonhilly simultaneously handles millions of international phone calls, e-mails and TV broadcasts. The purpose-built visitor centre offers a unique insight into the world of communications and has a variety of interactive displays. A licensed café and gift shop will make your trip complete.

stories and anecdotes   famous people   art and craft   entertainment and sport   walks

bend round the Earth's curvature. In 1903 Marconi was honoured with a visit by the future King George V and his wife, and in 1905 a daily news service for ships was inaugurated. In 1910 a message from Poldhu to the *SS Montrose* led to the arrest of the murderer Dr Crippen. A small granite obelisk, the **Marconi Monument**, was unveiled on the site of the wireless station by his daughter after the inventor's death.

Porthleven Harbour

Just a couple of miles inland, on the windswept heathland of **Goonhilly Downs**, is a monument to the very latest in telecommunications – **Future World @ Goonhilly** (see panel on page 49). It is the largest such station in the world and there have been few world events that have not been monitored through here since it opened in the 1960s. The guided tour around the station, which takes in all manner of telecommunications, including the internet and videophone links, is a fascinating and rewarding experience.

PORTHLEVEN
12 miles SW of Falmouth on the B3304

This pleasant fishing town developed from a small village in the 19th century. In 1811, London industrialists employed French prisoners-of-war to build a three-section harbour which is arguably the most impressive in Cornwall. They planned to export tin and china clay and import mining machinery, and also to protect the growing fishing fleet. Sadly, this scheme to establish Porthleven as a major tin-exporting centre failed, but today the harbour is still busy with small fishing boats landing their daily catch. A number of the town's old industrial buildings have been converted into handsome craft galleries, restaurants and shops, and the charming old harbour is overlooked by an assortment of attractive residential terraces and fishermen's cottages. A popular and attractive town. Porthleven is gaining a gastronomic reputation on account of the many excellent restaurants, cafés and inns to be found in such a small area. It also has a top quality fishmonger's shop located on the quayside.

LIZARD
14 miles SW of Falmouth on the A3083

🏃 South West Coast Path 🔄 Kynance Cove

Lizard is a place of craft shops, cafés and art galleries and lends its name to the **Lizard Peninsula,** the most southerly point of mainland Britain and also the country's warmest area. Just 14 miles by 14 miles, the peninsula's unique scenery has caused it to be designated an Area of Outstanding Natural Beauty. The **South West Coast Path** follows the coastline, much of which is in the hands of the National Trust, and provides many opportunities for walkers of all abilities. In particular, there is a nine-mile, sometimes strenuous, walk to Mullion that takes in some of the most spectacular scenery as well as passing lowland Britain's largest National Nature Reserve.

The Lizard is also known for its unique Serpentine rock, a green mineral that became fashionable in the 19th century after Queen Victoria visited Cornwall and ordered many items made from the stone for her house, Osborne, on the Isle of Wight. The village is still the centre for polishing and fashioning the stone into souvenirs and objets d'art.

Kynance Cove

To the south of the village is **Lizard Point**, the tip of the peninsula, whose three sides are lashed by waves whatever the season. There has been a form of lighthouse here since the early 1600s. The present **Lighthouse** was built in 1751 despite protests from locals who feared that they would lose a regular source of income from looting wrecked ships. It now houses a light that is one of the most powerful in the world.

Just to the northeast of Lizard is the very picturesque fishing village of **Cadgwith,** wedged in a rocky cove with fishing boats drawn up on the beach. With its cluster of pastel coloured thatched cottages and two shingle beaches, it is everyone's idea of a typical Cornish village. Life has not always been so peaceful here. Throughout the 19th century, this was a busy pilchard fishing centre. In 1904, a record catch of nearly 1.8 million pilchards was landed in just four days!

A small fleet of boats still sails from here, though their catch now is mainly lobster, crab, shark and mullet. Nearby is the curiously named Devil's Frying Pan, a collapsed sea cave with a spectacular blow-hole in the cliff.

To the northwest is the famous beauty spot, **Kynance Cove**, whose marvellous sandy beach and dramatic offshore rock formations have been a favoured destination ever since Prince Albert visited here with his children in 1846. The cove is the site of the largest outcrop of the Lizard Peninsula's curious Serpentine rock and there are caves to the west of the cove which can be explored, with care, at low tide.

WENDRON
8½ miles W of Falmouth on the B3297

🏛 Poldark Mine Heritage Complex

Close to this bleak village is one of the many mines that have been worked in this area since the 15th century. It has now re-opened as the **Poldark Mine Heritage Complex**. Visitors to this interesting attraction can take an underground tour of the tunnels, see the famous 18th century Poldark village and wander around the machinery exhibits, some of which are in working order. For a small charge, you can also try your hand at panning for real gold.

St Austell

⚜ St Austell Brewery Centre

🏛 Wheal Martyn China Clay Museum

"This strange white world of pyramid and pool," was Daphne du Maurier's response to the bizarre landscape around St Austell. The man ultimately responsible was William Cookworthy, a chemist from Plymouth, who discovered large deposits of kaolin, or china clay here in 1748. Cookworthy realised the importance of the china clay which is a constituent of many products including porcelain, glossy paper, textiles and pharmaceuticals. But for every ton of china clay extracted, another nine tons of spoil is created. Over the years, the waste material from the clay pits to the north and west of the town has been piled up into conical spoil heaps that led to these bare, bleached uplands being nicknamed the **Cornish Alps**. More recently the heaps and disused pits have been landscaped with acid-loving plants, such as rhododendrons, and they now have gently undulating footpaths and nature trails.

Although china clay has dominated St Austell since it was first discovered, and is still, despite fierce foreign competition, Cornwall's largest industry, the town is also the home of another important local business – the St Austell Brewery. Founded by Walter Hicks in 1851, the brewery flourished as the town expanded on the prosperity of the kaolin. Still thriving today, it remains a family business. The history of the company and an

insight into the brewing process can be found at the informative **St Austell Brewery Visitor Centre**, from where visitors are also taken on a guided tour of the brewery.

Just to the north of the town, in the heart of the Cornish Alps, is Wheal Martyn, an old clay works, now home to the **Wheal Martyn China Clay Country Park**. Set in 26 acres of woodland, this open air museum tells the 200-year story of the industry in Cornwall through a wide variety of displays. The land around this once busy mine has been replanted and it now has a unique range of habitats. The nature trail through the surrounding countryside offers visitors the opportunity to discover many different birds, small mammals, plants and insects.

Around St Austell

ST BLAZEY
3½ miles NE of St Austell on the A390

🌱 Eden Project

To the west of the village is the remarkable **Eden Project** which, since its opening in May 2001, has been a huge international success. The project aims to "promote the understanding and responsible management of the vital relationship between plants, people and resources." The brain-child of former record producer Tim Smit, back in 1994, the Project took over an abandoned, 50-metre deep china clay pit which now contains the largest conservatories in the world. Three of the world's climate zones (Biomes) have been chosen for interpretation: the Humid Tropics (Rainforests and Tropical Islands) and the Warm Temperate regions (the Mediterranean, South Africa & California) are contained within the two giant conservatories that have already captured the public imagination. The third, or Outdoor Biome, is our own Temperate zone that thrives on the climatic advantages that Cornwall has to offer. Currently (2008) under construction is The Edge, a landmark new building whose scale and ambition is designed to make it an international icon of sustainability, showing mankind is capable of amazing things. The building will be a model of cutting-edge architecture and technology, harvesting water and energy from the sun, wind., and rain to show how we all might live in the future.

CHARLESTOWN
1 mile SE of St Austell off the A390

| 🏠 Shipwreck & Heritage Centre |
| 🌿 Tregrehan Gardens |

This picturesque small fishing village, once named West Polmear, was transformed in the 1790s by Charles Rashleigh, a local mine owner, who built a harbour here to support the recently established china clay industry. Charlestown's harbour declined in the 19th century as other ports, such as Fowey and Plymouth, developed better facilities. However, what has been left is a harbour and village in a Georgian time capsule. As well as providing a permanent berth for square-rigged boats, it is a popular destination with holidaymakers and has been used as the location for TV series such as *Poldark* and *The Onedin Line*. Close to the docks is the **Charlestown Shipwreck and Heritage Centre**. This offers an insight into the town's history, local shipwrecks and the various devices that have been developed over the years for rescuing and recovering those in peril at sea. There are hundreds of artefacts recovered from more than 150 shipwrecks and the many and varied exhibitions reflect

village life in Charlestown, its history, shipwrecks and the once thriving China Clay industry. The exhibition shows a tremendous range of maritime history dating back to 1715 and one of the largest underwater diving equipment collections in the country, including various suits used for treasure seeking and naval purposes. A fairly recent addition is the "Heart of the Ocean" worn by Kate Winslet in the film *Titanic*.

Just to the northeast of Charlestown, close to Tregrehan Mills, is **Tregrehan Gardens**, where visitors can not only see many mature trees from as far afield as North America and Japan but also rhododendrons and a range of Carlyon hybrid camellias. The garden has been created over the years since the early 1800s by the Carlyon family who have lived here since 1565.

MEVAGISSEY
5 miles S of St Austell on the B3273

| 🏠 Mevagissey Folk Museum |
| 🚂 World of Model Railways |
| 🌿 Lost Gardens of Heligan |
| 🌿 Caerhays Castle Gardens |

Once aptly known as Porthilly, Mevagissey was renamed in the 14th century after the saints St Meva and St Issey. The largest fishing village in St Austell Bay, Mevagissey was an important centre of the pilchard industry and everyone who lived here was linked in some way with either the fishing boats or processing the catch. This has led to a labyrinth of buildings all within easy reach of the harbour. The Inner Harbour of today dates from the 1770s while the Outer Harbour, built to increase the size of the port, was finally finished at the end of the 19th century.

Elsewhere around the harbour, visitors can

World of Model Railways, Mevagissey

see the fascinating displays and models at the **World of Model Railways Exhibition.** It contains an impressive collection of 2,000 models and a working display featuring more than 30 trains travelling through varied landscapes including town, country, seaside and even an Alpine winter scene. The Mevagissey Aquarium features local sea life and is located in the old Lifeboat House just by the quay.

To the northwest of Mevagissey are the famous **Lost Gardens of Heligan** (see panel opposite), one of the country's most interesting gardens. Originally laid out in 1780, the gardens lay undisturbed, or 'lost', for 70 years before being rediscovered in 1990. The 200-acre estate contains Victorian pleasure grounds with spring-flowering shrubs; a Japanese Garden; a lush 22-acre 'sub-tropical' jungle with exotic foliage; a pioneering wildlife conservation project and woodland and farm walks.

BY THE BAY

9 Fore Street, Mevagissey, Cornwall PL26 6UQ
Tel: 01726 844600
e-mail: bythebay@btinternet.com
website: www.bythebaymeva.co.uk

June has lived in Cornwall for the past 25 years. Originally living in Boscastle she moved to the picturesque village of Mevagissey and opened her shop, **By the Bay**, three years ago. The shop is in the heart of the village and has views down Jetty Street to the harbour. June has worked with textiles most of her life making clothing for top class retailers in London, taking a City & Guilds course in upholstery, designing and producing top quality traditional Teddy Bears and now designing most of the textile range in her shop including cushions, door stops, bunting, tea cosies and aprons, nearly all of which are on short runs so designs are never widely available.

The shop itself has a wide and eclectic range of items for the home, which is constantly changing, with Emma Bridgewater tinware, Martin Gulliver ceramic range, Stubbs (Rather range) Mugs, nautical themed ware together with a range of decorative objects to compliment your home, whilst also always keeping a range of Cornish Dreckly clocks in stock.

 historic building 📷 museum and heritage 🏛 historic site ♈ scenic attraction 🌱 flora and fauna

BROCANTE

22a Fore Street, Mevagissey, Cornwall PL26 6UQ
Tel: 01726 842425
e-mail: brocanteltd@hotmail.co.uk
website: www.brocanteltd.com

Kieron Cockley opened **Brocante** in 2006, bringing to Mevagissey and Cornwall a shop with "something for yourself, your mum, your sister and your auntie!" Brocante is the French word for bric à brac so as you would expect, you will find an eclectic mix of items on sale. Kieron has personally hand-picked everything on display, choosing the items for their uniqueness, beauty - and value for money. Some of the brands featured include Green Gate, Gisela Graham, Garden Trading, Bombay duck and Two's Company.

Brocante occupies the ground floor of a delightful 18th century fisherman's cottage. Above the shop and to the rear of the building, Kieron has a self-catering cottage available to rent. The cottage is self-contained and approached from a courtyard at the back. There are three attractively furnished and decorated bedrooms, a living room with TV and DVD player, and a kitchen/ diner. With its proximity to the harbour, the apartment provides a delightful base for exploring Mevagissey and the surrounding area.

Gorran Haven, to the south of Mevagissey, was once a settlement to rival its neighbour. Those days were long ago and it is now an unspoilt village with a sandy beach, sheltered by **Dodman Point** – a prominent headland where the remains of an Iron Age defensive earthwork can be seen.

To the west of Mevagissey, **Caerhays**

Castle Gardens is an informal 60-acre woodland garden on the coast near Porthluney Cove. It was created in the late 1800s by JC Williams who sponsored plant-hunting expeditions to China to stock his grounds. The gardens are best known for their huge Asiatic magnolias which are at their most magnificent in March and April. The castle

The Lost Gardens of Heligan

Pentewan, St Austell, Cornwall PL26 6EN
Tel: 01726 845100
website: www.heligan.com

The award-winning restoration of productive gardens is only one of many features which combine to create a destination with a breadth of interest around the year: Victorian pleasure grounds with spring flowering shrubs, summerhouses, pools & rockeries; a sub-tropical jungle valley brimming with exotic foliage; woodland and farm walks through beautiful Cornish countryside, where sustainable management practices promote habitat conservation. Free access to parking, toilets, licensed restaurant/tearoom, Heligan Shop and Plant Sales.

PENGELLY PLANTS

Hewaswater, St Austell, Cornwall PL26 7JG
Tel: 01726 883757 Fax: 01726 882428
e-mail: sdanielppl@aol.com
website: www.pengellypurepleasure.co.uk

Sarah Daniel and Tracey Wilson established **Pengelly Plants** in 1993. Both originating from a strong Cornish background, Sarah and Tracey have much combined experience working in Cornwall's horticultural industries.

Pengelly Plants has a refreshingly different approach to a traditional garden centre. Walking around you almost feel that you are in a tropical garden as you notice the varieties of fruit tree, trace the upward progress of the climbing plants,

become dazzled by the bright flowers and admire the vibrantly coloured plant pots. The unique and interesting displays provide the customer with a captivating and truly inspirational experience.

After a leisurely stroll through Pengelly Plants, why not relax in the cosy and comfortable seating area and enjoy a homemade cake and a cup of freshly brewed tea or coffee.

Sarah and Tracey believe in a pro-active and hands on approach to their business. They are always available to offer guidance, advice and ideas to their customers regardless of how big or small their horticultural needs may be.

itself was built in the gothic style by John Nash between 1805 and 1807, and is open for conducted tours on certain days.

PROBUS
8 miles SW of St Austell off the A390

🌱 Trewithen House & Gardens

This large village is noted for having the tallest parish church tower in the county. Built of granite in the 16th century and richly decorated, it stands 124 feet high.

Just west of the village is **Trewithen House and Gardens**. The early Georgian house, whose name literally means 'house of the trees', stands in glorious woods and parkland and has gardens containing many rare species laid out in the early 20th century by George Johnstone. Of particular note are the magnificent collections of camellias, rhododendrons and magnolias. The interior of the house is filled with furniture and paintings collected by the Hawkins family over many years.

To the southeast of Probus lies **Tregony**, a small village that was an important river port long before Truro and Falmouth were developed; it is often called the 'Gateway to the Roseland Peninsula'. This indented tongue of land, which forms the eastern margin of the Fal estuary, is always known by its Cornish name **Carrick Roads**. It has a network of footpaths that take in not only the craggy cliffs with their nesting seabirds but also the grasslands dotted with wildflowers and the ruined military fortresses that go back to the time of the Armada and beyond.

TREGONY GALLERY

58 Fore Street, Tregony, Truro, Cornwall TR2 5RW
Tel/Fax: 01872 530505
website: www.tregonygallery.co.uk

In an un-missable location next to Tregonys' clock tower, **Tregony Gallery** marks the gateway to the Roseland Peninsula with the finest of Cornish contemporary arts and crafts. Now in its 10th year, the gallery is owned by local business woman Deanne Hornegger who worked on the premises before purchasing the gallery five years ago. Deanne is passionate about Cornwall and all the work displayed is predominantly, but not exclusively, Cornish.

The displays are endless and eclectic with ceramics by Charlotte Jones and Adrian Brough, pottery by Sue Binns, Nicholas Mosse spongewear, sculptures by Lawrence Murley and Teresa Gilder, Michael Storeys' bronze animals and contemporary jewellery by local artists. The delights continue with a range of local Seboni Spa products, and Tregony Gallery is also the exclusive Cornish retailer of Cath Collins designer toiletries. Among the artists currently represented in the gallery are John Brenton, Paul Lewin, Josep Pla, David Rust, Robert Jones, Amanda Hoskin, Alfred Adams, Julian Dyson, Richard Thorn, Michael Praed, John Piper, Lucie Bray and Michael Sanders. Many of these artists have featured in the annual exhibitions during May.

This friendly and intimate gallery provides a personal and obliging service to all who pass through its doors, and being situated on the widest street in Cornwall enables all visitors to park easily and browse until their hearts are content! Tregony Gallery is open throughout the year, Monday to Saturday, from 10am to 5pm in summer; 10am to 4pm in winter.

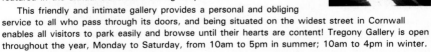

🎭 stories and anecdotes 🦅 famous people ✏ art and craft 🎪 entertainment and sport 🚶 walks

VERYAN

13 miles SW of St Austell off the A3078

🏚 Roundhouses

Set within a wooded hollow, this charming village is famous for the five **Roundhouses** that lie at its entrance. Built in the early 19th century for the daughters of the local vicar, the cottages' circular shape was believed to protect the residents from evil as there are no corners in which the Devil can hide.

Portloe Harbour

Eastwards, on the coast, is the unspoilt fishing village of **Portloe** whose tiny harbour is completely overshadowed by steep cliffs. To the south lies **Carne Beacon**, one of the largest Bronze Age burial mounds in the country.

Newquay

🗣 Huer's Hut   🏊 Trenance Leisure Park

🦜 Newquay Zoo   E Blue Reef Aquarium

🏊 Water World   🏛 Tunnels Through Time

🏊 Holywell Bay Fun Park

Washed by the warm waters of the Gulf Stream, Newquay is now the UK's top surfing resort with a choice of no fewer than 14 beaches. Fistral Beach faces the Atlantic head on, so when the wind is coming from the south-west the waves arrive after an unbroken 3,000-mile run – a worthy challenge for the top national and international surf riders. By contrast, the sheltered beaches at Towan, Great Western and Tolcarne provide a gentle

start for beginners on belly-boards.

This busy resort has a long history. There is evidence of an Iron Age coastal fort among the cliffs and caves of **Porth Island** – the outcrop connected to the mainland by an elegant suspended footbridge. For centuries, the harbour lay at the heart of this once important pilchard fishing village. The town takes its name from the 'New Kaye' that was built in the mid-15th century by the villagers who wanted to protect the inlet here. On Towan Headland, the **Huer's Hut** can still be seen; this was where the Huer would scan the sea looking for shoals of red pilchards. Once spotted, he would cry "hevva" to alert the fishing crews and then guide them to the shoals using a pair of bats known as 'bushes'. As the fishing industry declined, Newquay became a major port for both china clay and mineral exports. However, today, its beautiful rocky coastline and acres of golden sands has seen it develop into a popular seaside resort, famed throughout the world for its surfing.

Newquay's sheltered harbour is not just a working fishing port where you can buy freshly-caught shellfish and watch the daily activity, but also a pleasure area where visitors can compete in races or take sea-trips.

Huer's Hut, Newquay

Although there is some Regency architecture in Newquay, the rise of the town's fortunes in the 19th century saw a rapid expansion and many of the large Victorian hotels and residential houses still remain. The **Trenance Heritage Cottages**, Newquay's oldest dwellings were built in the 1700s but have stood empty since 2002. A group was formed in 2007 and is currently developing plans for their restoration.

Newquay is a traditional English resort and boasts a wide variety of attractions in and around the town. **Trenance Leisure Park** offers 26 acres of indoor and outdoor activities including bowling, boating, horse-riding, pitch & putt, crazy golf, horse-riding, ramp sports and a miniature railway. Also within the park is **Newquay Zoo** where conservation, education and entertainment go hand in hand, hundreds of animals can be seen in sub-tropical lakeside gardens. Siberian lynx are amongst the stars of the show but amongst the other residents are African lions, red pandas, sloths, tapirs, capybara and many more. Nearby, at the indoor **Water World** complex, the whole family can enjoy a range of pools and water activities in a tropical climate.

In Towan Bay, the **Blue Reef Aquarium** is home to a huge variety of Cornish and tropical species including octopi, giant crabs, clownfish, lobsters and many more. Some of them can be seen as you stroll among the colourful denizens of a coral reef through a spectacular underwater tunnel. There are more than 30 living displays including some graceful sharks and rays.

The characters and events that have shaped the history of this part of Cornwall can be discovered at **Tunnels Through Time**: more than 70 realistic life-size figures set in carefully constructed tableaux bring the days of smugglers and highwaymen, plague victims and miners, King Arthur and Merlin vividly to life. The scariest part is the Dungeon of Despair, where visitors can hear the screams of prisoners being tortured in the name of old-time 'justice'.

To the southwest of Newquay's famous beaches, Towan Beach and Fistral Beach, between the headlands of Pentire East and Pentire West, lies the quieter **Gannel**, home to notable populations of waders and wildfowl which feed off the mudflats and saltings. Just a short distance further on is the pretty hamlet of Holywell with its attractive beach, towering sand dunes and **Holywell Bay Fun Park** offering a whole range of activities for young and old.

BLUE BAY

Trenance, Mawgan Porth, Cornwall TR8 4DA
Tel: 01637 860324
e-mail: hotel@bluebaycornwall.co.uk
website: www.bluebaycornwall.co.uk

Enjoying superb views of the wild Atlantic and the serenity of the Vale of Lanherne, **Blue Bay** offers visitors the choice of self-catering or hotel accommodation. It occupies a beautiful position overlooking the golden sands, turquoise seas and scarlet sunsets of Mawgan Porth, "up where the gulls glide and rooks tumble", as owners James and Pippa McLuskie put it. The hotel, lodges, lounge, restaurant and most of the rooms all enjoy the wonderful panorama of the north Cornwall coastline.

The self-catering accommodation consists of four individually designed Cornish Lodges, family-owned and operated to cater for your individual needs. Each lodge is unique, with a character all of its own. All lodges are fully equipped, from dishwashers to TVs and DVDs. The Lodges are ideal for families, groups or short breaks.

The hotel's award-winning restaurant is open not only to residents but lodge guests and the public too. The chefs endeavour to use the freshest local ingredients and there's a varied wine list to complement your meal. The restaurant is open in the evenings from 7pm with last orders taken at 9pm. It can cater for up to 30 guests with a further 15 guests al fresco - as the weather permits.

CRANTOCK GALLERY

Langurroc Road, Crantock, Cornwall TR8 5RB
Tel: 01637 830212
e-mail: marionrowlanduk@yahoo.co.uk
website: www.crantockgallery.co.uk

Located next door to the Old Albion Inn in the picturesque village of Crantock, the purpose built **Crantock Gallery** was founded in 1994 and provides a showcase for original watercolours and prints by the artist Marion Rowland. Trained in art and design, Marion specialises in local views and wildlife, inspired by the beautiful scenery in Cornwall and a love of wildlife. She paints in a realistic, highly detailed style with some paintings taking months to complete.

Marion also paints commissioned paintings of much loved pets, people, houses and other subjects for which she has become much in demand.

Her many clients include The National Trust and the Bradford exchange plate collectors company. Marion's paintings have been exhibited several times at the Mall Galleries in London and her work was shortlisted for the *Daily Mail* "Not the Turner Prize" awards. Some examples of her distinctive works can be seen on her website. Crantock Gallery is open every day from 10am to 5pm, from April to October; during the winter months please phone as times vary.

Around Newquay

Crantock Beach

ST COLUMB MAJOR
7 miles E of Newquay off the A39

> 🍃 Hurling the Silver Ball

> 🏰 Castle-an-Dinas

> 🦅 Cornish Birds of Prey Centre

Once in the running for consideration as the site of Cornwall's cathedral, this small town has an unusually large and flamboyant parish church with monumental brasses to the influential Arundell family. In the 14th century Sir John Arundell was responsible for the town receiving its market charter. In 1850 the town's officials constructed a bishop's palace in anticipation of the county's cathedral being

STILTSKIN & WALRUS ANTIQUES

61 Fore Street, St Columb Major,
Cornwall TR9 6RH
Tel: 01841 520182
e-mail: janet92@talktalk.net

Set in the old Cornish market town of St Columb Major with its lovely church, ancient hill fort and some excellent pasties, is where you will find the antique shop with the weird name of **Stiltskin & Walrus.** "We wanted a name that was

unpredictable," says owner Janet Prescott. "Something that sounded like a Dickensian firm of solicitors, with a hint of fairytale, a bit of Alice in Wonderland... and of course some Beatles lyrics!" The shop also uses the tag line "Curios, Collectables and Cumberground". What is 'Cumberground'? It's an archaic work meaning something of no further use and in everyone's way - "Perfect for a shop like ours," says Janet. "I still dream of acquiring a huge stuffed bear to stand in one corner."

Her fascinating shop occupies a lovely old building of the 1750s which has narrow staircases, tiny doorways - "and the ghost of a woman pegging out washing!" adds Janet. Within the two floors you'll find a nostalgic wealth of china, glass, books, pictures, prints, postcards, furniture, curios and collectables. Definitely not to be missed!

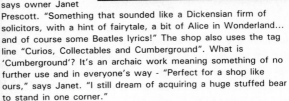

> 📖 stories and anecdotes   🦜 famous people   🎨 art and craft   🍃 entertainment and sport   🚶 walks

St Columb Major Parish Church

climbing to the gorse-covered remains will be rewarded with panoramic views over the leafy Vale of Mawgan to the northwest and the unearthly landscape created by china clay extraction to the south.

To the northeast of St Columb Major, at Winnards Perch, is the **Cornish Birds of Prey Centre** where visitors can see more than 50 hawks, falcons and buzzards fly freely during demonstrations. There are also waterfowl, ducks, pheasants, peacocks, emus, rheas, kookaburras, fallow deer, dwarf zebus and Shetland ponies. Also within the centre are three well-stocked fishing lakes, a tearoom and gift shop.

INDIAN QUEENS
8 miles E of Newquay off the A30

🐾 Screech Owl Sanctuary

Close to an area dominated by china clay quarries, this chiefly Victorian village is home to the **Screech Owl Sanctuary**, just to the northeast. A rehabilitation, conservation and education centre, the sanctuary has the largest collection of owls in the southwest of England – more than 170 owls of 46 different species. As well as offering visitors the chance to see hand-tame owls at close quarters, the centre runs courses on owl welfare. Harry Potter would approve.

built here. Now called the **Old Rectory**, it retains much of its grandeur though it does not play host to its originally intended guests.

Twice a year, the town plays host to **Hurling the Silver Ball**, a medieval game once common throughout Cornwall but now only played in St Columb and St Ives. It is played on Shrove Tuesday and then again on the Saturday 11 days later. The game involves two teams of several hundred people (the 'townsmen' and the 'countrymen') who endeavour to carry a silver ball made of apple wood to goals set two miles apart.

A couple of miles south-east of St Columb Major, on Castle Downs, are the remains of a massive Iron Age hill fort. **Castle-an-Dinas** was a major defence of the Dumnonia tribe who occupied this area around the 2nd century BC. The earthwork ramparts enclose an area of more than six acres. Anyone

KESTLE MILL
3m SE of Newquay on the A3058

🐾 DairyLand Farm World 🏛 Trerice

🏛 Lawnmower Museum

Just to the south of Kestle Mill is a family attraction that has welcomed more than two million visitors since opening in 1975. **DairyLand Farm World** is a working dairy farm where visitors can see the 120 cows being milked to music; try their hand at

🏛 historic building 📷 museum and heritage 🏛 historic site 🍃 scenic attraction 🐾 flora and fauna

TREVILLEY FARM SHOP

Lane, Newquay, Cornwall TR8 4PX
Tel/Fax: 01637 872310
e-mail: shop@trevilleyfarm.com   website: www.trevilleyfarm.com

Trevilley Farm Shop is a non-intensive traditional family-run farm which produces and sells delicious fine quality Cornish meat and produce. Owners Keith and Gill Barrett, the 5th generation of their family to farm here, believe in the value of good quality local produce and that is why they will only source products from within Cornwall. Opened in 2002, Trevilley Farm Shop now sells produce from over 60 Cornish suppliers as well as their own beef, lamb and vegetables. For Christmas they rear their own free-range bronze turkeys and free-range geese, as well as producing exquisite multi-bird rolls.

The on-site kitchen produces fresh produce daily, including bread, Cornish pasties, pies, cakes, ready meals and a variety of preserves.

The choice, variety and quality of their local produce is impressive and includes drinks (alcoholic and non-alcoholic), over 25 Cornish cheeses, other dairy produce, fine quality meat (including free-range chicken, pork, rabbit, venison, duck and game), ice-cream, fudge and much more.

The shop is open six days a week and the Barretts also offer the Trevilley Farm Produce Box Delivery Scheme - available to local homes and self-catering accommodation - UK wide mail order, Trevilley Farm Gift Hampers and they have a field available for hire for marquee events.

milking a life-size model cow; explore the nature trail and look around the Heritage Centre and Alternative Energy Centre.

Hidden away in the country lanes two miles west of Kestle Mill is the delightful small Elizabethan manor house, **Trerice** (National Trust). A real architectural gem, it was built in 1571 for the influential Arundell family. As well as the hint of Dutch styling in the gables and the beautiful window in the Great Hall with 576 small panes of 16th century glass, Trerice is noted for its huge, ornate fireplaces, elaborate plasterwork and fine English oak and walnut furniture. Several rooms contain superb English and Oriental porcelain, and among the more esoteric collections are clocks and drinking glasses. There are portraits by the renowned Cornish painter John Opie and an unusual set of early wooden skittles. Within the charming grounds, a small barn houses the **Lawnmower Museum** which traces the history of the lawnmower and contains more than 100 machines.

Trerice House, nr Kestle Mill

ST NEWLYN EAST
5 miles S of Newquay off the A3075

🚲 Lappa Valley Steam Railway

🏛 East Wheal Rose mine

A mile or so south of this sizeable village is the **Lappa Valley Steam Railway**. This narrow gauge railway (15 inch gauge) was opened in 1849 as a mineral line from Newquay, to East Wheal Rose and later became part of Great Western Railway's Newquay to Chacewater branch line. This line closed in 1963 but part of the track was re-opened in 1974 as a narrow gauge railway. Two steam locos, Muffin and Zebedee, work the line, running from Benny Halt on a two mile return journey to East Wheal Rose. The railway is open from the beginning of April to the end of September and runs between 7 and 11 trains a day, depending on the season.

At the northern terminus of the line are the imposing engine house and chimney stack of **East Wheal Rose** mine, Cornwall's richest lead mine that was the scene, in 1846, of the county's worst mining disaster. Following a flash flood caused by a sudden, unexpected cloudburst 39 miners were drowned. The village cockpit, where cockfighting had taken place for centuries, was restored as a memorial to the dead; the mine was re-opened a year after the tragedy but closed for good in 1885.

Wadebridge

🚲 Cornwall Folk Festival   🏹 Camel Trail

🏛 John Betjeman Centre

Attractively sited on the banks of the River Camel at its lowest bridging point, this ancient port and busy market town is now a

COUNTRYWISE

5 Eddystone Road, Wadebridge,
Cornwall PL27 7AL
Tel: 01208 812423

The classic country shop in Cornwall, **Countrywise**, stocks a full range of country clothing suitable for every kind of weather. It doesn't matter whether your home is in the town or the country, you will surely appreciate the range of quality clothing and accessories on sale here.

Bill Frisby and team sell a full range of Barbour and Musto clothing, surely two of the best known names among country people. They also stock R M Williams, Dubarry and Schofell amongst others. The North Face, Berghaus and Royal Robbins can be found on the first floor. Ladies will be enticed by the stylish handbags from Radley, Texier and The Bridge.

It used to be that countrymen - and country women - dressed in shapeless tweeds and were barely distinguishable from the shaggy retriever by their side. But with the clothes on sale at Countrywise you would not look out of place strolling through Hyde Park, Yet these very same clothes will keep you warm and dry as you tackle a windswept track of the South West Coastal Path.

The Royal Cornwall Show

Wadebridge, Cornwall PL27 7JE
Tel: 01208 812183
e-mail: info@royalcornwall.co.uk
website: www.royalcornwall.co.uk

Over three days each June, an event that involves and reflects all aspects of life in Cornwall takes place at a permanent site just outside Wadebridge. It's the **Royal Cornwall Show**. Besides being a truly Cornish event from the roots up, the show is a fantastic, multi-faceted spectacular which no visitor can afford to miss. Entertainment happens big-time at the Royal Cornwall Show.

The main ring programme changes each year and features the sort of acts you rarely get a chance to see altogether. Military bands, parachute teams, acts of daring, speed and skill combine to provide a truly enthralling display. Then there's the shopping. Hundreds of trade stands offering massive choices of thousands of products. Garden machinery, garden furniture, wonderful craft works, books, art, Wellington boots ... the list is endless. Food and drink is a feature of the show that every visitor must sample. Cornwall prides itself on the quality of its home-grown produce and the variety of eatables and drinkables on sale at the show is immense. Tempting aromas abound. See if you can resist!

There's a massive motor fair, extravagant steam fair, a flower show full of wonder and colour; in the NatWest Countryside Area conservation and country life provide a mix of fascination and tranquillity. Above all, the Royal Cornwall is an agricultural show. It is one of country's very best and for many people, the chance to wander round the cattle sheds, horse lines and sheep and pig pens is the highlight of their visit.

popular holiday centre which is not only attractive but also is renowned for its craftware. Linking the north and south coasts of Cornwall and the moorland with the sea, Wadebridge has always been a bustling place and its establishment as a trading centre began in earnest in the 15th century. The Rev Lovibond, the vicar of St Petroc's, was looking for a means of conveying his flock of sheep safely across the river and in the 1460s he built the 320-feet-long and now 14-arched bridge which can still be seen today. One of the longest bridges in Cornwall, it originally had 17 arches and it is said that this bridge, nicknamed the **Bridge on Wool**, was constructed on bridge piers that were sunk on a foundation of woolsacks. The bridge

still carries the main road that links the town's two ancient parishes.

With a permanent river crossing there was a steady growth in trade through the town and its port but the arrival of the railway in the 19th century saw Wadebridge really thrive. As a result, much of the town's architecture dates from the Victorian era.

Wadebridge maintains its links with farming and each June, to the west of the town centre, the **Royal Cornwall Agricultural Show** (see panel above) is held. Another popular annual event is the **Cornwall Folk Festival**, a feast of dance, music and fun that takes place over the August Bank Holiday weekend. The town's former railway station is now home to the **John Betjeman Centre**, dedicated to the life

📖 stories and anecdotes   🦆 famous people   🎨 art and craft   🎭 entertainment and sport   🚶 walks

SPRING GARDENS B&B

Bradfords Quay, Wadebridge, Cornwall PL27 6DB
Tel: 01208 813771
e-mail: springjent@aol.com
website: www.spring-garden.co.uk

Situated in the historic market town of Wadebridge in the heart or Cornwall, **Spring Gardens** provides the highest standard of accommodation in a friendly relaxed atmosphere. Spring Gardens is a former merchant's house comprising spacious beautifully furnished rooms in a pleasant setting and within walking distance of the local amenities.

The house, a Grade II listed building, is the home of Jenny and Steve Knightley who have been welcoming visitors to their handsome house since 1996. There are three guest bedrooms (two doubles and one family room), one of which has full en suite facilities, the others have a shower in the room. Breakfast at Spring Gardens is definitely something special with everything locally sourced wherever possible. The Cornish free range eggs come from Truro; the milk and juices come from a dairy in Delabole; bread and croissants from the Malcolm Barnecutt Bakery in Wadebridge; and the locally produced home-cured bacon and sausages from Gary Dutton Butchers, also in Wadebridge.

Spring Gardens provides the perfect base from which to discover the natural beauty of North Cornwall. Situated only two minutes walk from the famous Camel Trail and 10 minutes drive from the north Cornwall coast with its sandy beaches. Riverside walks, unique shopping, indoor and outdoor leisure facilities are all available nearby, and Wadebridge is also just 25 minutes from the Eden Project.

---

and work of the much-loved Poet Laureate. Among the tributes and intimate artefacts on display are the poet's desk, his chair and drafts of his books.

Although the railway line, which opened in 1899, closed in the 1960s, a stretch of the trackbed has been used to create the superb **Camel Trail**, a 17-mile traffic-free footpath and cycleway that leads up into the foothills of Bodmin Moor to the east and westwards, along the River Camel, to Padstow.

Just to the west of Wadebridge, close to the hamlet of St Breock, stands the **St Breock Downs Monolith**, a striking Bronze Age longstone that is also known as the Men Gurta (the Stone of Waiting). Other prehistoric remains, such as the Nine Maidens stone row, can also be found on St Breock Downs.

Around Wadebridge

PENCARROW
4 miles SE of Wadebridge off the A389

�____ Pencarrow

A fine Georgian country house completed in 1775, **Pencarrow** is the home of the Molesworth-St Aubyn family and has a Grade II* listed garden containing more than 600 varieties of rhododendron, along with rock and woodland gardens. A notable feature is the avenue of araucaria whose English name is said to have originated at Pencarrow in 1834 when a guest examined the prickly leaves and declared, "It would puzzle a monkey!" During the season, the gardens are open daily, and guided tours of the house with its superb

---

🏢 historic building   🏛 museum and heritage   🏚 historic site   ⌂ scenic attraction   🌿 flora and fauna

WOOD DESIGN

Tredannick, Sladesbridge,
Wadebridge, Cornwall PL27 6JE
Tel: 01208 813305
e-mail: sales@wooddesignfurniture.co.uk
website: www.wooddesignfurniture.co.uk

Wood Design has been creating beautiful objects in wood for some 35 years. Wood-turner Stephen Roberts attended Gravesend School of Art and Edinburgh College of Art and then left his native London to move to Cornwall in search of a quieter life and to pursue his love of creating works of art in wood. He produces original contemporary furniture in both native and foreign hardwoods, everything from tables, mirrors and storage cabinets to candlesticks, jewel cases and bowls.

The majority of Stephen's work is made to order, but his showroom displays ready-made high quality pieces, large and small. There's also a selection of his striking acrylic paintings on display. Stephen is always on hand in his workshop to discuss your ideas and is happy to accept commissions.

Wood Design is open daily throughout the year and the studio is easy to find - just follow the brown and white signs on the A389 Wadebridge to Bodmin Road.

collections of paintings, furniture, porcelain and antique dolls are available Sunday to Thursday.

PORTHCOTHAN

8 miles W of Wadebridge on the B3276

🦆 Trevose Head 🦆 Bedruthan Steps

This tiny village overlooks a deep, square, sheltered cove with a sandy beach which was once the haunt of smugglers but today is just one part of a stretch of coastline owned by the National Trust. A footpath over the southern headland leads to **Porth Mear**, another secluded cove beyond which, on a low plateau, is a prehistoric earthwork of banks and ditches. Further south again lie the **Bedruthan Steps** a curious beach rock formation that is best viewed from the grassy clifftops. The giant slate rocks have been eroded over the centuries and their uniform shape has caused them, according to local legend, to be thought of as the stepping stone used by the Cornish giant Bedruthan.

To the north, the South West Coast Path leads walkers around **Constantine Bay** and past a succession of sandy beaches which are ideal for surfing, but unfortunately the strong currents along this stretch make swimming hazardous. Beyond Constantine Bay lies the remote headland of **Trevose Head** from where there are wonderful views down the coast, taking in bay after bay. At the tip of the headland stands Trevose Lighthouse, which has been warning mariners away from its sheer granite cliffs since 1847 with a beam that, today, can be seen up to 27 miles away.

PADSTOW

6 miles W of Wadebridge on the A389

🏃 Saints Way   🦞 National Lobster Hatchery

🏛 Raleigh Cottage   🐦 Charles Dickens

🦋 May Day   🏛 Prideaux Place

Padstow's sheltered position, on the western side of the Camel estuary, has made it a welcome haven for vessels for centuries and the area has been settled by many different people over the years, including the prehistoric Beaker folk, Romans, Celtic saints and marauding Vikings. Originally named Petroc-stow, it was here that the Welsh missionary St Petroc landed in the 6th century and, before moving on to Bodmin Moor to continue his missionary work, founded a Celtic Minster. Beginning at the door of the town's 13th century parish Church of St Petroc, the **Saints' Way** is a 30-mile footpath that follows the route taken by travellers and pilgrims crossing Cornwall on their way from Brittany to Ireland.

The silting up of the River Camel in the 19th century and the evocatively named Doom Bar, which restricts entry into the estuary mouth, put paid to Padstow's hopes of continuing as a major port.

Today the picturesque harbour still teems with people and the influence of the sea is never far away. Since 1975, Padstow has been closely linked with the famous chef, restaurateur and ardent promoter of seafood, Rick Stein, whose empire now includes a seafood restaurant, a bistro café, a seafront delicatessen, fish & chip shop, a cooking school, accommodation and even a gift shop.

JACOB AND HIS FIERY ANGEL

7 Middle Street, Padstow, Cornwall PL28 8AP
Tel: 01841 533113/532130
e-mail: sales@tidingspadstow.co.uk
website: www.tidingspadstow.co.uk

The unusually named **Jacob and His Fiery Angel** is located beneath Padstow cinema in the quaint back streets of the town. Owner Debbie Morris-Kirby has always been interested in antiques and started going to, and selling at, antiques fairs. When, in 2000, the opportunity arose to have her own shop, she seized the chance whole-heartedly.

Her stock is very varied in character, ranging through antique furniture, cast iron garden furniture, French tables and lighting, ceramics and Nauticalia to a selection of new gifts and costume and vintage jewellery.

In April 2006, Debbie also took over the premises next door and opened Tidings Christmas Shop which is open all year round. Here she concentrates on quality Christmas decorations with a difference - you will not find any tinsel, or shatterproof baubles, but instead design-led individual decorations, most of which should provide many years enjoyment. Her stock includes designs from England, Germany, the Netherlands, America and Canada, and she is continually receiving new festive lines. The shop also stocks a selection of Easter decorations each spring, and halloween products during October.

More seafood is on display at the **National Lobster Hatchery** on South Quay. In 2005, the Hatchery released more than 15,000 juvenile lobsters into the sea – for just £1 you can adopt one of them, name it and receive a certificate and information pack. There's also a gift shop area with sea-life related goods and a range of books about marine life and Cornwall.

The Hatchery is close to the harbour which remains the town's focal point. Here can be found many of Padstow's older buildings including **Raleigh Cottage**, where Sir Walter Raleigh lived while he was Warden of Cornwall, and the tiny **Harbour Cottage**.

As well as the annual Fish and Ships Festival, Padstow continues to celebrate **May Day** in a traditional manner that has it roots back in pagan times. It begins at midnight on the eve of May Day and lasts throughout the next day. The townsfolk sing in the new morning and then follow the 'Obby 'Oss through the town until midnight when the 'Obby 'Oss dies.

It was while visiting Padstow in 1842 that **Charles Dickens** was inspired to write *A Christmas Carol* in which he mentions a lighthouse - the one at Trevose Head. His good friend, Dr Miles Marley, whose son, Dr Henry Marley, practised in Padstow for 51 years, provided the surname for Scrooge's partner, Jacob.

On the northern outskirts of the town and built on the site of St Petroc's monastery lies **Prideaux Place**, a magnificent Elizabethan mansion which has been the home of the ancient Cornish Prideaux-Brune family for more than 400 years. Along with family

Prideaux Place, Padstow

POLZEATH AND NEW POLZEATH

6 miles NW of Wadebridge off the B3314

▥ Rumps Cliff Castle

▦ Church of St Enadoc

🐦 Sir John Betjeman

Surfers and holidaymakers flock to these two small resorts as the broad west-facing beach is not only ideal for surf, but the fine sands, caves and tidal rock pools make it a fascinating place for children. This was also a place much loved by Sir John Betjeman. To the north of the villages is a beautiful coastal path that takes in the cliffs and farmland of Pentire Point and Rumps Point – where stands **Rumps Cliff**

portraits and memorabilia the house contains many artefacts illustrating the history of this area and the country. The mansion is surrounded by glorious gardens and parkland overlooking the Camel estuary that were laid out in Capability Brown style in the 18th century.

PORTEATH BEE CENTRE

St Minver, Wadebridge, Cornwall PL27 6RA
Tel: 01208 863718
Fax: 01208 862192
e-mail: porteathbeecentre@aol.com
website: www.porteathbeecentre.co.uk

Porteath Bee Centre was formed by Heather Jago and Edward Old in 1989 and really started as a hobby. Heather started keeping bees in 1970 when a local beekeeper sadly passed away and his wife wanted the bees gone. Heather being an accommodating person took them in and a home for the three hives was found. In 1987 she and Edward started a little shop underneath Porteath farmhouse calling themselves Porteath Bee Supplies, selling a range of bee supply equipment and making their own polishes and candles. Two years later the Porteath Bee Centre was built and the following year the Living Honey Bee Exhibition opened.

Then, in 1993, the shop was extended and in 1995 the Beehive Tearoom was opened where morning coffee, light lunches and cream teas are now served. In 2000 a honey room was built at the side of the centre to facilitate the 200 hives they now look after, stretching across the north of Cornwall from Port Isaac to St Agnes. Most of the honey is sold in their shop and also in a few other outlets, including the Eden Project.

ST KEW POTTERY

Hale Farmhouse, St Kew, Bodmin, Cornwall PL30 3HE
Tel: 01208 880836
e-mail: whitten@stkew.eclipse.co.uk
website: www.cornwallceramicsandglassgroup.co.uk

The **St Kew Pottery** occupies a large open plan studio in beautiful surroundings, in an award-winning, purpose built, green oak barn. Potter, Jon Whitten, who has a degree in the History of Art from UEA, studied with Bernard Leach's son, Michael, and Roger Cockram. Jon makes a wide variety of ceramics specialising in large, stoneware, wheel thrown pots, jugs, bowls and vases. He is a founder member and recent chairman of the Cornwall Ceramics and Glass Group. His work has been exhibited widely and can be found in collections in Europe, Japan, New Zealand and the USA. The studio gallery displays a large collection of Jon's work, which is available for sale and to order.

Jon has taught for 30 years and runs life drawing, still life classes, and pottery courses for local students, by appointment, and for holiday visitors staying in the restored, high quality holiday cottages at Hale Farm. From November to March guests staying in the holiday accommodation may attend art and pottery classes free of charge and at other times there is a small fee. Jon teaches at all ability levels, from the complete novice to the most advanced, and specialises in the teaching of throwing. Students have access to eight potters' wheels and work is fired in a large gas kiln in the studio. Please phone for further details of classes and look at the holiday accommodation on www.classic.co.uk (Properties 900, 1666, and 1680). The pottery is open daily from 10am to 6pm.

HALE FARM COTTAGES

Hale Farm, St Kew, Bodmin, Cornwall PL30 3HE
Tel: 01208 880836
e-mail: whitten@stkew.eclipse.co.uk
website: www.classic.co.uk (Property No's: 900. 1666 and 1680)

Hale Farm is set within 3.6 acres of fields, woodland, and landscaped gardens and is a tranquil wildlife and artists' haven. Just two miles inland from Port Isaac and a short walk from the famous St Kew Inn, this group of 19th century stone buildings, comprising the farmhouse, pottery studio, and three cottages, has been lovingly restored to the highest standards to provide high quality four star accommodation. Guests may be inspired to try throwing pots in the owners' green oak pottery studio or to paint and draw, joining art classes.

The owners are keen to promote sustainable tourism. Natural materials have been used throughout and Delabole slate and oak floors complement the original art work on the walls in each cottage. Wireless broadband is available in each cottage, as are TV, DVD player, CD player and radio. The Granary (Property 900) sleeps six + cot, Pottery Cottage (1680) and the Carriagehouse (1666) sleeps four + cot. Bookings can be made via the agent on www.classic.co.uk or direct with the owners on whitten@stkew.eclipse.co.uk or tel: 01208 880836.

The spectacular North Cornwall Coast is within 10 minutes drive, including the popular surfing beaches of Polzeath and Trebarwith Strand, and beautiful sandy beaches such as Daymer Bay and Rock, also renowned for windsurfing and sailing. The Camel trail is popular with cyclists and the coastal path and nearby Bodmin Moor attract keen walkers.

Castle, an Iron Age fortification. where the remains of four defensive ramparts can still be seen. The area is known for its wild tamarisk, an elegant flowering shrub that is more commonly found around the shores of the Mediterranean Sea. In the 1930s, Pentire Head was saved from commercial development by local fund raisers who bought the land and donated it to the National Trust.

This stretch of dramatic coastline that runs round to **Port Quin** includes sheltered bays and coves, ancient field patterns, old lead mines and Iron Age defensive earthworks. It is ideal walking country, and there are numerous footpaths taking walkers on circular routes that incorporate both coastal countryside and farmland.

The tiny hamlet of Port Quin suffered greatly when the railways took away the slate trade from its once busy quay and the demise was so swift that, at one time, outsiders thought that the entire population had been washed away by a great storm. Overlooking the now re-populated hamlet is Doyden Castle, a squat 19th century castellated folly that is now a holiday home.

To the southwest of Polzeath lies the delightful **Church of St Enodoc**, a Norman building that has on several occasions been virtually submerged by windblown sand. At these times the congregation would enter through an opening in the roof. The sand was finally cleared away in the 1860s when the church was restored, and the bell in the tower, which came from an Italian ship wrecked nearby, was installed in 1875. The beautiful churchyard contains many graves of shipwrecked mariners but what draws many people to this quiet place is the grave of the poet **Sir John Betjeman,** who is buried here along with his parents. Betjeman spent many of his childhood holidays in the villages and coves around the Camel Estuary, and his affection for the local people and places was the inspiration for many of his works. The church is reached across a golf course that is regarded as one of the most scenic links courses in the country.

Tintagel

🏛 Tintagel Castle 🏬 Old Post Office

🏬 King Arthur's Great Hall 💧 Rocky Valley

💧 Bossiney Haven

The romantic remains of **Tintagel Castle** (English Heritage), set on a wild and windswept headland that juts out into the Atlantic, are many people's image of Cornwall. Throughout the year, many come to clamber up the wooden stairway to **The Island** to see the castle that legend claims was the birthplace of King Arthur. If the great king was born at this spot, it was certainly not

Tintagel Castle

in this castle which was built in the 12th century. But in 1998 the discovery of a 6th century slate bearing the Latin inscription 'Artognov' – which translates as the ancient British name for Arthur – renewed the belief that Tintagel was Arthur's home.

The legends were first written down by Geoffrey of Monmouth in the mid-1100s and over the years were re-worked by many other writers, notably Sir Thomas Malory's *Morte d'Arthur* of around 1450, and Tennyson's epic poem *Idylls of the King* in 1859.

Tintagel village, of course, owes a lot to its Arthurian connections, so souvenir and 'themed' shops have proliferated along its main street. You might prefer to pass on the 'genuine Excaliburgers' on offer in one pub, but an oddity worth visiting is **King Arthur's Great Hall**. It was built in 1933 of Cornish granite by a group calling themselves the Knights of King Arthur. They furnished the vast halls with a Round Table and 72 stained glass windows depicting their coats of arms and some of their adventures.

However, there is more to Tintagel than King Arthur. In the High Street, is the weather-beaten **Old Post Office** – a 14th century small manor house that first became a post office in the 19th century. Purchased by the National Trust in 1903 for £100, the building is set within an enchanting cottage garden and still has its original stone-paved medieval hall and ancient fireplace along with the ground-floor office of the former postmistress.

To the north of the village lies the mile-long **Rocky Valley**, a curious rock-strewn cleft in the landscape which has a character all of its own. In the wooded upper reaches can be found the impressive 40-foot waterfall known as **St Nectan's Kieve**. This was named after the Celtic hermit whose cell is believed to have stood beside the basin, or kieve, at the foot of the cascade. Here, too, can be seen the **Rocky Valley Carvings**, on a rock face behind a ruined building. Though it is suggested that the carvings date from early Christian times, around the same time that St Nectan was living here, it is impossible to be accurate and other suggestions range from the 2nd century BC to the 17th century.

A little further north, and reached by a short footpath from the village of Bossiney is the beautiful, sheltered beach of **Bossiney Haven**, surrounded by a semi-circle of cliffs. The views from the cliff tops are spectacular but only the fit and agile should attempt to scramble down to the inviting beach below. Inland, at Bossiney Common, the outlines of ancient field patterns, or lynchets, can still be traced.

Old Post Office, Tintagel

Tintagel Castle

Distance: *3.8 miles (6.0 kilometres)*

Typical time: *170 mins*

Height gain: *100 metres*

Map: *Explorer 111*

Walk: *www.walkingworld.com ID:1095*

Contributor: *Dennis Blackford*

From Tintagel, take the Boscastle road for about 1 km until you come to Bossiney car park on your left. Look for the mast.

DESCRIPTION:

The walk takes us through the village of Tintagel and out along the cliff path to visit the legendary castle of King Arthur and Merlin's Cave. All along the path you will find wonderful views and a wealth of wildlife.

ADDITIONAL INFORMATION

There are toilets at the start point. Toilets, food and drink are available at Tintagel and the castle visitor centre.

FEATURES:

Hills or fells, sea, toilets, castle, National Trust/NTS, wildlife, birds, flowers, great views, butterflies, cafe, gift shop, food shop, public transport, restaurant, tea shop, ancient monument

WALK DIRECTIONS:

1 | After parking in the car park, turn right onto the main road and walk into Tintagel Village, about 0.7 kilometre away.

2 | Walk through the village until reaching the 'no through road' to 'Glebe Cliff' at the side of the 'Cornishman's Inn'. Turn into this road.

3 | Follow this road almost one kilometre down to the car park at the end. Follow the church wall around to the right and on to the coast path. The corner of the road may be cut off by going through the churchyard, which is being kept rough as a nature reserve.

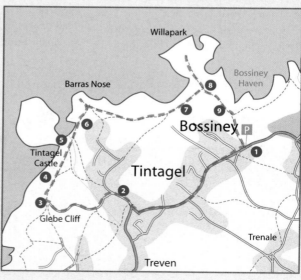

4 | After a few hundred metres you will be looking out over the ruins of the castle. Follow the path down.

5 | When you have reached the paved path to the castle, take the path to your right which zigzags down to the visitor centre. At low tide you can, with care, go to the beach and visit Merlin's Cave. Cross over the little bridge and up the steep flight of steps, or go past the café (which is an easier path) to continue on the coast path up the other side of the valley.

6 | 200 metres further on, after crossing a little wooden bridge, the path branches and you can go left or right; left goes up onto the point of 'Barras Nose' and is well worth the detour for a spectacular view over the cove and the castle. Continue on the coast path.

7 | About 1 km further on and you pass through a gate which will lead you to the headland known as 'Willapark'.

8 | After the path passes through the gap in the wall it branches. Left takes you out onto the point and is a very pleasant place to visit and relax before finishing your walk. After visiting the point, return to this junction and continue on the path to the right of the gap, which will take you down into the valley.

9 | Steps up the other side of the valley bring you to a stone stile. Cross the stile down to the track. Turn right to return to the starting point. Alternatively, turn left down into the secluded cove of Bossiney Haven, which is popular for swimming at low tide (the sand is covered at high tide).

Around Tintagel

PORT ISAAC
6 miles SW of Tintagel on the B3267

▥ Tregeare Rounds

🌿 Long Cross Victorian Gardens

A delightful fishing village that has retained much of its ancient charm, Port Isaac has become well-known to viewers of the ITV drama series, *Doc Martin*, for which it provides the major location as 'Port Wenn'. The town is surrounded by open countryside, Heritage Coast and an Area of Outstanding Natural Beauty. Port Isaac has been a busy port since the Middle Ages. During its heyday in the 19th century, fish along with cargoes of stone, coal, timber and pottery were loaded and unloaded on its quayside. Following the arrival of the railways, pilchards were landed here in great numbers, gutted and processed in the village's many fish cellars before being packed off to London and beyond by train. The centre of this conservation village is concentrated around the protected harbour where old fish cellars and fishermen's cottages line the narrow alleys and 'opes' that wend their way down to the coast.

Just to the east lies **Port Gaverne**, another busy 19th century fishing port where, in one season, more than 1,000 tons of pilchards were landed and processed in the village's fish cellars or 'pilchard palaces'. Today, most of the large stone buildings, including some of the old fish cellars, have been converted into holiday accommodation. Tourism has prospered as the village has one of the safest beaches along the North Cornwall coast.

Just inland from the village can be found the double ramparts of **Tregeare Rounds**. This Celtic hill fort was excavated in 1904.

THE LONG CROSS HOTEL & VICTORIA GARDENS

Trelights, Port Isaac, Cornwall PL29 3TF
Tel: 01208 880243
e-mail: info@longcrosshotel.co.uk
website: www.longcrosshotel.co.uk

An elegant country house hotel and the only public gardens in North Cornwall comprise the twin attractions of the **Long Cross Hotel & Victorian Gardens.** The hotel was originally built as a Victorian gentleman's residence and later converted to an hotel. Purchased by James and Sharon bishop in January 2005, the hotel has been beautifully refurbished with all the rooms receiving brand new bathrooms and interior design. Some of the rooms enjoy glorious sea views and many have the generous proportions, high ceilings and detailed features so favoured by the Victorians. The hotel has 14 elegant bedrooms, all with private bathrooms, central heating, colour TV and tea/coffee-making facilities. Many of the rooms have panoramic views. The hotel is able to cater for those who are less mobile with three rooms on the ground floor that are no more than four metres from the car park. The hotel boasts all modern creature comforts along with a stunning restaurant with terraces taking advantage of the expansive panoramic views.

Set in almost four acres of its own grounds and gardens overlooking the North Cornwall coast between Port Isaac and Port Quin, the Long Cross is in a perfect secluded location to enjoy a quiet, relaxing break yet is within easy striking distance of some of the area's best attractions. Rock and the Camel Estuary with their sailing and watersports and easy ferry access to Padstow; the championship golf course at St Enodoc, Daymer Bay and Polzeath; surfing beaches, historic Port Isaac fishing village; the local market town of Wadebridge with cycle hire

for the Camel Trail to Padstow; and the diversity of Bodmin Moor are all within a 20-minute drive. The Eden Project is 40 minutes away; Tate St Ives about an 80-minute drive.

Located adjacent to the hotel are Long Cross Victorian Gardens which were the subject of a TV documentary because of their unusual aspects. They were constructed primarily to overcome the difficulties of the local climate. North Cornwall is England's windiest area with strong winds laden with salt even in the summer, a fact that results in the garden receiving more than one hundredweight of salt per acre, per year. So most of the shrubs in the garden have shiny or leathery leaves to provide protection against the salt. Plants are available to buy at the gardens, including some of the 18 herbs that are grown here.

🏠 historic building 🏛 museum and heritage 🏚 historic site ♤ scenic attraction ↟ flora and fauna

Tregeare Rounds, nr Port Isaac

uninterrupted since Tudor times and it is known that, in around 2000BC Beaker Folk on Bodmin Moor used slate as baking shelves. The huge crater of **Delabole Slate Quarry** is over half a mile wide and 500 feet deep – making it the largest man-made hole in the country. Although the demand for traditional building materials declined during the 20th century, the quarry is still worked and there are occasional slate splitting demonstrations.

To the southwest of the village stands the first wind farm in Britain, **Delabole Wind Farm**, which became operational in 1991. It produces enough power each year to satisfy more than half the annual demands of both Delabole and Camelford. The 30m-tall turbines provide an unusual landmark and at the heart of the farm is the **Gaia Energy Centre** where visitors can learn all about the past, present and future of renewable energy. One of the many striking exhibits is a giant steel and glass waterwheel. The centre has a café and shop, a picnic area and easy access and facilities for disabled visitors.

Among the finds uncovered were pottery fragments thought to be more than 2,000 years old. It is believed to be the Castle Terrible in Thomas Malory's 15th century epic, *Morte D'Arthur*. Here Uther Pendragon laid siege and killed the Earl of Cornwall because he had fallen in love with the earl's beautiful wife, Igerna.

Just over a mile inland, close to the village of Trelights, lies the only public garden along this stretch of North Cornwall coast – **Long Cross Victorian Gardens** (see panel opposite), a real garden lover's delight. Located next to the Long Cross Hotel the gardens' imaginative planting and superb panoramic views make it a very special place. Other attractions here include a secret garden and a fascinating Victorian maze.

DELABOLE
3 miles S of Tintagel on the B3314

🏛 Gaia Energy Centre   ⛏ Delabole Slate Quarry

Home to the most famous slate quarry in Cornwall, Delabole is almost literally built of slate. It has been used here for houses, walls, steps and the church. The high quality dark blue slate has been quarried here

CAMELFORD
4 miles SE of Tintagel on the A39

🏛 North Cornwall Museum

🏛 British Cycling Museum

This small and historic old market town, on the banks of the River Camel, prospered on the woollen trade. Around its central small square are some pleasant 18th and 19th century houses. The **North Cornwall Museum and Gallery**, housed in a converted coach house, displays aspects of life in this

---

🎭 stories and anecdotes   🐦 famous people   🎨 art and craft   🎟 entertainment and sport   🥾 walks

area throughout the 20th century as well as the reconstruction of a 19th century moorland cottage. Just to the north of the town and housed in the former railway station is the **British Cycling Museum**, whose exhibits include more than 400 cycles, an old cycle repair shop, a gallery of framed cycling pictures, an extensive library and a history of cycling from 1818. Close by, on the riverbank at Slaughter Bridge, lies a 6th century slab that is said to mark the place where King Arthur fell at the Battle of Camlann in 539AD, defeated by his nephew Mordred. The **Arthurian Centre** houses the Land of Arthur exhibition and also contains an information room (including brass rubbing and a video presentation), a play area, a refreshment area and a shop stocked with Arthurian books and gifts.

BOSCASTLE

3 miles NE of Tintagel on the B3263

🏠 Museum of Witchcraft   🦢 Thomas Hardy

On August 16th, 2004, torrential rain fell on the hills above the picturesque fishing village of Boscastle and within hours its main street was filled with a turbulent torrent of water sweeping everything before it towards the sea. Vivid television pictures recorded the dramatic scenes as cars were jostled along like toys on the surging waves, and residents were winched by helicopters from their rooftops. Astonishingly, no-one died and no-one was seriously injured in the calamity, but most of the houses in the path of the flood were rendered uninhabitable. Insurance companies estimated that claims would exceed half a billion pounds.

Before this disaster, Boscastle was best known for its picture-postcard qualities and its associations with the novelist Thomas Hardy. The village stands in a combe at the head of a remarkable S-shaped inlet that shelters it from the Atlantic Ocean. The only natural harbour between Hartland Point and Padstow, Boscastle's inner jetty was built by the renowned Elizabethan, Sir Richard Grenville, when the village was prospering as a fishing, grain and slate port. The outer jetty, or breakwater, dates from the 19th century when Boscastle had grown into a busy commercial port handling coal, timber, slate and china clay. Because of the dangerous harbour entrance, ships were towed into it by rowing boats – a blowhole in the outer harbour still occasionally sends up plumes of spray.

Next to the slipway where the River Valency meets the sea is the **Museum of Witchcraft** (see panel opposite) which suffered badly in the floods of August 2004. It re-opened the following Easter and once again boasts the world's largest collection of witchcraft related artefacts and regalia. Visitors can also learn all about witches, their lives, their spells, their charms and their curses.

Boscastle Harbour

Even before the floods, Boscastle was becoming familiar to viewers of BBC2's documentary series, *A Seaside Parish,* which followed the arrival of a new vicar, the Revd Christine Musser, in the village and recorded her role in its various activities. The series later detailed the aftermath of the inundation which included visits by Prince Charles and the Revd Musser's fictional TV equivalent, Dawn French's *Vicar of Dibley.*

The spectacular slate headlands on either side of Boscastle's harbour mouth provide some excellent, if rather demanding, walking. This stretch of tortuous coastline is not only of ecological importance but also historic. An Iron Age earthwork can be seen across the promontory at Willapark, and there is a 19th century lookout tower on the summit.

From the village there is a footpath that follows the steep wooded Valency Valley to the hidden hamlet of **St Juliot** which appears as 'Endelstow' in one of **Thomas Hardy**'s novels. As a young architect, Hardy worked on the restoration of the church and it was here, in 1870, that he met his future wife, Emma Gifford, the rector's sister-in-law. Emma later professed that the young architect had already appeared to her in a dream and wrote how, on first meeting him, she was "immediately arrested by his familiar appearance". Much of the couple's courtship took place along this wild stretch of coastline between Boscastle and Crackington Haven. When Emma died more than 40 years later, Hardy returned to St

Museum of Witchcraft

The Harbour, Boscastle, Cornwall PL35 0HD
Tel: 01840 250111
e-mail: museumwitchcraft@aol.com
website: www.museumofwitchcraft.com

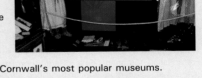

The **Museum of Witchcraft** in Boscastle houses the world's largest collection of witchcraft related artefacts and regalia. The museum has been located in Boscastle for over 40 years and despite severe damage in recent floods, it remains one of Cornwall's most popular museums.

The fascinating displays cover all aspects of witchcraft and include Divination, Sea Witchcraft, Spells and Charms, Modern Witchcraft, Herbs & Healing, Ritual Magic, Satanism and Hare & Shapeshifting.

One exhibit features the burial of Joan Wytte who was born in Bodmin, Cornwall, in 1775 and died of bronchial pneumonia in Bodmin Jail in 1813. She was a renowned clairvoyant and healer but became aggressive and impatient due to an untreated abscess in her tooth and people came to believe she was possessed by the devil. She became known as 'The Fighting Fairy Woman' and was imprisoned for grievous bodily harm.

Her skeleton came into the possession of the Museum of Witchcraft and was exhibited there for many years. Eight years ago the museum team believed she deserved a proper burial and Joan was finally laid to rest in 1998.

Among the other artefacts to be seen here are an amazing collection of figures and dolls, carved plates and stones, jewellery, cauldrons, weapons and unpleasant devices used for extracting confessions! A stair lift is available for those with limited mobility.

🎞 stories and anecdotes 🪶 famous people 🎨 art and craft 🎭 entertainment and sport 🚶 walks

THE EDGCUMBE

Summerleaze Crescent, Bude, Cornwall EX23 8HJ
Tel: 01288 353846 Fax: 01288 355256
e-mail: info@edgcumbe-hotel.co.uk
website: www.edgcumbe-hotel.co.uk

The Edgcumbe occupies a superb beach location enjoying panoramic views over Summerleaze Beach, the Downs and the valley of the river Neet. It is only a two-minute walk from the hotel to Bude town centre and other facilities in this attractive Cornish town. The Edgcumbe has undergone an exciting refurbishment to offer chic seaside style with relaxed and professional service.

The hotel is owned and run by Lee Norman, his wife Emma and his sister-in-law Jo Green who has been in the hotel business for some 11 years. The Edgcumbe has its own restaurant which is also open to non-residents and there is a separate bar. There are 12 ensuite guest bedrooms, (six doubles; two single; three triple; and one twin), all attractively furnished and decorated with modern accessories. Also available are a deluxe double suite with lounge and a deluxe double with luxury bathroom.

The Edgcumbe has a warm welcoming atmosphere and offers a comfortable tranquil base from which to enjoy one of the most spectacular stretches of coastline in Britain.

SUNRISE

Burn View, Bude, Cornwall EX23 8BY
Tel: 01288 353214
e-mail: sunriseguest@btconnect.com
website: www.sunrise-bude.co.uk

Ideally located in the heart of Bude, **Sunrise** is a beautifully refurbished Victorian house offering contemporary bed & breakfast accommodation. It has been awarded four stars and a Silver Award by Enjoy England for the quality of its service, food and accommodation.

The home of Lesley Sharratt, Sunrise has seven guest bedrooms, all en suite and with a choice of single, twin, triple, double and family rooms. One of the doubles is on the ground floor. All rooms are equipped with TV, video, hair dryer, radio, a well-stocked hospitality tray, toiletries, bath robes and even wine glasses and a corkscrew. After a restful night's sleep, guests can enjoy one of Lesley's renowned breakfasts which include traditional English, fish, vegetarian and continental, together with an extensive buffet bar of fruit, juices and yoghurts. Delicious home-cooked evening meals are available by arrangement.

Sunrise has wireless internet access, and well-behaved dogs are welcome. Golf breaks with discounted fees on local courses are available for one to five nights. Sunrise actually overlooks the golf course, is just a few moments walk from two beaches, one of them a Blue Flag beach, and is close to the numerous shops, restaurants and cafés of the town centre.

🏛 historic building 🏚 museum and heritage 🏯 historic site 🏞 scenic attraction 🌱 flora and fauna

Juliot to erect a memorial to her in the church. Following his death in 1928 a similar memorial was erected to Hardy.

CRACKINGTON HAVEN

7½ miles NE of Tintagel off the B3263

One of the most dramatic places along this remarkable stretch of coastline, this tiny port is overlooked by towering 400-foot cliffs, which make it Cornwall's highest coastal point. The small and narrow sandy cove is approached down a steep-sided wooded combe. It is difficult to see how sizeable vessels once landed here to deliver their cargoes of limestone and Welsh coal. Just to the south of Crackington Haven the path leads to a remote beach, curiously named **The Strangles**, where at low tide large patches of sand are revealed amongst the vicious looking rocks. During one year alone in the 1820s, some 20 ships were said to have come to grief here. The undercurrents are strong and swimming is always unsafe.

Bude Canal

Bude

| 🚶 Bude Canal Trail | 🏰 Bude Castle |
| 🏛 Town Museum | 🔭 Bude Light 2000 |

A traditional seaside resort with sweeping expanses of sand, rock pools and Atlantic breakers, Bude has plenty to offer holidaymakers and coastal walkers. A popular surfing centre, said to be where British surfing began, the town is a much favoured holiday destination in summer. However, during the winter, gales can turn this into a remote and harsh environment.

The **Bude Canal,** built in the early 1820s, was an ambitious project that aimed to connect the Atlantic with the English Channel via the River Tamar. However, the only stretch to be finished was that between Bude and Launceston. It was a remarkable feat of engineering as the sea lock at the entrance to the canal was the only lock even though it ran for 35 miles and rose to a height of 350 feet in six miles. In order to achieve the changes in level a series of inclined planes, or ramps, were used between the different levels and a wheeled tub boat was pulled up the ramps on metal rails. It finally closed to commercial craft in 1912 and now only two miles of the canal are passable. The **Bude Canal Trail** follows this tranquil backwater through some wonderfully peaceful and unspoilt countryside.

Close to the entrance to the canal stands **Bude Castle**, an unusually small fortification with no towers or turrets, designed by the local 19th century physician, scientist and inventor, Sir Goldsworthy Gurney. It is now an office building but is particularly interesting because it is thought to be the first building in Britain to be constructed on sand. The castle rests on a concrete raft - a technique developed by Gurney. Among his other

RANDOM

4 Lansdown Road, Bude, Cornwall EX23 8BH
Tel: 01288 256033
e-mail: randomcornwall@aol.com
website: www.randomartcornwall.com

Opened in November 2007, **Random** is a stylish art gallery owned and run by artist Susan Taylor who is Cornish through and through. She grew up in Polzeath and her own work is deeply influenced by the north Cornwall coast.

She has a degree in Art, Design and Media from the College of St Marks and St Johns and felt that there were few galleries in the very north of Cornwall dedicated to contemporary art. So she opened her own to promote the work of south-west artists, makers and craftspeople.

In addition to Susan's own striking pieces, the gallery is currently displaying the work of painters Ben Langton, Sally Hewitt, Sara Gilbert and Jess Jones; pottery by Caroline Curtis and the Welcombe Pottery; Angel ceramics from Devon; and jewellery from Cornish maker Carol Allen.

LOOKING 4 NEVALAND

27 Belle Vue, Bude, Cornwall EX23 8JL
Tel: 01288 354983
e-mail: claire@looking4nevaland.com
website: www.looking4nevaland.com

Inspired by JM Barrie's Peter Pan, **Looking 4 Nevaland** is a fascinating themed shop focussed around pirates, fairies and mermaids. Owner Claire Damree opened her shop in the autumn of 2007, having moved from Hampshire with the desire of wanting a change. She has filled the shop with a colourful range of items which, says Claire, are aimed at both children and adults.

Pirates of the Caribbean feature prominently, naturally, and a popular gift for children is a miniature pirate's chest. Here they can make up their own chest or choose from one of the gift sets that are available; filled with coins, jewels, necklaces, rings and even a One Million Dollar Gold Doubloon Bill.

Also popular are the fairy figurines by Amy Brown, fancy dress costumes, novelties, Jolly Roger flags, Charlotte Bird prints and cards, Nene Thomas figurines and Nevaland's own T-shirts. Harry Potter collectables are also available. As Claire says: "Our main aim is to keep children and adults young at heart!"

🏚 historic building 🏛 museum and heritage 🏛 historic site 🗺 scenic attraction 🌿 flora and fauna

inventions were a steam jet, a musical instrument consisting of glasses played as a piano, and the Bude Light, an intense light obtained by introducing oxygen into the interior flame and using mirrors. He used this to light his own house and also to light the House of Commons, where his invention replaced 280 candles and gave rise to the expression 'in the limelight'. The Bude Light served the House of Commons for 60 years and earned Gurney a knighthood.

Bude Bay

To celebrate the new millennium, Carole Vincent and Anthony Fanshawe designed the **Bude Light 2000**, the first large-scale public sculpture to combine coloured concrete with fibre optic lighting. It stands close to the castle and was officially opened in June 2000 by the Duke of Gloucester.

The history of the town and its canal can be

LANGFIELD MANOR

Broadclose, Bude, Cornwall EX23 8DP
Tel: 01288 352415
e-mail: langfieldmanor@btconnect.com
website:www.langfieldmanor.co.uk

Set next to the Bude and North Cornwall golf course, **Langfield Manor** is a fine Edwardian manor that has been converted into eight individual self-catering apartments. Three of these are on the ground floor, the remainder are on the first floor. The excellent facilities at the Manor are for the exclusive use of guests and include a covered, heated outdoor pool and a full size snooker table. Guests can also enjoy table tennis, pool or other games in the recreation room, and there is also a barbecue area for outside grilling. The conservatory and patio are real sun traps while the south-facing gardens are perfect for relaxing.

Each of the apartments has its own private entrance hall, lounge with widescreen TV and DVD player, and dining area. They have either one, two or three bedrooms and a well-fitted kitchen equipped with a fridge, microwave and conventional oven. All apartments have showers and five have baths and showers. There is a separate laundry room with two washing machines and a tumble dryer.

Langfield Manor is close to some of the finest beaches in the country and to the picturesque villages of Clovelly and Boscastle, while the Eden Project is within easy driving distance.

📰 stories and anecdotes 🐦 famous people 🎨 art and craft 🎭 entertainment and sport 🚶 walks

explored in the **Town Museum**, which stands on the canal side in a former blacksmith's forge. The story of Bude and the surrounding area, including shipwrecks, railways, farming and geology, is told in a series of vivid displays. One of the high spots in the Bude calendar is the annual jazz festival, held in August and featuring numerous performances, street parades, jazz workshops - even jazz church services.

Around Bude

STRATTON
2 miles NE of Bude on the A39

This ancient market town and one time port is believed to have been founded by the Romans. During the Civil War, the town was a stronghold of the Royalists and their commander, Sir Bevil Grenville, made **The Tree Inn** his centre of operations. (The inn is of interest in its own right as it is constructed from the timbers of wrecked ships). In May 1643, at the Battle of Stamford Hill, Grenville led his troops to victory over the Parliamentarians and the dead of both sides were buried in unmarked graves in Stratton churchyard. The battle is re-enacted in mid-May each year. The Tree Inn was also the birthplace of the Cornish giant, Anthony Payne, Sir Bevil's bodyguard who stood over seven feet tall. They fought together both here and later at Lansdown Hill, near Bath, where Grenville was killed. After helping Grenville's son lead the Royalists to victory, Payne carried his master's body back to Stratton. After the Civil War, Payne continued to live at the Grenville manor house until his death. When he died, the house had to be altered to allow his coffin to pass through the doorway.

LAUNCELLS
2½ miles E of Bude off the A3072

🏠 Church of St Swithin

Set in a delightful wooded combe, the 15th century **Church of St Swithin** was acclaimed by Sir John Betjeman as "the least spoilt church in Cornwall". It is notable for its fine Tudor bench-ends and for 15th century floor tiles made in Barnstaple. In the churchyard is the grave of the remarkable Sir Goldsworthy Gurney (1793-1875) whose inventions included a prototype of incandescent lighting, the high-pressure steam jet, and steam-driven coaches that achieved a steady 15mph.

KILKHAMPTON
4 miles NE of Bude on the A39

The tall and elegant Church of St James contains monuments to the local Grenville family, many of them the work of Michael Chuke, a local man and a pupil of Grinling Gibbons. Equally notable are the magnificent carved bench-ends, and the organ is one played by Henry Purcell when it was installed in Westminster Abbey.

MORWENSTOW
5 miles N of Bude off the A39

🗣 Revd Stephen Hawker   🏠 Rectory

🏠 Hawker's Hut

Used to taking the full brunt of Atlantic storms, this tiny village lies on the harshest stretch of the north Cornwall coast. Although it can sometimes seem rather storm-lashed, it is a marvellous place from which to watch the changing moods of the ocean. Not surprisingly, shipwrecks have been common along this stretch of coast. Many came to grief in storms, but it was not unknown for local criminals to lure unsuspecting ships onto

Morwenstow Church

Though a bizarre character, Hawker was also one of the first people to show concern at the number of ships coming to grief along this stretch of coastline. He spent hours monitoring the waves and would often climb down the cliffs to rescue shipwrecked crews or recover the bodies of those who had perished among the waves. After carrying the bodies back to the village he would give them a proper Christian burial. One of the many ships wrecked off Sharpnose headland was the *Caledonia*, whose figurehead stands above the grave of her captain in Morwenstow churchyard.

Hawker's other contribution to Morwenstow was the **Rectory**, which he built at his own expense and to his own design. As individual as the man himself, the chimneys of the house represent the towers of various churches and Oxford colleges; the broad kitchen chimney is in remembrance of his mother. His lasting contribution to the church was to reintroduce the annual Harvest Festival and his most famous poem is the rousing Cornish anthem, *The Song of Western Men*. The National Trust-owned land, between the church and the cliffs, is dedicated to this remarkable man's memory.

the rocks by lighting lanterns on the cliff tops or the shore.

The village's most renowned inhabitant was its eccentric vicar and poet, the **Reverend Robert Stephen Hawker**, who came here in 1834 and remained among his flock of "smugglers, wreckers and dissenters" until his death in 1875. A colourful figure dressed in a purple frock coat, fisherman's jersey, and fishing boots beneath his cassock, Hawker spent much of his time walking through his beloved countryside. When not walking he could often be found writing verses and smoking, opium by some accounts, in the driftwood hut that he built 17 steps from the top of the precipitous Vicarage Cliff. Now known as **Hawker's Hut**, it is the National Trust's smallest property.

To the north of the village is **Welcombe Mouth**, the graveyard of many ships that came to grief on its jagged rocks. Set back from the shore are the **Welcombe and Marsland Valleys** that are now a nature reserve and a haven for butterflies. To the south are the headlands, **Higher** and **Lower Sharpnose Points**. Rugged rocks, caused by erosion, lie above a boulder-strewn beach, while some of the outcrops of harder rock have begun to form tiny islands.

Lanhydrock House

Distance: *4.1 miles (6.5 kilometres)*
Typical time: *150 mins*
Height gain: *115 metres*
Map: *Explorer 107*
Walk: *www.walkingworld.com ID:1514*
Contributor: *Jim Grindle*

ACCESS INFORMATION:

The estate is just under two miles from Bodmin Parkway railway station from which the no. 55 bus runs. It is signposted from the A30, the A38 and the B3268.

DESCRIPTION:

This is an excellent walk for anybody with an interest in natural history. The trees in the parkland have on them over 100 species of lichens and there are also mosses, beetles and birds, including treecreeper, tawny owl, nuthatch and all three British woodpeckers. Nine of the 14 British bats can be found here and there is an abundance of grassland flowers. On the River

Fowey are otters and we saw lots of dippers and grey wagtails, more of the latter than I have seen anywhere else. You could spend a long time getting round. The walk is a mixture of woodland and river with a steady climb back up to the house.

ADDITIONAL INFORMATION

The National Trust describes the house as, "One of the most fascinating late 19th century houses in England, full of period atmosphere and the trappings of a high Victorian country house". There is enough time to visit the house and do this walk in a day, but obviously there is a lot to see both indoors and out.

FEATURES:

River, toilets, stately home, National Trust/ NTS, birds, flowers, butterflies, café, gift shop, good for kids, nature trail, restaurant, tea shop, woodland.

WALK DIRECTIONS:

1 | From the car park go back to its entrance and look for a path on the left. The low signpost directs you to reception and the house. Just out of sight is a gate giving access to a road. (There are toilets in the car park and a refreshment kiosk with limited opening hours.)

2 | From here you can see the award-winning reception building. Cross the road and pass to the right of it. You do not have to pay if you just intend doing the walk and you will be on a public footpath. Follow the main drive to the gatehouse outside the main house.

3 | Pass the gatehouse and follow the tarmac to the right where you will see a wooden gate in a corner.

4 | Go through and follow this drive. Don't take any of the smaller paths that join it,

including the one immediately to the left behind the gate. You will pass a house with the estate's kitchen gardens and go through a red gate. Almost 1km from this Waymark a track goes off to the right.

5 | Pass by it and where the main track curves right there is another which you also ignore. A few metres past this bend, though, a track joins from the left.

6 | This one you do want. Turn left and pass an old quarry as it leaves the wood to enter meadows. At the entrance to another wood is a gate.

7 | Go through and turn right. The track leads down, with more gates, to the banks of the River Fowey.

8 | Turn left and follow the river until you see a bridge. This is Kathleen Bridge, built in 1991 by the Royal Engineers. Cross and turn left following the river to an ancient stone bridge.

9 | Once over the bridge turn to the right into the car park and cross to a little footbridge.

10 | Go over the bridge onto Station Drive, a stone track. You will pass a large Giant Redwood just across the stream. Turn right and follow the track for 1km until you see a red, signposted metal gate on your left.

11 | Go through onto a lane and turn left - you will see a similar gate a few metres along on the far side of the road. This gives access to the wood. Turn left on any forks in the path - there are lots of yellow arrows on this stretch - so that you keep to the edge of the wood - you will be able to see the meadows outside for most of the way. When the path levels out it meets a forestry track at right angles. Turn left and follow it until you reach a road.

12 | Cross to the minor road directly opposite. Almost on the corner (on the right) is another of the red gates.

13 | Go through this - a path goes to the left, passing around the edge of a cricket field and then following a wall all the way round to the left to enter the back of the car park.

Bodmin Moor

BODMIN

10 miles SW of Bolventor on the A38

🏛 Castle Canyke   A St Petroc's Church

🏚 Bodmin Jail   ✎ Shire Hall Gallery

🏚 Lanhyrdrock House

🚲 Bodmin & Wenford Railway   ⚔ Saints' Way

Situated midway between Cornwall's two coasts and at the junction of two ancient trade routes, Bodmin has always been an important town used, particularly, by traders who preferred the overland journey to the sea voyage around Land's End. **Castle Canyke**, to the southeast, was built during the Iron Age to defend this important route. A few centuries later, the Romans erected a fort (one of a string they built to defend strategic river crossings) on a site here above the River Camel. The way-marked footpath, the **Saints' Way**, follows the ancient cross-country route. In the 6th century, St Petroc, one of the most influential of the early Welsh missionary saints, visited Bodmin. In the 10th century, the monastery he had founded at Padstow moved here as a protection against Viking raiders. The present **St Petroc's Church** is the largest parish church in Cornwall at 151ft long and 65ft wide. Part of the tower contains masonry of the Norman period, but most of the present building was built between 1469 and 1472. It is one of the few churches of the period of which building records survive almost complete. The Mayor's accounts are preserved at the County Records Office in Truro. The total recorded cost was £196 7s 4d (about half a million pounds today). The 'furniture' - pulpit, screens and seats - cost £92 under a separate contract with one Mathy More in 1491. The timber was bought in Wales and some of this original woodwork is incorporated in the present screens and priests' seats. In the churchyard can be found one of the many holy wells in Bodmin – **St Goran's Well** – which dates from the 6th century.

The only market town in Cornwall to appear in the Domesday Book, Bodmin was chiefly an ecclesiastical town until the reign of Henry VIII. However, this did not mean that it was a quiet and peaceful place. During the Tudor reign, it was the scene of three uprisings: against the tin levy in 1496, in support of Perkin Warbeck against Henry VII in 1597 and, in 1549, against the imposition of the English Prayer Book. The town's failure to flourish when the railways arrived in Cornwall was due to its decision not to allow the Great Western Railway access to the town centre. Not only did it fail to expand as other towns did but, when Truro became the seat of the new bishopric, Bodmin missed out again.

The Crown Jewels and the Domesday Book were hidden at **Bodmin Jail** during World War I and this former county prison, dating from 1776, is an interesting place to visit. The imposing Shire Hall, built in 1837, served as the County Court until 1988. Now restored, it brings to life in **The Courtroom Experience** the notorious murder in 1844 of Charlotte Dymond on lonely Bodmin Moor and the trial of Matthew Weeks for the crime. Visitors can participate in the drama of the trial as jurors and enter the chilling holding cells where convicted felons awaited their fate. The prison's gruesome history has attracted many paranormal investigations and it was recently a location for the popular Living TV's *Most Haunted* programme.

A second courtroom houses the **Shire Hall Gallery** which hosts a varied programme of Cornish and West County artists and craftspeople, as well as community exhibitions.

Bodmin Town Museum provides an insight into the town's past and that of the surrounding area. Just a short distance from the town centre is **Bodmin Beacon Local Nature Reserve**. From the beacon summit, on which stands the 114-foot Gilbert Memorial, there are splendid views over the town and moor. Also easily reached from Bodmin is the **Camel Trail**, a walking and cycling path along the River Camel to Padstow following the track bed of one of the country's first railways.

Housed in The Keep near the railway station in Bodmin, the **Duke of Cornwall's Light Infantry Regimental Museum** covers the military history of the County Regiment of Cornwall, The Duke of Cornwall's Light Infantry from its formation in 1702 to its eventual amalgamation with the Somerset Light Infantry in 1950. The Armoury contains a fine collection of small arms and machine guns. It also exhibits many of the colourful uniforms worn by the Regiment before 1914.

Nearby, Bodmin General Station is also the base for the **Bodmin and**

Bodmin and Wenford Railway

Wenford Railway, a former branch line of the Great Western Railway. The line closed to passenger traffic in 1963 but has been splendidly restored. Today, steam locomotives take passengers on a 13-mile round trip along a steeply graded line through beautiful countryside. There are occasional luncheon and dinner specials, and driving instruction is also available.

To the south of the town, near the village of Cutmadoc, stands one of the most fascinating late-19th century houses in England, the spectacular **Lanhydrock House** (National Trust - see walk on page 86). Surrounded by wonderful formal gardens, woodland and parkland, it originally belonged to Bodmin's Augustinian priory. The extensive estate was bought in 1620 by Sir Richard Robarts (who made his fortune in tin and wool) and his family lived here until the estate was given to the Trust in 1953. Although partially destroyed by fire in 1881, this mansion is probably the grandest in Cornwall. Visitors can see that many of the rooms combine the building's original splendour with the latest in Victorian domestic comforts and amenities. One special bedroom belonged to Tommy Agar-Robarts, who was killed at the Battle of Loos in 1915; it contains many of his personal possessions. The grounds are equally magnificent and are known for the fabulous springtime displays of rhododendrons, magnolias and camellias, a superb avenue of ancient beech and sycamore trees, a cob-and-thatch summer house and a photogenic formal garden overlooked by the small estate church of St Hydroc. In the woods are many unusual flowers and ferns as well as owls, woodpeckers and many other birds.

HELLAND BRIDGE POTTERY

Helland Bridge, Bodmin, Cornwall PL30 4QR
Tel: 01208 75240
e-mail: paul@paul-jackson.co.uk
website: www.paul-jackson.co.uk

Occupying a former chapel, **Helland Bridge Pottery** stands beside the River Camel and is home to three potters, each with a distinctive style. The unique character of Paul Jackson's work derives from two interrelated processes. Each piece is first thrown on the wheel, then subtly altered in form - giving the pot an individual character and strength defined by a journey of discovery. The journey continues during decoration, where the pot's elegance and sense of balance grow directly out of Paul's concern for harmony between form, colour, and the painted surface. The guiding force behind all of Paul's work is energy: sinuous forms creating sensations of movement and life, and the possibilities for change which are always present in the wet clay but are only revealed once the exploration has begun. Rosie Jackson's

work reflects her botanical interests and her fascinating ceramics include tulips and a magnolia design originally created for Caerhayes Castle. Jethro Jackson's pots focus on his love of the sea and estuary bird life and have a unique Japanese flavour. Jethro is also an accomplished artist, specialising in landscapes and paintings of birds. The Pottery does not have fixed opening times but can be visited by appointment.

Around Bodmin

BLISLAND
5 miles N of Bodmin off the A30

🏛 Church of St Protus

Hidden in a maze of country lanes, this moorland village has a tree-lined village green that has stayed true to its original Saxon layout – an unusual sight on this side of the River Tamar. The part-Norman parish **Church of St Protus and St Hyacinth,** was one of Sir John Betjeman's favourites, described by the poet as "dazzling and amazing". The church was restored with great sensitivity in the 1890s by the architect FC Eden who also designed the sumptuously coloured Gothic screen that dominates the interior.

On the moorland to the north of the village are numerous ancient monuments including the stone circle of Blisland Manor Common and Stipple Stone Henge Monument on Hawkstor Down.

BOLVENTOR
10 miles NE of Bodmin off the A30

🏛 Daphne du Maurier   🏛 Dozmary Pool
🏛 Museum of Smuggling   🏛 Roughtor
🏛 Museum of Curiosity   🏛 King Arthur

Right at the heart of Bodmin Moor, this scenic village is the location of the former coaching inn, immortalised by **Daphne du Maurier** in her famous novel, *Jamaica Inn* (1936). During the 18th and 19th centuries this isolated hostelry, on the main route across the bleak moorland, provided an ideal meeting place for smugglers and other outlaws as well as legitimate travellers journeying between

---

TORR HOUSE COTTAGES

Torr House, Blisland, Cornwall PL30 4JH
Tel: 01208 851601   Mobile: 07889 790815
e-mail: contact@torrhousecottages.co.uk
website: www.torrhousecottages.co.uk

Located in the delightful village of Blisland with its old granite cottages, church and pub nestling around the village green, **Torr House Cottages** offer luxury accommodation in a quiet away-from-it-all location, yet less than half an hour from outstanding beaches, coastal paths and popular visitor attractions. The cottages are set in more than 2 acres of peaceful, landscaped gardens with wonderful views stretching for miles and, being equi-distant from north and south coasts, are the perfect base for enjoying all that Cornwall has to offer.

Both of the four-star cottages are very well-appointed and fully equipped with central heating, TV/DVD, and CD/radio. Hollyhock Cottage is exceptionally spacious and is fully accessible for wheelchair users. There is a large and comfortable lounge opening onto the patio, a well-equipped kitchen together with a spacious dining area. The cottage has three bedrooms and can sleep up to six guests. Appletree Cottage is smaller and enjoys glorious views from both lounge and kitchen. It is accessed by stone steps from the original barn and is suitable for up to four people. Bed linen and towels are provided and there are cycles available to borrow. There's also a discrete play area for children.

🏛 historic building 🏛 museum and heritage 🏛 historic site 🏛 scenic attraction 🌿 flora and fauna

Cornwall and the rest of England. Today, as well as providing hospitality, the inn has a **Museum of Smuggling** "devoted to the arts of concealment and evasion" which the arch villain, Demon Darvey, the vicar of Altarnum demonstrates with the aid of tableaux. There's also a room dedicated to the memory of Daphne du Maurier which is full of memorabilia of the writer including her Sheraton writing desk on top of which is a packet of du Maurier cigarettes named after her father, the actor Gerald du Maurier. There's also a dish of Glacier Mints – Dame Daphne's favourite sweets.

Yet another attraction here is Mr Potter's **Museum of Curiosity**, a fascinating collection of some 10,000 items gathered by the Victorian taxidermist Walter Potter. Exhibits include the Death and Burial of Cock Robin, Victorian toys and dolls' houses, smoking memorabilia and a variety of strange oddities.

Bodmin Moor, the bleak expanse of moorland surrounding Bolventor, is the smallest of the three great West Country moors and an Area of Outstanding Natural Beauty. Its granite upland is characterised by saturated moorland and weather-beaten tors. From here the rivers Inny, Lynher, Fowey, St Neot and De Lank flow to both the north and south coasts of Cornwall. In this wild countryside roams the Beast of Bodmin, an elusive catlike creature which could be an escaped puma or panther – or just another creation of the fertile Cornish imagination.

At 1,377 feet, **Brown Willy** is the highest point of Bodmin Moor, and Cornwall, while, just to the northwest, rises **Roughtor** (pronounced 'row tor' to rhyme with 'now tor'), the moor's second highest point. Standing on National Trust-owned land, Roughtor is a magnificent viewing point and also the site of a memorial to the men of the Wessex Regiment who were killed during World War II.

Throughout this wild and beautiful moorland there are scattered Bronze Age hut circles and field enclosures and Iron Age hill forts. Many villages in and around the moor grew up around the monastic cells of Celtic missionaries and took the names of saints. Others were mining villages where ruined engine houses still stand out against the skyline.

To the south of Bolventor is the mysterious natural tarn, **Dozmary Pool**, a place firmly linked with the legend of **King Arthur**. Brought here following his final battle at Slaughter Bridge, the king lay dying at the water's edge, listening to *"the ripple washing in the reeds, and the wild water lapping on the crag"* as Tennyson described it in his poem *The Passing of Arthur*. Close to death, Arthur asked his friend, Sir Bedivere, to throw his sword Excalibur into the centre of the pool. As the knight did so a lady's arm *"clothed in white samite,*

Roughtor, Bodmin Moor

stories and anecdotes   famous people   art and craft   entertainment and sport   walks

mystic, wonderful" rose from the waters to receive the sword. Dozmary is not the only lake to claim the Lady of the Lake – Loe Pool at Mount's Bay, and Bosherstone and Llyn Llydaw in Wales are also put forward as alternative resting places for Excalibur.

This desolate and isolated place is also linked with Jan Tregeagle, the wicked steward of the Earl of Radnor whose many evil deeds included the murder of the parents of a young child whose estate he wanted. As a punishment, so the story goes, Tregeagle was condemned to spend the rest of time emptying the lake with a leaking limpet shell. His howls of despair are still said to be heard to this day.

By tradition, Dozmary Pool is bottomless, although it did dry up completely during a prolonged drought in 1869. Close by is the county's largest man-made reservoir, **Colliford Lake**. At 1,000 feet above sea level, it is the perfect habitat for long tailed ducks, dippers and grey wagtails, and rare plants such as the heath-spotted and frog orchids.

TREWINT
13 miles NE of Bodmin off the A30

John Wesley   Wesley Cottage

This handsome village often played host to **John Wesley**, the founder of Methodism, on his preaching tours of Cornwall. One of the villagers, Digory Isbell, built an extension to his house for the use of Wesley and his preachers, and **Wesley Cottage** is open for visits. The rooms, thought to be the smallest Methodist preaching place in the world, have been maintained as they were in the 18th century, and visitors can see the prophets' room and the pilgrims' garden. Digory Isbell and his wife are buried in Trewint churchyard.

ALTARNUN
14 miles NE of Bodmin off the A30

Cathedral of the Cornish Moors

This moorland village, charmingly situated in a steep-sided valley, is home to a splendid, 15th century parish church that is often referred to as the '**Cathedral of the Cornish Moors**'. Dedicated to St Nonna, the mother of St David of Wales, the church has a 108-feet pinnacled tower that rises high above the river. Inside, it is surprisingly light and airy, with features ranging from Norman times through to 16th century bench end carvings. In the churchyard stands a

Celtic Cross, Laneast

Celtic cross, thought to date from the time of St Nonna's journey here from Wales in around 527AD. The waters of nearby St Nonna's well were once thought to cure madness. After immersion in the waters, lunatics were carried into the church for mass. The process was repeated until the patient showed signs of recovery.

Just to the northwest, near the peaceful village of St Clether, is another holy well, standing on a bracken-covered shelf above the River Inny beside its 15th century chapel. To the north is **Laneast** where yet another of Bodmin Moor's holy wells is housed in a 16th century building, close to a tall Celtic cross and the village's original Norman church. Laneast was also the birthplace of John Adams, the astronomer who discovered the planet Neptune.

This Bronze Age temple comprising three circles takes its name from the ancient game of hurling, the Celtic form of hockey. Legend has it that the circles were men who were caught playing the game on the Sabbath. As a punishment, they were turned to stone. The **Cheesewring**, a natural pile of granite slabs whose appearance is reminiscent of a cheese press, also lies close to the village. Again, legends have grown up around these stones. One, which is probably true, involves Daniel Gumb, a local stonecutter who was a great reader and taught himself both mathematics and astronomy. He married a local girl and they supposedly made their home in a cave under the Cheesewring. Before the cave collapsed, numerous intricate carvings could be seen on

MINIONS
16 miles NE of Bodmin off the B3254

Minions Heritage Centre　Golitha Falls

Hurlers Stone Circle

Boasting the highest pub in Cornwall, this moorland village was a thriving mining centre during the 19th and early 20th centuries with miners and quarrymen extracting granite, copper and lead from the surrounding area. It was also the setting for EV Thompson's historical novel, *Chase the Wind*. One of the now disused mine engine houses has become the **Minions Heritage Centre**. It covers more than 4,000 years of life on the moorland, including the story of mining along with the life and times of much earlier settlers.

Close to the village stands the impressive **Hurlers Stone Circle**.

Cheesewring, Minions

stories and anecdotes　famous people　art and craft　entertainment and sport　walks

the walls, including the inscription "D Gumb 1735". Another story tells that the Cheesewring was once the haunt of a Druid who would offer thirsty passers-by a drink from a golden chalice that never ran dry. The discovery at nearby Rillaton Barrow, in 1890, of a ribbed cup of beaten gold lying beside a skeleton gave credence to the story. The chalice, known as the Rillaton Cup, is displayed in the British Museum.

Just to the northeast lies Upton Cross, the home of **Cornish Yarg Cheese**. Made since 1983 in the beautiful Lynher Valley, this famous cheese with its distinctive flavour comes wrapped in nettle leaves. The local delicacy reaches many of the best restaurants and delicatessen counters in the country. Visitors can watch the milking of the dairy herd and the cheese-making process, follow the pond and woodland trails and enjoy cheese tastings.

South of Minions and not far from the sizeable moorland village of St Cleer, is another holy well, **St Cleer's Holy Well**, also thought to have curative powers. There are several other reminders of the distant past. Dating back to Neolithic times, **Trethevy Quoit** is an impressive enclosed chamber tomb that originally formed the core of a vast earthwork mound. The largest such structure in Cornwall, this quoit is believed to be more than 5,000 years old. Just to the west stands a tall stone cross, **King Doniert's Stone**, erected in memory of King Durngarth, a Cornish king, believed to have drowned in the River Fowey in 875AD. Downstream from the Stone the River Fowey descends through dense broadleaved woodland in a delightful series of cascades known as **Golitha Falls**. This outstanding and well-known beauty spot is a National Nature Reserve.

WARLEGGAN
11 miles E of Bodmin off the A38

[f] Revd Frederick Densham   [flora] Cardinham Woods

Warleggan's most eccentric inhabitant was undoubtedly **Revd Frederick Densham**, who arrived at this tiny and remote hamlet in 1931. Immediately alienating his parishioners by closing the Sunday school, Densham continued by putting barbed wire around the rectory and patrolling the grounds with a pack of German Shepherd dogs. In response, his flock stayed away from his church and one record in the parish registry reads, "No fog. No wind. No rain. No congregation." Unperturbed, the rector fashioned his own congregation from cardboard, filled the pews and preached on as normal. It would, however, appear that Densham did have a gentler side to his nature, as he built a children's playground in the rectory garden.

To the north and west stretch the peaceful backwaters of **Cardinham Woods**, enjoyed by both walkers and cyclists. Acquired by the Forestry Commission in 1922, this attractive and varied woodland is a haven for a wide variety of wildlife as well as producing high quality Douglas Fir for the timber industry. In medieval times, the woods were the location of an important Norman castle belonging to the Cardinham family but all that remains today are an earthwork mound and a few traces of the original keep.

ST NEOT
11 miles E of Bodmin off the A38

[f] St Neot   [site] Carnglaze Slate Caverns

Once a thriving centre of the woollen industry, St Neot is famous for the splendid 15th century Church of St Anietus and, in particular, its fabulous early 16th century stained glass. Of the many beautiful scenes depicted here, perhaps the most interesting is that of **St Neot,** the diminutive saint after whom the village is named. Although only 15 inches tall, the saint became famous for his miracles involving animals. One story tells of an exhausted hunted doe which ran to St Neot's side. A stern look from the saint sent the pursuing hounds back into the forest while the huntsman dropped his bow and became a faithful disciple. Another tale depicted in the church window tells of an angel giving the saint three fish for his well and adding that as long as he only eats one fish a day there will always be fish to eat. Unfortunately, when St Neot fell ill, his servant took two fish and prepared them for his master. Horrified, Neot prayed over the meal, ordering the fish be returned to the well and, as they touched the water, they came alive again.

Tied to the tower outside the church is an oak branch that is replaced annually on Oak Apple Day. The ceremony was started by Royalists wishing to give thanks for the oak tree that hid Charles II during his flight from the country.

To the south of St Neot are the **Carnglaze Slate Caverns** where slate for use in the building trade was first quarried in the 14th century. Today, visitors can journey underground and see the large chambers that were once used by smugglers as rum stores and the subterranean lake that is filled with the clearest blue-green water.

LISKEARD

13 miles E of Bodmin on the B3254

🌲 Dobwalls Adventure Park 🐾 Looe Valley Line

Situated on the undulating ground between the valleys of the East Looe and Seaton Rivers, this picturesque and lively market town was one of Cornwall's five medieval stannary towns – the others being Bodmin, Lostwithiel, Truro and Helston. The name comes from the Latin for tin, '*stannum*', and these five towns were the only places licensed to weigh and stamp the metal. Liskeard had been a centre for the mining industry for centuries. However, by the 19th century, after the construction of a canal linking the town with Looe, vast quantities of copper ore and granite joined the cargoes of tin. In the 1850s, the canal was replaced by the Looe Valley branch of the Great Western Railway. An eight-mile long scenic stretch of the **Looe Valley Line** is still open today though the industrial wagons have long since been replaced with passenger carriages. The route hugs the steep-sided valley of the East Looe river and terminates in the coastal town of Looe.

Although it is a small town, Liskeard does boast some public buildings that act as a reminder of its past importance and prosperity. The Guildhall was constructed in 1859 while the Public Hall, opened in 1890, is still used as offices of the town council as well as being home to a local Museum. Adjacent to the Passmore-Edwards public library stands **Stuart House**, a handsome Jacobean residence where Charles I stayed in 1644 while engaged in a campaign against Cromwell at nearby Lostwithiel. Finally, in Well Street, is one of Liskeard's most curious features – an arched grotto that marks the site of Pipe Well, a medieval spring reputed to have had curative powers.

To the west of Liskeard is an attraction that will please all the family, **Porfell Animal Land Wildlife Park** at Trecongate. Within its 15 acres of fields bounded by streams and woodland, visitors can meet wallabies, marmosets, lemurs, zebra, meerkats and

PAINTERS

7 Fore Street, Liskeard, Cornwall PL14 3JA
Tel: 01579 347237
e-mail: shop@craft-box.com
website: www.craft-box.com

When you walk along (pedestrianised) Fore Street, in Liskeard, you will be pleasantly surprised to discover an emporium of art & crafts materials. Painters opened in 1998 and is striving to be one of the best art shops in the South West.

Louise Kidd runs the shop with a very enthusiastic and helpful team of staff all with diverse creative skills. As Louise is a trained textile artist, the shop specialises in textile art materials and is excellent for those taking City and Guilds or degrees, as there is so much under one roof - a wonderful range of dyes, paints, heat reactive materials, threads, fibres etc.

There is an excellent choice for the paper crafter with lots of card making products, including rubber stamps, ink pads and all sorts of embellishments, decoupage, pergamano supplies, scrapbooking papers and more.

There is a good range of patchwork fabrics and quilting supplies and an excellent selection of speciality knitting yarns from Designer Yarns, Noro, Colinette, Mission Falls and others. Also opal sock-knitting wool and felting fibres. Beads, charms and jewellery findings are ever-popular, with staff on hand to teach simple techniques at the counter.

The basement studio is a wonderful surprise where weekly classes are held in painting and sculpture as well as workshops and demonstrations of various crafts. It is also possible to shop online at www.craft-box.com.

The shop now caters for junior creativity, with a growing selection of children's art and craft materials, with kits, paints, modelling clays and facepaints. Upstairs there is a wonderful emporium of high quality toys and gifts.

Painters has teamed up with Ringinglow Toys, famous for their wonderful rocking horses (they are makers and restorers) and traditional wooden toys including sit-on motor bikes and dolls houses. The toys are designed and made with traditional fun in mind, the nursery playthings are a particular favourite along with the hand puppets and the rag dolls. Educational toys are also in stock; clocks, puzzles, shape toys,toolsets and rattles.

A special emphasis is placed on the high quality of manufacture, most of Ringinglows' toys are made in the EU and the UK, many of these items will become heirlooms to be passed down to future generations.

A magical place for children of all ages...1 to 101 years. Everyone is welcome.

HAYLOFT RISTORANTE

Lower Clicker Road, Menheniot, Liskeard,
Cornwall PL14 3PU
Tel/Fax: 01503 240241
website: www.hayloftristorante.co.uk

The well-respected head chef Vito Dell'Anno and his wife Lynda took over the **Hayloft Ristorante** in February 2006. Their restaurant occupies the former hayloft of Lower Clicker Farm and boasts impressive beamed ceilings and many character features. It looks particularly inviting when the room is candlelit.

Vito's extensive à la carte menu includes delicious traditional Italian and English cuisine created by Vito and his team of chefs. All dishes are freshly prepared to order using locally sourced meats, fresh fish and seafood, dairy produce and ice cream, fruits and vegetables. There is a children's menu and an excellent choice of vegetarian dishes and all of the delicious desserts are homemade too.

The Hayloft can cater for all your requirements, anything from intimate dinners and family gatherings to corporate functions, whether it be a full business luncheon or a simple buffet. Vito also offers a full outside catering service. The Hayloft is also Kernow's (Cornwall's) latest internet café, with internet access available via WiFi to your laptop. Full presentation facilities are also available, from flipcharts to flat screens.

HAYLOFT COURTYARD COTTAGES

Lower Clicker Road, Menheniot, Liskeard,
Cornwall PL14 3PU
Tel/Fax: 01503 240879
e-mail: courtyardcottage@btconnect.com
website: www.hayloftcourtyardcottages.com

The luxury four star **Hayloft Courtyard Cottages** are situated in a rural location just outside the village of Menheniot and only six miles from the popular resort of Looe. Nestled between the coast & moors they provide the perfect touring base from which to explore the many delights of Cornwall & West Devon. Cornish family run since 1988 the cottages have been lovingly converted from stone barns which once formed part of Lower Clicker Farm. They retain many original features including exposed beams & stonework and are well equipped with many "home from home" comforts.

There's a choice of either one, two or three bedroom properties which are available all year round. Rowan, Maple & Chesnut overlook the courtyard, whilst Pine, Elm & Walnut have views across the rolling Cornish countryside. All cottages are double-glazed and have central heating making them cosy & warm in the cooler months and all have newly fitted bathrooms with jacuzzi baths. Each cottage has digital flatscreen TV with DVD player, CD system and wireless broadband internet access. Within the 7 acre grounds there is a new heated outdoor swimming pool, hot tub, games room, children's play area & large field perfect for dog exercising. Arriving guests are greeted with a warm welcome & Cornish cream tea. Locally produced food hampers, delivered to the cottage are also available.

porcupines; feed the deer, goats, ducks and chickens, just stroll through the woods or relax in the tea room housed in an attractive old barn.

Looe

🏛 Old Guildhall Museum

🚶 Looe Valley Line Footpath

The tidal harbour at Looe, created by the two rivers the East Looe and West Looe, made this an important fishing and sea-faring port from the Middle Ages through to the 19th century. Originally, two separate towns on either side of the estuary, East and West Looe were first connected by a bridge in the early 15th century. In 1883, they were officially incorporated. The present day seven-arched bridge, dating from the 19th century, carries the main road and links the two halves of the town. Something of a jack-of-all-trades, over the years Looe has had a pilchard fishing fleet, it has served the mineral extractors of Bodmin Moor and is has also been the haunt of smugglers. However, it is only the fishing industry that remains from the town's colourful past. Looe is still Cornwall's second most important port with fish auctions taking place at East Looe's busy quayside market on the famous **Banjo Pier** which, actually part of the harbour wall with a circular area at its sea end, vaguely resembling a banjo.

Of the two distinct parts, East Looe, with its narrow cobbled streets and twisting alleyways, is the older. Here, housed in one of the town's several 16th century buildings, is the **Old Guildhall Museum**, where can be seen the old magistrates' bench and original cells as well as displays detailing much of Looe's history. After the opening of the Looe Valley Line to passengers in 1879, the development of the twin towns as a holiday resort began. Fortunately, the character of East Looe has been retained while West Looe is, essentially, a residential area.

The Looe Valley Line railway replaced the Liskeard to Looe canal and today the same journey can be made by following the **Looe Valley Line Footpath**. A distance of 10 miles, the walk takes in some of Cornwall's most beautiful woodlands as well as the 'Giant's Hedge', a seven-foot earth embankment.

More recently, Looe has established itself as Britain's major shark fishing centre and regularly plays host to an International Sea Angling Festival. Once a refuge for one of Cornwall's most notorious smugglers, Black Joan. **Looe Island**, just off the coast, is now a bird sanctuary. The island was made famous by the Atkins sisters who lived there and featured it in their books, *We Bought an Island* and *Tales from our Cornish Island*.

Looe Bridge

PAUL CORIN'S MAGNIFICENT MUSIC MACHINES

St Keyne Station, near Liskeard, Cornwall PL 14 4SH
Tel: 01579 343108
e-mail: paulcorinmusic@yahoo.co.uk
website: www.paulcorinmusic.co.uk

Just down the hill from the famous Well of St Keyne , by the old millstream of Lametton Mill which is mentioned in the text of Daphne du Maurier's novel *The King 's General* is the location of **Paul Corin 's Magnificent Music Machines** where one can step back in time with live musical tours from the era of steam trains, Austin Seven cars and the picture-palace with it's mighty

Wurlitzer Organ. This Mighty Wurlitzer was originally installed in the Regent Cinema, Brighton in 1929, it weighs five tons, has 693 organ pipes, real percussions such as xylophone, glockenspiel, drums, cymbals, sound effects for silent films and occupies as much space as a small house. Other popular exhibits include Player Pianos, with music rolls of the playing Grieg, Rachmaninov, and 1920s and 30s American Popular Pianists; Polyphon Musical Boxes from the 1890s; 1906 Edison Phonograph and 1920s Gramophones. The owners hope you will try your hand at turning the Berlin Street Barrel Organ.

Dog lovers should know that this is the most dog-friendly attraction in Cornwall, and if you are planning to stay in this lovely part of the county, there are two very high grade holiday cottages available for weekly lets, each for two adults. You can visit by train, as it is only two minutes walk from St Keyne Wishing Well Halt on the Looe Valley Line.

Around Looe

ST KEYNE

5 miles N of Looe on the B3254

▥ St Keyne's Well

♫ Paul Corin's Magnificent Music Machines

Named after one of the daughters of a Welsh king who settled here during the 5th century, St Keyne is home to the famous holy well – **St Keyne's Well** – that lies beneath a great tree about a mile outside the village. Newly married couples came here to drink – the first to taste the waters was said to be the one to wear the trousers in the marriage. Romanticised by the Victorians, the custom is still carried out by newly-weds today.

Though a small village, St Keyne sees many visitors during the year as it is home to **Paul Corin's Magnificent Music Machines** (see panel above), a wonderful collection that opened in 1967. Housed in the old mill buildings, where Paul was the last miller, this collection of mechanical instruments covers a wide range of sounds and music from classical pieces to musicals, and includes a Wurlitzer from the Regent Cinema, Brighton. Paul's collection has featured on numerous radio and TV programmes. Incidentally, Paul's grandfather was Bransby Williams, the only great star from the music hall days to have his own BBC TV show, in the early 1950s.

Just to the south of St Keyne, and in the valley of the East Looe river, is a **Stone Circle** of eight standing quartz stones, said to be older than Stonehenge.

▥ stories and anecdotes ♦ famous people ♫ art and craft ✎ entertainment and sport ☂ walks

ST GERMANS
7 miles NE of Looe on the B3249

🏛 St German's Church 　 🏛 Port Eliot

Before the Anglo-Saxon diocese of Cornwall was incorporated with Exeter in 1043, this rural village was a cathedral city. The present **St German's Church** stands on the site of the Saxon cathedral. Dating from Norman times, the present building was built as the great church for the Augustinian priory founded here in 1162. As well as curiously dissimilar towers dating from the 13th and 15th centuries, the church contains several striking monuments to the Eliot family, including one by Rysbrack commemorating Edward Eliot who died in 1722. Other treasures in the church include a glorious east window with stained glass by Burne-Jones, a superb Norman doorway as its west front and an old chair that bears a series of carvings depicting Dando, a 14th century priest from the priory. According to local stories, one Sunday Dando left his prayers to go out hunting with a group of wild friends. At the end of the chase, the priest called for a drink and was handed a richly decorated drinking horn by a stranger on a black horse. While quenching his thirst Dando saw the stranger stealing his game. Despite his calls, the horseman refused to return the game. In a drunken frenzy, Dando swore that he would follow the stranger to Hell in order to retrieve his prizes, whereupon the stranger pulled Dando up onto his horse and rode into the River Lynher. Neither the stranger on the horse nor the priest was ever seen again.

Adjoining the village is the **Port Eliot** estate, the home of the Earl and Countess St Germans. At the centre of the estate is the magnificent stately house with a history that goes back 937AD when it was built as an Augustinian Priory. At the dissolution of the monasteries it became the property of the Earl's ancestors. The present building has 100 rooms, 82 chimneys, 13 staircases and a kitchen almost 100 yards from the nearest dining room. The rooms are hung with family portraits, including some by Reynolds, Hoppner and Ramsey Robert. It is very much a lived-in house but a long period of neglect before the present earl inherited means that some of the furnishings and decoration are rather worn. As the present Countess has written: "Some may recoil at what might be described as the 'thread-bareness' of it all…some poetic friends consider the house to be a classic example of opulent and gilded decay".

The house is all but joined to a St Germans Church (see above) that was once the cathedral of Devon and Cornwall. Church and house stand on the banks of the Lynher estuary, surrounded by a semi-circle of densely planted woodland and a stunning landscaped park laid out by Humphrey Repton in the 1790s. The house and park are only open for 100 days from spring to early summer, an arrangement with the Treasury which cedes inheritance taxes in lieu of art treasures being made available to public viewing for certain periods each year.

SALTASH
11½ miles NE of Looe on the A38

🏛 Royal Albert Bridge 　 ⚲ Fore Street

🏛 Saltash Museum

A medieval port on the River Tamar, Saltash was once the base for the largest river steamer fleet in the southwest. Today, it remains the 'Gateway to Cornwall' for many holidaymakers who cross the river into Cornwall via one of the town's mighty bridges. Designed by Isambard Kingdom Brunel in 1859, the iron-built **Royal Albert Bridge** carries the railway while alongside is the much more slender **Tamar Bridge**, a suspension road bridge that was opened in 1961 replacing a ferry service that had operated since the 13th century.

Though older than Plymouth, on the other side of the Sound, Saltash is now becoming a suburb of its larger neighbour, following the construction of the road bridge. However, Saltash has retained much of its charm and Cornish individuality. There's an impressive 17th century **Guildhouse** which stands on granite pillars and is now home to the town council and tourist information centre. Close by is **Mary Newman's Cottage**, a quaint 15th century building that was the home of Sir Francis Drake's first wife. **Saltash Museum and Local History Centre** opened in 2000 and contains a small permanent display about the history and well-known characters of Saltash.

An interesting initiative by the local council and traders can be seen in **Fore Street** which served as the main retail hub of the town for many years. With the growth of out of town shopping, competition from Plymouth and increased use of motor vehicles, shops here were struggling. So it was decided to try and make some of the empty shop-fronts look more appealing. Local artist Emma Spring was commissioned to carry out the work and her colourful murals certainly brighten up this corner of the town.

TORPOINT
11½ miles E of Looe on the A374

🏛 Antony House 🌿 Antony Woodland Gardens

This small town grew up around a ferry service that ran across the **Hamoaze** (as the Tamar estuary is called at this point) to Devonport in the 18th century. From here there are excellent views over the water to the Royal Navy Dockyards and *HMS Raleigh*, the naval training centre for ratings and artificer apprentices. Commissioned in 1940, *HMS Raleigh* is also the home of the Royal Marine Band (Plymouth).

To the north of the town, overlooking the River Lynher as it meets the Tamar, is **Antony House** (National Trust), a superb example of a Queen Anne house. Built of pale silver-grey stone between 1711 and 1721, it has been the ancestral home of the influential Carew family for almost 600 years. It contains a wonderful collection of paintings (many by Sir Joshua Reynolds), tapestries and furniture. Surrounding

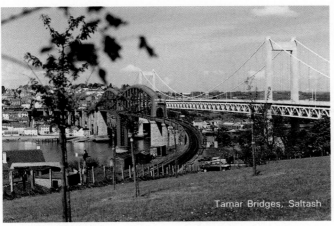

Tamar Bridges, Saltash

the house are the gardens and grounds landscaped by Humphry Repton in the late 18th century, including the delightful **Antony Woodland Gardens**, which are at their best in the spring and autumn. The formal gardens contain the National Collection of Day Lilies.

CREMYLL
12½ miles E of Looe on the B3247

🏠 Mount Edgcumbe House ⚓ Rame Head

Linked to Plymouth by a passenger ferry, Cremyll is an excellent place from which to explore **Mount Edgcumbe House**, the 16th century home of the Earls of Mount Edgcumbe. They moved here from Cotehele House after Piers Edgcumbe married Jean Durnford, an heiress with considerable estates including the Cremyll ferry. The gardens here, overlooking Plymouth Sound, have been designated as one of the Great Gardens of Cornwall. The 10 acres of grounds feature classical garden houses, statues, follies, an exotic Shell Seat, and the National Camellia Collection.

To the southwest of Cremyll are the two small and attractive villages of **Cawsand** and **Kingsand.** By some administrative quirk, for centuries they were placed in different counties: Cornwall and Devon respectively. Though it is hard to believe today, it was from here that one of the largest smuggling fleets in Cornwall operated. At the peak of their activities in the late 18th and early 19th centuries, thousands of barrels of

brandy, silk and other contraband were landed here in secret and transported through sleeping villages to avoid the attentions of the revenue men. It was also at **Cawsand Bay** that the Royal Navy fleet used to shelter before the completion of the **Plymouth Breakwater** in 1841, leaving the welcome legacy of a large number of inns.

Further southwest again and at the southernmost point of Mount Edgcumbe Country Park rises the spectacular **Rame Head** which guards the entrance into Plymouth Sound. From the 400ft-high cliffs there are superb views but this beautiful headland has its own special feature – the ruined 14th century St Michael's Chapel, from which a blazing beacon warned of the coming of the Armada. In the little hamlet of Rame itself is the older Church of St Germanus, which is still lit by candles; for centuries its west tower and spire acted as a landmark for sailors.

The **Eddystone Lighthouse**, which can be seen on a clear day, lies 10 miles offshore from Rame Head. It was from here, in July 1588, that the English fleet had their first encounter with the Spanish Armada.

Mount Edgcumbe House, Cremyll

WHITSAND BAY
8 miles E of Looe off the B3247

🐒 Monkey Sanctuary

Running between Rame Head and the hamlet of Portwrinkle, this bay has an impressive stretch of beach that is more a series of coves than one continuous expanse of sand. The seaside village of Portwrinkle developed around its medieval harbour. Further west along the coast, at the coastal village of Murrayton, is the famous **Monkey Sanctuary**, the world's first protected colony of Amazonian woolly monkeys. The sanctuary was set up in 1964 to provide a safe environment for monkeys rescued from zoos or abandoned as pets, and its inhabitants roam freely in the gardens of the outdoor enclosures. Plants for the monkeys to eat are grown in a forest garden, while the Tree Top Café takes care of hungry humans.

POLPERRO
3 miles SW of Looe off the A387

🏛 Museum of Smuggling

Polperro is many people's idea of a typical Cornish fishing village as its steep, narrow streets and alleyways are piled high with fisherman's cottages built around a narrow tidal inlet. All routes in this lovely village seem to lead down to its beautiful harbour. It is still a busy fishing port, where there is normally an assortment of colourful boats to be seen. For centuries dependent on pilchard fishing for its survival, Polperro also has a long association with smuggling. During the 18th century, the practice was so rife that nearly all of the inhabitants were involved in the shipping, storing or

transporting of contraband. To combat this widespread problem, HM Customs and Excise established the first 'preventive station' in Cornwall here in the 1800s. At the **Museum of Smuggling** a whole range of artefacts and memorabilia are used to illustrate the myths and legends surrounding the characters who dodged the government taxes on luxury goods. A model of *Lady Beatrice*, a traditional gaff-rigged fishing boat, can also be seen.

FOWEY
8 miles W of Looe on the A3082

🐒 Fowey Marine Aquarium   🖋 Daphne du Maurier

Guarding the entrance to the river from which it takes is name, Fowey (pronounced Foy – "to rhyme with joy") is a lovely old seafaring town with steep, narrow streets and alleyways leading down to one of the most beautiful natural harbours along the south coast. An

Polperro Harbour

important port during the Middle Agest, he town exhibits architectural styles ranging from Elizabethan to Edwardian. As a busy trading port, Fowey also attracted pirates and was the home of the 'Fowey Gallants', who preyed on ships in the Channel and engaged in raids on the French coast. Brought together during the Hundred Years War to fight the French, these local mariners did not disband at the end of the hostilities but continued to terrorise shipping along this stretch of coast and beyond. A devastating raid by the French in 1457, that saw much of Fowey burnt to the ground, was in direct retaliation for attacks made by the Gallants.

Later, in the 19th century, much of the china clay from St Austell was exported through Fowey. It is still a busy place as huge ships continue to call at this deep water harbour alongside fishing boats and pleasure craft. The town's **Museum,** housed in part of the medieval town hall, is an excellent place to discover Fowey's colourful past, from the days of piracy through to the china clay exports of the 19th century. Naturally, there are many inns here including the **King of Prussia**, named after Frederick the Great whose victories in the Seven Years War made him a popular figure in England; and the **Ship Inn**, originally a town house built by the influential Rashleigh family in 1570.

On the Town Quay, **Fowey Marine Aquarium** contains a collection of fish from the local waters around the town. Sinister conger eels, bass, turbot, mullet and colourful members of the wrasse family are on display,

BROCANTE

49a Fore Street, Fowey, Cornwall, PL23 1AH
Tel: 01726 833390
e-mail: brocanteltd@hotmail.co.uk
website: www.brocanteltd.com

Kieron Cockley opened **Brocante** in Mevagissey in 2006, bringing to Mevagissey and Cornwall a shop with "something for yourself, your mum, your sister and your auntie!" Brocante is the French word for bric à brac so as you would expect, you will find an eclectic mix of items on sale.

Located along the beautiful Fowey estuary and opened in May 2007, **Brocante** in Fowey, is the sister shop of Brocante in Mevagissey and opened in May 2007. Like its sister shop, it stocks an intriguing medley of items, all personally chosen by owner Kieron Cockley.

The premises here are larger than in Mevagissey so Kieron is able to stock larger pieces of furniture - anything from marble washstands and wardrobes to sofas, dressers and chandeliers. Like Mevagissey, this is a beautiful shop filled with unusual pieces that you won't be able to find in any ordinary high street outlet.

When you visit, you may well find Mini, Kieron's Italian greyhound, helping out!

FOWEY FISH & FOWEY WINES

37 Fore Street, Fowey, Cornwall PL23 1AH
Tel: 01726 832422 Fax: 01726 832887
e-mail: buyfish@foweyfish.com
website: www.foweyfish.com

Fowey Fish & Fowey Wines is a small and friendly family-owned business that was set up in April 1983 by Graham and Sue Giles. It began as just a fishmonger's shop with a few trade customers. Then in 2000 their daughter Karen joined the business and introduced the now very popular Mail Order service and a much larger selection of wines. The company now sends its fresh, locally caught fish and shellfish all over the UK from Monday to Thursday every week.

All the fresh fish comes in daily from the local fishing boats, mainly Looe Day Boats who catch and land the best and freshest fish in the country. Oysters and mussels come from the River Fowey while the lobsters and crabs are caught by a Newquay fisherman with more than 20 years of experience.

In the other half of the shop Karen formally set up Fowey Wines, although her parents sold wine on smaller scale before her arrival, the shop now boasts a selection of over 250 wine and champagnes, including the famous local Camel Valley wines, 25 locally produced beers and ciders and a small selection of spirits. The selection of her wines could be described as eclectic and covers New and Old World with enthusiasm. Staff are always on hand to give helpful advice whilst Karen has achieved qualifications to WSET Advanced Level 3.

together with an occasional octopus. There's also a range of lobsters and crabs, with a crab touch pool for children.

Fowey has two important literary connections. Sir Arthur Quiller-Couch (or 'Q'), who lived for over 50 years at **The Haven**, on the Esplanade just above the Polruan ferry. Sir Arthur was a Cambridge professor, sometime Mayor of Fowey, editor of the *Oxford Book of English Verse* and author of several books connected with Fowey – he called it Troy Town. He died in 1944 after being hit by a car and was buried in St Fimbarrus churchyard.

The second literary figure was the novelist **Daphne du Maurier** who lived at Gribbin Head. Each year in mid-May, a general arts and literature festival is held in her memory. A

'tented village' is set up overlooking the picturesque Fowey Estuary and the events include talks by a sparkling mix of star names, guided walks, drama, community events and free entertainment.

Another major event is the **Fowey Royal Regatta** which takes place in mid-August (usually the third full week). In addition to the sailing events there are fireworks displays on the Quay, Red Arrow displays, raft races, childrens events, live music on the Quay, grand draws and carnival processions.

To the south of Fowey is Readymoney Cove whose expanse of sand acts as the town's beach. Further along, **St Catherine's Castle** was part of a chain of fortifications built by Henry VIII to protect the harbours along the south coast. From Readymoney

📖 stories and anecdotes 🐿 famous people 🎨 art and craft 🎭 entertainment and sport 🚶 walks

Bodinnick Ferry

Fowey is the pretty hamlet of **Bodinnick** where the actor Gerald du Maurier bought a holiday home beside the landing slip. He named it Ferryside and it was here that his daughter Daphne lived before her marriage and where she wrote her first novel *The Loving Spirit*. The house is still owned by the Du Maurier family but not open to the public. If you arrive in Bodinnick by the ferry, you pass the gates to the house as you walk off the landing slip.

Sir Arthur Quiller-Couch is remembered by a monolithic memorial that stands on the coast facing Fowey. It was close to the site of this monument that, in 1644, Charles I narrowly escaped death from a sniper's bullet while making a survey of Cromwell's forces at Fowey. From the Bodinnick ferry there is a delightful walk across mainly National Trust land that leads up to the 'Q' memorial and then back via the Polruan ferry to Fowey.

Cove the **Coastal Footpath** is clearly marked all the way around to Polkerris and the walk takes in many fine viewpoints as well as the castle and the wonderful daymark on Gribbin Head. The beacon on Gribbin Head was built in 1832 to help seafarers find the approaches into Fowey harbour. But the craggy headland is best known as the home of Daphne du Maurier, who lived at the still private house of Menabilly, which featured as Manderley in her most famous novel *Rebecca* (1938).

Facing St Catherine's Castle across the mouth of the River Fowey and reached by ferry from Fowey, **Polruan** is an impossibly picturesque village. Tiny cottages cling to the steep hillside, threaded with winding steps, alleys and passageways. Life here revolves around the quay where the ferry lands. Beside the harbour, busy with pleasure craft and some industrial vessels, stands the late-15th century **Polruan Blockhouse**, one of a pair of artillery buildings constructed to guard the narrow entrance into Fowey.

Just to the north of Polruan and also facing

GOLANT
8 miles W of Looe off the B3269

Close to this delightful waterside village, which is home to yet another of Cornwall's many holy wells, are the **Castle Dore Earthworks**. This densely overgrown Iron Age lookout point is thought to be the site of King Mark's palace and is therefore linked with the legend of Tristan and Iseult.

Upriver and found in a sleepy creek is the quiet village of **Lerryn** that was once a busy riverside port. Those familiar with Kenneth Grahame's novel, *The Wind in the Willows*, may find the thickly wooded slopes of Lerryn Creek familiar as they are believed to have been the inspiration for the setting of this ever-popular children's story.

LOSTWITHIEL
10 miles NW of Looe on the A390

🏛 Lostwithiel Museum 🏰 Restormel Castle

Nestling in the valley of the River Fowey and surrounded by wooded hills, Lostwithiel's name – which means 'lost in the hills' – perfectly describes its location. This small market town was the 13th century capital of Cornwall. As one of the stannary towns, tin and other raw materials were brought here for assaying and onward transportation until the mining activity cause the quay to silt up and the port moved further down river.

Lostwithiel was also a major crossing point on the River Fowey and the bridge seen today was completed in Tudor times. Beside the riverbank lies the tranquil **Coulson Park**, named after the American millionaire, Nathaniel Coulson, who grew up in Lostwithiel. On the opposite bank of the river from the town lies **Bonconnoc Estate**, the home of the Pitt family who gave Britain two Prime Ministers: William Pitt the Elder and his son, William Pitt the Younger.

Throughout the town there are reminders of Lostwithiel's once important status. These

📖 stories and anecdotes 🦜 famous people 🎨 art and craft 🎭 entertainment and sport 🚶 walks

OLD PALACE ANTIQUES

Quay Street, Lostwithiel, Cornwall PL22 0BS
Tel: 01208 872909
website: www.oldpalaceantiques.co.uk

In 1997, Jeremy and Melanie Askew came to Cornwall on holiday and fell in love with the county. They acquired an antiques shop in Polperro before moving to Lostwithiel, the 'Antiques Capital of Cornwall', in 2003 and opening **Old Palace Antiques**. Here you will find an interesting selection of old and new furniture, available in pine, rustic oak and painted, 'shabby chic' style. You can also get the country look from their shop with TG Green's famous blue and white striped Cornish kitchen ware, displayed on a fabulous Victorian rustic pine dresser. For the ultimate 'shabby chic' appeal, you can furnish

your bedroom with a painted and distressed chest of drawers or a vintage teddy bear seated on a beautiful French chair.

You can also solve your storage problems in style with a selection of cupboards, chests of drawers, or a quirky mule chest. You can then add the finishing touches - a vintage hand-embroidered table runner, rustic chilli heart door hangers or a simple bowl of dried rosebuds. And do take time to browse around Melanie's stylish selection of fabrics and soft furnishings at Rhubarb Interiors. Old Palace Antiques is open from 9.30am to 5pm, Monday to Saturday.

WATTS TRADING

12 Fore Street, Lostwithiel, Cornwall PL22 0BW
Tel/Fax: 01208 872304
e-mail: enquiries@wattstrading.co.uk
website: www.wattstrading.co.uk

The grocer's shop advertising in the window of **Watts Trading**, left behind by a previous owner of this handsome Georgian Grade II listed building, is misleading. Today, the shop is stocked with an enormous variety of environmentally friendly products, a reflection of owner Denise Watts's philosophy and lifestyle. Her aim, she says, is "to use products that have not harmed the planet by their production, and that will rot back into the earth when they have reached the end of their useful life."

So you'll find bio-degradable cleaning products; one of the biggest selections of natural brushes in the country; organic pre-packaged food; local products from sea salt and organic fudge to natural soap and shampoo bars; Fair Trade

products, including some very beautiful baskets and bags; and much, much more. The shop also sells the amazing Earthborn claypaint, currently the only environmental paint sold in the UK with the European eco label.

Visitors and locals alike love the smell and atmosphere of the shop and are intrigued by the curved wall that hides the wonderful staircase. This is a great place to stock up on essential supplies and to buy those special gifts and treats.

CHARK COUNTRY HOLIDAYS

Chark Farm, Redmoor, Bodmin, Cornwall PL30 5AR
Tel: 01208 871118
e-mail: charkholidays@tiscali.co.uk
website: www.charkcountryholidays.co.uk

Chark Farm offers five four star country cottages converted from the original farm yard in a picturesque rural, yet easy to reach setting. The spacious and comfortable accommodation is tastefully furnished in country style having solid wooden floors with oak and beech kitchens and all have full central heating. The accommodation sleeps two to six people, larger parties can easily be accommodated in adjoining cottages. Single storey Mesyow Chy is fully wheelchair accessible, rated M3.

Outside there are large patio and lawned areas, an attractive courtyard and a play area with large trampoline. A haven for animal lovers, guests can enjoy the friendly farm animals in Pets Paddock including hens, ducks, goats and ponies. There are calves to bottle feed during the summer, and everyone can take a horse and cart ride around the scenic lanes. There is a wide variety of wildlife to spot in the fields and woodlands. Major local attractions include Eden Project, Lanhydrock House, Camel Trail, Bodmin Moor, and South Coast beaches – all within 15 minutes drive.

Everyone is welcome here from pre-school families to mature couples, and many of our guests return again and again to enjoy the relaxed atmosphere.

include the remains of the 13th century **Great Hall**, which served as the stannary offices, and the early 18th century **Guild Hall**. Built by Richard, Lord Edgcumbe, this building is now occupied by the **Lostwithiel Museum**. It tells the story of this interesting town as well as displaying photographs of everyday life from the late 1800s to the present day.

Lostwithiel's strategic position as a riverside port and crossing place led to the construction of **Restormel Castle** upstream from the town, high on a mound overlooking the wooded Fowey valley. The Black Prince stayed here in 1354 and 1365 but following the loss of Gascony soon afterwards, most of the contents of any value were removed and the castle was left to fall into ruin. In summer, the site is one of the best picnic spots in Cornwall, boasting stunning views of the peaceful surrounding countryside.

Restormel Castle, Lostwithiel

🎬 stories and anecdotes 🦜 famous people 🎨 art and craft 🎵 entertainment and sport 🚶 walks

LANREATH

5½ miles NW of Looe
off the B3359

🏛 Lanreath Folk & Farm Museum

This pretty village of traditional cob cottages is home to the **Lanreath Folk and Farm Museum**, found in Lanreath's former tithe barn. There are numerous vintage exhibits here, many of which can be handled, including old agricultural implements, mill workings, engines, tractors, a traditional farmhouse kitchen and a bric-a-brac shop. Craft workshops and a pets' corner complete the museum.

Launceston

🏛 St Mary Magdalene Church   🏛 Launceston Castle

🖼 Launceston Steam Railway

🎋 Tamar Valley Discovery Trail

Situated on the eastern edge of Bodmin Moor close to the county border with Devon, Launceston (pronounced locally Lawnson) is one of Cornwall's most pleasant inland towns and was a particular favourite of Sir John Betjeman. The capital of Cornwall until 1838, it guarded the main overland route into the county. Shortly after the Norman Conquest, William I's half-brother, Robert of Mortain, built the massive **Launceston Castle** overlooking the River Kensey. Visited by the Black Prince and seized by Cornish rebels in 1549, the castle changed hands twice during the Civil War before becoming an assize court and prison. George Fox, the founder of the Society of Friends was detained here in 1656. The court was famous for imprisoning and executing 'on the

nod'. Although now in ruins, the 12-foot thick walls of the keep and tower are still impressive.

The most striking building in the town however is **St Mary Magdalene Church**. Its walls of sturdy Cornish granite are covered with delicate carvings that include angels, roses, pomegranates and heraldic emblems. The church was built by a local landowner, Sir Henry Trecarrel, in the early 1500s. He had started building a manor house nearby when both his beloved wife and infant son died within days of each other. Overwhelmed with grief, Sir Henry abandoned the manor house and devoted the rest of his life to building this magnificent church in their memory.

Elsewhere in the town, the streets around the castle are filled with handsome buildings including the impressive **Lawrence House** that was built in 1753 for a wealthy local lawyer. Given to the National Trust to help

Launceston Steam Railway

preserve the character of the street, the house is home to a **Museum**, which dedicates its numerous displays to the history of the area. To the west of the town and running through the beautiful Kensey Valley, the **Launceston Steam Railway** takes visitors on a nostalgic and scenic journey back in time. Travelling in either open or closed carriages, passengers can enjoy a round trip along five miles of narrow-gauge track to Newmills and back. The locomotives used to haul the trains were built in the 1880s and 1890s by the famous Hunslet Engine Company of Leeds and once worked on the slate carrying lines high in the mountains of North Wales.

Launceston is also the start, or the finish, of the **Tamar Valley Discovery Trail**, a 30-mile footpath from here to Plymouth that takes in many of the villages scattered along the Cornwall-Devon border. Passing through old mining country, past market gardens and through ancient river ports, walkers of the trail will also see the wealth of bird, plant and wildlife that the varying habitats along the way support. In 1995, the Tamar Valley was designated an Area of Outstanding Natural Beauty.

Around Launceston

GUNNISLAKE
10 miles SE of Launceston on the A390

Often referred to as the first village in Cornwall, it was here in the 1520s that Sir Piers Edgcumbe built the **New Bridge** over the River Tamar that continues to serve as one of the major gateways into the county. In fact, this 180-foot-long granite structure remained the lowest crossing of the river by road right up until the 1960s when the massive

suspension bridge linking Saltash with Plymouth was opened. The 16th century bridge meant that this charming village also had an important strategic value. During the Civil War, it was the centre of bitter fighting. In the 18th and 19th centuries the village came alive with mining. Though the mines have closed, some of the mine buildings have been immortalised by Turner in his great painting, *Crossing the Brook*, that also captures Gunnislake's famous bridge. The River Tamar is tidal as far as the weir upstream near Newbridge and salmon fishermen continue to come to Gunnislake, as they have done since medieval times, to catch the fish as they travel up river to their spawning grounds.

CALSTOCK
12 miles SE of Launceston off the A390

🏠 Cotehele House

Well known for its splendid views of the Tamar Valley, the village of Calstock was an important river port in the 19th century when vast quantities of tin, granite and copper ore were brought here for loading on to barges to be transported down the Tamar to the coast. In the countryside surrounding Calstock the remains of old mine workings, along with the spoil heaps, can still be seen along with the remains of the village's boat-building industry. The decline of Calstock as a port came with the construction of the huge **Railway Viaduct**, which carries the Tamar Valley Line southwards to Plymouth. Completed in 1908, this giant 12-arched viaduct, the first in the country to be constructed of concrete blocks, stands 120 feet above the river. Probably one of Britain's most picturesque branch lines, the **Tamar Valley Line** can still be taken down to the coast. Though the river has lost most of its commercial traffic, it is a starting point for

Tamar River canoe expeditions.

Just to the southwest of the village **Cotehele** (see panel below) represents one of the best-preserved medieval estates held by the National Trust. Mainly built between 1485 and 1539, this low granite fortified manor house was the principal home of the Edgcumbe family until the mid-16th century when they moved their main residence to Mount Edgcumbe. Along with its Great Tudor Hall, fabulous Flemish and Mortlake tapestries and period furniture, the house incorporates some charming features such as the secret spy-hole in the Great Hall and a tower clock with a bell but no face or hands. Surrounding the house are, firstly, the grounds, containing exotic and tender plants that thrive in the mild valley climate and, beyond that, the estate with its ancient network of pathways that allow exploration of the valley.

The River Tamar runs through the estate and close to an old cider house and mill is **Cotehele Quay**, a busy river port in Victorian times. The quay buildings now house an outstation of the National Maritime Museum, an art and craft gallery and a licensed tea room. The restored Tamar sailing barge *Shamrock* is moored alongside the museum.

CALLINGTON
9½ miles S of Launceston on the A388

Situated on the fertile land between the rivers Tamar and Lynher, Callington is now rich fruit growing country. During the 19th century, the surrounding landscape was very different as it was alive with frantic mining activity. The area's heritage, landscape and character are depicted on many of the walls of the town's buildings, thanks to the interesting and unusual **Mural Project**.

About a mile outside the town, **Dupath Holy Well** is enclosed in a fine granite building of 1510. The water in the basin was believed to cure whooping cough.

Overlooking the River Lynher, southwest of this old market town, is **Cadsonbury Hillfort** – a massive Iron Age bank and ditch that are thought to be the remains of a local chief's

Cotehele

St Dominick, nr Saltash, Cornwall PL12 6TA
Tel: 01579 351346
e-mail: cotehele@nationaltrust.org.uk
website: www.nationaltrust.org.uk

At the heart of this riverside estate sits the granite and slatestone house of **Cotehele**, built mainly between 1485 and 1627 and a home of the Edgcumbe family for centuries. Intimate chambers feature large Tudor fireplaces and rich hangings. Outside, the formal gardens overlook the richly planted valley garden below, with medieval dovecote, stewpond and Victorian summer house. At the quay interesting old buildings house the Edgcumbe Arms tea-room and an outstation of the National Maritime Museum. The restored sailing barge Shamrock is moored alongside.

🏛 historic building   🏛 museum and heritage   🏛 historic site   🏵 scenic attraction   🌱 flora and fauna

home. To the northeast rises **Kit Hill**, now a country park, where a 19th century chimney stack built to serve one of the area's mines adds a further 80 feet to the hill's summit.

NORTH PETHERWIN
5 miles NW of Launceston off the B3254

🌿 Tamar Otter Sanctuary

Found above the River Ottery, this village is home to the **Tamar Otter Sanctuary,** a branch of the famous Otter Trust, dedicated to breeding young otters for release into the wild to prevent the species from becoming extinct in lowland England. Visitors can watch the otters playing in large natural enclosures, see them in their breeding dens, or holts, and watch the orphans in the rehabilitation centre. Also here are a dormouse conservation project, refreshment and gift shop, lakes with waterfowl and an area of woodland where fallow and Muntjac deer roam freely.

Tamar Otter Sanctuary

2 | Devon

Asked to describe the "ideal" English countryside, many people would conjure up a landscape of green rolling hills, of bright, fresh streams tumbling through wooded valleys, of white thatched cottages clustering around a venerable church, with a picturesque inn nestling beside it. Devon, of course, but only part of it. The whole of the Dartmoor National Park lies within its boundaries, a huge area of dome-shaped granite where the most frequently seen living creatures are the famous Dartmoor ponies which have roamed here since at least the 10th century.

The moor is notorious for its abundant rainfall – an annual average of 60 inches, twice as much as falls on Torbay, a few miles to the east. In some of the more exposed westerly fringes, an annual rainfall of 100 inches is common. In prehistoric times the climate was much drier and warmer. The moor then was dotted with settlements and this Bronze Age population left behind them a rich legacy of stone circles, menhirs, burial chambers, and single, double or even triple rows of stones.

Then there's the busy port of Plymouth with its proud maritime history and associations with Sir Francis Drake and the Pilgrim Fathers. The rugged coastline to the north contrasts with the almost Mediterranean character of Torbay – the "English Riviera". There are hundreds of picture postcard villages, of which Clovelly and Inner Hope are perhaps the most famous, and scores of delightful small towns such as Salcombe, Totnes and Dartmouth.

The county also boasts some outstanding buildings. The Gothic masterpiece of Exeter Cathedral has been described as "one of the supreme architectural pleasures of England", and it was a 14th century Bishop of Exeter who built the glorious parish church of Ottery St Mary. The sumptuous mansion of Saltram House near Plymouth contains fine work by Robert Adam, Sir Joshua Reynolds and Thomas Chippendale, while Buckland Abbey is famed as the home of the Drake family and their most famous son, Sir Francis. Arlington Court is notable for the eclectic collections amassed by its last owner, Rosalie Chichester, during the course of a long life, and the now redundant church at Parracombe is a "time warp" building still just as it was in the 18th century.

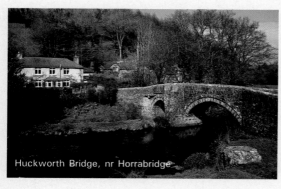

Huckworth Bridge, nr Horrabridge

Part of Devon's enormous charm derives from the fact that it is so lightly populated. Just over a million people, roughly equivalent to the population of Birmingham, occupy the third largest county in England, some 670,000 acres in all. And most of those million people live in towns and resorts along its coastline, leaving huge tracts of countryside where the villages, the lanes and byways are still magically peaceful.

LOCATOR MAP

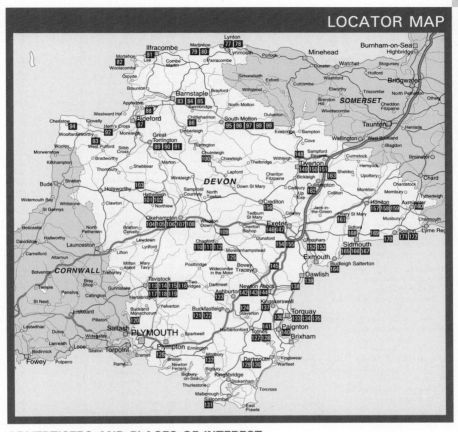

ADVERTISERS AND PLACES OF INTEREST

🎭 stories and anecdotes 🐦 famous people 🎨 art and craft 🎟 entertainment and sport 🚶 walks

🏛 historic building   🏛 museum and heritage   🏛 historic site   🔱 scenic attraction   ❦ flora and fauna

Lynton

Lynton and Lynmouth, though often mentioned in the same breath, are very different in character. Lynton is the younger of the two settlements and sits atop a great cliff 600ft high; Lynmouth, far below, clusters around the junction of the East and West Lyn rivers just before they reach the sea.

Lynton is a bright and breezy village, its houses and terraces mostly Victorian. The **Exmoor Museum**, housed in a restored 16th century house, has an interesting collection of the tools and products of bygone local craftsmen and other exhibits relating to the area.

If you are visiting Lynton in August, you won't be able to avoid the odd characters standing in gardens and doorways, sitting on roofs or shinning up drainpipes. Don't worry – they are just participating in the **Lynton & Lynmouth Scarecrow Festival**, a popular event that has become the largest and longest running such festival in the West Country.

To the west of Lynton, about a mile or so along a minor road, is one of the most remarkable natural features in Devon, the **Valley of the Rocks.** When the poet Robert Southey visited the area in 1800, he was most impressed by this natural gorge *"covered with huge stones...the very bones and skeletons of the earth; rock reeling upon rock, stone piled upon stone, a huge terrific mass"*. In *Lorna Doone*, the author RD Blackmore transforms the site into the "Devil's Cheesering" where Jan Ridd visits Mother Meldrun who is sheltering under "eaves of lichened rock". And it was after walking along the clifftop path, more than 1,300ft above the sea, in company with William Wordsworth and his sister Dorothy, that S.T. Coleridge was inspired to write his immortal *Rime of the Ancient Mariner*.

Valley of the Rocks, Lynton

THE LYN VALLEY ART & CRAFT CENTRE

Old Methodist Church, Lee Road, Lynton,
North Devon EX35 6HT
Tel: 01598 752549/753611
website: www.lynvalleycraftcentre.co.uk

Since it occupies the former Methodist church, (next to the Town Hall), **The Lyn Valley Art & Craft Centre** has adopted as its tag line "Stocked to the belfry with a fabulous collection of art and craft work from the locality".

Established in 1975 and now widely acclaimed as one of the best art and craft centres in the UK, it has everything from a 50p pottery mouse through to wrought iron, candles, glass, ceramics, wood turning, jewellery, cards, preserves, textiles. You'll also find mirrors, paintings, knit-wear and clothing. The myriad of paintings, art and crafts are all superbly presented; admission is free and dogs and buggies are welcome. New members producing good quality work are welcome to apply.

The centre is open seven days a week except from January to mid-February; most major debit and credit cards are accepted. For disabled visitors, four steps are unavoidable but the staff will do all they can to help. Also located within the old Methodist church, is the Lynton Cinema which is noted as one of the smallest public cinemas in the country with seating for a maximum of 80 people.

ROCKVALE

Lee Road, Lynton, Devon EX35 6HW
Tel: 01598 752279

Just a short walk from the rugged scenery of the Valley of the Rocks and commanding glorious views, **Rockvale** offers a peaceful haven with comfortable accommodation and a friendly atmosphere. It has a well-stocked bar with stunning views and a large choice of single malt whiskeys. In addition to breakfast, the attractively bright and airy dining room offers an array of tempting home-cooked evening meals.

There are eight pretty and attractively furnished bedrooms, all of which are either en suite or have their own private facilities.

An unusual attraction in the valley is its herd of feral goats, introduced here in the 1970s. A good time to see them is in January when the nannies give birth to their kids.

Around Lynton

LYNMOUTH
1 mile E of Lynton on the A39

🖋 Lynmouth Pottery   🗝 Watersmeet

🖋 Exmoor Brass Rubbing Centre

🎞 The *Louisa* lifeboat

Lynton is connected to its sister-village Lynmouth by an ingenious cliff railway which, when it opened on Easter Monday 1890, was the first of its kind in Britain. A gift from Sir George Newnes, the publisher and newspaper tycoon, the railway is powered by water, or rather by two 700-gallon water tanks, one at each end of the 450ft track. When the tank at the top is filled, and the one at the bottom emptied, the brakes are released and the two passenger carriages change place.

For centuries, the people of Lynmouth subsisted on agriculture and fishing, especially herring fishing and curing. By good fortune, just as the herring shoals were moving away to new waters, the North Devon coast benefited from the two new enthusiasms for "romantic" scenery and sea bathing. Coleridge and Wordsworth arrived here on a walking tour in the 1790s, Shelley wrote fondly of his visit in 1812, and it was Robert Southey, later Poet Laureate, who first used the designation "the English Switzerland" to describe the dramatic scenery of the area. The painter Gainsborough had already described it as "the most delightful place for a landscape painter this country can boast". One of the most picturesque villages in Devon, Lynmouth also has a tiny harbour surrounded by lofty wooded hills, a curious Rhenish Tower on the pier, and do seek out Mars Hill, an eye-ravishing row of thatched cottages.

Understandably, this lovely setting acts as a magnet for artists and craftspeople. People like Peter Allen, for example, whose **Lynmouth Pottery** is very much a pottery with a difference. For one thing, it's a working pottery and one of the few places where you can try out your own skills at the potter's wheel. (Children too are encouraged to have a go). If you're not totally ashamed of the result, Peter Allen will then fire the finished item and post it on to you. Many a visitor to Lynmouth Pottery has discovered an unsuspected talent for turning slippery clay into a quite presentable decorative piece.

More hands-on experience is offered at the **Exmoor Brass Rubbing and Hobby Craft Centre** on Watersmeet Road. The first collection of brass rubbings was made by a man named Craven Ord between 1790 and 1830. His collection is now housed in the British Museum but because of his method – pouring printer's ink into the engraved lines and then pressing a sheet of damp tissue paper on the brass – the results are often very poor. It was the Victorians who developed a process using heelball (shoemaker's black wax) and white paper that is still in use today. The Centre provides all the necessary materials and friendly instruction.

If you continue along Watersmeet Road you will come to the popular beauty spot of **Watersmeet,** where the East Lyn river and Hoar Oak Water come together. An 1832 fishing lodge, Watersmeet House, stands close by. A National Trust property, it is open during the season as a café, shop and information centre where you can pick up

South West Coast Path and Woody Bay

Distance: *6.0 miles (9.7 kilometres)*
Typical time: *180 mins*
Height gain: *200 metres*
Map: *Explorer OL9*
Walk: *www.walkingworld.com ID:309*
Contributor: *Bryan Cath*

ACCESS INFORMATION:

From the Ilfracombe direction go towards Combe Martin on the A399, continuing through Combe Martin and on up the winding road until it eventually straightens out. After a while the first turning on your left comes up, signposted to Hunters Inn. Take this road and keep on it all the way to Hunters Inn. Park in the car park opposite the toilets. From other directions, pick up the A399 Ilfracombe to South Molton road, and Hunters Inn is signed off this road above Combe Martin.

DESCRIPTION:

This walk will take you along a section of the South West Coast Path that is often considered to be one of the most scenic sections of its whole 630 miles. It starts by following the old coaching road giving easy walking and amazing views. On reaching the aptly-named Woody Bay, clothed mainly in sessile oak, you return via the lower coast path, locally known as the 'goat path', being narrow and closer to the sea and cliffs. You pass by one of the highest waterfalls along this section of the coast, overlook a rock arch and generally experience some wonderful coastal scenery.

FEATURES:

River, sea, pub, toilets, National Trust/ NTS, wildlife, birds, flowers, great views.

WALK DIRECTIONS:

1 | Having parked in the car park opposite the toilets and National Trust shop, walk back towards the Hunters Inn and take the road on the right of the inn, continuing ahead when the road turns right up the hill.

2 | Go through the facing gate and follow the sign to Woody Bay 2.75 miles, on the wider track ahead.

3 | This climb brings you above Heddon's Mouth, with glorious views over the valley.

4 | Follow this track all the way to Woody Bay, with wonderful coastal views, to reach the gate by a hairpin bend.

5 | Follow the road down, following the left-hand fork to the car park.

6 | Have a look at the National Trust information board on the area, then continue down the hill to the small road that goes hard back on the left down through the woods, signposted to Martinhoe Manor. Follow this

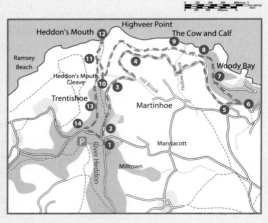

down through the woods, past Wringapeak House to the hairpin bend and carry on straight ahead through the gate, signposted Coastpath to Hunters Inn.

7 | Follow the sign to Hunters Inn, up through the woods, with views on your right (leaves permitting) of Lee Abbey and the Valley of Rocks, with Foreland Point lighthouse flashing in the distance.

8 | Carry on and over the stile, now being wary of the drop on your right!

9 | Soon you come to a high waterfall in a lovely valley. Carry on out to the point; a pause to look at the rock arch and surrounding scenery is most rewarding. Carry on up between the heather, around the next rocky point to more spectacular cliff scenery. Continue round the next two rocky points and down into the Heddon Valley.

10 | When the path reaches the Heddon Valley path, turn hard right and walk down by the river to Heddon's Mouth.

11 | Cross the bridge by the picnic area and continue down to reach the beach.

12 | Having visited the beach and newly-restored limekiln, return to the picnic area by the bridge and continue across it, with the river on your left. In a while ignore the path going down to your left.

13 | Pass through the gate and continue ahead, ignoring the signpost to Combe Martin up to the right, instead continuing along the level path.

14 | On reaching the gate by the road, pass through and turn left to follow the small road over the bridge and on back to Hunters Inn. Be aware of cars, particularly on the narrow bends.

leaflets detailing some beautiful circular walks, starting here, along the East Lyn valley and to Hoar Oak Water.

Lynmouth's setting beside its twin rivers is undeniably beautiful, but it has also proved to be tragically vulnerable. On the night of August 16th, 1952, a cloudburst over Exmoor deposited nine inches of rain onto an already saturated moor. In the darkness, the normally placid East and West Lyn rivers became raging cataracts and burst their banks. Sweeping tree trunks and boulders along with it, the torrent smashed its way through the village, destroying dozens of houses and leaving 34 people dead. That night saw many freak storms across southern England, but none matched the ferocity of the deluge that engulfed this pretty little village. The Flood Memorial Hall has an exhibition that details the events of that terrible night.

An earlier exceptional storm, in 1899, involved the Lynmouth lifeboat in a tale of epic endurance. A full-rigged ship, the *Forest Hall,* was in difficulties off Porlock, but the storm was so violent it was impossible to launch the lifeboat at Lynmouth. Instead, the crewmen dragged their three-and-a-half ton boat, the *Louisa,* the 13 miles across the moor. Along the way they had to negotiate Countisbury Hill, with a gradient of 1,000ft over two miles, before dropping down to Porlock Weir where the *Louisa* was successfully launched and every crew member of the stricken ship was saved.

MARTINHOE
4 miles W of Lynton on minor road off the A39

Hollow Brook Falls

Set amidst rolling fields above spectacular cliffs some 700ft high, the small village of Martinhoe was occupied in Roman times as a signal station keeping an eye out for any aggressive activity by the Silurian tribes of Wales on the other shore of the Bristol Channel.

Martinhoe boasts what some argue is the highest waterfall in the West Country - it all depends on how you define a waterfall. **Hollow Brook Falls** descend 600ft to the sea in a series of cascades, including two drops of 150ft each. Coastal waterfalls are quite

THE OLD RECTORY COUNTRY HOUSE HOTEL

Martinhoe, Exmoor National Park, North Devon EX31 4QT
Tel: 01598 763368   Fax: 01598 783567
e-mail: info@oldrectoryhotel.co.uk
website: www.oldrectoryhotel.co.uk

The Old Rectory Hotel is a sanctuary for wildlife, birds and guests. Once a charming Georgian Rectory serving the adjacent ancient 11th century church, the hotel is now a unique and elegant retreat within Exmoor National Park where relaxation, comfort and friendly informal service are the order of the day.

This secluded peaceful corner of Exmoor is fantastic walking country with access to the stunningly dramatic coastal path from the end of the garden. Nearby are several National Trust properties and Rosemoor RHS Garden. Good food and wine is important here and ingredients are sourced locally and wherever possible direct from the farm – the local Exmoor organic lamb and beef are just out of this world! Even the water comes from the hotel's own spring.

Nurtured by clergy past, The Old Rectory has three acres of glorious gardens full of birdsong and scent – feel free to enjoy a drink or afternoon tea to the sound of a babbling brook or curl up on a lounger in a quiet glade and read a book.

The eight comfortable bedrooms are tastefully appointed all with sparkling en suite bathrooms – one has a balcony overlooking the gardens.

HOLLOWBROOK COTTAGES

Martinhoe, Exmoor National Park EX31 4QT
Tel: 01598 763368
e-mail: info@oldrectoryhotel.co.uk
website: www.exmoorcottages.co.uk

Hollowbrook Cottages – stylish holiday homes nestling in the grounds of The Old Rectory Hotel, a peaceful haven on the stunning Exmoor Coast. A walker's paradise, there is access to the coast path from the end of the garden. Beautifully furnished to a high specification with large comfy sofas, woodburning stoves and luxury kitchens, the cottages have been sympathetically converted from the old stable block with retained original beams, exposed stonework and latch doors yet offering all mod cons including complimentary wi-fi.

common on the North Devon and Exmoor coast but unusual elsewhere in Europe apart from the Norwegian fjords.

Ilfracombe

Like Barnstaple, Ilfracombe takes its floral decorations very seriously – during the 1990s the town was a consistent winner of the Britain in Bloom Competition. Between June and October the town goes "blooming mad" with streets, parks and hotels awash with flowers. Ilfracombe also promotes itself as a "Festival Town" offering a wide variety of events. They include a Victorian Celebration in mid-June when local people don period costumes. A grand costume ball and a fireworks display all add to the fun. There's the National Youth Arts Festival in July, a Fishing Festival in early August, a Carnival Procession later that month, and many more.

A fairly recent addition to the town's amenities is **The Landmark Theatre**, a striking building with what look like two gleaming white truncated cooling towers as its main feature. This multi-purpose arts centre has a 480-seat theatre, cinema screening facilities, a spacious display area and a café-bar with a sunny, sea facing terrace. Next door to the Landmark

Theatre, in Runnnymede Gardens, is the **Ilfracombe Museum** (see panel on page 124) which opened in 1932 and has a variety of displays ranging from bats to Buddhas.

With a population of around 11,000, Ilfracombe is the largest seaside resort on the North Devon coast. Up until 1800, however, it was just a small fishing and market town relying entirely on the sea both for its living and as its principal means of communication. The boundaries of the old town are marked by a sheltered natural harbour to the north, and, half-a-mile away to the south, a part-Norman parish church boasting one of the finest medieval waggon roofs in the West Country.

The entrance to Ilfracombe harbour is guarded by Lantern Hill, a steep-sided conical rock which is crowned by the restored medieval **Chapel of St Nicholas**. For centuries, this highly conspicuous former fishermen's chapel has doubled as a lighthouse, the light being placed in a lantern at the western end of the building. St Nicholas must surely be the only ecclesiastical building in the country to be managed by the local Rotary Club – it was they who raised the funds for its restoration. From the chapel's hilltop setting there are

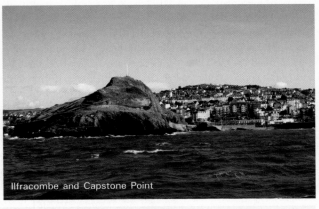

Ilfracombe and Capstone Point

Ilfracombe Museum

Wilder Rd, Ilfracombe, Devon EX34 8AF
Tel: 01271 863 541
website: www.devonmuseums.net

First opened in the 1930s and enlarged over the years, **Ilfracombe Museum** displays a fascinating range of exhibits that tell the story of the town and the surrounding area. Meanwhile, the Lundy Room gives visitors plenty of interesting background information on the island whilst, elsewhere, there are displays that cover all manner of subjects that highlight people's desire for collecting. Along with the memorabilia on display, the museum has, in its archive, back copies of the local newspaper from to the 1860s to the mid 20th century.

superb views of Ilfracombe, its busy harbour and the craggy North Devon coastline.

Like so many west country resorts, Ilfracombe developed in response to the early-19th century craze for sea bathing and sea water therapies. The **Tunnel Baths,** with their extravagant Doric façade, were opened in Bath Place in 1836, by which time a number of elegant residential terraces had been built on the hillside to the south of the old town.

The arrival of a branch railway line from Barnstaple in 1874 brought an even larger influx of visitors to Ilfracombe. Much of the town's architecture, which could best be described as "decorated Victorian vernacular", dates from this period, the new streets spreading inland in steeply undulating rows. Around the same time the harbour was enlarged to cope with the paddle steamers bringing in tourists from Bristol and South Wales. Today, visitors can take advantage of regular sailings from that harbour to Lundy Island, as well as cruises along the spectacular Exmoor coast.

Standing beside the harbour is the **Ilfracombe Aquarium,** housed in the former

lifeboat house. It contains an impressive collection of both freshwater and marine species in carefully re-created natural habitats. Worth a visit is the fun fish retail area here.

For walkers, the **South West Coast Path** from Ilfracombe provides some spectacular scenery, whether going west to Capstone Point, or east to Hillsborough Hill.

Just to the east of Ilfracombe, at Hele Bay, **The Old Corn Mill & Pottery** is unique in North Devon. Dating back to the 16th century, the mill has been lovingly restored from near dereliction and is now producing 100% wholemeal stone-ground flour for sale. In Robin Gray's pottery, you can watch him in action at the potter's wheel and try your own skill in fashioning slippery clay into a more-or-less recognisable object. If you really want to keep the result, the pottery will fire and glaze it, and post it on to you.

Half a mile or so south of the mill, set in a secluded valley, **Chambercombe Manor** is an 11th century mansion which was first recorded in the Domesday Book. Visitors have access to eight rooms displaying period furniture from Elizabethan to Victorian times, can peek into

Chambercombe Manor, nr Ilfracombe

the claustrophobic Priest's Hole, and test their sensitivity to the spectral presences reputed to inhabit the Haunted Room. The Coat of Arms bedroom was once occupied by Lady Jane Grey and it is her family's arms that are displayed above the fireplace. Outside, the four acres of beautiful grounds contain wildfowl ponds, a bird sanctuary and an arboretum.

BERRYNARBOR

3 miles E of Ilfracombe off the A399

🏠 St Peter's Church   🏰 Watermouth Castle

Nestling in a steep-sided combe, Berrynarbor is a wonderfully unspoilt village set around **St Peter's Church** which, with its 96ft high tower, is one of the grandest churches in North Devon. Inside, there's an interesting collection of monuments, many of them memorials of the Berry family, once the owners of the nearby 15th century manor house which later became the village school.

On the coast here is the pretty cove of Watermouth and the Victorian folly, **Watermouth Castle,** which has been transformed into a family theme park. In the castle's great hall, there's a collection of suits of armour and visitors can enjoy mechanical music demonstrations. Elsewhere, there are displays on Victorian life, antique pier machines, a room devoted to model railways and, down in the depths of the dungeon labyrinths, fairy tales come to life.

COMBE MARTIN

4 miles E of Ilfracombe on the A399

🏠 Combe Martin Museum   🐾 Exmoor Zoological Park

🐾 Wildlife & Dinosaur Park   🏰 Pack o' Cards Inn

Just a short distance from Berrynarbor, on the other side of the River Umber, is another popular resort, Combe Martin. There's a good sandy beach here and a short walk will take you to one of the secluded bays. An added attraction, especially for children, is the large number of rock pools amongst the bays. In the village itself, the main street is more than two miles long, reputed to be the longest in the country and featuring a wide selection of inns, cafés and shops. As well as the **Combe Martin Museum**, there is also the **Wildlife and Dinosaur Park** where life-sized animated dinosaurs lurk in the woods. The 25-acre site also shelters 250 species of real animals, including a large and lively collection of apes and monkeys. Within the park are animal handling areas, an "Earthquake Ride", a dinosaur museum and oriental gardens. There's an otter pool and daily sea lion shows and falconry displays, and if you book ahead you can experience the unique thrill of swimming with the sea lions.

A remarkable architectural curiosity in the village itself is **The Pack o' Cards Inn**, built by Squire George Ley in the early 18th century with the proceeds of a highly successful evening at the card table. This Grade II listed building represents a pack of cards with four decks, or floors, 13 rooms, and a total of 52 windows. Inside there are many features representing the cards in each suit.

About five miles to the east of Arlington Court, **Exmoor Zoological Park** is home to more than 170 species of unusual and exotic animals and birds. The residents of the 12 acres of gardens here range from pygmy marmosets to tarantulas, from penguins to catybara. Children can enjoy close encounters with many of the more cuddly animals, there are informative talks by the keepers but, as at any zoo, the most magnetic visitor attraction is the feeding time for the various animals.

PARRACOMBE

13 miles SE of Ilfracombe off the A39

🏛 Church of St Petroc

The redundant **Church of St Petroc** is notable for its marvellously unspoilt interior, complete with 15th century benches, 17th century box pews, a Georgian pulpit and a perfectly preserved musician's gallery. Perhaps most striking of all is the unique gated screen between the chancel and the nave which bears a huge tympanum painted with the royal arms, the Lord's Prayer, the Creed and the Ten Commandments. We owe the church's survival to John Ruskin who led the protests against its intended demolition in 1879 after another church was built lower down the hill.

Combe Martin Wildlife Park

MORTEHOE

4 miles W of Ilfracombe off the B3343

🗺 Barricane Beach   🏛 St Mary's Church

🏛 Mortehoe Heritage Centre

Mortehoe is the most north-westerly village in Devon and its name, meaning "raggy stump", reflects the rugged character of the Morte Peninsula. In this pretty stone-built village set on the cliff-top, Mortehoe's part-Norman **St Mary's Church** is certainly worth a visit. It's a small cruciform building with a 15th-century open-timbered waggon roof, an interesting early 14th century table tomb, a bell in the tower which may be the oldest in Devon, and a wonderful series of grotesquely carved Tudor bench ends. The church is also notable for the large mosaic of 1905 which fills the chancel arch. Designed by Selwyn Image, the Slade Professor of Art at Oxford, the mosaic was created by the same craftsmen who did the mosaics in St Paul's Cathedral.

In the village centre, the **Mortehoe Heritage Centre** occupies the Cart Linhay building and also serves as a local Tourist Information Centre. It contains a museum

---

🏛 historic building   🖼 museum and heritage   🏚 historic site   🗺 scenic attraction   🌱 flora and fauna

CRESCENT FOODS DELI & CAFÉ

3 The Crescent, Mortehoe, North Devon EX34 7DX
Tel: 01271 870688

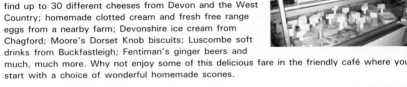

At **Crescent Foods Deli and Café** the emphasis is very definitely on top quality produce from local sources. You'll find up to 30 different cheeses from Devon and the West Country; homemade clotted cream and fresh free range eggs from a nearby farm; Devonshire ice cream from Chagford; Moore's Dorset Knob biscuits; Luscombe soft drinks from Buckfastleigh; Fentiman's ginger beers and much, much more. Why not enjoy some of this delicious fare in the friendly café where you can start with a choice of wonderful homemade scones.

which has sections dealing with the local farming communities, the railway and the history of shipwrecks in the area,

A short walk from Mortehoe village leads you to the dramatic coastline, mortally dangerous to ships, but with exhilarating views across to Lundy Island. Much of this clifftop area is in the guardianship of the National Trust which also protects nearby **Barricane Beach** (remarkable for being formed almost entirely of sea shells washed here from the Caribbean), and the three-mile stretch of Woolacombe Sands.

WOOLACOMBE
7 miles SW of Ilfracombe on the B3343

🖉 Once Upon a Time

The wonderful three-mile-long stretch of golden sands at Woolacombe is justifiably regarded as the finest beach in North Devon. This favoured resort lies between two dramatic headlands, both of which are now in the care of the National Trust. The sands and rock pools lying between these two outcrops are a delight for children, (along with the swing boats and donkey rides), and surfers revel in the monster waves rolling in from the Atlantic.

Back in the early 1800s, Woolacombe was little more than a hamlet whose few residents sustained a precarious livelihood by fishing. Then, suddenly, the leisured classes were seized by the craze for sea bathing initiated by George III at Weymouth and enthusiastically endorsed by his successor George IV at Brighton. Inspired by the economic success of those south coast towns, the two families who owned most of the land around Woolacombe, the Fortescues and the Chichesters, began constructing villas and hotels in the Regency style, elegant buildings which still endow the town with a very special charm and character. Many friends of the Fortescue and Chichester families regarded their initiative as a suicidally rash enterprise. Woolacombe was so remote and the roads of North Devon at that time still so primitive, little more than cart tracks. "Who," they asked, "would undertake such an arduous journey?" During the first few years only a trickle of well-to-do visitors in search of a novel (and comparatively inexpensive resort) found their way to Woolacombe. But their word of mouth recommendations soon ensured a steady flow of tourists, a flow which has swelled to a flood over subsequent years. The town recently won the England for Excellence Gold Award for best family resort, and was dubbed Best British Beach by the *Mail on Sunday*.

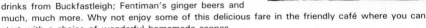

🖼 stories and anecdotes   🐦 famous people   🎨 art and craft   🖉 entertainment and sport   🚶 walks

Just outside the town, **Once Upon a Time** provides a huge variety of entertainment for younger children - indoor and outdoor play areas, crazy golf, a young scientist's room, children's driving school, train rides, animated fairy tales, an ocean of plastic balls to play through in the Wild Boar Adventure Trail, and much more.

Barnstaple

🏛 Pannier Market 🏛 St Ann's Chapel

🏛 Queen Anne's Walk 🏃 Tarka Trail

🏛 Butchers Row 🏛 Guildhall

Barnstaple enjoys a superb location at the head of the Taw estuary, at the furthest point downstream where it was possible to ford the river. The first bridge across the Taw was built in the late 1200s, but the present impressive structure, 700ft long with 16 arches, dates from about 1450 although it has been altered and widened many times.

Visitors will immediately realise that Barnstaple takes its floral decorations very seriously. The town began its association with the Britain in Bloom movement in 1991 and just five years later crowned its efforts by winning the Gold award for the "Prettiest Floral Town in Europe" in the Entente Florale Competition. Wherever you turn you may well find a magnificent display - a hay cart full of flowers outside the police station and civic centre, for example, a giant postage stamp modelled in blossoming plants outside the Post Office, or a stunning model of a train (again, all created in flowers) at the entrance to the railway station.

The town's love of floral exuberance may be one of its most endearing features but Barnstaple is also the administrative and commercial capital of the region, a pre-eminence it already enjoyed when the Domesday Book recorded the town as one of only four boroughs in the county. Back then, in 1086, Barnstaple had its own mint and, already, a regular market. More than nine centuries later, the town still hosts produce markets every Tuesday and Friday, but the **Pannier Market** is open every weekday. This huge, glass-roofed building covering some 45,000 square feet was built in 1855 and its grandiose architecture resembles that of a major Victorian railway station, (London's St Pancras springs to mind). The Market takes it name from the pannier baskets, (two wicker baskets connected by a leather strap draped across the back of a donkey, pony or horse), in which country people in those days would carry their fruit and vegetables to town.

River Taw, Barnstaple

Just across the road from the Pannier Market is **Butchers Row,** a quaint line of booth-like Victorian shops built

🏛 historic building 🏛 museum and heritage 🏛 historic site 🏵 scenic attraction 🌿 flora and fauna

ZENA'S RESTAURANT

1 Market Street, Barnstaple, Devon EX31 1BY
Tel: 01271 378844
e-mail: zburland@aol.com
website: www.zenasrestaurant.com

With its open air courtyard and Mediterranean style interior, **Zena's Restaurant** offers a truly cosmopolitan setting with a menu of innovative cuisine that fuses the global cultures of the Mediterranean and the Caribbean into an exciting culinary tour - a continental bistro where a passion for food is matched only by the friendly table service. Emerging as one of the south west's top dining destinations, Zena's is also notable for its live music every Saturday from noon until 3pm - usually a mix of blues and jazz -which adds to the chilled out atmosphere.

mostly of wood and with brightly painted wooden canopies. When they were built, back in 1855, they were occupied exclusively by butchers, but now you'll find a much wider variety of goods on sale – seaweed amongst them. Every week during the summer season at least 300lbs of this succulent algae are sold, most of it ending up as a breakfast dish, served with bacon and an egg on top.

In Barnstaple's High Street stands the rather austere **Guildhall,** built in the Grecian style in 1826 and now housing some interesting civic memorabilia – portraits, municipal regalia and silverware – which are occasionally on display. Nearby, the **Church of St Peter and St Paul** dates back to the early 1300s. After having its spire twisted by a lightning strike in 1810, it suffered even more badly later that century under the heavy hand of the Victorian restorer, Sir Gilbert Scott. Much more appealing are the charming 17th century **Horwood's Almshouses** nearby, and the 15th century **St Anne's Chapel** which served for many years as the town's Grammar School. During the late 17th century John Gay, author of *The Beggar's Opera,* was numbered amongst its pupils. The town has other literary

associations. William Shakespeare visited in 1605 and it was the sight of its narrow streets bustling with traders that inspired him to write *The Merchant of Venice.* The diarist Samuel Pepys

St Anne's Chapel, Barnstaple

🎦 stories and anecdotes 🐦 famous people 🎨 art and craft 🖌 entertainment and sport 🚶 walks

BOUTIQUE 28

Boutport Street, Barnstaple, North Devon EX31 1RP
Tel: 01271 377888
e-mail: joelleelmhirst@hotmail.co.uk
website: www.boutique-28.co.uk

Opened in 2005, **Boutique 28** stocks exclusive labels and brings new designers' collections to Barnstaple and, since February 2008, Taunton, giving individuality to customers. The mix of cosmopolitan, timelessly chic pieces and contemporary current trends, offers individual clothing for every woman.

Boutique 28 stocks Ispirato by Condici, Vera Mont, Marina Avraam, Libra, Joseph Ribcoff, Oui Set and Oui Moments, Avoca Renaissance, beautiful collections from the south of France with Zapa and Evalinka, Aftershock and Rene Derhy and many, many more. There are also hats by Walter Wright & Richard's Design & Fascinators, and a beautiful jewellery collection handpicked by Boutique 28's owner, Joelle Elmhirst. A beautifully handpicked selection of shoes by wonderful designers such as Valentino Russo, Esino and Aftershock, scarves and belts will help you to put the final touch to the look you desire.

Feel free to come and browse in the friendly and relaxed atmosphere where a dedicated team will help you to find the dream outfit for whatever occasion. With endless classics and a unique style, Boutique 28 offers you the perfect look for the perfect occasion.

PUSHKIN'S

63-64 Boutport Street, Barnstaple, North Devon EX31 1HG
Tel: 01271 346624
e-mail: dominic.rawling@virgin.net
website: www.pushkins.co.uk

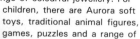

Located just off Barnstaple High Street, close to the town square and the river Torridge, **Pushkin's** offers an interesting mix of stylish clothing, toys and gifts. Owners Dominic and Kate Rawling took over the clothes shop in October 2007 and have introduced other lines with a wide appeal. The clothes on sale include casual wear, attractive summer dresses, colourful sweaters and cardigans from Ecuador, and some lovely jackets from India. Natural fibres are used and the sizes range from 10 to 18. Accessories include Natural Nomads Fair Trade bags from India and a striking range of colourful jewellery. For

children, there are Aurora soft toys, traditional animal figures, games, puzzles and a range of creative modern toys. Then there is the wide selection of greetings cards, including some by local artists and some featuring local scenes. Other local products include the range of bronzes made by the Running Dog Foundry at nearby East Buckland, and the decorative glass bowls from Holsworthy Dean. Pushkin's is open from 9.30am to 5pm, with longer opening hours during the summer.

🏛 historic building 🏛 museum and heritage 🏛 historic site ⌘ scenic attraction 🌿 flora and fauna

married a 15-year-old Barnstaple girl in 1655.

As at Tiverton, the 17th century well-to-do residents of Barnstaple were given to charitable endowments. As well as Thomas Horwood's almshouses, Messrs. Paige and Penrose both bequeathed substantial funds for almshouses, and in 1659 Thomas' wife, Alice, paid for the building in Church Lane of a school for "20 poor maids". It is now a coffee house.

A slightly later building of distinction is **Queen Anne's Walk**, a colonnaded arcade with some lavish ornamentation and surmounted by a large statue of the Queen herself. Opened in 1708, it was used by the Barnstaple wool merchants who accepted that any verbal bargain they agreed over the Tome Stone was legally binding. The building stands on the old town quay from which, in 1588, five ships set sail to join Drake's fleet against the Armada. The building is now home to the **Barnstaple Heritage Centre** where more can be found out about this ancient town and one of its most enduring industries, pottery, which has been made here continuously since the 13th century. As in those days, local Fremington red clay is used.

Barnstaple has two railway stations but only one is still functioning. This is the northern terminus of the **Tarka Line**, a lovely 39-mile route that follows the gentle river valleys of the Yeo and the Taw where Tarka the Otter had his home. The railway is actually the main line route to Exeter but has been renamed in honour of one of the area's major visitor attractions.

Walkers along the **Tarka Trail** will know Barnstaple well as the crossover point in this figure-of-eight long-distance footpath. Inspired by Henry Williamson's celebrated story of *Tarka the Otter*, the 180-mile trail wanders through a delightful variety of Devon scenery – tranquil countryside, wooded river valleys, rugged moorland, and a stretch of the North Devon coast, with part of the route taking in the Tarka Line railway in order to get the best views of the locations described in the novel.

Around Barnstaple

MUDDIFORD
4 miles N of Barnstaple on the B3230

🌿 Marwood Hill Gardens

From Barnstaple to Ilfracombe, the B3230 winds through a pretty valley, passing along the way through attractive small villages. Despite the rather unappealing name, Muddiford is one of them. The village really did get its name from the "muddy ford" by which medieval travellers used to cross the river here.

About two miles southwest of Muddiford, **Marwood Hill Gardens** offer visitors some 18 acres of trees and shrubs, many of them

Marwood Hill Gardens, Marwood

rare and unusual. The collection was started more than half a century ago and now includes an enormous number and variety of plants. The three lakes, linked by the largest bog garden in the West Country, are busy with ducks and multi-coloured carp. From spring, when camellias and magnolias are in bloom, through to the brilliant hues of autumn, the gardens provide a continuous spectacle of colour. The gardens are home to the national collections of astilbe, iris and tulbaghia.

ARLINGTON
6 miles NE of Barnstaple on the A39

🏛 Arlington Court

Arlington Court is an imposing National Trust property which was home to the Chichester family from 1534 until the last owner, Rosalie Chichester, died childless in 1949. (Sir Francis Chichester, famous as an aviation pioneer and as the first solo round-the-world sailor, was born two miles away at Shirwell). The present house was built in 1822 to an unambitious design by the Barnstaple architect, Thomas Lee, and extended some 40 years later by Sir Bruce Chichester who also added the handsome stable block. When he died in 1881, he left the house and its 2,775-acre park to his daughter Rosalie, along with a staggering mountain of debts. Only 15 years old when she inherited the estate, Rosalie managed to keep it intact and stayed on at Arlington Court until her death at the age of 83.

The interior today is really a museum reflecting Rosalie's varied interests. There are displays of her collections of porcelain, pewter, shells, snuff boxes, and more than a hundred model ships, some made by French soldiers captured during the Napoleonic wars.

Intriguingly, Rosalie never saw the most valuable work of art amongst her possessions. After her death, a watercolour by William Blake was discovered on top of a wardrobe where it had lain forgotten for over 100 years. It is now on display in the white drawing room.

During her lifetime, Rosalie Chichester transformed the grounds of Arlington Court into something of a nature reserve. She ordered the building of an eight-mile long perimeter fence to protect the native wildfowl and heron populations. The Shetland ponies and Jacob sheep grazing the fields today are descendants of those introduced by Rosalie. Another of her eclectic interests is evident in the 18th century stable block which houses a unique collection of horse-drawn carriages she saved from destruction.

LANDKEY
2 miles SE of Barnstaple off the A361

🐾 Miss Piggyland

Landkey boasts a fine church with some impressive memorials (well worth visiting) and also the distinction of being the only village bearing this name in Britain. Historians believe that it is derived from *Lan*, the Celtic word for a church, and the saint to which it was dedicated, Kea. An enduring legend claims that St Kea rowed over from Wales with his personal cow on board determined to convert the pagans of North Devon to Christianity. Sadly, these benighted people were not persuaded by his eloquence, so they chopped off his head. Not many public speakers could cope with that kind of negative response, but St Kea calmly retrieved his severed head and continued, head in hand, to preach the Gospel for many years.

Just outside the village, **Miss Piggyland, Rabbit World and Indoor Jungle World** has been trading as a farm park and rare breed centre since 1992 with the aim of providing an educational glimpse into times and lifestyles past. It is set in beautiful, unspoilt North Devon countryside, and centres around a Grade II listed, 15th century Devon farm house. There are more than 50 acres of lovely countryside and nature walks to explore, including lime kilns, badger sets, rivers and lakes. There are many animals to see and feed as well as activities for the young ones, whatever the weather.

SWIMBRIDGE
5 miles SE of Barnstaple on the A361

🐾 Revd "Jack" Russell 🏛 Church of St James

For almost half a century from 1833 this attractive village was the home of the **Rev. John "Jack" Russell,** the celebrated hunting parson and breeder of the first Jack Russell terriers. A larger than life character, he was an enthusiastic master of foxhounds and when his bishop censured him for pursuing such an unseemly sport for a man of the cloth, he transferred the pack into his wife's name and continued his frequent sorties. He was still riding to hounds in his late 70s and when he died in 1880 at the age of 87 hundreds of people attended his funeral. Russell was buried in the churchyard of St James', the church where he had been a diligent pastor. He was gratefully remembered for his brief sermons, delivered as his groom waited by the porch with his horse saddled and ready.

Mostly 15th century, the **Church of St James** is one of Devon's outstanding churches, distinctive from outside because of its unusual lead-covered spire. Inside, there is a wealth of ecclesiastical treasures: a richly carved rood screen spanning both the nave and the aisles, an extraordinary 18th century font cover in the shape of an elongated octagonal "cupboard", a fine 15th century stone pulpit supported by a tall pedestal and carved with the figures of saints and angels, and a wonderful nave roof with protective angels gazing down. Collectors of unusual epitaphs will savour the punning lines inscribed on a monument here to John Rosier, a lawyer who died in 1658:

> *Lo, with a Warrant sealed by God's decree*
> *Death his grim Seargant hath arrested me*
> *No bayle was to be given, no law could save*
> *My body from the prison of the grave.*

The village itself has some elegant Georgian houses and a pub which in 1962 was renamed after Swimbridge's most famous resident. Jack Russell societies from around the world frequently hold their meetings here.

COBBATON
6 miles SE of Barnstaple off the A377

🏛 Cobbaton Combat Collection

The hamlet of Cobbaton is home to the largest private collection of military vehicles and wartime memorabilia in the south west.

Cobbaton Combat Collection

HIGHER BIDDACOTT FARM

Chittlehampton, nr Umberleigh, Devon EX37 9PY
Tel/Fax: 01769 540222
e-mail: waterers@sosi.net
website: www.heavy_horses.net

Home to Jonathan and Fiona Waterer, **Higher Biddacott Farm** is a wonderful Grade II listed building dating back to the 12th century. It is surrounded by glorious unspoilt countryside and offers charming bed and breakfast accommodation in five delightful guest bedrooms, all en suite with bath. One of the bedrooms features an original 17th century ceiling by the Abbott brothers who were renowned for their plaster work in Devon at that time. There are also magnificent fireplaces in the residents' sitting room, and in the dining room where there's a log fire.

What makes High Biddacott extra special are the couple's heavy horses which they use to farm sustainably their 100 acres of land. Guests can sign up for one of the driving courses that Jonathan runs, watch the horses at work and also participate in various traditional farming activities. Another attraction is the Wildlife Trail around the farm which has been developed in conjunction with the Devon Wildlife Trust. The full trail extends for a little over a mile and takes in, en route, a large badger sett, flora such as wild garlic and bluebells in spring, wood avens and red campion later in the year, and a wildflower meadow.

In the evenings, three-course home-cooked meals are available - bring your own wine.

Owner Preston Isaac started the **Cobbaton Combat Collection** as a hobby but admits that "it got out of hand!" His schoolboy's box of treasures has grown to comprise more than 60 World War II military vehicles, including tanks and artillery, along with weapons and equipment from all over the world as well as thousands of smaller items. For visitors' convenience, a NAAFI truck is on duty to provide snacks and drinks and the Quartermaster's Stores offers a range of surplus uniforms, de-activated guns, militaria, books and souvenirs.

BISHOPS TAWTON
2 miles S of Barnstaple on the A377

Bishop's Tawton takes its name from the River Taw and the medieval Bishop's Palace that stood here until the reign of Henry VIII and of which a few fragments still stand. The village today is not over-endowed with listed buildings but it can boast a very unusual one, a sociable three-seater outside lavatory which has been accorded Grade II listed status. This amenity has not been used for 40 years or more (and the brambles which have invaded it would make it rather uncomfortable to do so) but it still looks perfectly serviceable.

ATHERINGTON
7 miles S of Barnstaple on the B3217

🏛 St Mary's Church

A landmark for miles around, **St Mary's Church** stands in the picturesque square of this hilltop village and is notable for a feature which is unique in Devon – a lavishly carved and alarmingly top-heavy rood loft. Created by two carvers from Chittlehampton in the 1530s, it is an exceptionally fine example of their craft. The church also contains striking effigies of Sir John Wilmington, who died in 1349, and his wife; a window of medieval glass; and well-preserved brasses of Sir John Basset, (died 1529), his two wives and 12 children.

HIGH BICKINGTON
8 miles S of Barnstaple on the B3217

Two miles south of Atherington is another hilltop village. Standing at almost 600ft above sea level, the village commands excellent views in all directions. It boasts a fine 16th century inn, The George, which is set amongst a delightful group of thatched cottages, and a parish church dating back to the 1100s which is renowned for its exceptional collection of carved bench and pew ends. There are around 70 of them in all: some are Gothic (characterised by fine tracery); others are Renaissance (characterised by rounded figures). More recent carving on the choir stalls depicts an appealing collection of animals and birds.

BRAUNTON
6 miles NW of Barnstaple on the A361

🏛 Braunton Great Field

Braunton claims the rather odd distinction of being the largest village in Devon. It is certainly a sizeable community, spreading along both sides of the River Caen, with some handsome Georgian houses and a substantial church reflecting Braunton's relative importance in medieval times. The church is dedicated to St Brannoc, a Celtic saint who arrived here from Wales in the 6th century. It's said that his bones lie beneath the altar of the present 13th century church, a story which

may well be true since the building stands on the site of a Saxon predecessor. What is certainly true is that the church contains some of the finest 16th century carved pews to be found anywhere in England. Many of the carvings depict pigs, a clear allusion to the ancient tradition that St Brannoc was instructed in a dream to build a church where he came across a sow and her litter of seven pigs. Arriving in North Devon the saint happily discovered this very scene at the spot where Braunton's church now stands.

There is further evidence of Saxon occupation of this area to be found in **Braunton Great Field**, just to the south west of the village. This is one of very few remaining examples of the Saxon open-field strip system still being actively farmed in Britain. Around 350 acres in total, the field was originally divided into around 700 half-acre strips, each of them a furlong (220yds) long, and 11yds wide. Each strip was separated by an unploughed "landshare" about one foot wide. Throughout the centuries, many of the strips have changed hands and been combined, so that now only about 200 individual ones remain.

CROYDE
9 miles NW of Barnstaple on the B3231

🐾 Braunton Burrows   🐾 Baggy Point

One of the prettiest villages in Devon, Croyde is renowned for its excellent beach with, just around the headland, another three-mile stretch of sands at Saunton Sands, one of the most glorious, family-friendly sandy beaches in the West Country. The sands are backed by 1,000 acres of dunes known as **Braunton Burrows.** The southern part of this wide expanse is a designated nature reserve noted for its fluctuating population of migrant birds

Baggy Point, Croyde

while in Norfolk but returned to Georgeham where he died in 1947. He is buried in the graveyard of St George's Church.

Bideford

🏛 Pannier Market
🏛 Royal Hotel
🏛 Burton Museum
🗺 Lundy Island

as well as rare flowers and insects.

Also noted for its abundant wildlife is **Baggy Point,** just northwest of Croyde. This headland of Devonian rock (so named because the rock was first identified in this county) is a popular nesting place for seabirds, including herring gull, fulmar, shag and cormorant. Grey seals can often be seen from here.

Running north westwards from the cliffs is a shoal known as Baggy Leap. In 1799, *HMS Weazle* was driven onto the shoal during a gale and all 106 souls on board perished.

GEORGEHAM
9 miles NW of Barnstaple off the B3231

🐿 Henry Williamson

It was in Georgeham that **Henry Williamson** settled in 1921 and where he wrote his most famous novel, *Tarka the Otter,* which was published in 1927. 'Tarka' lived in the land between the Taw and Torridge rivers and many of the small villages and settlements feature in the story. The writer lived a very simple life in a wooden hut that he built himself. After World War II, he farmed for a

Dubbed the "Little White Town" by Charles Kingsley, this attractive town set beside the River Torridge was once the third busiest port in Britain. The first bridge across the shallow neck of the Torridge estuary was built around 1300 to link Bideford with its aptly-named satellite village, East-the-Water. That bridge must have been very impressive for its time. It was 670ft long, and built of massive oak lintels of varying length which created a series of irregular arches between 12 and 25ft apart. These erratic dimensions were preserved when the bridge was rebuilt in stone around 1460, (the old bridge was used as scaffolding), and despite widening during the 1920s they persist to this day. Unusually, Bideford Bridge is managed by an ancient corporation of trustees, known as *feoffees,* whose income, derived from property in the town, not only pays for the upkeep of the bridge but also supports local charities and good causes. A high-level bridge a mile or so downstream, opened in 1987, has relieved some of the traffic congestion and also provides panoramic views of the town and the Torridge estuary.

🏛 historic building   🏛 museum and heritage   🏛 historic site   🗺 scenic attraction   🌱 flora and fauna

Bideford received its Market Charter from Henry III in 1272, (on May 25th to be precise) and markets still take place every Tuesday and Saturday. Since 1883 they have been held in the splendid **Pannier Market** building, reckoned to be one of the best surviving examples of a Victorian covered market. Along with local produce, there's a huge selection of gifts, crafts, and handmade goods on offer: "Everything from Antiques to Aromatherapy!"

Devon ports seemed to specialise in particular commodities. At Bideford it was tobacco from the North American colonies which brought almost two centuries of prosperity until the American War of Independence shut off supplies. Evidence of this golden age can still be seen in the opulent merchants' residences in Bridgeland Street, and most strikingly in the **Royal Hotel** in East-the-Water, a former merchant's house of 1688 with a pair of little-seen plasterwork ceilings which are perhaps the finest and most extravagant examples of their kind in Devon.

It was while he was staying at the Royal Hotel that Charles Kingsley penned most of *Westward Ho!* A quarter of a million words long, the novel was completed in just seven months. There's a statue of Kingsley, looking suitably literary, on Bideford Quay. Broad and tree-lined, the Quay stands at the foot of the narrow maze of lanes which formed the old seaport.

Just round the corner from the Quay, on the edge of Victoria Park, is the **Burton Museum & Art Gallery**, opened in 1994.

COOPERS FINE ANTIQUE JEWELLERY & PICTURES

47 Mill Street, Bideford,
North Devon EX39 2JR
Tel: 01237 477370
e-mail: coopergallery@freecell.co.uk

Located on a pedestrianised road parallel to Quay Street, **Coopers Fine Antique Jewellery & Pictures** is a well-established business with a fine reputation.

Owned and run by Jenny and David Bruce, Coopers specialises in fine antique and modern jewellery, silver, watches and pictures. Amongst the paintings you'll find scenes of Dartmoor and other local places, watercolours and oils of boats, in particular the famous tea clippers.

Notable artists featured include FJ Widgery and RD Sherrin. Coopers offers a seven-day wedding ring service as well as a quality reframing service.

The museum contains some interesting curios such as Bideford harvest jugs of the late 1700s, and model ships in carved bone made by French prisoners during the Napoleonic wars. The gallery has frequently changing exhibitions with subjects ranging from automata to kites, quilts to dinosaurs, as well as paintings by well-known North Devon artists. The museum also has a craft gallery, shop, workshop, lecture area and coffee shop.

Starting at the Burton Gallery, guided walks around the town are available.

One excursion from Bideford that should not be missed is the day trip to **Lundy Island** on the supply boat, the *MS Oldenburg*. Lundy is a huge lump of granite rock, three miles long and half a mile wide, with sheer cliffs rising 500ft above the shore. Its name derives from the Norse *lunde ey*, meaning puffin island, and these attractive birds with their multi-coloured beaks are still in residence, along with many other species. More than 400 different species of birds have been spotted on Lundy, and you might also spot one of the indigenous black rats which have survived only at this isolated spot. The island has a 13th century castle and a lighthouse, both offering accommodation, a church, a pub and a shop selling souvenirs and the famous stamps.

Around Bideford

WESTWARD HO!
2 miles NW of Bideford on the B3236

🐦 Northam Burrows Country Park

🍃 Pot Walloping Festival

Is there any other place in the world that has been named after a popular novel? Following the huge success in 1855 of Charles Kingsley's tale of Elizabethan derring-do, a company was formed to develop this spectacular site with its rocky cliffs and two miles of sandy beach. The early years were troubled. A powerful storm washed away the newly-built pier and most of the houses. When Rudyard Kipling came here in 1874 as a pupil at the United Services College he described the place as "twelve bleak houses by the shore". Today Westward Ho! is a busy holiday resort well worth visiting for its two miles of golden sands, recently awarded a Blue Flag, and the nearby **Northam Burrows Country Park,** almost 1,000 acres of grazed burrows rich in flora, fauna and migratory birds, and offering tremendous views across Bideford Bay.

An unusual event at Westward Ho! is the **Pot Walloping Festival** which takes place in late spring. Local people and visitors join together to throw pebbles which have been dislodged by winter storms back onto the

Needle Rock, Lundy Island

famous ridge, after which pots of a different kind also get a walloping.

NORTHAM
2 miles N of Bideford on the A386

🏛 Bloody Corner

Northam is said to have been where Hubba the Dane attacked Devon and was repelled by either Alfred the Great or the Earl of Devon. Another tale recounts that in 1069AD, three years after King Harold had been slain at the Battle of Hastings, his three sons landed at Northam in an attempt to regain their father's throne. They came from Ireland with an invasion force of more than 60 ships but their rebellion was mercilessly suppressed at a site just to the south of the town. To this day, it is known as **Bloody Corner**.

APPLEDORE
3 miles N of Bideford on the A386

🏛 North Devon Maritime Museum

🎨 Appledore Visual Arts Festival

Overlooking the Taw-Torridge estuary, Appledore is a delightful old-world fishing village of narrow winding lanes and sturdy fishermen's cottages from the 18th and 19th centuries. All types of fishing can be arranged here and you can even go crabbing from the quayside. The streets of the old quarter are too narrow for cars although not, it seems, for the occasional small fishing boat which is pulled up from the harbour and parked between the buildings.

It seems appropriate that the **North Devon Maritime Museum** should be located in this truly nautical setting. Housed in a former ship-owner's residence, the museum contains a wealth of seafaring memorabilia, a photographic exhibit detailing the military exercises around the estuary in preparation for the D-Day landings during World War II, a reconstructed Victorian kitchen, and much more.

A stroll along Bude Street is recommended. Art and craft galleries have gathered here amongst the Georgian style "Captains" houses, and it's particularly colourful during the **Appledore Visual Arts Festival** in late May-early June when one of the many events is a door decorating competition.

INSTOW
3 miles N of Bideford on the B3233

The older part of this delightful village lies inland from the Torridge estuary while, looking out over the magnificent beach, there are some early 19th century villas. Here, too, is

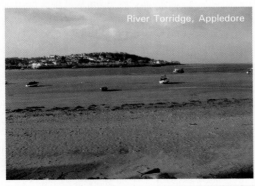
River Torridge, Appledore

the **Instow Signal Box** that was built in 1873 to control the crossing gates and the passing loop at Instow Station. It has been restored and is now the first Grade II listed signal box in the country. Visitors can see its machinery, gate wheel and instruments as well as 'pull off' a re-instated signal.

Just south of the village are **Tapeley Park Gardens,** some 35 acres of grounds on the eastern bank of the River Torridge. From here there are

🏛 stories and anecdotes 🎨 famous people 🎨 art and craft ✍ entertainment and sport 🚶 walks

WATERSIDE GALLERY

2 Marine Terrace, Instow, Bideford,
Devon EX39 4HZ
Tel/Fax: 01271 860786
e-mail: jmj@watersideart.co.uk
website: www.watersideart.co.uk

The seaside village of Instow, between Barnstaple and Bideford, enjoys glorious views across the Torridge Estuary to the old fishing community of Appledore. The **Waterside Gallery** occupies a superb position on the quayside at Instow, its large windows overlooking the water.

The Gallery showcases work by leading local artists, potters and craftsmen of the South West and also stages occasional exhibitions of individual artist's work – details can be found on the Gallery's website or if you wish to be included in its mailing list just let owner Judith James know.

Examples of work by artists such as Colin Albrook, Ken Doughty and Mary Tozer; pottery by Clive Pearson, Pat Armstrong and Phillip and Frannie Leach can also be seen on the website.

excellent views across the estuary and over to Lundy Island. Along with the lake reached by a woodland walk, there are masses of hydrangeas, rhododendrons and camellias. As well as the renovated Italian terraces and the restored walled kitchen garden, Tapeley has a new organic perm culture garden where fruit, vegetables, nuts and herbs are mixed together using companion planting. There is also a children's play area and a variety of animals and pets to entertain the youngsters. The Gardens are open daily, except Saturdays, from mid-March to the end of October.

GREAT TORRINGTON
7 miles SE of Bideford on the A386

🏛 Church of St Michael

💎 Dartington Crystal

🦋 May Fair   🌿 Rosemoor Garden

A good place to start exploring Great Torrington is at **Castle Hill** which commands

grand views along the valley of the River Torridge. (There's no view of the castle: that was demolished as long ago as 1228: its site is now a bowling green). On the opposite bank of the river is the hamlet of Taddiport where the tiny 14th century church by the bridge was originally the chapel of a leper hospital: its inmates were not permitted to cross over into Torrington itself.

Not many churches in England have been blown up by gunpowder. That was the fate however of the original **Church of St Michael and All Angels.** It happened during the Civil War when General Fairfax captured the town on February 16th, 1645. His Royalist prisoners were bundled into the church which they had been using as an arsenal. In the darkness, the 80 barrels of gunpowder stored there were somehow set alight and in the huge explosion that followed the church was demolished, 200 men lost their lives, and

🏛 historic building 🏛 museum and heritage 🏛 historic site 🔱 scenic attraction 🌿 flora and fauna

Fairfax himself narrowly escaped death. The present spacious church was built five years later, one of very few in the country erected during the Commonwealth years.

Today, the town's leading tourist attraction is **Dartington Crystal** where visitors can see skilled craftsmen blowing and shaping the crystal, follow the history of glass-making from the Egyptians to the present day, watch a video presentation, and browse amongst some 10,000 square feet of displays. The enterprise was set up in the 1960s by the Dartington Hall Trust to provide employment in an area of rural depopulation:

Great Torrington Castle

today, the beautifully designed handmade crystal is exported to more than 50 countries around the world.

Torrington's **May Fair** is still an important event in the local calendar, and has been since 1554. On the first Thursday in May, a Queen

THE SOAP KITCHEN

11a South Street, Great Torrington, Devon EX38 8AA
Tel: 01805 622221
website: www.thesoapkitchenplus.co.uk

Located close to the town centre, the wonderfully fragrant **Soap Kitchen** offers a huge choice of quality handmade soaps and toiletries. Owner Lesley Phillips began by making soaps and fragrances at the rear of the shop in 2001. She and her husband Richard now have their own factory and are supplying other shops throughout Devon. Their shop now stocks an alluring range of quality bath time accessories, including bath bombs, moisturising creams and gels, oils, beautiful handmade natural soaps, plus other handmade and hand-finished toiletries. In addition to its own products, the shop also stocks products from a selection of quality manufacturers.

The shop is not exclusively devoted to soaps and toiletries. It also stocks a range of fashion jewellery, scarves, pashminas, a selection of giftware, candles, greetings cards, gift bags, 'Made in Devon' wall plaques and other decorative designs. The Soap Kitchen is easy to find as it is near the main town square, just a very short walk from the main town centre car park.

RHS GARDEN ROSEMOOR

Rosemoor, Great Torrington, Devon EX38 8PH
Tel: 01805 624067   Fax: 01805 624717
e-mail: rosemooradmin@rhs.org.uk
website: www.rhs.org.uk

The Royal Horticultural Society Garden **Rosemoor** is acclaimed by gardeners throughout the world, but visitors do not have to be keen gardeners to appreciate the beauty and diversity of Rosemoor. Whatever the season, the garden is a unique and enchanting place that people return to time and time again. Situated on the west-facing slopes of the beautiful Torridge Valley, Rosemoor is undeniably one of the jewels in the West Country crown. Generously donated to the Society by Lady Anne Palmer in 1988, Rosemoor is now established as a garden of national importance, famous for its variety and planting.

To Lady Anne's collection of rare and interesting plants a wide range of varied features has been added. They include a formal garden, where the object is to display an enormous selection of plants and planting schemes. Then there is a series of individual gardens such as the renowned Rose Gardens, Foliage Gardens, the Cottage, Square and Spiral Gardens, and the Winter Garden which provides some stunning effects in the colder months. Other attractions include a lake, a bamboo and fern planted rock gully, an arboretum, three model gardens, and a marvellous fruit and vegetable garden.

Also on site is a Plant Centre and Shop which stocks a wealth of colourful, rare and beautiful plants. Each plant comes with a two-year guarantee. The shop stocks a delightful selection of beautiful gifts, local produce and drinks including Rosemoor's own apple juice produced from fruit in its own garden.

Round off your visit by sampling the fare on offer in the licensed Restaurant with its garden views, or in the Wisteria Tea Room. Visitors can use the restaurant, plant centre and shop all year round without having to pay a garden entry fee.

APARTMENTS AT ROSEMOOR

RHS Garden Rosemoor, Great Torrington,
Devon EX38 8PH
Tel: 01805 624067   Fax: 01805 624717

Apartments at Rosemoor offer quality self-catering accommodation in a delightful setting. Rosemoor House was built around the 1780s and was donated to the Royal Horticultural Society in 1988 along with the exquisite Rosemoor Garden. The three apartments are in the northern and western wings of the house. 'Magnolia', on the ground floor, can sleep two guests; 'Camellia' on the first floor also sleeps two; while 'Azalea', also on the first floor, can accommodate up to four people. All enjoy lovely garden views.

is crowned, there is maypole dancing in the High Street, and a banner proclaims the greeting *"Us be plazed to zee 'ee"*.

About a mile south of Great Torrington, the Royal Horticultural Society's **Rosemoor Garden** (see panel on page 142) occupies a breathtaking setting in the Torridge Valley. The 40-acre site includes mature planting in Lady Anne Palmer's magnificent garden and arboretum; a winding rocky gorge with bamboos and ferns beside the stream, and a more formal area which contains one of the longest herbaceous borders in the country. There are trails for children, a picnic area and an award-winning Visitor Centre with a licensed restaurant, plant centre and shop.

MONKLEIGH
5 miles S of Bideford on the A388

🎭 Sir William Hankford

Monkleigh parish church contains a striking monument, an ornate canopied tomb containing the remains of **Sir William Hankford** who was Lord Chief Justice of England in the early 1400s. He lived at nearby Annery Park and the story goes that having been troubled by poachers Sir William instructed his gamekeeper to shoot anyone he found in the park at night. The gamekeeper did indeed see a figure passing through the park, fired and discovered to his horror that he had killed his master.

WEARE GIFFARD
5 miles S of Bideford off the A386

🏠 Weare Giffard Hall

This appealing village claims to be the longest riverside village in England, straggling for almost two miles along the banks of the Torridge. Weare Giffard (pronounced *Jiffard*) has a charm all its own, suspended in time it seems to belong to the more peaceful days of half a century ago. The villagers have even refused to have full street lighting installed, so avoiding the "street furniture" that blemishes so many attractive places.

Another attraction in the village is a fine old 15th century manor house, **Weare Giffard Hall**. Although its outer walls were partially demolished during the Civil War, the splendid gatehouse with its mighty doors and guardian lions has survived. Inside, the main hall has a magnificent hammer-beam roof, and several of the other rooms are lined with Tudor and Jacobean oak panelling. For centuries, the house was the home of the Fortescue family and in the nearby church there is an interesting "family tree" with portraits of past Fortescues carved in stone.

WOOLFARDISWORTHY
11 miles SW of Bideford off the A39

🎭 Milky Way Adventure Park

Naturally, you don't pronounce Woolfardisworthy the way it looks. The correct pronunciation is *Woolsery*. The extraordinary name goes back to Saxon times when the land was owned by Wulfheard who established a *worthig*, or homestead, here.

A mile or so north of the village, alongside the A39, is another family entertainment complex, the **Milky Way Adventure Park**. The park includes a huge indoor play area (for both children and adults) where you can test your archery and laser target shooting skills, a Pets Corner where children are encouraged to cuddle the animals, a Bird of Prey Centre, a Sheep Dog Training and Breeding Centre, "Toddler Town" - a safe play area for very young children, a Sports Hall, a miniature railway, and a "Time Warp Adventure Zone".

FOXDOWN MANOR COTTAGES

Horns Cross, Bideford, North Devon EX39 5PJ
Tel: 01237 451325
e-mail: enquiries@foxdownmanorcottages.co.uk
website: www.foxdownmanorcottages.co.uk

Located in the 12-acre grounds of an elegant Victorian
Manor House, **Foxdown Manor Cottages** were originally the
Stables, Dairy, Bakery, Smithy and Byre. There are six
cottages in all, sleeping from two people to eight plus. These lovely old properties are all
comprehensively equipped, including colour TV with Freeview and a DVD player. In the
extensive grounds with its stream and woods, there's also a tennis court, an outside heated
swimming pool during July and August, weather permitting, and a sauna for which there is a
small charge. There is also a croquet lawn and dogs are welcome for a small charge.

BARTON FARM SHOP

South Stroxworthy Farm, Wolsery, nr Clovelly, North Devon EX39 5QB
Tel: 01237 431690
e-mail: bartonfarmshop@btinternet.com
website: www.bartonfarmshop.co.uk

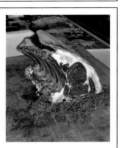

South Stroxworthy Farm has been in Steve Harding's family since 1959.
Barton Farm Shop sources as much as possible directly from this farm
and this is increasing all the time. All the rest is always sourced locally
from within North and Mid Devon, and North Cornwall. The shop is
well-established as suppliers of the finest quality home-reared beef and
lamb and locally sourced pork, chicken and home-grown vegetables. Also
available are homemade pies, pasties, Scotch eggs, quiches, chutneys and fresh bread. The shop
is open from 9am to 5pm, Monday to Friday; 9am to 2pm on Saturday.

CLOVELLY
12 miles SW of Bideford off the A39

🏠 Kingsley Exhibition 🏠 Fisherman's Cottage

⚱ Clovelly Pottery

Even if you've never been to Devon, you
must have heard of this unbelievably quaint
and picturesque village that tumbles down a
steep hillside in terraced levels. Almost every
whitewashed and flower-strewn cottage is
worthy of its own picture postcard and from
the sheltered little harbour there is an
enchanting view of this unique place. One
reason Clovelly is so unspoilt is that the village
has belonged to the Rous family since 1738
and they have ensured that it has been spared

such modern defacements as telegraph poles
and "street furniture".

The only access to the beach and the
beautifully restored 14th century quay is on
foot or by donkey, although there is a Land
Rover service from the Red Lion Hotel for
those who can't face the climb back up the
hill. The only other forms of transport are the
sledges which are used to deliver weekly
supplies. During the summer months there are
regular boat trips around the bay, and the
Jessica Hettie travels daily to Lundy Island with
timings that allow passengers to spend some
six hours there, watching the seals and
abundant wildlife.

The skipper of the *Jessica Hettie*, Clive

HARTLAND
15 miles SW of Bideford on the B3248

🏛 Church of St Nectan ⚓ Hartland Point

🏛 Hartland Abbey

This pleasant village with its narrow streets and small square was once larger and more important than Bideford. Hartland was a royal possession from the time of King Alfred until William the Conqueror and continued to be a busy centre right up to the 19th century. It was at its most prosperous in the 1700s and some fine Georgian buildings survive from that period. But the most striking building is the parish **Church of St Nectan** (see panel on page 146) which stands about 1.5 miles west of the village. This is another of Devon's "must-see" churches. The exterior is impressive enough with its 128ft high tower, but it is the glorious 15th century screen inside which makes this church one of the most visited in the county. A masterpiece of the medieval woodcarvers' art, its elegant arches are topped by four exquisitely fretted bands of intricate designs. The arches are delicately painted, reminding one yet again how colourful English churches used to be before the vandalism of the Puritan years.

In the churchyard is the grave of Allen Lane who, in 1935, revolutionised publishing by his introduction of Penguin Books, paperback books which were sold at sixpence (2.5p) each.

From the village, follow the signs to **Hartland Abbey.** Founded in 1157, the abbey was closed down in 1539 by Henry VIII who gave the building and its wide estates to William Abbott, Sergeant of the Royal wine cellars. His descendants still live here. The house was partly rebuilt in the mid-18th century in the style known as Strawberry Hill

Cobbled Street, Clovelly

Pearson, is also a potter. In 1992 he opened **The Clovelly Pottery** which displays an extensive range of items made by Cornish and Devon potters. In the nearby workshop, for a small fee, you can try your own hand at throwing a pot.

This captivating village has some strong literary connections. It features as "Steepway" in the story *A Message from the Sea* by Dickens and Wilkie Collins. Charles Kingsley (*The Water Babies; Westward Ho!*) was at school here in the 1820s and the **Kingsley Museum** explores his links with the village. Next door, the **Fisherman's Cottage** provides an insight into what life was like here about 80 years ago. And the award-winning Visitor Centre has an audio-visual show narrating the development of Clovelly from around 2000BC to the present day.

Hartland Point

recently visited the Alhambra Palace in Spain which he much admired. He asked Scott to design something in that style and the result is the elegant Alhambra Corridor with a blue vaulted ceiling with white stencilled patterns. The abbey has a choice collection of pictures, porcelain and furniture acquired over many generations and, in the former Servants' Hall, a unique exhibition of documents dating from 1160. There's also a fascinating Victorian and Edwardian photographic exhibition which includes many early photographs.

Gothic, and in the 1850s the architect George Gilbert Scott added a front hall and entrance. The abbey's owner, Sir George Stucley, had

The Church of St Nectan

Hartland, Devon
Tel: 01479 810000

St. Nectan, the patron saint of this church and parish, was one of many Celtic hermits and missionaries associated with early Christian sites in south west Britain, south Wales and Ireland in the 5th and 6th centuries.

The church as we have it is in the Perpendicular style of the 14th century, subject to restoration, particularly the windows, in 1848. Although situated some three kilometres from the village of Hartland, the centre of the manor, the church is one of the largest in this part of Devon, Hartland parish being in the top 10 percent of Devon parishes by population until the 17th century.

The only major addition in the 1848 restoration was an increase in the length of the chancel. The size is best appreciated from beneath the tower arch, being enhanced by the areas of clear glass, the exceptional height of the tower arch itself, and the width of the arches over the aisles. The piers of the arcades (four in the nave and one in the chancel) are of limestone and appear to be earlier than some other North Devon examples. The tower arch is over eight metres high; from an early date and up to 1848 it contained a musicians' gallery.

🏚 historic building 🏛 museum and heritage 🏛 historic site ♨ scenic attraction 🌾 flora and fauna

A mile further west is **Hartland Quay.** Exposed to all the wrath of Atlantic storms, it seems an inhospitable place for ships, but it was a busy landing-place from its building in 1566 until the sea finally overwhelmed it in 1893. Several of the old buildings have been converted into a comfortable hotel; another is now a museum recording the many wrecks that have littered this jagged coastline.

About three miles to the north of the Quay, reached by winding country lanes, is **Hartland Point.** On Ptolemy's map of Britain in Roman times, he names it the "Promontory of Hercules", a fitting name for this fearsome stretch of upended rocks rising at right angles to the sea. There are breathtaking sea and coast views and a lighthouse built in 1874.

South Molton

🏛 Town Museum

🐝 Quince Honey Farm

This pleasant old market town, thankfully now bypassed by the A361 North Devon link road, has been a focus of the local agriculture-based economy since Saxon times, and in common with many such towns throughout Devon was a centre of the wool trade in the late Middle Ages. The town still flourishes as a market town with a main market day on Thursday and an extra pannier market on Saturday.

Unusually, the town has two Royal Charters, one from Elizabeth I in 1590 and another from Charles II in 1684. They are commemorated each year with an Old English Fayre held in June. The original charters can both be seen in the **Town Museum** along with one of the oldest fire engines in the country. It was bought by the town in 1746 for £46.

In the heart of the old town lies Broad Street, so broad as to be almost a square, and distinguished by some handsome Georgian and Victorian civic architecture. Among the noteworthy buildings to be found here are the **Market Hall and Assembly Rooms,** the eccentric **Medical Hall** with its iron balcony and four Ionic columns, and the Palladian-style **Guildhall** of 1743 which overhangs the pavement in a series of arches. A useful Heritage Trail Guide, obtainable from the Tourist Information Centre, provides an excellent introduction to these notable buildings.

Just to the north of South Molton is **Quince Honey Farm** where the mysterious process of honey-making is explained in a series of

🎭 stories and anecdotes 🦅 famous people 🎨 art and craft ✐ entertainment and sport 🚶 walks

ENI

3a King Street, South Molton, Devon EX36 3BL
Tel: 01769 574441
e-mail: sales@eni-uk.co.uk   website: www.eni-uk.co.uk

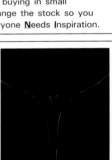

A finalist for the 'Best Retailer of the Year South West', **Eni** meaning precious gift is a independant boutique and lifestyle shop offering an enticing and inspirational range of gifts, clothing, babywear, home and living accessories that you are unlikely to find on the high street.

We have a passion for beautiful things - all irresistible and affordable. Choose from a stylish collection of clothing, co-ordinating accessories, purses, washbags and handbags as well as exquisite handmade jewellery adorned with freshwater pearls and precious stones. And for babies there are some wonderfully soft organic babywear, anything from striped rompers to pretty pyjamas as well as irresistible soft toys.

Eni also stocks hand embroidered photograph albums and journals made from vintage saris. You could pamper yourself with the world famous scents of Cote Bastide or La Compagnie de Provence, treat yourself to bath melts that look good enough to eat, or enjoy one of the range of hand poured scented candles. Browse the collection of French tableware, crystal tea lights and the unique handpainted bespoke furniture collection that would grace any home.

Eni lovingly sources products that are gorgeous, stylish and individual, buying in small quantities so each piece is unique to their customers. They constantly change the stock so you never know what you will find in the little shop of treasures, after all Everyone Needs Inspiration.

MELCHIOR CHOCOLATES

Tinto house, Pathfields Business Park,
Station Road, South Molton, Devon EX36 3LL
Tel: 01769 574442
website: www.melchiorchocolates.co.uk

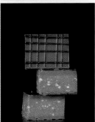

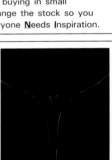

Melchior chocolates are luxurious hand-crafted chocolates made from the world's finest ingredients by Swiss chocolatier Carlo Melchior.

Based in the West Country, only 300m off the A361 near South Molton, Carlo's chocolates and chocolate truffles are each individually handmade to his own trusted Swiss recipe using the best ingredients available.

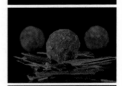

His award-winning chocolates range from a minimum of 60% cocoa solids up to 85% for the more adventurous palate. Carlo's passion and love for his authentic product has continued to grow since he started trading in 1977 as has his ever increasing and loyal customer base.

If you are looking for that special artisan gift or just fancy a luxurious treat, pop into the premises and showroom to see and sample the range of over 60 mouth watering flavours.

THE CORN DOLLY TEA SHOP

115a East Street, South Molton, Devon EX36 3DB
Tel: 01769 574249 Fax: 0845 644 5087
e-mail; kevin@corndollyteashop.com
website: www.corndollyteashop.co.uk

The award-winning **Corn Dolly Tea Shop** is well-established in
South Molton and since 1997 has been owned and run by
Kevin Venison. His menu offers an extensive choice of home-
cooked treats ranging from the Corn Dolly Breakfast through
salads, jacket potatoes, 'things on toast', sandwiches and specialities such as the Farmhouse
Tea and the Gamekeepers Tea - smooth venison, pheasant and duck pâté with a port topping
served with brown toast and butter. And make sure you don't miss out on the delicious homemade desserts such as the scrumptious Warm Chocolate Fudge Cake.

SOURCE FOR THE GOOSE

5 East Street, South Molton, Devon EX36 3BU
Tel: 01709 579483
e-mail: olivecottage@hotmail.com

Patricia Campbell opened **Source for the Goose** in
March 2007 and she sells an eclectic mix of
antique vintage furniture, some of it painted in
the French style, and country-style items of
furniture. You'll find beds, dressers, vintage
mirrors and rustic garden furniture, all of it
sourced locally. Patricia also stocks a range of
vintage and modern textiles, Persian rugs,
designer fabrics, kitchenalia and a range of unique cushions which are handmade locally.

displays and demonstrations. This is the world's
largest exhibition of living honey bees, their
hives all safely behind glass. A viewing gallery
gives an overhead view of the process of
honey-making and the shop offers a full range
of honey and honey products, including
delicious Devonshire honey ice cream.

Around South Molton

NORTH MOLTON
3 miles NE of South Molton off the A399

🏛 Church of All Saints

Tucked away in the foothills of Exmoor,
North Molton was once a busy wool and

mining town. At intervals from Elizabethan
times until the late 1800s, copper and iron
were extracted from the hills above the town
and transported down the valley of the River
Mole and on to the sea at Barnstaple.
Evidence of abandoned mine workings are
still visible around the town as well as remains
of the old Mole Valley tramway.

North Molton's 15th century parish
Church of All Saints reflects the small
town's former industrial importance. It's a
striking building with a high clerestory and a
100ft pinnacled tower which seems rather
grand for this rather remote community.
Several notable features have survived. There's
a part-medieval "wine-glass" pulpit complete

🎭 stories and anecdotes 🦢 famous people ✎ art and craft ✐ entertainment and sport 👣 walks

with sounding board and trumpeting angel, a rood screen, some fine Jacobean panelling, and an extraordinary 17th century alabaster monument to Sir Amyas Bampfylde depicting the reclining knight with his wife Elizabeth reading a book and their 12 sons and five daughters kneeling nearby. The figures are delightfully executed, especially the small girl with plump cheeks holding an apple and gazing wide-eyed at her eldest sister.

Also interesting is the church clock which was purchased in 1564 for the then exorbitant price of £16.14s 4d. However, it proved to be a sound investment since it remained in working order for 370 years before its bells chimed for the last time in 1934.

Just to the west of the church is a fine 16th century house, Court Barton (private). The iconoclastic biographer and critic Lytton Strachey (1880-1932) stayed here with a reading party in 1908. It seems that the eminent writer greatly enjoyed his stay, reporting enthusiastically on the area's "mild tranquillities", and a way of life which encompassed "a surplusage of beef and Devonshire cream,.....a village shop with bulls'-eyes,.....more cream and then more beef and then somnolence".

MOLLAND
6 miles E of South Molton off the A361

🏛 St Mary's Church

Hidden away in a maze of lanes skittering across the foothills of Exmoor, Molland is one of Devon's "must-visit" villages for anyone interested in wonderfully unspoilt churches. Following the sale of the village in the early 1600s, **St Mary's Church** stood within the estates of the Courtenay family. During and following the Commonwealth years, the Courtenays remained staunch

Catholics and showed no interest in restoring or modernising the Protestant parish church. So today you will still find a Georgian screen and tiers of box-pews, whitewashed walls, an elaborate three-decker pulpit crowned by a trumpeting angel and a colourful Royal Arms blazoned with the name of its painter, Rowlands. Despite their Catholic principles, three late-17th and early-18th century members of the Courtenay family are commemorated by some typically flamboyant monuments of the time. Also within Molland parish lies Great Champson, the farm where in the 18th century the Quartly family introduced and developed their celebrated breed of red North Devon cattle.

WEST ANSTEY
9 miles E of South Molton off the B3227

🚶 Two Moors Walk

The tiny hamlet of West Anstey lies just a mile or so from the Somerset border. **The Two Moors Way** passes by just a little to the east and the slopes on which the hamlet stands continue to rise up to the wilds of Exmoor. Despite being so small, West Anstey nevertheless has its own church, which boasts a fine Norman font and an arcade from the 1200s but is mostly 14th century. The area around West Anstey is one of the emptiest parts of Devon – grand open country dotted with just the occasional farm or a tiny cluster of cottages.

BISHOP'S NYMPTON
3 miles SE of South Molton off the A361

🏛 Lady Pollard

Bishop's Nympton, King's Nympton, George Nympton, as well as several Nymets, all take the Nympton or Nymet element of their names from the River Yeo which in Saxon and earlier times was known as the Nymet, meaning "river at a holy place". Bishop's Nympton has a long sloping main street, lined with thatched cottages, and a 15th century church whose lofty, well-proportioned tower is considered one of the most beautiful in Devon. For many years the church had a stained glass window erected in Tudor times at the expense of **Lady Pollard,** wife of Sir Lewis, an eminent judge and leading resident of the village. Sir Lewis told the author of *The Worthies of Devon,* John Prince, that he was away on business in London at the time and the details of the window's design were entrusted to his wife. At the time Sir Lewis left for town, he and his wife already had 21 children, 11 sons and 10 daughters. "But his lady caused one more child than she then had to be set there: presuming that, usually conceiving at her husband's coming home, she should have another. Which, inserted in expectation, came to pass in reality". The oddest thing about the story is that Lady Pollard not only correctly predicted the forthcoming child, but also its sex.

Chumleigh Church

CHULMLEIGH
8 miles S of South Molton off the A377

🌿 Eggesford Forest

With its narrow cobbled lanes, courtyards and quiet squares, Chulmleigh is a delight to explore. Sprawled across the hills above the leafy valley of the Little Dart river, it is one of several attractive small towns in mid-Devon which prospered from the wool trade in the Middle Ages and then declined into sleepy, unspoilt communities. Chulmleigh's prosperity

---

MESSRS. PJ LUCAS

Lakehead Farm, Chulmleigh, Devon EX18 7AG
Tel: 01769 580339
e-mail: leica@lakehead.freeserve.co.uk

A warm and welcoming family-run business, **Messrs PJ Lucas** offers its customers a selection of locally grown fruit and vegetables together with meat from the animals they raise on their 148 acres of mixed farming. The Lucas family farm lies within a conservation area with glorious views along the Taw Valley. Also on site is a Certified Camping, Caravan Club Hideaway site which is open from May to October. The shop itself is open from 9am to 5pm, Thursday, Friday and Saturday.

🎭 stories and anecdotes 🦜 famous people 🎨 art and craft ✒ entertainment and sport 🚶 walks

lasted longer than most since it was on the old wagon route to Barnstaple but in 1830 one of the newfangled turnpike roads was constructed along the Taw valley, siphoning off most of its trade. A quarter of a century later the Exeter to Barnstaple railway was built along the same route, the final straw for Chulmleigh as a trade centre. But this charming small town has been left with many original thatched cob cottages which cluster around a fine 15th century church noted for its lofty pinnacled tower and, inside, a wondrously carved rood screen that extends 50ft across the nave and aisles.

To the south of Chulmleigh is **Eggesford Forest** where, in 1919, the newly-formed Forestry Commission planted its first tree. This event is commemorated by a stone unveiled by the Queen in 1956. The stone also marks the planting of more than one million acres of trees by the Commission. There are two walks through the forest, each about one mile long, which provide visitors with the opportunity of seeing the red deer that live here.

LAPFORD
12 miles S of South Molton on the A377

Remarkably, this small community still has its own railway station. Passenger numbers have been much augmented since British Rail's rather prosaic "Exeter to Barnstaple route" was re-christened as the **"Tarka Line"**. The original name may have been lacklustre but the 39-mile journey itself has always been delightful as it winds slowly along the gentle river valleys of the Yeo and the Taw.

Lapford stands high above the River Yeo, its hilltop church a famous local landmark for generations: *"when yew sees Lapford church yew knaws where yew'm be"*. It's well worth a visit since the 15th century rood screen inside is regarded as one of the most exquisitely

fashioned in the country. There are five bands of the most delicate carving at the top and above them rise modern figures of the Holy Family, (Jesus, Mary and John), surmounted by the original ornamental ceiling with its carved angels gazing down from the nave roof.

WINKLEIGH
12 miles SW of South Molton on the A3124

This attractive village with its open views across to Dartmoor is believed to have been a beacon station in prehistoric times. When the Normans arrived they built two small castles, one at each end of the village. They were probably intended as bases for hunting in the nearby park – the only Devon park to be mentioned in the Domesday Book. For centuries Winkleigh was an important local trading centre with its own market, fair and borough court. Today, it's a peaceful little place with thatched cottages nestling up to the mainly 15th century church which has a richly carved and painted waggon roof where 70 golden-winged angels stand guard over the nave.

DOLTON
12 miles SW of South Molton on the B3217

Dolton clusters around its parish church of St Edmund's which boasts a real treasure, a Saxon font more than 1,000 years old. Its intricate carvings depict a fantastic menagerie of winged dragons and writhing serpents, with yet more dragons emerging from the upturned face of a man. Their relevance to the Christian message may be a little obscure but there's no denying their powerful impact.

MEETH
14 miles SW of South Molton on the A386

🏃 Tarka Walkway

A mile or so north of Hatherleigh, the A386

🏛 historic building   🏛 museum and heritage   🏛 historic site   🍃 scenic attraction   🌿 flora and fauna

crosses the River Torridge and a couple of miles further is the pleasant little village of Meeth whose Old English name means "the meeting of the streams". Indeed, a small brook runs down the hillside into the Torridge. From the early 1700s, Meeth and the surrounding area was noted for its "pipe" and "ball clay" products, generically known as pottery clay. There are still extensive clay works to the northwest of the village.

But for cyclists and walkers Meeth is much better known as the southern terminus of the **Tarka Trail Cycle / Walkway** which runs northwards through Bideford and Barnstaple.

NORTH TAWTON
16 miles SW of South Molton off the A3072

🎦 Bathe Pool

Well-known nowadays to travellers along the Tarka Trail, the small market town of North Tawton was once an important borough governed by a portreeve, an official who was elected each year until the end of the 19th century. This scattered rural community prospered in medieval times but the decline of the local textile industry in the late 1700s dealt a blow from which it never really recovered - the population today is still less than it was in 1750. The little town also suffered badly from the ravages of a series of fires which destroyed most of the older and more interesting buildings. However, a few survivors can still be found, most notably Broad Hall (private) which dates back to the 15th century.

In a field close to the town is **Bathe Pool,** a grassy hollow that is said to fill with water at times of national crises or when a prominent person is about to die. The pool reportedly filled at the time of the death of Nelson, the Duke of Wellington and Edward VII, and also just before the outbreak of World War I.

HATHERLEIGH
17 miles SW of South Molton on the A386

🏛 Church of St John the Baptist

🌳 Abbeyford Woods 🎨 Hatherleigh Pottery

🎨 Hatherleigh Arts Festival

This medieval market town, which has held a market every Tuesday since 1693, has been popular for many years as a holiday base for fishermen trying their luck on the nearby River Torridge and its tributary which runs alongside the small town.

A good starting point for an exploration of this attractive town with its cob and thatch cottages is the Tarka Country Information Point at **Hatherleigh Pottery** (see panel on page 154) where there are exhibits detailing the life and countryside in and around this 1,000-year-old town. You can also pick up leaflets to guide you around Hatherleigh's narrow streets. The Pottery itself has showrooms displaying colourful hand-thrown ceramics, textile items, original prints and greetings cards.

Hatherleigh was owned by Tavistock Abbey from the late 900s until the Dissolution of the Monasteries in the 1540s and the picturesquely thatched George Hotel is believed to have been built around 1450 as the abbot's court house. The London Inn also dates from around that time and the Old Church House is thought to be even older.

The town would have possessed an even finer stock of early buildings were it not for a devastating fire in 1840 which destroyed much of the old centre. Fortunately, the 15th century **Church of St John the Baptist** escaped the flames. Set high above the Lew valley, the church's red sandstone walls and sturdy tower still provide a striking focus for this pleasant rural community. Although the church survived the great fire of 1840, a century-and-a-half later hurricane force winds, generated during the storms of January 1990, swashed against its spindly tower and tossed it through the roof of the nave. Thankfully, nobody was in the church at the time.

In mid-July, the **Hatherleigh Arts Festival** takes place, consisting of four days of contemporary arts, including theatre, concerts, art exhibitions, street theatre and workshops. All year round art is visible in the various sculptures scattered around the town, notably the larger than life "Sheep" sculpture in the town's car park.

For a superb view of the surrounding countryside, make your way to the Monument erected in memory of Colonel William Morris, a hero of the Charge of the Light Brigade.

Until 1966, the Okehampton to Bude railway ran through Hatherleigh. In that year it was closed as part of the notorious "Beeching Cuts". Dr Richard Beeching, a successful businessman until then in the employ of the multi-national company ICI, was appointed in 1963 by Prime Minister Harold Macmillan, to sort out what the Conservative government of the day regarded as the mess created by the Labour party's nationalisation of the railways in 1948. Naturally, Dr Beeching's solution was to close every mile of line that did not produce a paper profit. The last train on the Hatherleigh to Bude line, a prized local amenity, steamed its way into Cornwall on May 16th, 1966, then to a

---

HATHERLEIGH POTTERY

20 Market Street, Hatherleigh, Devon EX20 3JP
Tel: 01837 810624
e-mail: hatherleighpots@aol.com
website: www.hatherleighpottery.co.uk

Located in a delightful and secluded cobbled courtyard off Market Street, **Hatherleigh Pottery** is owned and run by Jane Payne who has been a keen potter for more than 40 years. After retiring from teaching, she took a four-year course in ceramics and subsequently bought the pottery. Jane specialises in hand-thrown, practical domestic stoneware – jugs, mugs, bowls, dishes and the like. Much of her work is sgraffito decorated and her use of a wide range of glazes brings colour and variety to her wares. All Jane's pottery is trade-marked with a small fish imprinted near the base.

The light and airy showrooms at the pottery also feature work by other craftspeople such as Michael Taylor, a local potter who shows mugs, vases and casseroles in a style that makes an interesting contrast with Jane's work. Also on display are Jane Ritchie's ranges of shoulder bags and handbags, all delightfully designed and beautifully made in rich, colourful textiles; and Gill Salway's original prints using a variety of techniques. The pottery is open from Easter to New Year, Monday to Saturday, from 10am-5pm.

🏛 historic building   🏛 museum and heritage   🏛 historic site   🌄 scenic attraction   🌿 flora and fauna

SALAR GALLERY

*20 Bridge Street, Hatherleigh, nr Okehampton,
Devon EX20 3HY
Tel: 01837 810940
website: www.salargallery.co.uk*

The **Salar Gallery** opened in the centre of this market town in 1991 to provide an exhibition space for local artists and craftspeople. It displays and sells original work, mainly by Devon artists, much of it a celebration of the West Country - landscape, animals and rural subjects through the eyes of up to 60 artists and craftsmen.

The works include local scenes by Eileen Gold; landscapes by Pam Cox, Paul Hardy, Ken Hildrew and David Howell; seascapes by Harry McConville, railway scenes by Bernard Jones GRA, paintings on silk by Hermione Dunn, sculptures by Jean Buchanan, Jo Seccombe, Joanna Martins and Suzie Marsh. Also on display are photographs by Jen Bryant, woodcarvings by Colin Burlton, pottery by Mary Jane Carruthers, metalwork by Peach and Bill Shaw and glass by Jo Downs and Margaret Johnson.

The gallery also has prints of Dartmoor by Widgery; rural scenes from Michael Cooper; flowers by Anne Cotterill, plus a wide selection of cards, books, jewellery, church candles and so on. There are changing monthly exhibitions from April to December.

The gallery is in the centre of Hatherleigh on level ground, not far from the town car park. The gallery is open from 10am to 1pm and 2pm-5pm Tuesdays, Thursdays, Fridays and Saturdays.

---

siding, and then to rust. Long stretches of the old track bed of the railway now provide some attractive walking.

There's more good walking at **Abbeyford Woods,** about a mile to the east of the village, with a particularly lovely stretch running alongside the River Okement.

Holsworthy

 St Peter's Fair

Wednesday is a good day to visit Holsworthy. That's when this little town, just four miles from the Cornish border, holds its weekly market. This is very much the traditional kind of street market, serving a large area of the surrounding countryside and with locally-produced fresh cream, butter, cheese, and

vegetables all on sale. The town gets even livelier in early July when it gives itself over to the amusements of the three-day-long **St Peter's Fair.** The Fair opens with the curious old custom of the Pretty Maid Ceremony. Back in 1841, a Holsworthy merchant bequeathed a legacy to provide a small payment each year to a local spinster, under the age of 30 and noted for her good looks, demure manner and regular attendance at church. Rather surprisingly, in view of the last two requirements, the bequest still finds a suitable recipient each year.

Holsworthy's most striking architectural features are the two Victorian viaducts that once carried the railway line to Bude. The viaducts stride high above the southern edge of the town and, since they now form part

---

 stories and anecdotes   famous people   art and craft   entertainment and sport   walks

of a footpath along the old track, it's possible to walk across them for some stunning views of the area.

An interesting feature in the parish church is an organ built in 1668 by Renatus Hunt for All Saints Church, Chelsea. In 1723, it was declared worn out but was nevertheless purchased by a Bideford church. There it gave good service for some 140 years before it was written off once again. Removed to Holsworthy, it has been here ever since.

The area around Holsworthy is particularly popular with cyclists. There are three clearly-designated routes starting and finishing the town, and it also lies on the **West Country Way**, a 250-mile cycle route from Padstow to Bristol and Bath which opened in the spring of 1997.

Around Holsworthy

SHEBBEAR
7 miles NE of Holsworthy off the A388

🏛 Devils Stone

This attractive village is set around a spacious square laid out in the Saxon manner with a church at one end and a hostelry at the other. Lying in a hollow just outside St Michael's churchyard is a huge lump of rock, weighing about a ton, which is known as the **Devil's Stone**. According to local legend, the boulder was placed here by Old Nick who challenged the villagers to move it, threatening that disaster would strike if they could not. Every year since then, on November 5th (a date established long before the Gunpowder Plot

---

THE BEAD CELLAR

Broad Street, Black Torrington, Devon EX21 5PT
Tel: 01409 231442
e-mail: tohobeads@btinternet.com
website: www.thebeadcellar.co.uk

Established in 2006, The **Bead Cellar** offers a comprehensive range of Japanese seed beads and many other beautiful beads from around the world. Owned and run by Jill and Geoff Lockwood, the shop also stocks a huge range of findings, threads, tools and accessories. You'll find gems and freshwater pearls, pendants and drops, non-gemstone cabochons, shell and wooden beads, cat's eye and moon beads, porcelain faces, charms and bells. Accessories include organza bags and storage boxes, while the range of tools includes bead scoops, beading loom, beading design board, crochet hook, beeswax and a variety of glues. The shop also stocks a range of card-making components. All the products stocked can be ordered at The Bead Cellars' website which is continuously serviced.

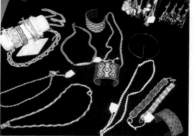

If you would like to learn more about this interesting craft, Jill and Geoff host regular day and evening workshops by appointment.

The Bead Cellar is open from 10am to 5pm, Tuesday to Friday, and from 10am to 1pm on Saturday.

🏛 historic building 🏛 museum and heritage 🏛 historic site 🌿 scenic attraction 🌿 flora and fauna

of 1605), a curious ceremony has taken place. After sounding a peal of bells, the bell ringers come out of the church and set about the stone with sticks and crowbars. Once they have successfully turned the stone over, they return in triumph to the bell tower to sound a second peal. The story is recounted in greater detail in the village hostelry, The Devils Stone Inn.

SHEEPWASH
9 miles E of Holsworthy off the A3072 or A386

Sheepwash Bridge

Sheepwash is yet another Devon community to have been devastated by fire. The conflagration here occurred in 1742 and the destruction was so great that for more than 10 years the village was completely deserted. Slowly, the villagers returned, built new houses in stone, and today if you want the essence of Devon distilled into one location, then the village square at Sheepwash is just about perfect. Along one side stands the famous Half Moon Inn, renowned amongst fishermen; on another, the old church tower rises above pink-washed thatched cottages, while in the centre, cherry trees shelter the ancient village pump.

Just south of the village, a minor road crosses the River Torridge and there's a rather heartening story about the bridge here, **Sheepwash Bridge.** Until well into the 1600s, the only way of crossing the river was by means of stepping stones. One day, when the river was in full spate, a young man attempting to return to the village was swept away and drowned. His father, John Tusbury, was grief-stricken but responded to the tragedy by providing money to build a bridge. He also donated sufficient funds for it to be maintained by establishing the Bridgeland Trust and stipulating that any surplus income should be used to help in the upkeep of the church and chapel. The Trust is still in operation and nowadays also funds outings for village children and pensioners.

NORTHLEW
10 miles SE of Holsworthy off the A3072 or A3079

As at Sheepwash, the thatched cottages and houses stand around a large central square which is dominated by a charming 15th century church standing on the hilltop above the River Lew. The church is noted for its Norman remains and the exceptional (mainly Tudor) woodwork in the roof, bench ends and screen. Also of interest is one of the stained glass windows which features four saints. St Thomas, to whom the church is dedicated, is shown holding a model of the church; St Augustine, the first Archbishop of Canterbury, holds the priory gateway, while St Joseph carries the Holy Grail and the staff which grew into the famous Glastonbury thorn tree. The fourth figure is simply clad in a brown habit and carries a bishop's crozier and a spade. This is St Brannock who is credited with being the first man to cultivate the wild lands of this area by clearing woodland and ploughing and could therefore be regarded as the patron saint of farmers.

CLAWTON
3 miles S of Holsworthy, on the A388

A good indication of the mildness of the Devon climate is the number of vineyards which have been established over the last 30 years or so. **Clawford Vineyard** in the valley of the River Claw is a good example. Set in more than 78 acres of vines and orchards, the vineyard's owners welcome visitors to sample their home-grown wines and ciders, and in the autumn to watch that year's vintage being produced.

In and Around Dartmoor

Okehampton

🏛 Okehampton Castle   📷 Museum of Dartmoor Life

🌿 Dartmoor Railway

The old travel-writer's cliché of a "county of contrasts" can't be avoided when describing the landscape around Okehampton. To the north and west, the puckered green hills of

North Devon roll away to the coast; to the south, lie the wildest stretches of Dartmoor with the great peaks of **High Willhays** and **Yes Tor** rising to more than 2,000ft. At this height they are, officially, mountains but quite puny compared with their original altitude: geologists believe that at one time the surface of Dartmoor stood at 15,000ft above sea level. Countless centuries of erosion have reduced it to a plateau of whale-backed granite ridges with an average height of around 1,200ft. After so many millions of years of erosion, the moor has become strewn with fragments of surface granite, or moorstone. It was because of this ready-to-use stone that Dartmoor became one of the most populous areas of early Britain, its inhabitants using the easily quarried granite to

---

ST JAMES STREET ANTIQUES

Okehampton, Devon EX20 1DW
Tel: 01837 659623

Occupying one of the oldest buildings in Okehampton, **St. James Street Antiques** is a small centre stocking an extensive range of antiques and decorative items.

Within its three rooms you will find an enticing selection that includes furniture from the 18th to 20th centuries, ceramics, pictures, glass, rugs, clocks, silver, jewellery and more. In addition to the stock on display both owner, Jo Catling, and fellow dealer, Sue Sibley, have a further selection of furniture stored in barns at their homes. Customers are welcome to view the items there by appointment. Jo also sells pieces that need restoring or re-upholstering which customers can buy at cost to 'do up' themselves.

Back to the shop and here you will almost certainly find some items with French provenance as Jo travels to France occasionally to buy the 'French Look'. Finally, if you are looking for a particular item let them know and they will endeavour to source it for you.

Local delivery is free and the shop is open Monday-Thursday 10.00am-4.30pm and Friday and Saturday till 5.00pm. They take all major credit and debit cards and are situated in the town centre behind the Clock Tower, next to the 'Piggies'.

🏛 historic building   📷 museum and heritage   🏛 historic site   🌿 scenic attraction   🌱 flora and fauna

create their stone rows, circles, and burial chambers. Stone was also used to build their distinctive hut-circles of which there are more than 1,500 scattered across the moor.

From Celtic times Okehampton has occupied an important position on the main route to Cornwall. Romantically sited atop a wooded hill and dominating the surrounding valley of the River Okement are the remains of **Okehampton Castle**. This is the largest medieval castle in Devon and the ruins are still mightily impressive even though the castle

---

THE ARTS GALLERY

7 Red Lion Yard, Okehampton, Devon EX20 1AW
Tel: 01837 55807
e-mail: yvette martin@btinternet.co.uk
website: www.theartsgallery.co.uk

Located in the busy Red Lion Yard, just off Okehampton High Street, is a vibrant and colourful place where selected local artists and crafts people exhibit and sell their work.

The arts gallery has more than 50 different exhibitors at one time including painters, sculptors, printmakers, photographers, potters, jewellers and even clothes designers which make it almost impossible not to find something of interest.

The Arts Gallery is also renowned locally for its unusual 'arts' clothing. These chic, colourful, well cut and stylish clothes reflect the gallery's image perfectly.

This gallery is brimming with bright and beautiful items that make visiting an absolute must.

HEATHER COTTAGE

129 Station Road, Okehampton, Devon EX20 1EH
Tel: 01837 658820
e-mail: yvettemartin@btinternet.com
website: www.lastminute-cottages.co.uk

Offering quality self-catering accommodation, **Heather Cottage** is situated in a delightful and very convenient location at the very edge of the lovely mid-Devon town of Okehampton. It boasts a large light and modern kitchen and a cosy sitting/dining room area with a gas wood-burner and modern comfortable sofa. The large and luxurious Victorian style bedroom has click and zip beds which means it can be a real double bed or two large comfortable singles. Just an eight-minute walk from the town centre and four minutes from Dartmoor National Park, the cottage stands in its own extremely sunny and locally planted 'abundant' garden.

📖 stories and anecdotes 🦐 famous people 🎨 art and craft 🎭 entertainment and sport 🚶 walks

ANGEL CASUAL AND OCCASIONAL WEAR

29 Fore Street, Okehampton, Devon EX20 1HB
Tel: 01837 659005

Opened in 2000, **Angel Casual and Occasional Wear** offers quality women's clothing. Many leading designers are featured on the racks here - Jackpot; In Wear; Fenn Wright and Manson; Joules and Sandwich, for example. You'll also find attractive items from Condici, Libra, Noli and John Charles among others. The clothes are available in a range of sizes that extends from 8 to 20. There's also an enticing range of accessories including matching bags, shoes and jewellery.

You'll find friendly and knowledgeable staff, light and airy changing rooms, and the whole premises are air-conditioned.

MASON JUDGE

33 Fore Street, Okehampton, Devon EX20 1HB
Tel: 01837 658530
website: www.mason-judge.co.uk

Offering a wide range of quality items for the home, **Mason Judge** will surely provide plenty of inspiration for adding style and distinction to your home.

Owners Sharon Mason and Meryl Coe moved their shop to the centre of this historic town in 2006, having previously been located in Hatherleigh. It has certainly lifted the profile of shops here, together with Angel Fashions next door but one.

Sharon and Meryl's stock includes table, oven and kitchenware from Maxwell and Williams, including their Allure cutlery; some lovely throws and quilts; gifts for christenings, weddings and anniversaries; adult and children's bags from Sally Hurst's Old Bag Company which is located in Devon. Then there are the acrylic wall paintings; Fair Trade Nkuku photo albums; Pioneros leather bags from Argentina; Durance fragrances and toiletries; Aspire handbags and beach bags by Bagali of Bath; fine jewellery and watches by Israeli jeweller Yaron Morheim; and costume jewellery by Cadari and Gemini.

With so many covetable items on display, allow yourself plenty of time to do a thorough browse!

🏛 historic building 🏛 museum and heritage 🏛 historic site ⌘ scenic attraction 🌿 flora and fauna

was dismantled on the orders of Henry VIII after its owner, the Earl of Devon, was convicted of treason.

A good place to start a tour of the town is the **Museum of Dartmoor Life,** housed in a former mill with a restored water wheel outside. In the surrounding courtyard, you will also find a gift shop and a tearoom. Amongst the town's many interesting buildings are the 15th century **Chapel of Ease,** and the **Town Hall**, a striking three-storey building erected in 1685 as a private house and converted to its current use in the 1820s. And don't miss the wonderful Victorian arcade within the shopping centre which is reminiscent of London's Burlington Arcade.

Okehampton is also the hub of the **Dartmoor Railway,** part of the former Southern Railway mainline from London to Plymouth and Cornwall. This was once the route of the famous Atlantic Coast Express and the Devon Belle Pullman. Okehampton Station has been restored to its 1950s appearance, complete with buffet and licensed bar. Sampford Courtenay Station, 3.5 miles to the east was re-opened in 2004 and provides access to pleasant walking routes, including

the Devon Heartlands Way footpath. To the west, Meldon Quarry Station is the highest station in southern England. It has two visitor centres, a buffet with licensed bar, a picnic area and a spectacular verandah giving wonderful views of Dartmoor's highest tors and the Meldon Reservoir dam.

Around Okehampton

SAMPFORD COURTENAY
5 miles NE of Okehampton

Prayer Book Revolt

A charming and unspoilt village with a fine medieval church, Sampford Courtenay is notable for its picturesque assortment of cottages, many of them thatched and built of cob. This local building material is created by mixing well-sieved mud with straw. This is then built up in sections. It was the local tradition to limewash the outside of the cottages at Whitsuntide, a process that helps to preserve the cob. This simple material is surprisingly durable and will last indefinitely provided it has a "good hat", that is, if the thatched roof is well looked after. Another unusual feature of the village is that every road out of it is marked by a medieval stone cross.

This peaceful and pretty village was the unlikely setting for the start of the **Prayer Book Revolt** of 1549. It was originally initiated as a protest against Edward VI's introduction of an English prayer book, but when the undisciplined countrymen marched on Exeter, it degenerated into a frenzy of looting and violence. Confronted by an army led by Lord Russell, the rioters were soon overwhelmed and several unfortunate ringleaders executed.

Okehampton Castle

STICKLEPATH
2 miles E of Okehampton off the A30

📷 Finch Foundry

The little village of Sticklepath boasts one of the most interesting exhibits of industrial archaeology in Devon. From 1814 to 1960, **Finch Foundry** (National Trust) was renowned for producing the finest sharp-edged tools in the West Country. The three massive waterwheels are now working again, driving the ancient machinery, and pounding rhythms of the steam hammer and rushing water vividly evoke that age of noisy toil.

SOUTH ZEAL
4 miles E of Okehampton off the A30

South Zeal is yet another of the many Devon villages which have good reason to be grateful for the major road-building undertakings of the 1970s. The village sits astride what used to be the main road from Exeter to Launceston

and the Cornwall coast, a road which as late as 1975 was still laughably designated on maps of the time as a "Trunk (major) Road". The "Trunk Road" was actually little more than a country lane but it was also the only route available for many thousands of holiday-makers making their way to the Cornish resorts. Today, the village is bypassed by the A30 dual carriageway.

Isolated in the middle of the broad main street stand a simple medieval market cross and St Mary's chapel, rebuilt in 1713. To the south of the village rises the great granite hump of Dartmoor. On its flanks, for the few years between 1901-9, the villagers of South Zeal found sorely needed employment in a short-lived copper mine.

WHIDDON DOWN
7 miles E of Okehampton off the A30

📷 Spinsters Rock

About a mile south of the village stands the **Spinsters' Rock**, the best surviving chambered tomb in the whole of Devon. According to legend, three spinsters erected the dolmen one morning before breakfast, an impressive feat since the capstone, supported by just three uprights seven feet high, weighs 16 tons.

BELSTONE
2 miles SE of Okehampton off the A30

📷 Nine Stones

Surrounded by the magnificent scenery of the Dartmoor National Park, Belstone is a picturesque village with a triangular village green, complete with stocks and a stone commemorating the coronation of George V, and a church dating back to the 13th century.

A path from Belstone village leads up to the ancient standing stone circle known as the

Belstone Stocks

Castle Drogo

Drewsteignton, near Exeter EX6 6PB
Tel: 01647 433306
e-mail: castledrogo@nationaltrust.org.uk

Castle Drogo (National Trust) is spectacularly sited on a rocky outcrop with commanding views out over Dartmoor and the Teign gorge. It was built for Sir Julius Drewe, a self-made millionaire, on land once owned by his Norman ancestor, Drogo de Teigne. Surrounding this

20th century dream country home, lies an equally impressive garden – the highest in the Trust.

The square shape of the castle and the large rotund croquet lawn exemplifies the simple ethos of the architect,

Lutyens, of "circles and squares". From spring bulbs in the formal garden, the rhododendron garden, the stunning herbaceous borders, the rose garden and the winter garden there is colour and interest here all year round.

Nine Stones, although there are actually well over a dozen of them. Local folklore asserts that these stones under Belstone Tor were formed when a group of maidens was discovered dancing on the Sabbath and turned to stone. The problem with this story is that the stone circle was in place long before the arrival of Christianity in England. It is also claimed that the mysterious stones change position when the clock strikes noon. What is certain is that the view across mid-Devon from this site is quite breathtaking.

Another path from Belstone leads south to a spot on the northern edge of Dartmoor where the ashes of the Poet Laureate, Ted Hughes, were scattered and where a granite stone was placed to his memory.

For lovers of solitude, this is memorable country, unforgettably evoked by Sir Arthur Conan Doyle in *The Hound of the Baskervilles*. Recalling the villain's fate in that book, walkers should beware of the notorious "feather beds" – deep bogs signalled by a quaking cover of brilliant green moss.

DREWSTEIGNTON

10 miles SE of Okehampton off the A30

🏰 Castle Drogo

This appealing village stands on a ridge overlooking the valley of the River Teign and the celebrated beauty spot near the 400-year-old Fingle Bridge. Thatched cottages and a medieval church stand grouped around a square, very picturesque and much photographed. To the south of the village, Prestonbury Castle and Cranbrook Castle are not castles at all but Iron Age hilltop fortresses. **Castle Drogo** (National Trust -

see panel on page 163) on the other hand, looks every inch the medieval castle but in fact was constructed between 1911 and 1930 – the last castle to be built in England. Occupying a spectacular site on a rocky outcrop 900ft above sea level, with commanding views over Dartmoor, it was built to a design by Lutyens for the self-made millionaire Sir Julius Drewe on land once owned by his Norman ancestor, Drogo de Teigne. Lutyens preliminary sketches envisaged a house of heroic size, but practicalities and the intervention of World War I caused the dimensions to be reduced by about two-thirds. Nevertheless, the granite castle, finally completed in 1930, is one of Lutyens' most remarkable works. It combines the grandeur of a medieval castle with the comforts of the 20th century.

Surrounding Sir Julius's dream home is an impressive garden which displays colour and interest all year round.

CHAGFORD
10 miles SE of Okehampton off the A382

🏛 Mary Whiddon

An ancient settlement and Stannary town, Chagford lies in a beautiful setting between the pleasant wooded valley of the North Teign river and the stark grandeur of the high moor. In the centre of the town stands the former **Market House**, a charming octagonal building erected in 1862. Around the square are some old style family shops providing interesting shopping and scattered around the town are distinctive old thatched granite buildings, many dating from the 1500s.

CHAGFORD GALLERIES

20 The Square, Chagford, Devon TQ13 8AB
Tel: 01647 433287
websites: www.chagfordgalleries.co.uk or www.devonsnatureinart.com

This beautiful and spacious art gallery is right in the centre of the picturesque Stannary town of Chagford on Dartmoor.

It is the home to "Devon's Nature In Art" which is a unique collection of artwork by the well known artist Eleanor Ludgate. It portrays the wildlife, flowers, birds, insects, views and nature of Devon. Eleanor has a studio at the back of the gallery and can often be seen at work there.

There are many original works of art in the gallery, something, we hope, to suit everyone. There is also a small gallery room with paintings of Provence. There is some striking and unusual hand crafted jewellery, pottery, bronzes etc, all made in Devon. Local views and prints, a wide range of greetings cards and plenty of smaller gift items.

Please visit the websites www.chagfordgalleries.co.uk and www.devonsnatureinart.com

The owners look forward to welcoming you, and are open all year round from 10am to 5pm including most Sundays during the summer months.

🏛 historic building 🏛 museum and heritage 🏛 historic site 🌿 scenic attraction 🌱 flora and fauna

SUSAN AT NUMBER TEN

10 High Street, Chagford, Devon TQ13 8AJ
Tel: 01647 433700
website: www.susanatnumberten.co.uk

Looking for something rather special to wear? Then a visit to **Susan at Number Ten** is strongly recommended. Opened in 2007, this stylish shop on Chagford's High Street specialises in quality women's clothing.

Owner Susan Powell has some 20 years experience in the fashion business, including three years in Canada with the fashion house Escada. Her own shop showcases items from leading designers such as Zucchero, Diktons, Claire.DK, Lui & Lei and Paddy Campbell. There are suede shoes from SalvadorSapena, handbags from Ripani, and scarves and ties from award-winning British textile designer Margo Selby. You'll find something for every occasion here - day or evening wear, sporty casual wear, or even garments and accessories for a day at the races.

As Susan says, what she is striving to offer is "fashion with pizzazz"! In addition to the

fashion wear, Susan also stocks art deco pieces such as objets d'art and glass tables. You'll find her fascinating shop directly opposite the village church and with views across to Castle Drogo. There's ample parking near the church.

St Michael's Church, mostly 15th century, has an elaborate monument to Sir John Wyddon who died in 1575. But the church is better known because of the tragic death of one of his descendants here in October 1641. **Mary Whiddon** was shot at the altar by a jilted lover as she was being married, an incident that is said to have inspired R.D. Blackmore's *Lorna Doone*. Her tombstone bears the inscription "Behold a Matron yet a Maid". Her ghost is thought to haunt Whiddon Park Guest House - a young woman dressed in black appeared there on the morning of a wedding reception due to take place later that day.

The famous Dartmoor guide, James Perrot, lived in Chagford between 1854 and 1895, and is buried in St Michael's churchyard. It was he

who noted that some of the farms around Chagford had no wheeled vehicles as late as 1830. On the other hand, Perrot lived to see the town install electric street lighting in 1891 making Chagford one of the first communities west of London to possess this amenity.

It was Perrot also who began the curious practice of letterbox stamp collecting. He installed the first letterbox at Carnmere Pool near the heart of the moor so his Victorian clients could send postcards home, stamped to prove they had been there. Today, there are hundreds of such letterboxes scattered all over Dartmoor.

To the west of Chagford, an exceptionally pleasant lane leads upstream from Chagford Bridge through the wooded valley of the North Teign river. (For 1.5 miles of its length,

📖 stories and anecdotes 🐦 famous people 🎨 art and craft 🎭 entertainment and sport 🚶 walks

BLACKS DELICATESSEN

28 The Square, Chagford, Devon TQ13 8AB
Tel: 01647 433545
website: www.blacks-deli.co.uk

A true food emporium and one of Devon's finest
delicatessens, **Blacks Delicatessen** offers a spectacular
range of quality foods. Chris and Catherine Mount have
filled their stylish shop with items that range from freshly
cooked honey roast hams and roast beefs to homemade
frozen meals such as lasagne, coq au vin and curries.
There are cheeses galore, organic chocolates, Italian oils,
30 different teas and much more. And if you phone ahead with your order, Blacks will happily
prepare a picnic hamper for you filled with their delicious goodies.

this lane is joined by the Two Moors Way, the
long-distance footpath which runs all the way
from Ivybridge on the southern edge of
Dartmoor to the Bristol Channel coast.) A
rock beside the river known as the **Holed
Stone** has a large round cavity. If you climb
through this, local people assure you, a host of
afflictions from rheumatism to infertility will
be cured.

The land to the south of Chagford rises
abruptly towards Kestor Rock and Shovel
Down, the sites of impressive Bronze Age
settlements and, a little further on, the
imposing Long Stone stands at the point
where the parishes of Gidleigh and Chagford
end and Duchy of Cornwall land begins.

LYDFORD
8 miles SW of Okehampton off the A386

🏛 Lydford Castle   🍃 Lydford Gorge

In Saxon times, there were just four royal
boroughs in Devon: Exeter, Barnstaple,
Totnes and, astonishingly, Lydford which is
now a pleasant small town still occupying the
same strategic position on the River Lyd
which made it so important in those days. In
the 11th century, the Normans built a
fortification here which was superseded 100
years later by the present **Lydford Castle**, an

austere stone fortress which for generations
served the independent tin miners of
Dartmoor as both a court and a prison. The
justice meted out here was notoriously
arbitrary. William Browne of Tavistock (1590-
1643) observed:

I oft have heard of Lydford law,
How in the morn they hang and draw
And sit in judgement after.

Lydford parish is the largest in England,
encompassing the whole of the Forest of
Dartmoor. For many centuries the dead were
brought down from the moor along the
ancient Lych Way for burial in St Petroc's
churchyard. A tombstone near the porch bears
a lengthy and laboriously humorous epitaph to
the local watchmaker, George Routleigh, who
died in 1802. The inscription includes the
statement that George's life had been

Wound up in hope of being taken in hand by his
Maker and of being thoroughly cleansed and repaired
and set going in the world to come.

To the southwest of the village, the valley
of the River Lyd suddenly narrows to form
the 1.5 mile long **Lydford Gorge** (NT), one
of Devon's most spectacular natural features.
Visitors can follow the riverside path to the
Devil's Cauldron, or wander along the two-
mile walk to the White Lady, a narrow 100ft

high waterfall. Back in the 17th century, the then remote Lydford Gorge provided a secure refuge for a band of brigands who called themselves the Gubbinses. Their leader was a certain Roger Rowle, (dubbed the "Robin Hood of the West"), whose exploits are recounted in Charles Kingsley's novel *Westward Ho!*

Tavistock

🍃 Goose Fair

This handsome old town is one of Devon's four stannary towns, so named from the Latin word for tin – *stannum*. These towns – the others are Ashburton, Chagford and Plympton – were the only places licensed to weigh and stamp the metal extracted from the moor.

For most of its recorded history, Tavistock has had only two owners. Tavistock Abbey and the Russell family. The Benedictine abbey was founded here, beside the River Tavy, in around 974, close to a Saxon stockade or *stoc*, now incorporated into the town's name. The town grew up around the abbey and, following the discovery of tin on the nearby moors in the 12th century, both flourished.

Then, in 1539, Henry VIII closed the Abbey and gave the building, along with its vast estates to John Russell whose family, as Earls and Dukes of Bedford, owned most of the town until 1911. The present town centre is essentially the creation of the Russell family, who after virtually obliterating the once-glorious abbey, created a completely new town plan. Later, in the 1840s, Francis the 7th Duke diverted some of the profits from his copper mines to build the imposing **Guildhall** and several other civic buildings. He also remodelled the Bedford Hotel, and

FUNKY FOOD DELI

15 The Market, Tavistock, Devon PL19 0AL
Tel: 01822 618595

Located on the edge of the famous Pannier Market in the historic Stannary Town of Tavistock, the **Funky Food Deli** specialises in local organic vegetables along with an extensive array of delicious treats and speciality foods.

Other locally sourced produce includes Beaworthy organic milk, Eversfield organic meat, artisan 'Bread of Devon', and organic carrots, leeks and cauliflowers from the Tamar Valley. The shop also offers 'Veggie Boxes' of assorted vegetables which can be delivered free within a 10-mile radius.

The shop also sells a wide variety of frozen dishes - lamb & rosemary bake, three cheese macaroni and sticky choccy pudding from the Red Earth kitchen, for example. There are also dishes from Flying Fish and organic meals for one or two people from the Dorset-based Manna company. The deli also sells various locally smoked delicacies, Stokes mayonnaise and tomato ketchup, Midfields granola cereals and much, much more. The deli is open from 9am to 5pm, Monday to Saturday.

📖 stories and anecdotes 🐦 famous people 🎨 art and craft 🍃 entertainment and sport 🥾 walks

AFTER EIGHT LINGERIE

The Old Dairy, Paddons Row, Tavistock, Devon PL19 0HF
Tel: 01822 615015

After Eight Lingerie has been providing quality lingerie and swimwear for 20 years now. Janie's major brands include Fantasie, Anita, Prima Donna, Triumph and Passionata while her swimwear brands include Fantasie, Christina and Sunflair. Hosiery is represented by pretty Polly, Levante and Aristoc and her nightwear designers include Miss Elaine, Pill and Damella. Janie also offers a personal bra-fitting service for sizes AA to JJ.

BRIGID FOLEY

8 Paddons Row, Tavistock, Devon PL19 0HP
Tel: 01822 612203

In the heart of Tavistock, in an offshoot of the main shopping street, is the unique clothing shop, **Brigid Foley**. This quiet and secluded backwater in a busy town is the perfect setting for this stylish boutique where the very individual designs of this world-renowned knitwear expert can be seen and purchased. Famous for her hand-embroidered and appliquéd sweaters and cardigans, Brigid has built up her reputation over the last 20 years.

KIDDIES KITCHEN

Lockyer House, Paddons Row, Tavistock, Devon PL19 0HF
Tel: 01822 611177   Fax: 01822 611499
e-mail: enquiries@kiddieskitchen.co.uk
website: www.kiddieskitchen.co.uk

Specialising in clothing and food for babies and toddlers up to five years of age, **Kiddies Kitchen** is a convenient 'one-stop shop' for busy parents. Owner Richard Tyler stocks a wide range of baby food, including Ella's Kitchen products, and a variety of nappies and wraps, including organic versions. His introduction of a secondhand baby goods agency, "hand-me-downs", has proved highly successful and provides parents with quality items at very reasonable prices.

WRIGHTSTYLE DEVON HATTERS

Paddons Row, Tavistock, Devon PL19 0HF
Tel: 01822 615117
e-mail: info@wrightstylehatters.com   website: www.wrightstylehatters.com

Operating from their specialist shop in the town's charming Paddons Row, **Wrightstyle Devon Hatters** supply quality headwear to discerning customers. Whether you are looking for a traditional tweed cap, a genuine hand-woven panama or a stylish hat for that special occasion, wedding or a visit to the races, Wrightstyle are sure to have a hat for you.

CRYSTAL WISDOM

1 Lockyer Mews, Paddons Row, Tavistock, Devon PL19 0HF
Tel: 01822 618073
e-mail: anita@granitadesigns.co.uk

Would you like some hand-crafted jewellery that is striking and unusual? **Crystal Wisdom** has the answer. Owner Anita and her partner Graham provide bespoke jewellery to your own design. This fascinating shop also sells hand selected crystals for both healers and collectors alike, angels, Tarot, cards, Native American and Celtic items, incense, CD's, Mountain T'shirts, and much more.

DOWNINGS THE BUTCHERS

12-13 Pannier Market, Tavistock, Devon PL19 0AL
Tel: 01822 618010
website: www.tavistockeatwise.co.uk

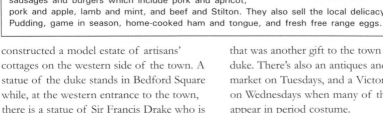

Downings the Butchers have been selling quality local meat for 19 years from their shop within Tavistock's famous Pannier Market. John and Simon Downing source their produce from farms in Lamerton, Brentor, Yelverton and Bickley, and are well-known for making their own sausages and burgers which include pork and apricot, pork and apple, lamb and mint, and beef and Stilton. They also sell the local delicacy Hog's Pudding, game in season, home-cooked ham and tongue, and fresh free range eggs.

constructed a model estate of artisans' cottages on the western side of the town. A statue of the duke stands in Bedford Square while, at the western entrance to the town, there is a statue of Sir Francis Drake who is believed to have been born at nearby Crowndale.

One of the legacies of the abbey is the annual three-day fair, granted in 1105, which has now evolved into **Goose Fair**, a wonderful traditional street fair held on the second Wednesday in October. Tavistock was also permitted to hold a weekly market which, more than 900 years later, still takes place every Friday in the Pannier Market, a building

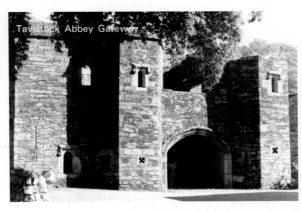

Tavistock Abbey Gateway

that was another gift to the town from the 7th duke. There's also an antiques and crafts market on Tuesdays, and a Victorian market on Wednesdays when many of the stallholders appear in period costume.

Around Tavistock

BRENT TOR
4½ miles N of Tavistock off the A386

 Church of St Michael of the Rocks

Brent Tor, an 1,100ft-high volcanic plug that rears up from the surrounding countryside is one of the most striking sights in the whole of Dartmoor. Perched on its summit is the **Church of St Michael of the Rocks**, the fourth smallest complete church in England. St Michael's is only 15 feet wide and 37 feet long and has walls only 10 feet high but three feet thick. Constructed of stone that was quarried from the rock beneath, the church is surrounded by a steep churchyard that contains a surprising number of graves considering its precarious and seemingly soil-less position. Sometimes lost in cloud, the scramble to the summit of Brent Tor is rewarded on a clear day with magnificent views of Dartmoor, Bodmin Moor and the sea at Plymouth Sound.

LEWDOWN
8 miles N of Tavistock off the A30

🐦 Revd. Sabine Baring-Gould

The completion of a bypass in the early 1990s took the main road between Exeter and Launceston away from the centre of this village, making Lewdown a much quieter and more enjoyable place to visit. The village lies within the parish of Lewtrenchard whose rector for 43 years, between 1881 and 1924, was the **Revd Sabine Baring-Gould**. Best known as the composer of the hymn, *Onward, Christian Soldiers*, Baring-Gould was also a prolific prose writer. He regularly produced two or three books a year – novels, historical works such as *Curious Myths of the Middle Ages*, and books on Devon legends and folklore. Baring-Gould nevertheless found time to restore St Peter's Church. His most remarkable success was the creation of a replica of a medieval screen that his

grandfather, also a rector here, had destroyed. The grandson found enough pieces remaining for the replica to be made. It is very impressive with an elaborate canopied loft decorated with paintings of 23 saints.

The Revd. Sabine scandalised Victorian society by marrying a Lancashire mill girl but the union proved to be a happy one and they had a huge family. One local story tells how, one day, emerging from his study, the rector saw a little girl coming down the stairs. "You look nice, my dear, in your pretty frock," he said, vaguely remembering that a children's party was under way. "Whose little girl are you?" "Yours, papa," she answered and burst into tears.

MARY TAVY
3 miles NE of Tavistock on the A386

🏛 Wheal Betsy

The twin villages of Mary Tavy and Peter Tavy lie on opposite banks of the River Tavy and each takes its name from the saint of its parish church. Roughly twice the size of its east bank twin, Mary Tavy stands in the heart of Dartmoor's former mining area. Just to the north of the village stands a survivor from those days. **Wheal Betsy**, a restored pumping engine house, was once part of the Prince Arthur Consols mine that produced lead, silver and zinc.

In the village, the grave of William Crossing, the historian of the moor whose magisterial guide first published in the early 1900s is still in print, can be found in the churchyard. Crossing

Wheal Betsy, nr Mary Tavy

Clapper Bridge, Postbridge

horses following the post road from Exeter into Cornwall.

Two miles along the road to Moretonhampstead, **Warren House Inn** claims to be the third highest tavern in England. It used to stand on the other side of the road but in 1845 a fire destroyed that building. According to tradition, when the present inn was built its landlord carried some still-smouldering turves across the road to the hearth of his new hostelry and that fire has been burning ever since. It's a pleasant enough sight in summer and must have been even more welcome in the winter of 1963. In that year, the Warren House Inn was cut off by heavy snow drifts some 20ft deep for almost three months and supplies had to be flown in by helicopter. Such a remote inn naturally generates some good tales. Like the one about the traveller who stayed here one winter's night and opening by chance a large chest in his room discovered the body of a dead man. "Why!", said the landlord when confronted with the deceased, "tis only feyther! 'Twas too cold to take 'un to the buryin', so mother salted 'un down!"

moved to Peter Tavy in 1909 and described it as "a quiet little place, with a church embosomed by trees, a chapel, a school and a small inn". Inside the impressive medieval church there is a poignant memorial to the five daughters of a 17th century rector. The oldest of them was less than a year when she died:

They breathed awhile and looked the world about
And, like newly-lighted candles, soon went out.

POSTBRIDGE
14 miles NE of Tavistock on the B3212

🏛 Clapper Bridge   📖 Warren House Inn

In prehistoric times, the area around Postbridge was the "metropolis" of Dartmoor as the wealth of Bronze Age remains bears witness. Today, the village is best known for its **Clapper Bridge** which probably dates back to the 13th century and is the best preserved of all the Devon clapper bridges. Spanning the East Dart River, the bridge is a model of medieval minimalist construction with just three huge slabs of granite laid across solid stone piers. Not wide enough for wheeled traffic, the bridge would originally have been used by pack

PRINCETOWN
9 miles E of Tavistock on the B3212

🏚 Dartmoor Prison Heritage Centre

Princetown, best known for its forbidding prison, stands 1,400ft above sea level in an area of the moor which is notorious for its atrocious climate. It gets doused with 80 to 100 inches of rain a year, more than three times the average for Exeter which is less than 20 miles away.

Dartmoor Prison, nr Princetown

That a settlement should be located here at all was the brainchild of one man, Sir Thomas Tyrwhitt, the owner of a local granite quarry. He proposed that a special prison should be built here to house the thousands of troops captured during the Napoleonic wars who were becoming too numerous and unruly for the prison ships moored in Plymouth Sound. The work was completed in 1809 by the prisoners themselves using granite from Sir Thomas' quarry. Paid at the rate of sixpence (2.5p) a day, they also built the main east-west road across the moor which is now the B3212. Yet another of their constructions was the nearby Church of St Mary, a charmless building in whose churchyard stands a tall granite cross in memory of all those prisoners whose bodies lie in unmarked graves. (The mortality rate of the inmates in the early 1800s was 50%). Since around 1900, prisoners' graves have been marked just with their initials and date of death. The lines of small stones are a gloomy sight.

At one time the prison held as many as 9,000 French and, later, American inmates but by 1816, with the cessation of hostilities, the prison became redundant and was closed. Princetown virtually collapsed as a result and

it wasn't until 1823 that its granite quarries were given a new lease of life with the building of the horse-drawn Dartmoor Railway, another of Sir Thomas Tyrwhitt's initiatives. The prison was eventually re-opened for long-serving convicts in 1850 and since then it has been considerably enlarged and upgraded. It is currently in use as a medium security prison with around 640 inmates. The **Dartmoor Prison Heritage Centre** has exhibits detailing the history of the institution.

Also in the town is the National Park's **Moorland Visitors' Centre** which contains some excellent and informative displays about the moor, and also stocks a wide range of books, maps and leaflets. The centre is housed in the former Duchy Hotel where Sir Arthur Conan Doyle stayed while writing some chapters of *The Hound of the Baskervilles,* much of which is set in Dartmoor.

DARTMEET
13 miles E of Tavistock off the B3357

Dartmeet is a picturesque spot where the boulder-strewn East and West Dart rivers join together. At their junction, a single-span packhorse bridge was built in the 1400s; its remains can still be seen just upstream from the more modern road bridge.

Rising in the boggy plateau of north Dartmoor, the Dart and its tributaries drain a huge area of the moor. The river then flows for 46 miles before entering the sea at Dartmouth.

In the days when the tin mines were working, this area was extremely isolated, lacking even a burial ground of its own. Local people had to carry their dead across the moor to Lydford – "Eight miles in fair weather, and 15 in foul". In good weather, this is grand walking country with a choice of exploring the higher moor, dotted with a wealth of prehistoric remains, or following the lovely riverside and woodland path that leads to the famous Clapper Bridge near Postbridge, about five miles upstream.

A Winters Day on Dartmoor

To the east of Dartmeet, and hidden among bracken and gorse, is the **Coffin Stone**, a large boulder on which it was customary for the bearers to rest the body while making the moorland crossing. A cross and the deceased's initials were carved into the stone while the bearers had some liquid refreshment and got back their breath before continuing on their journey.

YELVERTON
5 miles SE of Tavistock on the A386

🎭 Great Western Railway

In prehistoric times, the area around Yelverton must have been quite heavily populated to judge by the extraordinary concentration of stone circles and rows, hut and cairn circles, and burial chambers. The B3212 to Princeton passes through this once-populous stretch of moorland, part of which is now submerged beneath Burrator Reservoir.

Situated just inside the Dartmoor National Park, Yelverton itself is a large village with broad-verged streets which has caused it to be described as "rather like a thriving racecourse". The village is one of very few in the country to have had its name bestowed by the Board of Directors of a railway company. When the **Great Western Railway** opened a station here in 1859 the village was officially known as Elfordtown. The story goes that the London-based surveyors interpreted the Devon pronunciation of Elfordtown as Yelverton. So that was the name blazoned on the station signboard, and the name by which the village has been known ever since.

BUCKLAND MONACHORUM
5 miles S of Tavistock off the A386

🏛 Buckland Abbey   🌿 The Garden House

Tucked away in a secluded valley above the River Tavy, **Buckland Abbey** (National Trust - see panel on page 174) was founded in 1278 by Amicia, Countess of Devon, but became

Buckland Abbey

Buckland Monachorum, nr Yelverton,
Devon PL20 6EY
Tel: 01822 853607

Buckland's peaceful setting belies its exiting past as the home of Sir Francis Drake. Exhibitions reveal the secrets of medieval and monastic life, the Dissolution and the Armada. See Drake's Drum, the beautiful plasterwork of the Great Hall and the fascinating kitchen. A plasterwork ceiling has recently been sculpted in the Drake Chamber. Visit the box hedged herb garden, the Elizabethan garden, the massive Great Barn and estate walks. The three galleries have been redesigned with an exciting introductory film and computer interactives. Presented in association with the City of Plymouth Museum.

better known as the home of Sir Francis Drake. Drake purchased the former abbey in 1581 from his fellow-warrior (and part-time pirate), Sir Richard Grenville, whose exploits in his little ship, *Revenge* were almost as colourful as those of Drake himself. The house remained in the Drake family until 1947 when it was acquired by the National Trust. Of the many exhibits at the abbey, Drake's Drum takes pride of place – according to legend, the drum will sound whenever England is in peril. The drum was brought back to England by Drake's brother, Thomas, who was with the great seafarer when he died on the Spanish Main in 1596. (Rather ignominiously, of dysentery). Elsewhere at the abbey, visitors can see a magnificent 14th century tithe barn, 154ft long, housing an interesting collection of carts and carriages; a craft workshop and a herb garden.

In the village itself, on the site of a medieval vicarage, **The Garden House** is surrounded by a delightful garden created after World War II by Lionel Fortescue, a retired schoolmaster.

GULWORTHY
2 miles SW of Tavistock on the A390

This little village lies at the heart of an area that, in the mid-1880s, had a world wide reputation. A quarter of the world's supply of copper was extracted from this part of Devon and, more alarmingly, so was half of the world's requirements for arsenic. Mining for copper in this area has long been abandoned, due to the discovery of cheaper sources around the world, particularly in South America. Gulworthy's arsenic has also gone out of fashion as an agent of murder.

MILTON ABBOT
5½ miles NW of Tavistock on the B3362

🏠 Endsleigh House

Situated high above the Tamar Valley, Milton Abbot is home to the Regency masterpiece, **Endsleigh House,** that was designed for the Duke and duchess of Bedford by the architect Sir Jeffry Wyattville and the landscape designer Humphry Repton. Built in the *cottage orné* in about 1810, the house comprises the main building and a children's wing that are linked by a curved terrace. The formal gardens were designed to form a setting for the house as well as frame views out across the surrounding countryside. Along with the three terraces, which were restored in 1998, there are less formal garden areas that include a Rock Garden with a mysterious underground grotto that leads to the Diary Dell. Little altered since they were first created, the grounds also include an internationally famous arboretum containing more than 1,000 specimen trees. The house has recently been re-developed as an upmarket hotel.

River Tamar, Bere Alston

BERE ALSTON
5 miles SW of Tavistock on the B3257

🏛 Morwellham Quay

For centuries, Bere Alston was a thriving little port on the River Tamar from whence the products of Dartmoor's tin mines were transported around the world. All that commercial activity has long since gone but the river here is still busy with the to-ings and fro-ings of sleek pleasure craft. Just a few miles upstream from Bere Alston is one of the county's most popular visitor attractions, **Morwellham Quay**. The port fell into disuse following the arrival of the railway and by the 1980s it was a ghost harbour with the Tamar valley breezes whistling through its abandoned buildings. Now restored, this historic site faithfully recreates the busy atmosphere of the 1860s when half the world's copper came

through this tiny harbour. Visitors can journey through the mines on a riverside tramway, and another highlight is the restored Tamar ketch *Garlandstone*. Although Morwellham lies some 20 miles upstream from Plymouth, the Tamar river at this point was deep enough for 300-ton ships to load up with the precious minerals. Once known as the Devon Klondyke, Morwellham suffered a catastrophic decline when cheaper sources of copper were discovered in South America.

The quayside inn has also been restored. It was here that the dockside labourers used to meet for ale, food and the latest news of the ships that sailed from Morwellham. In those days, the news was chalked up on a blackboard and it still is. Though out of date, the stories nonetheless remain intriguing.

LIFTON
9 miles NW of Tavistock on the A30

🏛 Dingles Fairground Heritage Centre

Situated on the banks of the River Lyd, Lifton was, in medieval times, an important centre of the wool trade. Dartmoor sheep tend to have rather coarse fleeces, due to the cold pastureland, so the weavers of Lifton petitioned Henry VII, "by reason of the grossness and stubbornness of their district" to allow them to mix as much lambs' wool and flock with their wool "as may be required to work it".

Just to the east of Lifton is **Dingles Fairground Heritage Centre** where visitors can see one of the best working steam collections in the country including traction engines, steam rollers, fairground attractions and vintage machinery. There's also a collection of vintage road signs, play areas for children, a gift shop, café and riverside walks.

Ivybridge

🚶 Two Moors Way

The original bridge over the Erme at Ivybridge was just wide enough for a single packhorse and the 13th century crossing that

Bridge at Ivybridge

replaced it is still very narrow. When the railway arrived here in 1848, Brunel constructed an impressive viaduct over the Erme valley. It was made of wood, however, so that too was replaced in 1895 by an equally imposing stone structure. The town grew rapidly in the 1860s when a quality paper-making mill was established to make good use of the waters of the Erme and more recently Ivybridge has continued to grow as a commuter town for Plymouth.

Serious walkers will know Ivybridge as the southern starting point of the **Two Moors Way,** the spectacular but gruelling 103-mile path across both Dartmoor and Exmoor, finishing at Barnstaple. The trek begins with a stiff 1,000ft climb up Butterdon Hill, just outside Ivybridge – and that's the easy bit!

SOUTH BRENT
5 miles NE of Ivybridge off the A38

Standing on the southern flank of Dartmoor, just within the National Park, South Brent is a sizeable village of some 3,000 souls. It has a 13th century church with a massive Norman tower, set beside the River Avon, which was once the main church for a large part of the South Hams as well as a considerable area of Dartmoor. Alongside the River Avon are some attractive old textile mills recalling the days when South Brent was an important centre for the production of woollens. In Victorian times, one of the mills was managed by William Crossing whose famous *Crossing's Guide to Dartmoor* provides a fascinating picture of life on the moor in the late 1800s.

In the days of stagecoach travel the town was a lively place with two "posting houses" servicing the competing coaches. It was said that four horses could be changed in 45 seconds and a full-course meal served in 20

🏚 historic building 🏛 museum and heritage 🏛 historic site 🌄 scenic attraction 🌿 flora and fauna minutes. The most famous of the coaches, the *Quicksilver*, left Plymouth at 8.30 in the evening and arrived in London at 4 o'clock the following afternoon – a remarkable average speed of 11 mph, *including* stops.

BUCKFASTLEIGH
9 miles NE of Ivybridge off the A38

🦦 South Devon Railway   🏛 Valiant Soldier Museum

🦋 Buckfast Butterflies & Dartmoor Otter Sanctuary

🦦 Pennywell   🐦 Robert Herrick

A former wool town on the banks of the River Mardle. Several old mill buildings still stand and the large houses of their former owners lie on the outskirts. A unique insight into the lives of local folk is provided by an old inn that has been restored and now houses the **Valiant Soldier Museum and Heritage Centre.** When the Valiant Soldier pub was closed in the 1960s, everything was left in

place – even the money in the till. Rediscovered years later, this life-size time capsule features period public and lounge bars as well as domestic rooms including the kitchen, scullery, parlour and bedrooms.

Buckfastleigh is the western terminus and headquarters of the **South Devon Railway**, (formerly known as the Primrose Line - see panel below), whose steam trains ply the seven-mile route along the lovely Dart Valley to and from Totnes. The Dart is a fast flowing salmon river and its banks abound with herons, swans, kingfishers, badgers and foxes. The company also offers a combined River Rail ticket so that visitors can travel in one direction by train and return by boat. The railway runs regular services during the season with the journey taking about 25 minutes each way.

Another popular attraction close to the town is the **Buckfast Butterflies &**

SOUTH DEVON RAILWAY

The Railway Station, Buckfastleigh, Devon TQ11 0DZ
Tel: 0845 345 1420 e-mail: info@ southdevonrailway.org
website: www.southdevonrailway.org

One of the most delightful ways of exploring the Dart river valley is by taking a journey on the nostalgic **South Devon Railway.** It was originally built in 1872 as the Buckfastleigh, Totnes and South Devon Railway and became part of the Great Western Railway four years later.

The line provided much needed support to the local agricultural and woollen industries and continued to serve the local economy during two world wars. Declining traffic led to the line being closed to passengers in November 1958 and to freight traffic in 1962.

However, local enthusiasts managed to re-open the line in 1969 and the most scenic stretch, from Totnes to Buckfastleigh, survives today as the South Devon Railway. It follows the lovely Dart river valley for some six miles and the majority of the services are operated by steam engines.

There are regular daily services from mid-March to late October, with special services on other days. At Buckfastleigh Station, you will find an extensive railway museum, railway workshops, refreshment rooms serving hot and cold meals, a model railway and the Expressway model railway, gift and book shop.

🎭 stories and anecdotes   🦅 famous people   🎨 art and craft   🎭 entertainment and sport   🚶 walks

Dartmoor Otter Sanctuary (see panel below) where a specially designed tropical rain forest habitat has been created for the exotic butterflies. There's an underwater viewing area and both the butterflies and otters can be photographed, with the otters' thrice-daily feeding times providing some excellent photo-opportunities.

A couple of miles south of Buckfastleigh, **Pennywell** is a spacious all-weather family attraction which offers a wide variety of entertainments and activities. Winner of the West Country "England for Excellence" award in 1999, Pennywell also boasts the UK's longest gravity go-kart ride and promises that its hands-on activities provide something new every half hour.

Another mile or so south, the little church of Dean Prior stands beside the A38. The vicar here at the time of the Restoration was the poet and staunch royalist, **Robert Herrick** (1591-1674). Herrick's best known lines are probably the opening of *To the Virgins, to make*

Much of Time:

> *Gather ye rosebuds while ye may,*
> *Old Time is still a-flying*
> *And this same flower that smiles today*
> *Tomorrow will be dying.*

Herrick apparently found rural Devon rather dull and much preferred London where he had a mistress 27 years his junior. Perhaps to brighten up the monotony of his Devonshire existence, he had a pet pig which he took for walks and trained to drink beer from a tankard. Herrick died in 1674 and was buried in the churchyard where a simple stone marks his assumed last resting place.

BUCKFAST
10 miles NE of Ivybridge off the A38

🏛 Buckfast Abbey

Dominating this small market town is **Buckfast Abbey,** a Benedictine monastery built in the Norman and Gothic style between 1907 and 1938. If you've ever wondered how many people it takes to construct an abbey,

Dartmoor Otters & Buckfast Butterflies

Buckfastleigh, Devon TQ11 0DZ
Tel: 01364 642916
e-mail: contact@ottersandbutterflies.co.uk
website: www.ottersandbutterflies.co.uk

The tropical landscaped gardens at **Dartmoor Otters & Buckfast Butterflies** are home to a wide variety of exotic butterflies from around the world that live, breed and fly freely here along with small birds and other tropical creatures such as terrapins and leaf cutting ants.

Meanwhile, in specially designed outside landscape, three species of otter, including the native British otter, can be seen both on land and in the water. The otters, some of whom have been rescued and some that have been bred here, are fed three times a day and both they and the butterflies provide plenty of opportunity for budding wildlife photographers to hone their skills.

🏛 historic building   🏛 museum and heritage   🏛 historic site   🍃 scenic attraction   🌿 flora and fauna

the astonishing answer at Buckfast is just six. Only one of the monks, Brother Peter, had any knowledge of building so he had to check every stone that went into the fabric. A photographic exhibition at the abbey records the painstaking process that stretched over 30 years. Another monk, Brother Adam, became celebrated as the bee-keeper whose busy charges produced the renowned Buckfast Abbey honey. The abbey gift shop also sells the famous Buckfast Tonic Wine, recordings of the abbey choristers and a wide range of religious items, pottery, cards and gifts.

CORNWOOD

3 miles NW of Ivybridge off the A38

Cornwood is a pleasant village on the River Yealm, a good base from which to seek out the many Bronze Age and industrial remains scattered across the moor. One of the most remarkable sights in Dartmoor is the double line of stones set up on Stall Moor during the Bronze Age. One line is almost 550yds long; the other begins with a stone circle and crosses the River Erme before ending at a burial chamber some two miles distant. There are no roads to these extraordinary constructions, they can only be reached on foot.

If you approach Dartmoor from the south, off the A38, Cornwood is the last village you will find before the moors begin in earnest. Strike due north from here and you will have to cross some 15 miles of spectacular moorland before you see another inhabited place. (Her Majesty's Prison at Princetown, as it happens.)

Bovey Tracy

🏛 Riverside Mill 🐾 Becky Falls

This ancient market town takes its name from the River Bovey and the de Tracy family who received the manor from William the Conqueror. The best-known member of the family is Sir William Tracy, one of the four knights who murdered Thomas à Becket in Canterbury Cathedral. To expiate his crime, Sir William is said to have endowed a church here, dedicated to St Thomas. That building was destroyed by fire and the present church is 15th century with a 14th century tower. Its most glorious possession is a beautifully carved screen of 1427, a gift to the church from Lady Margaret Beaufort, the new owner of the manor and the mother of King Henry VII.

Bovey Tracy, unlike so many Devon towns and villages, has never suffered a major fire. This is perhaps just as well since its fire-fighting facilities until recent times were decidedly limited. In 1920, for example, the town did have an engine, and five volunteers to man it, but no horses to draw it. The parish council in that year issued a notice advising "all or any persons requiring the Fire Brigade with Engine that they must take the responsibility of sending a Pair of Horses for the purpose of conveying the Engine to and from the Scene of the Fire".

For such a small town, Bovey Tracy is remarkably well-supplied with shops as well as the **Riverside Mill** which is run by the Devon Guild of Craftsmen. This is also the South West's leading gallery and craft showroom with work selected from around 240 makers, many with national and international reputations. The Guild presents changing craft exhibitions and demonstrations and the mill also contains a study centre, gallery and a café with roof terrace..

Walkers will enjoy the footpath that passes through the town and follows the track bed of the former railway from Moretonhampstead to Newton Abbot, which runs alongside the

Haytor Ramble

Distance: *4.0 miles (6.4 kilometres)*
Typical time: *180 mins*
Height gain: *150 metres*
Map: *Explorer OL28*
Walk: *www.walkingworld.com ID:1589*
Contributor: *Dennis Blackford*

ACCESS INFORMATION:

On the B3387 Bovey Tracey to Widdecombe road. About 300 metres past the Haytor Vale & Ilsington turning you will pass the bottom car park (tarmac but hot and crowded) where the toilets are. Ignore this car park and continue on for about 200 metres to the middle car park (grass) and park here. There should be buses from Bovey Tracey.

DESCRIPTION:

This circular walk starts at Haytor car park and, after a visit to the scenic quarry with its lake, heads out over the moor to a secret pool that most walkers are unaware of as it is invisible from a distance. From the pool you walk through a gorse and heather part of the moor to Smallacombe Rocks, passing the stone circle sites of ancient round houses. After looking around the rocks with their spectacular outlook you head back towards Haytor and turn onto a Granite Railway to visit a wilder quarry before heading down to Becka Brook (lovely place to picnic). From the stream you return to Haytor by a different route, climbing up over the Tor itself before returning to the starting point.

ADDITIONAL INFORMATION:

Toilets at bottom car park. Ice cream vending van at bottom and top car parks. Park ranger and information at lower car park. This is wild, open moor so care and precautions should be taken. Strong walking boots or shoes, with good tread are strongly recommended. Conditions can change very quickly here so a wind and waterproof extra garment such as a kagoule is also recommended together with a map, compass, water and snack food. Even in mid-summer, it can get very cold on the moor. August and September are possibly the best time to see the gorse and heather in flower.

FEATURES:

Hills or fells, river, toilets, wildlife, birds, flowers, great views, butterflies, industrial archaeology, moor.

WALK DIRECTIONS:

1 | Park in the middle car park which has a firm grass surface and is always far less crowded than the others. Looking across the road, you will see the unmistakable shape of Haytor which can be seen for tens of kilometres in most directions. Leave the car park by the lower of the two entrances and cross the road. After crossing the road, follow the fairly wide path bearing diagonally to the right away from the Tor.

2 | After a few hundred metres, the path widens out and takes you directly to a wooden gate in a wire fence. Go through the gate into the scenic quarry, turn left on the hard dirt path.

3 | After looking around the quarry, follow the path around the left hand edge of the lakes.Follow the path up and over the wooden stile. Continue on the distinct path across the moor for a few hundred metres towards the distant rocky outcrop.

4 | The path crosses the granite railway where you can still see the tracks carved from stone. In the distance you can see the outcrop of

Smallacombe rocks. Do not take the path directly towards the rocks but look for the one diagonally to the right. Follow this path across the moorland (do not follow the railway).

5 | A few hundred metres will suddenly bring you to the secret pool hidden down a fold in the moor. Walk round the left hand edge of the pool and follow the small path through the gorse and heather towards Smallacombe Rocks. As you approach the outcrop, down in the bracken on your left, there are circles of stones with a depression in the centre. These are the remains of ancient roundhouses.

6 | After looking around the rocks and seeing the spectacular views over the valley, turn again towards Haytor and follow the wide path which is fairly clearly visible.

7 | When you reach the railway again, turn right and follow it for about 50 metres until you reach the 'points' in the track. Follow the branch to the right. The track goes downhill for about 800 metres to a rugged quarry with a 'spoil heap' projecting over the valley.

8 | Just before the track appears to end in a pile of rocks, look for a small path down to your right. The first part is a steep scramble down a rocky path (approx five metres) before it becomes a zig-zag path that heads for the trees at the bottom of the valley. Note: If you do not want to attempt this rough section of the walk, retrace your steps out of the quarry until you see the track up to your right and rejoin the walk at waymark 11.

9 | There is another scramble down a rocky path (approx six metres drop) to the lovely Becka Brook which is a great place for a picnic in the shade of the trees and the music of the river. When you have finished here, retrace your steps up the scramble. When you again see the wide path you came down on, look for a smaller branch to your left and

follow this path as it winds through the bracken and heather.

10 | The path is not always very definite so aim for the 'big' tree to the left of the rocks. After passing the tree, bear right to pass on the left of the pile of rocks from the quarry. The track ascends here to rejoin the railway at the entrance of the quarry.

11 | After reaching the railway, cross over and follow the wide track up hill, diagonally to your left.

12 | This path will bring you out to the upper railway track. Turn left on it for about 10 metres then turn diagonally right up the side track towards the rocks.

13 | After a few hundred metres, the path heads towards Haytor. Where the path appears to go down a little valley go to the right of the rocks and continue on the path which will again head towards the Tor.

14 | The path disappears in a boulder strewn grassy area. Head towards the massive rock to pass on its right.

15 | Having passed the Tor, bear left around a smaller outcrop of rock to follow the wide track back to the car park.

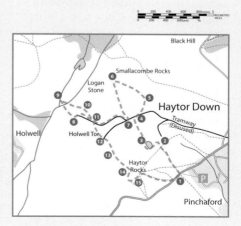

River Bovey for part of its length

Just to the north of Bovey Tracy is **Parke,** formerly the estate of the Tracy family but now owned by the National Trust and leased to the Dartmoor National Park as its headquarters.

Around Bovey Tracy

ILSINGTON
3 miles SW of Bovey Tracey off the B3387

Like so many Dartmoor communities, Ilsington was once an important centre of the wool industry. At the heart of the village is a characteristic trio of late medieval buildings – church, church house and inn. The interior of St Michael's Church is well worth seeing with its impressive array of arched beams and roof timbers which seem to hang in mid-air above the nave. The medieval pew ends are thought to be the only ones in Devon carved with the distinctive "poppy head" design; there's also a mid-14th century effigy of a woman; and an elaborately carved 16th century rood screen.

Entry to the churchyard is by way of an unusual lych gate with an upper storey which once served as the village schoolroom. The present structure is actually a replica of the original medieval gate which apparently collapsed when someone slammed the gate too energetically. The nearby church house, dating back to the 1500s, is now sub-divided into residential dwellings known as St Michael's Cottages.

This small village was the birthplace of the Jacobean dramatist John Ford (1586-1639) whose most successful play, *Tis Pity She's A Whore* (1633), is still occasionally revived.

Ilsington is a sizeable parish and includes the three well-known tors of Rippon, Saddle and Haytor Rocks. The latter is perhaps the most dramatic, especially when approached from the west along the B3387, and with a height of almost 1,500ft provides a popular challenge for rock climbers.

In the early 1800s, the shallow valley to the north of Haytor Rocks was riddled with quarries which supplied granite for such well-known buildings as London Bridge, the National Gallery and the British Museum.

ASHBURTON
7 miles SW of Bovey Tracey off the A38

🏛 Ashburton Museum

This appealing little town lies just inside the boundary of the Dartmoor National Park, surrounded by lovely hills and with the River Ashburn splashing through the town centre.

THE FISH DELI

7 East Street, Ashburton, Devon TQ13 7AD
Tel: 01364 654833
e-mail: information@thefishdeli.co.uk
website: www.thefishdeli.co.uk

The only dedicated fishmonger's in South Devon, **The Fish Deli** was set up in 2004 and is run by Nick and Michele Legg who share a passion for fish sourced from local day boats and selected with marine conservation in mind. All the fished is sourced in Devon and Cornwall and include scallops from Start Bay and oysters from the River Teign estuary. The shop is a feast for all the senses. There are delicious smells of cooking food, outstanding olives, delicious deli, inspired cooked fish dishes to take home, and lots of interesting and innovative things.

🏛 historic building 🏛 museum and heritage 🏛 historic site 🍃 scenic attraction 🌿 flora and fauna

Municipal history goes back a long way here, to 821AD in fact, when the town elected its first Portreeve, the Saxon equivalent of a mayor. The traditional office continues to the present day, although its functions are now purely ceremonial. But each year, on the fourth Tuesday in November, officials gather to appoint not just their Portreeve but also the Ale Tasters, Bread Weighers, Pig Drovers and even a Viewer of Watercourses.

In medieval times, Ashburton's prosperity was based on tin. As one of Devon's four stannary towns, it benefited from the trade generated by the Dartmoor tinners who were obliged to come here to have their metal weighed and stamped, and to pay the duty. Later, the cloth industry was the town's main money-spinner, with several fulling mills along the banks of the Ashburn producing cloth which the East India Company exported to China.

The town is characterised by its many attractive houses and shops, with distinctive slate hung front elevations. Housed in the former home and workshop of a brushmaker, **Ashburton Museum** offers a fascinating insight into the history of this stannary town as well as the domestic and rural life of Dartmoor down the centuries. The collections include old farming implements, Victorian toys, a model of the old Market Hall and Native American artefacts donated by Paul Endicott, whose parents had left Ashburton for Oklahoma at the beginning of the 1900s.

HILL HOUSE NURSERY & GARDENS

Landscove nr Ashburton, South Devon TQ13 7LY
Tel: 01803 762273
e-mail: sacha@hillhousenursery.co.uk
website: www.hillhousenursery.co.uk

Built in 1850 as the vicarage for the adjacent village church, the house now stands in the centre of **Hill House Nursery & Garden**. Owned and run by Ray Hubbard and his son Matthew, this exceptional garden was originally established by Edward Hyams, the gardening correspondent of the *Illustrated London News* and *The Spectator*.

Now beautifully restored by the Hubbards, the garden is open to the public and is a must for any budding horticulturalist. The adjacent Nursery has flourished as a well known venue for serious and casual gardeners. Featuring a combination of the more exotic plants and the everyday variety, Hill House Nursery caters for all levels and tastes of gardeners. And as one customer remarked: "The staff here know about plants and planting. You get good advice with good service". The plant prices are extremely competitive and are sometimes up to 50% cheaper than London.

During the summer months, you can round off your visit by sampling the fare on offer in the tearoom which serves cream teas and light lunches. With the choice of outdoor or indoor tables, you can enjoy the sunshine in summer and enjoy the warmth of the tearoom with its coal fire on cold days.

GATE HOUSE

North Bovey, Moretonhampstead,
Devon TQ13 8RB
Tel: 01647 440479
Fax: 01647 440479
e-mail: srw.gatehouse@btinternet.com
website: www.gatehouseondartmoor.com

Dating back to around 1460, **Gate House** is set in the heart of the beautiful conservation village of North Bovey with its old granite packhorse bridge and thatched cottages. As you open the gate into the large country garden where roses, lavender and heather scent the air, you will catch your first glimpse of this charming medieval home with its thatched roof and quaint widows tucked under the eaves.

This Grade II* Devonshire hall house is very special indeed. Not simply because it has witnessed the passing of 25 English monarchs, along with plagues and civil wars, but because it is also a much loved and restored home where guests can experience ancient history alongside modern comforts.

On arrival, guests pass through the old-fashioned porch way into the beamed sitting rooms with their huge granite fireplaces with bread oven. Here you can begin to relax - perhaps with tea and homemade cake in front of a warming fire in winter. If you prefer to soak up the sunshine and magnificent moorland views, take tea by the swimming pool in a sheltered corner of the garden.

Each of the bedrooms at Gate House reflects a country style elegance and charm, and enjoy lovely views of the garden or moors beyond. There are three double guest bedrooms, each with private bath/shower room and charmingly furnished. Each morning, before descending the winding staircase to a splendid breakfast of local produce, relax with your early morning tea and enjoy the stillness that is Dartmoor. Traditional, whole food and vegetarian meals as requested, using organically grown produce when available. B&B is available from £38 pppn based on two people sharing a double room.

After a hearty breakfast, there are even more choices to be made. A visit to one of the many nearby National Trust properties, perhaps, or to one of the glorious Devon gardens. Perhaps you would prefer to walk along the banks of the River Teign, hike on open moorland, or creep through sheltered woodland listening to the birds and wildlife. The more active may wish to finish that round of golf, or set off on the mysterious Sherlock Holmes trail. Whatever you decide, you can be sure that the day will be one to remember!

WIDECOMBE IN THE MOOR
6 miles W of Bovey Tracey off the B3212

🏠 Cathedral of the Moors   🏠 Church House

🌿 Widecombe Fair   ⬚ Grimspound

This pleasing village enjoys a lovely setting in the valley of the East Webburn river and its grand old church, with a massive 120ft high granite tower rising against a backdrop of high moorland, has understandably been dubbed the **"Cathedral of the Moors"**. Dedicated to St Pancras, the church was built with funds raised by tin miners in the 14th century, and enlarged during the next two centuries. A panel inside the church records the disastrous events of 21st October 1638. A sizeable congregation had gathered for a service when a bolt of lightning struck the tower, dislodging huge blocks of masonry on to the worshippers. Four were killed and a further 60 badly injured. (Local legend maintains that the Devil had been spotted earlier that day spitting fire and riding an ebony stallion across the moor).

In addition to the church, two other buildings are worth mentioning. Glebe House is a handsome 16th century residence which has since been converted to a shop, and **Church House** is an exceptional colonnaded building which was originally built around 1500 to accommodate those travelling large distances across the moor to attend church services. It was later divided into almshouses then served in succession as a brewery and a school. It is now a National Trust shop and information centre.

The famous **Widecombe Fair** to which Uncle Tom Cobleigh, his boisterous crew and the old grey mare, were making their way is still held here on the second Tuesday in September and although it is no longer an agricultural event, remains a jolly affair. A succession of real-life Tom Cobleighs have lived around Widecombe over the centuries but the song probably refers to a gentleman who died in 1794. An amorous bachelor, this Uncle Tom Cobleigh had a mane of red hair and he refused to maintain any babies that did not display the same characteristic.

From Widecombe, a country lane leads to **Grimspound** which is perhaps the most impressive of all Dartmoor's Bronze Age survivals. This settlement was occupied between 1800BC and 500BC and is remarkably well-preserved. There are 24 hut circles here, some of them reconstructed, and it's still possible to make out the positions of door lintels and stone sleeping shelves. Today, the area around Grimspound is bleak and moody, an atmosphere which recommended itself to Sir Arthur Conan Doyle who had Sherlock Holmes send Dr Watson into hiding here to help solve the case of *The Hound of the Baskervilles*.

NORTH BOVEY
6 miles NW of Bovey Tracey off the B3212

In any discussion about which is the "loveliest village in Devon", North Bovey has to be one of the leading contenders. Set beside the River Bovey, it is quite unspoiled, with thatched cottages grouped around the green, a 15th century church and a delightful old inn, the Ring of Bells, which like many Devon hostelries was originally built, back in the 13th century, as a lodging house for the stonemasons building the church.

LUSTLEIGH
3 miles NW of Bovey Tracey off the A382

Lustleigh is one of Dartmoor's most popular and most photographed villages. Placed at all angles on the hillside, are a ravishing assortment of 15th and 16th century deeply-thatched, colour-washed cottages, picturesquely grouped around the church. Appropriately for such a genuinely olde-worlde village, Lustleigh keeps alive some of the time-honoured traditions of country life, enthusiastically celebrating May Day each year with a procession through the village, dancing round the maypole, and the coronation of a May Queen. From the village there are some delightful walks, especially one that passes through Lustleigh Cleave, a wooded section of the steep-sided Bovey valley. Also close by is the **Becky Falls Woodland Park**, with its waterfalls, rugged landscape and attractions for all the family. Here, too, is **Yarner Wood Nature Reserve**, home to pied flycatchers, wood warblers and redstarts.

MORETONHAMPSTEAD

7 miles NW of Bovey Tracey on the A382

🏚 St Michael's Church   🏚 Almshouses

🐾 Miniature Pony Centre

Moreton, as this little town is known locally, has long claimed the title of "Gateway to east Dartmoor", a rôle in which it was greatly helped by the branch railway from Newton Abbot which operated between 1866 and 1964. This is the gentler part of Dartmoor, with many woods and plantations, and steep-sided river valleys. Within easy reach are picture-postcard villages such as Widecombe in the Moor, striking natural features like Haytor, and the remarkable Bronze Age stone hut-circle at Grimspound.

The best approach to Moreton is by way of the B3212 from the southwest. From this direction you are greeted with splendid views of the little hilltop town surrounded by fields and with the tower of **St Andrew's Church** piercing the skyline. Built in Dartmoor granite during the early 1400s, the church overlooks the Sentry, or Sanctuary Field, an attractive public park. In the south porch are the tombstones of two French officers who died here as prisoners of war in 1807. At one point during those years of the Napoleonic Wars, no fewer than 379 French officers were living in Moreton, on parole from the military prison at Princetown. One of them, General Rochambeau, must have sorely tested the patience of local people. Whenever news arrived of a French success, he would don his full-dress uniform and parade through the streets.

One of the most interesting buildings in Moreton is the row of **Almshouses** in Cross Street. Built in 1637, it is thatched and has a striking arcade supported by sturdy granite columns. The almshouses are now owned by the National Trust but are not open to the public. Just across the road from the almshouses is **Mearsdon Manor Galleries,** the oldest house in Moreton, dating back to

Moretonhampstead Almshouses

the 14th century. The ground floor of the manor is now a very pleasant traditional English tearoom. In total contrast, the remaining rooms contain an astonishing array of colourful, exotic artefacts collected by the owner, Elizabeth Prince, on her trips to the Far East. There are Dartmoor-pony-sized wooden horses, Turkish rugs, Chinese lacquered furniture, finely-carved jade – a veritable treasury of Oriental craftsmanship.

Two miles west of Moretonhampstead on the B3212, the **Miniature Pony Centre** is home to miniature ponies, donkeys and other horse breeds, as well as pygmy goats, pigs, lambs and many other animals. There are pony rides for children aged nine and under, a daily birds of prey display, indoor and outdoor play areas and a cafeteria.

Plymouth

🏛 Plymouth Hoe   🏛 The Citadel

🏛 Mayflower Steps   🏛 Eddystone Lighthouse

🐦 National Marine Aquarium

With around a quarter of a million inhabitants, Plymouth is now the largest centre of population in the south west peninsula but its development has been comparatively recent. It wasn't until the late 1100s that the harbour was recognised as having any potential as a military and commercial port. Another 300 years passed before it was established as the main base for the English fleet guarding the western channel against a seaborne attack from Spain.

Perhaps the best way of getting to know this historic city is to approach **Plymouth Hoe** on foot from the main shopping area, along the now-pedestrianised Armada Way. It was on the Hoe on Friday, July 19th, 1588,

that one of the most iconic moments in English history took place. Commander of the Fleet, and erstwhile pirate, Sir Francis Drake was playing bowls here when he was informed of the approach of the Spanish Armada. With true British phlegm, Sir Francis completed his game before boarding *The Golden Hind* and sailing off to harass the Spanish fleet. A statue of Sir Francis, striking a splendidly belligerent pose and looking proudly to the horizon, stands on the Hoe which is still an open space, combining the functions of promenade, public park and parade ground.

Just offshore, the striking shape of **Drake's Island** rises like Alcatraz from the deep swirling waters at the mouth of the River Tamar. In its time, this stark fortified islet has been used as a gunpowder repository, (it is said to be riddled with underground tunnels where the powder was stored), a prison, and a youth adventure centre.

Two miles from the Hoe, Plymouth's remarkable **Breakwater** protects the Sound from the destructive effects of the prevailing south-westerly winds. Built by prisoners between 1812 and 1840, this massive mile-long construction required around four million tons of limestone. The surface was finished with enormous dovetailed blocks of stone, and the structure rounded off with a lighthouse at one end.

On a clear day, it's possible to see the famous **Eddystone Lighthouse,** 12 miles out in the Channel. The present lighthouse is the fourth to be built here. The first, made of timber, was swept away in a huge storm in 1703 taking with it the man who had built the lighthouse, the ship-owner Winstanley. In 1759, a much more substantial structure of dovetailed granite blacks was built by John

🎬 stories and anecdotes 🦢 famous people 🎨 art and craft 🖋 entertainment and sport 🏃 walks

Smeaton's Tower, Plymouth Hoe

the Civil War, Charles' Citadel has a number of gun ports bearing directly on the city. The Citadel is still a military base, but there are guided tours every afternoon from May to September.

Close by the Citadel is Plymouth's oldest quarter, the **Barbican.** Now a lively entertainment area filled with restaurants, pubs, and an innovative small theatre, it was once the main trading area for merchants exporting wool and importing wine.

Close by are the **Mayflower Steps** where the Pilgrim Fathers boarded ship for their historic voyage to Massachusetts. The names of the Mayflower's company are listed on a board on nearby Island House, now the tourist information office. Many other emigrants were to follow in the Pilgrim Fathers' wake, with the result that there are now more than 40 communities named Plymouth scattered across the English-speaking world.

A number of interesting old buildings around the Barbican have survived the ravages of time and the terrible pasting the city received during World War II. **Prysten House,** behind St Andrew's Church, is a 15th century priest's house; the **Elizabethan House** in New Street has a rich display of Elizabethan furniture and furnishings, and the **Merchant's House** in St Andrew's Street, generally regarded as Devon's finest Jacobean building, is crammed full of interesting objects relating to Plymouth's past. A particularly fascinating exhibit in the Merchant's House is the **Park Pharmacy,** a genuine Victorian pharmacy complete with its 1864 fittings and stocked with such preparations as Ipecacuanha Wine ("one to two tablespoonfuls as an emetic") and Tincture of Myrrh and Borax, "for the teeth and gums". Another vintage shop is **Jacka's**

Smeaton. It stood for 120 years and even then it was not the lighthouse but the rocks on which it stood which began to collapse. The lighthouse was dismantled and re-erected on the Hoe where, as **Smeaton's Tower,** it is one of the city's most popular tourist attractions. From the top, there are good views of Millbay Docks, Plymouth's busy commercial port which was once busy with transatlantic passenger liners. Today, the docks handle a variety of merchant shipping, including the continental ferry services to Brittany and northern Spain. To the east, the view is dominated by **The Citadel,** a massive fortification built by Charles II, ostensibly as a defence against seaborne attack. Perhaps bearing in mind that Plymouth had resisted a four-year siege by his father's troops during

Bakery which claims to be the oldest commercial bakery in the country and is reputed to have supplied the *Mayflower* with ship's biscuits.

Also in the Barbican area is the **National Marine Aquarium**, located on the Fish Quay. The Aquarium experience comprises a total of 50 live exhibits including three massive tanks, the largest of which – Britain's deepest tank – holds 2.5 million litres of water. More than 4,000 animals from 400 species are displayed in realistic habitats from local shorelines to coral reefs. The virtual reality tour includes encounters with brilliantly coloured fish, seahorses and even Caribbean sharks. A recently opened aquarium zone, Explorocean, focuses on ocean exploration and sustainability through innovative, interactive exhibits.

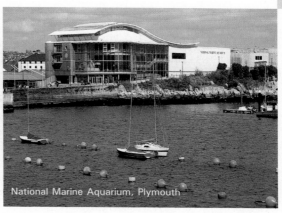
National Marine Aquarium, Plymouth

Locally, the Tamar estuary is known as the Hamoaze, (pronounced ham-oys), and it's well worth taking one of the boat trips that leave from the Mayflower Steps. This is certainly the best way to see Devonport Dockyard, while the ferry to Cremyll on the Cornish bank of the Tamar drops off passengers close to Mount Edgcumbe Country Park and the old smuggling village of Cawsand.

The blackest date in Plymouth's history is undoubtedly March 21st, 1941. On that night, the entire centre of the city was razed to the ground by the combined effects of high-explosive and incendiary bombs. More than 1,000 people were killed; another 5,000 injured. After the war, the renowned town planner Sir Patrick Abercrombie was commissioned to design a completely new town centre. Much of the rebuilding was carried out in the 1950s, which was not British architecture's golden age, but half a century later the scheme has acquired something of a period charm. Abercrombie's plan included some excellent facilities, like the first-rate **Museum and Art Gallery,** the **Theatre Royal** with its two auditoria, the **Arts Centre**, and the **Pavilions** complex of concert hall, leisure pool and skating rink.

Plymouth's best-known export has to be **Plymouth Gin** which has been produced in the city since 1793. At the company's Black Friars Distillery visitors can take a guided tour and learn about the art of making this famous tipple. In the Refectory Bar here, it is said, the Pilgrim Fathers spent their last night before setting sail in the *Mayflower*. There's also a café and a shop.

Around Plymouth

PLYMPTON
4 miles E of Plymouth on the B3416

🏛 Saltram House

Plympton boasts one of Devon's grandest mansions, **Saltram House** (National Trust).

Plym Valley Railway

Marsh Mills Station, Coypool Road,
Plympton, Devon PL7 4NW
Tel: 01752 330881
website: www.plymrail.co.uk

The object of the **Plym Valley Railway** is to
relay and restore a short section of the
former Great Western Railway branch line
from Plymouth to Launceston via
Tavistock and, in particular, the section
that runs from Marsh Mills, Plympton to the local beauty spot of Plym Bridge, a distance of
around a mile and a quarter. A series of heritage steam and diesel locomotives from the
1950s and 1960s operate the services that run on Sundays and there is also a buffet and
souvenir shop at Marsh Mills.

Built during the reign of George II for the
Parker family, this sumptuous house occupies
a splendid site overlooking the Plym estuary.
In the 1760s Robert Adam was called in, at
enormous expense, to decorate the dining
room and "double cube" saloon, which he
accomplished with his usual panache. There
are portraits of the Parkers by the locally born
artist Sir Joshua Reynolds, and amongst the
fine furniture, a magnificent four-poster bed
by Thomas Chippendale. Other attractions
include the great kitchen with its fascinating
assortment of period kitchenware, an
orangery in the gardens, and the former
chapel, now a gallery displaying the work of
West Country artists. Saltram House appeared
as Norland House in the 1995 feature film of
Jane Austen's *Sense and Sensibility* starring
Emma Thompson and Hugh Grant.

TURNCHAPEL

1 mile SE of Plymouth off the A379

Enjoying views across Cattewater to
Plymouth, the village of Turnchapel is strung
along the waterside. The village was declared a
Conservation Area in 1977 and, with its two

pubs, church, and waterfront, is a pleasant
place to wander around. Nearby, there are ex-
RAF Catalina flying boats to admire; and from
Mountbatten Peninsula grand vistas open up
over to Plymouth Hoe and Drake's Island. It
was at RAF Mountbatten that Lawrence of
Arabia served as a humble aircraftman for
several years.

A short distance to the south is a stretch of
coastline known as **Abraham's Garden**. The
story goes that, during the fearful plague of
1665, a number of Spanish slaves were buried
here. In their memory, it is said, the shrubbery
always remains green, even in winter.

WEMBURY

6 miles SE of Plymouth off the A379

Wembury church provides a dramatic
landmark as it stands isolated on the edge of
the cliff, and the coastal path here provides
spectacular views of the Yealm estuary to the
east, and Plymouth Sound to the west (see
walk on page 192). The path is occasionally
closed to walkers when the firing range is in
use, so look out for the red warning flags. **The
Great Mew Stone** stands a mile offshore in

Wembury Bay. This lonely islet was inhabited until the 1830s when its last residents, the part-time smuggler Sam Wakeham and his family, gave up the unequal struggle to make a living here. The Mew Stone is now the home of seabirds who surely can't take kindly to its use as

Newton Ferrers

a target from time to time by the HMS Cambridge gunnery school on Wembury Point.

NEWTON FERRERS
9 miles SE of Plymouth on the B3186

A picturesque fishing village of whitewashed cottages sloping down to the river, Newton Ferrers is beloved by artists and is also one of the south coast's most popular yachting centres. Part of the village sits beside the River Yealm (pronounced "Yam"), the rest alongside a large creek. When the creek dries out at low tide, it is possible to walk across to Noss Mayo on the southern bank. (When the tide is in, a ferry operates, but only during the season.)

The South Hams

"The frutefullest part of all Devonshire." said an old writer of this favoured tract of land lying south of Dartmoor, bounded by the River Dart to the east and the River Erme to the west. The climate is exceptionally mild, the soil fertile and the pastures well watered. But

the rivers that run off Dartmoor to the sea, slicing north-south through the area, created burdensome barriers to communications until fairly recent times. This comparative isolation kept the region unspoilt but also kept it poor.

There are few towns of any size – only Totnes, Kingsbridge and Modbury really qualify, along with the picturesque ports of Dartmouth and Salcombe. For the rest, the South Hams is a charmed landscape of drowsy villages linked by narrow country lanes running between high banks on which wildflowers flourish: thanks to an enlightened County Council, the verges were never assaulted with massive quantities of herbicides as in other areas.

The area has been known as the South Hams, the 'homesteads south of Dartmoor', since Saxon times, but one town at least claims a history stretching much further back in time. We begin our exploration of the South Hams at Totnes which is the second oldest borough in England. The town sent its first Member of Parliament to London in 1295, and elected the first of its 630-odd Mayors in 1359.

📷 stories and anecdotes 🐿 famous people 🎨 art and craft 🖉 entertainment and sport 🚶 walks

Wembury

Distance: *4.8 miles (7.6 kilometres)*

Typical time: *120 mins*

Height gain: *200 metres*

Map: *Explorer OL20*

Walk: *www.walkingworld.com ID:2072*

Contributor: *Dave Pawley*

ACCESS INFORMATION:

From the Plymouth direction as you drive into Wembury you will pass the Odd Wheel pub on your right, a few yards along the road turn left and 100 yards on turn left again into Barton Close and at the end of the road are playing fields and a large car park. There are buses from Plymouth bus station to Wembury for those who wish to use public transport.

DESCRIPTION:

A walk with a bit of everything, footpaths through fields, views of Dartmoor at one point, the sea and the lovely river Yealm. It includes a section of the South West Coastal path and even the start of the Devon version of the Coast to Coast path. The walk takes you from the large

village of Wembury out across fields and roads to high above the river Yealm and a loop down to the very edge of the river and the ferry across it. From there up again to take the coastal path west along to Wembury Beach where there is a church, car park, toilets and a shop and the start of the coast to coast walk. The route is then up a splendid valley and along footpaths and a small amount of road walking to near Knighton before returning to the car park.

ADDITIONAL INFORMATION:

The Great Mewstone Island was once inhabited, if only by a man once employed as a warrener on the island. There is an excellent signpost right by Wembury beach which indicates just how long the SW coastal path is and the distance of the coast to coast path which runs from Wembury Beach up to Lynmouth in the North. At Waymark 10 the Odd Wheel is well worth a visit and, as with almost all pubs these days, food is served. The Jazz is very good, every Thursday evening.

FEATURES:

Hills or fells, river, sea, pub, toilets, play area, church, wildlife, birds, flowers, great views, food shop, marine centre.

WALK DIRECTIONS:

1 | Leave the car park at Barton Close near the Odd Wheel public house and follow the track along at the rear of the childrens play area and tennis courts and descend along the track beside the field hedge until you come to some houses on your left. Almost opposite the second house there are stone steps to your right up through the hedge leading into a field.

2 | Turn right and walk up the steps and follow the track across a field, through kissing gates and along the side of another field to emerge by a lovely small manor house over a stile onto a road. Head south east slightly uphill along the road then on through a stile by a gate onto a rough

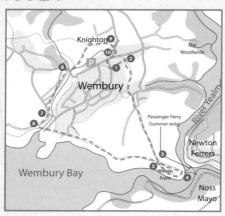

track. After about half a mile you will come to a gate with a house to the left hand side and just beyond the gate there are three tracks, one ahead, one to the left and the other to the right. This walk takes you along all three!

3 | Go through the gate and just by the gatehouse turn left and follow the footpath which will loop you right down to the very edge of the very scenic River Yealm. As you descend, there is a newly opened linear track through Thorn Woods off to your left, not incorporated into this walk so continue south east heading down an increasingly steep path until you are just above river level where, during the summer months, the passenger ferry departs for the short hop to the other bank.

4 | Continue along the loop, walking to the left of a lovely waterside house and then follow the track back steeply uphill until you reach the gate house /gate again. The main coastal path is off to your left.

5 | Turn left though a gate and onto the coastal path which leads you along overlooking the mouth of the Yealm. Continue along parallel to the mouth of the river below and do not take the track leading inland at a junction. After about a mile you will pass a couple of houses on your right. About 20 metres beyond the houses, turn left and follow the track which descends towards the sea and you will pass a church to your right. Descend to the car park and there is a new Wembury Marine Centre building which is well worth a brief visit. Then make your way down to the beach, passing between a small shop and toilets.

6 | Cross over a small bridge just above the beach. By the signpost turn inland from the coastal path and start the coast to coast walk. Make your way up a valley. The track leads you up and over a stile to a road after 250 metres. Turn left on the road and a few metres on, the road joins another road where you will see a

path sign on the left hand side directing you on up the valley, initially along a concreted path below a house.

7 | Turn right onto the track which continues east up the valley. At the far end of the gardens of the house there are two parallel tracks, take the upper permissive footpath marked with the coast to coast logo, the lower bridlepath is very, very muddy. The track eventually emerges over a stile and onto a road. Turn left and walk down the road for 100 yards or more and you will see a sign pointing up by some renovated houses, showing Langdonand Train Road.

8 | Follow the wide track up with a house to your left and right. Just beyond the second house take a narrow track which leads you steeply uphill up through trees, over a stile and into a field. Walk uphill along the field edge, keeping the hedge to your right, until you come to the first wide gap in the hedge. Go through the gap and walk diagonally across the next field along a broad track with clear signposting. Ignore the signed footpath off to your left at the top corner, pass through a gap in the hedge and continue diagonally along another broad track heading east north east to the corner of the second field where you go through a yet another wide gap in the hedge.

9 | Just beyond the wide gap in the hedge, the path turns slightly right to lead you diagonally across a field as it descends. Again the track is narrow through the cultivated field. At the far corner there is a stile leading out to a narrow lane. Turn right and follow the road which leads you downhill then directly up to the Odd Wheel Pub.

10 | Just beyond the Odd Wheel Pub is the main road you travelled along to reach the car park. Turn right onto the road and where the road turns into Mewstone Ave there is a narrow pedestrian only track off to your left which leads you up by a school to your left and directly back into Barton Close and the car park.

Totnes

🏛 Totnes Castle   🏛 Guildhall   📷 Bowden House

📷 Totnes Elizabethan Museum   🌱 Rare Breeds Farm

This captivating little town claims to have been founded by an Ancient Trojan named Brutus in 1200BC. The grandfather of Aeneas, the hero of Virgil's epic poem *The Aeneid,* Brutus sailed up the River Dart, gazed at the fair prospect around him and decided to found the first town in this new country which would take its name, Britain, from his own. The **Brutus Stone,** set in the pavement of the main shopping street, Fore Street, commemorates this stirring incident when both the town and a nation were born.

The first recorded evidence of this town, set on a hill above the highest navigable point on the River Dart, doesn't appear until the mid-10th century when King Edgar established a mint at Totnes. The Saxons already had a castle of sorts here, but the impressive remains of **Totnes Castle** are Norman, built between the 1100s and early 1300s. Towering over the town, it is generally reckoned to be the best-preserved motte and bailey castle in Devon.

A substantial section of Totnes' medieval town wall has also survived. The superb **East Gate**, which straddles the steep main street is part of that wall.

Just a little way down the hill from East Gate is the charming **Guildhall** of 1553, a remarkable little building with a granite colonnade. It houses both the Council

---

PAPERWORKS

63 High Street, Totnes, Devon TQ9 5PB
Tel: 01803 867009
Fax: 01803 866515
e-mail: shop@paperworkstotnes.com
website: www.paperworkstotnes.com

Unusual and handmade paper and stationery is the speciality of **PaperWorks** which is owned and run by partners Heidrun and David Guest. Heidrun is an accomplished artist and the partners design and make many of the cards, books and albums themselves.

Their highly individual shop is a paradise for lovers of paper and original design with an amazing range of papers available for all kinds of art, craft and decorative uses. This fascinating High Street shop, fronted by Heidrun's colourful and often witty window displays, also sells greetings cards, gift wrap and decorated stationery as well as an extensive selection of paper-related gifts and craft materials. Many of the papers are handmade; recycled papers are another speciality.

PaperWorks also stocks a wide range of artists' products including pens, pastels and watercolours. This is a place tailor-made for browsing and enjoying the wealth of colour and visual stimulation on offer.

🏛 historic building   📷 museum and heritage   🏚 historic site   🌳 scenic attraction   🌱 flora and fauna

VINTAGE LIVING

61 High Street, Totnes, Devon TQ9 5PB
Tel: 01803 863999
Also at; 13 Broad Street, Bath, BA1 5LJ
Tel: 01225 335068
website: www.vintageliving.co.uk

Specialising in stylish French country interiors, Vintage Living offers a wide selection of painted furniture and decorative accessories to adorn your home. Usually in stock are a selection of rustic country dining tables and dining chairs, together with French buffets. Also, a range of antique and new sofas, armchairs and upholstered furniture. Specially featuring lots of storage ideas for your home with chest of drawers, wardrobes, pigeon hole units and lots more. Customers are welcomed with the sound of old French café music and scented roses wafting through the air. Once inside, there are a feast of delights and customers can imagine that they've just landed in rural France. Diana Warszawski, the owner travels extensively to find her unique mix of vintage and characterful new stock which shows 'years of wear', even if it's new!

Vintage Living is a stockist of Kate Forman lampshades, inspired by 19th century French designs, Lene Bjerre lace curtain panels, and Le Comptoir De Famille home accessories. These two highly individual shops make the people who visit both Totnes and Bath want to spread their discovery to lots of their friends. Many customers now make a weekly visit to not miss out.

Chamber (which is still in use) and the underground Town Gaol (which is not). The cells can be visited, as can the elegant Council Chamber with its plaster frieze and the table where Oliver Cromwell sat in 1646.

Almost opposite the Guildhall is another magnificent Elizabethan building, currently occupied by Barclays Bank. It was built in 1585 for Nicholas Ball who had made his fortune from the local pilchard fishery. When he died, his wife Anne married Sir Thomas Bodley and it was the profit from pilchards that funded the world-famous Bodleian Library at Oxford University.

The town's Elizabethan heritage really comes alive if you are visiting on a Tuesday in summer. You will find yourself stepping into a pageant of Elizabethan colour, for this is when the people of Totnes array themselves in crisp, white ruffs and velvet gowns for a charity market which has raised thousands of pounds for good causes since it began in 1970. In August, the Elizabethan Society organises the **Orange Race** which commemorates a visit to the town by Sir Francis Drake during which he presented "a fair red orange" to a small boy in the street. Today, contestants chase their oranges down the hill.

The parish church of Totnes is **St Mary's.** It was entirely rebuilt in the 15th century when the town's cloth industry was booming – at that time Totnes was second in importance only to Exeter. The church's most glorious possession is a rood-screen delicately carved in stone from the quarry at Beer.

Close by at 70 Fore Street is the **Totnes Elizabethan Museum**, housed in an attractive half-timbered Elizabethan building whose upper floors overhang the street. One of the fascinating exhibits here honours a distinguished son of Totnes, Charles Babbage (1791-1871) whose 'Analytical Machine' is universally acknowledged as the forerunner of the electronic computer. The museum display records his doomed struggle to perfect such a calculator using only mechanical parts. A little further up the hill, in High Street, the **Butterwalk** and **Poultrywalk** are two ancient covered shopping arcades whose upper storeys rest on pillars of granite, timber or cast iron.

In recent years, Totnes has earned the title of 'Natural Health Capital of the West Country'. The first Natural Health Centre was established here in 1989. Visitors will find specialist shops offering natural medicines, organic food, aromatherapy, relaxation tapes and books on spiritual healing. A variety of craft and antique shops all add to the town's allure for shopaholics.

For centuries, Totnes was a busy river port and down by **Totnes Bridge**, an elegant stone structure of 1828, the quay was lined with warehouses, some of which have survived and been converted into highly desirable flats. Nearby, on the Plains, stands a granite obelisk to the famous explorer William Wills, a native of the town who perished from starvation when attempting to re-cross the Australian desert with Robert Burke in 1861.

One excursion from Totnes not to be missed is the breathtakingly beautiful river trip to Dartmouth, 12 miles downstream. This stretch of the river has been called the

"English Rhine" and the comparison is no exaggeration. The river here is well away from roads, making it an ideal location for seeing wading-birds, herons, cormorants, and even seals. During the summer, there are frequent departures from the quay by the bridge.

Another memorable journey is by steam train along the seven-mile stretch of the **South Devon Railway,** also known as the Primrose Line, which runs through the glorious scenery of the Dart Valley to Buckfastleigh. Most of the locomotives and carriages are genuine Great Western Railway stock and are painted in the GWR's famous chocolate and cream livery.

Next door to the railway, the **Rare Breeds Farm** includes a hedgehog rescue centre, some spectacular owls, red squirrels, goats, sheep, birds and much more. It also has a Garden Café with views of working steam trains and Totnes Castle.

Even that list of attractions isn't exhaustive. The **Devonshire Collection of Period Costume** is housed in one of the town's most interesting 16th century houses,

Around Totnes

BERRY POMEROY
2 miles E of Totnes off the A385 or A381

🏛 Berry Pomeroy Castle

For the last 1,000 years this small village has been owned by just two families. The de la Pomerais dynasty arrived with William the Conqueror and held the land for almost 500 years. In the early 1300s they built **Berry Pomeroy Castle** in a superb position on a wooded promontory above the Gatcombe Brook. Substantial remains of the castle still stand, including sections of the curtain wall

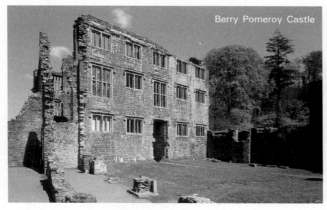

Berry Pomeroy Castle

STOKE GABRIEL
5 miles SE of Totnes off the A385

A charming village of narrow lanes and alleys, Stoke Gabriel stands on a hillside above a tidal spur of the River Dart. A weir was built across the neck of the creek in Edwardian times and this traps the water at low tide, giving the village a pleasant lakeside atmosphere. The part-13th century church of St Gabriel has a restored late-medieval pulpit and a truncated screen with some good wainscot paintings. In the churchyard are the rather forlorn remains of an oak tree reputed to be more than 1,500 years old. To the west of the village, a lane leads to the riverside hamlet of Duncannon where, by general consent, the River Dart is at its most lovely.

DITTISHAM
11 miles SE of Totnes off the A3122

🏛 Greenway House   ✐ Barn Gallery

The best way to reach the pretty yachting village of Dittisham is by passenger ferry from Dartmouth. The major attraction here is **Greenway,** the home of Dame Agatha Christie for the last 30 years of her life. Her daughter now lives there and the house is currently not open to the public, but the lovely gardens overlooking the river are open Wednesday to Sunday inclusive, with gardener's guided walks every Friday. The house itself is expected to open to the public in 2009. Also within the grounds is the **Barn Gallery** which mounts exhibitions of contemporary art by local artists.

and the 14th century gatehouse. In 1548 the Pomeroys, as they were now known, sold the estate to Sir Edward Seymour whose sister, Jane, had been the third wife of Henry VIII. Sir Edward built a three-storey Tudor mansion within the medieval fortifications but this too is now a shell. Although the castle is still owned by Sir Edward's descendant, the Duke of Somerset, it is administered by English Heritage and open to the public daily during the season. In the village itself, St Mary's Church contains some interesting monuments to the Pomeroys and Seymours, as well as an outstanding rood screen.

ASHPRINGTON
2 miles SE of Totnes off the A381

Set in a stunning location above the River Dart, **Sharpham Vineyard and Cheese Dairy** offers two gastronomic experiences. Visitors can sample the international award-winning red and white wines, and watch the dairy cheese being made. The entrance fee includes complimentary tastings. An attractive way of visiting the vineyard is by taking one of the ferry boats along the River Dart which will stop at Sharpham on request.

🔲 stories and anecdotes   🍴 famous people   ✐ art and craft   🖉 entertainment and sport   🚶 walks

Dartmouth Harbour

DARTMOUTH

14 miles SE of Totnes on the A3122

- Dartmouth Castle
- Dartmouth Museum
- Britannia Royal Naval College
- Dartmouth Regatta

For centuries, this entrancing little town clinging to the sides of a precipitous hill was one of England's principal ports. Millions of casks of French and Spanish wine have been offloaded onto its narrow quays. During the 1100s Crusaders on both the Second and Third Crusades mustered here, and from here they set sail. In its sheltered harbour, Elizabeth's men o'war lay in wait to pick off the stragglers from the Spanish Armada. In 1620, the *Mayflower* put in here for a few days

for repairs before hoisting sail on August 20th for Plymouth and then on to the New World where the pilgrims arrived three months later. The quay from which they embarked later became the major location for the BBC TV series, *The Onedin Line,* and was also seen in the feature film *Sense and Sensibility* starring Emma Thompson and Hugh Grant.

Geoffrey Chaucer visited the town in 1373 in his capacity as Inspector of Customs and is believed to have modelled the 'Schipman of Dertemouthe' in his *Canterbury Tales* on the character of the then Mayor of Dartmouth, John Hawley. Hawley was an enterprising merchant and seafarer who was also responsible for building the first **Dartmouth Castle** (English Heritage). Dramatically sited, it guards the entrance to the Dart estuary and was one of the first castles specifically designed to make effective use of artillery. In case the castle should prove to be an inadequate deterrent, in times of danger a heavy chain was strung across the harbour to Kingswear Castle on the opposite bank. (Kingswear Castle is now owned by the Landmark Trust and available for holiday rentals.)

historic building   museum and heritage   historic site   scenic attraction   flora and fauna

BAXTERS GALLERY

12 Foss Street, Dartmouth,
Devon TQ6 9DR
Tel: 01803 839000
e-mail: info@baxtersgallery.co.uk
website: www.baxtersgallery.co.uk

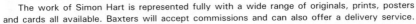

Baxters was established in July 2006 when Sarah Duggan took over Hartworks Gallery. After too many years of saying "one day, I'll own a gallery", Sarah decided that Dartmouth and Baxters would be where she would enjoy life and her passion for the arts.

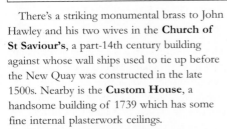

The bright and airy space of Baxters on the corner of Foss Street and Flavel Street shows off the best in contemporary art, printmaking, craft and jewellery. The atmosphere is relaxed and hopefully inspiring, allowing you to take your time in choosing from established and new artists. Several themes are evident, a strong inspiration from the Devon & Cornwall coastline captured by many artists. Other works reflect a subtle sense of humour or the quirkiness of animal-life. A programme of changing exhibitions and introduction of new work ensures an interesting visit for art lovers. Check out their fun website for details of what exhibitions are coming up.

The work of Simon Hart is represented fully with a wide range of originals, prints, posters and cards all available. Baxters will accept commissions and can also offer a delivery service.

There's a striking monumental brass to John Hawley and his two wives in the **Church of St Saviour's**, a part-14th century building against whose wall ships used to tie up before the New Quay was constructed in the late 1500s. Nearby is the **Custom House**, a handsome building of 1739 which has some fine internal plasterwork ceilings.

Also worth seeking out are **The Butterwalk**, a delightful timber-framed arcade dating from 1640 in which the **Dartmouth Museum** occupies the ground floor. The museum has a fine collection of model ships, ships in bottles and a nostalgic selection of vintage photographs of the town. In one of the galleries King Charles II held court whilst stormbound in Dartmouth in 1671. Some of the unique features of this magnificent room

are the original panelling and the superb plaster ceiling.

Two other buildings in Dartmouth should be mentioned. One is the railway station, possibly the only one in the world which has never seen a train. It was built by the Great Western Railway as the terminus of their line from Torbay and passengers were ferried across to Kingswear where the railway actually ended. The station is now a restaurant. The other building of note is the **Britannia Royal Naval College** (guided tours during the season). This sprawling red and white building, built between 1899 and 1905, dominates the northern part of the town as you leave by the A379 towards Kingsbridge.

Near the eastern boundary of the South Hams flows the enchanting River Dart, surely

---

The Butterwalk, Dartmouth

one of the loveliest of English rivers. Rising in the great blanket bog of the moor, the Dart flows for 46 miles and together with its tributaries drains the greater part of Dartmoor. Queen Victoria called the Dart the "English Rhine", perhaps thinking of the twin castles of Dartmouth and Kingswear that guard its estuary. It was her ancestor, Alfred the Great who developed Dartmouth as a strategic base and the town's long connection with the senior service is reflected in the presence here of the Royal Naval College. The spectacular harbour is still busy with naval vessels, pleasure boats and ferries, and particularly colourful during the June **Carnival** and the **Dartmouth Regatta** in late August.

The most picturesque approach to the town is to drive to Kingswear and then take one of the two car ferries for the 10 minute trip across the river. Parking space in Dartmouth is severely restricted and it is strongly

recommended that you make use of the Park & Ride facility located just outside the town on the A3122.

STOKE FLEMING
16 miles SE of Totnes on the A379

🞅 Blackpool Sands

Stoke Fleming is one of the most delightful villages in the South Hams, perched high on the cliffs 300ft above Start Bay and with a prominent church that has served generations of mariners as a reassuring landmark. Inside is a brass of 1351 which is reckoned to be one of the oldest in Devon and another which commemorates the great-grandfather of the celebrated engineer, Thomas Newcomen. Less than a mile from the village are the misleadingly-named **Blackpool Sands,** a broad crescent of sandy beach overhung by Monterey pines, which boasts a Blue Flag Award for its safe and healthy bathing.

HARBERTON
2 miles SW of Totnes off the A2381

🏛 St Andrew's Church

This delightful village is regarded as absolutely typical of the South Hams, a place where those two traditional centres of English village life, church and inn, sit comfortably almost side by side. **St Andrew's Church,** which is famous for its amazing, fantastically-carved, 15th century altar screen, has been closely linked to the village hostelry for almost 900 years. Church House Inn, as the name suggests, was originally built to house the masons working on the church around 1100AD. Harberton was then a major centre for church administration and a much more important place than Totnes. The inn became the Chantry House for the monks, the civil servants of their time, and what is now the bar comprised their Great Hall, chapel and workshop where they would congregate for a glass of wine.

In 1327 the Abbot handed the property over to the poor of the parish but it was not until 1950 that it passed out of the Church's hands altogether. During restoration work ancient plaster was removed to reveal massive beams of fluted mellow oak and a fine medieval screen. Other treasures discovered then, and still in place, were a Tudor window frame and a latticed window containing priceless panes of 13th century handmade glass. The inn's ecclesiastical connections are enhanced even more by the old pews from redundant churches which provide some of the seating.

DARTINGTON
2 miles NW of Totnes on the A384

🏛 Dartington Hall 🏛 High Cross House

When Leonard and Dorothy Elmhirst bought **Dartington Hall** and its estate in 1925 the superb Great Hall had stood roofless for more than a century. The buildings surrounding the two large quadrangles laid out in the 1390s by John Holand, Earl of Exeter, were being used as stables, cow houses and hay lofts. The Elmhirsts were idealists and since Dorothy (*née* Whitney) was one of the richest American women of her time, they possessed the resources to put their ideals into practice. They restored the Hall, re-opened it as a progressive school, and set about reviving the local rural economy in line with the ideology of the Indian philosopher, Rabindranath Tagore. The Elmhirsts were closely involved in the creation of the famed Dartington Glass. Sadly, long after their deaths, their school closed in 1995 as a consequence of financial problems and a pornography scandal. But the headmaster's residence, **High Cross House**, a classic Modernist building of the early 1930s has now been converted into an art gallery. Visitors are welcome here and also to wander around the 26-acre gardens surrounding the Hall. There is no charge for entry to the quadrangle and Great Hall, but donations for its upkeep are welcomed. Guided tours are available by appointment.

Dartington Hall hosts more than 100 music performances each year during its International Summer School, a season which attracts musicians and artistes of the highest calibre from all over the world. All year round, even more visitors are attracted to the **Dartington Cider Press Centre,** a huge gallery on the edge of the estate which displays a vast range of craft products – anything from a delicate handmade Christmas or birthday card to a beautifully modelled item of pottery.

Kingsbridge

🏛 Cookworthy Museum of Rural Life

The broad body of water to the south of Kingsbridge is officially known as **Kingsbridge Estuary**, although strictly speaking it is not an estuary at all – no river runs into it – but a ria, or drowned valley. Whatever the correct name, it provides an attractive setting for this busy little town, an agreeable spot in which to spend an hour or two strolling along the quayside or through the narrow alleys off Fore Street bearing such graphic names as Squeezebelly Lane.

In Fore Street is St Edmund's parish church, mostly 13th century, and well known for the rather cynical verse inscribed on the

Dartington

Distance: *4.8 miles (7.5 kilometres)*

Typical time: *120 mins*

Height gain: *65 metres*

Map: *Explorer 110*

Walk: *www.walkingworld.com ID:1782*

Contributor: *Dennis Blackford*

ACCESS INFORMATION:

By car take the A385 from Totnes to Shinners Bridge, turn right at the roundabout for about 100 metres and the Cider Press is clearly marked on your right. Park in the upper 'overflow' car park in the summer or main car parks in winter.

DESCRIPTION:

Starting from the Cider Press Craft Centre walk along a quiet country lane in the Dartington Hall Estate to the gardens of the hall. After an optional look around the hall itself travel down the long, tree lined main drive of the hall with extensive views over the

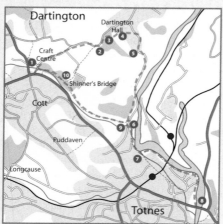

River Dart to the ancient Water Meadow. There is an optional detour along the river bank to the historic town of Totnes with its castle and museum. Return back along the river bank to the water meadow and follow its side to a woodland track back to the Cider Press.

ADDITIONAL INFORMATION:

Refreshments and toilets at the Cider Press, Dartington Hall and Totnes. The walking is generally good with wide tracks and country roads so is very pushchair friendly.

FEATURES:

River, pub, toilets, museum, church, castle, wildlife, birds, flowers, great views, butterflies, cafe, gift shop, food shop, industrial archaeology, public transport, restaurant, tea shop, woodland.

WALK DIRECTIONS:

1 | From the car parks - leave at the far end and turn left up the path. Cross the road and walk up the lane past the overflow car parks. Follow the country lane to the junction with the access road to Dartington Hall. Turn right along the tarmac footpath on the right hand side of the road.

2 | Where the footpath ends at a large white signpost, go to the right and through the gate into the gardens of Dartington Hall.

3 | Follow the wide drive down through the gardens or detour through any of the woodland paths to the left. Near the end of the drive, look for the wide, paved path on the right leading down to the swan fountain. Follow this path to the end. Turn left along the hedged pavement and then right, through the hedge and along the terrace in front of the buildings. Note: the grass area used to be used for jousting tournaments.

4 | At the end of the terrace, go up the first flight of steps, then turn right down another flight to the grass. Note: If you wish to look around the buildings or visit the toilets, continue up the steps turning left at the top for 100 metres then left past the restaurant into the quadrangle. Go out through the arched gateway and turn left on the road, then left again along the wide path to pass the tranquil Zen Mediation garden. Go on through the church yard to rejoin the terrace again.

5 | At the bottom of the steps, turn left along the lawn and walk down to its end. Go through the gate at the bottom of the field and turn right onto the tree lined drive following it down to the gate house.

6 | Pass the gatehouse and through the gates to turn left onto the river walk. Follow along the bank of the river. Note: The meadow seen just before the gatehouse is the water meadow and will be the way back to the Cider Press for those who wish to shorten the walk - missing out the river walk and Totnes.

7 | Just past the weir, cross the wooden bridge to follow along the bank of the river. Note: The wide path passing the bridge brings the walker a little outside the top of Totnes.

8 | The river path ends at Brutus Bridge. Go up the steps to the bridge and turn right into the town.

9 | After visiting the town, return along the river, past the gatehouse to the Water Meadow mentioned in Waymark 6 and follow the cycle path along the right hand side of it.

10 | When you see the water mill - either take the wide path along the side of the road, or go up the steps on the woodland path. They join a few hundred metres further along and after passing some old lime kilns, you return to the Cider Press Centre.

gravestone of Roger Phillips who died in 1798:

Here lie I at the chancel door
Here lie I because I'm poor
The further in the more you pay
Here lie I as warm as they.

Nearby is **The Shambles**, an Elizabethan market arcade whose late-18th century upper floor is supported on six sturdy granite pillars. Above the church, the former Kingsbridge Grammar School, founded in 1670, now houses the **Cookworthy Museum of Rural Life,** named after William Cookworthy who was born at Kingsbridge in 1705. Working as an apothecary at Plymouth, William encountered traders from the Far East who had brought back porcelain from China. English pottery makers despaired of ever producing such delicate cups and plates, but Cookworthy identified the basic ingredient of porcelain as kaolin, huge deposits of which lay in the hills just north of Plymouth. Ever since then, the more common name for kaolin has been China clay.

During the season, a popular excursion from Kingsbridge is the river cruise to Salcombe. Coastal cruises and private charter boats are also available.

Around Kingsbridge

TORCROSS
7 miles E of Kingsbridge on the A379

Normally, the four-mile stretch of sand and shingle beach near Torcross is too extensive to ever become crowded but back in 1943 things were very different. The beach had been selected by the Allied Commanders for a "dress rehearsal" of the impending D-Day invasion of Normandy. The area was swarming with troops, and because live ammunition was being used in the training exercise, all the local people were evacuated, more than 3,000 of them from seven coastal villages.

Those D-Day preparations are recalled at Torcross where a Sherman tank recovered from the sea in 1984 is on display in the car park. While the exercises were in progress, an enemy E-boat attacked the landing forces and more than 600 Allied servicemen lost their lives. Beside the tank are memorial tablets to the men who died during this little-publicised military tragedy, and to the many who later perished on the Normandy beaches.

SLAPTON
8 miles E of Kingsbridge off the A379

🌿 Slapton Ley Field Study Centre

To the south of Slapton, the A379 runs for 2.5 miles along the top of a remarkable sand and shingle bank which divides the salt water of Start Bay from the fresh water of Slapton Ley, the largest natural lake in Devon. Continually replenished by three small rivers, this shallow body of water is a designated Nature Reserve and home to large numbers of freshwater fish, insects, water-loving plants and native and migrating birds. The **Slapton Ley Field Study Centre**, located in Slapton village, has leaflets detailing the delightful circular nature trails through this fascinating Site of Special Scientific Interest.

An obelisk on the beach near Slapton, presented in 1954 by the US Army authorities to the people of the South Hams, commemorates the period in 1943 when the beach was used by Allied troops as a "dress rehearsal" for the D-Day landings. The story is well told in Leslie Thomas's novel *The Magic Army*.

CHIVELSTONE
7 miles SE of Kingsbridge off the A379

Even in Devon it would be hard to find anywhere further away from the madding crowd than Chivelstone, an unassuming village hidden away in a maze of country lanes in the extreme southwest of the county and well worth seeking out. It's the tranquil rural surroundings that make Chivelstone so appealing but the village also has a fine parish church, the only one in England dedicated to the 4th century pope, St Sylvester. Historically, Sylvester is a misty figure but an old tradition claims that his saintly ministrations cured the Roman emperor, Constantine, of leprosy. Chivelstone church was built at a time (the 15th century) when this disfiguring disease was still common in England: it seems likely the parishioners hoped that by dedicating their church to him, St Sylvester would protect them from the ravages of a deeply feared illness which, once contracted, imposed total social exclusion on its innocent victims.

BEESANDS
8 miles SE of Kingsbridge off the A379

Beesands lies little more than a mile due south of Torcross and can easily be reached on foot along the coast path. By car, a four mile detour is required. If you don't want to walk, it's well worth negotiating the narrow Devon lanes to reach this tiny hamlet, just a single row of old cottages lining the foreshore of Start Bay. Less than 100 years ago, Beesands was a busy little fishing village. There are photographs from the 1920s showing fishermen who have drawn their boats laden with lobster, crab and mullet up the beach virtually to their cottage doors. Sadly, the fishing fleet is no longer operating but the mile-long shingle beach is as appealing as ever.

🏛 historic building   🏛 museum and heritage   🏛 historic site   🌿 scenic attraction   🌿 flora and fauna

HALLSANDS
11 miles SE of Kingsbridge off the A379

South of Beesands, the only way to follow the coastline is by a well-trodden footpath. It's part of the South West Coast Path and the route takes you through the ruined village of Hallsands which was almost completely demolished by a violent storm in January 1917. Another mile or so further brings you to the lighthouse at **Start Point,** built in 1836, and open to visitors from Monday to Saturday during daylight hours. And if you want to be able to boast that you once stood at the most southerly point in Devon, continue along the Coast Path for about five miles to **Prawle Point**, an ancient lookout site where today there is a Coastguard Station.

MALBOROUGH
5 miles S of Kingsbridge on the A381

🏠 Yarde

For anyone travelling this corner of the South Hams, the lofty spire of Malborough's 15th century church is a recurrent landmark. It's a broach spire, rising straight out of the low tower. Inside, the church is wonderfully light, so much so that the splendid arcades built in Beer stone seem to glow.

About half a mile to the east of Malborough, just off the A381, is an outstanding example of a medieval farmhouse. **Yarde** is a Grade I listed manor farm with an Elizabethan bakery and a Queen Anne farmhouse. This is a privately owned working farm but Yarde can be visited on Sunday afternoons from Easter to the end of September, and by groups at any time by arrangement.

SALCOMBE
7 miles S of Kingsbridge, on the A381

🌱 Overbecks 🏛 Salcombe Maritime Museum

Standing at the mouth of the Kingsbridge "estuary", the captivating town of Salcombe enjoys one of the most beautiful natural settings in the country. Sheltered from the prevailing westerly winds by steep hills, it also basks in one of the mildest micro-climates in England. In the terraced gardens rising from the water's edge, it's not unusual to see mimosa, palms, and even orange and lemon trees bearing fruit. The peaceful gardens at **Overbecks** (National Trust), overlooking Salcombe Bar, have an almost Mediterranean character. Otto Overbeck, who lived in the charming Edwardian house here between 1918 and 1937, amassed a wide-ranging collection that includes late-19th century photographs of the area, local shipbuilding tools, model boats, toys and much more.

Salcombe Ferry and Boarding Tractor

🎭 stories and anecdotes   🕊 famous people   🎨 art and craft   🏌 entertainment and sport   🚶 walks

AMELIA'S ATTIC

66a Fore Street, Salcombe, South Devon TQ8 8ET
Tel: 01548 844 445
e-mail: karen@ameliasattic.co.uk
website: www.ameliasattic.co.uk

Located in the heart of glorious Salcombe, **Amelia's Attic** is
a wonderful shop filled with, quite simply, beautiful
things...clothes, boots, shoes, jewellery, gifts, toiletries,
pictures, candles, and bits and pieces for the home.
Everything in the Attic has been carefully chosen and
sourced by owner Karen Woodley from some of the best makers and
suppliers from around Devon, the UK and the world. Among the most
popular ranges are 'Love Lammie' bags and accessories, designed and
handmade in Devon by Victoria Lammie from a mixture of vintage and
contemporary textiles. The collection consists of handbags featuring
beautiful embroidered appliqués, wristlets and make-up bags perfect
for every occasion. Each piece is totally unique! Then there's a
stunning range of silk lingerie from Coco Ribbon; Amelia's Attic
exclusive range of Hoodies, T-shirts and Salcombe Babe pants;
jewellery by Philippe Ferrandis, Sam Ubhi and Claudia Bradby as well
as bangles, beads and freshwater pearls. E. Coudray fragrances from
Paris; Meli Melo Italian leather bags; True Grace organic candles;

handmade cowhide bags and belts from the Columbian Fair Trade
Organisation, Artisan Life; French Sole ballet pumps, NuggZ cowhide Ugg boots from New
Zealand; wallets, filofaxes and bags from Ipa Nima; jewel coloured twin sets by Palace of
London; pretty dresses and cardigans by Avoca and a range of books of particular interest to
women. A wonderful place in which to find the unusual, beautiful and exclusive treat for the
woman you love, the woman you are.

Like other small South Devon ports,
Salcombe developed its own special area of
trading. Whilst Dartmouth specialised in
French and Spanish wine, at Salcombe high-
sailed clippers arrived carrying the first fruits
of the pineapple harvest from the West Indies,
and oranges from the Azores. That traffic has
ceased, but pleasure craft throng the harbour
and a small fishing fleet still operates from
Batson Creek, a picturesque location where
the fish quay is piled high with lobster creels.
The town's seafaring history is interestingly
evoked in the **Salcombe Maritime & Local
History Museum** in the old Customs House
on the quay.

The coastline to the south and west of
Salcombe, some of the most magnificent in

Britain, is now largely owned by the National
Trust. Great slanting slabs of gneiss and schist
tower above the sea, making the clifftop walk
here both literally and metaphorically
breathtaking.

HOPE COVE
6 miles SW of Kingsbridge off the A381

There are two Hopes here: Outer Hope, which
is more modern and so gets less attention, and
Inner Hope which must be one of the most
photographed villages in the country. A
picturesque huddle of thatched cottages
around a tiny cobbled square, Inner Hope once
thrived on pilchard fishing but nowadays only a
few fishermen still operate from here, bringing
in small catches of lobster and crab.

THURLESTONE

5 miles W of Kingsbridge off the A381

One of the most attractive coastal villages, Thurlestone can boast not just one, but two beaches, separated by a headland. Both beaches are recommended, especially the one to the south with its view of the pierced, or "thyrled", stone, the offshore rock from which the settlement gets its name and which was specifically mentioned in a charter of 846AD. The village itself stands on a long, flat-topped ridge above the beaches and is an attractive mixture of flower-decked cottages, old farm buildings and long-established shops and inns.

BANTHAM

6 miles SW of Kingsbridge off the A379

One mile to the north of Thurlestone (as the crow flies) is another fine sandy beach, at Bantham. This small village has a long history since it was a centre of early tin trading between the ancient Britons and the Gauls. By the 8th century, Anglo-Saxons were well-established here, farming the fertile soil. The sea also provided a major source of income in the form of pilchard fishing. Bantham continued to be a busy little port until the early 1900s with sailing barges bringing coal and building stone for the surrounding area.

BIGBURY ON SEA

10 miles W of Kingsbridge on the B3392

🏝 Burgh Island

This popular family resort has a stretch of National Trust coastline and extensive sands. The most interesting attraction here though is **Burgh Island** which is actually only a part-time

island. When the tide is out, it is possible to walk across the sandbar linking it to the mainland. At other times, visitors reach the island by a unique "Sea Tractor", specifically designed for this crossing. It can operate in 7ft of water, in all but the roughest conditions, and it's well worth timing your visit to enjoy this novel experience.

The whole of the 28-acre island, complete with its 14th century Pilchard Inn, was bought in 1929 by the eccentric millionaire Archibald Nettlefold. He built an extravagant art deco hotel which attracted such visitors as Noel Coward, the Duke of Windsor and Mrs Wallis Simpson, and Agatha Christie. The "Queen of Crime" used the island as the setting for two of her novels, *Ten Little Niggers,* (later renamed *And Then There Were None*), and *Evil Under the Sun.* The hotel, which has been described as "a white art deco cruise liner beached on dry land" is still in operation, its wonderful 1930s décor meticulously renovated in the 1990s.

AVETON GIFFORD

5 miles NW of Kingsbridge on the A379

🖐 Robert Macey

Pronounced "Awton Jiffard", this pleasant small village, little more than one main street,

Burgh Island Tractor, Bigbury-on-Sea

🎞 stories and anecdotes 🦜 famous people 🎨 art and craft 🏌 entertainment and sport 🚶 walks

TOP O' THE STEPS

5 Church Street, Modbury,
Devon PL21 0QW
Tel: 01548 830072   Fax: 01548 831005
e-mail: mandyrolt@hotmail.com
website: www.modburychamberofcommerce.com

With its Georgian inns and houses and steep main street, Modbury is one of the most enchanting of Devon's small towns. It lies in a hollow surrounded by the rolling hills of the South Hams just a few miles from some of the most beautiful unspoilt beaches and wonderful coastal walks.

In the heart of the town, **Top o' the Steps** is an outstanding gift and coffee shop, owned and run by Amanda Rolt. Amanda has always had an interest in finding stylish and unusual gifts and her quest for distinctive but value-for-money items has taken her to various parts of France and Italy.

You'll find a dazzling range of imaginative items ranging from delicate jewellery to Emma Bridgewater china; from quality greetings cards to a range of clothes and handbags. The extensive choice also includes pocket-money pieces for younger visitors. Goods can be gift wrapped to add that extra touch of distinction. Round off your visit with coffee, lunch, delicious homemade cakes or a Devon cream tea in the licensed coffee shop.

One thing: don't expect to have your purchases handed to you in a plastic bag - since May 1st 2007 all the traders in the town have made their shops plastic bag-free areas.

Opening hours are 9.30am to 5.30pm,
Monday to Saturday.

🏚 historic building 🏛 museum and heritage 🏛 historic site 🝔 scenic attraction 🌿 flora and fauna

had one of the oldest churches in Devon until it was almost completely destroyed by a German bomb in 1943. The modern replacement is surprisingly satisfying. The village's most famous son was born here in 1790, the son of a mason. After learning his father's trade, **Robert Macey** also studied as an architect. He then walked all the way to London where he successfully established himself and was responsible for designing many hospitals, factories, churches and theatres, of which the most notable were the Adelphi and the Haymarket.

At the southern end of the village, just before the three-quarter-mile long medieval causeway, a lane on the right is signposted to Bigbury. This very narrow road runs right alongside the River Avon and is very beautiful, but be warned – the river is tidal here and when the tide is in the two fords along the way are impassable.

LODDISWELL
3 miles NW of Kingsbridge off the A379

🌱 Loddiswell Vineyard 🐟 Judhel of Totnes

After the Norman Conquest, Loddiswell became part of the 40,000 acre estate of **Judhel of Totnes**, a man with an apparently insatiable appetite for salmon. Instead of rent, he stipulated that his tenants should provide him with a certain number of the noble fish: Loddiswell's contribution was set at 30 salmon a year.

The benign climate of South Devon has encouraged several viticulturists to plant vineyards in the area. The first vines at **Loddiswell Vineyard** were planted in 1977 and since then its wines have been laden with awards from fellow wine-makers and consumer bodies. Visitors are welcome, Monday to Saturday.

MODBURY
9 miles NW of Kingsbridge on the A379

🏛 St George's Church 🐟 Rebecca Hoskins

Modbury's main street climbs steeply up the hillside, its pavement raised above street level and stepped. The many Georgian buildings give this little town an air of quiet elegance and the numerous antique, craft and specialist shops add to its interest. **St George's Church** contains some impressive, if damaged, effigies of the Prideaux and Champernowne families; the White Hart and Assembly Rooms are 18th century, the Exeter Inn even older. Once a coaching inn, this inviting old pub dates back to the 1500s. Modbury's Fair Week in early May is a jolly affair, though perhaps not as riotous as it was in the 19th century when it lasted for nine days and the town's 10 inns stayed open from morning to night.

In May 2006 this quiet little town sparked off a green campaign that attracted national attention. It was master-minded by **Rebecca Hoskins**, a young Modbury-born-and-raised wildlife camerawoman who was appalled by the appalling plastic bag pollution she found in remote parts of the Pacific Ocean. On her return to Devon she found the sea equally infested. She called a meeting of all 43 Modbury shopowners, showed them her film, and convinced them to stop handing out plastic bags to customers. More than two years later, the town is still a plastic-bag-free area.

Torbay

The most extensive conurbation in Devon, Torbay includes the three major towns of Torquay, Paignton and Brixham, strung around the deep indentation of Tor Bay. The excellent beaches and leisure facilities here have made it

---

🎭 stories and anecdotes 🐟 famous people 🎨 art and craft 🏃 entertainment and sport 🚶 walks

the county's busiest resort area with a host of indoor and outdoor attractions on offer. Torquay is the more sophisticated of the three, with elegant gardens, excellent shops and a varied nightlife. Paignton prides itself as being "unbeatable for family fun", and Brixham is a completely enchanting fishing town where life revolves around its busy harbour.

If you think Torbay's claim to be "The English Riviera" is a mite presumptuous, just take a look at all those palm trees. You see them everywhere here: not just in public parks and expensively maintained hotel gardens, but also giving a Mediterranean character to town house gardens, and even growing wild. They have become a symbol of the area's identity, blazoned on tourism leaflets, brochures, T-shirts, shop fronts, key-rings and hats.

The first specimen palm trees arrived in Britain in the 1820s and it was soon discovered that this sub-tropical species took kindly to the genial climate of South Devon. Today, there are literally thousands of them raising their spiky tufted heads above the more familiar foliage of English gardens. To the uninitiated, one palm tree may look much like another, but experts will point out that although the most common variety growing here is Cordyline Australis (imported from New Zealand), there are also Mediterranean Fan Palms, Trachycarpus Fortunei from the Chusan Islands in the East China Sea, and Date Palms from the Canary Islands. The oldest palm tree on record in the area is now over 80 years old and more than 40ft high.

The Mediterranean similarities don't end there. Torquay, like Rome, is set on seven hills and the red-tiled roofs of its Italianate villas, set amongst dark green trees, would look equally at home in some Adriatic resort. The resemblance is so close that in one film in the

Roger Moore TV series, *The Saint,* a budget-conscious producer made Torquay double for Monte Carlo.

Torquay

🐦 Edward VI🖉   🏛 Torre Abbey

🐦 Agatha Christie   🏛 Torquay Museum

🏚 Kents Cavern   🏛 Bygones   🍃 Living Coasts

🍃 Occombe Farm Project   🍂 Cockington Village

🏯 Babbacombe Model Village

In Victorian times, Torquay liked to be known as "The English Naples", a genteel resort of shimmering white villas set amongst dark green trees and spread, like Rome, across seven hills. It was indisputably the West of England's premier resort with imposing hotels like the Imperial and the Grand catering for "people of condition" from across Europe. At one time,

Torre Abbey, Torquay

the town could boast more royal visitors to the square mile than any other resort in the world. **Edward VII** came here on the royal yacht *Britannia* and anchored in the bay. Each evening he would be discreetly ferried across to a bay beneath the Imperial Hotel and then conducted to the first floor suite where his mistress, Lily Langtry, was waiting.

The town's oldest building is **Torre Abbey,** founded in 1195 but largely remodelled as a Georgian mansion by the Cary family between 1700 and 1750. Within its grounds stand the abbey ruins and the Spanish Barn, a medieval tithe barn so named because 397 prisoners from the Spanish Armada were detained here in 1588. Torre Abbey was sold to Torbay Council in 1930 and, together with its extensive gardens, was open to the public until 2004 when the building was closed for major refurbishment. It is expected to re-open in the summer of 2008.

One of the abbey's most popular attractions was the **Agatha Christie Memorial Room** in the Abbot's Tower, which contained fascinating memorabilia loaned by her daughter. Dame Agatha was born in Torquay in 1890 and the town has created an **Agatha Christie Mile** which guides visitors to places of interest that she knew as a girl and young woman growing up in the town.

Torquay Museum also has an interesting exhibition of photographs recording her life, as well as a pictorial record of Torquay over the last 150 years, and displays chronicling the social and natural history of the area. Amongst the museum's other treasures are many items discovered at **Kents Cavern**, an astonishing complex of caves regarded as

BRANTWOOD HOTEL

Rowdens Road, Torquay TQ2 5AZ
Tel: 01803 297241
e-mail: brantwood.hotel@unicombox.co.uk
website: www.thebrantwood.co.uk

Located in the heart of beautiful Torquay, the **Brantwood Hotel** is a small and friendly family-run business offering comfortable accommodation and excellent food. The hotel is owned and run by Chris and Catharine: Chris has been a professional chef for some 20 years, and Catharine has wide experience in the hospitality business.

Built in 1950, the hotel has recently been extended and the licensed restaurant has also been newly refurbished. The accommodation comprises a choice of en suite rooms, some of which are on the ground floor. Family rooms are available and all rooms are provided with TV and hospitality tray. Cots, baby monitors and high chairs are all available.

The hotel has its own peaceful garden with decking and there is a private car park. It is only 500 yards from either Torquay or Torre train stations and pick-ups from these are available by arrangement. Located at the end of a tree-lined cul-de-sac, the Brantwood is also just 500 yards of level walking from the magnificent sea front.

HALDON PRIORS

Meadfoot Sea Road, Torquay TQ1 2LQ
Tel: 01803 213365
website: www.haldonpriors.co.uk

This charming Victorian villa is situated in a peaceful location of Torquay, Devon, set in three quarters of an acre of beautifully landscaped gardens and just 200 yards from Meadfoot beach.

Noted for its warm hospitality, Haldon Priors provides a uniquely relaxing ambience for guests to unwind and restore a sense of well-being.

There is a magnificent 35' heated swimming pool which has an original Roman end, surrounded by sub-tropical gardens and, after a long swim, why not enjoy the comfort of a relaxing sauna!

"one of the most important archaeological sites in Britain". Excavations here in the 1820s revealed a remarkable collection of animal bones – the remains of mammoths, sabre-toothed tigers, grizzly bears, bison, and cave lions. These bones proved to be the dining-room debris of cave dwellers who lived here some 30,000 years ago, the oldest known residents of Europe. The caves are open daily, all year, offering guided tours, a sound and light show, a gift shop and refreshment room.

Another popular attraction is **Bygones** in Fore Street where visitors can wander back in time through a real olde worlde street complete with ironmongers, sweet shop, apothecary's shop, forge and pub. There are many original Victorian artefacts and other attractions include a giant model railway and railwayana collections; a children's fantasy land; a World War I exhibit, tearoom and shop.

A fairly new attraction is **Living Coasts** which opened in 2003 on Torquay Harbour. It is operated by the same wildlife trust that runs Paignton Zoo and is best described as a coastal zoo which provides a natural habitat for seals, penguins, puffins, auks and sea ducks with the emphasis on the coast and environmental issues. There's a café and a restaurant with grand views across Tor Bay.

Opened in the spring of 2006, the **Occombe Farm Project** is a 150-acre organic demonstration farm and educational venture. It incorporates a nature trail, a working farm, a butcher's, a baker's, a shop selling local produce and an educational centre.

JACK & JILL

30 Old Mill Road, Chelston,
Torquay TQ2 6AU
Tel: 01803 690888
Fax: 01803 612537
e-mail: sales@kiddistore.co.uk
website: www.kiddistore.co.uk

Jack and Jill is the kind of nursery shop that every parent of young children will give heartfelt thanks. The family-run business has gathered together an extraordinary range of items both practical and decorative for children up to the age of eight. There are toys suitable from birth, an extensive selection of clothing (including designer labels), gift sets, nappy 'cakes' and even wedding 'cakes'.

Recently they have added personalised candles, which you can order for weddings, christenings, birthdays etc., wedding accessories (including the finest wedding confectionery for wedding favours), disposable cameras, confetti and bridal accessories. You can even have a canvas made from your favourite photograph.

Jack and Jill is a must to visit whether you are local or just visiting the beautiful town of Torquay. Jack and Jill is open from 1pm to 5pm, Tuesday to Friday and from 9am to 3pm on Saturday. If you cannot wait to visit the shop then you can order online at www.candles-unique.com; www.the-bride-to-be.com or www.canvas-unique.com

🎭 stories and anecdotes 🦜 famous people 🎨 art and craft 🍃 entertainment and sport 🚶 walks

COCKINGTON FORGE GIFTS AND BRASSWARE

Cockington Lane, Cockington, Torquay TQ2 6XA
Tel: 01803 605024
website: www.cockingtonforge.com

Dating back to the 11th century, Cockington Forge stands at the heart of the impossibly picturesque village of that name. The old thatched building is now home to Cockington Forge Gifts and Brassware which stocks a remarkable range of products of which the most famous are its miniature good luck horseshoes which are made on site. But the variety on sale here ranges from martingales and horse brasses, through copperware to fridge magnets and star sign brasses, along with practical items such as kettles, coal scuttles, hand bells and candle holders.

Just a mile or so from Torquay town centre is **Cockington Village**, a phenomenally picturesque rural oasis of thatched cottages, a working forge, and the Drum Inn designed by Sir Edward Lutyens and completed in 1930. From the village there's a pleasant walk through the park to **Cockington Court**, now a Craft Centre and Gallery. Partly Tudor, this stately old manor was for almost three centuries the home of the Mallock family. In the 1930s they formed a trust to preserve "entire and unchanged the ancient amenities and character of the place, and in developing its surroundings to do nothing which may not rather enhance than diminish its attractiveness". The Trust has been spectacularly successful in carrying out their wishes.

About a mile north of Torquay is another village but this village is one-twelfth life size. **Babbacombe Model Village** contains some 400 models, many with sound and animation. Created by Tom Dobbins, a large number of the beautifully crafted models have been given entertaining names: "Shortback & Sydes", the gents' hairdresser, for example, "Walter Wall Carpets" and "Jim Nastik's Health Farm". The site also contains some delightful gardens, including a collection of more than 500 types of dwarf conifer, a 1,000ft model railway, an ornamental lake stocked with koi carp and much more.

KNITTING YARNS AT THE GARDEN GATE

7 Fore Street, Kingskerswell, nr Torquay, Devon TQ12 5HT
Tel: 01803 873534

Knitting Yarns at the Garden Gate vary from two ply to extra chunky, passing through baby yarns in either man-made or natural fibres to pure merino wool to basic double knit, Aran and Chunky; then on to fashion yarns which only need a knowledge of stocking stitch to create an attractive result.

For those knitters who prefer natural fibres they stock pure new wool, cotton and linen and UK Alpaca, whilst fashion yarns come in various fibres, textures and colour combinations. Accompanying leaflets are available, as are knitting needles, buttons etc.

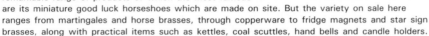

🏚 historic building 🏛 museum and heritage 🏛 historic site ♧ scenic attraction ❦ flora and fauna

Around Torquay

COMBETEIGNHEAD
3 miles N of Torquay off the A380 or A379

🐦 John Keats

Standing across the river from Bishopsteignton, Combeteignhead is a charming village which **John Keats** came to know well when he was staying with his consumptive brother Tom at nearby Teignmouth in 1818. In a letter to his family he often enclosed scraps of "happy doggerel" like this:

> *Here all the summer I could stay,*
> *For there's Bishop's Teign*
> *And King's Teign*
> *And Coomb at the clear Teign head -*
> *Where close by the stream*
> *You may have your cream*
> *All spread upon Barley bread.*

SHALDON
7 miles N of Torquay on the A379

🐦 Shaldon Wildlife Trust

Set on the southern bank of the Teign estuary, Shaldon's Marine Parade provides a grand viewpoint for watching the busy traffic sailing in and out of the river. A goodly number of Regency houses add architectural dignity to the town, a reminder of the era when affluent Londoners, unable to holiday in a Europe dominated by Napoleon, began to discover the gentle charms of south-western England. A more recent attraction for visitors is the **Shaldon Wildlife Trust's** breeding centre for rare small mammals, reptiles and exotic birds, just to the north of the town.

TEIGNMOUTH
9 miles N of Torquay on the A381 & A379

Teignmouth has something of a split personality. On the coastal side is the popular holiday resort with its two miles of sandy beaches, a splendid promenade almost as long, and a pier. There's also a 25ft-high lighthouse which serves no apparent purpose apart from looking rather fetching. The residential area contains much fine Regency and Georgian building. Particularly noteworthy are the **Church of St James** with its striking octagonal tower of 1820, and the former **Assembly Rooms**, a dignified colonnaded building which now houses the Riviera Cinema. Teignmouth's Georgian past is recalled on Wednesdays during the season when local people dress up in 18th century costume.

MARTINA'S GUEST HOUSE

1 Glendarash Road, Teignmouth, Devon TQ14 8PH
Tel: 01626 772316
website: www.martinasguesthouse.co.uk

Located just a minute or two from the town centre, railway station and beaches, **Martina's Guest House** is a handsome Edwardian house where Martina and Derrick Hancock offer comfortable four-star en suite accommodation. There are two doubles and one twin room available, some with sea views. All are attractively furnished and decorated, and equipped with Freeview TV, clock radio and hospitality tray. A hearty English breakfast is included in the tariff and both gluten-free and vegetarian diets can be catered for. The guest house is open all year round.

🗽 stories and anecdotes 🐦 famous people 🎨 art and craft 🏞 entertainment and sport 🚶 walks

On the river side of the town is the working port, approached by the narrowest of channels. The currents here are so fast and powerful that no ship enters the harbour without a Trinity House pilot on board. **The Quay** was built in 1821 with granite from the quarries on Haytor Down. This durable stone was in great demand at the time. Amongst the many buildings constructed in Haytor granite were London Bridge, (the one now relocated to Lake Tahoe in California), and the British Museum. Teignmouth's main export nowadays is potter's clay, extracted from pits beside the River Teign, but boat building also continues, albeit on a small scale.

DAWLISH

12 miles N of Torquay on the A379

🌿 The Lawn   🌿 Dawlish Warren

🏛 Atmospheric Railway

This pretty seaside resort, which boasts one of the safest beaches in England, has the unusual feature of a main railway line separating the town from its sea front. The result is, in fact, much more appealing than it sounds. For one thing, the railway keeps motor traffic away from the beachside, and for another, the low granite viaduct which carries the track has weathered attractively in the century and a half since it was built. The arches under which beach-goers pass create a kind of formal entrance to the beach and the Victorian station has become a visitor attraction in its own right.

By the time Brunel's railway arrived here in 1846, Dawlish was already well-known as a fashionable resort. John Keats, with his convalescent brother, Tom, had visited the town in 1818. The great poet was inspired to pen the less-than-immortal lines:

Over the hill and over the Dale
And over the bourne to Dawlish
Where Gingerbread wives have a scanty sale
And gingerbread nuts are smallish.

Other distinguished visitors included Jane Austen, (one of whose characters cannot understand how one could live anywhere else in Devon but here), and Charles Dickens, who, in his novel of the same name has Nicholas Nickleby born at a farm nearby. All of these great literary figures arrived not long after the first houses were built along the Strand. That had happened in 1803. Up until then, Dawlish was just a small settlement beside the River Daw, located about a mile inland in order to be safe from raiders. This is where the 700-year-old church stands, surrounded by a small group of thatched cottages.

At the time of John Keats' visit, the town was being transformed with scores of new villas springing up along the Strand. Earlier improvers had already "beautified" the River Daw, which flows right through the town, by landscaping the stream into a series of shallow waterfalls and surrounding it with attractive gardens like **The Lawn.** Until Regency times, The Lawn had been a swamp populated by herons, kingfishers and otters. Then in 1808, the developer John Manning filled in the marshy land with earth removed during the construction of Queen Street. Today, both The Lawn and Queen Street still retain the elegance of those early-19th century days.

A couple of miles northeast of the town is **Dawlish Warren,** a mile-long sand spit which almost blocks the mouth of the River Exe. There's a golf course here and also a 55-acre Nature Reserve, home to more than 450 species of flowering plants. For one of them, the Jersey lily, this is its only habitat in mainland England. Guided tours of the Reserve, led by

DELI DELICIOUS AND TOO DELICIOUS

18 The Strand, Dawlish, Devon EX7 9PS
Tel: 01626 888656

Deli Delicious was opened by Simon and Charley in June 2005 and sells local and continental cheeses, locally cooked hams, smoked fish, pâté, large range of antipasti and ambient products such as jam, chutney, chocolates, fresh coffee etc. Most product ranges have won taste awards from the Guild of Fine Foods. There are lots of local products - jams from Bishopsteignton, local honey, gluten free cakes by Kay in Dawlish as well as continental products such as organic Greek olive oil, Spanish cheeses, salamis and chorizo.

Simon and Charley say, "We encourage people to taste the products where possible - it makes them feel excited about new taste sensations." There are take away sandwiches, paninis etc available all day and hampers are made to order. There is an outside catering service available - whether for a business function or a picnic in the park. They also sell fresh fish from Brixham to order.

Too Delicious, the café and bistro, provides good food at affordable prices using, where possible, local produce. The style ranges from British to fusion food with gourmet breakfasts, light lunches and bistro style evening meals all cooked fresh to order. The café is licenced and regularly has special events such as tapas nights, Greek nights etc. Parties can be catered for. The friendly staff, who are excited and knowledgeable about food, will be happy to help you.

the warden, are available during the season.

Railway enthusiasts will want to travel a couple of miles further to the village of Starcross to see the last surviving relic of Isambard Kingdom Brunel's **Atmospheric Railway**. The great engineer had intended that the stretch of railway between Exeter and Totnes should be powered by a revolutionary new system. The train would be attached to a third rail which in fact was a long vacuum chamber, drawing the carriages along by the effects of air pressure. His visionary plan involved the building of 10 great Italianate engine houses at three mile intervals along the line. Sadly, the project was a failure, partly for financial reasons, but also because the leather seals on the vacuum pipe were quickly eaten away by the combined forces of rain, salt and hungry rats. The exhibition at Starcross displays a working model, using vacuum

cleaners to represent the pumping houses, and volunteers are even propelled up and down the track to demonstrate the viability of the original idea.

Brunel had to fall back on conventional steam engines but the route he engineered from Exeter to Newton Abbot is one of the most scenic in the country, following first the western side of the Exe estuary, then hugging the seaboard from Dawlish Warren to Teignmouth before turning inland along the north bank of the River Teign.

PAIGNTON
3 miles SW of Torquay on the A379

🏠 Oldway Mansion   🐾 Paignton Zoo

🚢 Quaywest   🚂 Paignton & Dartmouth Railway

Today, Torquay merges imperceptibly into Paignton, but in early Victorian times Paignton

🎭 stories and anecdotes 🦚 famous people 🎨 art and craft 🎢 entertainment and sport 🚶 walks

ALPENROSE HOLIDAY APARTMENTS

20 Polsham Park, Paignton,
Devon TQ3 2AD
Tel: 01803 558430
e-mail: alpenrose@blueyonder.co.uk
website: www.alpenrose.myby.co.uk

Alpenrose Holiday Apartments are perfectly located just a few moments level walk from the town centre shops, superb sandy beach, harbour and the South West Coastal Footpath. There's an excellent choice of restaurants, pubs, theatre cinema and entertainment within easy reach, and the bus, coach and mainline railway station are a short walk away.

The house itself is a unique example of Victorian grandeur designed by the renowned architect George Souden Bridgeman. It has been sympathetically transformed into modern, spacious, exceptionally well-equipped and tastefully furnished one and two bed-roomed self-contained apartments. They are spacious, individually designed, and tastefully and comfortably furnished. Each has a modern kitchen with full size electric cooker, refrigerator and microwave oven. A remote controlled 29" colour TV with Teletext is provided and there is a guest payphone for outgoing calls. Each apartment is allocated a parking space and additional street parking is available nearby.

The large landscaped grounds are a delight at any time of the year and a perfect place to relax. This elegant residence nestles peacefully in an idyllic Conservation Area bordering onto Victoria Park with its duck ponds, tennis courts and lawned areas.

was just a small farming village, about half a mile inland, noted for its cider and its "very large and sweet flatpole cabbages". The town's two superb sandy beaches, ideal for families with young children, were to change all that. A pier and promenade add to the town's appeal, and throughout the summer season there's a packed programme of specials events, including a Children's Festival in August, fun fairs and various firework displays.

The most interesting building in Paignton is undoubtedly **Oldway Mansion,** built in 1874 for Isaac Singer, the millionaire sewing-machine manufacturer. Isaac died the following year and it was his son, Paris, who gave the great mansion its present exuberant form. Paris added a south side mimicking a music pavilion in the grounds of Versailles, a hallway modelled on the Versailles hall of

mirrors, and a sumptuous ballroom where his mistress Isadora Duncan would display the new, fluid kind of dance she had created based on classical mythology. Paris Singer sold the mansion to Paignton Borough Council in 1946 and it is now used as a Civic Centre, but many of the splendid rooms (and the extensive gardens) are open to the public free of charge and guided tours are available.

An experience not to be missed in Paignton is a trip on the **Paignton and Dartmouth Steam Railway**, a seven mile journey along the lovely Torbay coast and through the wooded slopes bordering the Dart estuary to Kingswear where travellers board a ferry for the ten-minute crossing to Dartmouth. The locomotives and rolling stock all bear the proud chocolate and gold livery of the Great Western Railway, and on certain services you can wine

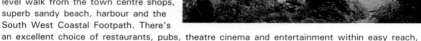
historic building   museum and heritage   historic site   scenic attraction   flora and fauna

and dine in Pullman style luxury in the "Riviera Belle Dining Train". During the peak season, trains leave every 45 minutes or so.

Paignton and Dartmouth Steam Railway

Another major attraction in the town is **Paignton Zoo**, set in 75 acres of attractive botanical gardens and home to some 300 species of world animals. A registered charity dedicated to protecting the global wildlife heritage, the zoo is particularly concerned with endangered species such as the Asiatic lions and Sumatran tigers which are now provided with their own forest habitat area. Orang utans and gorillas roam freely on large outdoor islands, free from cages. The route of the Jungle Express miniature railway provides

---

NEWBARN FARM

Totnes Road, Paignton, Devon TQ4 7PT
Tel: 01803 553602 Fax: 01803 553603
e-mail: info@newbarnfarm.com
website: www.newbarnfarm.com

Awarded four.4 stars by Visit Britain Quality in Tourism in 2008, **Newbarn Farm** offers outstanding self-catering accommodation in delightful surroundings. Richard and Catherine Soley have managed the farm since 2005, living on site with their two young children. They have worked hard in renovating the cottages and surrounding land to create the beautiful haven Newbarn Farm represents.

There are eight.8 luxury cottages, all renovated and refurbished to an exceptionally high standard and sleeping from two to a maximum of 12 people. Although very similar in design, each cottage takes on its own persona. The accommodation is spread over two buildings - Cottage Terrace and the Old Farmhouse which has apartment style cottages with walls two feet thick - very cosy! Each has a kitchen equipped with everything to conjure up a gourmet meal. If you don't want to cook, there are award-winning restaurants in the locality or just phone in a take-away. Guests are encouraged to explore the 42 acres of woodland and pasture which command wonderful panoramic views of Dartmoor. Also within the grounds are six coarse fishing lakes/ponds, two outdoor play areas to occupy children of all ages, and there is free unlimited use of the neighbouring heated swimming pool, sauna, steam room and gym.

---

good views of these and many other animals.

Located on Goodrington Sands, **Quaywest** claims to be Britain's "biggest, best, wildest and wettest waterpark", with the highest water slides in the country. Other amusements include go-karts, bumper boats, and crazy golf and the site also offers a choice of bars, restaurants and cafés.

BRIXHAM
8 miles S of Torquay on the A3022

🐦 Battery Gardens   🦅 Revd. Lyte

🐦 Berry Head Country Park

In the 18th century, Brixham was the most profitable fishing port in Britain and fishing is still the most important activity in this engaging little town, although the trawlers now have to pick their way between flotillas of yachts and tour boats. On the quay there are stalls selling freshly caught seafood and around the harbour a maze of narrow streets where you'll find a host of small shops, tearooms and galleries. From the busy harbour, there are regular passenger ferries to Torquay and coastal cruises in the 80-year-old Brixham-built yacht *Vigilance* and other craft.

It was at Brixham that the Prince of Orange landed in 1688 to claim the British throne as William III; an imposing statue of him looks inland from the harbour. And in 1815, all eyes were focussed on the *Bellerophon*, anchored in the bay. On board was Napoleon Buonaparte, getting his only close look at England before transferring to the *Northumberland* and sailing off to his final exile on St Helena.

A short walk from the quay brings you to **Battery Gardens,** so named because an Emergency Coastal Defence Battery was established here in World War II. It is now a Scheduled Monument with many of the buildings and structures from that time still

standing. A museum on site tells their story.

Also close to the harbour is All Saints' Church where the **Revd Henry Francis Lyte** was Vicar from 1823 until his death in 1847. During his last illness, the Revd Lyte composed what is perhaps the best known and best loved English hymn – *Abide with me*. The church bells play the tune each evening.

To the west of the town is **Berry Head Country Park** which is noted for its incredible views (on a good day as far as Portland Bill, 46 miles away), its rare plants, (like the white rock-rose), and its colonies of sea birds such as fulmars and kittiwakes nesting in the cliffs. The park also boasts the largest breeding colony of guillemots along the entire Channel coast. A video camera has been installed on the cliffs to relay live close-up pictures of the guillemots and other seabirds. Within the park is a lighthouse which has been called "the highest and lowest lighthouse in Britain". The structure is only 15ft high, but it stands on a 200ft high cliff rising at the most easterly point of Berry Head.

In the town itself, the **Strand Art Gallery** was founded in 1972 and showcases the work of local artists. There are more than 300 original paintings on display and visitors can see the artists at work, either in the gallery or on the slipway outside.

KINGSWEAR
10 miles S of Torquay off the A379

🐦 Coleton Fishacre

Kingswear sits on the steeply rising east bank of the River Dart, looking across to the picturesque panorama of Dartmouth stretched across the hillside on the opposite bank. The town is the terminus for the Paignton and Kingswear steam railway and passengers then join the ferry for the 10-minute crossing to Dartmouth. There's also a vehicle ferry. Above the town stand the impressive remains of Kingswear Castle which is now owned by the Landmark Trust and has been converted to holiday flats. Together with its twin across the river, Dartmouth Castle, the fortresses guarded the wide estuary of the Dart. If an invasion seemed imminent, a huge chain was strung across the river from Dartmouth as an additional deterrent.

Compton Castle

About three miles to the east of Kingswear, **Coleton Fishacre** (NT) is a delightful coastal garden basking in a mild climate that is ideal for growing exotic trees and shrubs. The garden was created between 1925 and 1940 by Lady Dorothy D'Oyly Carte whose grandfather had produced the Gilbert and Sullivan comic operas. Lady Dorothy introduced a wonderfully imaginative variety of plants. The 20-acre site, protected by a deep combe, contains formal gardens, wooded areas with wild flowers, tranquil pools and secret paths weaving in and out of glades.

COMPTON
4 miles W of Torquay off the A381

🏰 Compton Castle

Dominating this small village, **Compton Castle** (NT) dates back to the 1300s and in Elizabethan times was the home of Sir Humphrey Gilbert, Walter Raleigh's half brother and the coloniser of Newfoundland in 1583. Complete with battlements, towers and portcullis, the castle also boasts an impressive

Great Hall, a solar and an ancient kitchen. The castle is still occupied by the Gilbert family although owned by the National Trust.

NEWTON ABBOT
7 miles NW of Torquay on the A380

🗣 William II 🖋 Racecourse 🏰 Bradley Manor
🏰 Tuckers Maltings

An ancient market town, Newton Abbot took on a quite different character in the 1850s when the Great Western Railway established its locomotive and carriage repair works here. Neat terraces of artisans' houses were built on the steep hillsides to the south; the more well-to-do lived a little further to the north in Italianate villas around Devon Square and Courtenay Park.

The town's greatest moment of glory was on November 5th, 1688 when William, Prince of Orange, "the glorious defender of the Protestant religion and the liberties of England" was first proclaimed king as **William III.** This climactic moment of the "Glorious Revolution" took place in front of St Leonard's Church of which only the medieval tower now remains. The new king had landed at Brixham and was on his way to

MAGPIES

"FOR SOMETHING SPECIAL"

11 Wolborough Street,
Newton Abbot, Devon, TQ12 1JR
Tel: 01626 353456
Fax: 01626 335391
e-mail: carol.rick@btopenworld.com
website: www.magpies-gifts.co.uk
or www.charliebearsuk.com
or www.rivegollies.co.uk

Located close to Newton Abbot's famous clock tower, **Magpies** is stocked with a huge variety of gifts and covetable items for the home. Owners Carol and Richard Handley-Collins started the business in 1999 and have gathered together a fascinating collections of distinctive items distributed around the shop. There are stylish contemporary gifts which include pictures, handbags, hat boxes, Russian dolls, frames, clocks, lamps, fountains, mirrors, ornaments, glassware, ceramics, necklaces, scarves, bracelets and collectable bears from Charlie Bears which are based in Holsworthy, Devon, Bearington bears from the USA and Brigette Rive collectable Gollies. The shop also stocks small furnishings, garden ornaments and furniture.

Particularly attractive are the Swarowski crystals set in gold and silver. Every item is either 22k gold plated and/or rhodium, a member of the platinum family. It is stronger than sterling silver and will not tarnish.

Clothing accessories for men and women are also on sale and upstairs is **Mrs B's Bonnets** where you'll find a wonderful collection of some 100 varieties of hats for sale or hire. Just the place to select a hat for the races at Newton Abbot's Racecourse.

Remember also that Magpies' Christmas scene attracts people from miles around and is well worth a visit. Spend some time browsing through their collection of unusual gifts and then why not visit Magpies' sister establishment The Nest Café for a tasty treat situated at the back of Magpies, all under one roof!

🏛 historic building 🏛 museum and heritage 🏛 historic site 🏞 scenic attraction 🌱 flora and fauna

THE NEST CAFÉ AND RESTAURANT

"HOMEMADE IS OUR SPECIALITY"

11 Wolborough Street, Newton Abbot, Devon, TQ12 1JR
Tel: 01626 353456   website: www.thenestcafe.co.uk

At The Nest Café you can treat yourself to some marvellous home-made food. The café serves all day breakfasts, lunches and afternoon cream teas, plus homemade cakes and speciality ice cream. At lunchtime there are daily specials such as Brixham crab salad or chicken casserole served in a giant yorkshire. The café has recently been redecorated in a striking blend of burgundy and strawberry wallpaper. Customers can also enjoy their refreshments at tables outside on the rear patio. The Nest is open from 9.15am to 3.30pm, Mon-Sat.

London. Stopping off in Newton Abbot, he stayed at the handsome Jacobean manor, Forde House, which is now used as offices by the District Council.

To the south of the town is a delightful attraction in the shape of the Hedgehog Hospital at Prickly Hill Farm – where else?

On the northern outskirts of the town is **Newton Abbot Racecourse** where National Hunt racing takes place from the spring through to the autumn. For the rest of the year, the site is used for country fairs and other events.

On the western edge of the town stands **Bradley Manor** (NT), a notable example of medieval domestic architecture. Most of it dates from around 1420 and includes a chapel,

Solar, Great Hall and porch. By the mid-1750s this quaint style of architecture was decidedly out of fashion and the building became a farmhouse with poultry occupying the chapel. The house was given to the National Trust in 1938 by the then owner, Mrs AH Woolner. Her family continue to live here and manage the property.

Newton Abbot also boasts the only traditional working malthouse open to the public. **Tuckers Maltings** has been malting in Newton Abbot for more than 100 years and claims to offer the finest selection of bottled beers to be found in Devon. The speciality beer shop is open throughout the year and guided tours of the maltings are available during the summer months.

THE CRAFT ROOM

57 Queen Street, Newton Abbot, Devon TQ12 2AU
Tel: 01626 336171
e-mail: craftroom@btconnect.com
website: www.craftroomonline.co.uk

The Craft Room is a fascinating and colourful shop full of interesting and varied items for card making, paper crafts, rubber stamping, scrapbooking, jewellery making and more. It is the major UK stockist and distributor for Paplins Quilling papers, tools and accessories, including fringing machines for both straight and 45 degree cuts for flowers and leaves. Owner Jo Grand regularly holds classes for up to 10 people covering lots of different techniques – from beginners to advanced. Booking is essential.

CHUDLEIGH
14 miles NW of Torquay off the A38

🏛 Ugbrooke House

Activists who oppose the building of new roads will find little sympathy in this former coaching town on what used to be the main thoroughfare between Exeter and Plymouth. By the 1960s, the volume of traffic had reached unbearable levels, especially during the holiday season. Mercifully, the dual carriageway A38 now bypasses the little town and it is once again possible to enjoy Chudleigh's 14th century church, containing some fine memorials to the Courtenay family, and its former Grammar School nearby which was founded in 1668. (It is now a private house). It was at the coaching inn here that William of Orange stayed after his landing at Torbay. From one of its windows, the new

king addressed the good people of Chudleigh. The Dutchman's English was so bad however they were unable to understand what he was saying. They cheered him anyway.

Clifford Street is named after Sir Thomas Clifford, Lord Treasurer to Charles II and a member of the king's notorious Cabal, his secretive inner Cabinet. As was the custom then, Sir Thomas used his official position to amass a considerable fortune. This was later put to good use by his grandson who employed Robert Adam and Capability Brown to design **Ugbrooke House and Park,** a couple of miles southwest of Chudleigh and well worth visiting. Dating from the mid-1700s and replacing an early Tudor manor house, Ugbrooke is named after the Ug Brook that flows through the estate and was dammed to create three lakes in the beautifully

---

DANDELION

6 Fore Street, Chudleigh, nr Exeter,
Devon TQ13 0HX
Tel: 01626 859333
e-mail: gabi@dandeliondevon.co.uk
website: www.dandeliondevon.co.uk

Located in the heart of the pretty village of Chudleigh on the old A38, Dandelion offers a unique variety of gifts, jewellery, designer fashion, handmade cards, ceramics and art. When Gabi Ginsberg established Dandelion in 2006, quality, service and integrity were the most important characteristics in her mind. Gabi is constantly on the lookout for new talent and many of Dandelion's products are directly sourced from local artists and designers, including beautiful silver and gold jewellery made in Devon and luxurious knitwear from Somerset. She always knows the source of what the shop sells and can make absolutely sure that all items

are made ethically. Around 80% of the products on sale have been sourced in the UK, and about 60% of them are locally made.

Dandelion offers a truly warm, friendly shopping atmosphere. It is a place where customers can feel at home. Whether you seek unique and inspired gifts for friends, family or that special someone, or just want to treat yourself, Dandelion is the place for you. The shop is open from 10am–5pm, Monday to Saturday.

🏛 historic building   🏛 museum and heritage   🏛 historic site   🏝 scenic attraction   🌱 flora and fauna

Ugbrooke House Dining Room, Chudleigh

landscaped grounds. In the 1930s, the 11th Lord Clifford abandoned the estate as he could not afford to live there. During World War II, Ugbrooke was used as a school for evacuated children and as a hostel for Polish soldiers. In the 1950s, some of the ground floor rooms were used to store grain but today the house has been beautifully restored by the present Lord and Lady Clifford. It is noted for its collections of paintings, dolls, military uniforms and furniture.

Exeter & the Exe Valley

Exeter

🏛 Roman Bath House	🏰 Rougemont Castle
🏰 St Peter's Cathedral	🏰 St Nicholas' Priory
🏰 Guildhall	🏰 Tucker's Hall	🏛 Piazza Terracina
🏛 Underground Passages	🏛 Sculpture Walk
🐟 Seahorse Nature Aquarium	🏛 Exeter Ship Canal

A lively and thriving city with a majestic Norman cathedral, many fine old buildings, and a wealth of excellent museums, Exeter's history stretches back for than two millennia. Its present High Street was already in place some 200 years or more before the Romans arrived, part of an ancient ridgeway striking across the West Country. The inhabitants then were the Celtish tribe of the Dumnonii and it was they who named the river Eisca, "a river abounding in fish".

The Romans made Isca their south-western stronghold, surrounding it with a massive defensive wall. Most of that has disappeared, but a spectacular *caldarium,* or **Roman Bath House** was uncovered in the Cathedral Close in 1971.

In the Dark Ages following the Roman withdrawal, the city was a major ecclesiastical centre and in 670AD King Cenwealh founded an abbey on the site of the present cathedral. That, along with the rest of Exeter, was ransacked by the Vikings in the 9th century. They occupied the city twice before King Alfred finally saw them off.

The Normans were next on the scene, although it wasn't until 20 years after the Battle of Hastings that William the Conqueror finally took possession of the city after a siege that lasted 18 days. He ordered the construction of **Rougemont Castle,** the gatehouse and tower of which still stand at the top of Castle Street.

During the following century, the Normans began building **St Peter's Cathedral,** a work not completed until 1206. Half a century later, however, everything except the two sturdy towers was demolished and the present cathedral took shape. These years saw the development of the Decorated style, and Exeter is a sublime example of this appealing form of church architecture. In the 300ft long nave, stone piers rise 60ft and then fan out into sweeping arches. Equally impressive is the west front, a staggering display of more than 60 sculptures, carved between 1327 and 1369. They depict a curious mix of Biblical characters, soldiers, priests and a royal flush of Saxon and Norman kings.

Other treasures include an intricately-carved choir screen from about 1320, an astronomical clock built in 1376 which is one of the oldest timepieces in the world, a minstrels' gallery with a wonderful band of heavenly musicians, a monumental organ, and a colossal throne with a canopy 59ft high, carved in wood for Bishop Stapledon in 1316.

Another strange carving can be found beneath the misericord seats in the choir stalls where, amongst other carvings, there is one of

an elephant. However, as the carver had no model to work from he has given the animal tusks that look like clubs and rather eccentric feet. It has been suggested that the carving was based on the first elephant to come to Britain as a gift to Henry III in 1253. The carver had probably heard stories of the creature and made up the rest.

In 1941 much of the old part of the city was destroyed by a German air raid and, although the cathedral survived, it was badly damaged. When restoration work began in 1943, a collection of wax models was discovered hidden in a cavity. Including representations of human and animal limbs, the complete figure of a woman and a horse's head, they are thought to have been brought here by pilgrims who would place their wax

🏛 historic building 🏛 museum and heritage 🏚 historic site ✤ scenic attraction 🌱 flora and fauna

INSPIRATIONS HANDICRAFT SHOP

5 Central Station, Queen Street,
Exeter, EX4 3SB
Tel: 01392 435115
website: www.inspirationsuk.net

Housed in what was once a railway station waiting room, **Inspirations Handicraft Shop** really lives up to its name. With the wealth of materials on display here, a myriad of ideas will surely be sparked off.

The handsome double-fronted building has been a handicraft shop since 1949 but it is now owned and run by Cherry Whitaker who, together with her warm and welcoming staff, provide a friendly and personal service to their customers. The shop is packed to the ceiling with an astonishing variety of materials for knitting, cross-stitching, patchwork and embroidery, along with a huge selection of beads, buttons and much more.

All the staff are craftspeople themselves so they are able to give knowledgeable advice and information on all the various processes involved. Over the years, the shop has built up a loyal clientele from far and wide, and, says Cherry, they have become friends. Inspirations is open from 9.30am to 5pm, Monday to Saturday.

models on the tomb of Bishop Edmund Lacy. By placing a model of an injured or withered limb on the tomb the pilgrims believed that they would be cured of their affliction.

Such is the grandeur of the cathedral that other ecclesiastical buildings in Exeter tend to get overlooked. But it's well worth seeking out **St Nicholas' Priory**, an exceptional example of a small Norman priory. The Priory re-opened to the public in April 2008 after a two-year programme of conservation work. Adorned with quality replica furniture and painted in the bright colours of the period, the Priory is now presented as the 1602 home of the wealthy Hurst family. Visitors can experience Tudor life including Elizabethan music, costume, food, games and stories. And view the original Priory cellar with its chunky Norman pillars, the 15th century kitchens, and

the parlour with its original Tudor plaster ceiling. The church of **St Mary Steps** also repays a visit just to see its beautifully-preserved Norman font, and its ancient "Matthew the Miller" tower clock, named after a medieval miller noted for his undeviating punctuality. The church stands in Stepcote Hill, a narrow cobbled and stepped thoroughfare which until as late as 1778 was the main road into Exeter from the west.

The remarkable **Guildhall** in the High Street has been in use as a Town Hall ever since it was built in 1330, making it one of the oldest municipal buildings in the country. Its great hall was remodelled around 1450, and the Elizabethans added a striking, if rather fussy, portico but the interior is still redolent of the Middle Ages.

Another interesting medieval building is

Exeter Guildhall

The Tucker's Hall in Fore Street, built in
1471 for the Company of Weavers, Fullers
and Shearmen. Inside there is some
exceptional carved panelling, a collection of
rare silver, and a huge pair of fulling shears
weighing over 25lbs and almost 4ft long.
Nearby Parliament Street claims to be the
world's narrowest street.

Exeter's one-time importance as a port is
reflected in the dignified **Custom House,**
built in 1681, and now the centrepiece of
Exeter Historic Quayside, a fascinating
complex of old warehouses, craft shops,
cafés, and the **Seahorse Nature Aquarium**
which is specially dedicated to these beautiful
and enigmatic creatures. There are riverside
walks, river trips, Canadian canoes and cycles
for hire, and a passenger ferry across the
river to the **Piazza Terracina** which
explores five centuries of Exeter's trading
connections around the world. The museum

contains an extraordinary collection of boats,
amongst them an Arab dhow, a reed boat
from Lake Titicaca in South America, and a
vintage steam launch. A special attraction of
the museum is that visitors are positively
encouraged to step aboard and explore in
detail the many craft on show.

Other excellent museums in the city
include the **Devonshire Regiment
Museum** (regimental history); the
Rougemont House Museum near the
castle which has a copious collection of
costumes and lace; and the Bill Douglas
Centre for the History of Cinema and
Popular Culture.

One of the city's most unusual attractions
lies beneath its streets: the maze of
Underground Passages constructed in the
14th and 15th centuries to bring water from
springs beyond the city walls. A guided tour
of the stone-vaulted caverns is an experience
to remember.

Although Exeter is linked to the sea by the
River Exe, the 13th century Countess of
Devon, with a grudge against the city, built a
weir across the river so that boats could sail
no further upstream than Topsham. Some
300 years passed before action was taken by
the city and the world's first ship canal was
constructed to bypass the weir. Originally
only three feet deep, this was changed to 14
feet over the years and the **Exeter Ship
Canal** continued to be used until the 1970s.
However, the M5 motorway, which crosses
the canal on a fixed height bridge too low to
allow big ships to pass, finally achieved what
the Countess of Devon began so many
centuries ago.

Exeter University campus is set on a hill
overlooking the city, and the grounds, laid
out by Robert Veitch in the 1860s, offer

superb views of the tors of Dartmoor. The landscape boasts many rare trees and shrubs, and the University has followed Veitch's example by creating many new plantings, including areas devoted entirely to Australasian plants. **Exeter University Sculpture Walk** comprises more than 20 sculptures, including works by Barbara Hepworth and Henry Moore, set out both in the splendid grounds and within the university buildings.

To the southwest of the city lies the **Devon and Exeter Racecourse**, one of the most scenic in the country and one that is considered to be Britain's favourite holiday course.

Around Exeter

CADBURY
10 miles N of Exeter off the A3072

🏰 Cadbury Castle 🏠 Fursdon House

To the north of this delightful hamlet is **Cadbury Castle**, actually an Iron Age fort. It was built high on the hilltop, about 700ft above sea level, and it's claimed that the views here are the most extensive in Devon. On a good day Dartmoor and Exmoor are in full view, and the Quantocks and Bodmin Moor can also be seen. A little more than a mile away stands **Fursdon House** which has been lived in by the Fursdon family since around 1260. The varied architecture reflects the many additions made over the centuries. Some fascinating family memorabilia, including old scrapbooks, are on display, there's an excellent collection of 18th century costumes and textiles, and amongst the family treasures is a letter from Charles I written during the Civil War. Opening times are restricted.

BICKLEIGH
12 miles N of Exeter on the A396

🏰 Bickleigh Castle 🏛 Devon Railway Centre

Running due north from Exeter, the Exe Valley passes through the heart of what is known as "Red Devon". The soil here has a distinctive colour derived from the red Permian rocks that underlie it. Unlike most land in Devon, this is prime agricultural land, fertile, easily-worked and, for some reason, particularly favourable to growing swedes to which it gives a much sought-after flavour.

One of the most charming villages in the Exe Valley is Bickleigh. With its riverside setting and picturesque thatched cottages with lovingly-tended gardens, Bickleigh is one of Devon's most photographed villages. It also boasts two of the area's most popular attractions. Bickleigh Mill has been developed as a craft centre and farm stocked with rare breeds, while across the river is **Bickleigh Castle,** actually a moated and fortified manor house with an impressive gatehouse dating back to the late 1300s. Even older is the detached chapel which was built in the 11th century. Exhibits include Tudor furniture, (including a massive four-poster), some fine oil paintings, and a Civil War Armoury. The nearby 17th century farmhouse is very atmospheric with its inglenook fireplaces, oak beams and ancient bread ovens. The castle is open daily from the late spring Bank Holiday until the first Sunday in October, and at any time for pre-booked groups.

Railway buffs will enjoy the **Devon Railway Centre** housed in the Victorian station buildings. It has 15 different working model railway layouts and various museum collections, and provides unlimited train rides on two railways. There's also a riverside picnic area, crazy golf and refreshments.

🎭 stories and anecdotes 🕊 famous people ✐ art and craft ✍ entertainment and sport 🚶 walks

THE HARTNOLL HOTEL

Bolham, Tiverton, Devon EX16 7RA
Tel: 01884 252777
e-mail: thehartnollhotel@btinternet.com
website: www.thehartnollhotel.com

Nestling amidst the rolling hills of the Exe Valley, **The Hartnoll Hotel** is located in the tiny village of Bolham on the outskirts of the thriving market town of Tiverton. Claire Carter bought the hotel in 2007 and has refurbished the bar and all the guest bedrooms to a very high standard. The 15 bedrooms are all en suite, fitted with top quality Egyptian cotton sheets, goose down duvets and pillows, luxury towels and fully equipped with remote control TV, direct dial telephone and hospitality tray. The cottage style bedrooms in the annexe are particularly suited for pet owners or guests wishing to avoid stairs. And the bridal suite boasts a luxurious four-poster bed, perfect for those special occasions.

The hotel's restaurant overlooks a mill stream and serves a variety of delicious à la carte dishes. It is open for lunch and dinner seven days a week. For more informal dining, the cosy bar offers a selection of freshly prepared meals based on the finest local produce. A wide variety of fine wines and locally brewed real ales and cider is available to complement your meal. The hotel also has an oak-panelled banqueting suite with its own private bar and open log fireplace.

DANE-T'S LITTLE TREASURES

40 Gold Street, Tiverton, Devon EX16 6PY
Tel: 01884 251117
e-mail: jan@dane-t-s.co.uk
website: www.dane-t-s.co.uk

Opened in November 2005, **Dane-T's Little Treasures** is a family run business specialising in dolls houses and miniatures. Owners Jan and Alan Thorne are constantly being complimented on their wide choice of goods, the large selection of handcrafted items available and the overall quality and variety of dolls houses and miniatures that they have in their shop. The displays are changing constantly and Jan and Alan are always looking for new and innovative ideas to enhance their products and services. They offer a building, lighting and decorating service and pay great attention to the interior and exterior design of houses to ensure our customers receive the houses of their dreams. They also do home visits for that extra personal touch to discuss projects with their customers - "If our customers are happy, then so are we," they say.

Visitors to Dane-T's Little Treasures were used to being greeted by the Thorne-s 16 year old cat Brodie and their new addition Munchkin (pictured above) but unfortunately since moving to larger premises the cats now have to stay at home and are not in the shop all day. says Jan " People still ask where they are but finally we can build our window displays and know they are not going to get destroyed by fluffy feet!" For those cat lovers amongst us pictures of Brodie and Munchkin can still be seen on the website.

🏛 historic building   🏛 museum and heritage   🏛 historic site   ⌖ scenic attraction   🌿 flora and fauna

TIVERTON
16 miles N of Exeter on the A396

🏚 Tiverton Castle 🏚 St Peter's Church

🏚 St George's Church 🏚 Knightshayes Court

🏛 Museum of Mid-Devon Life

The only town of any size in the Exe valley is Tiverton, originally Twyfyrde, or two fords, for here the Exe is joined by the River Lowman. The town developed around what is now its oldest building, **Tiverton Castle,** built at the command of Henry I in 1106. Unfortunately, the castle found itself on the wrong side during the Civil War. General Fairfax himself was in charge of the successful onslaught in 1645. A few years later Parliament decreed that the castle should be "slighted", destroyed beyond any use as a fortification. Cromwell's troops observed the letter of their instructions, sparing those parts of the castle which had no military significance, and leaving behind them a mutilated, but still substantial, structure.

During the Middle Ages, the citizens of Tiverton seem to have had a very highly-developed sense of civic and social responsibility. Throughout the town's golden age as a wool town, from the late 1400s until it reached its zenith in the 18th century, prosperous wool merchants put their wealth to good use. Around 1613, George Slee built himself a superb Jacobean mansion in St Peter Street, the **Great House,** and in his will bequeathed the huge sum of £500 to establish the **Slee Almshouses** which were duly built right next door. Later almshouses, founded by

LANTIC GALLERY

38 Gold Street, Tiverton, Devon EX16 6PY
Tel : 01884 259888
e-mail: info@lanticgallery.co.uk
website: www.lanticgallery.co.uk

Lantic Gallery opened in 2004 as a platform for contemporary quality art works. It has a fine selection of the best studio pottery and sculpture together with paintings, glass, wood and jewellery. Lantic Gallery is Arts Council approved and offers the 'Own Art' 0% interest scheme on purchases. There are a number of exhibitions throughout the year and more details can be found on the website.

The continuing displays are by well established ceramic artists such as Laurel Keeley, John Maltby, John Wheeldon, Lawson Rudge, Rod Hare, Jenny Southam, Nancy Wells, Isobel Merrick and Nic Harrison – between them all providing both dynamic sculptural and functional work.

Painters and printmakers include John Hoar, Mary Sumner, Jo Whiteland, Lester Halhead, Mark Abdey and Pam Pebworth; from watercolours to wood engravings which sit alongside the vibrant and colourful glass of Nic Orsler and straw silk work of Margaret Johnson.

The gallery has an excellent selection of jewellery, featuring the gold and silversmith Les Grimshaw for specialised occasion rings and the colourful beaded work of Nina Parker; when you add scarves, bags and cards, you have a stylish mixture which makes a visit to Lantic Gallery a must.

The Gallery is open: Monday to Friday 10am to 5pm and Saturday 10am to 4pm

📖 stories and anecdotes 🕊 famous people 🎨 art and craft 🎭 entertainment and sport 🥾 walks

John Waldron (in Welbrook Street), and John Greenway (in Gold Street) are still in use. As well as funding the almshouse, John Greenway also devoted another sizeable portion of his fortune to the restoration of **St Peter's Church** in 1517. He added a sumptuous porch and chapel, their outside walls richly decorated with carvings depicting sailing ships of the time.

Peter Blundell chose a different method of demonstrating his beneficence by endowing Tiverton with a school. It was in the **Old Blundell's School** building of 1604, by the Lowman Bridge, that the author R.D. Blackmore received his education. He later used the school as a setting for the first chapter of his novel, *Lorna Doone*. Now a highly-regarded public school, "Blundell's"

moved to its present location on the edge of town in 1880.

The **Tiverton Museum of Mid Devon Life** is one of the largest social history museums in the southwest, containing some 15 galleries in all. It's particularly strong on agriculture – it has a nationally important collection of farm wagons - and the Great Western Railway. One entire gallery is devoted to John Heathcoat's original lace-making machine.

The more one reads of Devon in the early to mid 18th century, the more one becomes convinced that there must have been a serial arsonist abroad. So many Devonshire towns during this period suffered devastating fires. Tiverton's conflagration occurred in 1731, but one happy outcome of the disaster was the

---

THE PAINTED DOOR

36 Gold Street, Tiverton, Devon EX16 6PY
Tel: 01884 256694

Occupying a fine old Victorian property built around 1870, **The Painted Door** provides a whole range of inspirations for interior decoration, gifts and garden items.

The shop has kept its original Victorian display window which runs almost the whole length of the frontage and is filled with a wide variety of covetable pieces. Inside, owner Helena Hawksley has gathered together a veritable Aladdin's cave of colourful, useful and well-crafted items. A former nurse, Helena clearly has a natural flair for discovering the desirable and unusual.

Whatever your taste in interior design you will surely find much here to suit. The Painted Door is open from 9.30pm to 5pm, Tuesday to Saturday.

🏛 historic building   🏛 museum and heritage   🏛 historic site   🏞 scenic attraction   🌱 flora and fauna

Knightshayes Court, Tiverton

National Trust, who were given the building by the builder's son in 1973. The house is surrounded by extensive grounds that include a water-lily pond, topiary and some rare shrubs.

BAMPTON
21 miles N of Exeter on the B3190/ B3227

🌿 Exmoor Pony Sale

building of **St George's Church,** by common consent the finest Georgian church in the county, furnished with elegant period ceilings and galleries.

A quay on the south eastern edge of Tiverton marks the western end of the Grand Western Canal which was built in the early 1800s with the idea of linking the River Exe to Bridgewater and the Bristol Channel. It was never fully completed and finally closed in 1920. In recent years, an attractive stretch from Tiverton quay to the Somerset border has been restored and provides a pleasant easy walk. Horse-drawn barge trips along the canal are also available.

A few miles north of Tiverton, up the Exe Valley, is **Knightshayes Court** a striking Victorian Gothic house designed by William Burges in 1869. It remains a rare survivor of his work. The grand and opulent interiors, blending medieval romanticism with lavish Victorian decoration, became too much for the owner, Sir John Heathcoat-Amory, the lace manufacturer. So he sacked Burges and employed the less imaginative but competent John Diblee Crace. Covered over during the time of the backlash against the High Victorian style, the rooms have been returned to their original grandeur by the

In medieval times Bampton was quite an important centre of the wool trade but it's now best known for its annual **Exmoor Pony Sale,** held in late October. Throughout the rest of the year, though, it's a wonderfully peaceful place with some handsome Georgian cottages and houses, set beside the River Batherm, a tributary of the Exe. To the north of the village, a tree-crowned motte marks the site of Bampton Castle. Bampton's parish church of St Michael and All Angels is popular with collectors of unusual memorials. A stone on the west side of the tower replicates a memorial of 1776 which records the strange death of the parish clerk's son who was apparently killed by a falling icicle. The inscription is remarkably insensitive and reads:

Bless my I I I I I I (eyes),
Here he lies,
In a sad pickle,
Killed by an icicle.

BROADCLYST
5½ miles NE of Exeter on the B3181

🏛 Killerton

Just to the north of the village and set within the fertile lands between the Rivers Clyst and Culm, lies the large estate of **Killerton,** centred around the grand 18th century mansion house that was the home of the

DARTS FARM

Topsham, nr Exeter, Devon, EX3 0QH
Tel: 01392 878200
e-mail: shop@dartsfarm.co.uk   website: www.dartsfarm.co.uk

Darts Farm near the historic estuary town of Topsham is fortunate to be situated in a region that is rich in high quality artisan food producers. With all this wonderful local produce on the doorstep and still with their own working farm it's easy to understand why The Guardian described Darts Farm as..

'like finding Selfridges Food Hall dumped in the middle of a field'

Visit the deli, the cider maker, the florist or sample a bit of everything in the restaurant which uses the food hall as its larder with the chefs preparing fresh dishes everyday letting the good basic ingredients speak for themselves. This philosophy runs throughout Darts Farm whether it be the master butchers – Gerald David and family with their locally reared, naturally fed meat or The Fish Shed which only sells locally caught fish straight off the day boats. The choice is yours, either beautiful wet fish to take home and cook or try their famous fish and chips also open in the evenings for takeaway.

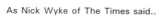

Combine all this with the Aga shop, Fired Earth, Orange Tree and the unusual design led gifts for the home and garden, florist, children's clothes, toys, The Treatment Loft beauty salon, Cotswold Outdoor and the RSPB shop and you will understand why your first visit won't be your last.

As Nick Wyke of The Times said..

'I've seen the future of shopping and it's not in London, Manchester or Edinburgh but on a road that runs alongside the Exe Estuary in Devon, a few miles south of Exeter.'

Acland family. Furnished as a comfortable family home, the house contains a renowned costume collection and a Victorian laundry. While the house provides some interest it is the marvellous grounds laid out by John Veitch in the 1770s that make a visit here special. Veitch introduced many rare trees to the arboretum along with rhododendrons, magnolias and herbaceous borders, and in the parkland are several interesting structures including a 19th century chapel and the Dolbury Iron Age hill fort. Here, too, can be found **Marker's Cottage** dating from the 15th century and containing 16th century paintings, and **Forest Cottage**, originally a gamekeeper's cottage. Circular walks around the grounds and estate provide ample opportunity to discover the wealth of plant, animal and birdlife that thrives in this large estate.

CLYST ST MARY
4 miles E of Exeter on the A376/A3052

> Crealy Park

A couple of miles east of Clyst St Mary is **Crealy Park,** a large all-weather entertainment centre offering a wide range of attractions for children, including the largest indoor PlayZone in the country, bumper boats and go-karts, a farm nursery and pony rides.

TOPSHAM
3 miles SE of Exeter off the A376

It's not surprising to find that the whole of the old town of Topsham has been declared a conservation area. Its narrow streets are lined with fine examples of 17th and 18th century merchants' houses, many built in the Dutch style with curved gable ends. There's a wealth

---

TOPSHAM JEWELLERS

63 Fore Street, Topsham, Exeter,
Devon EX3 0HL
Tel: 01392 823180

Set beside the estuary of the River Exe, Topsham is famed for the wealth of splendid 17th and 18th century buildings - indeed, the whole of the old town has been declared a conservation area. One of these fine old Grade II listed houses is now occupied by **Topsham Jewellers**, a highly respected firm which has been serving the town for 12 years.

The building is double-fronted with traditional small-paned windows and inside the elegant décor is full of character. The various cabinets display an exciting selection of jewellery and gifts which definitely have the "Wow" factor! Whether you want designer chic or traditional elegance, a striking silver necklace or an enviable diamond ring, Topsham Jewellers provides a refreshing alternative to the conventional High Street jewellers, combining quality and individuality with good honest prices.

A member of the National Association of Goldsmiths, Topsham Jewellers is staffed by friendly assistants who have been trained to Diploma level and are able to help and advise on all levels. The shop is open from 9.30am to 5pm, Monday to Saturday.

---

of specialist and antique shops, and some stunning views over the Exe estuary with its extensive reed beds, salt marshes and mud banks. These provide an important winter feeding ground and summer breeding area for birds from all over the world. The estuary is also home to the largest winter flocks of avocets in the county. There are walks along the banks of the estuary that lead right from Exeter to the coast at Exmouth.

WOODBURY
7 miles SE of Exeter on the B3179

☘ Woodbury Common

St Swithin's Church at Woodbury has achieved a rather sad kind of fame because of the Revd. J. Loveband Fulford who in 1846 cut great chunks out of its medieval rood screen so that his parishioners could see him more clearly. Fortunately he left untouched the fine 15th century font made from Beer stone, the Jacobean pulpit, and the interesting memorials.

A mile or so to the east of the village is the famous **Woodbury Common** viewpoint. More than 560ft high, it provides spectacular

vistas across the Exe estuary to Dartmoor, and along the south Devon coast. It's easy to understand why an Iron Age tribe chose this spot to build their massive fort whose huge ramparts lie close to the viewpoint.

LYMPSTONE
8 miles SE of Exeter off the A376

Set beside the estuary of the River Exe, Lympstone looks across the water to the impressive outline of Powderham Castle. There's a tiny harbour with a slipway and, on the beach, an Italianate clock tower erected in 1885 by a Mr W. H. Peters in commemoration of his wife, Mary Jane, who was noted for her good works amongst the poor of the village. It's a delight to wander around the old part of Lympstone with its narrow streets, small courts and ancient cottages.

POWDERHAM
7 miles S of Exeter off the A379

🏛 Powderham Castle

Set in a deer park beside the River Exe, **Powderham Castle** has been the home of the Courtenay family, Earls of Devon since

Powderham Castle

1390. The castle stands in a beautiful setting in an ancient deer park alongside the River Exe and is at the centre of a large traditional estate of about 4,000 acres. The present building is mostly 18th century and contains some fine interiors, a breathtaking Grand Staircase, and historic family portraits – some of them by Sir Joshua Reynolds, a Devon man himself.

KENTON

7 miles S of Exeter on the A379

🏛 All Saints Church

Founded in Saxon times, this picturesque village is famed for its glorious 14th century **All Saints Church**. The tower stands over 100ft high and is decorated with a wonderful assortment of ornate carvings. Inside, there is more rich carving in the south porch and in the Beer stone arcades of the nave. The pulpit is a 15th century original which was rescued and restored after it was found in pieces in 1866, and the massive rood screen, one of the finest in Devon, is a magnificent testimony to the 15th century woodcarver's art.

DUNCHIDEOCK

7 miles SW of Exeter off the A30

A beautifully located village, Dunchideock hugs the sides of a deeply-sloping combe. At the northern end, the modest red sandstone church of St Michael has an unusual number of noteworthy internal features. There's a medieval font, a set of carved pew ends and a richly-carved rood screen which at one point makes a surprising diversion around three sides of an octagonal roof column. Amongst the monuments is one to Major-General Stringer Lawrence, the "Father of the Indian Army", who in 1775 left a legacy of £50,000 to his lifelong friend, Sir Robert Palk. Palk

TAVERNERS FARM SHOP

Lower Brenton, Kennford, nr Exeter EX6 7YL
Tel: 01392 833776
e-mail: elephants@tavernersfarm.co.uk
website: www.tavernersfarm.co.uk

Set on a working family farm, **Taverners Farm Shop** specialises in fine, local, seasonal and organic produce, including their own organic South Devon beef. The shop also sells handmade sausages, burgers and other meat from its own butchery, free range eggs, regional cheeses, salads, vegetables and delicious local honey. Visitors can also wander around the kitchen garden growing fresh seasonal produce and get close to the herd of South Devon cows known as Orange Elephants!

ORANGE ELEPHANT ICE CREAM PARLOUR

Lower Brenton, Kennford, nr Exeter EX6 7YL
Tel: 01392 833776

Set below the Haldon Belvedere Tower just off the A38 at Kennford, the **Orange Elephant Ice Cream Parlour** provides an enjoyable food haven for the whole family. The Taverners have been farming for four generations and their farm is home to pedigree South Devons, known as Orange Elephants because of their large size, long faces and rusty coloured coats. Theirs is the only farm still milking South Devons, producing rich milk which is used to make the delicious Orange Elephant Ice Cream which comes in a range of 18 wonderful flavours.

proceeded to build himself a mansion, Haldon House, half a mile to the south, along with a folly in memory of his benefactor. Known locally as Haldon Belvedere, or Lawrence Castle, this tall triangular structure stands on the summit of Haldon Ridge and can be seen for miles around.

CREDITON
8 miles NW of Exeter on the A377

🐦 St Boniface   🏛 Church of the Holy Cross

Very few Britons have managed to become fully-fledged Saints, so Crediton is rather proud that one of this small and distinguished group, **St Boniface,** was born here in 680. The infant was baptised with the name Wynfrith but on becoming a monk he adopted the name Boniface. He rose swiftly through the ranks of the Benedictine Order and in 731

was sent by the Pope to evangelise the Germans. Boniface was remarkably successful, establishing Christianity in several German states. At the age of 71, he was created Archbishop of Mainz but three years later, he and 53 members of his retinue were ambushed and murdered. They were on their way to the great monastery at Fulda in Hesse which Boniface had founded and where he was now laid to rest.

Boniface was greatly revered throughout Germany and a few years later the Pope formally pronounced his sanctification, but it was to be almost 1,200 years before the town of his birth accorded him any recognition. Finally, in 1897, the people of Crediton installed an east window in the town's grand, cathedral-like **Church of the Holy Cross** depicting events from his life. A few years

---

TRELOAR'S DELICATESSEN

38 High Street, Crediton, Devon EX17 3JP
Tel: 01363 772332

Guy Garrett, the owner of **Treloar's Delicatessen** in Crediton's High Street, has been in the delicatessen business for some 20 years. After finishing university he was offered a job in his family's restaurant 'Food for Thought' in London. He later married and moved to the West Country bringing ideas he had gathered at the restaurant. His delicatessen occupies a fine 18th century building in a well-preserved part of this ancient market town.

The day at Treloar's starts with a major baking session - all the pies, pasties, quiches, savouries, cakes and desserts on sale are made on the premises, as well as a range of tasty oven-ready meals. Cheese lovers are well-catered for with a choice of more than 50 varieties including local farmhouse, unpasteurised and imported cheeses. Also on display is a wide range of relishes, conserves, jams, honey and much more.

The staff are friendly, welcoming and knowledgeable about all the items on sale. No wonder this outstanding deli has received many awards including Best Independent Food Shop in Devon, 2007.

🏛 historic building   🏛 museum and heritage   🏛 historic site   🍃 scenic attraction   🌿 flora and fauna

later, a statue of the saint was erected in the gardens to the west of the church.

The interior of the early 15th century church is especially notable for its monuments which include one to Sir John Sully who fought alongside the Black Prince and lived to the age of 105, and another to Sir William Peryam, a commissioner at the trial of Mary, Queen of Scots. Most impressive of all, though, is the richly ornamented arch in memory of Sir Henry Redvers Buller, commander-in-chief during the Boer War and the hero of the Relief of Ladysmith. Also of interest is the Lady Chapel of 1300 which housed Crediton's famous grammar school from the time of Edward VI until 1859 when it moved to its present site at the western end of the High Street.

Church of the Holy Cross, Crediton

East Devon

No less a traveller than Daniel Defoe considered the landscape of East Devon the finest in the world. Acres of rich farmland are watered by the rivers Axe, Otter and Madford, and narrow, winding lanes lead to villages that are as picturesque and interesting as any in England. Steep-sided hills rise towards the coastline where a string of elegant Regency resorts remind the visitor that this part of the coast was one of the earliest to be developed to satisfy the early 19th century craze for sea bathing.

Bounded by the rolling Blackdown Hills to the north, and Lyme Bay to the south, much of the countryside here is designated as of Outstanding Natural Beauty. The best, and for much of the route, the *only* landward way to explore the glorious East Devon coastline is to follow the South West Coast Path, part of the 600-mile South West Peninsula Coast Path which starts at Minehead in Somerset and ends at Shell Bay in Dorset.

East Devon's most famous son is undoubtedly Sir Walter Raleigh who was born at Hayes Barton near Yettington in 1552 and apparently never lost his soft Devon burr – a regional accent regarded then by 16th century London sophisticates as uncouth and much mocked by Sir Walter's enemies at the court of Elizabeth I. The Raleighs' family pew can still be seen in Yettington parish church. The famous picture by Sir John Everett Millais of *The Boyhood of Raleigh* was painted on the beach at Budleigh Salterton with the artist using his two sons and a local ferryman as the models.

🎞 stories and anecdotes 🦜 famous people 🎨 art and craft 🎭 entertainment and sport 🎿 walks

Honiton

🏛 Allhallows Museum   🏛 Thelma Hulbert Gallery

🍃 Dumpdon Hill

Honiton is the "capital" of east Devon, a delightful little town in the valley of the River Otter and the "gateway to the far southwest". It was once a major stopping place on the Fosse Way, the great Roman road that struck diagonally across England from Lincoln to Exeter. Honiton's position on the main traffic artery to Devon and Cornwall brought it considerable prosperity, and its broad, ribbon-like High Street, almost two miles long, testifies to the town's busy past. By the 1960s, this "busyness" had deteriorated into appalling traffic congestion during the holiday season. Fortunately, the construction of a by-pass in the 1970s allowed Honiton to resume its true character as an attractive market town with a street market held on the High Street every Tuesday and Saturday.

Surrounded by sheep pastures, Honiton was the first town in Devon to manufacture serge cloth, but the town became much better known for a more delicate material, Honiton lace. Lace-making was introduced to east Devon by Flemish immigrants who arrived here during the early years of the reign of Elizabeth I. It wasn't long before those who could afford this costly new material were displaying it lavishly as a signal of their wealth and status. By the end of the 17th century, people were engaged in the lace-making

PERJINKS GIFT GALLERY

77 High Street, Honiton, Devon EX14 1PG
Tel: 01404 43926
e-mail: perjinks@btconnect.com

Located on the High Street of the charming small town of Honiton, **Perjinks Gift Gallery** is indeed a gift of a place for anyone looking for an inspired present. With its striking bold yellow and black awning outside and its light and spacious interior, this is an eye-catching place both inside and out. The shop's displays are brimming with lovely and unusual items - gifts galore for one and all!

There's local pottery by Colin Kellam and Colin Horne, Irish pottery from Paul Maloney and Kiltrea, Scottish pottery by Highland Stoneware, along with other pottery giftware. For glassware, check out the spectacular pieces from the Jonathan Harris Studio, Heritage Crystal Irish cut glass, as well as a wealth of other glass giftware. Particularly striking items are the French candles created in the most unique shapes. Also in stock are wrought iron wine racks and other giftware, candlesticks, gorgeous blankets and throws, luxurious scarves and serapes! You'll also find an interesting range of picture frames and much, much more. Most products on sale are hand-crafted or hand finished - hence their individuality.

Oh, and if you're wondering about the name, Perjinks is Old Scottish for trim, neat, and in a manner minutely attentive to detail!

🏚 historic building   🏛 museum and heritage   🏛 historic site   🍃 scenic attraction   🌿 flora and fauna

YARROW ANTIQUES & INTERIORS

155-157 High Street, Honiton,
Devon EX14 1LJ
Tel: 01404 44399
e-mail: info@yarrow155.com
website: www.yarrow155.com

Yarrow Antiques & Interiors occupies two handsome late-Georgian town houses on Honiton's main street. The 12 main showrooms on two floors are individually decorated in a number of styles and many of the rooms are decorated with *trompe l'oeil*, hand-painted, and block-printed walls. To the rear of the showrooms is an extensive garden with numerous courtyards, terraces, pergolas, follies and a summerhouse.

Both the garden and showrooms are full of unique and one-off items of furniture, statuary and objects of virtue, collected and commissioned by owners James Yarrow and Sarah Wolfe. At 45, James has already spent more than 25 years travelling and buying in Asia and the Orient; Sarah is an accomplished artist, with an acute sense of colour.

Yarrow Antiques is open six days a week and has its our own private parking at the rear of the shop which is accessible from the main Lace Walk car park - head for the tourist information bureau, then drive in to the yard just to the left of the T I B. Walk down the garden to the shop.

industry, most of them working from their own homes making fine "bone" lace by hand. Children as young as five were sent to "lace schools" where they received a rudimentary education in the three Rs of Reading, (W)Riting, and (A)Rithmetic, and a far more intensive instruction in the skills of lace-making. Almost wiped out by the arrival of machine-made lace in the late 1700s, the industry was given a new lease of life when Queen Victoria insisted upon Honiton lace for her wedding dress and created a new fashion for lace that persisted throughout the 19th century. The traditional material is still made on a small scale in the town and can be found on sale in local shops, and on display in **Allhallows Museum.** This part-15th century building served as a school for some 300 years

but is now an interesting local museum housing a unique collection of traditional lace and also, during the season, giving daily demonstrations of lace making.

Allhallows Schoolroom was one of the few old buildings to survive a series of devastating fires in the mid-1700s. However, that wholesale destruction had the fortunate result that the new buildings were gracious Georgian residences and Honiton still retains the pleasant, unhurried atmosphere of a prosperous 18th century coaching town.

Another building which escaped the flames unscathed was Marwood House (private) in the High Street. It was built in 1619 by the second son of Thomas Marwood, one of Queen Elizabeth's many physicians. Thomas achieved great celebrity when he managed to

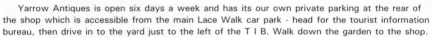

stories and anecdotes   famous people   art and craft   entertainment and sport   walks

cure the Earl of Essex after all others had failed. (He received his Devonshire estate as a reward). Thomas was equally successful in preserving his own health, living to the extraordinary age of 105.

Honiton boasts the only public art gallery in East Devon. The **Thelma Hulbert Gallery** occupies Elmfield House, an attractive Grade II listed late Georgian/early-Victorian town house which was the home and studio of the artist Thelma Hulbert (1913-1995). Now owned by East Devon District Council, the gallery has strong links with the Hayward Gallery in London which enables it to exhibit works by artists such as David Hockney, Andy Warhol and Roy Lichenstein.

Some buildings on the outskirts of the town are worth a mention. **St Margaret's**

Hospital, to the west, was founded in the middle ages as a refuge for lepers who were denied entry to the town itself. Later, in the 16th century, this attractive thatched building was reconstructed as an almshouse. To the east, an early 19th century toll house known as **Copper Castle** can be seen. The castellated building still retains its original iron toll gates. And just a little further east, on Honiton Hill, stands the massive folly of the **Bishop's Tower**, erected in 1842 and once part of Bishop Edward Copplestone's house.

On the northern edge of Honiton rises the National Trust-owned **Dumpdon Hill**, an 850ft high steep-sided outcrop which is crowned by a sizeable late-Iron Age fort. Both the walk to the summit and the views over the Otter Valley are breathtaking.

CHAMPERS

7 New Street, Honiton, Devon EX14 1HA
Tel: 01404 42589
e-mail: champersdeli@yahoo.co.uk

More than just a delicatessen, **Champers** is an old-fashioned traditional shop specialising in West Country products. The cheese counter boasts one of the largest selections of West Country cheeses to be found in the area. The Deli counter has a range of local meats including Cornish salamis, Devonshire smoked meats and, of course, Champers own traditional ham on the bone which has been cooked on the premises in the same way for well over 30 years.

The beauty of Champers is that all of the delicatessen produce can be enjoyed in the relaxing licensed café which has seating inside throughout the year and outside from April to October. Customers can enjoy everything from traditional café fare such as bacon sandwiches, to more specialist dishes such as Spanish platters and Greek salads. And why not enjoy a glass of wine, or a bottle of local beer or cider with your lunch as the café is now fully licensed.

🏛 historic building   🏛 museum and heritage   🏛 historic site   ⚘ scenic attraction   🌿 flora and fauna

Around Honiton

DUNKESWELL
5 miles N of Honiton off the A30

🏚 Dunkeswell Abbey

🏛 Dunkeswell Memorial Museum

A pleasant country lane leads past **Dunkeswell Abbey**, of which only the 15th century gatehouse survives, the rest of the site now occupied by a Victorian church of no great charm. A couple of miles further and the road climbs up the hillside to Dunkeswell itself. This little village lies in the heart of the Blackdown Plateau and its main claim to fame is a 900-year-old Norman font in St Nicholas' Church on which is carved a rather crude depiction of an elephant, the earliest known representation of this animal in England. Almost certainly the stonemason had never seen such a beast, but he made almost as good a fist of it as he did with his satirical carvings of a bishop and a doctor. The font was originally located in Dunkeswell Abbey.

To the west of the village, **Dunkeswell Memorial Museum** stands on the site of the only American Navy air base commissioned on British soil during World War II. It is dedicated to the veterans of the US Fleet Air Wing 7 and RAF personnel who served at the base.

DALWOOD
6 miles E of Honiton off the A35

🏚 Loughwood Meeting House   🏚 Shute Barton

🏚 St Michael's Church   🌿 Burrow Farm Gardens

By some administrative freak, until 1842 the little village of Dalwood, despite being completely surrounded by Devon, was actually part of Dorset. Its other main claim to fame is as the home of the **Loughwood Meeting House,** one of the earliest surviving Baptist chapels in the country. When the chapel was built in the 1650s, the site was hidden by dense woodland, for the Baptists were a persecuted sect who could only congregate in out of the way locations. Under its quaint thatched roof, this charming little building contains a simple whitewashed interior with early 18th century pulpits and pews. The chapel was in use until 1833, then languished for many years until it was acquired by the National Trust in 1969. It is now open all year round with admission by voluntary donation.

About three miles south of Dalwood is another National Trust property, **Shute Barton**, an exceptional example of a medieval manor house which dates from the 1380s. Only two wings of the original building have survived, but they include some remarkably impressive features such as the Great Hall with its massive beamed ceiling, and the ancient kitchen with a huge range capable of roasting an ox whole. Entry is by way of a Tudor gatehouse. Shute

Shute Barton, nr Dalwood

🎭 stories and anecdotes   🦜 famous people   🎨 art and craft   🎭 entertainment and sport   🚶 walks

Barton was owned by the Pole family, a local dynasty which is commemorated by some grand monuments in **St Michael's Church.** Amongst them is an overbearing memorial to Sir William Pole which depicts the Master of the Household to Queen Anne standing on a pedestal dressed in full regalia. More appealing is the 19th century sculptured panel, seven feet high and framed in alabaster, which shows Margaret Pole greeting her three little daughters at the gates of heaven.

Close by are **Burrow Farm Gardens**, beautifully landscaped gardens that provide a peaceful place for a relaxing afternoon's outing as well as plenty of interest for keen gardeners.

AXMINSTER
10 miles E of Honiton on the A35/A358

🎞 Thomas Whitty 🏛 Axminster Museum

This little town grew up around the junction of two important Roman roads, the Fosse and the Icknield, and was important in medieval times because of its Minster beside the River Axe. Its name has entered the language as the synonym for a very superior kind of floor-covering which first appeared in the early 1750s. Wandering around London's Cheapside market, an Axminster weaver named **Thomas Whitty** was astonished to see a huge Turkish carpet, 12 yards long and 8 yards wide. Returning to the sleepy little market town where he was born, Thomas spent months puzzling over the mechanics of producing such a seamless piece of work. By 1755 he had solved the problem, and on midsummer's day that year the first of these luxurious carpets was revealed to the world. The time and labour involved was so prodigious that the completion of each carpet was celebrated by a procession to St Mary's Church and a ringing peal of bells. Ironically, one distinguished purchaser of an Axminster carpet was the

---

SPOTTY CHICKEN

3 Miltons Yard, West Street,
Axminster, Devon EX13 5FE
Tel: 01297 34209
website: www.spottychicken.co.uk

You'll understand why owners Julie Hall and Hannah West named their colourful gift shop **Spotty Chicken** when you step inside their inviting shop. You'll see quite a lot of spotty chickens in various forms amidst the huge choice of gift items on display. Many of the pieces have been made in the West Country and include some very inventive and desirable objects. There's china by Gabriella Miller, an enticing range of contemporary jewellery including pieces made in the west country, Fair Trade bags, handmade Rocky point bags, Jelly Cat soft toys and greeting cards. As well as an extensive selection of stylish accessories, the Spotty Chicken also stocks a wide range of bath and body products that are organic, Fair Trade and vegan approved. Whether you are looking for something unusual for a family member or friend, or something for yourself, you can be sure of finding something that more than satisfies your needs in this fascinating and friendly emporium. The Spotty Chicken is open from 10am to 5pm, Monday to Friday; and from 10am to 4.30pm on Saturday.

🏛 historic building   🏛 museum and heritage   🏚 historic site   🏞 scenic attraction   🌿 flora and fauna

Sultan of Turkey who in 1800 paid the colossal sum of £1,000 for a particularly fine specimen. But the inordinately high labour costs involved in producing such exquisite hand-tufted carpets crippled Whitty's company. In 1835, their looms were sold to a factory at Wilton. That was the end of Axminster's pre-eminence in the market for top-quality carpets, but echoes of those glorious years still reverberate. **St Mary's Church** must be the only house of worship in Christendom whose floor is covered with a richly-woven carpet.

Opposite the church is the former courthouse which is now home to the **Axminster Museum** where the old police cells can be visited and there are collections of vintage agricultural tools and Axminster carpets.

COLYTON
7 miles SE of Honiton off the A3052

🏛 Church of St Andrew

The tramway that starts at Seaton runs by way of Colyford to this ancient and very appealing small town of narrow winding streets and interesting stone houses. Throughout its long history, Colyton has been an important agricultural and commercial centre with its own corn mill, tannery, sawmill and iron foundry.

Many of the older buildings are grouped around the part-Norman **Church of St Andrew,** a striking building with an unusual 15th century octagonal lantern tower, and a Saxon cross brilliantly reconstructed after its broken fragments were retrieved from the tower where they had been used as building material. Nearby is the Vicarage of 1529, and the Old Church House, a part-medieval building enlarged in 1612 and used as a Grammar School until 1928.

OTTERY ST MARY
7m SW of Honiton on the B3177

🏛 Church of St Mary   🕊 Samuel Taylor Coleridge

🏛 Cadhay   🌿 Escot Park

The glory of Ottery St Mary is its magnificent 14th century **Church of St Mary.** From the outside, St Mary's looks part mini-Cathedral, part Oxford college. Both impressions are justified since, when Bishop Grandisson commissioned the building in 1337, he stipulated that it should be modelled on his own cathedral at Exeter. He also wanted it to be "a sanctuary for piety and learning", so accommodation for 40 scholars was provided.

The interior is just as striking. The church's

🎭 stories and anecdotes   🌰 famous people   🎨 art and craft   🎟 entertainment and sport   🚶 walks medieval treasures include a brilliantly-coloured altar screen, canopied tombs, and a 14th century astronomical clock showing the moon and the planets which still functions with its original machinery.

Cadhay Manor, nr Ottery St Mary

Ottery's Vicar during the mid-18th century was the Rev. John Coleridge whose 13th child became the celebrated poet, **Samuel Taylor Coleridge.** The family home near the church has since been demolished but in one of his poems Samuel recalls

> *"my sweet birth-place, and the old church-tower*
> *Whose bells, the poor man's only music, rang*
> *From morn to evening, all the hot Fair-day"*

A bronze plaque in the churchyard wall honours Ottery's most famous son. It shows his profile, menaced by the albatross that features in his best-known poem, *The Ancient Mariner.*

It's a delight to wander around the narrow, twisting lanes that lead up from the River Otter, admiring the fine Georgian buildings amongst which is an old wool manufactory by the riverside, a dignified example of early industrial architecture.

An especially interesting time to visit Ottery is on the Saturday closest to November 5th. The town's Guy Fawkes celebrations include a time-honoured, if rather alarming, tradition of rolling barrels of flaming tar through the narrow streets.

About a mile northwest of Ottery, **Cadhay** is a beautiful Tudor mansion built around

1550 but incorporating the Great Hall of an earlier mansion built between 1420 and 1470. The house was built for a Lincoln's Inn lawyer, John Haydon, whose great-nephew Robert Haydon later added the exquisite Long Gallery thus forming a unique and attractive courtyard. Opening times are restricted.

Close by is **Escot Park and Gardens** where visitors can see an arboretum and rose garden along with a collection of wildlife that includes wild boar, pot-bellied pigs, otters and birds of prey. The original gardens in this 1,200-acre estate were set out by Capability Brown and have been restored by the land artist and television gardener, Ivan Hicks.

BLACKBOROUGH
10 miles NW of Honiton off the A373

Most of the villages in this corner of East Devon nestle in the valley bottoms, but Blackborough is an exception, standing high on a ridge of the Blackdown Hills. It's a comparatively new settlement which sprang up when whetstone mining flourished here for a period in the early 1800s. RD Blackmore's novel *Perlycross* presents a vivid picture of life in these makeshift mining camps where the amenities of a comfortable life were few and far between.

UFFCULME

13 miles NW of Honiton off the A38

🏭 Coldharbour Mill

In medieval times, the charming little village of Uffculme, set beside the River Culm, was an important centre for the wool trade. Profits from this booming business helped build the impressive parish church of St Mary around 1450 and to install its splendid rood screen, believed to be the longest in Devon.

Coldharbour Mill, to the west of the village, is one of the few surviving reminders of the county's industrial wool trade. It closed down in 1981 but has since been converted into a

---

THE KINGS HEAD

High Street, Cullompton, Devon EX15 1AF
Tel: 01884 32418
e-mail: info@kings-head-cullompton.co.uk
website: www.kings-head-cullompton.co.uk

Conveniently located close to junction 27 of the M5, **The Kings Head** is a fine old English hostelry serving excellent food and a wide choice of beverages that includes up to nine real ales. The inn opens at 10am each day and from 11.30am offers an enticing choice of lunches and light bites. In the afternoon, Cream Teas are served and from 6pm the evening menu is available.

WEIR MILL FARM B&B

Jaycroft, Willand, Cullompton, Devon EX15 2RE
Tel: 01884 820803
e-mail: rita@weirmill-devon.co.uk
website: www.weirmill-devon.co.uk

Located just three miles from junction 27 of the M5, **Weir Mill Farm B&B** is surrounded by 100 acres of farmland and has a large garden with ample parking. Luxurious rooms, beautiful views of the Culm Valley and a peaceful setting make Weir Mill a very special experience.

The farmhouse offers spacious accommodation which consists of an en suite family room (one double and two single beds, or let as a twin), a double en suite and a double room with en-suite bathroom. Each room has colour TV, tea making facilities, electric blanket, hair dryer and heating. Guests have the use at all times of a comfortable lounge with colour TV. Breakfast is served in the dining room any time before 9am.

For other meals, there are three pubs which all serve food within a three mile radius of Weir Mill, one of which is in walking distance. Weir Mill Farm's proximity to the M5 provides easy access to many places of interest, including the Cathedral City of Exeter, and the lovely East Devon seaside resorts which are only half an hour's drive away.

🎭 stories and anecdotes 🦜 famous people 🎨 art and craft 🎭 entertainment and sport 🚶 walks

Working Wool Museum where visitors can watch the whole process of woollen and worsted manufacture, wander around the carpenter's workshop, a weaver's cottage and the dye room. On most Bank Holidays, the massive 300 horsepower engine in the boiler house is "steamed up"- a spectacular sight. Conducted tours are available and the complex also includes a Mill Shop and a waterside restaurant.

CULMSTOCK
14 miles NW of Honiton on the B3391

🐿 RD Blackmore   🏛 Hemyock Castle

Lovers of **RD Blackmore's** novel *Lorna Doone* will be particularly interested in Culmstock since it was here that the author lived as a boy during the years that his father was the Vicar. One of his playmates in the village was Frederick Temple, another bright boy, and the two friends both went on to Blundell's School at Tiverton where they shared lodgings. Blackmore was to become one of the most successful novelists of his time; Temple entered the church and after several years as Headmaster of Rugby School reached the pinnacle of his profession as Archbishop of Canterbury.

In the centre of the village stands Culmstock's parish church with its famous yew tree growing from the top of the tower. The tree has been growing there for more than 200 years and, despite the fact that its only nourishment is the lime content of the mortar in which it is set, the trunk has now achieved a girth of 18 inches. It's believed that the seed was probably carried up in the mortar used to repair the tower when its spire was demolished in 1776. The church's more traditional kind of treasures include a magnificently embroidered cope of the late

1400s, now preserved in a glass case; a remarkable 14th century tomb rediscovered during restoration in the 19th century; and a richly-coloured memorial window designed by Burne-Jones.

About three miles east of Culmstock is **Hemyock Castle**, built around 1380. Four turrets, a curtain wall, a moat with mallard and moorhen in residence, and a dungeon are all that remains of the Hidon family's sturdy manor house, but it is a peaceful and evocative place. The castle stands behind the church in beautiful grounds and, since it lies close to the head of the lovely Culm valley, is very popular as a picnic spot. Opening times are limited.

The Jurassic Coast

🐾 East Devon Way

The coastal stretch to the east of Exmouth has been named the Jurassic Coast because it was formed during the Jurassic period some 185 million years ago. England's first natural World Heritage Site, the 95 miles of coastline from Exmouth to Studland in Dorset is spectacularly beautiful.

Three river valleys, those of the Axe, the Sid and the Otter, cut through the hills of east Devon to meet the sea at Lyme Bay. They provide the only openings in the magnificent 20-mile long stretch of rugged cliffs and rocky beaches. Virtually the only settlements to be found along the seaboard are those which developed around the mouths of those rivers: Seaton, Sidmouth and Budleigh Salterton. The intervening cliffs discouraged human habitation and even today the only way to explore most of this part of the coast is on foot along the magnificent **East Devon Way,** part of the South West Coast Path. Signposted by a foxglove, the footpath travels through the county to Lyme Regis just over the county border in Dorset. Four other circular paths link in with the East Devon Way providing other options for walkers to enjoy and explore the quieter and more remote areas away from the coast.

For centuries the little towns along the coast subsisted on fishing and farming until the early 1800s when the Prince Regent's fad for sea bathing brought an influx of comparatively affluent visitors in search of healthy relaxation. Their numbers were augmented by others whose accustomed European travels had been rendered impossible by Napoleon's domination of the Continent. Between them, they transformed these modest little towns into fashionable resorts, imbuing them with an indefinable "gentility" which still lives on in the elegant villas, peaceful gardens and wide promenades.

Exmouth

🏛 World of Country Life   🏛 A La Ronde

🏛 Exmouth Museum

With its glorious coastal scenery and splendid beach, Exmouth was one of the earliest seaside resorts to be developed in Devon, "the Bath of the West, the resort of the tip-top of the gentry of the Kingdom". Lady Byron and Lady Nelson came to stay and found lodgings in The Beacon, an elegant Georgian terrace overlooking the Madeira Walk and Esplanade. This early success suffered a setback when Brunel routed his Great Western line along the other side of the estuary, (incidentally creating one of the most scenic railway journeys still possible in England), and it wasn't until a branch

line reached Exmouth in 1861 that business picked up again. The town isn't just a popular resort. Exmouth Docks are still busy with coasters and in summer a passenger ferry crosses the Exe to Starcross. There are also services to Dawlish Warren.

Exmouth's major all-weather attraction is **The World of Country Life** which offers an Adventure Exhibition Hall, a collection of vintage cars, a Victorian Street, safari train, pirate ship, pets centre and restaurant.

Occupying converted 18th century stables and an adjoining cottage, **Exmouth Museum** provides fascinating insights into the town's rich history and its strong maritime links.

While in Exmouth, you should make a point of visiting what has been described as "the most unusual house in Britain". **A La Ronde** (National Trust) is a fairy-tale thatched house built in 1765 by the sisters Jane and Mary Parminter who modelled it on the church of San Vitale in Ravenna. Despite its name, the house is not in fact circular but has 16 sides with 20 rooms set around a 45ft high octagon. The sisters lived here in magnificent feminist seclusion, forbidding the presence of any male in their house or its 15 acres of grounds.

A La Ronde, Exmouth

🎭 stories and anecdotes   🦜 famous people   🎨 art and craft   🎵 entertainment and sport   🚶 walks

THE ROWAN TREE

7 Fore Street, Budleigh Salterton, Devon EX9 6NG
Tel: 01395 446066
website: www.rowantreegifts.co.uk

Located in the charming seaside resort of Budleigh Salterton, **The Rowan Tree** is the perfect place to find that extra special gift, something to decorate your home or just to treat yourself! Owner Karen Ritchie specialises in home and garden gifts and accessories. She stocks everything from quality pottery to greetings cards, designer bags to clocks, pictures to jewellery and a lot more besides.

There are clocks from Roger Lascelles of London; Liz Cox handbags; Jersey Pottery; Burleigh china; colourful cushions and fabrics from Linum, and a good selection of art prints, notelets and books. The stock is continually changing as Karen is constantly searching for new and exciting items for her loyal customers. And she always ensures that she keeps up-to-date with the latest seasonal collections from top brands such as Gisela Graham and other leading names.

All purchases can be gift-wrapped in tissue and ribbon; handy for those last minute presents or as an extra helping hand before Christmas. Whether you're shopping for presents, searching for quality decorations and ornaments or simply wanting to treat yourself to a special something, The Rowan Tree will have the solution to your needs – and there's a convenient car park situated directly behind the shop.

SORBUS

32 Fore Street, Budleigh Salterton, Devon EX9 6NH
Tel: 01395 445958

Karen Ritchie gained valuable experience managing large shops in London and Bath before starting out on her own. **Sorbus** is Karens second shop in Budleigh Salterton and is a fantastic showcase for her great passion for contemporary design. Inside, there is a distinctively modern feel to the space. Avant garde lighting company Innermost supplies most of the truly spectacular lamps and chandeliers which immediately catch the eye as you come in. A comprehensive collection of designer homewares from top names such as Alessi, Guzzini and Eva Solo sit alongside modern table and glassware. Also in Sorbus are clever kitchen gadgets and cookware accessories from award winning design company Joseph and Joseph.

There are many more interesting and delightful items available. An ever changing collection of prints and clocks adorn the walls, jewellery from Carrie Elspeth catches the glow from the elaborate lighting, funky trinkets sit atop the contemporary oak furniture and bathroom accessories nestle amongst the soft furnishings.

Sorbus has a fantastic range of products that are forever useful whilst also bringing a sense of fun and imaginative style into your home.

What, therefore, no gentleman saw during the lifetime of the sisters, was the wonderfully decorated interior that the cousins created. These fabulous rooms, common in Regency times, are rare today. Due to their delicacy, the feather frieze and shell-encrusted gallery can be seen only via closed circuit TV. Throughout the house the vast collection of pieces that the ladies brought back from their extensive travels is on display.

East of Exmouth

BUDLEIGH SALTERTON
4 miles E of Exmouth on the B3180

🏛 Fairlynch Museum

With its trim Victorian villas, broad promenade and a spotlessly clean beach flanked by 500ft high red sandstone cliffs, Budleigh Salterton retains its 19th century atmosphere of a genteel resort. Victorian tourists "of the better sort" noted with approval that the two-mile long beach was of pink shingle rather than sand. (Sand, apparently, attracted the rowdier kind of holiday-maker). The steeply-shelving beach was another deterrent, and the sea here is still a place for paddling rather than swimming.

One famous Victorian visitor was the celebrated artist Sir John Everett Millais who stayed during the summer of 1870 in the curiously-shaped house called **The Octagon.** It was beside the beach here that he painted his most famous picture *The Boyhood of Raleigh*, using his two sons and a local ferryman as the models. Raleigh's birthplace, Hayes Barton, lies a mile or so inland and remains virtually unchanged.

Found on the town's seafront is

Fairlynch Museum, one of a very few thatched museums in the country. It houses numerous collections covering all aspects of life through the ages in the lower Otter Valley.

The name Budleigh Salterton derives from the salt pans at the mouth of the River Otter which brought great prosperity to the town during the Middle Ages. The little port was then busy with ships loading salt and wool, but by 1450 the estuary had become blocked by a pebble ridge and the salt pans flooded.

YETTINGTON
7 miles NE of Exmouth off the B3178

🕊 Sir Walter Raleigh   🕊 Bicton Park

Just to the south of the village of Yettington is Hayes Barton (private), a fine E-shaped Tudor house in which **Sir Walter Raleigh** was born in 1552. The Raleighs' family pew can still be seen in All Saints' Church, dated 1537 and carved with their (now sadly defaced) coat of arms. The church also contains a series of more than 50, 16th century bench-ends which were carved by local artisans into weird and imaginative depictions of their various trades.

A mile or so in the other direction is **Bicton Park,** best known for its landscaped gardens which were laid out in the 1730s by Henry Rolle to a plan by André Le Nôtre, the designer of Versailles. There is also a formal

Bicton Park and Gardens, Yettington

🕮 stories and anecdotes   🕊 famous people   ✏ art and craft   ✐ entertainment and sport   🕭 walks

Italian garden, a remarkable palm house known as The Dome, a world-renowned collection of pine trees, and a lake complete with an extraordinary summer house, The Hermitage. Its outside walls are covered with thousands of tiny wooden shingles, each one individually pinned on so they look like the scales of an enormous fish. Inside, the floors are made from deer's knucklebones. The Hermitage was built by Lady Louise Rolle in 1839 as an exotic summer-house; any occupation during the winter would have been highly inadvisable since the chimney was made of oak.

OTTERTON
7 miles NE of Exmouth off the B3178

🏚 Otterton Mill

This delightful village has a charming mix of traditional cob and thatch cottages, along with other buildings constructed in the distinctive local red sandstone, amongst them the tower of St Michael's parish church. Nearby stands a manor house which was built in the 11th century as a small priory belonging to Mont St Michel in Normandy. It is now divided into private apartments.

The Domesday Book recorded a mill on the River Otter here, almost certainly on the site of the present **Otterton Mill**. This handsome, part-medieval building was restored to working order in the 1970s by Desna Greenhow, a teacher of Medieval Archaeology, and visitors can now buy packs of flour ground by the same methods that were in use long before the compilers of the Domesday Book passed through the village. The site also includes a craft centre, shop and restaurant.

An interesting feature of this village of white thatched cottages is the little stream that runs down Fore Street. At the bottom of the

hill, this beck joins the River Otter, which at this point has only a couple of miles to go before it enters the sea near Budleigh Salterton. There's a lovely riverside walk in that direction, and if you go northwards the path stretches even further, to Ottery St Mary some nine or ten miles distant.

HARPFORD
11 miles NE of Exmouth off the A3052

🐦 Revd Augustus Toplady   🌿 Aylesbeare Common

Attractively located on the east bank of the River Otter with wooded hills behind, Harpford has a 13th century church with an impressive tower and, in its churchyard, a memorial cross to the **Revd Augustus Toplady** who was vicar of Harpford for a couple of years in the mid-1700s. In 1775 Augustus wrote the hymn *Rock of Ages, cleft for me*, which has proved to be one of the most durable contributions to English hymnody.

If you cross the footbridge over the river here and follow the path for about a couple of miles you will come to **Aylesbeare Common**, an RSPB sanctuary which is also one of the best stretches of heathland in the area. Bird watchers may be lucky enough to spot a Dartford warbler, stonechats, or tree pipits, and even hear the strange song of the nightjar.

SIDMOUTH
11 miles NE of Exmouth on the A375

🐦 Duke of Kent   🏛 Sidmouth Museum

🏚 Old Chancel   🎐 International Folk Festival

Sidmouth's success, like that of many other English resorts, had much to do with Napoleon Buonaparte. Barred from the Continent and their favoured resorts by the Emperor's conquest of Europe, the leisured classes were forced to find diversion and entertainment within their own island fortress.

🏚 historic building   🏛 museum and heritage   🏚 historic site   🐦 scenic attraction   🌿 flora and fauna

At the same time, sea bathing had suddenly become fashionable so these years were a boom time for the south coast, even as far west as Sidmouth which until then had been a poverty-stricken village dependent on fishing.

Sidmouth's spectacular position at the mouth of the River Sid, flanked by dramatic red cliffs soaring to over 500ft and with a broad pebbly beach, assured the village's popularity with the newcomers. A grand Esplanade was constructed, lined with handsome Georgian houses, and between 1800 and 1820 Sidmouth's population doubled as the aristocratic and well-to-do built substantial "cottages" in and around the town. Many of these have since been converted into impressive hotels such as the Beach House, painted strawberry pink and white, and the Royal Glen which in the early 19th century was the residence of the royal **Duke of Kent**. The duke came here in 1819 in an attempt to escape his numerous creditors, and it was here that his infant daughter, Princess Victoria, later Queen Victoria, saw the sea for the first time.

Attempting to evade his many creditors, the Duke had his mail directed to Salisbury. Each week he would ride there to collect his letters but in Sidmouth itself he couldn't conceal his delight in his young daughter. He would push Victoria in a little carriage along the mile-long Regency Esplanade, stopping passers-by to tell them to look carefully at the little girl – "for one day she would be their Queen". Half a century later, his daughter presented a stained-glass window to Sidmouth parish church in dutiful memory of her father.

One of the town's early visitors was Jane Austen, who came here on holiday in 1801 and, according to Austen family tradition, fell in love with a clergyman whom she would

HAYMAN'S

6 Church Street, Sidmouth, Devon EX10 8CT
Tel: 01395 512877   Fax: 01395 579489
e-mail: stewart.hayman@haymansbutchers.co.uk
website: www.haymansbutchers.co.uk

In 2007, **Hayman's** celebrated one hundred years of providing top quality meat to the good people of Sidmouth and the surrounding area. Stewart and Shirley Hayman run a very modern and progressive butchery business with a growing range of products that Stewart reckons his grandmother, Lilian Irene Hayman would have been proud of. Lilian Irene was the driving force behind much of the business in its earlier days. Her recipe for pork brawn is still in use, unchanged, today. In 2003 it won the Q Guild's Supreme Award - the ultimate accolade and later, as a result, the shop featured on BBC "Rick Stein's Food Heroes".

The Haymans try to source all of their meat locally. Most of the beef comes from Houghton Farm which is owned by Mervyn Hayman. The cattle are slaughtered by his brother, Philip Hayman, in nearby Ottery St Mary and hung for a minimum of fourteen days.

Over the years, Hayman's has diversified by producing a wide range of pasties, pies, cooked meats and ready meals, many of which have been awarded national prizes. In 1996 a bakery section was opened and now Hayman's has become as well known for its pies and pasties as it is for its sausages and brawn!

📖 stories and anecdotes   🍽 famous people   🎨 art and craft   🎭 entertainment and sport   🚶 walks

have married if he had not mysteriously died or disappeared. Later, in the 1830s, William Makepeace Thackeray visited and the town featured as Baymouth in his semi-autobiographical work *Pendennis* (published in 1848). During the Edwardian age, Beatrix Potter was a visitor on several occasions.

A stroll around the town reveals a wealth of attractive Georgian and early-Victorian buildings. Amazingly for such a small town, Sidmouth boasts nearly 500 listed buildings. Curiously, it was the Victorians who let the town down. Despite being the wealthiest nation in the world at that time, with vast resources at its command, its architects seemed incapable of creating architecturally interesting churches and the two 19th century Houses of the Lord they built in Sidmouth display a lamentable lack of inspiration. So ignore them, but it's worth seeking out the curious structure known as the

Old Chancel, a glorious hotch-potch of styles using bits and pieces salvaged from the old parish church and from just about anywhere else, amongst them a priceless window of medieval stained glass.

Also well worth a visit is **Sidmouth Museum**, near the sea-front, which provides a vivid presentation of the Victorian resort, along with such curiosities as an albatross's swollen foot once used as a tobacco pouch. There's also an interesting collection of local prints, a costume gallery and a display of fine lace. One of the most striking exhibits in the museum is the "Long Picture" by Hubert Cornish which is some eight feet (2.4 metres) long and depicts the whole of Sidmouth seafront as it was around 1814.

The town also boasts one of the few public access observatories in Britain: the **Norman Lockyer Observatory**. It has a planetarium

---

SIDMOUTH TRAWLERS

Fisherman's Yard, The Ham, Port Royal, Sidmouth, Devon EX10 8BG
Tel: 01395 512714

Tucked away in Fisherman's Yard at the far eastern end of the Esplanade is **Sidmouth Trawlers**, a fishmonger well known in the area for the excellent quality of its locally caught fish and shellfish. Established in the 1960s by Stan Bagwell, from a long line of fishermen, this family-run business maintains the highest standards in endeavouring to provide for all lovers of seafood a large variety of fish and shellfish sourced from local fishermen.

The family take great pride in the various national craftsmanship awards they have won over the years, and filleting and preparation is all part of the service. No one coming to Sidmouth should miss the opportunity to visit this superb fishmonger's. Insulated packaging is available to take home a selection of the freshest seafood - from brill, Dover sole, mackerel and scallops to freshly cooked lobster and crab - to be found anywhere in the country. A ready-to-eat service is also available for whelks, cockles, mussels, prawns and crabmeat, and generously filled sandwiches are made to order.

🏛 historic building   🏚 museum and heritage   🏛 historic site   ⌘ scenic attraction   🌱 flora and fauna

TRUMPS WEST COUNTRY CAFÉ

8 Fore Street, Sidmouth, Devon EX10 8AQ
Tel: 01395 512446
website: www.trumpsofsidmouth.co.uk

As in the rest of the UK, retailers and independent traders in Devon are suffering from the multiple national giants squeezing the traditional high street retailers out of business by harsh competition. Sidmouth is fortunate in having one of the most famous establishments in the county, **Trumps West Country Café**, which has been a fixture on the town's main shopping street since 1813.

It is not just a fine café but also a quality delicatessen selling a wide range of local meats, cheeses, fresh bread from Otterton Mill, and West Country beers and ciders. The extensive choice is displayed on grand Victorian mahogany shelving.

In the café, Trumps offers customers the finest local traditionally prepared foods of the highest quality. There's a choice of fresh home-made scones each day, pâtés from Budleigh Salterton, delicious home-made cakes and much more. And if you are planning a picnic on the nearby beach, why not choose from the wide range of quiches and pies or a freshly made sandwich. Trumps is open from 9am to 5pm, Monday to Saturday; and from 11am to 4.30pm on Sundays.

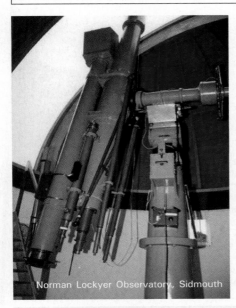

Norman Lockyer Observatory, Sidmouth

and large telescopes, and a radio station commemorating the contribution of Sir Ambrose Fleming, a local hero, to the invention of the radio valve.

Demure though it remains, Sidmouth undergoes a transformation in the first week of August each year when it plays host to the **International Folklore, Dance and Song Festival**, a cosmopolitan event which attracts a remarkable variety of morris dancers, folk singers and even clog dancers from around the world.

SIDBURY

12 miles NE of Exmouth on the A375

🏰 Sidbury Castle

St Peter & St Giles' church at Sidbury boasts the unique amenity of a Powder Room. In fact, the room over the porch

🎞 stories and anecdotes 🍴 famous people 🎨 art and craft 🎭 entertainment and sport 🚶 walks

THE BLUE BALL AT SIDFORD

Stevens Cross, Sidford,
Devon EX10 9QL
Tel: 01395 514062
e-mail: rogernewton@blueballinn.net
website: www.blueballinn.co.uk

Located in the picturesque village of Sidford, **The Blue Ball at Sidford** has a history dating back to 1385. It looks very inviting with its thatched roof over cob and flint walls, and the interior has the atmosphere of a bygone age. Remarkably, the original inn was destroyed in March 2006 but has been faithfully rebuilt with tender care and re-opened in September 2007.

The inn has been run by the Newton family for five generations since 1912 and although alterations to the dining room, kitchen and bedrooms have been undertaken over the years, it still retains its old world charm with features such as the large open fires. There's a central bar that serves the three main seated areas and in good weather, customers can take their drinks into the attractive and spacious garden. The Blue Ball is noted for its good food and offers an extensive selection of traditional meals with a speciality of the house being its locally caught fish dishes.

The inn also offers good, competitively priced accommodation, with all of the rooms en suite and one of them accessible for disabled guests. Another major amenity is the function room which can seat up to 70 people and has its own bar, skittle alley and a drop-down projector.

THE BULSTONE HOTEL

Higher Bulstone, Branscombe,
Devon EX12 3BL
Tel: 01297 680446 Fax: 01297 680000
e-mail: bulstone@aol.com
website: www.childfriendlyhotels.com

Located close to the dramatic East Devon Jurassic Coast, **The Bulstone Hotel** dates back to 1620 and stands in just over three acres of its own grounds, surrounded by fields. There are glorious beaches close by and many local attractions offering exciting days out for children and grown-ups alike. Good food is a priority at the Bulstone. The menu changes daily and uses fresh local produce wherever possible. There is always a vegetarian option and specials diets can be catered for. To accompany your meal, the licensed bar is stocked with a range of fine wines, spirits and local cider.

A family-friendly hotel, the Bulstone has seven family suites, each comprising two bedrooms and a bathroom. All bedrooms are furnished and decorated to a very high standard. A guest kitchen is available and the hotel offers a laundry service at a small charge. Guests also have the use of a sitting room which is in the original building and has low beams, thick walls, and built-in window seats.

Branscombe itself is a magical village largely owned by the National Trust where dramatic cliffs tower over one of the best beaches in Devon.

🏛 historic building 🏛 museum and heritage 🏚 historic site ♨ scenic attraction 🌿 flora and fauna

contained not cosmetics, but gunpowder which was stored there by the military during the fearful days when Napoleon was expected to land in England at any moment. The church is also notable for its Saxon crypt, rediscovered during restoration in 1898. It's a rough-walled room just nine feet by 10 located under the chancel floor. Other treasures include a remarkable 500-year-old font with a square iron lock intended to protect the holy water in the basin from witches, and a number of curious carvings on the Norman tower.

Above the village to the southwest stands **Sidbury Castle**, not a castle at all but the site of a hilltop Iron Age fort from which there are some spellbinding views of the coastline extending from Portland Bill to Berry Head.

BRANSCOMBE
14 miles NE of Exmouth off the A3052

🏭 Branscombe Manor Mill 🎬 MSC Napoli

The coastal scenery near Branscombe is some of the finest in the south west with great towers of chalk rising from overgrown landslips. The village itself is a picturesque scattering of farmhouses and thatched cottages with an interesting National Trust property within its boundaries – **Branscombe Manor Mill, Old Bakery and Forge.** Regular demonstrations are held at the Manor Mill which is still in working order. The water-powered mill provided flour for the adjacent bakery which, until 1987, was the last traditional bakery operating in Devon. Its vintage baking equipment has been preserved and the rest of the building is now a tearoom. The Forge is still working and the blacksmith's ironwork is on sale to visitors.

The land around Branscombe's beach with its long expanse of pebbles and painted coastal huts, is also owned by the National

Trust. The beach entered the national consciousness in January 2007 when a container ship, the *MSC Napoli* got into difficulties during a gale and was grounded about 100 yards from the beach. Some of the ship's containers broke open and their contents were washed on to the beach. The flotsam included barrels of wine, shoes, hair care products, beauty cream, steering wheels, exhaust pipes, gearboxes, nappies, foreign language bibles and even BMW motorbikes. As the word spread, the beach was invaded by scavengers, many of whom made away with rich pickings until the police closed the beach 24 hours after the *Napoli* had grounded. It was not until seven months later that the stricken ship was taken by tug to a dry dock at the Harland and Wolff shipyard in Belfast.

BEER
16 miles NE of Exmouth on the B3174

🎭 Pecorama 🏛 Beer Quarry Caves

Set between the high white chalk cliffs of Beer Head and Seaton Hole, this picturesque fishing village is best known for the superb white freestone which has been quarried here since Roman times. Much prized for carving, the results can be seen in countless Devon churches, and most notably in the cathedrals at Exeter, Winchester, and St Paul's, as well as at the Tower of London and in Westminster Abbey. Conducted tours around the vast, man-made complex of the **Beer Quarry Caves** leave visitors astonished at the sheer grandeur of the lofty halls, vaulted roofs and massive supporting pillars of natural stone. Not surprisingly, this complex underground network recommended itself to smugglers, amongst them the notorious Jack Rattenbury who was a native of Beer and published his *Memoirs of a Smuggler* in 1837.

MARINE HOUSE AT BEER

Fore Street, Beer, nr Seaton, Devon EX12 3EF
Tel: 01297 625257
e-mail: info@marinehouseatbeer.co.uk
website: www.marinehouseatbeer.co.uk

The centre for arts and crafts in Devon, **Marine House at Beer** opened in 1998, followed by the Steam Gallery four years later. In that time, Beer has become the centre on the Devon and Dorset coasts between Bournemouth and Dartmouth for paintings, sculpture, pottery, studio glass, hand-made jewellery and limited edition prints.

The galleries are informal and friendly, and are open seven days a week in summer and six days a week in winter. They are always open on Saturday and Sunday. Over the years, the galleries have carefully built up strong relationships with leading British artists and craftspeople. With work by more than 100 people to choose from, many of whom live and work in the Southwest, there is a wide choice with prices ranging from a few pounds to pictures commanding five-figure sums.

Some of the most notable artists include Michael Morgan RI. His carefully drafted landscapes and original technique has truly revitalised the watercolour medium. Beer-based Andrew Coates has built a world-wide following with his fine portrayal of local river and sea scenes, often with translucent water and dramatic skies. And Amanda Popham has risen to celebrity status with her magnificently inventive sculptural pottery.

SILK STOCKING

14 Fore Street, Seaton, Devon EX12 2CA
Tel: 01297 24440
e-mail:shirley@bras4u.net   website: www.bras4u.net

Based in the pretty seaside town of Seaton, just a stone's throw from the beach, **Silk Stocking** offers a wide selection of lingerie "for the pretty petite to the beautiful larger lady". Owner Shirley Bailey, who has many years experience in the retail trade, has gathered together a huge choice of garments from a host of leading lingerie designers. You'll find exquisite creations from Aubade Lingerie; Lepel of Italy; Change from Scandinavia; Charnos; Ballet; Triumph; Fantasie; Sloggi; Berlei; Rigby & Peller; Naturana; Playtex; Silhouette; Faveo; Gossard and more. Silk Stocking also stocks an extensive selection of swimwear, including swim hats and shower caps. Stockings, glamourous nightwear, saucy underwear, sport and maternity wear, and mastectomy bras are all available. Shirley and her friendly and helpful team also offer a fitting and made to

measure service. And if you can't get to visit her spacious shop, you can find full details of the numerous items available and see photographs of them being modelled, just log on to Silk Stocking's website.

A family attraction here is **Pecorama** which sits on the cliff tot high above the village and has an award-winning miniature railway, spectacular Millennium Gardens, the Peco Model Railway Exhibition, play areas and superb sea views.

SEATON
17 miles NE of Exmouth on the B3172

🦢 Seaton Tramway   🚶 South West Coast Path

Set around the mouth of the River Axe, with red cliffs on one side and white cliffs on the other, Seaton was once a quite significant port. By the 16th century, however, the estuary had filled up with stones and pebbles, and it wasn't until moneyed Victorians came and built their villas (and one of the first concrete bridges in the world, in 1877) that Seaton was accorded a new lease of life. The self-confident architecture of those times gives the little town an attractive appearance which is enhanced by its pedestrianised town centre and well-maintained public parks and gardens.

From Seaton, an attractive way of travelling along the Axe Valley is on the **Seaton Tramway,** whose colourful open-topped tramcars trundle through an area famous for its bird life to the villages of Colyford and Colyton. The three-mile route follows the course of the River Axe which is noted for its abundant wild bird life. Really dedicated tram fans, after a short lesson, are even permitted to take over the driver's seat.

From Seaton, eastwards, the **South West Coast Path** follows the coastline uninterruptedly all the way to Lyme Regis in Dorset. Considered by naturalists as the last and largest wilderness on the southern coast of England, this area of unstable cliffs, wood and scrub is also a haven for wildlife.

DANIEL-ALEXANDER INTERIORS

37 Queen Street, Seaton, Devon EX12 2NY
Tel: 01297 22115
e-mail: info@daniel-alexander.co.uk
website: www.daniel-alexander.co.uk

Based in the coastal town of Seaton, Devon, **Daniel-Alexander Interiors** aim to offer its customers a truly unique and pleasurable experience when visiting their boutique shop which showcases a carefully selected range of luxury homewares and giftwares, as well as a full interior design service run in-house. These services include home-makeovers, colour consultations, special paint effects, murals, trompe l'oeil, gilding, marbling, commissioned artworks and hand painted furniture. With their knowledge of style and creative flair for colour coordination, they draw on more than a decade of experience working with high profile clients, both in the UK and abroad, to find the perfect design solutions, tailor made to suit the most discerning of tastes. Large or small projects are always treated with the same integrity and dedication, leading to high quality results every time. If you are looking for something that you can't find, they will strive to source anything unique or individual as quickly as they can. If you're searching for a gift, interested in talking to them about any of the services they offer, or looking for that special something for your home or business, they look forward to welcoming you to their shop.

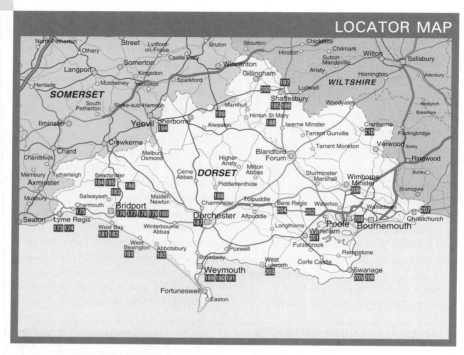

LOCATOR MAP

ADVERTISERS AND PLACES OF INTEREST

🏛 historic building   🏛 museum and heritage   🏛 historic site   ❧ scenic attraction   ❦ flora and fauna

3| Dorset

"Dorset has no high mountains and no coal. Everything else of beauty and almost everything of utility can be found within its borders." This was Ralph Wightman's description of one of England's most enchanting counties. Twenty-five miles of the county's spectacular coastline has been awarded World Heritage Site status by UNESCO for its outstanding geology, an accolade that ranks it alongside the Grand Canyon and the Great Barrier Reef. The glorious coastal scenery includes beautiful Lulworth Cove, the strange natural formations of Durdle Door and the 10-mile long stretch of pebbles known as Chesil Beach. South of Weymouth, the Isle of Purbeck – famous for the marble which has been quarried here since Roman times – falls like a tear-drop into the English Channel. To the west is the charming resort town of Lyme

Neville Ford, Fifehead

Regis, famous for its curved harbour wall, The Cobb, its associations with Jane Austen and for the remarkable fossils discovered in what is now known as the Jurassic Coast.

🎭 stories and anecdotes   🦜 famous people   🎨 art and craft   🎪 entertainment and sport   🚶 walks

Inland, gently rolling hills, woodlands and gentle river valleys epitomise the charms of unspoilt rural England. Delightful old market towns like Shaftesbury, Bridport, Blandford Forum and Sherborne have a settled graciousness, while villages such as Milton Abbas, Cranborne and Breamore are almost impossibly picturesque.

The county has more than its fair share of historic castles. Corfe Castle, set high on a hill, is one of the most impressive man-made sights in the southwest; Sherborne Castle was the home of Sir Walter Raleigh and Portland Castle is the best-preserved of Henry VIII's coastal fortresses. Stately homes range from the Tudor gem of Athelhampton House, through the splendour of Kingston Lacy House with its outstanding collection of Old Masters, to Parnham House near Beaminster, a restored Tudor manor house which is now a powerhouse of contemporary craftsmanship. Then there are the magnificent abbeys of Wimborne Minster, Forde and Sherborne, and the fine church at Bere Regis, famed for its superbly carved and painted roof, and the priory at Christchurch with its imposing Norman exterior and wealth of tombs and chantries.

Coast at Kimmeridge

Dorchester, one of England's most appealing county towns, stands at the heart of 'Hardy Country' – most of the scenes in Thomas Hardy's novels are set within a dozen or so miles of the town. Hardy was born in the nearby village of Higher Bockhampton; the humble house where he grew up is open to the public. He spent the last four decades of his life in Dorchester at Max Gate, a modest villa he designed himself which is now a National Trust property. Many of Dorset's most striking features – the Cerne Abbas hill carving of a naked giant, for example – feature in Hardy's novels, either as themselves or lightly disguised.

Lyme Regis

- The Cobb ⚓ Golden Cap
- South West Coast Path 🌱 Jane Austen Garden
- Lyme Regis Museum 🏛 Dinosaurland
- Town Mill 🖌 Regatta & Carnival

Known as "The Pearl of Dorset", Lyme Regis is a captivating little town enjoying a setting unrivalled in the county, an Area of Outstanding Natural Beauty where the rolling countryside of Dorset plunges to the sea. The town itself is a maze of narrow streets with many charming Georgian and Regency houses, and the picturesque harbour will be familiar to anyone who has seen the film *The*

French Lieutenant's Woman, based on the novel by Lyme resident, John Fowles. The scene of a lone woman standing on the wave-lashed Cobb has become one of cinema's most enduring images.

The Cobb, which protects the harbour and the sandy beach with its clear bathing water from south-westerly storms, was first recorded in 1294 but the town itself goes back at least another 500 years to Saxon times when there was a salt works here. A charter granted by Edward I allowed Lyme to add 'Regis' to its name but during the Civil War the town was staunchly anti-royalist, routing the forces of Prince Maurice and killing more than 2,000 of them. Some 40 years later, James, Duke of Monmouth, chose Lyme as his landing place to start the ill-fated rebellion that would end with ferocious reprisals being meted out to the insurgents by the notorious Judge Jeffreys. Happier days arrived in the 18th century when Lyme became a fashionable resort, famed for its fresh, clean air. Jane Austen and her family visited

The Cobb, Lyme Regis

POP GOES THE WEASEL

32a Broad Street, Lyme Regis, Dorset DT7 3QE
Tel: 01297 443393
website: www.hpgtw.co.uk

Alison Tutcher is an accomplished milliner with some 20 years experience in the business. She came to Lyme Regis in 1990 and opened her colourful shop, **Pop Goes The Weasel**, in 1992. To begin with, the shop also doubled as her workshop where she created and sold hats for special occasions. Over the years, Alison has added a sumptuous range of eye-catching hats for every occasion and in all sizes, along with bags, gloves & scarves and other stylish and practical accessories. Alison has recently expanded and opened another shop in Honiton in Devon.

📖 stories and anecdotes 🦜 famous people 🎨 art and craft 🎭 entertainment and sport 🚶 walks

THE LYME REGIS FOSSIL SHOP

4 Bridge Street, Lyme Regis, Dorset DT7 3QA
Tel: 01299 442088
e-mail: info@fossil-shop.co.uk
website: www.lymeregis.com/lymefossilshop

Established more than 30 years ago, **The Lyme Regis Fossil Shop** stocks a huge variety of local fossils – probably the largest selection in Britain. Their professional palaeontologist visitors frequently tell them that is the best fossil shop in the UK. The Titchener family are constantly travelling the world to find the best specimen fossils or minerals.

So you'll find a wide choice of amber and copal from the Baltic, Dominican Republic, Columbia and Madagascar, many of them with inclusions of insects. There's also a huge variety of fish plates with specimens originating in America, France, Germany, China, Lebanon and Brazil.

The shop is also well known for its vast range of local fossils with prices ranging from 99p to £1,500. Another interesting fossil available here is the Portland Titanites Gigantus, the largest ammonite in the world, and the very similar Moroccan Agadir ammonites –   these range in price from £45 to £400. The shop doesn't confine itself to fossils and minerals. It also sells dinosaur toys, sea shells, carved stone products in soapstone, coal, and onyx, as well as jewellery which is mostly handmade with either sterling silver or 9ct and 18ct gold.

Dinosaurland & Fossil Museum

in 1803 and part of her novel *Persuasion* is set in the town. The **Jane Austen Garden** commemorates her visit.

A few years after Jane's visit, a 12-year-old girl called Mary Anning was wandering along the shore when she noticed bones protruding from the cliffs. She had discovered the first ichthyosaur to be found in England. Later, as one of the first professional fossil collectors, she also unearthed locally a plesiosaur and a pterodactyl. The six-mile stretch of coastline on either side of Lyme is world famous for its fossils and some fine specimens of local discoveries can be seen at the award-winning **Lyme Regis Museum** in Bridge Street and at **Dinosaurland & Fossil Museum** in Coombe Street which also runs guided 'fossil walks' along the beach. The museum is housed in a magnificent Grade I listed building which was once a church where Mary Anning was

🏛 historic building 🏛 museum and heritage 🏛 historic site ◀ scenic attraction 🌿 flora and fauna

baptised and where she used to worship.

Just around the corner from Dinosaurland, in Mill Lane, you'll find one of the town's most interesting buildings. It was in January 1991 that a group of Lyme Regis residents got together in an effort to save the old **Town Mill** from destruction. There has been a mill on the River Lim in the centre of the town for many centuries, but most of the present buildings date back to the mid-17th century when the mill was rebuilt after being burned down during the Civil War siege of Lyme in 1644. Today, back in full working order, Town Mill is one of Lyme's major attractions, incorporating two Art Galleries which stage a wide range of exhibitions, concerts, poetry readings and other live performances. There is also a stable building which houses craft workshops and a café/bistro.

If you enjoy walking, the **South West Coast Path** passes through Lyme: if you follow it eastwards for about five miles it will bring you to **Golden Cap** (617ft), the highest point on the south coast with spectacular views from every vantage point. Or you can just take a pleasant stroll along Marine Parade, a traffic free promenade stretching for about a mile from the Cobb.

For its size, Lyme Regis has an extraordinary range of activities on offer, too many to list here although one must mention the famous week-long **Regatta and Carnival** held in August. Bands play on the Marine Parade, there are displays by Morris Men and folk dancers, and an annual Town Criers Open

Championship. Lyme has maintained a town crier for more than 1,000 years without a break and the current incumbent in his colourful 18th century costume can be seen and heard throughout the town during the summer months.

Around Lyme Regis

CHARMOUTH
2 miles NE of Lyme Regis off the A35

🏛 Charmouth Heritage Coast Centre

What better recommendation could you give the seaside village of Charmouth than the fact that it was Jane Austen's favourite resort? "Sweet and retired" she called it. To quote Arthur Mee, "She loved the splendid sweep of country all round it, the downs, the valleys, the hills like Golden Cap, and the pageantry of the walk to Lyme Regis." Charmouth remains an attractive little place with a wide main street lined with Regency buildings, and a quiet stretch of sandy beach that gradually merges into shingle. This part of the coast has yielded an amazing variety of fossils, many of which can be seen at the **Charmouth**

Charmouth Coast Heritage Centre

📖 stories and anecdotes 🐿 famous people 🎨 art and craft 🖋 entertainment and sport 🚶 walks

WOOD FARM CARAVAN PARK

Axminster Road, Charmouth, Dorset DT6 6BT
Tel: 01297 560697 Fax: 01297 561243
e-mail: holidays@woodfarm.co.uk
website: www.wood farm.co.uk

Enjoying spectacular views over Lyme Bay and the Marshwood Vale, **Wood Farm Caravan Park** offers a variety of accommodation and an outstanding range of facilities. If you are touring with your own caravan or motor caravan, the Park has individual all-weather hard standings, electric hook-ups and provision for awnings. There are some premium pitches with their own individual water hook-up and grey waste drainage points. For those who are camping, the grass tent field is level, terraced, situated in a sheltered location and offers electric hook-ups.

The Park also offers luxury holiday homes which have two bedrooms, one double and one twin, and can sleep up to six persons using a make-up bed in the lounge area. Then there is The Poplars, a two bedroomed (one double and one twin) self-catering flat, sleeping up to four persons and a baby (under two years of age). It has a lounge, bathroom and kitchen/dining area, all decorated to a very high standard.

The amenities at Wood Park include a superb indoor swimming pool, an all weather tennis court, a children's Play Field, recreation hall, laundry, shop and tourist

Heritage Coast Centre. Two large aquariums house a variety of local marine life, while a computerised display enables you to 'dive' into Lyme Bay and explore the secrets of the underwater world. The centre is run by three wardens who, throughout the season, organise a series of guided fossil-hunting walks along this scenic stretch of the Jurassic Coast.

WHITCHURCH CANONICORUM
4 miles NE of Lyme Regis off the A35

🏚 Church of St Candida 🥀 St Wite ⓖ Georgi Markov

Clinging to the steep hillside above the valley of the River Char, Whitchurch Canonicorum is notable for its enchanting setting and for its **Church of St Candida and the Holy Cross**. This noble building with its Norman arches

and an imposing tower built around 1400 is remarkable for being one of only two churches in England still possessing a shrine to a saint. (The other is that of Edward the Confessor in Westminster Abbey). St Candida was a Saxon woman named Wite – the Anglo-Saxon word for white, which in Latin is Candida. She lived as a hermit but was murdered by a Viking raiding party in AD831. During the Middle Ages a major cult grew up around her memory. A large shrine was built of golden Purbeck stone, its lower level pierced by three large ovals into which the sick and maimed thrust their limbs, their head or even their whole body, in the hope of being cured. The cult of **St Wite** thrived until the Reformation when all such "monuments of feigned miracles" were swept away. That

🏚 historic building 🖼 museum and heritage 🏛 historic site 🍃 scenic attraction 🌿 flora and fauna might have been the end of the story of St Wite but during the winter of 1899-1900 the foundations of the church settled and cracked open a 13th century tomb chest. Inside was a lead casket with a Latin inscription stating that "Here rest the relics of St Wite" and inside the casket the bones of a small woman about 40 years old. The shrine still attracts pilgrims today, the donations they leave in the openings beneath the tomb now being devoted to causes which aid health and healing.

A martyr of a different kind lies in the churchyard with English words on one side of his stone and Bulgarian on the other. In 1978, **Georgi Markov,** "Bulgaria's most revered dissident", was assassinated on Waterloo Bridge by a communist agent using a gas-gun disguised as an umbrella to inject him with a pin-sized pellet of the lethal toxin ricin.

BROADWINDSOR
9 miles NE of Lyme Regis on the B3163

Just to the south of this pretty terraced village is a trio of hill forts, Pilsdon Pen, Lambert's Castle and Coney's Castle (all National Trust). They are connected by a network of paths and all provide magnificent views out across Marshwood Vale to the sea. William Wordsworth took a house on Pilsdon Pen for a while and declared that there was no finer view in England.

FORDE ABBEY
11 miles N of Lyme Regis off the B3162

🏛 Forde Abbey

About as far west as you can get in Dorset, **Forde Abbey** enjoys a lovely setting beside the River Axe. Founded as a Cistercian monastery more than 800 years ago, it is now the home of the Roper family. The abbey church has gone but the monks of those days would still recognise the chapter house, dormitories, kitchen and refectories. The Upper Refectory is particularly striking with its fine timbered roof and carved panelling. After the Dissolution of the Monasteries, the abbot's residence became a private house and was greatly extended in 1649 by Cromwell's Attorney-General, Sir Edmond Prideaux. The mansion's greatest treasures are the superb Mortlake tapestries of around 1630 which are based on cartoons by Raphael and have borders probably designed by Rubens. Gardens extending to 30 acres and with origins in the early 1700s, are landscaped around this enchanting house.

Bridport

🏛 Town Hall ⚗ Purbeck Brewery

🐦 Charles II 🏛 Bridport Museum 🏛 Mangerton Mill

With its broad streets, (from the days when they were used for making ropes), Bridport is an appealing little town surrounded by green hills and with a goodly number of 17th and 18th century buildings. Most notable amongst these are the stately Georgian **Town Hall** of 1786, and the pleasing collection of 17th century houses in the street running south from the Town Hall. An even older survivor is the medieval Prior's House. If you visit the town on a Wednesday or Saturday you'll find its three main streets chock-a-block with dozens of stalls participating in the regular Street Market. The Town Council actively encourages local people who produce goods at home and not as part of their regular livelihood to join in. So there's an extraordinary range of artefacts on offer, anything from silk flowers to socks, fossils to fishing tackle. Another popular attraction is **Palmers Brewery** in West Bay Road.

FRUITS OF THE EARTH

2a Victoria Grove, Bridport, Dorset DT6 3AA
Tel: 01308 425827
e-mail: sales@fruitsoftheearth.co.uk
website: www.fruitsoftheearth.co.uk

Sue and Mike English have been running **Fruits of the Earth** for some 22 years now. There are many more products on display than when they started but otherwise, they say, little has changed. The secret of their success, they believe, has been "personal service, local knowledge and happy customers!"

They are both environmentally aware so you'll find a wide choice of organic whole foods, organic local vegetables and ingredients for special diets. The shop stocks eco cleaning products and refills, and even eco-friendly nappies. Manager Sue Williams also has a Diploma in Phytotherapy so is very knowledgeable about herbal remedies, homoeopathy, supplements and flower essence products.

More conventional products are well-represented in the array of grains, dried fruit, nuts, herbs and spices on display, along with teas and coffees, organic wines, beers and spirits. Old fashioned glass jars contain a variety of goodies and if you are looking for something rather exotic, try browsing around the Japanese food ingredients on display in one corner!

COUNTRY SEATS

18 South Street, Bridport, Dorset DT6 3NG
Tel: 01308 427968   Fax: 01308 422729
e-mail: country-seats@btconnect.com
website: www.countryseats.co.uk

Voted as one of the best shops in Bridport by the *Sunday Telegraph,* **Country Seats** offers a full service covering all aspects of interior design. Owner Martin Ball heads the team of interior designers and their assistants, and offers a free interior design and measuring service, no matter what size a job is.

The service is complemented by the company's state-of-the-art library of fabric and wallpaper books. Customers can borrow these or have individual samples sent direct to their homes. "We are quite unique," says Martin, "in that we have our own workshop, run by my partner Katherine Hayball, where all our soft furnishings are handmade to a very high standard. We also run a re-upholstery and loose covering service."

Leading suppliers of fabrics include Zoffany, Sanderson, Colfax & Fowler, Villa Nova, Brunschwig & Fils, Pierre Frey and many others. Country Seats also stocks an extensive range of home-related gifts and furniture, in both contemporary and vintage styles. When you visit the shop, your sense of smell will be stimulated by the aromatic ambience provided by the wonderfully scented candles from St Eval.

🏛 historic building   🏛 museum and heritage   🏛 historic site   🏞 scenic attraction   🌿 flora and fauna

BRIDPORT LIGHTING CENTRE

52 South Street, Bridport, Dorset DT6 3NN
Tel: 01308 422318

Occupying a handsome Grade II listed building, the **Bridport Lighting Centre** is known to many visitors as Aladdin's Cave because of the huge range of lighting. The Centre, originally established in 1986, was taken over by its present owners in 2005. The shop displays and stocks a very wide range of domestic lighting and includes both traditional and modern styles. At any one time, the products of up to 25 different manufacturers

are on display. These include Franklite; Interiors 1900, Endon, Elstead and many more. A wide and varied selection of shades is also available. And if you are looking for

something really distinctive, the Centre can supply hand-made silk lampshades made to your specifications by Lotus Lampshades, a company based in Wales.

Established in 1794, part of the brewery is still thatched. During the season, visitors are welcomed on Tuesdays and Wednesdays for a tour of the historic brewery, the charge for which includes a commemorative certificate and also a glass or two of beer.

The focal point of the town is the oddly-named Bucky Doo Square which has at its centre a magnificent carved centrepiece of Portland and Purbeck stone by a local stone mason, Karl Dixon. The octagonal piece has 8 bas relief panels depicting aspects of the town's past, present and future.

Bridport Museum is good on local history and family records and also has an interesting collection of dolls. You can also learn about two distinguished visitors to the town. One was Joan of Navarre who landed at Bridport in 1403 on her way to become queen to Henry IV; the other, **Charles II**

who arrived in the town after his defeat at the Battle of Worcester in 1651. He was fleeing to France, pretending to be the groom in a runaway marriage. As he attended to his horses in the yard of an inn, an ostler approached him saying, "Surely I know you, friend?" The quick-thinking future monarch asked where the ostler had been working before. When he replied "In Exeter," Charles responded "Aye, that is where we must have met." Charles then excused himself and made a speedy departure from the town. If the ostler's memory for faces had been better, he could have claimed the £1000 bounty for Charles' capture and subsequent English history would have followed a very different course.

Just to the north of Bridport, **Mangerton Mill** is a working 17th century watermill in a peaceful rural setting. On the same site is a

HEADFUL

5b South Street, Bridport, Dorset DT6 3NR
Tel: 01308 458844

For that special present **headful** is a fabulous find in central Bridport. Owner Denise Revy and her daughter Jesa have stocked this gem of a gift shop with the sort of presents that anyone would be pleased to receive, from tots to teens to grannies.

There is fabulous jewellery by Johnny Loves Rosie, aromatherapy candles and room sprays by Natural Magic, and a range of melamine picnic and party ware for children and adults.

Denise and Jesa have thought of everything for the discerning present shopper. Whether it's a gift for a friend or family member, or a treat for yourself, headful has something. There's nothing more decadent than an indulgent soak in an aromatic bath, a facial and an all over skin treatment from Neal's Yard or the Dr Hauschka range – all available in this treasure of a gift shop. With Bridport such a haven for artisans and craftspeople, headful stocks a range of locally made quirky jewellery, bags and cards.

headful is right in Bridport's Bucky Doo Square, just to the left when facing the Arts Centre. Off street parking is available on South Street or just behind the Tourist Information Centre.

GROVES NURSERY AND GARDEN CENTRE

West Bay Road, Bridport, Dorset, DT6 4BA
Tel: 01308 422654
website: www.grovesnurseries.co.uk

The Groves family have their roots firmly established in the Dorset countryside, from the original nursery clinging to the steep slopes of the Piddle Valley to the present day, fully stocked, modern garden centre in Bridport, run by the fifth and sixth generation of Groves. The plants and various garden ornaments are attractively displayed amongst Koi ponds, stone pergolas, rose beds and there is even an experimental potager garden, complete with Solar Dome.

Many of the plants are grown in their own nurseries in Bridport and in Beaminster (just seven miles north). The Beaminster nursery is called 'Little GROVES' and also retails directly to the public. It specialises in rare and aromatic plants and herbs, which are set out amongst a small landscaped garden. Groves Nurseries are especially noted for their Hardy Violet collection, which has the NCCPG National Collection status. These have appeared in many national magazines and on TV. The collection is displayed at the garden centre throughout the flowering season, from Jan-April in the Solar Dome.

The Garden Centre boasts of a café, clothed with mature plants from walls to ceiling, where they bake their own delicious homemade cakes on the premises, also hot snacks and homely Sunday roasts. Roses are another speciality and over 5,000 are potted each year in the nursery. These can be purchased from the garden centre all year round or online during their dormant season.

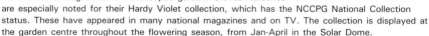

🏚 historic building 🏛 museum and heritage 🏛 historic site ♖ scenic attraction 🌿 flora and fauna

Museum of Rural Bygones, a tearoom and craft shop.

In recent years, the area around Bridport has featured extensively in TV chef Hugh Fearnley-Whittingstall's popular "live off the land" cookery series, *Return to River Cottage*.

WEST BAY
1 mile S of Bridport off the A35

🏛 Harbour Life Exhibition

When Bridport's own harbour silted up in the early 1700s, the townspeople built a new one at the mouth of the River Brit and called it West Bay. During the 19th century, hundreds of ships docked here every year, and West Bay had its own shipbuilding industry until 1879.

The little town never became a fashionable resort but the beach, backed by 100ft high sandstone cliffs, is much enjoyed by holiday-makers, and there's still a stall at the little harbour where you can treat yourself to a tub of cockles. From the harbour you can take a mackerel boat round the bay or go for the deeper waters in search of cod, conger, skate or pollock – and keep a lookout for one of the friendly dolphins.

Close to the harbour is the Bridport Arms Hotel, an historic old thatched building which in parts dates back as far as the 1500s. The inn's picturesque qualities earned it two rôles in the BBC-TV series *Harbour Lights* starring Nick Berry and Tina Hobky. The inn appeared

THE RIVERSIDE RESTAURANT
West Bay, Bridport, Dorset, DT6 4EZ
Reservations: 01308 422011
website: www.fishrestaurant-westbay.co.uk

The Riverside Restaurant, overlooking the River Brit and with views of the harbour, is Dorset's long-established and famed seafood restaurant. It has been under the same ownership and management since 1964 – Arthur & Janet Watson. It began life as a café providing roasts and cream teas but always being supporters of using local produce from local suppliers, Arthur & Janet soon started to put locally-caught fish, crabs and lobsters on the menu... and have not looked back...their world-wide reputation speaks for itself.

You can enjoy the freshest and best fish and shellfish from local waters... crab, scallops, lobster, brill, mackerel. a seafood platter or Lyme Bay dover sole simply grilled is typical. Everything is cooked for you at time of order by Head Chef, George Marsh and his chefs. The menu changes daily according to what is available from the market and local landings that day. As well as fish there are always daily vegetarian and meat dishes. The dessert menu is vast and mouth-watering with homemade specials such as 'crisp fig & pistachio frangipane tart with cardamom ice cream' prepared by pastry chef, Natalie Andrews; alongside old favourites such as knickerbockers glory and banana split. The wine list is extensive too, and is specially selected to complement the menu.

Whether it is a celebration, a romantic meal for two or simply a meal out with family and friends [children welcome] it is the aim of the general manager, Neil Chilcott and his team, to give you an enjoyable dining experience in an atmosphere that always puts you first.

🎞 stories and anecdotes   🦢 famous people   🎨 art and craft   🎭 entertainment and sport   🚶 walks

SLADERS YARD

**Contemporary British Art,
Furniture and Craft,
Boatyard and Café**

*West Bay Road, West Bay,
Bridport, Dorset DT6 4EL*
Tel: 01308 459511
e-mail: info@itrefurniture.co.uk website: www.sladersyard.co.uk

Sladers Yard was built in 1805 as a maritime warehouse
serving the busy harbour at West Bay. It has been used ever since as a working building
without modernisation, making it a beautiful, original setting for the top quality artworks now
shown here. The yard itself offers a flower-filled sunny seating area for the café inside which
serves delicious organic light lunches, ice cream, coffees, cakes, and cream teas.

The spearhead for Sladers Yard is award-winning designer/maker Petter Southall who has been
making his distinctive furniture at the i tre studio outside Bridport since 1991. (i tre is Norwegian
for in wood.) With a highly skilled team of apprentices, Petter makes his designs by hand, using
both boat building and fine cabinet-making techniques. The studio works in solid oak, ash and
elm often steam bending it into arches, rings and twists. The galleries of the old warehouse are
now sensitively converted to form a showroom for Petter's furniture with a changing programme
of selling exhibitions by very good contemporary painters and artists in mixed media. As well as
the exhibitions, Sladers Yard offers a range of gift and domestic ware made by leading British
designers and makers, many of whom are local to Bridport. These include ceramics, turned wood,
pleated silks, woven textiles, scarves, throws and cushions, linen clothes, jewellery, lamps,
mirrors, trays, leatherware, photography and baskets, as well as cards and prints.

SLAPE HILL BARN

Waytown, nr Netherbury, Bridport, Dorset DT6 5LQ
Tel: 01308 488429
website: www.slapehillbarn.co.uk

Gill Clarke has been running her four star B&B for 10 years,
and the high number of return visits and recommendations
are testimony to its comfort, quality and beautiful situation.
Slape Hill Barn stands in four acres of grounds with superb
views over the hills and valleys of Dorset. Nearby lies the
quiet picturesque village of Netherbury and beyond it the small
country town of Beaminster. South west Dorset is a delight at any
time of the year; beaches, fine coastal scenery, country walking,
many National Trust houses, superb gardens and pretty hamstone
villages are all within easy reach. Guests can enjoy the many
galleries, craft centres, studios and workshops as well as the wide
range of pubs, tea shops and restaurants in the area.

Guests at Slape Hill Barn are welcomed with afternoon tea and homemade cakes served in
the garden, weather permitting, or in the comfortable drawing-room where a wood-burning stove
keeps guests snug on chillier days. The bedrooms - one twin with ensuite shower room, one
double with bath and over-bath shower - are prettily decorated and comfortable with lovely
views. A full English cooked breakfast is provided, with fresh fruit and fruit juices, cereals,
toast, honey and marmalade, fresh coffee and tea, to give your day a good start.

Slape Hill Barn offers its guests the warmest of welcomes, every attention to their needs,
good food, comfort and care in this loveliest of surroundings.

as both The Piers Hotel and the Bridehaven public house.

The **Harbour Life Exhibition** has exhibitions and displays on the history of this small settlement which is known as the Gateway to the Jurassic Coast – a coast where fossils formed 200 million years ago are continuously being revealed as the cliffs erode.

BEAMINSTER
5 miles N of Bridport on the A3066

🏛 Beaminster Museum 🏛 Parnham House

🐾 Horn Park Gardens 🐾 UK Llamas

In Hardy's novel, when Tess Durbeyville arrives in Beaminster, ("Emminster" in the novel), she finds a delightful little market town. Visitors today will find that remarkably little has changed. The whole of the town centre is a conservation area and contains an impressive 200 listed buildings. The 17th century almshouse, the majestic church tower in gold-tinted Hamstone, the 16th century Pickwick's Inn, and the charming Market Square with its stone roofed market cross are all much the same as Hardy knew them. What have disappeared are the many small industries that thrived in those days – rope and sailcloth, embroidered buttons, shoes, wrought ironwork and clock-making were just some of the artefacts produced here. Housed in the former Congregational Chapel of 1749, **Beaminster Museum** displays objects relating to the life of the town from medieval times to the present day.

Visitors to Beaminster's imposing 15th century church tend to be overwhelmed by the grandiose, over-lifesize sculptures of the Strode family who lived at Parnham House, a

---

WEST COUNTRY INTERIORS / THE LITTLE ART GALLERY

2 Church Street, Beaminster, Dorset DT8 3AZ
Tel: 01308 863131

Located in the rural west Dorset town of Beaminster, **The Little Art Gallery** is a complete gem. Occupying the first floor above West Country Interiors, the gallery provides a warm, vibrant and accessible space, It has several exhibitions throughout the year, largely featuring the extraordinary talent of local artists. Regular gallery artists include Royal Academy summer show exhibitor, wood engraver Howard Phipps, ceramics from Miranda Berrow, linocuts by Liz Somerville and wildlife studies by Aviva Halter Hurn. An absolute must for anyone visiting West Dorset and interested in visual art.

On the ground floor, **West Country Interiors** is a 'complete treasure trove of a shop', stocking fabrics, paints and wallpapers such as Colefax & Fowler, Zoffany, Designers Guild, Manuel Canova and Osborne & Little, to name just a few. West Country Interiors offer a complete interior design service specialising in the making of curtains, Roman blinds, upholstery and loose covers. The friendly staff have a wealth of experience and are able to advise on all aspects of interior design. The shop also has a large range of unusual gifts and interior accessories, lamps and cushions.

🎬 stories and anecdotes 🍴 famous people 🎭 art and craft 🎟 entertainment and sport 🚶 walks

CILLA & CAMILLA

2 The Square, Beaminster, Dorset DT8 3AS
Tel/Fax: 01308 861120
e-mail: cillcam@yahoo.co.uk

Need to buy a gift for someone special and looking for inspiration? Then make your way to the centre of the pretty market town of Beaminster and to **Cilla & Camilla** where you'll find a ravishing display of quality gifts, children's toys, books and jewellery, scarves, candles, greeting cards and much more.

The shop occupies a lovely 18th century Grade II listed building and its three display rooms are bursting with a cornucopia of attractive and desirable objects. As well as buying gifts for somebody else,

you'll almost certainly want to buy something for yourself!

Cilla and Camilla is open from 9.30am to 5.30pm, Monday to Saturday.

gem of Tudor architecture about a mile south of the town. Unfortunately this house is now closed to the public as a result of its recent sale into private ownership.

A mile or so to the north of Beaminster, **Horn Park Gardens** are set around a house built in 1910 by a pupil of Sir Edwin Lutyens. The gardens enjoy a magnificent sea view and are full of unusual shrubs and trees, with terraced lawns, lovely herbaceous and rose borders, water gardens and natural wildflower meadows.

For a rather different mode of exploring rural Dorset, drop in at **UK Llamas** just outside the town. Guided llama trekking tours are available and the owners will also modify the tours to suit your individual requirements and pace. A full day's trek starts at approximately 10:30am with a stop for lunch and there's a variety of routes throughout the area.

MAPPERTON
5 miles NE of Bridport off the A3066

🏛 Mapperton

It's not surprising to find that the house and gardens at **Mapperton** (see panel opposite) have featured in three three major films – *Tom Jones, Emma* and *Restoration*. Home of the Earl and Countess of Sandwich, this magnificent Jacobean mansion set beside a lake is stunningly photogenic. The Italianate upper gardens contain some impressive topiary, an orangery, dovecote and formal borders descending to fish ponds and shrub gardens. The house stands in an Area of Outstanding Natural Beauty with some glorious views of the Dorset hills. The gardens are open during the season; tours of the house only by appointment.

🏛 historic building   📷 museum and heritage   🏛 historic site   � scenic attraction   🌷 flora and fauna

Mapperton Gardens

Beaminster, Dorset DT8 3NR
Tel: 01308 862645 Fax: 01308 863348
e-mail: office@mapperton.com
websitewww.mapperton.com

Two miles from Beaminster, five miles from Bridport, **Mapperton Gardens** surround a fine Jacobean manor house with stable blocks, a dovecote and its own Church of All Saints. The grounds, which run down a gradually steepening valley, include an orangery and an Italianate formal garden, a 17th century summer house and a wild garden planted in the 1960s. The gardens, which are open to the public from March to October, are a natural choice for film location work, with *Emma* and *Tom Jones* among their credits.

Dorchester

🏛 Maumbury Rings 🏛 Roman Town House

🏛 Dorset County Museum 🏛 Church of Our Lady

🏛 Tutankhamun Exhibition 🦅 Thomas Hardy

🏛 Terracotta Warrior 🏛 Dinosaur Museum

🏛 Dorset Teddy Bear Museum 🏛 Court & Cells

🏛 The Keep Military Museum 🏛 Max Gate

🦅 Judge Jeffreys

One of England's most appealing county towns, Dorchester's known history goes back to AD74 when the Romans established a settlement called Durnovaria at a respectful distance from the River Frome. At that time the river was much broader than it is now and prone to flooding. The town's Roman origins are clearly displayed in its street plan, in the beautiful tree-lined avenues known as The Walks which follow the course of the old Roman walls, at **Maumbury Rings**, an ancient stone circle which the Romans converted into an amphitheatre, and in the well-preserved **Roman Town House** behind County Hall in Colliton Park. As the town's most famous citizen put it, Dorchester

"announced old Rome in every street, alley and precinct. It looked Roman, bespoke the art of Rome, concealed dead men of Rome". **Thomas Hardy** was in fact describing 'Casterbridge' in his novel *The Mayor of Casterbridge* but his fictional town is immediately recognisable as Dorchester. One place he describes in great detail is Mayor Trenchard's House, easily identified as what is now Barclays Bank in South Street and bearing a plaque to that effect. Hardy made his home in Dorchester in 1883 and two years later moved into **Max Gate** (National Trust) on the outskirts of the town, a strikingly unlovely 'two up and two down' Victorian villa designed by Hardy himself and built by his brother at a total cost of £450. Here Hardy entertained a roll-call of great names – Robert Louis Stevenson, GB Shaw, Rudyard Kipling and HG Wells amongst many others.

The most accessible introduction to the town and the county can found at the excellent **Dorset County Museum** in High Street West. Designated Best Local History Museum in the 1998 Museum of the Year Awards, the museum houses a comprehensive range of exhibits spanning the centuries, from

NUMBER 19

High East Street, Dorchester DT1 1HH
Tel: 01305 268595

Owned and run by Jane Wheeler, **Number 19** offers customers an attractive collection of womens' fashions in a light and spacious ambience and a warm and welcoming atmosphere. This beautiful boutique stocks an eclectic mix of labels that includes Ispirato, Michele and St James and offers garments for every kind of occasion. Experienced and friendly staff add to the pleasure of a visit here. In addition to the extensive range of clothing, Number 19 also stocks an alluring selection of accessories and jewellery.

a Roman sword to a 19th century cheese press, from dinosaur footprints to a stuffed Great Bustard which used to roam the chalk uplands of north Dorset but has been extinct in this country since 1810. Founded in 1846, the museum moved to its present site in 1883, into purpose-built galleries with lofty arches of fine cast ironwork inspired by the Great Exhibition of 1851 at the Crystal Palace. The building was designed by GR Crickmay, the architect for whom Thomas Hardy worked in 1870. The great poet and novelist is celebrated here in a major exhibit which includes a fascinating reconstruction of his study at Max Gate, his Dorchester home. The room includes the original furnishings, books, pictures and fireplace. In the right hand

corner are his musical instruments, and the very pens with which he wrote *Tess of the d'Urbervilles, Jude the Obscure,* and his epic poem, the *Dynasts.* More of his possessions are displayed in the Gallery outside – furniture, his watch, music books, and some of his notebooks. Also honoured in the Writers Gallery is William Barnes, the Dorset dialect poet, scholar and priest, who was also the first secretary of the Dorset Natural History and Archaeological Society which owns and runs the museum.

Just outside the museum stands the **Statue of William Barnes** and, at the junction of High Street West and The Grove, is the **Statue of Thomas Hardy**. There are more statues outside St George's Church, a group of lifesize models by Elizabeth Frink representing Catholic martyrs who were hung, drawn and quartered in the 16th century.

Opposite the County Museum, the Antelope Hotel and the 17th century half-timbered building beside it (now a tearoom) were where **Judge Jeffreys** (1648-89) tried 340 Dorset men for their part in Monmouth's Rebellion of 1685. As a result of this 'Bloody Assize', 74 men suffered death by being hung, drawn and quartered. A further 175 were transported for life. Jeffreys' ferociousness has been attributed to the agony he suffered from gallstones for which doctors of the time could provide no relief. Ironically, when his patron James II was deposed, Jeffreys himself ended up in the Tower of London where he died. A century and a half after the Bloody Assize, another infamous trial took place in the Old Crown Court nearby. Six farm labourers who later became known as the Tolpuddle Martyrs were condemned to transportation for their part in organising a 'Friendly Society' – the first agricultural trade union. The **Court and Cells** are now open to the public where they are invited to "stand in the dock and sit in the dimly-lit cells...and experience four centuries of gruesome crime and punishment".

There can be few churches in the country with such a bizarre history as that of **Our Lady, Queen of Martyrs, & St Michael**. It was first erected in Wareham, in 1888, by a Roman Catholic sect who called themselves the Passionists, a name derived from their obsession with Christ's passion and death. When they found that few people in Wareham shared their fixation, they had the church moved in 1907, stone by stone to Dorchester where it was re-assembled and then served the Catholic community for almost 70 years. By the mid-1970s the transplanted church had

become too small for its burgeoning congregation. The Passionists moved out, ironically taking over an Anglican church whose communicants had become too few to sustain it. A decade later, their abandoned church was acquired by an organisation called World Heritage which has transformed its interior into the **Tutankhamun Exhibition**. The life, death and legacy of Tutankhamun exerts an abiding fascination present and the exhibition pulls all the various strands of the extraordinary tale together. The Exhibition has won international renown and has been featured in most major TV documentaries.

Also owned by World Heritage is the **Dinosaur Museum**. Dorchester is just seven miles from Dorset's world famous coastline and in the heart of dinosaur country. The award-winning museum is the only one on mainland Britain dedicated to dinosaurs.

Under the same ownership are two more museums. For those who want to get in touch with their softer side a visit to the **Dorset Teddy Bear Museum** is a must. Marvel at the evocative and atmospheric displays of the history of the teddy bear, featuring examples from the very earliest about a century ago up to the present day. Famous bears such as Rupert Bear, Winnie the Pooh, and Paddington are on display, along with bears representing the signs of the zodiac. Many collectors, limited editions, and artists bears are also present. In Teddy Bear House meet Edward Bear and his extended family of human sized teddy bears as they busy themselves or relax around their Edwardian style home. A gem of a museum is **The Terracotta Warriors Museum**. It is the only museum outside China devoted to the terracotta warriors who are now regarded as the 8th wonder of the Ancient World.

Featured are unique replicas of the warriors, plus reconstructions of costumes and armour, and multimedia presentations. For further information on these four museums phone 01305 269741.

Also well worth a visit is **The Keep Military Museum** housed in an interesting, renovated Grade II listed building. Audio technology and interactive computerised displays tell the remarkable story of those who have served in the regiments of Dorset and Devon. An additional bonus is the spectacular view from the battlements across the town and surrounding countryside.

An oddity in the town is an 18th century sign set high up in a wall. It carries the information that Bridport is 15 miles distant and Hyde Park Corner, 120. Apparently, the sign was placed in this position for the convenience of stage-coach drivers, although one would have thought that they, of all people, would have already known the mileage involved.

On the western outskirts of Dorchester, less than a mile from the town centre, is **Poundbury**, the Prince of Wales'

controversial experiment in creating a new community based on old principles. The prince wanted to show how traditional quality architecture and modern town planning could combine to create urban life in a rural setting. One objective was to make it possible for no-one to be more than 10 minutes away from his or her workplace. The enterprise began in 1993 and when completed will consist of four different quarters, each with its own public buildings, shops, pubs, offices and workshops. The enterprise has attracted much scorn from 'cutting edge' architects who deride the whole concept as 'living in the past' but the traditionally-built properties are much sought after.

Around Dorchester

CHARMINSTER
1 mile N of Dorchester on the A52

🏛 Wolfeton House

An attractive town on the River Cerne, Charminster has a 12th century church with an impressive pinnacled tower added in the 1400s. Inside are some striking memorials to the Trenchard family whose noble mansion, **Wolfeton House,** stands on the northern edge of the town. A lovely medieval and Elizabethan manor house, it is surrounded by water meadows near the meeting of the rivers Cerne and Frome. The house contains a great stone staircase, remarkable plaster ceilings, fireplaces and carved oak

Poundbury Hill Fort, nr Dorchester

Wolfeton Manor, Charminster

was originally the village smithy. According to tradition, Charles II happened to stop here to have his horse shod. Feeling thirsty, the king asked for a glass of ale and was not best pleased to be told that as the blacksmith had no licence, no alcoholic drink was available. Invoking the royal prerogative, Charles granted a licence immediately and this tiny hostelry has been licensed ever since. Given the cramped interior, elbow-bending at the Smith's Arms can be a problem at busy times, but fortunately there is a spacious terrace outside.

panelling – all Elizabethan – some good pictures and furniture. Opening times are restricted. There is also a cider house here from which cider can be purchased.

GODMANSTONE
4 miles N of Dorchester on the A352

🏠 Smith's Arms

Dorset can boast many cosy, intimate pubs, but the **Smith's Arms** at Godmanstone is in a class of its own, claiming to be the smallest inn in the country with a frontage just 11 feet wide. This appealing 14th century thatched building

PIDDLETRENTHIDE
6 miles N of Dorchester on the B3143

Mentioned in the Domesday Book, this village is named after the river beside which it stands and the '30 hides' of land for which it was assessed. A beautiful place in a beautiful location, Piddletrenthide is believed to have been the home of Alfred the Great's brother, Ethelred.

LONGPUDDLE

4 High Street, Piddlehinton, Dorchester, Dorset DT2 7TD
Tel: 01300 368532
e-mail: ann@longpuddle.co.uk
website: www.longpuddle.co.uk

Set midway between Sherborne and Dorchester in the Piddle Valley, **Longpuddle** is a charming 400-year-old thatched cottage which is well placed for exploring Thomas Hardy's Dorset. The accommodation, which enjoys a four-star Highly Commended rating from the AA, comprises three spacious and tastefully decorated guest bedrooms, two doubles and one twin, all of them en suite. Guests have the use of a large, comfortable lounge with a colour TV and views over the garden and paddocks through which the River Piddle flows. Breakfast at Longpuddle consists of local produce cooked personally by owner Ann Lamb.

🎬 stories and anecdotes 🍴 famous people 🎨 art and craft 🎭 entertainment and sport 🚶 walks

Pitchmarket House, Cerne Abbas

CERNE ABBAS
7 miles N of Dorchester on the A352

🏛 Cerne Abbey 🏛 Cerne Abbas Giant

This pretty village beside the River Cerne takes its name from **Cerne Abbey**, formerly a major Benedictine monastery of which an imposing 15th century gatehouse, a tithe barn of the same period, and a holy well still survive, all well worth seeing. So too are the lofty, airy church with grotesque gargoyles and medieval statues adorning its west tower, and the old Market House on Long Street. In fact, there is much to see in this ancient village where cottages dating back to the 14th century still stand.

But the major visitor attraction is to be found just to the north of the village – the famous **Cerne Abbas Giant** (National Trust), a colossal 180ft-high figure cut into the chalk hillside. He stands brandishing a club, naked and full-frontal, and there can be absolutely no doubt about his maleness. An ancient tradition asserts that any woman wishing to become pregnant should sit, or preferably sleep the night, on the giant's huge erect penis, some 22ft long. The age of this extraordinary carving is hotly disputed but a consensus is

emerging that it was originally created by ancient Britons as a fertility symbol and that the giant's club was added by the Romans. (There are clear similarities between the giant and the representation of Hercules on a Roman pavement of AD 191, preserved at Sherborne Castle.) As with all hill-carvings, the best view is from a distance, in this case from a layby on the A352. A curious puzzle remains. The giant's outlines in the chalk need a regular scouring to remove grass and weeds. Should this be neglected, he would soon fade into the hillside. In medieval centuries, such a non-essential task of conservation could only have been authorised by the locally all-powerful Abbots of Cerne. What possible reason did those Christian advocates of chastity have for carefully preserving such a powerful pagan image of virility?

MINTERNE MAGNA
9 miles N of Dorchester, on the A352

🌿 Minterne Gardens

A couple of miles north of the Cerne Giant, Minterne Magna is notable for its parish church, crowded with memorials to Napiers, Churchills and Digbys, the families who once owned the great house here and most of the Minterne valley. The mansion itself, rebuilt in the Arts & Crafts style around 1900 is not open to the public but its splendid **Minterne Gardens** are. The gardens are laid out in a horseshoe below the house and landscaped in the 18th century style of Capability Brown. They contain an important collection of

Minterne Gardens

his relatives), which played from a gallery at the back of the church. The gallery was demolished in Hardy's lifetime, but many years later he drew a sketch from memory which showed the position of each player and the name of his instrument. A copy of this drawing is on display in the church, alongside a tablet commemorating the Hardys who took part.

Although Thomas Hardy was cremated and his ashes buried in the Poets' Corner of Westminster Abbey, his heart was brought to Stinsford to be interred in a graveyard tomb here. According to a scurrilous local tradition, it is shared with the village cat which had managed to eat the heart before it was buried.

Also buried in the churchyard is the former Poet Laureate Cecil Day Lewis (1904-72)

Just to the east of the village, **Kingston Maurward Gardens** are of such historical importance that they are listed on the English Heritage Register of Gardens. The 35 acres of classical 18th century parkland and lawns sweep majestically down to the lake from the stately Georgian house. The formal Edwardian Gardens include a croquet lawn, rose garden, herbaceous borders and a large display of tender perennials, including the National Collection of Penstemons and Salvias. There's also an Animal Park with an interesting collection of unusual breeds, a lovely ornamental lake, nature trails, plant sales and the Old Coach House Restaurant serving morning coffee, lunches and teas.

Himalayan rhododendrons and azaleas, along with cherries, maples and many other fine and rare trees. The gardens are open daily from March to early November.

On Batcombe Hill, to the west of the village, stands a stone pillar known as the Cross and Hand which is said to date from the 7th century. Its purpose is unknown but in *Tess of the d'Urbervilles*, Hardy relates the local legend that the pillar marks the grave of a criminal who was tortured and hanged there, and whose mournful ghost appears beside the column from time to time.

STINSFORD
1 mile NE of Dorchester, off the A35

🐦 Thomas Hardy 🐑 Kingston Maurward Gardens

It was in St Michael's Church at Stinsford that Thomas Hardy was christened and where he attended services for much of his life. He sang hymns to the accompaniment of the village band, (amongst whom were several of

HIGHER BOCKHAMPTON
2 miles NE of Dorchester off the A35

🏠 Hardy's Cottage 🐦 Thomas Hardy

In the woods above Higher Bockhampton, reached by a series of narrow lanes and a 10-minute walk, is a major shrine for devotees of

Hardy's Cottage, Higher Bockhampton

Thomas Hardy. **Hardy's Cottage** is surrounded by the trees of Puddletown Forest, a setting he evoked so magically in *Under the Greenwood Tree*. The delightful thatched cottage and gardens are now owned by the National Trust and the rooms are furnished much as they would have been when the great novelist was born here in 1840. Visitors can see the very room in which his mother gave birth only to hear her child proclaimed still-born. Fortunately, an observant nurse noticed that the infant was in fact breathing and so ensured that such classics of English literature as *Tess of the d'Urbervilles* and *The Return of the Native* saw the light of day. This charming cottage was Hardy's home for the first 22 years of his life until he set off for London to try his luck as an architect. In that profession his record was undistinguished, but in 1871 his first novel, *Desperate Remedies,* was published. An almost farcical melodrama, it gave few signs of the great works that would follow but was sufficiently successful for Hardy to devote himself thereafter to writing full time.

PUDDLETOWN
5 miles NE of Dorchester off the A35

🏛 Athelhampton House

Originally called Piddletown ('piddle' is the Saxon word for 'clear water') the village's name was changed by the sensitive Victorians. It was at Piddletown that Hardy's grandfather and great-grandfather were born. Renamed 'Weatherbury' it features in *Far From the Madding Crowd* as the place where Fanny's coffin was left out in the rain, and Sergeant Troy spends the night in the porch of the church after covering her grave with flowers.

Just to the east of Puddletown, **Athelhampton House** is a delightful, mostly Tudor house surrounded by a series of separate, 'secret' gardens. It's the home of Sir Edward and Lady du Cann and has the lived-in feeling that adds so much interest to historic houses. One of the finest houses in the county, Athelhampton's most spectacular feature is its magnificent Great Chamber built during the reign of Elizabeth I. In the grounds are topiary pyramids, fountains, the Octagonal Garden designed by Sir Robert Cooke in 1971, and an unusual 15th century circular dovecote. It is almost perfectly preserved, with its 'potence', or revolving ladder used to collect eggs from the topmost nests, still in place and still useable.

MORETON
7 miles E of Dorchester off the B3390

🍃 T.E. Lawrence 🏛 Cloud's Hill

Thomas Hardy may be Dorset's most famous author, but in this small village it is another distinguished writer, (also a scholar, archaeologist and military hero), who is remembered. In 1935 **T.E. Lawrence,** "Lawrence of Arabia", left the RAF where he was known simply as Aircraftsman TE Shaw and retired to a spartan cottage he had bought 10 years earlier. It stands alone on the heath outside Moreton village and here Lawrence lived as a virtual recluse, without cooking facilities and with a sleeping bag as his bed. He was to enjoy this peaceful, if comfortless, retreat for only a few weeks. Lawrence loved speeding along the Dorset lanes on his motor-cycle and one sunny spring day his adventurous driving led to a fatal collision with a young cyclist. The King of Iraq and Winston Churchill attended the hero's burial in the graveyard at Moreton and the home Lawrence occupied for such a short time, **Cloud's Hill** (National Trust), is now open to the public.

WINTERBORNE CAME
2 miles SE of Dorchester off the A352

🐦 William Barnes

This tiny hamlet is a place of pilgrimage for admirers of Dorset's second most famous man of letters who is buried in the graveyard here. **William Barnes** was Rector of Winterborne Came from 1862 until his death in 1886 and in the old Rectory (not open to the public) he entertained such luminaries of English literature as Alfred Lord Tennyson and Hardy himself. Although Barnes was highly respected by fellow poets, his pastoral poems written in the distinctive dialect of the county never attracted a wide audience. At their best, though, they are marvellously evocative of the west Dorset countryside:

> *The zwellen downs, wi' chalky tracks*
> *A-climmen up their zunny backs,*

> *Do hide green meads an zedgy brooks...*
> *An' white roads up athirt the hills.*

Winterborne Came's unusual name, incidentally, derives from its position beside the River Winterborne and the fact that in medieval times the village was owned by the Abbey of Caen in France.

OWERMOIGNE
6 miles SE of Dorchester off the A352

🏛 Mill House Cider Museum

🏛 Dorset Collection of Clocks

Just north of the village is a dual attraction in the shape of the **Mill House Cider Museum** and the **Dorset Collection of Clocks**. Housed in a mill that featured in Hardy's *The Distracted Preacher*, the Cider Museum has a collection of 18th and 19th century cider-making mills and presses, reflecting the importance of cider as a main country drink in bygone days. The Collection of Clocks showcases numerous timepieces ranging from longcase clocks to elaborate turret clocks. Visitors get the opportunity to see the intricate movements that are usually hidden away in the large clocks found on churches and public buildings.

MAIDEN CASTLE
2 miles SW of Dorchester off the A35

🏰 Maiden Castle

Maiden Castle is one of the most impressive prehistoric sites in the country. This vast Iron Age fortification covering more than 45 acres dates back some 4,000 years. Its steep earth ramparts, between 60 and 90 feet high, are nearly two miles round and together with the inner walls make a total of five miles of defences. The settlement flourished for 2,000 years until AD44 when its people were defeated by a Roman army under Vespasian.

🎭 stories and anecdotes 🐦 famous people 🎨 art and craft ✎ entertainment and sport 🚶 walks

Maiden Castle Earthworks

ancient barrows, amongst which are the **Nine Stones**, Dorset's best example of a standing stone circle. Not the best location, however. The circle lies beside the busy A35, isolated from the village to the west and surrounded by trees. Despite the constant din of passing traffic, the circle somehow retains an air of tranquillity.

Excavations here in 1937 unearthed a war cemetery containing some 40 bodies, one of which still had a Roman arrowhead embedded in its spine. The Romans occupied the site for some 30 years before moving closer to the River Frome and founding Durnovaria, modern Dorchester. Maiden Castle was never settled again and it is a rather forbidding, treeless place but the extensive views along the Winterborne valley by contrast are delightful.

WINTERBOURNE ABBAS

4 miles W of Dorchester

🏛 Nine Stones

The village of Winterbourne Abbas stands at the head of the Winterborne valley, close to the river which is notable for running only during the winter and becoming a dry ditch in summer. The second part of the name, Abbas, comes from having been owned by the abbots of Cerne. The village is surrounded by

Weymouth

🏛 Timewalk Journey	🏛 Brewers Quay
🏛 Museum of Coastal Defence	🍃 Nothe Gardens
🏛 Nothe Fort	🍃 Lodmoor Country Park
🏛 Deep Sea Adventure	🏛 Model World

No wonder the good citizens of Weymouth erected a **Statue of George III** to mark the 50th year of his reign in 1810. The troubled

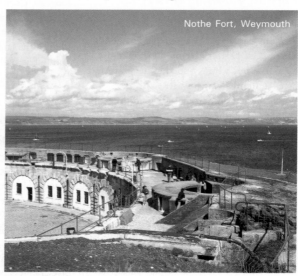

Nothe Fort, Weymouth

WEYMOUTH DELI

3 Frederick Place, Weymouth, Dorset DT4 8HQ
Tel: 01305 774268
e-mail: lian@weymouthdeli.co.uk
website: www.weymouthdeli.co.uk

Located near the sea front, close to the statue of George III, the **Weymouth Deli** stocks a huge range of quality produce. Owned and run by Lian Berry who used to make sausages here before taking over the business. The deli is noted especially for its homemade items - faggots, quiches, pies, sausages and much more, all made from scratch and based wherever possible on locally sourced produce. The deli also home cooks all its ham, turkey, beef and pork.

You'll find a large selection of local, English and Continental cheeses; smoked salmon; traditional locally baked bread and cakes; local dairy farm ice cream; coffee beans and loose leaf teas. Some of the more unusual items include biltong, fois gras, pickled quails eggs, Patum Peperium, organic Fairtrade chocolate, olives, sun-dried tomatoes, Turkish Delight and organic sesame seed bars.

The deli also stocks a wide selection of Country Wines from Gales Brewery in Horndean, rice wine, cider brandy, West Country liqueurs, Perry's somerset cider, a traditional ale "Boondoggle", made by Ringwood Brewery; River Cottage Ale - an organic ale made from nettles at the Badger Brewery at Blandford; vintage port and a small selection of good quality wines.

king had brought great kudos and prosperity to their little seaside resort by coming here to bathe in the sea water. George had been advised that sea-bathing would help cure his 'nervous disorder' so, between 1789 and 1805, he and his royal retinue spent a total of 14 holidays in Weymouth. Fashionable society naturally followed in his wake and left as its legacy the wonderful seafront of Georgian terraces. Not far away, at the head of King Street, George's granddaughter Victoria is commemorated by a colourful **Jubilee Clock** erected in 1887, the 50th year of her reign.

Nearby, the picturesque harbour is always busy – fishing boats, paddle steamers, pleasure boats, catamarans servicing the Channel Islands and St Malo in France and, if you're lucky, you may even see a Tall Ship or two.

One of the town's premier tourist venues is **Brewers Quay** (see panel on page 286), an imaginatively redeveloped Victorian brewery offering an enormous diversity of visitor attractions within a labyrinth of paved courtyards and cobbled streets. There are no fewer than 22 different establishments within the complex, ranging from craft shops and restaurants through a fully automated ten pin bowling alley to the **Timewalk Journey** which promises visitors that they will "See, hear and smell over 600 years of Weymouth's spectacular history".

From Brewers Quay, a path leads through **Nothe Gardens** to **Nothe Fort**, built between 1860 and 1872 as part of the defences of the new naval base being established on Portland. Ten huge guns face

Brewers Quay

Old Harbour, Weymouth, Dorset DT4 8TR
Tel: 01305 777622 Fax: 01305 761680
website: www.brewers-quay.co.uk

Brewers Quay is an imaginatively converted Victorian brewery in the heart of the picturesque Old Harbour. Amid the paved courtyards and cobbled alleys is a unique under-cover shopping village with over 20 specialist shops and attractions.

The Timewalk tells the fascinating story of the town as seen through the eyes of the brewery cat and her family, and in the Brewery Days attraction, Hope Square's unique brewing heritage is brought to life with an interactive family gallery, audio-visual show and Victorian-style Tastings Bar.

Weymouth Museum contains an important record of local and social history; its latest exhibition is called Marine Archaeology and Associated Finds from the Sea. The Discovery Hands-on Science Centre has over 60 interactive exhibits, and this entertaining complex also has a bowling alley, gift shops, a traditional pub and a self-service restaurant.

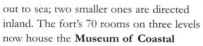

out to sea; two smaller ones are directed inland. The fort's 70 rooms on three levels now house the **Museum of Coastal Defence** which has many interesting displays illustrating past service life in the fort, history as seen from the Nothe headland, and the part played by the people of Weymouth in World War II. Nothe Fort is owned and operated by the Weymouth Civic Society which also takes

care of **Tudor House,** just north of Brewers Quay. One of the town's few remaining Tudor buildings, the house originally stood on the edge of an inlet from the harbour and is thought to have been a merchant's house. It's now furnished in the style of an early-17th century middle class home and the guided tour gives some fascinating insights into life in those days.

Only yards from the waters of Weymouth Bay, **Lodmoor Country Park** is another popular attraction. Access to most of the park is free and visitors can take advantage of the many sport and recreation areas, wander around the footpaths and nature reserve, or enjoy a picnic or barbecue.

A major family attraction is **Deep Sea Adventure** with two separate attractions under one roof. Deep Sea Adventure tells

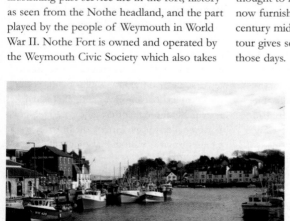

🏛 historic building 🏛 museum and heritage 🏛 historic site 🝔 scenic attraction 🐦 flora and fauna

THE CHANNEL HOTEL

93 The Esplanade, Weymouth,
Dorset DT4 7AY
Tel: 01305 785405
e-mail: channel.hotel@googlemail.com

The Channel is a beautiful Grade II listed Georgian town house, originally built in 1797, and located on Weymouth's famous Esplanade, opposite the sandy beach and looking out into Weymouth Bay, a view which has to be experienced to be fully appreciated. The owners say, "as a family run guest house we're here to provide a warm welcome in comfortable surroundings and to make your experience within the house and in Weymouth a memorable experience that will have you wanting to come back again and again." The visitor book has many entries that tell how comfortable the stay was, how good the food was and that it was like a "home from home".

The house has 11 bedrooms comprising of a mix of single, double and family rooms to suit the range of guests regularly welcomed into the house. The hotel is family friendly and welcomes children of all ages. All of the sea view rooms have unobstructed views over Weymouth bay, and for those special occasions you may want to try the four poster room. Family rooms all comprise one double bed and two single beds.

As part of the cost of your accommodation the hotel offers complimentary parking permits and wireless internet access. Some of the parking permits also allow free parking at local visitor attractions around Weymouth and the surrounding areas. For those travelling by rail or coach the hotel is ideally placed just a few moments walk from the railway station and coach stop. The hotel holds a three star rating from Visit Britain and Associate Guest House rating from The AA, and has recently won a Silver Award from Weymouth & Portland borough council for its food hygiene standards. The hotel is also awaiting grading by the Green Tourism Business Scheme, to assess its success in the reduce, reuse and recycle activities that it already follows, together with other green business practices.

the story of underwater exploration and marine exploits from the 17th century through to the modern day. This entertaining and educational exhibition fills three floors of an imposing Victorian Grain Warehouse with a wealth of animated and interactive displays recounting compelling tales of shipwreck survival and search and rescue operations, a "Black Hole" in which you can experience what it is like to be a deep sea diver, and a unique display which tells the epic story of the Titanic in the words of the officers, crew and survivors, along with the original Titanic signals and one of the largest models of the doomed ship in the world. A fairly recent addition to Deep Sea Adventure is Sharky's, a

huge, all-weather adventure play area for children of all ages, (with a height limit of 5ft), and with a separate area for toddlers.

OSMINGTON
3 miles NE of Weymouth on the A353

⚐ White Horse 🏨 Smugglers Inn

There are several 'White Horses' carved into hillsides around the country, but the **White Horse** near Osmington, apart from being one of the largest, (354ft high and 279ft wide), is the only one which also has a rider. The horse was created in 1807; the rider was added about three years later. Wearing a tall cocked hat and carrying a whip, the horseman represents George III. The king was a frequent visitor to nearby Weymouth and his royal patronage naturally attracted many free-spending courtiers to the town. The town fathers of Weymouth decided to express their appreciation by paying the local militia to add the royal rider. The result was an unrecognisable, if undoubtedly loyal, tribute to His Majesty. Like all the other White Horses in England, it looks much better when seen from a few miles away; close up, it is meaningless.

A mile south of Osmington, at Osmington Mills, the area's notorious history in trading contraband liquor lingers in the name of The **Smugglers Inn.** Unlike many similarly-named hostelries, this one really was a regular haunt for smugglers. Dating back to the 13th century, this former fisherman's cottage enjoyed a secluded position and the nearby beach provided safe landing. The inn's landlord in the early 1800s was Emmanuel Carless who, together with his French partner, Pierre Latour or 'French Peter', ran a thriving business importing thousands of gallons of brandy each year. Unfortunately, the liquor was so inferior locals refused to drink it and the spirit had to be carried inland on stage coaches, disguised as luggage, to be distilled again.

ISLE OF PORTLAND
4 miles S of Weymouth, on the A354

✤ Tout Quarry Sculpture Park	🏛 Portland Castle	
🏛 St Andrew's Avalanche Church	⋔ The Fleet	
⋒ Chesil Beach	🏛 Portland Museum	

Portland is not really an island at all, but a 4.5 mile long peninsula, well known to devotees of shipping forecasts and even more famous for the stone from its quarries. Numerous buildings in London are constructed of Portland stone, amongst them St. Paul's

Cathedral, Inigo Jones' Banqueting Hall in Whitehall, and Buckingham Palace. The stone was also favoured by sculptors such as Henry Moore. The quarries still provide the renowned stone and are also used as study centres. In the **Tout Quarry Sculpture Park** some 50 pieces in the local stone are on display – watch out for Anthony Gormley's figure of a man falling down the rock face.

The island's most famous building is **Portland Castle** (English Heritage), one of the finest of Henry VIII's coastal fortresses. Its active role lasted for 500 years, right up to World War II when it provided a D-Day embarkation point for British and American forces. Oliver Cromwell used the castle as a prison and in Victorian times it was the residence of Portland's governors. Visitors can try on the armour, meet 'Henry VIII' in the Great Hall, and enjoy the special events that are held regularly throughout the year. The battlements command superb views of Portland Harbour whose breakwaters were

Bill of Portland Lighthouse

constructed by convict labour to create the second largest man-made harbour in the world. On the highest point of the island is Verne Citadel which was a base for troops defending Portland and Weymouth. It became a prison in 1950.

At Southwell, near the tip of Portland Bill, **St Andrew's Avalanche** church was built in 1879 chiefly as a memorial to those who perished when the clipper *Avalanche* sank off the Portland coast at the beginning of a passage to New Zealand. Also in Southwell is the **Portland Museum** which was founded by the birth control pioneer Marie Stopes who lived on the island. Housed in a charming pair of thatched cottages, the museum tells the story of life on the island from smuggling and shipwrecks to traditions and customs. One of the cottages inspired Thomas Hardy to centre his novel *The Well-Beloved* around it, making it the home of 'Avice', the heroine of the story.

At the southernmost tip of the island, the Bill of Portland, the first lighthouse to be built here is now a base for birdwatchers. The current Portland Bill Lighthouse offers guided tours during the season and also has a visitor centre. Nearby are some particularly fascinating natural features: the tall, upright Pulpit Rock which can be climbed, and some caves to explore.

The Isle provides some good cliff-top walks with grand views of **Chesil Beach**, a vast bank of pebbles worn smooth by the sea which stretches for some 10 miles to Abbotsbury. Inexplicably, the pebbles are graded in size from west to east. Fishermen reckon they can judge whereabouts on the beach they are landing by the size of the

Chesil Beach

pebbles. In the west they are as small as peas and usually creamy in colour; at Portland they have grown to the size of cooking apples and are more often grey. The long, narrow body of water trapped behind the beach is known as **The Fleet.** It is now a nature reserve and home to a wide variety of waterfowl and plants, as well as fish that can be viewed by taking a trip in a glass-bottomed boat.

CHICKERELL
3 miles NW of Weymouth off the 3157

🌱 Water Gardens

A pretty village of thatched cottages, Chickerell is best known for its **Water Gardens** which were created in 1959 by Norman Bennett. He began by growing water lilies in the disused clay pits of a brickworks. The gardens are now home to the National Collection of Water Lilies. Within the gardens is a museum telling the story of the village which featured in the *Domesday Book*.

PORTESHAM
6 miles NW of Weymouth on the B3157

🏛 Hardy's Monument 🌱 Great Dorset Maize Maze

On the Black Downs northeast of Portesham stands **Hardy's Monument** (National Trust)

🎦 stories and anecdotes 🐦 famous people ⚘ art and craft 🖉 entertainment and sport 🦶 walks

Abbotsbury

Abbotsbury Tourism Ltd, West Yard Barn,
West Street, Abbotsbury, Dorset DT3 4JT
Tel: 01305 871130 Fax: 01305 871092
e-mail: info@abbotsbury-tourism.co.uk
website: www.abbotsbury-tourism.co.uk

Surrounded by hills, with the sea close at hand, **Abbotsbury** is one of the county's most popular tourist spots and by any standards one of the loveliest villages in England. Very little remains of the Benedictine Abbey that gives the village its name, but what has survived is the magnificent Great Abbey Barn, a tithe barn almost 250ft long that was built in the 14th century to house the Abbey's tithes of wool, grain and other produce.

The village's three main attractions, which bring the crowds flocking in their thousands to this lovely part of the world, are the **Swannery**, the **Sub-Tropical Gardens** and the **Tithe Barn Children's Farm**. The most famous of all is Abbotsbury Swannery, which was established many centuries ago, originally to provide food for the monks in the Abbey. For at least 600 years the swannery has been a sanctuary for a huge colony of mute swans. The season for visitors begins in earnest in March, when the swans vie for the best nesting sites. From May to the end of June cygnets hatch by the hundred and from then until October the fluffy chicks grow and gradually gain their wings. Cygnets who have become orphaned are protected in special pens until strong enough to fend for themselves. By the end of October many of the swans move off the site for the winter, while other wildfowl move in. An audio-visual show is run hourly in the old swanherd's cottage, and a few lucky visitors are selected to help out at the spectacular twice-daily feeding sessions. The swans' feed includes eelgrass from the River Fleet. In May of this year the Swanherd, who has looked after the colony for 40 years, Dick Dalley, retired. When he first started the birds were still being raised for the table, but today, the 159 breeding pairs - including two black swans - are protected by law. Also on site are a shire horse and cart service, a gift shop and a café housed in a delightful building that was converted from Georgian kennels.

At the western end of the village, Abbotsbury Sub-Tropical Gardens, established by the first Countess of Ilchester as a kitchen garden for her nearby castle, occupy a 20-acre site close to Chesil Beach that's largely protected from the elements by a ring of oak trees. In this micro-climate a huge variety of rare and exotic plants and trees flourish, and the camellia groves and the collections of rhododendrons and hydrangeas are known the world over.

There's a woodland trail, a children's play area, visitor centre, plant nursery, gift shop and restaurant with a veranda overlooking the sunken garden. Most of the younger children will make a beeline for the Tithe Barn Children's Farm, where they can cuddle the rabbits, bottle feed the lambs, race toy tractors, feed the doves and meet the donkeys and horses. The Farm's latest attraction is the Smugglers Barn, where the little ones can learn and play at the same time.

🏠 historic building 🏛 museum and heritage 🏚 historic site 🦢 scenic attraction 🌿 flora and fauna

which commemorates, not Thomas Hardy the great novelist of Wessex, but Sir Thomas Hardy the flag-captain of *HMS Victory* at Trafalgar to whom the dying Lord Nelson spoke the immortal words, "Kiss me, Hardy", (or possibly, "Kismet, Hardy"). Sir Thomas was born in Portesham and, like his novelist namesake, was descended from the Hardys of Jersey. After Trafalgar, he escorted Nelson's body back to London and soon afterwards was created a baronet and, eventually, First Sea Lord. Sir Thomas's stunningly graceless memorial has been variously described as a "huge candlestick", a "peppermill", and most accurately as a "factory chimney wearing a crinoline". But if you stand with your back to it, there are grand views over Weymouth Bay.

Just to the east of Portesham, an unusual attraction, the **Great Dorset Maize Maze,** challenges visitors to 'crack' the world-class maze with its fiendishly intricate design. Popular with families, the site also gives youngsters the opportunity to mingle with farm animals, and to have fun on the trampolines and pedal go-carts, or in the indoor fun barns.

ABBOTSBURY
8 miles NW of Weymouth on the B3157

🏛 St Catherine's Chapel	🦢 Abbotsbury Swannery
🏛 Great Abbey Barn	
🌿 Abbotsbury Sub-tropical Gardens	

Surrounded by hills, picturesque Abbotsbury is one of the county's most popular tourist spots (see panel opposite) and by any standards one of the loveliest villages in England. Its most striking feature as you approach is the 14th century **St Catherine's Chapel,** perched on the hill-top. Only 45ft by 15ft, it is solidly built to withstand the Channel gales with walls more than four feet thick. St Catherine was believed to be particularly helpful in finding husbands for the unmarried and in medieval times spinsters would climb the hill to her chapel chanting a dialect jingle which concludes with the words *"Arn-a-one's better than narn-a-one"* – anyone is better than never a one.

Abbotsbury takes its name from the important Benedictine Abbey that once stood here but was comprehensively cannibalised after the Reformation, its stones used to build the attractive cottages that line the village streets. What has survived however is the magnificent **Great Abbey Barn**, 247ft long and 31ft wide, which was built in the 1300s to store the abbey's tithes of wool, grain and other produce. With its thatched roof, stone walls and a mightily

Hardy's Monument, nr Portesham

🏛 stories and anecdotes 🦢 famous people 🌿 art and craft 🖊 entertainment and sport 🚶 walks

TAMARISK FARM

West Bexington, Dorchester DT2 9DF
Tel: 01308 8977784
e-mail: holidays@tamariskfarm.com
website: www.tamariskfarm.co.uk

Offering quality self-catering accommodation, **Tamarisk Farm** is located in West Bexington, a small coastal village between Abbotsbury and Burton Bradstock. The village stands on a slope running down to the unspoilt Chesil Beach and enjoys some magnificent views. The farm is operated organically and within its 600 acres are a flock of Dorset Down sheep, a herd of North Devon Ruby Red beef cattle and calves, Shire mares, Welsh ponies and a few of the rare breed Hebridean and Shetland sheep.

There are six properties available to rent, in various locations around the village. They range in size from Granary Lodge which sleeps seven people, to The Fossil and the Cross which sleeps four. All are comprehensively equipped and all boast either a four or three-star rating from Visit Britain.

The owners of the farm also have a small market garden with fruit and vegetables, and about 35 acres of arable crops. They mill their own home-grown wheat and rye, producing wholemeal, stoneground flour. Hampers of vegetables in season are available on request and you can order flour and meat before you arrive.

impressive entrance it is one of the largest and best-preserved barns in the country.

About a mile south of the village is the famous **Abbotsbury Swannery**, established in Saxon times to provide food for the abbey during the winter months. Up to 600 free-flying swans have made their home here and visitor figures rocket from the end of May to the end of June – the baby swans' hatching season. Quills from the fully-grown swans are still sent to Lloyds of London where they have been used for centuries to write the names of ships lost at sea in their official insurance records. There's also a children's Ugly Duckling Trail and the oldest known duck decoy still working.

Just to the west of the village, **Abbotsbury Sub-Tropical Gardens** enjoy a particularly well-sheltered position and the 20 acres of grounds contain a huge variety of rare and exotic plants and trees. Other attractions include an 18th century walled garden, beautiful lily ponds and a children's play area.

Sherborne

🏛 Sherborne Abbey   🏛 Sherborne Old Castle

🏛 Sherborne New Castle   🏛 Sherborne Museum

🏛 Almshouses   🏛 Sandford Orcas Manor House

🏛 Conduit House   🌿 Pageant Gardens

One of the most beautiful towns in England, Sherborne beguiles the visitor with its serene atmosphere of a cathedral city, although it is not a city and its lovely **Abbey** no longer enjoys the status of a cathedral. Back in AD705 though, when it was founded by St Aldhelm, the abbey was the Mother Cathedral for the whole of southwest England. Of that original Saxon church only minimal traces remain: most of the present building dates back to the mid-1400s which, by happy chance, was the most glorious period in the history of English ecclesiastical architecture. The intricate tracery of the fan vaulting above the nave of the abbey looks like the supreme culmination of a long-practised art: in fact, it is one of the earliest examples in England. There is much else to admire in this majestic church: 15th century misericords in the choir stalls which range from the sublime, (Christ sitting in majesty on a rainbow), to the scandalous, (wives beating their husbands); a wealth of elaborate tombs amongst which is a lofty six-poster from Tudor times, a floridly baroque late-17th century memorial to the 3rd

Earl of Bristol, and another embellished with horses' heads in a punning tribute to Sir John Horsey who lies below alongside his son.

As well as founding the abbey, St Aldhelm is also credited with establishing Sherborne School which numbered amongst its earliest pupils the two elder brothers of King Alfred, (and possibly Alfred himself). Later alumni include the Poet Laureate Cecil Day-Lewis and the writer David Cornwell, better known as John le Carré, author of *The Spy Who Came in from the Cold* and many other thrillers.

Perhaps the best-known resident of Sherborne however is Sir Walter Raleigh. At a time when he enjoyed the indulgent favour of Elizabeth I he asked for, and was granted, the house and estate of **Sherborne Old Castle** (English Heritage). Sir Walter soon realised

🎭 stories and anecdotes   🐦 famous people   🎨 art and craft   ✒ entertainment and sport   🚶 walks

Sherborne

Distance: *5.0 miles (8.0 kilometres)*

Typical time: *120 mins*

Height gain: *75 metres*

Map: *Explorer 129*

Walk: *www.walkingworld.com ID:582*

Contributor: *Pat Mallet*

Park in Sherborne station car park.

A delightful walk through fields, woods and farms with views of Sherborne's two famous castles and their lake as well as panoramas of the gentle hills of Dorset. It is mainly undulating countryside with just one short hill.

Lake/loch, castle, great views

1 | From the station car park, cross the railway tracks and walk up Gas House Hill to the main road at the top.

2 | From the top of Gas House Hill, turn left at the waymarked path up the gentle slope to the swing-gate at the top.

3 | Follow the well-walked path through the fields with Sherborne Castle and beautiful lake on your left in the distance.

4 | Go through the gate and continue in the same direction, along the path straight ahead. You climb a little here, towards the deer-park at the top of the hill.

5 | Go through the high deer-gate, past a boarded-up thatched gatehouse and on up the hill. Look for the deer in the trees.

6 | Exit the deer park at the top of the hill and follow the path as it goes through the woods past the overgrown foundations of a World War II army camp. You reach some corrugated iron farm buildings after about ½km.

7 | Turn right in the middle of the group of farm buildings, along a tarmac road. Continue to a small crossroads, about 200m away.

8 | Turn sharp left here so that you are facing a farm cottage up the track. Walk towards the cottage as far as the waymark on the side of the road and there turn right, only about 50 metres. Follow the edge of the field with the fence on your left, to a stile on your left. Climb the stile and follow the path (sometimes muddy) through the trees to another deer-gate.

9 | You are now back in the deer-park. Follow the telegraph poles down the hill towards Pinfold Farm, straight ahead in the valley. Apart from the farm, can you see another building? Keep a straight line for the farm, across a stile and a wooden bridge over the River Yeo. On your left, you may see just the end of the artificial lake created by Capability Brown in the grounds of the castle.

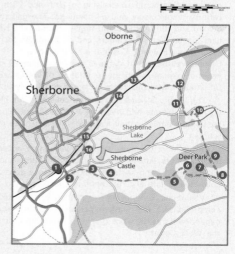

10 | At the waymark on the gate to the left of the main farm buildings, turn left and walk along the farm road for about 100 metres, through another gate with a waymark just beyond on a post on the right. Turn right here and walk through the field towards the two imposing stone gate pillars up the slope.

11 | Walk between the gate pillars and take the second path on the left, through the trees. Immediately turn right and follow a narrow path in the trees, NOT the obvious track which veers left. Follow the path until it reaches a stile, coming out of the woods.

12 | Climb the stile, go straight ahead across the fields towards the railway line, setting your sights on the rail track lights in the distance. The tunnel under the railway line lies to the right of the rail lights. Go through the tunnel, keeping to the right and look for a stile, which at times is hidden behind a farm manure pile.

13 | Climb the stile, go up to the main road and turn left. A detour can be made here to the tiny village of Oborne (signposted from the road).

14 | Walk back towards Sherborne along the main road for a distance of about ¼km, then take the left fork onto the B3145. Continue along the road past the Castleton Waterwheel on the left (sometimes open for tours).

15 | Fork left here towards the castle, cross the bridges over the railway and the River Yeo and see the next waymark on a gate to the right.

16 | Turn through the gate and follow the river back to the station and the car park. As a pleasant extension to the walk, take a stroll through the gardens opposite the station. Veering left, exit the gardens on the north west side, walk up Digby Road to the Abbey (about 200m) and visit this 1,000-year-old church. From there it is a short stroll to the delightful shops and teashops of Sherborne.

that the medieval pile with its starkly basic amenities was quite unsuitable for a courtier of his sophistication and ambition. He built a new castle alongside it, **Sherborne New Castle**, a strange three-storeyed, hexagonal structure which must rate, from the outside, as one of the most badly-designed, most unlikeable mansions to be erected in an age when other Elizabethan architects were creating some of the loveliest buildings in England. Inside Sir Walter's new castle, it is quite a different story: gracious rooms with elaborately-patterned ceilings, portraits of the man who single-handedly began the creation of the British Empire, and huge windows which at the time Sir Walter ordered them proclaimed a clear message that its owner had the wealth to pay the enormous cost of glazing such vast expanses. After Sir Walter's execution, the castle was purchased in 1617 by Sir James Digby and it has remained with his descendants ever since. They added exquisite gardens designed by Capability Brown and in the late 1800s re-decorated the interior in Jacobean style. Amongst the castle's greatest treasures is the famous painting by Robert Peake depicting Elizabeth I on procession, being carried on a litter and surrounded by a sumptuously dressed retinue. The old cellar of the castle is now a museum housing an eclectic display of items, most gruesome of which is the skull of a Royalist soldier killed in the seige of 1645. A bullet is still lodged in his eye socket. Sherborne New Castle, incidentally, is one of several locations claiming to be the genuine setting for the old story of Sir Walter enjoying a pipe of tobacco and being doused with a bucket of water by a servant who believed his master was on fire. Sherborne Castle is open from April to October, and also offers visitors an attractive lakeside tearoom, a well-stocked gift shop, and

Sherborne Castle

striking building is the former Abbey Gatehouse which frames the entrance to Church Lane where the **Sherborne Museum** has a collection of more than 15,000 items relating to local history. Particularly notable are two major photographic collections recording events and people in the town since 1880.

To the south of the town, near the railway station, **Pageant Gardens** were established in 1905 using funds raised by a great pageant of that year celebrating the 1,200th anniversary of the founding of the town by St Aldhelm.

various special events throughout the year.

This appealing small town with a population of around 8,500 has much else to interest the visitor. The **Almshouse of Saints John the Baptist and John the Evangelist**, near the abbey, was founded in 1437 and the original buildings, completed in 1448, are still in use as an almshouse, accepting both men and women. The almshouse chapel boasts one of the town's greatest treasures, a late-15th century Flemish altar tryptich which can be viewed on afternoons during the summer. Close by, the **Conduit House** is an attractive small hexagonal building from the early 1500s, originally used as a lavatorium, or washroom, for the abbey monks' ablutions. It was moved here after the Reformation and has served variously as a public fountain and a police phone box. The Conduit House is specifically mentioned in Hardy's *The Woodlanders* as the place where Giles Winterborne, seeking work, stood here in the market place "as he always did at this season of the year, with his specimen apple tree". Another

About two miles north of Sherborne, **Sandford Orcas Manor House** is a charming Tudor building with terraced gardens, topiary and herb garden. Since it was built in honey-coloured Ham Hill stone in the 1550s, only three different families have lived here. The present owner, Sir Mervyn Medlycott, whose family has lived here for more than 250 years, personally conducts guided tours that take in the manor's Great Hall, stone newel staircases, huge fireplaces, fine panelling, Jacobean and Queen Anne furniture and family portraits.

Shaftesbury Abbey Museum

Around Sherborne

MELBURY OSMOND

6 miles SW of Sherborne off the A37

It was in the Church of St Osmund in this pretty village that Thomas Hardy's parents, Jemima Hand and Thomas Hardy, were married in 1839. At the northern end of the footpath through the churchyard is a thatched house where Hardy's mother is thought to have lived as a child.

In Hardy's novels the village appears as Great Hintock which provides the setting for *The Woodlanders*. Melbury Osmond is still unspoilt and picturesque with many oak trees – do find time to walk down from the church to the water splash, and beyond to some 17th century thatched stone cottages.

Shaftesbury

🏛 Abbey Museum 🏛 Local History Museum

🐚 Gold Hill 🎭 Shaftesbury Arts Centre

🐑 Dorset Rare Breeds Centre

Set on the side of a hill 700ft high, Shaftesbury was officially founded in 880AD by King Alfred who fortified the town and also built an abbey of which his daughter was first Prioress. A hundred years later, the King Edward who had been murdered by his stepmother at Corfe Castle was buried here and the abbey became a major centre of pilgrimage. A few remains of Shaftesbury Abbey have survived – they can be seen in the walled garden of the **Abbey Museum** which contains many interesting artefacts excavated from the site.

BELL STREET CAFÉ

Bell Street, Shaftesbury, Dorset SP7 8AR
Tel: 01747 850022
website: www.bellstreetcafe.co.uk

A café by day and a restaurant at night, the **Bell Street Café** is owned and run by Nicola and Ben Rutter who believe that good food and ethical principles should go hand in hand. They take great care in sourcing top quality produce from local suppliers who are mainly organic. They try to be as environmentally friendly as possible and only use products manufactured by eco friendly manufacturers; from the paint on the walls to their cleaning products from Ecover.

The food style here is "Rustic Chic" and based on a series of Theme Menus made from recipes from France, Italy and Spain and cuisines such as Arabesque, Creole & Cajun, Basque & Persian. As Nicola and Ben put it: "Good food, inspired by legends, created by mortals!" To accompany your meal, there's a good selection of European wines to choose from.

Theme and Live Music evenings are held throughout the year celebrating notable dates,

events, culinary rendezvous or introductions to new gastronomic pleasures from around the world. Music is generally of a 'jazzy' nature with offerings from Trad Jazz and Gypsy Jazz/Manouche bands after Django Reinhardt, classical and Spanish guitar with occasional Irish & Scottish folk evenings.

🎭 stories and anecdotes 🍴 famous people 🎨 art and craft 🎶 entertainment and sport 🚶 walks

GREEN ROCK CAFÉ

Swans Yard, High Street, Shaftesbury,
Dorset SP7 8JQ
Tel: 01747 858550

In a quiet courtyard just off Shaftesbury High Street, you will find **Green Rock Café**. Situated within easy walking distance of many of Shaftesbury's individual and unique shops, it is the ideal place to take a break from shopping or rest after tackling the steepness of Gold Hill! Established over six years ago, during the last 18 months new owners Terri Wiltshire and Stephen Angell have created a friendly, contemporary café where you can enjoy a wide variety of homemade fare.

Sit back in the comfortable chairs or relaxing sofas and choose from a huge selection of sandwiches, baguettes, paninis and toasties all freshly made on the premises from locally sourced and Fair Trade produce wherever possible.

For those wanting a more substantial bite, a delicious range of hot meals are available with vegetarians also catered for. Alternatively you can simply enjoy a cup of freshly ground local coffee and some homemade cake whilst admiring the mural of Old Town Shaftesbury in the courtyard seating area. All are catered for at Green Rock Café. It is not just the deliciously tempting array of freshly made food but with disabled access and facilities, baby changing facilities and breastfeeding mothers made welcome, all customers from the elderly to the very youngest will want to return again and again!

DAIRY HOUSE ANTIQUES

Station Road, Semley, Shaftesbury, Dorset SP7 9AN
Tel: 01747 853317
e-mail: mail@dairyhouseantiques.co.uk
website: www.dairyhouseantiques.co.uk

Situated approximately three miles north of Shaftesbury, just off the A350 Warminster road, **Dairy House Antiques**, established in 1998, is housed in the old Semley Dairy. Visitors should take the turn signed to Semley Industrial Estate where you will find the three-storey building just a few hundred yards from the turn. Seventeen dealers currently display their stock in this wonderful old building with its black and white tiled upstairs floors.

The Dairy offers a large and regularly-changing selection of competitively-priced antique and decorative furniture dating from the 17th to the 20th century to suit your home, whatever its size. A selection of pine and painted English and Continental furniture is generally available and other dealers specialise in lighting, rugs and carpets, linen and textiles, pictures, kitchenalia and decorative items. In addition china and glass, together with other small collectables, are displayed in cabinets.

There is plenty of parking right outside, and a warm welcome awaits customers old and new. Open: Monday-Saturday 10am - 5pm; Sunday 11am - 4pm

Shaftesbury is a pleasant town to explore on foot. In fact, you *have* to walk if you want to see its most famous sight, **Gold Hill**, a steep, cobbled street, stepped in places and lined with 18th century cottages. Already well-known for its picturesque setting and grand views across the Vale of Blackmoor, Gold Hill became even more famous when it was featured in the classic TV commercial for Hovis. Also located on Gold Hill is the **Shaftesbury Town Museum** which vividly evokes the story of this ancient market town.

The 17th century Ox House, which is referred to in Thomas Hardy's *Jude the Obscure*, is just one of a number of interesting and historic buildings in the town. Others include the Church of St Peter, the Tudor-style Town Hall dating from the 1820s, and the Grosvenor Hotel, a 400-year-old coaching inn.

Shaftesbury boasts one of the liveliest arts centres in the country, the **Shaftesbury Arts Centre** which, remarkably, is completely owned by its membership and administered entirely by volunteers. The results of their efforts are anything but amateur, however. The centre's Drama Group is responsible for three major productions each year, performed in the well-equipped theatre which also serves as a cinema for the centre's Film Society,

screening a dozen or more films during the season. One of the most popular features of the centre is its Gallery which is open daily with a regularly changing variety of exhibitions ranging from paintings, etchings and sculpture, to batiks, stained glass, embroideries and quilting.

Around Shaftesbury

ASHMORE
5 miles SE of Shaftesbury off the B3081

🏛 Compton Abbas Airfield

To the northwest of Ashmore is **Compton Abbas Airfield** which is generally considered to be the most picturesque airfield in the country. Situated at more than 800ft above sea level, the airfield is surrounded by an Area of Outstanding Natural Beauty and 50% of the airfield is organically farmed. One of the most popular displays is the collection of famous aeroplanes, special effects and memorabilia from film and TV productions. For the more adventurous, flights are available with a qualified instructor for a trip over this scenic part of the county; training courses for a full pilot's licence are also conducted here. The airfield hosts regular events throughout the

---

VALE HOLIDAYS

Vale Farm, Sutton Waldron, nr Blandford Forum, Dorset DT11 8PG
Tel: 01747 811286
e-mail: valeholidays@tiscali.co.uk website: www.valeholidays.co.uk

Jon Drake and family welcome visitors to Vale Farm in the heart of the beautiful Blackmore Vale, the home of **Vale Holidays**.
Their luxury four-star barn conversions are set in outstanding countryside and the area has been described as "the prettiest pocket of Dorset". Visitors are welcome to watch the cows being milked, feed the calves, walk the two puppies and enjoy staying on a farm. The properties are close to a golf driving range, a super sports centre, riding stables and two village shops/post offices, one with a delicious in-store bakery for freshly baked bread, croissants and pies.

📖 stories and anecdotes 🦢 famous people 🎨 art and craft 🖋 entertainment and sport 🚶 walks

year, including aerobatic displays; there's a shop selling a range of stunt and power kites; a bar and restaurant.

To the west of Ashmore are Fontwell and Melbury Downs, two estates that cover an important stretch of chalk downland that is cut by steep-sided valleys. Both areas are owned by the National Trust and evoke the landscapes described by Thomas Hardy – they are also notable for their population of butterflies.

MARNHULL
7 miles SW of Shaftesbury on the B3092

🏠 Tess's Cottage

The scattered village of Marnhull claims to be the largest parish in England, spread over a substantial area with a circumference of 23 miles. The village itself is well worth exploring for its part-Norman St Gregory's church with a fine 15th century tower, and who knows what you might find along Sodom Lane? This now-prosperous village appears in *Tess of the d'Urbervilles* as 'Marlott', the birthplace of the heroine. The thatched **Tess's Cottage** (private, but visible from the lane) is supposedly the house Hardy had in mind, while the Crown Inn (also thatched) is

still recognisable as the "Pure Drop Inn" in the same novel.

STALBRIDGE
9 miles SW of Shaftesbury on the A357

🏠 Market Cross

The 15th century church here has a striking 19th century tower which provides a landmark throughout the Vale of Blackmoor. Perhaps even more impressive is the town's **Market Cross** standing 30ft high and richly carved with scenes of the Crucifixion and Resurrection. Just outside the town, Stalbridge Park (private) sheltered Charles I after his defeat at Marston Moor. The house (now demolished) was built by Richard Boyle, 1st Earl of Cork, and it was here that his 7th son, the celebrated physicist and chemist Robert Boyle carried out the experiments that eventually led to his formulation of Boyle's Law.

STURMINSTER NEWTON
11 miles SW of Shaftesbury on the A357

🏠 Riverside Villa   🏠 Newton Mill

This unspoilt market town – the 'capital' of the Blackmore Vale – is an essential stop for anyone following in Thomas Hardy's

---

GUGGLETON FARM ARTS PROJECT

Station Road, Stalbridge, Dorset DT10 2RQ
Tel: 01963 363456 or 01963 370219

The **Guggleton Farm Arts Project** was founded within converted stone farm buildings during 1995 for recently graduated young artists to have studio space and a gallery from which to show their work.

These small beginnings have developed into a full programme of arts related subjects for the community to participate in. As well as the gallery and studios thre is a

large workshop and dutch barn from which the courses are run. The programme includes stone carving, sculpture, painting, drawing, picture framing and children's courses. Contact Isabel de Pelet (9am-5pm) for the full programme, or for details of hiring studio, workshop or Gallery space.

🏠 historic building   🏛 museum and heritage   🏚 historic site   🌀 scenic attraction   🌿 flora and fauna

footsteps. It was at Sturminster Newton that he and his first wife Emma had their first real home together. From 1876 until 1878, they lived in "a pretty cottage overlooking the Dorset Stour, called **Riverside Villa**". Here, Hardy wrote *The Return of the Native* and he often referred later to their time at Sturminster Newton in his poems. It was, he said, "our happiest time". The house is not open to the public but is visible from a riverside footpath.

Sturminster Newton Mill

Until Elizabethan times, Sturminster and Newton were separate villages standing on opposite sides of the River Stour. Shortly after the graceful Town Bridge linked the two communities, a mill was built some 250 yards upstream. Once again restored to working order, **Newton Mill** offers guided tours explaining the milling process, and the delightful setting attracts many amateur and professional artists and photographers. Incidentally, the fine old six-arched bridge still bears a rusty metal plaque carrying the dire warning: "Any person wilfully injuring any part of this county bridge will be guilty of felony and upon conviction liable to be transported for life by the court. P. Fooks."

LYDLINCH
13 miles SW of Shaftesbury on the A357

The small hamlet of Lydlinch in the Vale of Blackmore features in a poem by the Dorset dialect poet, William Barnes. He recalls as a young boy hearing the sound of Lydlinch church bells wafting across meadows to his home in nearby Bagber:

Vor Lydlinch bells be good vor sound,
And liked by all the neighbours round.

The five bells he heard still hang in the tower of the 13th century church.

EAST STOUR
4 miles W of Shaftesbury on the A30

🐦 Henry Fielding

East Stour's literary connections are not with Dorset's omnipresent Thomas Hardy but with the man who has been dubbed 'Father of the English Novel', **Henry Fielding.** When he was three years old, Fielding's family moved to the Manor House here which stood close to the church. Fielding spent most of his childhood in the village before leaving to study at Eton and Leyden. He then spent a few years in London writing plays before returning to East Stour in 1734 with his new young wife, Charlotte Cradock. She was to provide the model for Sophia Western in his most successful novel, *Tom Jones.* By the time that book was published in 1749, Charlotte was dead, Fielding was seriously ill and he was to die just five years later while visiting Lisbon in an attempt to recover his health.

LE CHANTERELLE

Sherbourne Causeway, Shaftesbury,
Dorset SP7 9PX
Tel: 01747 852821

Conveniently located on the A30 two miles west of Shaftesbury, **Le Chanterelle** was opened by the mother and son team of Susan and Ryan Lamb in April 2007 and since then has been quietly forging a reputation for serving some of the finest food in the area.

The interior décor of the charming 17th century cottage is superb with leather sofas around an inglenook fireplace in the bar area, and crisp white tablecloths, gleaming cutlery and glasses in the dining room. Head Chef Ryan trained in Lyndhurst and Winchester and brings from his background a high standard of Anglo-French cuisine.

A full à la carte menu is available as well as a lighter lunch option. Everything served here is homemade on the premises - including the bread, ice cream and sorbets. Children eight years and above are welcome, and Susan and Ryan are happy to cater for private functions.

Dazzling food, smooth service and the elegant décor make dining at Le Chanterelle an experience to remember with pleasure. The restaurant is open from noon until 3pm, Wednesday to Sunday; and from 7pm to 9pm, Wednesday to Saturday. The restaurant has ample parking.

GILLINGHAM

4 miles NW of Shaftesbury on the B3081

🏛 Gillingham Museum

The most northerly town in Dorset, Gillingham was once an important centre for the milling of silk and the manufacture of the distinctive Victorian red-hot bricks. The parish church has a 14th century chancel but the rest of the building, like much of the town, dates from after the arrival of the railway in 1859. **Gillingham Museum** charts the history of the town and the surrounding villages from prehistoric times; an interesting exhibit here is a manual fire engine dating from 1790.

Blandford Forum

🏛 Church of St Peter & St Paul

🏛 Blandford Museum

🏛 Cavalcade of Costume Museum

🏛 Royal Signals Museum

Blandford Forum, the administrative centre of North Dorset, is beautifully situated along the wooded valley of the River Stour. It's a handsome town, thanks mainly to suffering the trauma of a great fire in 1731. The gracious Georgian buildings erected after that conflagration, most of them designed by local architects John and William Bastard, provide the town with a quite unique and soothing sense of architectural harmony. Three important ancient buildings escaped the fire of 1731: the **Ryves Almshouses** of 1682, the **Corn Exchange,** and the splendid 15th century **Old House** in The Close which was built in the Bohemian style to house Protestant refugees from Bohemia. The old parish church did not survive the fire, but its 18th century replacement, the **Church of St Peter & St Paul**, crowned by an unusual cupola, now dominates the market-place. It's well worth stepping inside the church to see the box pews, an organ presented by George III, the massive columns of Portland stone, and the elegant pulpit, designed by Sir Christopher Wren, removed here from St Antholin's Church in the City of London.

In front of the church, the **Fire Monument** (known locally as Bastard's Pump) has a dual purpose – to provide water for fire fighting and as a public drinking fountain. Opposite the church, the **Blandford Museum** features a diorama of the Great Fire along with a wonderful collection of artefacts illustrating many aspects of life in and around Blandford over the years.

Housed in one of the fine town houses designed by the Bastard brothers, the **Cavalcade of Costume Museum** displays a fantastic collection of costumes from the 1730s through to the 1950s. Originally amassed by the late Mrs Betty Penny, the collection comprises more than 500 items. The museum also has a garden, shop and tea room.

Just outside the town centre, at Blandford Camp, the **Royal Signals Museum** explores the arcane world of military communications with displays featuring spies, codes and code-breaking, the ENIGMA machine, and Dorset's involvement in the preparations for D-Day.

Around Blandford Forum

IWERNE MINSTER
6 miles N of Blandford Forum on the A350

Unusually for Dorset, the church at Iwerne Minster has a spire. It also has one of the few examples of a Victorian church restoration that was actually an improvement. The Lady Chapel here was reconstructed by the architect JL Pearson in elaborate Gothic style, roofed with a stone vault and decorated with intricate floral bosses. The beautiful stained glass is a reproduction of 16th century Flemish glass.

The old village was completely rebuilt in the early 1900s by a very wealthy Lord of the Manor and is notable for its varied cottages all built of red brick.

TARRANT HINTON
5 miles NE of Blandford Forum on the A354

Great Dorset Steam Fair

This small village is the setting for the **Great Dorset Steam Fair**, held in late-August/early September. Occupying a huge 600-acre site, this is one of the world's largest international steam events, attracting some 200 steam engines and more than 220,000 visitors. The annual extravaganza includes working engine displays, an old-time steam funfair, demonstrations of rural crafts, displays of working Shire horses and live music.

TARRANT GUNVILLE
7 miles NE of Blandford Forum off the A354

A tablet in the church here commemorates the death in 1805 of Thomas Wedgwood, son of the famous potter Josiah. Thomas's own claim to fame is as a pioneer of photography. He treated a sheet of white paper with a solution of nitrate of silver, placed a fern leaf on it and exposed the sheet to the sun. The resulting image, according to historians of photography, qualifies as possibly the first photograph ever made.

CHETTLE
7 miles NE of Blandford Forum off the A354

🏛 Chettle House

A picturesque village with a charming manor house, **Chettle House,** designed by Thomas Archer in the English baroque style and completed in 1720. Archer's work includes the north front of Chatsworth and the Church of St John in Smith Square and his buildings are typified by lavish curves, inverted scrolls and their large scale, a style that owed much to the Italian architects Bernini and Borromini. Chettle House was bought in 1846 by the Castleman family who added an ornate ceiling. The house contains portraits of the Chafin family, earlier owners, and the beautifully laid out gardens include herbaceous borders, a rose garden and croquet lawn.

BLANDFORD ST MARY
1 mile SW of Blandford Forum off the A354

🐾 Badger Brewery

The main attraction here is the **Badger Brewery** which was founded at Ansty near Dorchester in 1777 but moved to its present site here beside the River Stour in 1899. The original brewery was founded by Charles Hill, a farmer's son who learnt the brewing art along with farming. The brewery expanded quickly thanks to a contract to supply ale to the Army during the Napoleonic Wars. It is still thriving and visitors can take a tour of the premises.

MILTON ABBAS
6 miles SW of Blandford Forum off the A354

🏛 Abbey Church

This picture postcard village of thatched cottages was created in the 1770s by Joseph Damer, 1st Earl of Dorchester. The earl lived in the converted former abbey from which the village takes its name but he decided to demolish the medieval buildings, and build a more stately mansion surrounded by grounds landscaped by Capability Brown. The earl's ambitious plans required that the small town that had grown up around the abbey would have to go, so more than 100 houses, four pubs, a brewery and a school were razed to the ground. The residents were moved more than a mile away to the present village for which Brown had made the preliminary plans. The earl's new mansion is now a private school and the only part of the abbey that survived is the **Abbey Church** which contains some wonderful Pugin glass and an extraordinary tomb to the earl and his wife Caroline designed by Robert Adam. Exquisitely carved by Agostino Carlini, the monument shows the earl propped up on one elbow gazing out across his beautiful wife.

MILBORNE ST ANDREW
9 miles SW of Blandford Forum on the A354

🎭 John Morton

An attractive village in the valley of a tributary of the River Piddle, Milborne St Andrew was owned in medieval times by the Morton family. One of them gave his name to the expression 'Morton's Fork'. As Lord Chancellor to Henry VII (and Archbishop of Canterbury), **John Morton** devised a system of parting the rich, and the not-so-rich, from their money. He proposed the thesis that if a man was living in grand style he clearly had money to spare; if he lived frugally, then he obviously kept his wealth hidden away. This ingenious argument became known as Morton's Fork and many a citizen was caught on its vicious prongs. However, the system enriched and delighted the king who made Morton a Cardinal in 1493. Morton spent his remaining years spending lavishly on the building and restoration of churches, most notably in the magnificently carved and painted roof of Bere Regis church.

Wareham

🏛 Church of St Mary　🏛 Wareham Museum

🦅 TE Lawrence Memorial　𝒫 Rex Cinema

Situated between the rivers Frome and Piddle, Wareham is an enchanting little town lying

within the earthworks of a 10th century encircling wall. Standing close to an inlet of Poole Harbour, Wareham was an important port until the River Frome clogged its approaches with silt. Then, in 1726, a devastating fire consumed the town's timber buildings, a disaster which produced the happy result of a rebuilt town centre rich in handsome Georgian stone-built houses.

Wareham's history goes back much further than those days. Roman conquerors laid out its street plan: a stern grid of roads which faithfully follows the points of the compass. Saxons and Normans helped build the **Church of St Mary**, medieval artists covered its walls with devotional paintings of remarkable quality. It was in the grounds surrounding the church that King Edward was buried in 879AD after his stepmother, Queen Elfrida, contrived his murder at Corfe Castle.

THE CREATIVE GALLERY

St John's Hill, Wareham, Dorset BH20 4NB
Tel: 01929 551700
e-mail: gallery@creative-studios.com
website: www.creative-studios.com/gallery

The Creative Gallery in St John's Hill, Wareham features paintings, ceramics and photography by Dorset artists. This is an open studio where you can meet the artists and see them working. It displays local contemporary artwork and photography by brothers Cliff and Graham Towler who have a keen interest in nature and all its moods, especially landscapes. Their love of Dorset's Jurassic coastline inspires this current collection of works of acrylic and oil on canvas, watercolour and limited edition prints. There are also displays of work by old art school colleagues Jeremy Hammick, Ian Hargreaves and Lance Nation.

Established ceramic artists Andrew Davidson, Jack Doherty, Rosemarie James, Karen Harrison, Fiona Kelly, Bryony Burn and David Brown display works in stoneware and porcelain, making one-off strong sculptural forms with a distinctive variety of glazes, colours and textural surfaces. There are limited edition fine art prints by travel photographer David Jackson featuring seascapes, landscapes and classic cityscapes from his rapidly expanding west country and worldwide collection, Affinity Image Library (tel: 01929 551555). The gallery is open from 10am to 5pm, Monday to Saturday.

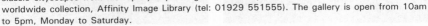

🎭 stories and anecdotes　🦅 famous people　𝒫 art and craft　🎣 entertainment and sport　🚶 walks

GOLDY'S FARM SHOP

Bere Farm, Lytchett Matravers, Dorset BH16 6ER
Tel: 01202 625777
e-mail: info@goldysfarmshop.com
website: www.goldysfarmshop.com

Winner of the prestigious FARMA Environmental Farm Shop of the Year, 2008, **Goldy's Farm Shop** aims to provide the very best local and organically produced food. The shop also sells a wide variety of foods including beautiful freshly baked bread and cakes from its own in-shop bakery. Goldy's bakery is different because the bakers use traditional, time honoured, often long forgotten methods to produce their bread. They do not use or add Es or improvers that the majority of modern breads are made with these days. And they use slower production methods and natural fermentation processes which take extra time, but means that the bread has greater taste. As well as their range of wholemeal, rye and white breads, the shop also has a range of speciality breads including pumpkin seed, seaweed, cheese & onion, olive, date & walnut and a variety of focaccia breads. The range of cakes changes each week as does the selection of homemade biscuits. The bakery also produces a range of homemade traditional pies and pasties either in the hot cabinet to take away, or chilled and frozen for home cooking.

The farm shop's butchery can provide you with beautifully prepared, quality meat, poultry and game. The butchers use innovative traditional skills to present the tasty local and organic meats, to suit modern cooking styles and palates. The chicken is free range and locally sourced, and the majority of the meat has been locally raised using organic methods. It is prepared and packaged in-house to help preserve fresh flavour and quality. The shop is licensed to sell game and it offers a lovely selection of fresh fish and delicious seafood, often caught in the waters off the beautiful Dorset coast.

You will find all of your everyday needs at Goldy's. All groceries are sourced locally and made to the highest standards, and organically where possible. There's also a wide variety of teas and instant and freshly ground coffee. And if you want to choose from a wide and exotic range of cheeses then you need go no further than Goldy's. Here you will find everything from Denhay cheddar or cheddar with spring or pickled onion, to smoked Brie, Somerset camembert and white Stilton and apricot. The shop also sells sheep's cheese and several goats' cheeses.

🏛 historic building   🏛 museum and heritage   🏛 historic site   ⌘ scenic attraction   🌱 flora and fauna

Elfrida added insult to injury by having the late king buried outside the churchyard, in unhallowed ground.

Occupying the 12th century Holy Trinity Church near the quay, the Purbeck Information & Heritage Centre offers copious information about the town; while in East Street, **Wareham Museum** has some interesting displays and artefacts illustrating the town's history.

In the Saxon St Martin's Church, notable for its early medieval wall paintings, there's a striking memorial to what appears at first glance to be a medieval crusader dressed in Arab robes, holding an Arab dagger and resting his head on a camel's saddle. This is a **memorial to TE Lawrence**, 'Lawrence of Arabia', who is actually buried at Moreton.

Wareham boasts one building that is unique – the privately owned **Rex Cinema** which was built pre-1914 and is the only gas-lit cinema in the country. The original antique carbon arc projectors are still used to show the latest blockbusters.

An even more ancient survival is the custom of the Court Leet. In Norman times these courts were the main judicial institution in many parts of the country. On four evenings in November, strangely dressed men visit the town's inns to check the quality and quantity of the food and ale on offer. The officials include ale-tasters, bread weighers and 'carnisters' who sample the meat. Although they have no powers nowadays, it is a quaint tradition.

Around Wareham

ORGANFORD
3 miles N of Wareham off the A35

🐑 Farmer Palmer's

The tiny village of Organford stands on the edge of the tree-covered expanses of Gore Heath. The settlement is so small it doesn't possess either a church or a pub, but it does have a Manor House which enjoys a wonderfully quiet and secluded position surrounded by woods. It's also home to **Farmer Palmer's Farm Park** where children can feed lambs and goats, watch cows being milked, enjoy a wild trailer ride, drive pedal tractors or work off some energy in the bouncy castles and soft play zone.

FURZEBROOK
4 miles S of Wareham off the A351

🏞 Blue Pool

If you are interested in natural curiosities, follow the brown and white signs for the **Blue Pool**. Here, in what was originally a clay pit, tiny particles of clay in the pool diffract light

The Blue Pool, Furzebrook

Worth Matravers

experiment until 1796 – 22 years after Benjamin's.

Standing high on the cliffs of St Aldhelm's Head, a couple of miles south of the village and accessible only by a bridleway, the **Chapel of St Aldhelm** stands alone. It is one of the oldest churches in Dorset, a low square building with a fine Norman doorway and one solitary window. Uniquely, the chapel has no east wall as the corners of the walls are aligned to the points of the compass. In its dank, dim interior the stonework is bare of decoration, just a central column from which eight ribs extend to the walls. According to legend, the church was built in 1140 by a local man in memory of his newly-married daughter and her husband. He was watching from this clifftop as the boat in which they were sailing to a new home was caught in a sudden squall and capsized. All on board perished.

and create an astonishing illusion of colour, varying from sky blue to deepest azure. There's a tea house, shops and museum here and the tree-lined shore is a popular picnic place.

WORTH MATRAVERS
7 miles SE of Wareham off the B3069

🎞 Benjamin Jesty   🏛 Chapel of St Aldhelm

In the graveyard of St Nicholas' Church is the grave of a local farmer, **Benjamin Jesty,** whose tomb inscription is worth quoting in full:

An upright and honest man, particularly noted for having been the first person known that introduced the Cow Pox by inoculation, and who, from his great strength of mind, made the experiment from the cow on his wife and two sons in the year 1774.

His family's "great strength of mind" might also have been noted since the inoculation was made using a knitting needle. The man usually credited with discovering inoculation, Edward Jenner, didn't make his first successful

WINFRITH NEWBURGH
9 miles SW of Wareham off the A352

🍃 Lulworth Cove 🍃 Durdle Door
🏛 Lulworth Castle

The charming little village of Winfrith Newburgh stands on a minor road that leads to one of the county's best-known beauty spots, **Lulworth Cove.** An almost perfectly circular bay, the Cove is surrounded by towering 440ft cliffs. Over the centuries, the sea has gnawed away at a weak point in the limestone here, inadvertently creating a breathtakingly beautiful scene. Best to visit out of season, however, as parking places nearby are limited.

🏛 historic building 🏛 museum and heritage 🏛 historic site 🍃 scenic attraction 🌿 flora and fauna

About a mile to the west of Lulworth Cove stands another remarkable natural feature which has been sculpted by the sea. **Durdle Door** is a magnificent archway carved from the coastal limestone. There's no road to the coast at this point, but you can reach it easily by following the South West Coast Path from Lulworth Cove. Along the way, you will also see another strange outcrop, a forest of tree-stumps which have become fossilised over the centuries.

A couple of miles inland, **Lulworth Castle** (English Heritage) looks enormously impressive from a distance: close-up, you can see how a

Cliffs near Lulworth Cove

CROMWELL HOUSE HOTEL

Lulworth Cove, West Lulworth, nr Wareham BH20 5RT
Tel: 01929 400253
Fax: 01929 400566
e-mail: catriona@lulworthcove.co.uk
website: www.lulworthcove.co.uk

Standing just 200 yards from Lulworth Cove, the **Cromwell House Hotel** provides guests with spectacular views across the cove and the Stair Hole. Built in the late-Victorian era, this family hotel is owned and personally run by Catriona and Alistair Miller. Together with their small and dedicated staff they have created a relaxed and friendly atmosphere that is reminiscent of a country house. Offering a high standard of luxury and service, the hotel has 18 guest bedrooms, along with a self-catering flat and a disabled-friendly ground floor room.

The hotel's reception rooms are spacious and attractive, many of them enjoying glorious views out over the sea, and the Millers pride themselves on the delicious food served in the dining room that faces the terrace and garden. Over the years, Catriona's cuisine has developed a style of its own, based on traditional English cooking but influenced by her years spent abroad. The dishes are freshly prepared using

only the finest local ingredients, with lobsters, crabs and scallops from Lulworth Cove's fishermen taking pride of place on the menu. The restaurant also serves a marvellous Dorset cream tea which can be enjoyed either inside or out on the south-facing patio. Other amenities included a heated outdoor swimming pool during the season.

disastrous fire in 1929 destroyed most of it. Amongst the remains, though, is a curious circular building dating from 1786: the first Roman Catholic church to be established in Britain since Henry VIII's defiance of the Pope in 1534. Sir Thomas Weld was given permission to build this unique church by George III. The king cautiously added the proviso that Sir Thomas' new place of worship should not offend Anglican sensibilities by looking like a church. It doesn't, and that's a great part of its appeal. The castle's other attractions include indoor and outdoor children's play areas; an animal farm; pitch & putt; woodland walks; café and shop.

BOVINGTON CAMP
6 miles W of Wareham off the A352

🏛 Tank Museum 🌿 Monkey World

It was at Bovington Camp that TE Lawrence served as a private in the Royal Tank Corps. Today, the camp is home to the **Tank Museum** which has more than 150 armoured vehicles on display dating from World War I to the present day. Audio tours are available, there's a children's play area, restaurant and gift shop, and during the summer tanks take part in live action displays. Also here is **Jumicar**, a children's fun and educational activity where road awareness skills are taught using real junior sized cars on a mini road layout complete with traffic lights and zebra crossings. Open every weekend and school holiday except December and January.

A very different kind of attraction, to the east of the camp, is **Monkey World** whose 65 acres are home to more than 160 rescued primates. The site also includes the largest children's adventure play area on the south coast, an education centre, woodland walk, pets corner, café, picnic areas and full disabled facilities.

BERE REGIS
7 miles NW of Wareham on the A35

🏛 Church of St John

Most visitors to the **Church of St John** at Bere Regis are attracted by its associations with Hardy's *Tess of the D'Urbervilles*. They come to see the crumbling tombs of the once-powerful Turberville family whose name Hardy adapted for his novel. It was outside the church, beneath the Turberville window, that Hardy had the homeless Tess and her family set up their four-poster bed. A poignant fictional scene, but the church itself is definitely worth visiting for its unique and magnificent carved and painted wooden roof. Large figures of the 12 Apostles (all in Tudor dress) jut out horizontally from the wall and there are a number of humorous carvings depicting men suffering the discomforts of toothache and over-indulgence. There's also a carving of Cardinal Morton who had this splendid roof installed in

Bovington Tank Museum

PAMPERED PIGS

Rye Hill Farm, Rye Hill, Bere Regis,
Wareham, Dorset BH20 7LP
Tel: 01929 472327

Meat with real "old-fashioned" flavour is the promise made by **Pampered Pigs**. A traditional farm shop selling its own pork, beef and lamb, along with a wide range of other locally produced meat, organic and GM-free groceries, locally grown fruit and vegetables, dairy products and even some local crafts. Amanda and Kevin Crocker's Rye Hill Farm in the picturesque Bere Valley is home to the beef herd consisting of traditional breeds of Angus and Hereford. This cross of old breeds gives the meat a distinct marbled appearance and hanging the carcasses for three to four weeks before cutting makes the beef wonderfully succulent. The pig herd, consisting of traditional English breeds such as British Saddlebacks,

large White, Berkshire and Gloucester Oldspots, resides at Tolpuddle in the Piddle Valley.

Over the years, the Crockers have expanded their range of products, including extending the variety of sausages and burgers made on the premises. Their menagerie of small animals has also grown and now includes rabbits, guinea pigs and pygmy goats as well as the more usual farmyard creatures. Bluebell and woodland walks can be followed, there's a café serving light lunches and cream teas, and also a plant centre.

1497. The church's history goes back much farther than that. In Saxon times, Queen Elfrida came here to spend the remainder of her days in penitence for her part in the murder of young King Edward at Corfe Castle in 979. Further evidence of the church's great age is the fact that around 1190 King John paid for the pillars of the nave to be "restored".

TOLPUDDLE

11 miles NW of Wareham on the A35

 Martyr's Museum

The small village of Tolpuddle is a peaceful little place today but in the early 19th century, Tolpuddle was far sleepier than it is now. Not the kind of place you would expect to foment a social revolution, but it was here that six ill-paid agricultural labourers helped lay the foundations of the British Trade Union

Movement. In 1833, they formed a "confederation" in an attempt to have their subsistence wages improved. The full rigour of the landowner-friendly law of the time was immediately invoked. All six were found guilty of taking illegal oaths and sentenced to transportation to Australia for seven years. Even the judge in their case was forced to say that it was not for anything they had done, or intended to do, that he passed such a sentence, but "as an example to others". Rather surprisingly, public opinion sided with the illegal "confederation". Vigorous and sustained protests eventually forced the government to pardon the men after they had served three years of their sentence. They all returned safely to England, honoured ever afterwards in trade union hagiography as the "Tolpuddle Martyrs". The **Martyrs' Museum** at Tolpuddle tells an inspiring story, but it's

 stories and anecdotes famous people art and craft entertainment and sport walks

CANDLEWORLD

14 High Street, Swanage, Dorset BH19 2NT
Tel: 01929 421611
e-mail: candleworld@mac.com
website: www.candleworld.co.uk

A well-established business, **Candleworld** has been supplying its customers with quality candles for more than a quarter of a century. Owner Vicky Clarke was a costumier based in London before taking over here. Her flair has been thoroughly utilised with the introduction of new lines which have enhanced the range on offer. Candleworld now stocks top quality candles from companies such as Woodwicks, Colony, St Eval, Broste, Spaas and Gisela Graham. The shop also offers accessories produced by Think Pink, Faerie Flames and Glide papers.

Candleworld provides lighting for all occasions, whether it be household interiors with different ranges dependent on the season and including lanterns, mobiles and outdoor lights. You'll also find organic bath products, greeting cards, bunting and a range of paper products for all occasions. The shop stands on Swanage's main street and its window displays change throughout the year based on themes such as Halloween, Christmas or the beach. Candleworld's products are also available by mail order and from its website.

EARTHLIGHTS

36 High Street, Swanage, Dorset BH19 2NU
Tel: 01929 422266
e-mail: sara@clairvoyant.co.uk   website: www.earthlights.co.uk

Ideally located in the busy high street in a grade II listed building designed by George Crickmay is **Earthlights**. Established in 2002, the premises were previously a new age book and crystal shop and that new age feel has been maintained by Mother and Daughter Sara and Sophie who own and run this busy and popular café restaurant.

Walking in, you are guaranteed a warm and friendly welcome by Sara who runs the front of house. Sophie's domain is the kitchen where she creates an exciting range of culinary delights made predominantly from locally sourced and organic produce. There is a distinctly Mediterranean feel to the food on offer; among the starters to choose from is houmous & pitta bread with Spinach & Ricotta Cannelloni to follow perhaps with a Greek salad. There is also more traditional fare available with home-made soup of the day, freshly baked jacket potatoes, pizzas and a large range of home-made cakes, biscuits and muffins. Cream teas are a speciality. To drink there is fair-trade tea and coffee available alongside a choice of fruit juices.

The café comfortably seats 30 people and is available to book for parties. Earthlights are open seven days a week, all year, and until late in the summer months.

🏛 historic building   🏛 museum and heritage   🏚 historic site   🗻 scenic attraction   🌿 flora and fauna

depressing to realise that the seven-shilling (35p) weekly payment those farm-workers were protesting against actually had more buying power in the 1830s than the current legally-enforced minimum wage.

Swanage

🐦 Durlston Country Park   ✎ Swanage Railway

🏫 Town Hall   🏫 King Alfred Column

📏 Great Globe   ⛰ Studland Bay

Picturesquely set beside a broad, gently curving bay with fine, clear sands and beautiful surrounding countryside, Swanage is understandably popular as a family holiday resort. A winner of Southern England in Bloom, the town takes great pride in the spectacular floral displays in its parks and gardens. The town's other awards include the prestigious European Blue Flag for its unpolluted waters, and the Tidy Britain Group's "Seaside Award". Swanage offers its visitors all the facilities necessary for a traditional seaside holiday, including boat-trips, (with sightings of bottle-nosed dolphins if you're lucky), water-sports, sea angling and an attractive, old-fashioned pier and bandstand. The Mowlem Theatre provides a seasonal programme of films, shows and plays, and on Sunday afternoons the Recreation Ground resounds to the strains of a brass band. On the clifftops, **Durlston Country Park** covers some 260 acres of delightful countryside; on the front, the Beach Gardens offer tennis, bowls and putting, or you can just rent a beach hut or bungalow and relax.

One attraction not to be missed is a ride on the **Swanage Railway** along which magnificent steam locomotives of the old Southern Railway transport passengers some six miles through lovely Dorset countryside to Norden, just north of Corfe Castle.

In the town itself, the **Town Hall** is worth seeing for its ornate façade, the work of Christopher Wren. Wren didn't build it for Swanage, however. It was originally part of Mercers Hall in Cheapside, London. When the Mercers Hall was being demolished, a Swanage man named George Burt scavenged the fine frontage and rebuilt it here. He also brought the graceful little Clock Tower which stands near the pier but once used to adorn the Surrey end of London Bridge; a gateway from Hyde Park for his own house; and cast-iron columns and railings from Billingsgate Market. No wonder older residents of the town refer to Swanage as "Little London".

There is, however, one monument that is purely Swanage – the **King Alfred Column** on the seafront. This commemorates the king's victory here over a Danish fleet in

Swanage Lifeboat

877AD. The column is topped by cannonballs that would have been of great assistance to Alfred had they been invented at the time.

Collectors of curiosities will want to make their way to Tilly Whim Hill, just south of Swanage, which is also well-known for its murky caves. High above the caves stands the **Great Globe,** a huge round stone, some 10 feet in diameter and weighing 40 tons, its surface sculpted with all the countries of the world. At its base, stone slabs are inscribed with quotations from the Old Testament psalms, Shakespeare and other poets. They include moral injunctions such as, "Let prudence direct you, temperance chasten you, fortitude support you", and the information that, "if a globe representing the sun were constructed on the same scale, it would measure some 1,090 feet across".

A couple of miles north of Swanage, **Studland Bay** offers a lovely three-mile stretch of sandy beach, part of it clearly designated as an exclusive resort for naturists only.

Around Swanage

LANGTON MATRAVERS
2 miles W of Swanage, on the B3069

🏛 Purbeck Stone Industry Museum

🐾 Putlake Adventure Farm

Before tourism, the main industry around Swanage was quarrying the famous Purbeck stone that has been used in countless churches, cathedrals and fine houses around the country. **The Purbeck Stone Industry Museum** at Langton Matravers tells the story of Purbeck Marble, a handsome and durable material which was already being cut and polished back in Roman times. This sizeable village

is also home to **Putlake Adventure Farm** where visitors are encouraged to make contact with a variety of friendly animals, bottle feed the lambs, or have a go at milking cows. There are pony and trailer rides, picnic and play areas, a farm trail, gift shop and tea room.

CORFE CASTLE
5 miles NW of Swanage on the A351

🏛 Corfe Castle   🏞 Model Village

One of the grandest sights in the country is the impressive ruin of **Corfe Castle** (National Trust) standing high on a hill and dominating the attractive grey stone village below. Once the most impregnable fortress in the land, Corfe dates back to the days of William the Conqueror, with later additions by King John and Edward I. The dastardly John threw 22 French knights into the castle dungeons and left them to starve to death. Later, Edward II was imprisoned here before being sent to Berkeley Castle and his horrible murder.

Corfe Castle remained important right up until the days of the Civil War when it successfully withstood two sieges before it fell into Parliamentary hands through treachery. A month later, Parliament ordered the castle to be 'slighted' – rendered militarily useless.

Although Corfe now stands in splendid ruin, you can see a smaller, intact version at

Corfe Castle

🏛 historic building 🏛 museum and heritage 🏛 historic site 🏞 scenic attraction 🐾 flora and fauna

the **Model Village** in West Street. This superbly accurate replica is built from the same Purbeck stone as the real thing and the details of the miniature medieval folk going about their daily business are wonderful. Surrounded by lovely gardens, this intriguing display is well worth a visit. You might also want to explore the local museum which is housed in the smallest Town Hall building in the country.

NORDEN
7 miles NW of Swanage, on the A351

  🖉 Swanage Railway

About half a mile north of Corfe Castle, Norden Station is the northern terminus of the **Swanage Railway** and there's a regular bus service from the station to the castle. The hamlet of Norden itself is actually another mile further to the northeast, a delightful place surrounded by pine trees and heathland.

Bournemouth

🏛 Pier	🏛 Russell-Cotes Art Gallery & Museum
🏛 St Peter's Church	🖉 Bournemouth Eye
🏛 Casa Magni Shelley Museum	🐟 Oceanarium
🏛 Rothesay Museum	🏛 Teddy Bear Museum
🏛 Bournemouth Aviation Museum	
🖉 Alice in Wonderland Family Park	

It's been calculated that Bournemouth has "more nightclubs than Soho" as well as a huge range of hotels, shops, bars, restaurants and entertainment venues. The town also supports two symphony orchestras. In July 2005, in the hope of attracting more of Britain's 250,000 surfers to the town, Bournemouth council announced the construction of a 1,600ft-long artificial reef capable of producing breakers up to 16ft high. Beach users will also benefit

as the reef will create a peaceful lagoon.

Already, some 5.5 million visitors each year are attracted to this cosmopolitan town which has been voted the greenest and cleanest resort in the UK – there are more than 2,000 acres of Victorian parks and gardens, and the town centre streets are washed and scrubbed every morning.

Two hundred years ago, the tiny village of Bourne was a mere satellite of the bustling port of Poole, a few miles to the west. The empty coastline was ideal for smugglers and Revenue men were regularly posted here to patrol the area. One of them, Louis Tregonwell, was enchanted by Bourne's glorious setting at the head of three deep valleys, or chines. He and his wife bought land here, built themselves a house and planted the valleys with the pines that give the present-day town its distinctive appearance. Throughout Victorian times, Bournemouth, as it became known, grew steadily and the prosperous new residents beautified their adopted town with wide boulevards, grand parks, and public buildings, creating a Garden City by the Sea.

They also built a splendid **Pier** (1855) and, around the same time, **St Peter's Church** which is much visited for its superb carved alabaster by Thomas Earp, and the tomb in which Mary Shelley, the author of *Frankenstein*, is buried along with the heart of her poet-husband, Percy Bysshe Shelley. The **Casa Magni Shelley Museum**, in Shelley House where the poet's son lived from 1849 to 1889, is the only one in the world entirely devoted to Shelley's life and works. Other museums include the **Russell-Cotes Art Gallery & Museum**, based on the collection of the globe-trotting Sir Merton Russell-Cotes; the **Rothesay Museum** which follows a mainly nautical theme but also has a display of more

Hengistbury Head

Distance: *3.8 miles (6.0 kilometres)*
Typical time: *95 mins*
Height gain: *35 metres*
Map: *Explorer OL22*
Walk: *www.walkingworld.com ID:719*
Contributor: *Peter Salenieks*

ACCESS INFORMATION:

Cars can be parked in Hengistbury Head Car Park. This is approached from the A35, turning south onto the B3059 and then east onto the Broadway to the west of Tuckton. Hengistbury Head is also accessible by bus during the summer months. Open Top Coastal Service 12 runs between Sandbanks and Christchurch Quay. It is possible to shorten the walk by catching the Land Train which runs between the Ranger Office and Sandspit. Whilst the service is operating, land trains run from 10am to 4pm. For a longer day, consider combining this walk with a ferry boat trip from Sandspit to Mudeford Quay.

DESCRIPTION:

Hengistbury Head has witnessed 11,000 years of human history, including a Stone Age camp on Warren Hill, an Iron Age port and 18th century quarrying. Nowadays it is a popular tourist spot, including a Local Nature Reserve which is home to a variety of birds, insects and small mammals.

This walk starts at the Ranger Office and Land Train terminus. There are good views of Christchurch Harbour and Christchurch Priory. In clear weather, the Purbecks can be seen across Poole Bay, with the Needles and the Isle of Wight lying to the south-east. The walk reaches the southern tip of Hengistbury Head, before descending to the beach. The return passes Holloway's Dock, a SSSI. The

walk includes a short, optional detour to the wildlife pond in the quarry. A cafe and toilets are situated at the end of the walk.

FEATURES:

Sea, toilets, wildlife, birds, great views, nature trail, ancient monument

WALK DIRECTIONS:

1 | Start with the Ranger Office and Land Train terminus behind you and walk about 50 metres east along the tarmac road, until you reach a junction with the track just before the Double Dikes. Bear right (south) and go along the track, which runs parallel to the Double Dikes, until you reach the seaward end of the dikes.

2 | Turn left (east) at the seaward end of the Double Dikes and walk along a tarmac path that goes along the clifftop towards Hengistbury Head. The path takes you towards Warren Hill, passing Barn Field and two paths on your left. Ascend steadily, keeping the wildlife pond on your right, to reach the triangulation pillar on top of Warren Hill.

3 | Continue east along a gravel track, passing a toposcope to reach the coastguard lookout station.

4 | The track continues beside the coastguard lookout station, passing a path junction on the left, to reach a crossroads. Ahead, the Isle of Wight can be seen in the distance.

5 | Turn right at the crossroads and follow the track along the clifftop, passing the southern end of the wildlife pond in the old quarry on your left. The track takes you to the southern tip of Hengistbury Head, before turning north-east to reach broad steps that lead down to the beach. There are several seats where you can sit and admire the view.

6 | Descend the steps and bear left to pick up a broad path which leads inland from the beach huts at Sandspit. Follow the broad path about

100 metres north-west from the beach huts, until you reach the road.

7 | Turn right (east) and follow the road towards Sandspit. Pass the Land Train terminus and the pontoon for the ferry boat to Mudeford Quay on your left. When you reach The Hut Cafe, cross between it and the beach office to reach the seaward side of Sandspit and walk north towards the end of the spit, where Avon Run marks the outflow from Christchurch Harbour into the sea. Do not enter the water as there are very strong currents.

8 | Retrace your route from Avon Run to Waymark 7 and go west along the road, passing Holloway's Dock (a Site of Special Scientific Interest) on your right. Pass a track on your left before entering woodland and continue until you see a wooded track on your left which leads gently uphill.

9 | Follow the track uphill for about 50 metres to reach the wildlife pond (this detour can be omitted if you are short of time). Retrace your route back to the road and turn left. Walk about a kilometre west to reach the Land Train terminus and Ranger Office.

10 | The walk ends at the Ranger Office and Land Train terminus. There are toilets and you can buy snacks at The Hiker Cafe.

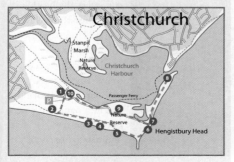

than 300 vintage typewriters; the **Teddy Bear Museum** in the Expocentre; and, north of the town, the **Bournemouth Aviation Museum** at Bournemouth International Airport, home to a collection of vintage jet aircraft – including the last flying Sea Fury fighter – which are flown on a regular basis.

Opposite the airport and set in seven acres of landscaped grounds, the **Adventure Wonderland,** (formerly the Alice in Wonderland Family Park) is designed for children aged 2-12 and offers a wide variety of rides and attractions, a huge Alice Maze, indoor play centre, and a daily panto-style Storyline.

Back in town, the **Oceanarium**, located alongside the Pier, explores the wonders of the natural world beneath the surface of seas, lakes and rivers. Displays include life under the Amazon, the Caribbean and the lagoons of Hawaii. A popular feature here is Turtle Beach, home to rescued green turtles.

And if you're looking for a novel experience, and a really spectacular aerial view of the town and coastline, **Bournemouth Eye,** in the Lower Gardens near the pier, offers day or night ascents in a tethered balloon which rises up to 500ft.

Around Bournemouth

CHRISTCHURCH
5 miles E of Bournemouth on the A35

🚶 Blue Plaques Millennium Trail	🚶 Double Dykes
🏛 Christchurch Priory	🏛 Christchurch Castle
🏚 St Michael's Loft Museum	🏚 Place Mill
🏚 Red House Museum	🏚 Museum of Electricity

An excellent way of exploring Christchurch is to follow the **Blue Plaques Millennium Trail** which commemorates sites around the town from Neolithic times to the 20th century. A booklet detailing this trip through time is available from the tourist information centre in the High Street.

Pride of place on the trail goes to **Christchurch Priory**, a magnificent building begun in 1094 and reputedly the longest parish church in England, extending for 311ft. It has an impressive Norman nave, some superb medieval carving, and a vast 14th century stone reredos with a Tree of Jesse. Other treasures include the magnificent Salisbury Chantry, some fine misericords and, in the beautiful Lady Chapel, a pendant vault believed to be the earliest of its kind in the country. From the Lady Chapel, a stairway of 75 steps leads to St Michael's Loft, originally a school for novice monks and later a grammar school for boys. It now houses **St Michael's Loft Museum** which tells something of the long history of the priory. Another stairway – a spiral one of 176 steps – winds its way up the tower of the church; from the top there are extensive views over the town and harbour.

Just north of the priory are the remains of **Christchurch Castle**, built in the late 11th

century and slighted (rendered militarily useless) after the Civil War. The site here contains the Constable's Hall which boasts the oldest Norman chimney in Britain, constructed around 1150.

Other nearby attractions include the **Red House Museum & Gardens** which is housed in a former Georgian workhouse and provides some interesting local history as well as a peaceful enclave in the heart of the town; and the **Museum of Electricity**, which occupies a stately Edwardian power station and has something for everyone – from dozens of early domestic appliances to a pair of boot warmers.

On Town Quay, at the meeting of the rivers Stour and Avon, is **Place Mill** which dates back to Anglo-Saxon times and was mentioned in the Domesday Book. The mill has been restored and although it is unable to grind corn, you can still see the wheel turning when tidal conditions are right. The body of the mill is now an art gallery with changing exhibitions by local artists, interesting displays of artefacts, and a gift shop.

To the south of Christchurch are the ancient ditches known as **Double Dykes**, an area that offers great walking along with superb views. The dykes cut across the heathland of **Hengistbury Head** (see walk on page 316) which forms the southern side of the town's large natural harbour. The headland is now a nature reserve, one of the few uninhabited parts of

Christchurch Harbour

this otherwise built-up stretch of coastline.

Not far from Double Dykes, in 1910, Britain's first air show took place. It was attended by some of the greatest names of early aviation, amongst them Wilbur Wright, Blériot, and the Hon. Charles Rolls (of Rolls-Royce fame) who was killed when his plane crashed at this event.

MUDEFORD
7 miles E of Bournemouth off the A337

Standing at the entrance to Christchurch Harbour, Mudeford has a picturesque quay with piles of lobster pots, a fresh fish stall, fishermens' cottages and an old inn. It is still the centre of the local fishing industry and the quay provides a great vantage point for watching yachts and windsurfers as they come up "The Run" into the harbour. The beach here is clean and sandy with a lifeguard service during the summer months when beach huts, deck chairs and canoes can all be hired, and ferry services cross the harbour to Mudeford Sandbank. Day cruises to the Needles and Yarmouth on the Isle of Wight are also available.

HIGHCLIFFE
9 miles E of Bournemouth on the A337

🏰 Highcliffe Castle

The most easterly community in Dorset, Highcliffe has a fine beach and views of the eastern tip of the Isle of Wight. The bustling village centre hosts a Friday market but the major attraction here is **Highcliffe Castle** (English Heritage), an imposing mansion of gleaming white stone originally built between 1831 and 1835. It was damaged by fire in the 1960s but the exterior was restored in the 1990s although most of the interior remains unrepaired. Guided tours are available every Tuesday afternoon during the summer; the grounds, visitor centre, galleries and gift shop are open all year round.

POOLE
4 miles W of Bournemouth, on the A35/A350

🏛 Waterfront Museum   ⚱ Poole Pottery

🌿 Compton Acres   ⚔ Brownsea Island

Once the largest settlement in Dorset, Poole is now a pleasant, bustling port. Its huge natural harbour, actually a drowned river

---

🎭 stories and anecdotes   🍃 famous people   ⚗ art and craft   🎪 entertainment and sport   ⚔ walks

YEATES QUALITY BUTCHERS

451 Poole Road, Branksome, Poole,
Dorset BH12 1DH
Tel: 01202 761964

Yeates Quality Butchers have been supplying quality meats to their customers for more than 100 years. All the beef and pork on sale is sourced locally in Dorset; their lamb is either from the county or from New Zealand. The shop is noted for its homemade sausages and it also sells home-cooked ham, special recipe burgers, the best faggots in Dorset, Wiltshire bacon, poultry, venison, haggis, black pudding and wild rabbits, as well as a selection of cheeses such as the tasty Dorset Blue Vinney.

valley, has a shoreline of some 50 miles and is the most extensive anchorage in Europe with a history going back well beyond Roman times. A 33ft long Logboat, hollowed from a giant oak tree and dating back to around 295 BC, has been found off Brownsea Island, the largest of several islands dotting the harbour. Poole's extensive sandy beaches boast more Blue Flag awards than any other UK strand, and every Thursday evening in August there's a beach party with sports, calypso bands, barbecues and a spectacular firework finale.

The Quay is a great place to relax with a drink and watch people "just messing about in boats" or participating in one of the many watersports available. Nearby is the **Waterfront Museum**, which celebrates 2,000 years of maritime heritage, and the internationally famed **Poole Pottery** which has been producing high-quality pottery for more than 125 years. Its visitor centre stands on the site of the old factory. Here, visitors can watch a 12-minute video summarising two millennia of ceramic production, see the age-old processes under way, and children can have a go themselves at this tricky craft. The Pottery Shop offers factory-direct prices and special savings on seconds, there are superb

displays of the Pottery's distinctively designed creations, and a brasserie and bar overlooking the harbour.

Poole is well-provided with public parks offering a wide range of activities, and the town also boasts one of the county's great gardens, **Compton Acres,** which was created in the 1920s by Thomas William Simpson who spent the equivalent of £10 million in today's money. Amongst its varied themed areas, which include a lovely Italian Garden, the Japanese Garden enjoys an especially fine reputation. Japanese architects and workmen were brought over to England to create what is reputed to be the only completely genuine Japanese Garden in Europe, an idyllic setting in which only the most troubled spirit could not find solace. Magnificent sculptures enhance the grounds which also contain restaurants, a delicatessen, model railway exhibition and shops. From the Colonnade viewpoint there are grand views over Poole Harbour to the Purbeck hills beyond.

From Poole Quay there are regular cruises along the coast and ferries to **Brownsea Island** (National Trust), where there are quiet beaches with safe bathing. Visitors can wander through 500 acres of heath and woodland which provide one of the few remaining refuges for Britain's native red squirrel. In 1907, General Robert Baden-Powell carried out an experiment on the island to test his idea of teaching boys from all social classes the scouting skills he had refined during the Boer Wars. Just 20 boys attended that first camp: in its heyday during the 1930s, the world-wide Scouting Movement numbered some 16 million members in more than 120 countries.

CORFE MULLEN
7 miles NW of Bournemouth off the A31

With a population of more than 10,000, Corfe Mullen has a good claim to be the largest village in the country. Much of it is modern housing for commuters to Poole and Bournemouth but the old village beside the River Stour has retained its charm. The ancient mill, mentioned in the Domesday Book, has had its wheel rebuilt and is turning once again, albeit inside a glass case at the centre of a tearoom. There's a medieval church whose first rector, Walter the Clerk, was installed in 1162; a delightful 300-year-old manor house (private); and a traditional pub with a flagstone floor in one of the bars.

WIMBORNE MINSTER
7 miles NW of Bournemouth on the A349/A31

🏛 Wimborne Minster	🌿 Knoll Gardens & Nursery
🎨 Wimborne Model Town	🏛 Stapehill Abbey
🌿 Honeybrook Country Park	🏛 Kingston Lacy
🏛 Museum of East Dorset Life
🌿 Dean's Court Garden

Happily, the A31 now by-passes this beguiling old market town set amongst meadows beside the rivers Stour and Allen. The glory of the town is **Wimborne Minster** which, in 2005, celebrated 1,300 years of ministry. It's a distinctive building of multi-coloured stone boasting some of the finest Norman architecture in the county and is also notable for its 14th century astronomical clock, and the 'Quarterjack', a life-sized figure of a grenadier from the Napoleonic wars, which strikes the quarter hours on his bells. Inside, the unique Chained Library, founded in 1686, contains more than 240 books, amongst them a 14th century manuscript on vellum.

In the High Street, the Priest's House is a lovely Elizabethan house set amidst beautiful gardens. It houses the **Museum of East Dorset Life** which recreates 400 years of history in a series of rooms where the decoration and furnishings follow the changing fashions between Jacobean and Victorian times. There's also an archaeology gallery with hands-on activities, a Gallery of Childhood, delightful walled garden and summer tea room.

In King Street you can see Wimborne as it was in the early 1950s – but at one tenth the size. **Wimborne Model Town** presents a meticulous miniature version of the town, complete with an Old English fair and a working small-scale model railway.

Also close to the town centre, **Dean's Court Garden** is a 13-acre expanse of partly wild gardens surrounding an old house that was once the Deanery to the Minster. There are many fine specimen trees, lawns and borders, as well as a fascinating old kitchen garden stocked with some of the oldest varieties of vegetables.

On the outskirts of Wimborne, **Honeybrook Country Park** has a family yard with lots of pure breed animals, dray and pony rides, an adventure playground, a period

JUST B INSPIRED

47 High Street, Wimborne, Dorset BH21 1HS
Tel: 01202 840640
e-mail: fiona@justbinspired.co.uk

Stocked with an extraordinary variety of stylish gifts for all occasions, **Just B Inspired** should surely solve all your needs for interesting and unusual gifts at one stroke. Owner Fiona Hammick, who purchased the shop in 2005, has put together a remarkably diverse collection of items that includes the whole range of Burleigh China, clocks by Roger Lascelles, Portmeirion china and tableware, Aspire silk handbags, Kath Kidston china, and cards from Alex Clark. Then there's a wide selection of soft furnishings, occasional furniture, glassware, lighting, fashion accessories, jewellery, photo frames, christening gifts and gifts for babies. This treasure trove of gift ideas is open from 9.30am to 5pm, Monday to Saturday.

Just B Inspired is located in the heart of the delightful and historic town of Wimborne. Its jewel in the crown is the glorious Minster which boasts some of the finest Norman architecture in the county. It's also famous for its 14th century astronomical clock which is distinguished by its 'Quarterjack', a life-sized figure of a grenadier from the Napoleonic wars which strikes the quarter hours on the bells.

farmhouse, a natural maze, river and countryside walks, farm shop, tea room and picnic areas. The park also hosts events such as country sports days, tug-of-war competitions, beer tasting and barn dances.

A mile or so northwest of Wimborne, **Kingston Lacy** (National Trust) is an imposing 17th century mansion which has been the home of the Bankes family for more than 300 years and exerts an irresistible attraction for anyone who loves the paintings of such Old Masters as Brueghel, Titian, Rubens and Van Dyck. Apart from those owned by the queen, the pictures on display here are generally acknowledged by experts as forming the finest private collection in the country. Kingston Lacy's fabulous gilded-

leather Spanish Room and elegant Grand Saloon, both with lavishly decorated ceilings, and a fascinating exhibit of Egyptian artefacts dating back to 3000 BC, all add to the interest of a visit. Outside, you can wander through 250 acres of wooded parkland which contains a genuine Egyptian obelisk of c.150BC and is also home to a herd of splendid Red Devon cattle. A fairly recent addition was the Edwardian Japanese Tea Garden which follows traditional Japanese design with features such as a waiting pavilion, a dry stream raked with gravel, and a thatched tea house. Also within the grounds of the Kingston Lacy estate are Badbury Rings, an Iron Age hill fort reputedly the site of a great campaign by King Arthur.

🏚 historic building   🏛 museum and heritage   🏛 historic site   🦢 scenic attraction   🌿 flora and fauna

A couple of miles to the east of Wimborne, **Stapehill Abbey** was built in the early 1800s as a Cistercian nunnery providing a peaceful place for retreat and contemplation. Visitors can enjoy the serenity of the restored Nuns' Chapel, stroll around the cloisters and enjoy the glorious

Kingston Lacy House

award-winning gardens. Inside, there are reconstructions of a Victorian parlour, kitchen and washroom, and an outstanding Countryside Museum recording rural life in the area. Stapehill is also home to a group of working craftspeople, special events are held throughout the year, and the site contains a licensed coffee shop and picnic areas.

Just to the east of Stapehill are **Knoll Gardens & Nursery** whose gardens were planted more than 30 years ago and are famous for the mature trees and shrubs that provide a wealth of colour throughout the seasons. The gardens specialise in grasses and perennials but in all there are more than 6,000 plant species, including many fine trees. Tumbling waterfalls and ponds in an informal English setting add to the appeal.

HORTON
12 miles NW of Bournemouth off the B3078

Just outside the village stands Horton Tower (private), a six-storey triangular folly built in the mid-1700s by Humphrey Sturt, the lord of the manor, as an observatory from which

he could watch the movement of deer. The tower appeared in the film *Far From the Madding Crowd*.

WIMBORNE ST GILES
15 miles NW of Bournemouth off the B3081

🏛 Church of St Giles

A pretty village set beside the River Allen, Wimborne St Giles is notable for its **Church of St Giles**. It was rebuilt after a fire by the distinguished architect Sir Ninian Comper who also contributed the fine stained glass. Also worth seeing are the marvellous monuments, notably to Sir Anthony Ashley and to the 7th Earl of Shaftesbury (who is even more memorably honoured by the statue of Eros in Piccadilly Circus, London).

VERWOOD
12 miles N of Bournemouth on the B3081

🐎 Dorset Heavy Horse Centre

🦌 Verwood Heathland Heritage Centre

Located in the heart of the town, **Verwood Heathland Heritage Centre** has permanent displays of the local Verwood pottery

📷 stories and anecdotes 🦆 famous people 🎨 art and craft 🎭 entertainment and sport 🚶 walks

CRANBORNE STORES

1 The Square, Cranborne, Wimborne,
Dorset BH21 5PR
Tel: 01775 517210
e-mail: s.hurley@cranborne.co.uk
website: www.cranborne.co.uk

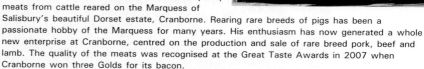

Chosen by Rick Stein as one of his "Food Heroes", **Cranborne Stores** is stocked with quality meats from cattle reared on the Marquess of Salisbury's beautiful Dorset estate, Cranborne. Rearing rare breeds of pigs has been a passionate hobby of the Marquess for many years. His enthusiasm has now generated a whole new enterprise at Cranborne, centred on the production and sale of rare breed pork, beef and lamb. The quality of the meats was recognised at the Great Taste Awards in 2007 when Cranborne won three Golds for its bacon.

The estate has gone back to the traditional way of rearing pigs "free range" in the estates' woods and downland where the pigs are allowed to mature slowly. They are fed with a mixture of home-grown barley with a significant portion of their diet coming from free grazing and rooting between the trees. Indeed, while they are in the woods, the pigs provide a service to the foresters by reducing the weed population and allowing the trees to thrive. These rearing methods result in the finest old-fashioned pork from the best traditional breeds, particularly Middle Whites, Large Blacks, Berkshires and Tamworths. Customers and potential customers are actively encouraged to visit the estate to see the operation for themselves, and the Store is happy to produce bespoke products such as sausages and burgers to your own recipe.

The estate also rears White Park and Aberdeen Angus/Sussex cross cattle to produce well-flavoured beef which is hung for a minimum of four weeks. They supplement their beef production with beef from Bob Hall at Moorland Court Farm in Bridgwater. This beef is grass fed and hung in the same way. Lambs are reared on the estate's behalf by a tenant grazier, as its the mutton, both to the organic standards of the Soil Association. Tender venison and other wild game are also available in season.

At the estate's retail outlet, Cranborne Stores, you'll find their own meats along with a range of local and international foods sourced to deliver maximum flavour. There's bread, fruit and vegetables from local producers, as well as pickles, jams, marmalades and all of the other usual farm shop fayre. The store is open seven days a week: from 6am to 6pm, Monday to Saturday; from 9am to 5pm on Sunday.

industry. The centre occupies a former pottery drying shed and visitors may get the opportunity to throw a pot or two themselves.

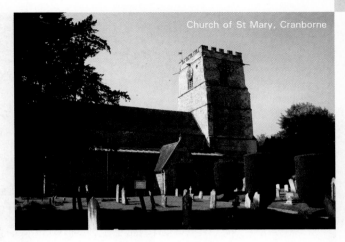
Church of St Mary, Cranborne

Just north of Verwood village, **The Dorset Heavy Horse Centre** offers a real hands-on experience with these mighty beasts. You can drive a horse and wagon, or a vintage tractor, or have a go at logging or ploughing with the heavy horses. Suitable for all ages and weather conditions, the centre also has a display of gypsy caravans, animal feeding and handling, pedal tractors and go carts, a straw slide barn and a resident menagerie of donkeys, llamas, kune kune pigs, miniature ponies and pigmy goats. There's also a café, picnic area and gift shop.

CRANBORNE
15 miles N of Bournemouth on the B3078

 Church of St Mary   Cranborne Manor

Edmonsham House & Gardens

A picturesque village in a glorious setting, Cranborne sits on the banks of the River Crane with a fine church and manor house creating a charming picture of a traditional English village. The large and imposing **Church of St Mary** is notable for its Norman doorway, 13th century nave, and exquisite 14th century wall-paintings. **Cranborne Manor** was built in Tudor and Jacobean times and acquired by Robert Cecil, Elizabeth I's

Chief Minister, and is lived in today by his descendant, Viscount Cranborne. The house is not open to the public but visitors can explore the gardens on Wednesdays during the season, and the Cranborne Manor Garden Centre, which specialises in old fashioned roses, is open all year. The present manor house stands on the site of a royal hunting lodge built by King John for his hunting forays in Cranborne Chase. Much of the huge forest has disappeared but detached areas of woodland have survived and provide some splendid walks.

To the south of the village lies **Edmonsham House & Gardens,** a superb Tudor manor house with Georgian additions that has been owned by the same family since the 1500s. Guided tours of the house are conducted by the owner. The grounds contain a walled organic garden, a six-acre garden with unusual trees and spring bulbs, and a stable block that is a fine example of Victorian architecture.

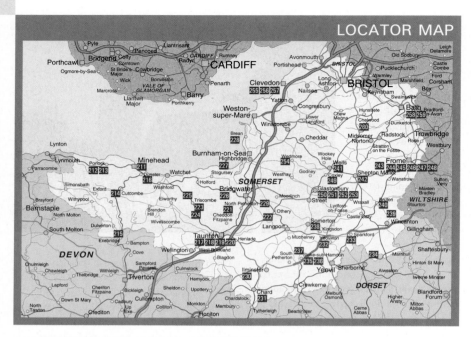

LOCATOR MAP

ADVERTISERS AND PLACES OF INTEREST

🏛 historic building 🏛 museum and heritage 🏛 historic site 🐾 scenic attraction 🌱 flora and fauna

4 Somerset

Was Cadbury Castle really King Arthur's Camelot? Did Joseph of Arimathea really walk through England's green and pleasant land to plant a thorn from Christ's crown of thorns at Glastonbury, where it blossomed once a year on the day of Christ's resurrection? Was it really at Athelney that King Alfred, deep in thought, allowed the cakes to burn? Myth and legend seem to be as integral to Somerset as its cider orchards and Cheddar cheese, its free-roaming ponies on Exmoor and the olde-worlde pubs with their skittle alleys.

Many literary luminaries found inspiration here. Exmoor provided the setting for RD Blackmore's great historical romance *Lorna Doone*; Wordsworth and Coleridge both lived in the county for several years and it was during their countless walks over the Somerset hills that they fashioned their *Lyrical Ballads*, a new kind of plain speaking verse that inspired the Romantic Revolution. Tennyson was a frequent visitor to the county and it was for his Clevedon friend, Arthur Hallam, that he spent 17 years perfecting his great lyrical poem *In Memoriam*.

🎭 stories and anecdotes 🦜 famous people 🎨 art and craft 🎟 entertainment and sport 🚶 walks

Fishing on River Hunspill

Tintinhull House Gardens, that were planted, or influenced by, the early-20th century landscape gardener, Gertrude Jekyll.

A wealth of prehistoric remains have been found within the county, but two of the area's most popular and famous attractions are both natural – Cheddar Gorge and the caves at Wookey Hole. With cliffs over 400 feet high on either side of the road that runs through the bottom of the gorge, Cheddar is indeed a spectacular sight, while the caves at Wookey Hole, from which the River Axe emerges, are famous for their echos and for their fantastic stalagmite and stalactite formations.

Somerset also contains the smallest city in England, Wells. It is also one of the country's most delightful cities, clustered around its superb cathedral. This magnificent building boasts a truly wonderful Astronomical Clock which was installed in the 14th century and is still functioning perfectly.

Hallam was a member of the Elton family whose great house, Clevedon Court, is just one of many fine mansions within the county borders. Others include the late-medieval stone manor house of Lytes Cary, the Palladian Hatch Court and the exquisite Montacute House, built in the late 16th century for Elizabeth I's Master of the Rolls. The fine houses are sometimes overshadowed by their gardens. There are some splendid examples here particularly those, such as Barrington Court, Hestercombe Gardens and

To the north of the Mendip Hills lies the city of Bath, which in the 18th century became the most fashionable spa town in the country. Some 1,600 years earlier, it was equally fashionable among the Romans. Close by is the West Country's largest city, Bristol, Sir John Betjeman's favourite English city which, he asserted, had "the finest architectural heritage of any city outside London".

Minehead

- North Hill Nature Reserve
- West Somerset Railway

Award-winning floral displays and gardens, a tree-lined avenue leading to a recently constructed promenade and a sandy beach, a wide range of shops, pubs, restaurants and open-air cafés, and an extensive choice of family attractions and amusements – Minehead has everything you expect of a successful English seaside resort. There are still thatched cottages in the picturesque Higher Town and the unspoilt acres of the Exmoor National Park stretch away to the west and south.

Despite sounding like a product of the industrial age, Minehead is an attractive and popular seaside town, lying at the foot of the wooded promontory known as North Hill. It is one of the oldest settlements in Somerset.

A busy Bristol Channel port since the time of the Celts, the old harbour lies in the lee of North Hill, making it one of the safest landing places in the West Country. At one time, ships arrived here with wool and livestock from Ireland, crops from the plantations of Virginia, coal from the South Wales valleys and day trippers from Cardiff and Bristol. The merchants and paddle steamers have gone and nowadays the harbour is the peaceful haunt of sailing dinghies and pleasure craft.

There is a good view of the old port from the **North Hill Nature Reserve**, and a three-mile-walk starting near the lifeboat station on the harbour side is an excellent way to explore this area of Minehead and its surroundings. The 14th century parish Church of St Michael stands in a prominent position below North Hill. For centuries, a light was kept burning in its tower to help guide ships into the harbour. Inside, the church contains a number of unusual features, including a rare medieval

West Somerset Railway

The Railway Station, Minehead, Somerset TA24 5BG
Tel: 01643 704996
website: www.west-somerset-railway.co.uk

Why not unwind as the steam trains of the **West Somerset Railway** take you on a leisurely 20-mile journey between Bishops Lydeard (near Taunton) and Minehead, taking in the sights, sounds and even the unique smells of the golden age of rail travel. As your train makes its

way along, the glorious Somerset countryside offers constantly changing views through the windows. The intimacy of the Quantock Hills country, Exmoor in the distance and views from the Exmoor coast across the sea to South Wales all feature at different times. Ten stations, lovingly restored and maintained by volunteers offer a whole range of things to do. Historic buildings, seaside, country walks, the choices are there for you to make.

🎬 stories and anecdotes 🐦 famous people ✒ art and craft 🍃 entertainment and sport 🚶 walks

prayer book, or missal, which once belonged to Richard Fitzjames, a local vicar who went on to become Bishop of London in 1506.

The decline of Minehead as a port was offset by its gradual expansion as a seaside resort and the town went to great lengths to attract a suitably respectable clientele. So much so, in fact, that there was a local bylaw in force until 1890 that forbad anyone over 10 years of age from swimming in the sea "except from a bathing machine, tent or other effective screen". The arrival of the railway in 1874 failed to trigger the rapid expansion experienced by some other seaside resorts. Nevertheless, during World War I, Minehead was able to provide an escape from the ravages of war at timeless establishments like the Strand Hotel, where guests were entertained by such stars as Anna Pavolva and Gladys Cooper. Changes to Minehead over the years have been gradual but the most momentous change came in 1962 when Billy Butlin opened a holiday camp at the eastern end of the esplanade. Now updated, this popular attraction has done much to transform present-day Minehead into an all round family resort.

The town is also the northern terminus of the **West Somerset Railway** (see panel on page 329), the privately-owned steam railway that runs for 20 miles between the resort and Bishop's Lydeard, just northwest of Taunton. Vintage locomotives up to 80 years old trundle along the route that follows the coast as far as Blue Anchor, which has a station next to the beach and a small Great Western Railway museum, then on to Watchet which has a Victorian station with a small gift shop. The route then turns inland and travels through peaceful countryside to Bishop's Lydeard.

Around Minehead

SELWORTHY
3 miles W of Minehead off the A39

🌿 Holnicote Estate

🌿 Horner & Dunkery National Nature Reserve

🏛 Allerford Museum

This picturesque and much photographed village is situated on the side of a wooded hill. Just to the northwest rises Selworthy Beacon, one of the highest points on the vast **Holnicote Estate.** Covering some 12,500 acres of Exmoor National Park, the estate includes a four-mile stretch of coastline between Minehead and Porlock Weir. There are few estates in the country that offer such a variety of landscape. There are north-facing cliffs along the coast, traditional villages and hamlets of cottages and farms and the **Horner and Dunkery National Nature Reserve** where **Dunkery Beacon**, the highest point on Exmoor, rises to 1,700 feet. Virtually the full length of the Horner Water lies within the estate, from its source on the high moorland to the sea at Bossington Beach, one of the best examples of a shingle storm beach in the country. The whole area is noted for its diversity of wildlife and the many rare plant species to be found.

This National Trust-owned estate has more than 100 miles of footpaths through fields, moors and villages for walkers to enjoy. The South West Coast Path curves inland at Hurlstone Point to avoid landslips in the soft Foreland sandstone. Among the settlements in the estate is the village of Selworthy created by Sir Thomas Dyke-Acland to house his estate workers. West of this model village is

---

🏛 historic building 🏛 museum and heritage 🏛 historic site 🏞 scenic attraction 🌿 flora and fauna

another estate village, Allerford, which has an elegant twin-arched packhorse bridge. In Allerford's old school is a **Museum** dedicated to the rural life of West Somerset. Among its many imaginatively presented displays are a Victorian kitchen, a laundry and dairy, and an old school room complete with desks, books and children's toys.

PORLOCK
7 miles W of Minehead off the A39

🏠 Dovery Manor   ⛰ Porlock Hill

An ancient settlement once frequented by Saxon kings, in recent decades Porlock has become a popular riding and holiday centre. The charming village is filled with lovely old

---

MYRTLE COTTAGE BED & BIG BREAKFAST

High Street, Porlock, Somerset TA24 8PU
Tel: 01643 862978
e-mail: bob.steer@virgin.net
website: www.myrtleporlock.co.uk

Myrtle Cottage is a fully modernised 17th century thatched cottage just a short walk away from the sea. It offers comfortable three stars ensuite accommodation with tea & coffee making facilities, television, radio and courtesy tray. There is a patio seating area available for residents. Myrtle cottage is renowned for its 'Big' breakfast in size and quality as they use only the best local produce. Vegetarians are also catered for. Myrtle Cottage is open all year round and there are many activities that can be enjoyed in the local area.

HARTSHANGER HOLIDAYS

Toll Road, Porlock, Somerset TA24 8JH
Tel: 01643 862700
e-mail: hartshanger@ lineone.net
website: www.hartshanger.com

Hartshanger Holidays are based in the lovely and lively village of Porlock on the north Somerset coast. Hartshanger is an Edwardian gentleman's residence set above the village in the heart of the Exmoor National Park. The top floor of the main house and the coach house have been converted into beautiful self-catering accommodation. High Hanger is a second floor flat with its own private entrance of stone steps to the entrance door at first floor level. An interior flight of stairs leads to the upper floor. High Hanger has one double room and a twin room with a view of the sea. The sitting room has a patio door to an outside balcony and there's a ladder up to a roof terrace with sun loungers. There are glorious views over Porlock Bay and the Bristol Channel. Little Hanger sleeps five plus a baby with two double

rooms and a single room with a cot. From the sitting room a large patio door gives access to a private garden. Both flats have well-equipped kitchens, TV, video and radio alarm clock. Guests have the use of an all weather hard tennis court and there are five acres of wooded hillside to explore around the house.

Culbone Church, Porlock

buildings, most notably the 15th century **Dovery Manor** with its striking traceried hall window, and the largely 13th century parish church that lost the top section of its spire during a thunderstorm in the 17th century. Porlock has the feel of a community at the end of the world as it lies at the foot of **Porlock Hill**, a notorious incline where the road rises 1,350 feet in less than three miles, with a gradient of 1 in 4 in places.

PORLOCK WEIR
9 miles W of Minehead off the A39

🏛 Culborne Church 🌿 Submerged Forest

Today this hamlet has a small tide-affected harbour full of pleasure craft but Porlock Weir was once an important seaport. The Danes sacked it on a number of occasions in the 10th century. In 1052, Harold, the future king of England, landed here from Ireland to begin a short-lived career that ended at the Battle of Hastings in 1066. A pleasant and picturesque place, Porlock Weir offers a number of interesting attractions, including a working blacksmith's forge and museum, and a glass studio where visitors can see lead crystal being made in the traditional manner. A short distance offshore a **Submerged Forest**, a relic of the Ice Age, can be seen at low tide.

From Porlock Weir an attractive one-and-a-half-mile walk leads up through walnut and oak trees to **Culbone Church**, arguably the smallest church in regular use in England, and certainly one of the most picturesque. A true hidden treasure, measuring only 33 feet by 14 feet, this superb part-Norman building is set in a wooded combe that once supported a small charcoal burning community and was at other times home to French prisoners and lepers.

OARE
11 miles W of Minehead off the A39

🐾 RD Blackmore

Set deep in a secluded valley, Oare is one of the highlights for pilgrims following the Lorna Doone Trail. According to **RD Blackmore's** novel, it was in the narrow little 15th century church here that his heroine was shot at the wedding altar by the villainous Carver Doone. Blackmore knew the church well since his grandfather was rector here in the mid-1800s. A placard inside the church indicates the most likely window used by Carver Doone to fire

East Lyn River, Oare

🏛 historic building 🖼 museum and heritage 🏚 historic site 🌿 scenic attraction 🌱 flora and fauna

the shot that almost proved fatal to the novel's heroine, and a memorial to the author RD Blackmore is set into the wall of the church beside the south door.

LISCOMBE
13 miles SW of Minehead off the B3223

🏛 Tarr Steps

Just west of the moorland village of Liscombe is an extraordinary survival from prehistoric times. **Tarr Steps** is the longest clapper bridge anywhere in the world, its huge stone slabs supported by low stone pillars extending 180ft across the River Barle. It's a mystery where the stones slabs came from since there are no similar rocks anywhere near.

Geologists believe they were probably left here by retreating glaciers at the close of the Ice Age.

WINSFORD
7 miles S of Minehead off the A396

One of the prettiest villages in Exmoor, with picturesque cottages, a ford and no fewer than seven bridges, including an old packhorse bridge. On a rise to the west of the village stands the medieval church with a handsome tall tower that dominates both the village and the surrounding area. This idyllic spot was the birthplace of the firebrand Ernest Bevin, founder of the Transport & General Workers Union, World War II statesman and Foreign Secretary in the post-war Labour government.

EXMOOR HOUSE

EXMOOR HOUSE

Wheddon Cross, Exmoor National Park, Somerset TA24 7DU
Tel: 01643 841432
e-mail: info@exmoorhouse.com
website: www.exmoorhouse.com

Formerly a tailor's shop, **Exmoor House** is a beautifully characterful Edwardian property in Exmoor's highest village, near Dunkery Beacon, ideally situated for exploring Somerset's fantastic countryside.

Named best hotel on Exmoor by the Guardian in July 2007, Exmoor House offers 5 high quality en-suite rooms decorated in a contemporary yet comfortable style. There is a cosy guest sitting room and residents may also enjoy the patio area on finer evenings. Exmoor House is truly a place to escape from daily life; there are no televisions in any of the rooms and mobile phones rarely work here. Be as active or relaxed as you

choose, with many walks to be enjoyed in the local area (you can order picnic lunches to take with you) and interesting towns and villages to visit.

The food is of an exceptional quality. Nominated for the *2007 & 2008 UKTV Food Local Hero Award*, the imaginative menu genuinely does source much of its produce locally. For breakfast, enjoy top-notch sausages and bacon, free-range eggs, or perhaps Dartmouth kippers, as well as home-made bread and preserves. The dinner menu changes daily and non-residents can also enjoy the outstanding cuisine – booking is essential. To complement your meal there's a good range of wines, local beers and Somerset ciders.

Exmoor House has a car park and is rated 4 stars by Visit Britain for the guest accommodation. The hotel also has the Walkers Welcome and Cyclists Welcome awards and it is a member of the Green Tourism Business Scheme - working towards accreditation at the present time.

🎭 stories and anecdotes 🐦 famous people 🎨 art and craft 🎵 entertainment and sport 🚶 walks

Wimbleball Lake

Distance: *4.4 miles (7.0 kilometres)*

Typical time: *105 mins*

Height gain: *200 metres*

Map: *Explorer OL9*

Walk: *www.walkingworld.com ID:1346*

Contributor: *Paul Edney*

ACCESS INFORMATION:

Pay and Display car park at the South West Lakes Trust site off the A396 Minehead to Tiverton Road.

DESCRIPTION:

The only road walking, a short section on a quiet lane, is got out of the way at the start. Be sure to leave time for a refreshing pot of tea here after your walk but please note the seasonal opening times. You are soon off the road and gain an impressive view of Wimbleball dam as you round a corner. You can also now see Haddon Hill above you. Once through a short section of Haddon Wood and out on to the open heath the views all around but especially behind you over Wimbleball Lake are superb and get even better as you gain height. Take plenty of breaks to admire these views up to the triangulation point.

This is the highest part of the walk. The descent is gentle at first with the views over the lake on your left as you cross the heath. When you leave the heath and go downhill through the trees the going becomes steeper but nowhere is it uncomfortably so. This short section of woodland is quite open and gives a good opportunity for bird spotting. Through the trees and you are now almost at the lake

and will stay in contact with it nearly all the way back to the car park.

Once over the dam the path stays close to the lakeside and heads back to the sailing club adjacent to the start. This path comprises a mixture of woodland and open grassland with an occasional wooden bench on which to sit and look across the water before that pot of tea from the café in the car park.

ADDITIONAL INFORMATION:

Tea shop, picnic tables, grass play area, toilets, phone and children's play area at the start. Toilets at the Haddon Hill car park just off route at waypoint 7.

FEATURES:

Lake/loch, toilets, play area, birds, great views, café

WALK DIRECTIONS:

1 | Leave the car park by the gate to the left of the tearoom back onto the road and turn left. At the sailing club sign, 200 metres up the road, keep straight on up the No Through Road.

2 | At the sharp left-hand bend take the track on the right past the farm buildings, through a gate and down a paved track.

3 | At the Y junction go through the left-hand gate and down the concrete road towards the dam. When you reach the dam turn right across the dam wall. Once over the dam go right at the T-junction signed Bury '2½ miles'.

4 | After about 150 metres, take the steep steps in a gap in the wall on the left signed 'Footpath to Haddon Hill'.

5 | The path through the trees ends at a stile over a wire fence. Over the stile turn right on the wide gravel path for 10 metres then take

the faint path on the left onto the heath land. Head up the hill following the faint path. At times there are choices of paths but it does not really matter which ones you choose as long as you continue to head up, zig zagging towards the highest point in front of you where you will find the Hadborough triangulation point.

6 | The triangulation point is set back beyond the main path, crossing in front of you, in a patch of heather and gorse bushes. Turn left here and follow the wide path gently down hill across the heath with superb views of Wimbleball Lake on your left.

7 | Pass Haddon Hill car park and toilets on your right, keeping ahead on the main path until you reach the tarmacked road. Cross here onto the path. After only about 20 metres turn left at this faint cross-roads. The path heads down hill, initially alongside gorse bushes, narrow at first then opening up slightly when it starts going through sparse woodland. Cross the wider path when you meet it and continue on the other side on the narrow path downhill though the trees.

8 | Near the bottom of the hill, just above the lake, you meet the wide bridleway that runs between Bury and Upton. Turn left here signed 'Bridleway to Dam and Bury'.

9 | The bridleway joins the road, the same one you crossed at the top of the hill, by these large boulders. Turn right here and take the road down the hill signed 'Wimbleball Dam and Bury'.

10 | Turn right across the dam. At the far side of the dam turn right, over the stile and follow the grassy path above the lake.

11 | The path goes through trees above the lake, across fields then over a little bridge. Ignore the gate for the farm on the left and follow the grassy path heading off to the right.

12 | Keep following the grass path until you reach the sailing club that you pass on the left. At the gate above the sailing club turn left on the track ahead, past the children's play area on your right, up to the gate onto the main road which you passed at waypoint 2. Turn right here for the 200 metres back to the start.

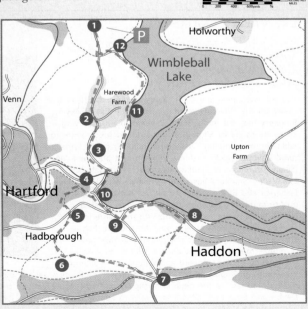

DULVERTON
12 miles S of Minehead on the B3222

📷 Guildhall Heritage & Arts Centre

Dulverton is a lively little town set in the wooded valley of the River Barle on the southern edge of Exmoor. Small though it is, the town boasts a surprising variety of attractions and in recent years has come to challenge Dunster in popularity. The Exmoor National Park has an excellent Visitor Centre here, housed in what used to be the local workhouse. Close by is the **Guildhall Heritage & Arts Centre** which has displays on Dulverton's history over the past century and is also home to the Exmoor Photographic Archive which stages special exhibitions throughout the year. An integral part of the centre is Granny Baker's Cottage with its authentic Victorian kitchen. There's also a gallery which provides a showcase for the work of local artists and craftspeople. The Centre is open from mid-April to the beginning of November.

It's a pleasure to stroll around the town with its ancient bridge, traditional hostelries, cosy tearoom and family-run shops selling anything from antiquarian books to country clothing, gifts to old-fashioned fish and chips. Regular community markets offer a wide range of local crafts, while the highlights of the year in Dulverton are the Carnival, held on the first Saturday in October, and "Dulverton by Starlight" on the first Sunday in December.

DUNSTER
2 miles SE of Minehead on the A396

🏛 Dunster Castle 🏛 Dunster Working Watermill

🏛 Dunster Priory 🏛 Luttrell Arms 🏛 Dovecote

Although Dunster is one of the most popular of Exmoor's villages, this ancient settlement is

---

EXE VALLEY SMOKERY

Exe Valley Fisheries, Exebridge, Dulverton, Somerset TA22 9AY
Tel: 01398 323895
website: www.exevalleysmokery.co.uk

Tucked away near the quiet headwaters of the River Exe valley on the Devon/Somerset border, the **Exe Valley Smokery** has, for more than 22 years, been supplying a complete range of all-natural oak-smoked foods with no additives or colouring. The range includes trout, salmon, tuna, halibut, chicken, duck, venison and pheasant, all locally sourced and smoked over untreated oak chips. Exe Valley Smokery has recently joined with Exe Valley Fisheries and El Pescadero to deliver not only the highest quality smoked game but can now supply fresh and frozen fish to your requirements. All the game is supplied locally from quality sources and the fish is supplied daily from either the markets in Brixham, Devon or direct from the source. Jacqui Young has taken over the running of the smokery and brings with her a great

knowledge of supplying only the best quality products - Jacqui is now branching out to supply quality products to the general public by participating at various shows and events in both Devon and Somerset. She is also able to supply hampers which include any of the smoked fish and game as well as some other high quality dishes.

🏛 historic building 📷 museum and heritage 🏛 historic site 🍃 scenic attraction 🕊 flora and fauna

also one of the least typical as it lies in the fertile valley of the River Avill. No visitor will be surprised to learn that this landscape inspired Mrs Alexander to compose the hymn *All Things Bright and Beautiful*. The village is dominated by **Dunster Castle** standing outside the village on the top of the wooded Conygar Hill. Founded by William de Mohun on this natural promontory above the River Avill, just a few years before the Domesday Book was completed in 1089, the castle passed into the hands of the Luttrell family in 1379. It remained in that family until it was

Dunster Working Windmill

given to the National Trust in 1976 by Lt Col GWF Luttrell. The medieval castle was remodelled in 1617 by William Arnold. During the English Civil War, Dunster Castle was one of the last Royalist strongholds in the West Country to fall. The garrison only surrendered after a siege lasting 160 days. While several Jacobean interiors have survived, the castle underwent major alterations during the latter part of the 17th century. Some of the finest features date from that period, in particular the superb plasterwork in the dining room and the magnificent balustraded main staircase with its delicately carved flora and fauna. However, the overall medieval character of the exterior of the present day castle is due to restoration work undertaken by Anthony Salvin in the 1860s when the castle was transformed into a comfortable and opulent country mansion. The steeply terraced gardens with their striking collection of rare shrubs and subtropical plants were also laid out around this time and the castle and gardens are

surrounded by a 28-acre deer park through which there are several footpaths, as well as the 'Arbutus Walk' through the National Collection of strawberry trees.

The parkland of Dunster Castle is also home to another National Trust property, **Dunster Working Watermill,** built in the 18th century on the site of a pre-Norman mill. Now restored to working order, the mill, which is run as a private business, has a shop selling mill flour, muesli and mill souvenirs and a tearoom by the riverside.

Remnants of the ancient feudal settlement that grew up in the shelter of the castle can still be seen in the village today, particularly in the wide main street. At the north end of this street stands a small octagonal building, which is the former Yarn Market. This was erected by the Luttrells in the early 17th century when the village was an important cloth trading centre. Such was Dunster's influence in this trade that a type of woollen cloth, renowned for its quality and strength, bears the village's name. The nearby **Luttrell Arms**, converted

THE CROOKED WINDOW GALLERY

7 High Street, Dunster, Somerset TA24 6SF
Tel: 01643 821606
e-mail: info@thecrookedwindow.co.uk
website: www.thecrookedwindow.co.uk

Opening Times:
Mon-Sat 10.30am-5.30pm
Sunday variable - please enquire
Other times by appointment

The Crooked Window Gallery is situated in Dunster's picturesque High Street and is so named because the movement in its timber framed construction has caused one of the shops bay windows to become distorted and bowed. The building dates from the 15th century and is unusual for its decorative 18th century plasterwork, or 'pargeting', a feature quite untypical of this area.

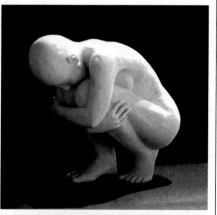

The gallery is owned and run by Robert and Margaret Ricketts. Robert buys, sells, collects and lectures on antiques. You might be surprised to find such an impressive collection of ancient Chinese ceramics - not normally seen outside London.

Margaret is an artist specialising in intricately detailed oil paintings of animals - especially horses, and landscapes. She also works in clay producing original ceramic sculptures.

Within the atmospheric interior you will find an exciting range of jewellery in gold, silver, precious and semi-precious stones. There are quality crafts from other artists as well as interesting and   unusual antique items - all eminently suitable as gifts.

🏘 historic building 🏛 museum and heritage 🏛 historic site ⊕ scenic attraction ⚘ flora and fauna

from a private residence into an inn in the mid-1600s, is more than 100 years older. Distinguished by its fine 15th century porch, the inn is one of the few places in the country where the once common custom of burning the ashen faggot is still observed. On Christmas Eve, the faggot, a bundle of 12 ash branches bound with green ash bands, is burnt in the inn's great fireplace. As each band burns through, another round of hot punch is ordered from the bar. While the ash is burning, the company sings the ancient Dunster Carol and when the faggot is finally consumed a charred remnant is taken from the embers ready to light the following year's fire.

The inn once belonged to Cleeve Abbey while the village's principal religious house, **Dunster Priory**, was an outpost of Bath Abbey. Now largely demolished, the only parts of the priory to survive are the splendid priory church and an unusual 12th century dovecote that can be seen in a nearby garden. It still contains the revolving ladder once used to reach the roosting birds. The priory church, rebuilt by the monks in a rose pink sandstone as early as 1100, is one of the most impressive of Somerset's parish churches. The church tower was added in the 15th century but its most outstanding feature is undoubtedly the fan-vaulted rood screen that extends across the nave and aisles. At 54ft it is the longest in England and was built in 1498 after a squabble between the priory and the townspeople. The magnificent screen served to separate the monk's choir from the parish church.

Another striking medieval survival is the 13th century **Dovecote** which has a revolving wooden ladder inside which gave access to the 500 nesting boxes and their eggs. The squabs, or fledgling doves, provided a staple element of the medieval monk's diet.

On the southern edge of the village, the ancient Gallox Bridge, a medieval packhorse bridge, spans the River Avill.

CARHAMPTON
3 miles SE of Minehead on the A39

🎞 Madam Carne

A small inland village that was the site of a Viking victory in the 9th century. Carhampton's original village church was named after St Carantoc, an early Celtic missionary from across the Bristol Channel. He is reputed to have chosen this site for his ministry by throwing his stone altar overboard and following it to the shore. The present church building, though much restored, contains a remarkable 15th century painted screen that extends across the entire church. The old inn, near the churchyard lych gate, has the date 1638 set into its cobbled floor in sheep's knuckle bones.

Carhampton Church & Cross

Each January, the residents of Carhampton re-enact the ancient custom of **wassailing the apple trees.** A toast is made to the most productive apple tree in the district and cider is poured on to its trunk in a charming ceremony that probably has pagan origins. Local folklore tells of a mysterious woman from the village, **Madam Carne,** who died in 1612 having done away with three husbands. According to legend, her ghost returned home after her funeral to prepare breakfast for the mourners.

WASHFORD
6 miles SE of Minehead on the A39

🏛 Cleeve Abbey   🌱 Tropiquaria

🏛 Radio Museum

This village is spread out across Vallis Florida, the flowery valley dedicated to 'Our Blessed Lady of the Cliff'. Washford is dominated by **Cleeve Abbey,** the only monastery in Somerset that belonged to the austere Cistercian order founded in 1198 by the Earl of Lincoln. This abbey is fortunate in that it was not allowed to fall into disrepair after the Dissolution of the Monasteries in 1539 like many great monastic houses. The cloister buildings at Cleeve were put to domestic use and they are now among the most complete in the country. Although the cruciform abbey church has been reduced to its foundations, the refectory, chapter house, monks' common room, dormitory and cloisters remain. Most impressive of all is the great hall, a magnificent building with tall windows, a wagon roof decorated with busts of crowned angels and medieval murals, and a unique set of floor tiles with heraldic symbols. The curved dormitory staircase has particularly fine archways and mullion windows, while the combined gatehouse and almonry, the last

building to be constructed before the Dissolution, makes an imposing entrance to the abbey precinct.

A short distance northeast of the village is a more recent attraction, **Tropiquaria,** a wildlife park featuring a wide range of tropical animals. There is an aquarium here as well as an aviary and visitors are offered the chance to stroke snakes, tickle tarantulas and to get in touch with their wilder side. Children can swarm over the full-size pirate ships or work off some energy in the indoor play castle; grown-ups may be more interested in the **Radio Museum** which is housed within an old radio transmitting station. There are hundreds of vintage radios to look at as well as a wealth of other radio memorabilia

WATCHET
7 miles SE of Minehead on the B3191

🏛 Florence Wyndham

In the 6th century, St Decuman is said to have landed here from Wales with a cow that he brought along to provide sustenance. The town's name is derived from the Welsh for 'under the hill'. Charles I was once described as wearing a waistcoat of Watchet blue, possibly taken from the very distinctive colour of the cliffs here that were worked for their alabaster. By the 10th century, the Saxon port and settlement here were important enough to have been sacked by the Vikings on at least three separate occasions and Watchet today remains the only port of any significance in Somerset. During the mid-19th century thousands of tons of iron ore from the Brendon Hills were being exported through the docks each year. Unlike many similar sized ports that fell into disuse following the arrival of the railway, Watchet is now a thriving marina for yachts and boats. It was from

Watchet that Coleridge's imaginary crew set sail in *The Rime of the Ancient Mariner*, the epic poem written while the poet was staying at nearby Nether Stowey.

The scale of Watchet's parish church reflects the town's long-standing importance and prosperity. It is set well back from the town centre and contains several fine tombs belonging to the Wyndham family, the local lords of the manor who did much to develop the potential of the port. There is a local story that suggests that one 16th century member of the family, **Florence Wyndham,** had to be buried twice. The day after her first funeral the church sexton went down into church vaults secretly to remove a ring from her finger. When the coffin was opened, the old woman suddenly awoke. In recent years, the town has become something of a coastal resort and one of its attractions is the small museum dedicated to local maritime history.

WILLITON
7 miles SE of Minehead on the A39/A358

🏛 Bakelite Museum

The large village of Williton was once a Saxon royal estate. During the 12th century the manor was the home of Sir Reginald FitzUrse, one of the knights who murdered Thomas à Becket. To atone for his terrible crime, Sir Reginald gave half the manor to the Knights Templar. The other half of the property remained in the FitzUrse family until the death of Sir Ralph in 1350 whereupon it was divided between his daughters. The village today is the home of the diesel locomotive workshops of the West Somerset Railway and the **Bakelite Museum,** a fascinating place providing a nostalgic look at the

'pioneer of plastics'. Housed within an historic watermill, the museum displays the largest collection of vintage plastics in Britain, with thousands of quirky and rare items, including spy cameras, monstrous perming machines and even a Bakelite coffin.

MONKSILVER
8 miles SE of Minehead on the B3188

🏠 Combe Sydenham Hall   🎞 Drake's Cannonball

🏠 Nettlecombe Court   🌲 Brendon Hills

This pretty village of charming old houses and thatched cottages has, in its churchyard, the graves of Elizabeth Conibeer and her two middle-aged daughters, Anne and Sarah, who were murdered in June 1775 in the nearby hamlet of Woodford. Their tombstone bears a message to the unidentified murderer:

> *Inhuman wretch, whoe'er thou art*
> *That didst commit this horrid crime,*
> *Repent before thou dost depart*
> *To meet thy awful Judge Divine.*

Just to the south of the village is a particularly handsome manor house, **Combe Sydenham Hall,** built in the middle of the

Combe Sydenham Country Park

reign of Elizabeth I by George Sydenham on the site of a monastic settlement. Above the entrance, there is a Latin inscription that translates as "This door of George's is always open except to ungrateful souls". This was also the home of Elizabeth Sydenham, George's daughter, who was to become the second wife of Sir Francis Drake. After becoming engaged, Sir Francis left his fiancée to go off looting for Spanish gold. Elizabeth grew so weary waiting for her betrothed to return that she resolved to marry another gentleman. According to local stories, she was on her way to the church, when a meteorite flew out of the sky and smashed into the ground in front of her. Taking this as a sign that she should wait for Sir Francis she called off the wedding and, eventually, the couple were reunited. The meteorite, now known as **'Drake's Cannonball',** is on display in the great hall; it is said to bring good luck to those who touch it. The 500-acre grounds around the hall have been designated a country park and they contain a working corn mill complete with waterwheel, a herb garden, a peacock house and a herd of fallow deer. The estate also incorporates a modern trout farm that stands on the site of a fully restored Tudor trout hatchery dating from the end of the 16th century.

A mile or so to the west stands another ancient manor, **Nettlecombe Court**, once the home of the Raleigh family, relations of another great Elizabethan, seafarer Sir Walter Raleigh. Later, the manor passed by marriage to the Cornish Trevelyan family and it is now a field studies centre open only by appointment.

To the southwest of the village are the **Brendon Hills**, the upland area within the Exmoor National Park from where, in the mid-19th century, iron ore was mined in significant quantities. The ore was then carried down a steep mineral railway to the coast for shipment to the furnaces of South Wales. At one time the Ebbw Vale Company employed almost 1,000 miners here. The company was a strictly Nonconformist concern and imposed a rigorous teetotal regime on its workers. Those wanting a drink had to walk across the moor all the way to Raleigh's Cross. The company also founded a miners' settlement with a temperance hotel and three chapels that became renowned for the achievements of its choir and fife and drum band. Those walking the slopes of the hills can still see sections of the old mineral railway. A two-mile stretch of the track bed leading down to the coast at Watchet is now a pleasant footpath.

EAST QUANTOXHEAD
11 miles SE of Minehead off the A39

🏛 Court House   🏛 Trendle Ring   🗺 Beacon Hill

This is a picturesque village of thatched cottages with a mill and millpond and a handsome old manor house, **Court House**, standing on a rise overlooking the sea. The original owner's family bloodline can be traced back to the 11th century and the Domesday Book but, in the 13th century, the manor passed by marriage to the Luttrell family, who were also to become the owners of Dunster Castle. The manor house seen today dates from the 16th and 17th centuries and was constructed by successive generations of the same family.

From the village there is a pleasant walk to the southeast, to **Kilve**, where the ruins of a medieval chantry, or college of priests, can be found. From here a track can be taken from the churchyard down to a boulder-strewn beach reputed to be a favourite haunt of glats

---

🏛 historic building   📷 museum and heritage   🗺 historic site   🗺 scenic attraction   🌿 flora and fauna

Kilve Chantry Ruins

Taunton, the county town of Somerset, has only been its sole centre of administration since 1935. Before that date, both Ilchester and Somerton had served as the county town. By Norman times the Saxon settlement had grown to have its own Augustinian monastery, a minster and a **Castle** – an extensive structure whose purpose had always been more as an administrative centre than as a military post. However, this did not prevent the castle from being the focus of two important sieges during the English Civil War. A few years later, the infamous Judge Jeffreys sentenced more than 150 followers of the Duke of Monmouth to death here during the Bloody Autumn Assizes. Even today, the judge's ghost is said to haunt the castle grounds on September nights.

The castle now houses the **Somerset County Museum**, a highly informative museum that contains a large collection of exhibits on the archaeology and natural and human history of the county. The **Somerset Military Museum** and some medieval almshouses are also to be found at the castle site. Another of the town's old buildings is still making itself useful today. Somerset's County Cricket Ground occupies part of the priory grounds that once extended down to the river. A section of the old monastic gatehouse, known as the Priory Barn, can still be seen beside the cricket ground. Now restored, this medieval stone building is home to the fascinating **Somerset County Cricket Museum**.

Soaring above the town is the exquisite

– conger eels up to 10-feet long that lie in wait among the rocks near the shore. Once known as 'St Keyna's serpents', local people used to search for them using trained 'fish dogs'.

Further to the southeast lies the village of Holford, in the Quantocks, and a track from here leads up to the large Iron Age hill fortification known as Dowsborough Fort. Close by are also the dramatic viewpoints **Beacon Hill** and Bicknoller Hill. On the latter is another Iron Age relic, a livestock enclosure known as **Trendle Ring**. This is one of many archaeological sites in this area, which lies within the Quantock Hills Site of Special Scientific Interest.

TAUNTON

- 🏛 Taunton Castle 🏛 Somerset County Museum
- 🏛 Somerset Military Museum ⚜ Bath Place
- 🏛 Somerset County Cricket Museum
- 🍃 Vivary Park 🍃 Taunton Racecourse
- 🏛 St Mary Magdalene Church
- 🚶 Bridgwater & Taunton Canal

Despite a settlement being founded here by the Saxon King Ine in the 8th century,

---

🎬 stories and anecdotes 🦜 famous people ⚜ art and craft 🍃 entertainment and sport 🚶 walks

ALPHA

2 The Courtyard, St James Street, Taunton,
Somerset TA1 1JR
Tel: 01823 324488
website: www.alpha clothing.co.uk

Looking to upgrade your wardrobe? Then the place to check out is **Alpha** in Taunton which stocks a wide range of stylish garments for both men and women. Amongst the leading designers of women's clothing featured are Ralph Lauren, Stills, Marc O' Polo, Turnover, Pink Soda Boutique, 120% Linen, James Jeans, Karen Cole and Caliban. For men, the choice includes Gant, Polo Ralph Lauren, Hackett, Duchamp, Delsiena,1...like no other and Quba Sails.

The shop also stocks an extensive range of quality accessories. There are cufflinks, ties and socks from Duchamp, fragrances by Gant, underwear from Polo Ralph Lauren and Honeydew, jewellery by About Face and Artisan, belts from Hamilton Davies and bags from Lupo Barcelona.

Andrew, Giri and their staff at Alpha warmly invite you into the friendly environment of the shop where you are able to browse and shop at your leisure.

BOUTIQUE 28

7 St James Street, Taunton, Somerset TA1 1JH
Tel: 01823 287613
e-mail: joelleelmhirst@hotmail.co.uk
website: www.boutique-28.co.uk

Opened in 2005, **Boutique 28** stocks exclusive labels and brings new designers' collections to Barnstaple and, since February 2008, Taunton, giving individuality to customers. The mix of cosmopolitan, timelessly chic pieces and contemporary current trends, offers individual clothing for every woman.

Boutique 28 stocks Ispirato by Condici, Vera Mont, Marina Avraam, Libra, Joseph Ribcoff, Oui Set and Oui Moments, Avoca Renaissance, beautiful collections from the South of France with Zapa and Evalinka, Aftershock and Rene Derhy and many, many more. There are also hats by Walter Wright & Richard's Design & Fascinators, and a beautiful jewellery collection handpicked by Boutique 28's owner, Joelle Elmhirst. A beautifully handpicked selection of shoes by wonderful designers such as Valentino Russo, Esino and Aftershock, scarves and belts will help you to put the final touch to the look you desire.

Feel free to come and browse in the friendly and relaxed atmosphere where a dedicated team will help you to find the dream outfit for whatever occasion. With endless classics and a unique style, Boutique 28 offers you the perfect look for every occasion.

🏛 historic building 🏛 museum and heritage 🏛 historic site ⌬ scenic attraction 🌠 flora and fauna

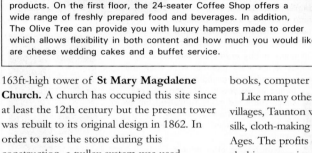

THE OLIVE TREE

10 The Bridge, Taunton, Somerset TA1 1UG
Tel: 01823 353707 website: www.theolivetreetaunton.co.uk

An outstanding delicatessen and licensed coffee shop, **The Olive Tree** offers quality produce to enjoy on the premises or to take away. The well-stocked delicatessen on the ground floor displays an extensive selection of fine cheeses, olives, chutneys, jams, oils, dressings, filled baguettes made to order and many artisan products. On the first floor, the 24-seater Coffee Shop offers a wide range of freshly prepared food and beverages. In addition, The Olive Tree can provide you with luxury hampers made to order which allows flexibility in both content and how much you would like to spend. Also available are cheese wedding cakes and a buffet service.

163ft-high tower of **St Mary Magdalene Church.** A church has occupied this site since at least the 12th century but the present tower was rebuilt to its original design in 1862. In order to raise the stone during this construction, a pulley system was used, operated by a donkey walking down Hammet Street. When the work was completed, the builders hauled the donkey to the top of the tower so that it could admire the view it had helped to create. The main body of the church is medieval and its interior distinguished by a host of carved saints, apostles and gilded angels floating above the congregation. The road leading to the church, Hammet Street, retains an impressive number of original Georgian houses.

Ardent shoppers will want to seek out **Bath Place,** a delightful narrow street of cottages mixed with an assortment of individual shops offering a huge range of goods and services. In medieval times when this street was owned by the Bishop of Winchester it was called Swains Street and was well known for its brothels, one of the few services not on offer here today. But you can have your hair done, your body pierced, lunch or dine in a choice of restaurants, and shop for arts and crafts, jewellery, glassware,

books, computer games and much more.

Like many other West Country towns and villages, Taunton was a thriving wool, and later silk, cloth-making centre during the Middle Ages. The profits earned by the medieval clothiers went into buildings. Here their wealth was used in the construction of two huge churches: St James' and St Mary's. The rest of the town centre is scattered with fine buildings including the timber-framed Tudor House in Fore Street. Taunton is still a thriving place with an important commercial centre, a weekly market and a busy light industrial sector that benefits from some excellent transport links with the rest of the country.

Today, the **Bridgwater and Taunton**

Somerset County Museum, Taunton

[K] stories and anecdotes   famous people   art and craft   entertainment and sport   walks

FINE FABRICS

Magdalene Lane, Taunton, Somerset TA1 1SE
Tel: 01823 270986
website: www.finefabrics.co.uk

Located in central Taunton, **Fine Fabrics** have been suppliers of high quality fabrics for 27 years. With an extensive range of dress patterns, including those from 'Vogue' and many beautiful fabrics to choose from, you can find all you need to accomplish that special and individual bridal gown or evening dress. As a haberdashery, you can find everything you need to make your outfit and a wide selection of accessories are also available to complete your look.

Fine fabrics are stockists of many hobby craft materials including cross-stitch, embroidery and tapestry materials together with wool and knitting accessories. They are also suppliers of daylight and needlework

lamps to aid you in your chosen past-time. There are many furnishing fabrics in stock and a variety of curtain accessories to meet you home furnishing requirements.

Fine fabrics offer private appointments to give customers professional advice with each stage of the dress making process, from choosing the patterns and selecting the fabrics,

Canal towpath has been reopened following an extensive restoration programme and it provides pleasant waterside walks along its 14 miles. A relative latecomer, the canal first opened in 1827 and was designed to be part of an ambitious scheme to create a freight route between Exeter and Bristol to avoid the treacherous sea journey around the Cornwall peninsula. For many years, the canal was the principal means of importing coal and iron from South Wales to the inland towns of Somerset and of exporting their wool and agricultural produce to the rest of Britain.

Taunton's major open space is the extensive **Vivary Park,** located at the southern end of the High Street and approached through a magnificent pair of Victorian ornamental gates. Fully restored with lottery money in 2002, the 70-acre park is home to the Vivary Golf Course, the Taunton Bowling Club and

Taunton Deane Cricket Club. Other features include tennis courts, a wildlife lake, a model boat pond, a bandstand, an ornate fountain commemorating Queen Victoria, a model train track and children's play areas.

Taunton's attractive **National Hunt Racecourse** lies on the opposite side of the motorway from the town and the combination of good facilities, excellent racing and glorious location make it one of the best country racecourses in Britain.

Around Taunton

CHEDDON FITZPAINE
3 miles N of Taunton off the A358

🌿 Hestercombe Gardens

Spreading across the south-facing lower slopes of the Quantock Hills, **Hestercombe**

🏛 historic building 🏛 museum and heritage 🏛 historic site 🌳 scenic attraction 🌿 flora and fauna

CLAVELSHAY BARN RESTAURANT

Clavelshay, North Petherton,
Somerset TA6 6PJ
Tel: 01278 662629
website: www.clavelshaybarn.co.uk

Clavelshay Barn Restaurant is an exciting new country restaurant which opened in Spring 2005. The restaurant has been converted from a traditional stone barn on a family run dairy farm on the edge of the Quantock Hills. Although in a beautiful rural setting, the restaurant is within easy reach of Taunton, Bridgwater and the M5 motorway.

Owners Bill and Sue Milverton are second generation tenant farmers of the Crown Estate. Their 260-acre farm is still run as a working dairy farm with about 110 milking cows, 70 followers and beef cattle.

Sue has run a successful Bed & Breakfast business in the farmhouse for the past 14 years and enjoyed cooking for and looking after guests. She is passionate about using fresh local food and realised that her guests appreciated "real food". Starting a restaurant in the barn using local produce seemed a logical, if huge, extension to the existing business. Sue is also a qualified photographer and her black and white photographs are displayed in the barn. She is keen to display artwork by other local artists in the future.

The restaurant specialises in fresh local food, including the farm's own home-reared beef. All dishes are made at Clavelshay Barn (except ice-cream and sorbet which is sourced locally). Bread is made daily and even the water on the table is from the farm's own spring. There is a fully licensed bar and an interesting wine list courtesy of Quantock Abbey Wine Cellars of Crowcombe.

The kitchen is run by an experienced Head Chef, Jon McAteer who uses the best local ingredients to produce country cooking with a contemporary feel. The menu is small but perfectly formed and is changed monthly to make best use of seasonal produce. Somerset has some of the best produce in the country and the restaurant is committed to selecting the very best local growers and suppliers for its food.

Gardens form part of an estate that has been in existence since Saxon times. In 1872 the estate was acquired by the 1st Viscount Portman and it was his grandson, the Hon. Edward Portman, who commissioned Sir Edwin Lutyens to create a new formal garden that was planted by Gertrude Jekyll between 1904 and 1908. Within the 40-acre site are temples, streams and lakes, formal terraces, woodlands, cascades and some glorious views. Of all the gardens designed by the legendary partnership of Lutyens and Jekyll, Herstercombe is regarded as the best preserved.

STOKE ST GREGORY
7 miles NE of Taunton off the A378

🌱 Willows & Wetlands Visitor Centre

A straggling village in the heart of the Somerset Levels, Stoke St Gregory provides

an appropriate location for the **Willows and Wetlands Visitor Centre** which was established by the Coates family which has more than 170 years experience in the willow industry. Their 80 acres of willow provide the natural material for craftsmen to weave a wide variety of baskets, furniture and garden items for sale. Guided tours are available.

BURROW BRIDGE
9 miles NE of Taunton on the A361

🌾 Somerset Levels Basket & Craft Centre

🏞 Burrow Mump   🏢 Maunsel House

This village, on the River Parrett, is home to one of several pumping stations built in Victorian times to drain the Somerset Levels. The Pumping Station is open to the public occasionally throughout the year. Burrow Bridge is also the home of the **Somerset Levels Basket and Craft Centre**, a

---

GALLERY AT THE GRANARY

Lyng Road, Burrowbridge, Somerset TA7 0SG
Tel: 01823 690096
e-mail: sue@silkstudio.co.uk   website: www.silkstudio.co.uk

The Gallery at the Granary is located in an easy to find position, next to the Willow and Craft Centre, on the A361 between Taunton and Glastonbury. The gallery is a showcase for owner Susan Aitkenheads original hand-painted silk clothing. The entire range is stocked including 'Ties the Limit', 'A Vested Interest' and 'Brace Yourself'. The colourful hangings, cushion covers, pictures and lampshades from the 'Cascade' range are also available.

However Susan's work isn't all that is resident in her gallery. There are many other contributions from the art world including bright fruit & vegetable pictures from Sarah Thomson-Engels, and 'Cow Art' from Alison Jacobs. Other featured artists include Richard Cox, Amy Morse and Kay Stones. Aside from the paintings and silks, there are a variety of alternative local gifts. The full range of Jane Maddern's goats milk soap and beauty products are stocked along with many locally produced foodstuffs. For that extravagant gift there is a beautiful collection of necklaces, bracelets and earrings from 'House of Bethamiee' stained glass and work by a local photographer.

The gallery at the Granary welcomes all to explore its varied range of arts and crafts and is open daily from 10am to 5.30pm.

🏢 historic building 📷 museum and heritage 🏛 historic site 🏞 scenic attraction 🌱 flora and fauna

workshop and showroom stocked with handmade basket ware.

Rising dramatically from the surrounding wetlands is the conspicuous conical hill, **Burrow Mump** (National Trust). Situated at a fording point on the River Parrett, this knoll has at its summit the picturesque remains of an unfinished chapel to St Michael begun in 1793 but for which funds ran out before its completion. Burrow Mump is located in the heart of the low lying area known as **King's Sedge Moor**, an attractive part of the Somerset Levels drained by the Rivers Cary and Parrett. A rich area of wetland, the moor is known for its characteristic pollarded willows, whose straight shoots, or withies, have been cultivated on a substantial scale ever since the taste for wicker developed during the 19th century. The traditional craft of basket-weaving is one of Somerset's oldest commercial activities and it once employed thousands of people. Although the industry has been scaled down over the last 150 years, it is still alive and currently enjoying something of a revival.

The isolated Burrow Mump is reputed to be the site of an ancient fortification belonging to King Alfred, King of Wessex. He is said to have retreated here to escape from invading Vikings. It was during his time here that he is rumoured to have sought shelter in a hut in the nearby village of Athelney. While sitting at the peasant's hearth, absorbed in his own thoughts, legend has it he allowed the cakes that the housewife had been baking to burn. Not recognising the king, the peasant boxed his ears for ruining all her hard work. In the 19th century, a stone was placed on the site recalling that in gratitude for his hospitality, King Alfred founded a monastery on the Isle of Athelney.

Just to the west of Burrow Bridge, the **Bridgwater and Taunton Canal** winds its way through some of the most attractive countryside in the Somerset Levels. The restored locks, swing bridges, engine houses and rare paddle gearing equipment add further interest to this picturesque walk. The canal also offers a variety of recreational facilities including boating, fishing and canoeing while the canal banks are alive with both bird and animal life. At the canal's southern end, boats have access to the River Tone via Firepool Lock in the heart of Taunton.

North Newton, one of the pretty villages along the canal, is home to the magnificent country manor of **Maunsel House** which dates back to the 13th century. The house is set in 100 acres of stunning parkland at the heart of a sprawling 2,000 acre Estate, comprising farms, lakes, woodlands, walnut groves, orchards, Somerset wetlands, cottages and ancient barns. The house can boast such visitors as Geoffrey Chaucer, who wrote part of the Canterbury Tales whilst staying here. Occasionally open to the public, the house is always available for functions such as weddings and conferences.

HATCH BEAUCHAMP
5½ miles SE of Taunton on the A358

🏛 Hatch Court

Hatch Beauchamp is a pleasant village that has managed to retain much of its rural atmosphere despite being on the major route between Ilminster and Taunton. Its name originates from *Hache*, a Saxon word meaning gateway and this refers to the ancient forest of Neroche whose boundary was just to the north and west. The Beauchamp element comes from the Norman family who owned the local manor and whose house stood on the land now occupied by one of the finest country houses in the area, **Hatch Court**.

John Collins, a rich local clothier, commissioned the Axbridge architect, Thomas Prowse, to design the house. Built of attractive honey coloured limestone the resulting magnificent Palladian mansion was completed in 1755. Among its finest features are the hall with its cantilevered stone staircase, the curved orangery with its arched floor-to-ceiling windows and the semicircular china room with its elegant display of rare porcelain and glass. There is also a fine collection of 17th and 18th century English and French furniture, 19th and 20th century paintings and a small military museum commemorating Britain's last privately raised regiment, the Princess Patricia's Canadian Light Infantry. The extensively restored grounds incorporate a walled kitchen garden, rose garden, arboretum and deer park.

PITMINSTER
3 miles S of Taunton off the B3170

🏛 Poundisford Park

Recorded as Pipeminster in the Domesday Book, although there is no evidence of a minster ever having been built here, the village does have an old church containing 16th century monuments to the Colles family. Just to the north of Pitminster is **Poundisford Park**, a small H-shaped Tudor mansion standing within a delightful, wooded deer park that once belonged to the bishops of Winchester. The house is renowned for its fine plasterwork ceilings and the grounds incorporate a formal garden laid out in the Tudor style.

BRADFORD-ON-TONE
4 miles SW of Taunton off the A38

📷 Sheppy's Cider

Sheppy's Cider has been making its renowned ciders since the early 1800s and now boasts more than 200 awards, including two gold medals. Visitors can stroll through the orchards with their wide variety of apples, visit the museum for an insight into the farming of yesteryear, watch a video following the cider-maker's year, and sample the finished product in the shop. Professional guided tours are available for parties of 20 or more. Other amenities on site include a licensed tearoom, picnic area and children's play area.

WELLINGTON
6 miles SW of Taunton on the A38

🏛 Town Hall   🏛 Wellington Monument

This pleasant old market town was once an important producer of woven cloth and serge and it owes much of its prosperity to Quaker entrepreneurs and, later, the Fox banking family. Fox, Fowler and Co was the last private bank in England to issue its own notes and they only ceased in 1921 when they were taken over by Lloyds. The broad streets around the town centre are peppered with fine Georgian buildings, including the neoclassical **Town Hall**. At the eastern end of the town, the much altered church contains the ostentatious tomb of Sir John Popham, the judge who presided at the trial of Guy Fawkes.

To the south of the town stands the **Wellington Monument**, a 175-foot obelisk erected not long after the duke's great victory at Waterloo. The foundation stone was laid in 1817 by Lord Somerville but the monument was only completed in 1854. The duke himself visited the site and the town from which he took his title only once, in 1819.

WIVELISCOMBE
9 miles W of Taunton on the B3227

🏛 Gaulden Manor

This is an ancient and isolated village where

the Romans once had a fort and a quantity of 3rd and 4th century coins have been uncovered in the area. Later, in medieval times, the local manor house was used as a summer residence of the bishops of Bath and Wells. The remains, including a striking 14th century archway, have now been incorporated into a group of cottages. During World War II, the church's crypt was used to store priceless historic documents and ecclesiastical treasures brought here from other parts of Somerset that were more at risk from aerial attack.

Gaulden Manor, nr Wiveliscombe

To the northeast of Wiveliscombe, close to the village of Tolland, is the delightful **Gaulden Manor,** an estate that dates from the 12th century although the present house is largely 17th century. This is very much a lived-in house with guided tours conducted by the owner. It contains some outstanding early plasterwork, fine furniture, and many examples of embroidery by the owner's wife. The interesting gardens include a herb garden, old fashioned roses, a bog garden and a secret garden beyond the monks' fish pond. Gaulden Manor once belonged to the Turberville family whose name was adapted by Thomas Hardy for use in his novel, *Tess of the D'Urbervilles* .

To the north and west of Wiveliscombe, below the Brendon Hills, are two reservoirs, Wimbleball and Clatworthy, which offer excellent facilities for picnickers, anglers and water sports enthusiasts.

NORTON FITZWARREN
2 miles NW of Taunton on the B3227

Large finds of Roman pottery have been excavated in and around this village, helping to confirm that Norton Fitzwarren was the Roman settlement of Theodunum. The village's name comes from the Saxon 'north tun' (meaning north farm) and the Norman family who were given the manor here after the Conquest. Norton Fitzwarren's antiquity and former importance gave rise to the old rhyme "When Taunton was a furzy down, Norton was a market town". Today, although the village has all but been consumed by its much larger neighbour, it has still managed to retain some of its individuality.

The land around Norton Fitzwarren is damp and fertile and, for hundreds of years, cider apples have been grown here. Cider made here is now transported all over the world, but until the early 19th century cider was a beverage very much confined to Somerset and the West Country. It was the Revd Thomas Cornish, a local clergyman, who first brought cider to the attention of the rest

THE BLUE BALL INN

Triscombe, Taunton, Somerset TA4 3HE
Tel: 01984 617242
e-mail: info@blueballinn.co.uk   website: www.blueballinn.co.uk

With its thatched roof, mellow stone walls and colourful window boxes and plants, **The Blue Ball Inn** looks irresistibly inviting. This lovely old hostelry is just one of a handful of buildings in the hamlet of Triscombe at the foot of the Quantock Hills. It lies just off the A358 and is easily accessible from junction 25 of the M5, Taunton and Minehead.

The interior of the inn is as captivating as the outside. There's a wealth of old beams, oak dividers separate the tables and the bar occupies a kind of wooden barn. Owners Gerald and Sue Rogers have made the Blue Ball well-known as one of the best rural venues for dining. The award-winning restaurant offers an outstanding à la carte menu that changes for each meal. "We pride ourselves," says Gerald, "on preparing our dishes from only fresh ingredients to give our customers a memorable and unhurried dining experience, whether for lunch or dinner". A typical lunchtime menu might offer cajun fillet of wild salmon with caesar salad and white anchovies, or ginger & lemon scented breast of free range chicken, white rice and sugar snaps as main courses. For lighter appetites, ploughman's and crusty rustic rolls with a choice of fillings are also available.

The dinner menu offers an equally extensive choice, again with many dishes based on local produce - the Blue Ball signature sirloin sliced over rossti with shallots, wild fungi, creamy leek & jus, for example, or a vegetarian saffron & leek risotto with spinach, red onion comfit, infused truffle oil & butter. Such is the reputation of the Blue Ball's cuisine that booking a table in advance is strongly recommended, especially at weekends.

The inn also has accommodation available in two cottages which are let on a bed & breakfast basis. Stag Cottage features an inglenook fireplace with gas effect fire, plus an upstairs bathroom with separate shower and Victorian style free-standing bath. Pheasant Cottage is equally comfortable and its amenities include an en suite shower and bath.

of the nation, when he produced a drink so appetizing that it found great favour with Queen Victoria. Close to one of the largest cider breweries in the area are the remains of an early Bronze Age bank and ditch enclosure, and artefacts excavated from here can be seen in the county museum in Taunton.

BISHOP'S LYDEARD
5 miles NW of Taunton off the A358

 West Somerset Railway   St Mary's Church

Bishop's Lydeard Mill

This large village is the southern terminus of the **West Somerset Railway,** a nostalgic enterprise that recaptures the era of the branch line country railway in the days of steam. This privately operated steam railway runs to Minehead on the Bristol Channel coast

and, extending for nearly 20 miles, is the longest line of its kind in the country. It was formed when British Rail's 100-year-old branch line between Taunton and Minehead closed in 1971. There are ten stations along the line and services operate between Easter and the end of October. The railway's special attractions include a first class Pullman dining car and the *Flockton Flyer* locomotive which is named after the 1970s children's drama series of that name which centred on the adventures of a family running a preserved railway.

St Mary's Church has a magnificent tower built of local red stone around 1450. Fortunately, it was spared any insensitive Victorian restoration of the interior. Look out for the 'hunky punks' on the outside of the tower. Hunky punk is the local term for the

---

FOUR SEASONS B&B
Seven Ash, Bishops Lydeard, Somerset TA4 3EX
Tel. 01823 430337 Contact: Heather Rose
e-mail: info@fourseasonsbedbreakfast.co.uk
website: www.fourseasonsbedbreakfast.co.uk

A warm welcome awaits you at the newly refurbished Four Seasons, situated in an ideal position for exploring West Somerset and the surrounding areas. Overlooking the rolling hills of the Quantocks, Britain's first designated Area of Outstanding Natural Beauty, this B&B witnesses the ever-changing colours of the heather-clad moorland. To the rear of the property are far-reaching views of the Brendon Hills leading on to Exmoor.

Offering high quality accommodation whether visiting overnight on business, seeking a relaxing well-earned break or, for the more energetic amongst you, an activity-based holiday amongst this exhilarating and beautiful landscape. If you prefer to explore the area on foot there are a number of gentle, scenic walks via public footpaths from the front door. Maps are available and the owners can also provide you with a delicious packed lunch to take with you for when you find that perfect spot for a rest.

All rooms have luxury en-suite facilities together with tea/coffee-making facilties, remote LCD TV with multi-channels, hairdryer, Wi-Fi access and local tourist maps/information. Start the day with a hearty breakfast which includes a choice of fruit juice, cereals, muesli, yoghurt, fruit together with the traditional English, using good quality local produce. For your evening meal there is a good selection of restaurants and cosy inns within a five mile radius.

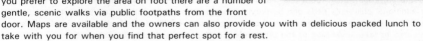

   stories and anecdotes   famous people   art and craft   entertainment and sport   walks

THE CAREW ARMS

Crowcombe, Taunton, Somerset, TA4 4AD
Tel: 01984 618631
e-mail: contact@thecarewarms.co.uk
website: www.thecarewarms.co.uk

Situated at the foothills of the Quantocks, The Carew Arms is a traditional 16th Century Inn where you can take the opportunity to relax and enjoy yourself. Whether you are looking for a Somerset pub that offers a great selection of locally brewed real ales, a truly special dining experience featuring expertly prepared local dishes and a wide selection of fine wines, or comfortable accommodation with glorious views, The Carew Arms is top of the list.

Ther is a choice of venue for eating. The well-appointed restaurant has views over the garden and surrounding countryside while the original flagstone bar with deep inglenook fireplace is muddy boot friendly for tired walkers! Whichever you choose, you will experience a warm welcome from the friendly staff. In addition, there is a private dining room available, which may also be used for meetings if required.

The range of food is updated with the seasons and always includes freshly prepared and locally sourced fish dishes, as well as sumptuous local meats prepared sympathetically and imaginatively by the Head Chef and Manager, Helen Holden. If your visit includes a Friday evening, why not take advantage of our pretty gardens and enjoy fish and chips served on paper watching the sun set over the fields? Or why not book an evening's fun playing skittles? There is a traditional skittle alley with buffet style food on request. Please check the Special Events page on the website for upcoming events.

If you are looking for accommodation, there are six well-appointed rooms, which offer a high level of comfort. There are three double rooms and three twin rooms, all with views over the garden or beautiful local scenery. Five of the rooms have en-suite facilities, and the sixth has its own private bathroom. Each room has tea and coffee making facilities and digital freeview TV. Cots or additional children's beds can be provided on request. Reservations can be made directly over the telephone or by email and all bookings require a 20% deposit. Whether you are visiting the area to take advantage of the outstanding walking or cycling trails, or just to enjoy the stunning scenery on the Quantock Hills, The Carew Arms is ideally placed.

Set within England's first designated Area of Outstanding Natural Beauty, The Carew Arms has been the centre of village life in Crowcombe for over 400 years. Owners Iain and Emma Kirkpatrick warmly welcome you to come and visit.

Open 7 days a week 12 noon to 3.00 pm and 5.00 pm to 11.00 pm

---

🏛 historic building   🏛 museum and heritage   🏛 historic site   ♣ scenic attraction   🌱 flora and fauna

carved creatures which, unlike gargoyles that carry off rainwater, serve no useful function. St Mary's has five hunky punks – the one on the south-west corner of a dragon with a stone in its mouth looks particularly menacing.

The Grade II listed **Bishop's Lydeard Mill** has been painstakingly restored over many years by the Back family and is now fully working. Among the many traditional trades and crafts displayed here are a wheelwright's shop, transported from Devon and preserved exactly as it was left on the day the owner shut up shop, and an equally authentic blacksmith's shop. Other attractions include fun interactive displays; a gift shop and Dusty Miller's tearoom.

BRIDGWATER

- 🏛 Blake Museum
- 🏛 Somerset Brick & Tile Museum
- 🎨 Carnival 🎨 Somerset Space Walk

Situated at the lowest bridging point of the River Parrett, Bridgwater is an ancient inland port and industrial town. Despite having been fortified since before the Norman Conquest, the settlement that grew up around the castle remained little more than a village until an international trade in wool, wheat and other agricultural products began to develop in the late Middle Ages. Bridgwater grew and, at one time, was the most important town on the coast between Bristol and Barnstaple. For a short period, it was the fifth busiest port in the country. The largely 14th century parish church, with its disproportionately large spire, is the only building to remain from that prosperous medieval era. The castle was dismantled after the English Civil War and the 13th century Franciscan friary and St John's Hospital disappeared long ago. Although the street layout here is still medieval, the

buildings in the area between King Street and West Quay are some of the best examples of domestic Georgian architecture in the county.

Bridgwater's most famous son is the celebrated military leader, Robert Blake, who was born here in 1598. When in his 40s, Blake became an important officer in Cromwell's army and twice defended Taunton against overwhelming Royalist odds. Just a decade later, he was appointed General at Sea and went on to win a number of important battles against the Dutch and the Spanish. In so doing, he restored the nation's naval supremacy in Europe. The house in which he was born is now home to the **Blake Museum** which contains a three-dimensional model of the Battle of Santa Cruz, one of Blake's most famous victories, along with a collection of his personal effects. Blake was not the only military leader connected with Bridgwater. During the late 1600s, the Duke of Monmouth stayed here before his disastrous defeat at the nearby Battle of Sedgemoor. The museum suitably illustrates this decisive battle in the duke's quest for the English throne. This is also a museum of local history with a large collection of locally discovered artefacts on display that date from Neolithic times right up to World War II.

The highlight of Bridgwater's events calendar is its **Carnival** commemorating Guy Fawkes' Day. Believed to be the largest such event in the world, the celebration involves hundreds of themed 'carts', each ablaze with as many as 25,000 light bulbs, which join a procession more than two miles long, accompanied by various town bands. Following the procession, "squibs", or giant fireworks, are carried through the town and set alight in the High Street.

An attractive amenity of the town is the **Bridgwater and Taunton Canal** which was

🎭 stories and anecdotes 🕊 famous people 🎨 art and craft ☕ entertainment and sport 🚶 walks

LISA'S

11 High Street, Bridgwater, Somerset TA6 3BE
Tel/Fax: 01278 450896

If knitting is your hobby, then **Lisa's** on Bridgwater's High Street is the place to indulge it to the full. When visiting you will be greeted by friendly, approachable and knowledgeable staff who are happy to help. Lisa's stocks 2,3 and 4-ply, double knit, chunky and aran weight. It also sells a good selection of knitting patterns and accessories, anything from knitting needles and stitch holders to bags to help keep you organised.

Lisa's haberdashery department offers a kaleidoscope of ribbons in satin and sheers, lace, upholstery braids and a selection of buttons which, says Lisa, "is second to none - or so we have been told!" Also available is an assortment of scissors, needles and pins, tape in two widths and in various colours, curtain heading tape, patches, repair tape, bra extenders and bikini clasps - the list is almost endless. Cross stitch and tapestries are always in stock, along with a full range of top name embroidery silks.

Lisa's also stocks a selection of gifts for the "not so crafty element amongst you". Credit and debit cards are accepted; the shop is wheelchair accessible and also offers a postal service.

CHESTNUT FARM CIDER

Edithmead, Highbridge, Somerset TA9 4HB
Tel: 01278 785376

Formerly known as Bennett's Cider, **Chestnut Farm Cider** is made by the Bennett family of whom five generations have been involved in the business.

Like his father Tom Bennett, who won more than 150 prize cards in 15 years, Viv Bennet has won a whole string of prizes at the Bath and West Show as well as at the Devon County Show and believes that he has now caught up with his father!

Chestnut Farm is a working farm and the cider is made in the traditional way from apples grown in the orchards here. If you visit in the autumn you can see the apples being pressed and breathe in the heady aroma of the fresh juice.

And if you visit in January you can watch the Wassailing Ceremony which is designed to ward off evil spirits from the apple trees and produce an abundant harvest.

The farm can be found just off the M5 at Junction 22, on the B3140. Go towards Burnham and the farm is on the left after half a mile, opposite a minor road, Stoddens Lane, leading to the entrance to a large caravan/camping site. If you go over the railway bridge, you've gone too far.

🏛 historic building 🏚 museum and heritage 🏛 historic site 🐸 scenic attraction 🐦 flora and fauna

completed in 1827 and can still be explored on water by canoe, trail boat or narrow boat, or along the towpath on foot or by cycle. Before the construction of a canal dock, the ships arriving at Bridgwater used to tie up on both sides of the river below the town's medieval bridge. Here, too, can be seen the last remnant of the medieval castle, The Water Gate, on West Quay.

The arrival of the canal gave a great boost to local industries. The manufacture of Bridgwater glass, which had begun the previous century, expanded greatly. The river mud that caused the decline of the town's port also proved to have hidden benefits, because when baked in oblong blocks it was found to be an excellent scourer. As Bath Brick, it was used for nearly a century to clean grates and stone steps. The canal terminus, where the brickworks also stood, was finally closed in 1970 but has now been restored as a fascinating area of industrial archaeology.

More of the county's industrial heritage can be explored at the **Somerset Brick & Tile Museum** on East Quay. The last surviving kiln at the former Barham Brother's yard is a poignant reminder of the brick and tile industry which was once so important in the county. The kiln has been repaired by Somerset County Council and now provides the centrepiece of the museum.

An interesting feature on the canal is based at Lower Mounsel Locks, about five miles south of Bridgwater. **The Somerset Space Walk** uses the 13-mile length of the canal to represent the solar system with scale models of each of the planets. The sun is placed at the locks with the inner planets nearby; Pluto can be found on the outskirts of Taunton.

Around Bridgwater

HIGHBRIDGE
6 miles N of Bridgwater on the A38

🐾 Alstone Wildlife Park

The small coastal town of Highbridge was once a busy port on the Glastonbury Canal. Today its main visitor attraction is **Alstone Wildlife Park,** a small non-profit making, family-run park which devotes all its proceeds to the welfare and upkeep of the animals. Open daily from Easter to November, the park is home to a variety of animals including Theadore the camel, a herd of red deer, wallabies, owls, pigs, emus and ponies.

BURNHAM-ON-SEA
7 miles N of Bridgwater on the B3140

🏛 St Andrew's Church 🏛 Low Lighthouse

🏞 Brent Knoll

A traditional seaside resort as well as a thriving market town, Burnham-on-Sea has acres of sandy beach, a fine Edwardian Esplanade, a Pier Pavilion and a 15th century church that was built close by the shore. This turned out to be a not very good idea. Because of the sandy foundations, the 80ft tower of **St Andrew's Church** now leans three feet from the vertical. But the structure is apparently quite stable and has not shifted for many decades. Inside are parts of a massive altarpiece designed by Inigo Jones and carved by Grinling Gibbons. Originally installed in James II's Whitehall Palace, it survived the great fire that destroyed the palace and was re-installed in Westminster Abbey. But when the abbey was being prepared for the coronation of George IV the huge structure was deemed out of place and surplus to requirements. Somehow, the vicar of Burnham learned of its impending fate and managed to acquire it for his country church. The parts are now dispersed over various parts of the chancel.

In the early 1800s, the local curate, the Revd Davies, discovered mineral springs in the gardens of Burnham Hall. An attempt was made to turn Burnham into a spa town to rival Cheltenham and Bath. A series of buildings was erected around the springs, the most notable of them being the Bath House, now Steart House, on the Esplanade. Unfortunately, the waters were too sulphurous and stinking for most convalescents to endure and the venture fizzled out. The town would have to depend on its wide sandy beach to attract visitors.

A distinctive feature on the beach is the unique nine-legged **Low Lighthouse,** a curious square structure raised above the beach on tall stilts. An earlier lighthouse, the High Lighthouse, erected in 1750, still stands inland behind the dunes but because of the huge rise and fall of tides in the Severn estuary, its light was ineffective at low tides. Hence the need for the Low Lighthouse.

To the northeast of Burnham rises **Brent Knoll**, a conspicuous landmark that can be seen from as far away as South Wales. Before the Somerset Levels were drained, this isolated hill would almost certainly have been an island. As with many other natural features that appear out of place in the landscape, there are several stories that suggest that the knoll owes its existence to the Devil. The 445-foot summit is crowned with the remains of an Iron Age hill fort. The summit, which can be reached by footpaths beginning near the churches at East Brent and Brent Knoll, offers walkers a spectacular view out over the Bristol Channel, the Mendips and the Somerset Levels.

BREAN
11 miles N of Bridgwater off the A370

🐾 Animal Farm Adventure Park

This elongated, mainly modern resort village is sheltered, to the north, by the 320ft high **Brean Down** (National Trust), an imposing remnant of the Mendip hills that projects out into the Bristol Channel. Another fragment can be seen in the form of the offshore island **Steep Holm**. A site of settlement, ritual and defence for thousands of years, the remains of an Iron Age coastal fort and a Roman temple have both been found on the down along with some medieval 'pillow' mounds. The tip of the promontory is dominated by the Palmerston fort of 1867, built as part of

---

THE OLD RECTORY

Church Road, Brean, Nr Burham on Sea, Somerset TA8 2SF
Tel: 01278 751447
e-mail: info@oldrectorybrean.co.uk
website: www.oldrectorybrean.co.uk

The Old Rectory is just 150 yards from beautiful sandy beaches and enjoys views over open countryside. Many of its 18 rooms are on the ground floor making the hotel accessible for disabled visitors. The rooms are mostly ensuite with all having tea & coffee making facilities and colour televisions. Breakfast is cooked using locally produced food and is served in the conservatory allowing guests to enjoy views of the award winning garden and coi carp pond. In the afternoons, cream-teas, light snacks and home-made cakes are served in the tea garden.

🏭 historic building   🏛 museum and heritage   🏚 historic site   🝈 scenic attraction   🐾 flora and fauna

the defences to protect the Bristol Channel. There are also some 20th century gun emplacements. As well as its archaeological and geological interest, this peninsula has been designated a Site of Special Scientific Interest because of its varied habitats. Oystercatcher and dunlin can be seen along the foreshore and estuary; the scrubland is an important habitat for migrating birds such as redstart, redpoll and reed bunting; rare plants take root in the shallow and exposed soil, and the south-facing slopes are home to a variety of butterflies. Subject to one of the widest tidal ranges in Europe, the currents around the headland can be dramatic and very dangerous.

About a mile inland from Brean Sands beach, **Animal Farm Adventure Park** promises fun for all the family with a mix of domestic and rarer animals, including llamas, alpacas and emus; adventure play areas, ride-on tractors and a miniature railway.

WESTONZOYLAND
3½ miles SE of Bridgwater on the A372

🏛 Battle of Sedgemoor   🏭 Pumping Station

Just to the northwest of the village and on the southern bank of what is now the King's Sedgemoor Drain is the site of the last battle to be fought on English soil. In July 1685, the well-equipped forces of James II heavily defeated the followers of the Duke of Monmouth in the bloody **Battle of Sedgemoor**. This brought an end to the ill-fated Pitchfork Rebellion that aimed to

---

MUSGROVE WILLOWS

Lakewall, Westonzoyland, Bridgwater, Somerset TA7 0LP
Tel: 01278 691105
e-mail: info@musgrovewillows.co.uk
website: www.musgrovewillows.co.uk

Musgrove Willows is a family run business founded in the early 1930s. Michael Musgrove is the third generation to continue the family tradition of willow growing and has accumulated many years of specialised knowledge and experience handed down to him by his father and grandfather. Michael, Somerset's youngest willow grower, together with his wife Ellen, now grow over 70 acres of more than 60 different varieties of willow, still in the traditional Somerset style.

Musgrove Willows grew and supplied the willow for the Willow Man on the M5 and also for a giant otter which can be found on the Pembrokeshire Coast. Their willow is used by independent basket makers, schools, willow sculptors & hurdle makers, and for lantern parades and art projects.

Musgrove Willows can be found on the outskirts of the historic village of Westonzoyland. To discover more about willow growing and the traditional practices still in operation, tours around the working willow farm are available from April - October; Tuesdays, Thursdays & Saturdays at 11am. Places must be booked in advance. Customers always welcome.

If you would like to learn a new skill, weave a traditional basket or enhance your garden with a living arbour, Musgrove Willows runs a variety of courses throughout the year covering basket making, garden structures, hurdles & plant climbers. Living willow is also available from November to March.

🎭 stories and anecdotes   🐦 famous people   🎨 art and craft   🎪 entertainment and sport   🚶 walks

replace the Catholic King James with the Protestant Duke of Monmouth, an illegitimate son of Charles II. Around 700 of Monmouth's followers were killed on the battlefield while several hundred survivors were rounded up and taken to Westonzoyland churchyard, where many of them were hanged. The duke himself was taken to London where, 10 days after the battle, he was executed on Tower Hill. However, it was during the infamous Judge Jeffrey's 'Bloody Assizes' that

Battle of Sedgemoor, Westonzoyland

the greatest terror was inflicted on the surviving followers of the duke when well over 300 men were condemned to death. A further 600 were transported to the colonies. Today, a stark memorial marks the site of the lonely battlefield.

The village lies in the Somerset Levels and a steam-powered **Pumping Station** was built here in the 19th century to drain the water from the levels into the River Parrett. The oldest pumping station of its kind in the area, the engine on show here was in operation from 1861 until 1952. Now fully restored, it can be seen in steam at various times throughout the year. The station itself is a grade II listed building. Also on the site is a small forge, a tramway and a number of other exhibits from the steam age.

ENMORE
4 miles SW of Bridgwater off the A39

⚘ Quantock Hills 🏠 Fyne Court 🎦 Andrew Cross

To the west of Enmore the ground rises up into the **Quantock Hills**, an Area of Outstanding Natural Beauty that runs from

near Taunton to the Bristol Channel at Quantoxhead. Rising to a high point of 1260 feet at **Wills Neck**, this delightful area of open heath and scattered woodland supports one of the country's last remaining herds of wild red deer. The exposed hilltops are littered with Neolithic and Bronze Age remains, including around 100 burial mounds, many of which now resemble nothing more than a pile of stones. The richer soil in the south sustains arable farms and pockets of dense woodland and this varied landscape offers some magnificent walking with splendid views over the Bristol Channel, the Vale of Taunton Deane, the Brendon Hills and Exmoor. It was this glorious classical English landscape that the poets Wordsworth and Coleridge so admired while they were living in the area.

Southwest of Enmore in one of the loveliest areas on the southern Quantocks is **Fyne Court** (National Trust) which houses both the headquarters of the Somerset Wildlife Trust and a visitor centre for the Quantocks. The main house here was built in the 17th century by the Crosse family. It was largely destroyed by fire in the 1890s and the only surviving parts are the library and music room that have been converted into the visitor centre. The grounds, which incorporate a walled garden, two ponds, an arboretum and a lake, have been designated a nature reserve. The most renowned occupant of the house was **Andrew Cross**, an early-19th century scientist who was a pioneer in the field of electrical energy. Known locally as the 'thunder and lightning man', one of Crosse's lightning conductors can still be seen on an oak tree in the grounds. Local stories tell how, during one of his electrical experiments, Crosse created tiny live insects. It was this claim that helped to inspire Mary Shelley to write her Gothic horror story, *Frankenstein*, in 1818.

NETHER STOWEY
10 miles W of Bridgwater off the A39

🏚 Stowey Court 🏚 Coleridge Cottage

🚶 Quantock Forest Trail 🦅 Samuel Taylor Coleridge

This attractive village of 17th and 18th century stone cottages and houses is best known for its literary connections but Nether Stowey has a much longer history. At one time, it was a small market town. A castle was built here in Norman times and the earthwork remains can be seen to the west of the village centre while its substantial manor house, **Stowey Court**, stands on the eastern side of the village. The construction of the manor house was begun by Lord Audley in 1497 shortly before he joined a protest against Henry VII's taxation policy. Sadly, he was not able to see the project through to completion as he was executed soon afterwards.

In 1797, a local tanner, Tom Poole, lent a dilapidated cottage at the end of his garden to his friend, **Samuel Taylor Coleridge**, who stayed here for three years with his wife and child. So began Nether Stowey's association with poets and writers. It was here that Coleridge wrote most of his famous works, including *The Rime of the Ancient Mariner* and the opium-inspired *Kubla Khan*. When not writing, he would go on long walks with his friend and near neighbour William Wordsworth who had moved close to Nether Stowey from a house in Dorset at around the same time. Other visitors to the cottage included Charles Lamb. But it was not long before Coleridge's opium addiction and his rocky marriage began to take their toll. These were not the only problems for the poet as local suspicion was growing that he and Wordsworth were French spies. The home in which the Coleridges lived for three years is now **Coleridge Cottage,** a National Trust property where mementoes of the poet are on display.

A lane leads southwest from the village to the nearby village of Over Stowey and the starting point of the Forestry Commission's **Quantock Forest Trail**, a three-mile walk lined with specially planted native and imported trees.

Ilminster

🏚 Dillington House

One of Somerset's most beguiling towns, Ilminster is perched on the side of a hill with its main street running round, rather than up and down the slope. For centuries, it stood on the main London to Exeter route; today the A303 bypasses the town allowing its special charm to be enjoyed in comparative peace.

A church was founded here by the Saxon King Ine in the 8th century and by the time of the Domesday Book in 1089, the borough had grown considerably – it was recorded as having a market and three mills. During the

A TOUCH OF ELEGANCE

5 West Street, Ilminster, Somerset TA19 9AA
Tel: 01460 55992
e-mail: sue@atouchofelegance.org.uk
website: www.atouchofelegance.org.uk

Sue Woodbury developed her love of interiors after renovating a Somerset cottage and in 2000 she established **A Touch of Elegance**, a home interiors shop supplying furnishings of the highest quality. There is a vast range of contemporary and traditional wooden, glass and bespoke furniture from companies including 'Zoffany' and 'Duresta'.

The collections of high quality designer fabrics come from suppliers such as 'Colefax & Fowler' and 'Robert Allen' among others lending themselves to the beautiful scatter cushions, bedspreads, curtains and the many curtain trimmings and accessories available. Old furniture can be revamped with quality upholstery and curtains and blinds can be made to measure with a choice of luxurious fabrics.

No part of the room is forgotten in A Touch of Elegance. With paints from 'The little green paint company' and 'Zoffany' and a wide range of wall coverings in a variety of designs and colours, there is something for every taste. To add interest, complete the room with one of the beautiful wall, ceiling or standing lights or choose from the collections of smaller ornamental pieces and giftware.

Sue's aim is to deliver a complete interior design service and that said her comfortable showroom is awash with colour, texture and inspiration.

Middle Ages, it expanded further into a thriving wool and lace-making town. This period of prosperity is reflected in the town's unusually large parish church, whose massive multi-pinnacled tower is modelled on that of Wells Cathedral. Any walk around the old part of Ilminster will reveal a number of delightful old buildings, many constructed in golden Hamstone, including the chantry house, the old grammar school and a colonnaded market house. Another, the George Inn, proudly displays a sign proclaiming that it was first hotel that Queen Victoria stayed at, as Princess Victoria, in 1819. The future queen was on her way with her parents to Sidmouth in Devon.

On the outskirts of Ilminster is another lovely old building, the handsome part Tudor mansion, **Dillington House.** It is now owned by Somerset County Council and used as a Residential Centre for Adult Education, but it was originally the home of the Speke family. In the time of James II, John Speke was an officer in the Duke of Monmouth's ill-fated rebel army that landed at Lyme Regis in 1685. Following the rebellion's disastrous defeat at the Battle of Sedgemoor, Speke was forced to flee abroad, leaving his brother, George, who had done no more than shake the duke's hand, to face the wrath of Judge Jeffreys. The infamous 'hanging judge' sentenced George to death, justifying his

decision with the words, "His family owes a life and he shall die for his brother."

Around Ilminster

BARRINGTON
3 miles NE of Ilminster off the B3168

🏠 Barrington Court

To the east of the village is the beautiful National Trust-owned **Barrington Court,** famous for its enchanting garden influenced by the great 20th century garden architect Gertrude Jekyll. This estate originally belonged to the Daubeney family but it passed through several hands before becoming the property of William Clifton, a wealthy London merchant, who was responsible for building the house in the mid-16th century. In 1907, the by then dilapidated Barrington Court became the first country house to be purchased by the National Trust. It was restored in the 1920s by Col AA Lyle, to whom the Trust had let the property. The garden, too, was laid out during this time in a series of themed areas including an iris garden, a lily garden, a white garden and a fragrant rose garden. Gertrude Jekyll was brought in to advise on the initial planting and layout and the garden remains the finest example of her work in the Trust's care. There is also an exceptionally attractive kitchen garden with apple, pear and plum trees trained along the walls that, in season, produces fruit and vegetables for the licensed restaurant that can be found here.

DOWLISH WAKE
2 miles SE of Ilminster off the A303 or A358

🪶 John Hanning Speke   🍎 Perry's Cider Mills

In the parish church of this attractive village

can be seen the tomb of **John Hanning Speke,** the intrepid Victorian explorer who journeyed for more than 2,500 miles through Africa to confirm that Lake Victoria was, indeed, the source of the River Nile. After his epic journey, Speke returned to England a hero but, tragically, on the very morning of the day that he was due to report his findings to the British Geographical Association he accidentally shot himself while on a partridge shoot.

This picturesque village is also the home of **Perry's Cider Mills** where the cider presses are installed in a wonderful 16th century thatched barn. If you visit in the autumn you can see the cider making in progress but the presses and an interesting collection of vintage farm tools and equipment are on view all year round. The full range of ciders, including cider brandy, is available in the shop and can be sampled from the barrel before you buy. The shop also stocks a huge range of country style pottery, stone cider jars, baskets, terracotta kitchenware, country jams and pickles and much more.

HINTON ST GEORGE
11 miles SE of Ilminster off the A356

🪶 Sir Amyas Poulett   🌳 Lower Severalls

This wonderfully unspoilt former estate village has a broad main street, thatched houses, a medieval village cross and a striking 15th century church. For centuries the village was owned by the Poulett family and it is thanks to them that Hinton St George has been left virtually untouched. The Pouletts arrived here in the 15th century and the house that they rebuilt then, Hinton House, now forms the main structure of the present day mansion. Although this has now been converted into apartments, the building is still said to be haunted by the ghost of a young Poulett woman who died of a broken heart after her father shot dead the man with whom she was planning to elope. Several ostentatious monuments to members of the Poulett family can be seen in the village's 15th century Church of St George. Commemorated by a superb alabaster memorial is the most famous member of the family, **Sir Amyas Poulett**. A loyal and honourable courtier of Elizabeth I, Sir Amyas fell out of favour when he declined to act on the queen's suggestion that he murder Mary, Queen of Scots who was in his custody. "A dainty and precise fellow," was the queen's scornful response to the knight's over-scrupulous behaviour.

On the last Thursday in October, called 'Punkie Night', it is traditional for Hinton children to beg for candles to put inside their intricately fashioned turnip and pumpkin lanterns. It is considered very unlucky to refuse to give a child a candle as each lantern is thought to represent the spirit of a dead person who, unless illuminated, will rise up at Hallowe'en.

Hinton seems to have a special interest in light. It was the first village in England to install gas street lighting in 1863 and recently its modern street lighting scheme received an award from the International Dark Skies Association because its street lamps minimise light pollution.

To the east of the village, **Lower Severalls** has an enchanting and original garden set in front of an 18th century Hamstone farmhouse. The garden has an informal style with profuse herbaceous borders around the house and innovative features that include a living dogwood basket, a wadi and a scented garden.

CREWKERNE
13 miles SE of Ilminster on the A30/A356

🏛 Church of St Batholomew   🍃 Windwhistle Hill

📷 Crewkerne & District Museum

🌿 Clapton Court Gardens   🚶 River Parrett Trail

Another delightful small town, noted for its antiques and book shops, and the famous auction house of Lawrence's which is housed in a restored linen yard. A thriving agricultural centre during Saxon times, Crewkerne even had its own mint in the decades leading up to the Norman invasion. Evidence of this ancient former market town's importance and wealth can still be seen in the magnificence of its parish **Church of St Bartholomew**, built using money generated by the late medieval boom in the local wool industry. A building of minster-like proportions, this is one of the grandest of the many fine Perpendicular churches to be found in south Somerset. Unlike many other towns in Wessex, whose textile industries suffered an almost total decline in later years, Crewkerne was rejuvenated in the 18th century when the availability of locally grown flax led to an expansion in the manufacture of sailcloth and canvas webbing. Among the many thousands of sails made here were those for *HMS Victory*, Admiral Nelson's flagship at the Battle of Trafalgar. Nelson's captain in that engagement was Sir Thomas Hardy, educated at Crewkerne grammar school. Hardy's career is celebrated at the **Crewkerne and District Museum,** recently relocated in a beautifully restored 18th century house.

The economic boost provided by the flax industry was further fuelled by the development of the London to Exeter stage coach route. This led to the rebuilding of Crewkerne with elegant Georgian buildings, many of which can still be seen. The main areas, around Church and Abbey Streets, have now been designated an Area of Outstanding Architectural Interest.

To the west of Crewkerne rises the aptly named **Windwhistle Hill**, a high chalk-topped ridge from the top of which there are dramatic views on a clear day, southwards to Lyme Bay and northwards across the Somerset Levels to the mountains of South Wales. The town also lies close to the source of the River Parrett. From here the 50-mile **River Parrett Trail** follows the river through some of the country's most ecologically sensitive and fragile areas, the Somerset Levels and Moors. Old mills, splendid churches, attractive villages and ancient monuments as well as orchards, peaceful pastureland and traditional industries such as cider-making and basket-weaving can all be found along the route.

Just a couple of miles southwest of Crewkerne, close to the village of Clapton, are the varied and interesting **Clapton Court Gardens**. Among the many beautiful features of this 10-acre garden are the formal terraces, the rose garden, the rockery and a water garden. The grounds incorporate a large wooded area containing a massive ash tree that, at over 230 years old and 28 feet in girth, is believed to be the oldest and the largest in mainland Britain. There is also a fine metasequoia that is already over 80 feet tall although it was only planted in 1950, from a seed brought back from China.

HASELBURY PLUCKNETT
14 miles SE of Ilminster on the A3066

🏠 Haselbury Bridge

This delightfully named and particularly pretty village has a large part-Norman church whose churchyard contains a series of unusual 'squeeze stones', narrow entrances formed by two large slabs of stone. Just to the west of the village the lovely **Haselbury Bridge**, a medieval packhorse bridge, crosses the still young River Parrett.

CHARD
6 miles S of Ilminster on the A30

🏛 Chard Museum   🏚 Hornsbury Mill
🌱 Chard Reservoir Nature Reserve

The borough of Chard was first established in 1235 and during the Middle Ages became a prosperous wool centre with its own mayor, or portreeve, and burgesses. However, few buildings date from before 1577, when a devastating fire raged through the town and left most of it as ashes. One building that did survive the destruction was the fine Perpendicular parish church. The town was rebuilt and, today, many of these 16th and 17th century buildings remain, including the courthouse and the old grammar school. Chard also has some striking Georgian and Victorian buildings. On the outskirts of the town the unusual round toll house, with its conical thatched roof, is a picturesque relic of the days of stagecoaches and turnpike roads.

Chard has expanded rapidly since World War II; its population has more than doubled. Nevertheless the centre of this light industrial town still retains a pleasant village-like atmosphere that is most apparent in its broad main shopping street. At the western end of the town's High Street, housed in the attractive thatched Godworth House, is the award-winning **Chard Museum** amongst whose exhibits are displays celebrating two very inventive former residents. James Stringfellow produced the first steam-powered aeroplanes in the 1840s, and James Gillingham pioneered artificial limbs a few decades later. Also featured is Margaret Bonfield who was the first female British cabinet member as Minister of Labour in 1929.

To the northwest of the town is a 200-year-old corn mill, **Hornsbury Mill**, whose impressive water wheel is still in working order. It stands in five acres of beautiful informally landscaped water gardens. The old buildings have been given a new lease of life and now incorporate a restaurant and bed & breakfast guest rooms, and also provides a popular venue for weddings, special events and conferences.

To the northeast, **Chard Reservoir Nature Reserve** is a conservation area where kingfishers, great crested grebes and other rare species of birds have made their home in and around the lake. The nature reserve also has a two-mile circular footpath that takes in rustling reed beds, broad-leaved woodland and open hay meadows.

Forde Abbey

Chard, Somerset TA20 4LU
Tel: 01460 220231 Fax: 01460 220296

Originally founded by Cistercian monks in the 12th century, **Forde Abbey** lay empty for over 100 years after the Dissolution of the Monasteries before its was sold to Edmund Prideaux, Oliver Cromwell's Attorney General in 1649.

The remains of the abbey were incorporated into the grand private house of the Prideaux family – the old chapter house became the family chapel – and later additions include the magnificent 17th century plaster ceilings and the renowned Mortlake Tapestries that were brought over from Brussels by Charles I. Today, Forde Abbey is the home of the Roper family and it stands at the heart of this family run estate.

Along with the collection of tapestries, period furniture and paintings to see in the house, there is the refectory and dormitory that still survive from the time of the medieval monastery whilst the abbey is also home to the famous Eeles Pottery exhibition.

Meanwhile, the house is surrounded by wonderful gardens and they have been described by Alan Titchmarsh as "one of the greatest gardens in the West Country". There are sloping lawns, herbaceous borders, a bog garden, lakes and a working kitchen garden that supplies the abbey's restaurant with produce whilst rare and unusual plants are for sale at the Plant Centre. The estate is also known for its pedigree herd of cattle and the house, with its restaurant and tearoom, can be visited between April and October whilst the gardens and grounds are open all year round.

🏛 historic building 🏛 museum and heritage 🏛 historic site 🏞 scenic attraction 🌱 flora and fauna

TATWORTH
8 miles S of Ilminster off the A358

🏛 Forde Abbey

To the northeast of this village lies a meadow watered by springs that rise on its borders. This meadow is the last remaining vestige of common land that was enclosed in 1819. Changes in the ownership of the land during the 1820s allowed too many farmers grazing rights on the land, and the meadow suffered from being over-stocked. Therefore, in 1832, the holders of those rights met and, calling their meeting 'Stowell Court', they auctioned off the meadow for one year and shared the proceeds. So an annual tradition was born and the Stowell Court still meets on the first Tuesday after April 6th every year. Although many more customs have been added over the years, the auction proceedings are unique. They begin when a tallow candle of precisely one inch in length is lit and they end with the last bid before the candle goes out. Today, Stowell Mead is managed as a Site of Special Scientific Interest and, as the land is not treated with fertilisers, pesticides or herbicides, it is home to many rare plants. There is no right of way across the land but it can be seen from the road.

A short distance to the southeast of Tatworth, just over the county border in Dorset, is **Forde Abbey** (see panel opposite), founded in the 12th century by Cistercian monks after they had made an unsuccessful attempt to found an abbey in Devon. For more details, see the entry in the Dorset chapter of this book.

CRICKET ST THOMAS
9 miles S of Ilminster off the A30

🐾 Cricket St Thomas Wildlife & Leisure Park

This former estate village is now home to the

Cricket St Thomas Wildlife and Leisure Park, Today, the attractions include stables, a children's adventure fort, wildlife world and a varied assortment of theme park crowd-pleasers designed to attract the young. The central building, Cricket House, was once the family home of the great 18th century naval commander Admiral Sir Alexander Hood and, later, of the Bristol chocolate manufacturer, FJ Fry. The estate also incorporates the tiny St Thomas's Church with its impressive monument to Admiral Hood, who was later to become Viscount Bridport.

WAMBROOK
8 miles SW of Ilminster off the A30

🐾 Ferne Animal Sanctuary

Visitors interested in animal welfare will be keen to visit the **Ferne Animal Sanctuary** at Wambrook. Originally founded in 1939 by the Duchess of Hamilton and Brandon while she was living at Berwick St John near Shaftesbury, the sanctuary moved to its present position in the valley of the River Yarty in 1975. This pleasant 51-acre site incorporates a nature trail, conservation area, dragonfly pools and picnic areas.

Yeovil

🏛 Church of St John the Baptist

🏛 Museum of South Somerset

Yeovil takes its name from the River Yeo, sometimes called the River Ivel. There was a Roman settlement here but the town really began to develop in the Middle Ages when a market was established that continues to be held every Friday. Yeovil's parish **Church of St John the Baptist** is the only significant medieval structure to survive as most of its other early buildings were destroyed by the

🎭 stories and anecdotes   🦜 famous people   🎨 art and craft   🖋 entertainment and sport   🚶 walks

series of fires that struck the town in the 17th century. A substantial building, with a solid-looking tower, the church dates from the late 14th century and has a surprisingly austere exterior given its exceptional number of windows. It has so many windows that it is sometimes referred to as the 'Lantern of the West'.

During the 18th century, Yeovil developed into a flourishing coaching centre due to its strategic position at the junction of several main routes. Industries such as glove-making, leather working, sailcloth making and cheese producing were established here. This rapid expansion was further fuelled by the arrival of the railway in the mid-1800s. Then, in the 1890s, James Petter, a local ironmonger and pioneer of the internal combustion engine, founded a business that went on to become one of the largest manufacturers of diesel engines in Britain. Although production was eventually transferred to the Midlands, a subsidiary set up to produce aircraft during World War I has since evolved into a helicopter plant.

Today, Yeovil retains its geographical importance and is south Somerset's largest concentration of population. It is a thriving commercial, shopping, and market town best known perhaps as the home of Westland Helicopters. Situated in Wyndham House, the **Museum of South Somerset** documents the social and industrial history of the town and surrounding area, from prehistoric times to the present. Amongst other intriguing exhibits is one that explains how a patent stove was the basis for the town's world-leading helicopter industry.

Fleet Air Arm Museum

RNAS Yeovilton, near Ilchester, Somerset BA22 8HT
Tel: 01935 840565 Fax: 01935 842630
e-mail: info@fleetairarm.com
website: www.fleetairarm.com

The Fleet Air Arm Museum is one of the world's largest aviation museums and visitors can come and experience the exciting development of Britain's Flying Navy through a succession of superb exhibits. However, this is much more than just a hanger full of vintage aircraft, and the highly imaginative collection on display also tells the stories of the men and women of naval aviation.

For those wishing to know just what it is like on an aircraft carrier, visitors can be 'flown' aboard the museum's own carrier where they can tour its nerve centre and experience close at hand the thrills and noises of a working flight deck. Meanwhile, through the use of touch screen interactive displays, dramatic lighting and vivid sound, the history and atmosphere of many of the museum's exhibits can be explored further. And, for those who have always wanted to experience the adrenaline rush as a pilot successfully completes his challenging mission, the Merlin Experience has been specially designed to allow visitors to act out their long held flying fantasies. Along with a children's adventure playground, a large book and souvenir shop, restaurant, airfield viewing galleries and a picnic area, this museum has much to offer visitors of all ages and interests whatever the weather.

🏠 historic building   🏛 museum and heritage   🏛 historic site   🏞 scenic attraction   🌿 flora and fauna

Around Yeovil

ILCHESTER
7 miles N of Yeovil off the A37

🏛 Ilchester Museum

In Roman times, the settlement here stood at the point where the north-south route between Dorchester and the Bristol Channel crossed the Fosse Way. However, it was during the 13th century that Ilchester reached its peak as a centre of administration, agriculture and learning. Like its near neighbour Somerton, this was, for a time, the county town of Somerset. Three substantial gaols were built here, one of which remained in use until the 1840s. Another indication of this town's former status is the 13th century Ilchester Mace, England's oldest staff of office. Up until recently, the mace resided in the town hall but today a replica can be seen here, while the original mace is on display in the County Museum at Taunton.

The tiny **Ilchester Museum** is in the centre of the town, by the Market Cross, and here the story of the town from pre-Roman times to the 20th century is told through a series of exhibits that include a Roman coffin and skeleton. Ilchester was the birthplace, in around 1214, of the celebrated scholar, monk and scientist, Roger Bacon, who went on to predict the invention of the aeroplane, telescope and steam engine although he was eventually imprisoned for his subversive ideas.

YEOVILTON
7 miles N of Yeovil

🏛 Fleet Air Arm Museum

Yeovilton boasts one of the world's largest aviation museums, the **Fleet Air Arm Museum** (see panel opposite) which owns a unique collection of aircraft of which around half are on permanent display. Concorde is here along with a hangar full of fragile vintage aircraft. Visitors can 'fly' aboard the museum's own carrier; use interactive displays to explore the history and atmosphere of many of the aircraft stored here, and undertake the Merlin Experience that replicates a challenging flying mission. Other attractions include a children's adventure playground, a large book and souvenir shop, restaurant, airfield viewing galleries and a picnic area.

CHARLTON MACKRELL
9 miles N of Yeovil off the A37

🏛 Lytes Cary Manor

A couple of miles southeast of the town stands the charming manor house of **Lytes Cary Manor** (National Trust). This late medieval stone house was built by succeeding generations of the Lyte family, the best known member of which was Henry Lyte, the Elizabethan herbalist who dedicated his 1578 translation of Dodoen's *Cruydeboeck* to Queen Elizabeth "from my poore house at Lytescarie". After the family left the house in the 18th century it fell into disrepair but in 1907 was purchased and restored by Sir Walter Jenner, son of the famous Victorian physician. Notable features include a 14th century chapel and Tudor Great Hall. The present garden is an enchanting combination of formality and eccentricity. There is an open lawn lined with magnificent yew topiary, an orchard filled with quince, pear and apple trees and a network of enclosed paths that every now and then reveal a view of the house, a lily pond or a classical statue.

🏛 stories and anecdotes   🦅 famous people   🎨 art and craft   🎭 entertainment and sport   🚶 walks

THE FABRIC BARN

Clock House, Queen Camel, Yeovil, Somerset, BA22 7NB
Tel: *01935 851025*
website: www.thefabricbarn.co.uk

Established 10 years ago The Fabric Barn specialises in clearance designer soft furnishing fabrics sold at greatly reduced prices. Set in a barn conversion in the grounds of Camel Farm in Queen Camel there are 100s of rolls of top quality fabrics suitable for curtains, upholstery, loose covers, cushions and other soft furnishing requirements.

With the owners sourcing fabrics from many of the top names, stock is constantly changing and this keeps the Fabric Barn fresh and inspiring every time you walk through the door. Ample parking, a relaxed atmosphere and the opportunity to see the whole roll of fabric rather than a small sample makes choosing so much easier.

Quality fabrics with fantastic savings!

Expert help is available for estimating how much fabric you will need, and accessories such as thread, lining, interlinings, curtain tape, feather cushion pads and many other soft furnishing items can be purchased. In addition, details of interior designers and curtain makers within the local area can be recommended.

The Fabric Barn is open from 10am until 4pm Tuesday through to Friday and on Saturday by appointment. Situated approximately a quarter of a mile outside Queen Camel on the A359 towards Yeovil (come off the A303 at the Sparkford Roundabout). Tel 01935 851025 or check the website www.thefabricbarn.co.uk

WAYNE PULLEN

6 High Street, Milborne Port, nr Sherborne,
Dorset DT9 5AG
Tel: *01963 250222*

The town of Milborne Port is fortunate in having an excellent traditional family butcher in **Wayne Pullen** who began his career as a butcher in this very shop back in 1986. Taken on as a 'Saturday lad', his very first job was boning sides of bacon. He was taken on full time when he left school the following year and served a five-year apprenticeship before leaving in 1993 to further his butchery career. He joined Loders of Yeovil and worked at their Yeovil branch for 13 years with Master Butcher Graham Loder. Then, in September 2006, he returned to Milborne Port to purchase the shop where his career had started.

His guiding principle, he says, "is that by buying only the finest quality local stock, I can guarantee total customer satisfaction." Customers can choose from a wide selection. There's Ruby Red Devon beef, local free range pork, free range chickens, ducks, and geese, Wiltshire dry-cured bacon (sliced on the premises to your requirements), homemade pies, homemade sausages and home-cooked meats - Wayne's gammon ham is his speciality.

Cadbury Castle during Excavations

century fortification on the hilltop. This particular discovery ties the castle in with King Arthur who, at around that time, was spearheading the Celtic British resistance against the advancing Saxons. If Cadbury Castle had been Arthur's Camelot, it would have been a timber fortification rather than the turreted stone structure of the storybooks.

SPARKFORD
8 miles NE of Yeovil on the A359

🏛 Haynes International Motor Museum

🏰 Cadbury Castle

The **Haynes International Motor Museum is** thought to hold the largest collection of veteran, vintage and classic cars and motorbikes in the United Kingdom. A living and working museum, it cares for more than 340 cars and bikes ranging from nostalgic classics to the super cars of today. The site contains 11 huge display halls; one of the UK's largest speedway collections; a kids' race track; adventure play area; gift shop and restaurant.

Just to the southeast of the village rises **Cadbury Castle**, a massive Iron Age hill fort first occupied more than 5,000 years ago and believed by some to be the location of King Arthur's legendary Camelot. The Romans are reputed to have carried out a massacre here in around 70AD when they put down a revolt by the ancient Britons. A major excavation in the 1960s uncovered a wealth of Roman and pre-Roman remains on the site as well as confirming that there was certainly a 6th

This easily defended hilltop was again fortified during the reign of Ethelred the Unready in the early 11th century. The poorly-advised king established a mint here in around 1000. Most of the coinage from Cadbury was used to buy off the invading Danes in an act of appeasement that led to the term Danegeld. As a consequence, most of the surviving coins from the Cadbury mint are now to be found in the museums of Scandinavia.

The mile-long walk around Cadbury Castle's massive earthwork ramparts demonstrates the site's effectiveness as a defensive position. This allowed those at the castle to see enemy's troop movements in days gone by and it now provides spectacular panoramic views for today's visitors.

BARWICK
2 miles S of Yeovil off the A37

🏛 Barwick Park

Pronounced 'barrik', this village is home to **Barwick Park**, an estate littered with bizarre follies, arranged at the four points of the compass. The eastern folly, known as Jack the Treacle Eater, is composed of a rickety stone arch topped by a curious turreted room. According to local stories, the folly is named after a foot messenger who ran back and forth between the estate and London on a diet of nothing more than bread and treacle. The estate also possesses a curious grotto and a handsome church with a Norman font and an unusual 17th century transeptal tower.

WEST COKER
3 miles SW of Yeovil off the A30

🏛 Brympton d'Evercy Manor

Close to the village of West Coker is the magnificent **Brympton d'Evercy Manor House** dating from Norman times but with significant 16th and 17th century additions. (The house is not normally open to the public but is available for civil weddings and other functions).The superb golden Hamstone south wing was built in Jacobean times to a design by Inigo Jones. It boasts many fine internal features including the longest straight single span staircase in Britain and an unusual modern tapestry depicting an imaginary bird's eye view of the property during the 18th century. When viewed from a distance, the mansion house, the little estate church and the nearby dower house make a delightful lakeside grouping.

In the church at nearby East Coker were buried the ashes of the poet and playwright TS Eliot. This village, is where his ancestors lived before emigrating to America in the mid-1600s, and provides the title for the second of his *Four Quartets*. Its opening and closing lines are engraved on a plaque in the church:

> *In my beginning is my end.*
> *In my end is my beginning.*

MONTACUTE
4 miles W of Yeovil off the A3088

🏛 Montacute House   📷 TV & Radio Museum

This charming village of golden Hamstone houses and cottages is also home to the magnificent Elizabethan mansion, **Montacute House** (National Trust), built in the 1590s for Edward Phelips, Queen Elizabeth's Master of the Rolls. The architect is believed to be William Arnold who also designed Wadham College, Oxford. There have been alterations made to the house over the centuries, most notably in the late 1700s when the west front was remodelled by the fifth Edward Phelips. In the 19th century the fortunes of the Phelips family began to decline and the house was leased out. In the 1920s, following a succession of tenants, the house was put up for sale. A gift from Ernest Cook (the grandson of the travel agent Thomas Cook) enabled the National Trust to purchase this wonderful Elizabethan residence. Constructed of Hamstone, the house is adorned with characteristic open parapets, fluted columns, twisted pinnacles, oriel windows and carved statues. The long gallery, one of the grandest of its kind in Britain, houses a

Montacute House

fine collection of Tudor and Jacobean portraits on permanent loan from London's National Portrait Gallery. Other noteworthy features include magnificent tapestries and samplers on display from the Goodhart Collection; the stone and stained glass screen in the great hall and Lord Curzon's bath, an Edwardian addition concealed in a bedroom cupboard. An established story tells of how Curzon, a senior Tory politician, waited at Montacute in 1923 for news that he was to be called to form a new government. The call never came. The house stands within a magnificent landscaped park that incorporates a walled formal garden, a fig walk, an orangery and a cedar lawn formally known as 'Pig's Wheaties's Orchard'.

Some 500 years before Montacute House was built, a controversial castle was erected on the nearby hill by Robert, Count of Mortain. The count's choice of site angered the Saxons as they believed the hill to be sacred because King Alfred had buried a fragment of Christ's cross here. In 1068, they rose up and attacked the castle in one of many unsuccessful revolts against the Norman occupation. Ironically, a subsequent Count of Mortain was found guilty of treason and forced into donating all his lands in the area to a Cluniac priory on the site now occupied by Montacute village. The castle has long since disappeared, as has the monastery, with the exception of its fine 16th century gatehouse, now a private home, and a stone dovecote.

The village is also home to the **Montacute TV and Radio Museum** where a vast collection of vintage radios, wireless receivers and TV sets, from the 1920s through to the present day, is on display. It developed from the keepsakes hoarded by Dennis Greenham who had been in the electrical business since 1930. The huge collection of radio and TV

memorabilia includes toys, books and games. There are also tearooms, gardens and a museum shop.

TINTINHULL
4 miles NW of Yeovil

🌱 Tintinhull House Garden

A couple of miles to the east of Martock is another enchanting National Trust property, **Tintinhull House Garden**, set in the grounds of an early 17th century manor house. The house itself, which is not open to the public, overlooks an attractive triangular green that forms the nucleus of the sprawling village of Tintinhull. This is home to a number of other interesting buildings: a remodelled, part-medieval rectory, Tintinhull Court; the 17th century Dower House; and St Margaret's parish church, a rare rectangular single-cell church.

Despite the age of the house, Tintinhull House Gardens were laid out between 1933 and 1961 in a series of distinctive areas, divided by walls and hedges, each with its own planting theme. There is a pool garden with a delightful pond filled with lilies and irises, a kitchen garden and a sunken garden that is cleverly designed to give the impression it has many different levels.

STOKE SUB HAMDON
5 miles NW of Yeovil off the A303

🏚 Stoke sub Hamdon Priory   🌲 Ham Hill

The eastern part of this attractive village is dominated by a fine Norman church; the western area of the village contains the remains of a late medieval priory. **Stoke sub Hamdon Priory** (National Trust) was built in the 14th and 15th centuries for the priests of the now demolished chantry chapel of St Nicholas. It was later converted into a house

CAROLINE J. SPIERS

11 North Street Workshops, Stoke sub Hamdon,
Somerset TA14 6QR
Tel/Fax: 01935 825485
e-mail: carolinejspiers@aol.com

Caroline J. Spiers was first established in 1978 offering a frame making and restoration service. The firm obtained a Duchy of Cornwall workshop in 1985 and since that time has expanded considerably. In the company's two Somerset workshops, work is undertaken from all over the UK and abroad. It now employs craftsmen who specialise in archival wash line mounting, frame making and frame restoration, as well as conservation of works of art on paper, canvas and other related materials. In recent years the firm has worked on paintings and drawings by a number of masters including John Constable RA, Pablo Picasso, Sir Edwin Landseer RA, and many more.

Frames are designed, constructed and also restored in the workshops using traditional processes little changed since medieval times. A variety of woods are selected and prepared to take applications of gesso, bole and gold leaf. Moulds are made for restoration, cast in plaster or carved in wood prior to gilding. Veneered and ebonised finishes are also applied.

The company also offers two-day workshop courses for small groups in either Oil & Watergilding, or in Botanical Watercolour & Drawing.

WESSEX ANTIQUE BEDSTEADS

Percombe (A303), Stoke Sub Hamdon,
Somerset, TA14 6RD
Tel: 01935 829 147 Fax: 01935 829 148
email: info@wessexbeds.com
website: www.wessexbeds.com

This is one of the largest and most varied collections of brass, iron and wooden bedsteads in the UK from the Victorian and Edwardian Era's with always more than 2,000 bedsteads in stock.

The owners are able to offer quality made to measure, mattresses and bases in any shape or size and also offer a full restoration service and carry a wide range of bed spares. Nationwide delivery and worldwide shipping is available. Easy to find and very accessible right next to the A303.

Opening hours are
Monday to Friday, 9am– 5pm
& Saturday 10am– 5 pm.

🏚 historic building 🏛 museum and heritage 🏚 historic site 🝣 scenic attraction 🌿 flora and fauna

with a very impressive Great Hall.

South of the village rises the 400ft-high **Ham Hill** (or Hamdon Hill), the source of the beautiful honey-coloured stone used in so many of the surrounding villages. This solitary limestone outcrop rises abruptly from the Somerset plain and provides breathtaking views of the surrounding countryside. A substantial hill fort, built here during the Iron Age, was subsequently overrun by the invading Romans. The new occupants built their own fortification to guard their major route, the Fosse Way, and its important intersection with the road between Dorchester and the Bristol Channel at nearby Ilchester.

It was the Romans who discovered that the hill's soft, even-grained limestone made a flexible and highly attractive building material and they used it in the construction of their villas and temples. Later, the Saxons and then the Normans came to share this high opinion of Hamstone. By the time quarrying reached its height in the 17th century, a sizeable settlement had grown up within the confines of the Iron Age fort though, today, only a solitary inn remains. A war memorial to 44 local men who died during World War I stands on the summit of Ham Hill. Now designated a country park, the combination of the view, the old earthwork ramparts and the maze of overgrown quarry workings make this an attractive place for recreation and picnics.

MARTOCK
6 miles NW of Yeovil on the B3165

🏛 Treasurer's House   🏛 Pinnacle Monument

This attractive, small town is surrounded by rich arable land and the area has long been renowned for its prosperous land-owning farmers. Martock's long-established affluence is reflected in its impressive part-13th century parish church. A former abbey church that once belonged to the monks of Mont St Michel in Normandy, the church boasts one of the finest tie-beam roofs in Somerset with almost every part of it covered in beautiful carvings.

The old part of Martock is blessed with an unusually large number of fine buildings. Amongst these can be found the **Treasurer's House** (National Trust), a small medieval house of two storeys built in the late 13th century for the Treasurer of Wells Cathedral who was also rector of Martock. Visitors can see the Great Hall, an interesting wall painting and the kitchen added to the building in the 15th century. Close by is the Old Court House, a parish building that served as the local grammar school for 200 years. To the west is Martock's 17th century Manor House, once the

Stoke sub Hamdon Priory

YANDLES

Hurst Works, Martock, Somerset TA12 6JU
Tel: 01935 822207   Fax: 01935 824484
e-mail: info@yandles.co.uk
website: www.yandles.co.uk

Yandles was established in 1860 and has been
supplying timber and woodworking paraphernalia for
nearly 150 years. Its award-winning Woodcentre attracts
visitors from all over the UK and Europe. Here you can
admire timbers from around the world and select from
displays which exhibit the natural colour and grain of
exotic wood. Also featured is a unique variety of
machinery, accessories and tools suitable for any
woodworking project. Yandles also offers courses which
allow participants to learn new skills and receive training
in routing and turning which will give them the
professional edge. An online store caters for regular
shoppers who need supplies delivered to their door. The
Woodcentre is open from 8.30am to 5pm, Monday to
Saturday; and from 9.30am to 1.30pm on Sunday.

Also at Yandles is the Hobbycentre which is packed
full of ideas and projects for numerous hobbies. The
centre offers a wide choice of products, displayed over
two floors, all at unbeatable prices. Helpful staff are on
hand to advise and assist with purchases. Whether you
are young or old, starting out a new skill or stocking up
with tools and accessories, you can be confident of
finding what you need at the Hobbycentre. The
Hobbycentre and Gift Shop are open from 9am to 5pm,
Monday to Saturday; and from 9.30am to 4pm on
Sunday.

A third attraction on the site is the 303 Gallery, a
bright modern space with a huge range of exceptional
handmade art and crafts. There's work here to suit all
tastes, from traditional elegance to fun, funky ideas.
You'll find art and pottery for the home, silk and
jewellery for the individual, all at prices to suit your
pocket. This is a place to be inspired and to admire the
craftswork and innovation of local and world-renowned
artists. The Gallery is open from 10am to 5pm, Monday

to Saturday; and
from 11am to 4pm
on Sunday.

And if you like
taking a break during your visit, why not settle down in
the Cedar Tree Café for a morning coffee and pastry, a
fresh lunch or an afternoon tea? You can also enjoy your
refreshments outdoors on the terrace. The café is open
from 10am to 4.30pm, Monday to Saturday; and from
11am to 3pm on Sunday.

🏚 historic building   🏛 museum and heritage   🏛 historic site   ♧ scenic attraction   🌢 flora and fauna

home of Edward Parker, who exposed the Gunpowder Plot after Guy Fawkes had warned him against attending Parliament on that fateful night.

East Lambrook Manor Garden

Outside the Market House stands the **Pinnacle Monument,** an unusual structure with four sundials arranged in a square on top of its column, the whole finished with an attractive weather-vane.

EAST LAMBROOK
8 miles NW of Yeovil off the A303

🦚 East Lambrook Manor Garden

Just west of this charming hamlet is **East Lambrook Manor Garden** which was planted with endangered species by the writer and horticulturist, Margery Fish, who lived at the medieval Hamstone manor house from 1937 until her death in 1969. Her exuberant planting and deliberate lack of formality created an atmosphere of romantic tranquillity that is maintained to this day. Now Grade I listed, the garden is also the home of the National Collection of the cranesbill species of geranium.

The low-lying land to the north of East Lambrook is criss-crossed by a network of drainage ditches or rhines (pronounced reens) that eventually flow into the rivers Parrett, Isle and Yeo. Originally cut in the early 19th century, the ditches are often lined with double rows of pollarded willows, a sight that has come to characterise this part of Somerset. Despite having to be cleared every few years, the rhines provide a valuable natural habitat for a wide variety of bird, animal and plant life.

MUCHELNEY
12 miles NW of Yeovil off the A372

🏛 Muchelney Abbey 🏛 Midelney Manor

This village's name means 'the Great Island' and it dates from the time when this settlement rose up above the surrounding marshland, long since drained to provide excellent arable farmland. Muchelney is also the location of an impressive part-ruined Benedictine monastery thought to have been founded by King Ine of Wessex in the 8th century. This claim was, in part, confirmed when, in the 1950s, an archaeological dig unearthed an 8th century crypt. During medieval times **Muchelney Abbey** (English Heritage) grew to emulate its great rival at Glastonbury. After the Dissolution in 1539, the buildings, dating mainly from the 15th and 16th centuries, gradually fell into disrepair. Much of its stone was removed to provide building material for the surrounding village. In spite of this, a substantial part of the original structure, including the south cloister and abbot's lodge, can still be seen today.

Opposite the parish church, which its noted

for is remarkable early 17th century illuminations, stands the **Priest's House** (National Trust), a late-medieval hall house built by the abbey for the parish priest. Little has changed since the 17th century when the building was divided. The interesting features to see include the Gothic doorway, the beautiful tracery windows and a massive 15th century stone fireplace.

Priests House, Muchelney

Although it is still a dwelling, the house is opened on a limited basis.

Just to the west of the village, near Drayton, stands the privately-owned **Midelney Manor**, originally an island manor belonging to Muchelney Abbey. A handsome manor house with architectural features from the 16th, 17th and 18th centuries, this has been in the hands of the Trevilian family since the early 1500s. The estate incorporates a heronry, a series of delightful gardens, a unique 17th century falcon's mews and woodland walks. Although the house is not normally open to the public, there are self-catering cottages available on the estate.

LANGPORT

12 miles NW of Yeovil on the A378

🏛 Langport Gap   🏛 Stembridge Tower Mill

🏛 Langport & River Parrett Visitor Centre

The old part of this former market town stands on a rise above an ancient ford across the River Parrett. A short distance downstream from this point, the river is joined by the Rivers Isle and Yeo. Defended by an earthwork rampart during Saxon times, by 930 Langport was an important commercial centre that minted its own coins. The only surviving part of the town's defences is the East Gate incorporating a curious 'hanging' chapel that sits above the arch on an upper level. It is now a Masonic Lodge and rarely open to the public. The impressive tower of the church at nearby Huish Episcopi can be seen through the barrel-vaulted gateway.

During the 18th and 19th centuries, Langport flourished as a banking centre and the local independent bank, Stuckey's, became known for its impressive branches, many of which can still be seen in the surrounding towns and villages although the bank has long since been taken over by NatWest. At the time of this amalgamation in 1909, Stuckey's had more notes in circulation than any other bank in the country save for the Bank of England. Stuckey's original head office is now Langport's branch of NatWest.

Throughout history, the **Langport Gap** has been the site of a number of important military encounters. Two of the most significant occurred more than 1,000 years apart. In the 6th century, Geraint, King of the Dumnonii, was involved in a battle here while, in July 1645, the Parliamentarian victory at the Battle of Langport gave Cromwell's forces almost total control of the West Country during the English Civil War.

More about life, past and present, on the Somerset Levels and Moors can be discovered at the **Langport and River Parrett Visitor Centre** through its series of hands-on exhibits and displays. Cycles are available for hire along with suggested cycle routes.

Just to the east, at **Huish Episcopi**, one of the finest examples in the country of a late medieval Somerset tower can be found at the village's church. At its most impressive in high summer when it can be viewed through the surrounding greenery, this ornate structure is adorned with striking tracery, pinnacles and carvings. The church also has an elaborate Norman doorway, which still shows signs of the fire that destroyed much of the earlier building in the 13th century. A window in the south chapel was designed by Edward Burne-Jones, the 19th century Pre-Raphaelite.

The church at Aller, just northwest of Langport, was the scene of another historic event. It was here, in 878, that King Alfred converted Guthrum the Dane and his followers to Christianity following a battle on Salisbury Plain. The low wooded rise to the east of Aller is criss-crossed by a network of ancient country lanes which pass through some pleasant hamlets and villages including

Stembridge Tower Mill, Langport

High Ham, the home of the last thatched windmill in England. Dating from 1822 and overlooking the Somerset levels, **Stembridge Tower Mill** (National Trust) continued to operate until 1910.

SOMERTON
13 miles NW of Yeovil on the B3151

🏛 Church of St Michael   🎨 Home Gallery

This small town gave the county its name and for 100 years between 1250 and 1350 was also its administrative centre. The prosperity this brought to the town is reflected in the fine **Church of St Michael** which was later enhanced even further by the installation of a magnificent roof. Carved by monks from Muchelney Abbey around 1500, the gloriously coffered structure is supported by tie beams on which rest pairs of Wessex wyverns, or dragons. These gradually increase in size as they near the altar, culminating in two ferocious monsters snarling across the aisle at each other.

📖 stories and anecdotes   🐦 famous people   🎨 art and craft   🎭 entertainment and sport   🚶 walks

ESCAPE

1 Brandon House, West Street, Somerton,
Somerset TA11 7PS
Tel: 01458 272282
e-mail: escapeinsomerton@hotmail.co.uk

Opened in June 2006, **Escape** is an
enchanting gift shop offering products for all
tastes and every occasion at very reasonable
prices. The shop is owned and run by Carole
and Tilly Landon, two local ladies who are
also sisters-in-law. They have created an
enticing shopping experience with a copious
choice of fine quality, exquisite and unique
accessories and gifts from all over the world,
including Fair Trade and locally sourced
products. There are toys for all ages,
handbags, jewellery, toiletries, candles,
gadgets, clocks - and even wellies! The shop
is clean, uncluttered and welcoming, with
room to browse and shop at your leisure. It
is centrally located, opposite free parking
and the Unicorn pub.

Somerton itself is a pleasant place to
explore. It gave the county of Somerset its
name and for, 100 years between 1250 and
1350, was the county's administrative
centre. The prosperity of that period is
reflected in its old stone buildings, unusual Market Cross, and a medieval church with a
magnificent roof on which Wessex wyverns, or dragons, rest in pairs, gradually increasing in size
as they get nearer the altar.

Somerton today is a place of handsome old
stone houses, shops and inns. The general
atmosphere of mature prosperity is enhanced
by the presence of a number of striking
ancient buildings, most notably the 17th
century Hext Almshouses. Broad Street leads
into the picturesque market place with its
distinctive octagonal covered Market Cross
and Town Hall. Between 1278 and 1371,
Somerton was the location of the county gaol
and the meeting place of the shire courts as
well as continuing to develop as a market
town, reflected in the delightfully down-to-
earth names of some of its streets such as
Cow Square and Pig Street (now Broad Street).

Castle Cary

🏛 Round House   🏛 Castle Cary District Museum

🏛 War Memorial   🌱 Hadspen House Gardens

🗲 John Boyd Textiles

This lovely little town, surrounded by
meadows and woods, has an atmosphere of
mature rural calm as well as some interesting
old buildings, many of them built in the local
Hamstone that radiates a golden glow. There
is a strikingly handsome 18th century post
office, a tiny 'pepper pot' lock-up gaol called
the **Round House** dating from 1779, and a
splendid Market House with a magnificent

17th century colonnade. Largely constructed in 1855, the Market House is now the home of the **Castle Cary District Museum**. Perhaps the most interesting site here is the town's **War Memorial**, which stands in the middle of a pond said to be part of the old castle moat. It was used for many years as a drive-through bath for muddy horses and carts, for washing horsehair and as a convenient place for ducking scolds and witches.

Just to the west of the town at Higher Flax Mills is an interesting survival from earlier days. **John Boyd Textiles** have been weavers of horsehair fabric since 1837 and are still using looms that were first installed in 1870. Horsehair was especially popular in Victorian times because of its durability, value and being easy to clean. Furniture designers such as Chippendale, Hepplewhite, Lutyens and

Charles Rennie Mackintosh all used horsehair fabrics and they were also used for Empire and Biedermeier furniture. Guided tours of the mill are available by arrangement.

Also worth visiting is the beautiful **Hadspen House Gardens** situated just to the southeast of the town. Penelope Hobhouse, who lived at Hadspen until 1979, restored and enlarged the earlier garden and made her work here the subject of her first book *The Country Gardener*. Since 1986 the Canadian gardeners, Sandra and Nori Pope, have continued this tradition, transforming the Upper and Walled Garden with entirely new planting schemes and a bold use of colour, incorporating a quarter of a mile of old brick walls.

Around Castle Cary

BRUTON
4 miles NE of Castle Cary on the A359

🏠 Sexey's Hospital　🏠 Patwell Pump

🏠 The Dovecote

This remarkably well-preserved former clothing and ecclesiastical centre, clinging to a hillside above the River Brue, is more like a small town than a village. In the middle of the High Street is the 17th century **Sexey's Hospital** with a beautiful quadrangle providing a stunning view across the Brue valley. It has a small, candle-lit chapel with dark Jacobean oak pews and pulpit. The hospital was founded by Hugh Sexey, a courtier of Elizabeth I and James I. It still accommodates the elderly and also has a school that is one of the few state boarding schools in England.

A priory was first established at Bruton in the 11th century and although much of this

Bruton Dovecote

🎭 stories and anecdotes　🦉 famous people　🎨 art and craft　✒ entertainment and sport　🚶 walks

KIMBER'S FARM SHOP AND BARROW LANE FARM COTTAGES

Barrow Lane, Charlton Musgrove, Wincanton, Somerset BA9 8HJ
Tel: 01963 33177 or 01963 33217
website: www.kimbersfarmshop.co.uk
or www.barrowlanefarm.com

Nestled in the Somerset countryside, just two miles off the A303 trunk road is a family farming business with a fantastic specialist farm shop and four holiday cottages.

Farm Shop

Both farms lie in the lea of King Alfred's Tower. The Kimber family have farmed this land for 300 years, where the fields provide good pasture for the free range livestock. The farm shop stocks a full range of home produced meats, including Aberdeen Angus cross beef, welfare friendly rose veal, Gloucester Old Spot pork, dry cured bacon, and sausages, lamb and when in season mutton and hogget, chickens, ducks, bronze turkeys and Christmas geese. Unpasturised milk from the Friesian and Shorthorn dairy herd is now available. Also stocked is a wide range of other local products including; Keens unpasturised cheddar cheese, and other local specialist cheeses, locally made preserves, condiments and cakes, Dorset Down mushrooms, Mendip Moments ice cream and locally produced ciders, wines and beers. Seasonal vegetables, eggs and a selection of fish are always available. The owners also sell local crafts. Open Tuesday to Saturday, call for opening times. Ordering Service available for the holiday cottages.

Holiday Cottages

Have you ever dreamed of a holiday that is far enough from home to leave your daily routine behind but close enough to ensure that within a few hours you have arrived to be greeted with a cheery welcome, comfortable stylish accommodation and local food in the cupboards?   Then look no further; These four cottages are available and sleep between two and seven people. Two of the cottages have wood burning stoves for cosy evenings in the cooler

months. For balmy long summer nights there is a garden and patio with BBQ overlooking views of rolling countryside and the Selwood forest beyond. The cottages are equipped to a high standard with professionally laundered sheets to ensure a good nights sleep. The location is well suited for walks, NT properties, Longleat, the cities of Bath, Wells and Salisbury (all within 40 minutes) and the Dorset Jurassic coast. There are many more attractions for all ages. A good country pub, The Bull Inn, serves excellent food and is within 25 minutes walk along country lanes. Well behaved dogs are welcome.

🏚 historic building 🏛 museum and heritage 🏚 historic site ⚘ scenic attraction 🌱 flora and fauna

PHILLIPS & SKINNER

19 High Street, Bruton, Somerset BA10 0AH
Tel: 01749 813221
e-mail: ameliaskinner@aol.com
website: www.phillipsandskinner.com

A former teacher in London, Amelia Skinner moved to Bruton and opened **Phillips & Skinner** in December 2007 with a vision of providing the town and surrounding area with a unique place to buy an eclectic mix of goods - anything from retro penny sweets to 1930s leather chairs.

The front of the shop is laid out like a sitting room with leather sofas where you can sit and enjoy a coffee whilst taking in the background music and admiring the slate flooring, handmade fireplaces and book-lined walls. The fireplaces are made by local stonemasons which Amelia can source for interested customers.

A fabulous hanging chair made from Somerset willow and offering comfort and style can also be made to order.

Elsewhere in the shop is a selection of antiquarian books, retro furniture, vintage clothing by Natasha Yearley, vinyl supplied by Glory Boy Records, distinctive giftware, stylish greetings cards, and a range of homeware.

has disappeared the former priory church is now the parish church. The Church of St Mary has a rare second tower built over the north porch in the late 1300s. The light and spacious interior contains a number of memorials to the Berkeley family, the local lords of the manor who also owned the land on which London's Berkeley Square now stands.

Across the river from the church is the **Patwell Pump**, a curious square structure that was the parish's communal water pump and remained in use until well into the 20th century. Further downstream a 15th century packhorse bridge still serves pedestrians. However, **The Dovecote** is arguably Bruton's most distinctive building. Now roofless, it can be seen on the crest of a hill to the south of the bridge. Built in the 15th century, the dovecote is thought to have doubled as a watchtower.

WINCANTON

5 miles SE of Castle Cary off the A303

🦫 Wincanton Racecourse 🦉 Discworld Emporiun

Wincanton's broad main street is flanked by substantial houses and former coaching inns, a faint echo of the era when as many as 17 coaches a day would stop here, pausing about halfway between London and the long-established naval base at Plymouth. At that time, the inns could provide lodging for scores of travellers and stabling for more than 250 horses. A former cloth-making centre, the oldest part of this attractive town stands on a draughty hillside above the River Cale. An impressive number of fine Georgian buildings, some of which were constructed to replace earlier buildings destroyed in a fire in 1747, can be found here.

Modern day Wincanton is a peaceful light industrial town whose best known attraction,

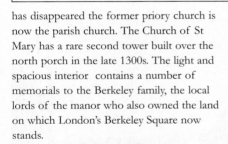

🎭 stories and anecdotes 🦅 famous people 🎨 art and craft 🎟 entertainment and sport 🚶 walks

Wincanton National Hunt Racecourse, harks back to the days when horses were the only form of transport. Horse-racing began in the area in the 18th century and the racecourse moved to its present site to the north of the town centre in 1927. Wincanton is remembered as the course where the great *Desert Orchid* had his first race of each season during his dominance of steeple-chasing in the 1980s. For golf enthusiasts, the racecourse incorporates a challenging nine-hole pay and play course, which is open throughout the year.

Wincanton also has the distinction of being home to the only shop in the known universe devoted to artefacts inspired by the writings of Terry Pratchett, author of the *Discworld* novels which have sold more than 40 million copies worldwide. At **The Cunning Artificer's Discworld Emporium** devotees will find all manner of wonderful objects ranging from the Mystic Prawn Medallion to the Dibbler Pie – "A culinary delight that will act as not just a superb paperweight, but also an appetite depressant".

TEMPLECOMBE
8 miles SE of Castle Cary on the A357

🏛 Gartell Light Railway

🏛 Templecombe Railway Museum

To the east of the village is the unusual **Gartell Light Railway**, a rare two-foot gauge line that runs for around a mile through the beautiful countryside of Blackmore Vale on the track bed of the Somerset and Dorset Railway, closed more than 30 years ago. The trains run every 15 minutes from Common Line Station, which also has a visitor centre, refreshment room and shop. The nearby **Templecombe Railway Museum** houses a fascinating collection of artefacts, photographs and models that tell the story of

the nearby station, once a busy junction where some 130 railwaymen worked.

Wells

🏛 Cathedral of St Andrew   ☄ Astronomical Clock

🏛 Bishop's Palace   🏛 Penniless Porch

🏛 Wells & Mendip Museum

This ancient ecclesiastical centre derives its name from a line of springs that rise up from the base of the Mendips and deliver water at the rate of some 40 gallons per second. The first church here is believed to have been founded by King Ine in around 700; the present **Cathedral of St Andrew** was begun in the 12th century. Taking more than three centuries to complete, this magnificent cathedral demonstrates the three main styles of Gothic architecture. Its 13th century west front, with more than 170 statues of saints,

Chain Gate, Wells

🏛 historic building 🏛 museum and heritage 🏛 historic site ☄ scenic attraction 🌱 flora and fauna

CADEAUX & CO.

5 High Street, Wells, Somerset BA5 2AA
Tel: 01749 672332

Opened in 2007, **Cadeaux & Co.** offers a wide choice of beautiful contemporary gifts sourced from all over the world. Owner Kristan Miller has gathered together an enticing range that includes gifts for the home, jewellery, fragrances from Ortigia and the Australian company Abode Aroma; scented candles from True Grace and Geodesis, soft furnishings, cards, stationery and a selection of garden accessories. There are soaps and herbal products from Heyland & Whittle; perfumes by La Compagnie de Provence and Nougat; and interior furnishings

from Parlane, Big Tomato, Gabriella Miller and Spaceform.

The shop occupies a handsome Grade II listed building close to the Market Square and its front showrooms are devoted to items for adults while the room at the back contain a huge range of products intended for children. These include a pin bowling set, spinning tops, puzzle alarm clocks, musical mills and much more. Suppliers include Little Pals, Petit Jour and Tyrrell Katz.

angels and prophets gazing down on the cathedral close, is generally acknowledged to be its crowning glory. There used to be twice as many statues, all painted in glowing colours. Following the Civil War, Puritan fanatics mutilated or destroyed as many as they could and 700 years of exposure to the Somerset weather has scoured away the colours. A few, including the central figure of Christ in His Glory, have been replaced with faithful copies.

Inside the cathedral there are many superb features including the beautiful and unique scissor arches and the great 14th century stained glass window over the high altar. However, the cathedral's most impressive sight is its 14th century **Astronomical Clock**, one of the oldest working timepieces in the world, that shows the minutes, hours and

phases of the moon on separate inner and outer dials and marks the quarter hours with a lively battle between knights.

The large cathedral close is a tranquil city within a city and for centuries the ecclesiastical and civic functions of Wells have remained separate. The west front of the cathedral has an internal passage with pierced apertures and there is a theory that choirboys might have sung through these openings to give the illusion to those gathered on the cathedral green that the then lifelike painted statues were singing.

To the south of the cathedral's cloisters is the **Bishop's Palace**, a remarkable fortified medieval building which has been the home of the bishops of Bath and Wells since 1206. The palace is enclosed by a high wall and surrounded by a moat fed by the springs that give the city its name. A pair of mute swans on the moat can often be seen at the Gatehouse, ringing a bell for food. Swans were trained to do this in the 19th century and the present pair continue the tradition, passing it on to their young.

In order to gain access to the palace from the Market Place, visitors must pass under a 13th century stone arch known as the Bishop's Eye and then cross a drawbridge that was last raised for defensive purposes in 1831. Although it is still an official residence of the Bishop of Bath and Wells, visitors can tour the palace's chapel, the 13th century Great Hall and the beautiful gardens where many of the fine trees were planted in 1821. On the northern side of the cathedral green is the Vicar's Close, completed in 1363. This picturesque cobbled thoroughfare was built to house the cathedral choristers.

The cathedral green is surrounded by a high wall breached at only three castellated entrance points. One of these, the gateway into the Market Place, is known as **Penniless Porch**. It was here that the bishop allowed the city's poor to beg for money from those entering the cathedral close. Set in the pavement here is a length of brass that extends over the prodigious distance leapt by local girl Mary Rand when she set a world record for the long jump.

There is, of course, much more to Wells than its ecclesiastical buildings and heritage. A visit to the **Wells and Mendip Museum**, found near the west front of the cathedral, explains much of the history of the city and surrounding area through a collection of interesting locally found artefacts. Amongst these are some Roman coins and lead ingots, geological remains some 180 million years old when the Mendip Hills were a tropical paradise, and the remains of the 'Witch' of Wookey Hole.

The city also remains a lively market centre, with a street market held every Wednesday and Saturday. For a grand view of Wells from a distance, follow the attractive footpath that starts from the Moat Walk and leads up the summit of Tor Hill.

Around Wells

STRATTON-ON-THE-FOSSE
9 miles NE of Wells on the A367

🏛 Downside Abbey

This former coal mining village is home to the famous Roman Catholic boys' public school, **Downside Abbey**, which occupies the site of a monastery founded in 1814 by a group of English Benedictines. The steady expansion of the school during the 20th century encouraged the monks to move to a new site on higher ground near the existing abbey church, an impressive building that took over 70 years to complete and numbered among its architects Sir Giles Gilbert Scott.

MIDSOMER NORTON
10 miles NE of Wells on the B3355

🏛 Radstock, Midsomer North & District Museum

The history of the area around this town is one of mining, with coal being hewn from nearby Norton Hill until as recently as the 1970s. In the churchyard of the town's parish church is a memorial to the 12 miners who were killed in an accident at Wellsway coal works in 1839. The surrounding countryside is beautiful and the sights and sounds of collieries have long since been replaced with that of open farmland. Midsomer Norton itself is a pleasant mix of old and new. There are excellent shopping facilities along with attractive Georgian buildings and a late medieval tithe barn.

🏛 historic building 🏛 museum and heritage 🏚 historic site 🏞 scenic attraction 🌿 flora and fauna

At the interesting **Radstock, Midsomer North and District Museum**, housed in a converted 18th century barn, more information can be sought about the Somerset coalfield as the museum is devoted to the people of the local coal mines along with other exhibits relating to the railways, farms and schools of the area.

CAMELEY
10 miles NE of Wells off the A37

🏠 St James's Church

This attractive village is home to a church referred to by John Betjeman as "Rip Van Winkle's Church". When the village of Cameley was moved to nearby Temple Cloud in the 1700s, **St James's Church** was left alone on its low hill. Its old box pews are still in place and seem to have been custom made for their owners. Those who couldn't afford their own box could worship from the gallery along the south wall which bears the legend "for the free use of the inhabitants, 1819". A row of hat pegs was also conveniently provided. In the 1960s a remarkable series of medieval wall paintings was discovered here, under layers of whitewash. The murals are believed to have been painted between the 11th and the 17th centuries and feature such diverse images as the foot of a giant St Christopher stepping through a fish and crab infested river, a charming 14th century jester complete with harlequin costume and a rare coat of arms of Charles I.

MELLS
13 miles NE of Wells off the A362

🏠 John Horner

Mells was at one time on the easternmost limit of the lands belonging to Glastonbury Abbey. In the 15th century the Abbot of Glastonbury drew up plans to rebuild the village in the shape of a St Anthony's cross, with four arms of equal length. However, only one street, New Street, was ever completed. This architectural gem can still be seen to the south of St Andrew's parish church. While the exterior of the church is certainly imposing, the main interest lies inside where there is a remarkable collection of monuments designed by masters such as Lutyens, Gill, Munnings and Burne-Jones. One of the memorials is to Raymond, the eldest son of Herbert Asquith, the Liberal Prime Minister. Raymond was killed in the First World War. Raymond's sister was Violet Bonham Carter, whose grave is in the churchyard. Another memorial in the churchyard honours the pacifist and poet Siegfried Sassoon.

According to legend, the Abbot of Glastonbury, in an attempt to stave off Henry VIII's Dissolution of the Monasteries, dispatched his steward, **John Horner,** to London with a gift for the king consisting of a pie into which was baked the title deeds of 12 ecclesiastical manor houses. However, rather than attempting to persuade the king, Horner returned to Somerset the rightful owner of three of the manors himself. He paid a total of £2,000 for Mells, Nunnery and Leigh-upon-Mendip. This blatant act of disloyalty is, supposedly, commemorated in the nursery rhyme *Little Jack Horner* that describes how Jack 'put in his thumb and pulled out a plum'. The manor house at Mells remained in the hands of the Horner family until the early 20th century, when it passed to the Asquith family by marriage.

LULLINGTON
19 miles NE of Wells off the B3090

🏠 Orchardleigh Park

A footpath leads southwards from this peaceful riverside village to **Orchardleigh**

🎦 stories and anecdotes   🐟 famous people   🎨 art and craft   🌿 entertainment and sport   🚶 walks

ONE CRAFT GALLERY

1 High Street, Shepton Mallet, Somerset, BA4 5AA
Tel: 01749 343777
website: www.onecraftgallery.co.uk

In the heart of Shepton Mallet, opposite the Market Cross, is One Craft Gallery. A visit there is always worthwhile, be it to find a unique gift, treat yourself to some original artwork or simply enjoy what is on show.

Set up by local artists and makers in 2001, One Craft Gallery is becoming a leading venue for craft in Somerset. It is run co-operatively, showcasing the members' work and displaying a wide choice of creative and decorative pieces. The range includes ceramics, jewellery, glass, textiles, painting and printmaking, turned wood and furniture. Within each discipline the work is varied and complementary.

You will find salt glaze pottery, attractive domestic ware and painted earthenware, while the jewellers specialise in forged silver, enamels and textured gold. Regular exhibitions by guest artists are held and this, together with new members' work and new pieces by established members, ensures there is something different to discover with every visit.

The members share in the stewarding of the Gallery and are familiar with each others' work, so there is ample opportunity to meet the makers, chat about the pieces and even discuss commissions. For a preview of what is on offer and to find out about guest artists visit the website. The gallery is open 10am-5pm Monday to Saturday.

SHUTE FARM STUDIO

Downhead, nr Shepton Mallet, Somerset BA4 4LQ
Tel: 01749 880746
e-mail: mail@shutefarmstudio.org.uk
website: www.shutefarmstudio.org.uk

Shute Farm Studio is an Art Education Centre situated on the edge of the East Mendip Hills in Somerset. It is part of a working dairy farm and is accessible to adults, children and those with special needs. Old agricultural buildings have been converted to create studios for teaching traditional art skills; stone and wood carving, wood engraving, wire, willow and stem sculpture, ceramics, painting, drawing, bronze casting, mould making, modelling and casting and printing are some of the many art forms explored at the studio. Individual tuition is given to small groups of students by practising artists with excellent teaching experience. An accessible garden, designed by Kevin McCloud of *Grand Designs*,

as a gift to the Studio, represents Downhead's past, creating landscape features that relate to local Iron Age settlements. The Studio promotes the link between art and agriculture. Farm visits are available to encourage a greater understanding of rural life. The Studio is renowned for its tranquil environment, feeding the spirit as well as the mind. It may be hired as a venue for the pursuit of the arts by groups, schools and organisations and has a directory of specialist tutors available. The Studio reinvests any profit into the promotion of art education.

🏛 historic building   🏛 museum and heritage   🏛 historic site   ♨ scenic attraction   🌱 flora and fauna

BROOKOVER FARM

Orchardleigh, Frome, Somerset BA11 2PM
Tel: 01373 462706

Offering AA three-star quality bed & breakfast accommodation, **Brookover Farm** is a handsome traditional period farmhouse with well-maintained gardens set beside a river. The house has three double bedrooms, two of which are en suite, the third has its own bathroom. The beds are unusually large and can be split to provide a twin room. All rooms are equipped with TV with Freeview, and a hospitality tray. An attractive amenity here is a good local restaurant you can walk to in 10 minutes. Brookover Farm also provides livery for horses.

Park, an imposing Victorian mansion built in the mid-1800s and now a popular venue for civil weddings and conferences. In the 550 acres of parkland surrounding the house is a lake with an island on which is a small church whose churchyard contains the grave of Sir Henry Newbolt, the author of *Drake's Drum*.

SHEPTON MALLET
6 miles E of Wells on the A371

🏛 Market Cross   🏛 The Shambles

🌿 Mid-Somerset Show   🌱 Pilton Manor

🏛 Tithe Barn   🌿 Royal Bath & Wells Show

Situated on the banks of the River Sheppey, just to the west of Fosse Way, this old market town has been an important centre of communications since before the time of the Romans. The settlement's name is Saxon and it means, quite simply, 'sheep town'. This reveals its main commercial activity from before the Norman Conquest to the Middle Ages, when Shepton Mallet was, firstly, a centre of woollen production and then weaving. The industry reached its peak in the 15th century. It was around this time that the town's most striking building, its magnificent parish church, was constructed. Other reminders of

Shepton Mallet's past can be seen around its market place where there is a 50ft **Market Cross**, dating from around 1500 and restored in Victorian times. There is also **The Shambles**, a 15th century wooden shed where meat was traded. After the Duke of Monmouth's ill-fated Pitchfork Rebellion, several of his followers were executed at the Market Cross in 1685 on the orders of the infamous Judge Jeffreys. Although it is a relatively nondescript building, Shepton Mallet's old prison, built in 1610, was thought to be so well away from the threat of enemy bombing that it was here that the Domesday Book was hidden during World War II. It was also used during that period by the US forces as a military prison.

Today, Shepton Mallet is a prosperous light industrial town that has a good selection of shopping and leisure activities. Each year the town plays host to two agricultural shows. The **Royal Bath and West Show,** which has a permanent showground to the southeast of the town. Takes place in late May/early June, followed in August by the **Mid-Somerset Show**.

To the southwest of the town stands a

THE GOLDEN GOOSE

1 Stony Street, Frome,
Somerset BA11 1BU
Tel: 01373 466681
website: www.thegoldengoose.co.uk

Located in the heart of the historic town of Frome, **The Golden Goose** offers a selection of quality gifts and accessories for every occasion. Owners Mary and Tony Gibson came to Frome in 2002, both with many years of experience as designers.

They aim to offer customers both a wonderful selection of gifts and home accessories, and an enjoyable shopping experience. Their range of high quality gifts is carefully selected for good design and craftsmanship and they are always looking for something just that little bit different to add to their stock. All their goods are Fairly traded, and Mary and Tony try to source them from the UK and Europe where possible. As a result their friendly shop is full of beautiful things that are a delight either to give or to receive.

They have selected a range of gifts and toys for children which are sourced mainly in France and Germany, which represent excellent value for parents' peace of mind.

There are also ranges of gifts selected for babies and infants; which include bright pram toys, rattles and comforters, along with beautiful organic boxed gifts and toys.

Gifts and accessories for the home include lovely textiles, candles, table settings etc that will bring a wonderful sense of style to any home. There is also a sophisticated range of jewellery, lovely toiletries and cards and books on the nice things in life. Recently a range of great gifts for men has been added.

Visitors are welcome to browse at the Golden Goose which is open from 9.30am to 5pm, Monday to Saturday. Frome itself is well worth taking time to explore. It has more listed buildings than any other town in Somerset and is the perfect place to combine historic interest with an enjoyable shopping experience.

🏛 historic building   🏛 museum and heritage   🏛 historic site   ⌖ scenic attraction   🐾 flora and fauna

former residence of the abbots of Glastonbury, **Pilton Manor**, whose grounds have been planted with vines, mostly of the German Riesling variety. Visitors are encouraged to stroll around the estate and also take the opportunity of sampling the vineyard's end product. Another legacy of Glastonbury Abbey can be found at **Pilton** village where there is a great cruciform tithe barn that stands on a hill surrounded by beech and chestnut trees. Unfortunately, the barn lost its arch-braced roof when it was struck by lightning in 1963 but has since been restored.

At Croscombe, to the west of Shepton Mallet, is another fine 15th century **Tithe Barn,** a reminder of the days when the local tenant farmers paid a proportion of the crops each year to their ecclesiastical landlords.

NUNNEY
12 miles E of Wells off the A361

🏰 Castle

This picturesque old market town is dominated by its dramatic moated **Castle** begun in 1373 by Sir John de la Mare on his return from the French wars. Thought to have been modelled on the Bastille, the fortress consists of four solidly built towers that stand on an island formed by a stream on one side and a broad water-filled moat on the other. The castle came under attack from Parliamentarian forces during the English Civil War and, despite having a garrison of only one officer, eight men and a handful of civilian refugees, held out for two days. However, the bombardment damaged the building beyond repair and it had to be abandoned, leaving the romantic ruins that can still be seen today. One of the 30-pound cannonballs that were used by Cromwell's forces can be seen in the village's 13th century church.

FROME
17 miles E of Wells off the A361

🏠 Blue House   🏠 Longleat House

The 4th largest settlement in Somerset, Frome is an attractive town built on steep hills with cobbled streets and boasting more listed buildings than anywhere else in Somerset.

The town developed beside the river from which it takes its name, its first recorded building being a mission station founded in 685 by St Aldhelm, the Abbot of Malmesbury. Such was the expansion around St Aldhelm's stone Church of St John that, by the time of the Domesday Book, the settlement had a market which suggests that it was already a place of some importance. General markets still take place every Wednesday and Saturday.

Frome continued to prosper during the Middle Ages on the back of its cloth industry until competition from the woollen towns of the north in the 19th century saw the industry begin to decline. The trade in Frome died out completely in the 1960s. Since then other industries, printing in particular, have flourished and the population has doubled to more than 20,000.

Fortunately, this new growth has not spoilt the charm of the town's old centre. Best explored on foot, the town's old quarter is an attractive conservation area where, amidst the interesting shops, cafés and restaurants, can be found the **Blue House**. Built in 1726 as an almshouse and a boy's school, it is one of the town's numerous listed buildings. Another is the fine bridge across the River Frome, a contemporary of Bath's Pulteney Bridge dating from 1667, and unusual in having buildings along its length.

A popular excursion from Frome is to **Longleat House,** about five miles to the

MARSAILI MACKENZIE

5 Cheap Street, Frome, Somerset BA11 1BN
Tel: 01373 455044
website: www.marsaili.fsnet.co.uk

Found down a delightful old medieval street, in the heart of this market town, is **Marsaili Mackenzie**, an interesting and unusual shop and gallery owned and personally run by the lady herself. The light and airy feel of the shop is provided by the varnished wooden floor and the subtle cream of the walls and here, on the ground floor, this creates the perfect environment in which to view the exciting range of jewellery. Contemporary in nature, the jewellery ranges from large, elaborate pieces to small, discreet items and the pieces are made from both precious and non-precious metals and stones. Here, too, is a range of colourful hats and fashion accessories that would certainly add the finishing touch to any outfit.

The stairs to the first floor of this charming old building lead to a fine collection of designer clothes that all share the same theme of simplicity and style. Flax, Terry Macey and Oska designs rub shoulders with other casualwear and knitwear labels and these garments, all of which are made from natural fibres, are ideal for anyone looking for something chic and different. The lower ground floor of Marsaili Mackenzie, with its low ceiling and black and white tiled floor, is home to a small and intimate but select gallery that concentrates on holding exhibitions of contemporary art throughout the year.

ANTIQUES AND COUNTRY LIVING

43-44 Vallis Way, Frome, Somerset, BA11 3BA
Tel: 01373 463015

Since it's establishment in 1994, Frome's Antiques & Country Living has built an esteemed reputation for good quality antiques and collectables. Always understanding the changes to interior fashions and designs, Antiques & Country Living has cleverly sourced a selection of new furniture and soft furnishings to complement its range of antiques.

French-style painted furniture, and luxurious silk upholstered gilt chairs harmonise beautifully with the rich dark wood of the period pieces of furniture. Opulent throws, cushions and tassels are just a few of the new soft furnishings range on offer to marry the mix of old and new together. You will be spoilt for choice with the large selection of decorative mirrors and beautiful lamps and the individual accessories for your home.

Lighting is a speciality, from Baccarat crystal wall lights to large antique French chandeliers, the selection will have you dazzled. Feel free to browse, and feel inspired with the eclectic delights of gifts and furnishings you will find. Antiques and Country Living is open seven days a week 9.30am to 5.30pm. You will find it in Frome on the A362. Free parking available outside.

🏠 historic building   📷 museum and heritage   🏛 historic site   🏞 scenic attraction   �___ flora and fauna

FIAT LUX

8 Bath Street, Frome, Somerset BA11 1DH
Tel: 01373 473555
e-mail: info@fiatlux.co.uk
website: www.fiatlux.co.uk

Fiat Lux is a specialist lighting retailer, supplying an eclectic mix of both modern and traditional lighting for the home. Owners Nick and Lesley Lanham-Cook have gathered together an extensive range of cool, funky and designer lighting in their showroom.

Nick has been in the lighting industry for more than a quarter of a century and looks at lighting with a more critical eye than most, taking the view that, "if we would not have it in our own home (because of the quality) why should we expect to sell it to others." They tend to look for design led products, statement pieces that you wouldn't find easily elsewhere. At Fiat Lux they are always happy to help by talking through your lighting projects and lighting dilemmas.

Situated in the Historic Market town of Frome, (which is approximately 16 miles south of Bath and 13 miles north of the A303). Fiat Lux is easy to find, Bath Street is on the main route through the centre of Frome. The showroom is located next to St John's church.

south and just across the county border in Wiltshire. The magnificent home of the Marquess of Bath was built by his ancestor, Sir John Thynne, in a largely symmetrical style in the 1570s. The interior is a treasure house of Old Masters, Flemish tapestries, exquisite furniture, rare books and the present Lord Bath's racy murals. The superb grounds were landscaped by Capability Brown and now contain one of the country's best-known venues for a marvellous day out. In the famous Safari Park the 'Lions of Longleat', first introduced in 1966, have been followed by a veritable Noah's Ark of exotic creatures, including rhinos, zebras and white tigers. The park also offers safari boat rides, a narrow-gauge railway, a children's amusement area, a garden centre, and the largest hedge maze in the world.

BALTONSBOROUGH
9 miles S of Wells off the A37

🐦 St Dunstan

Baltonsborough was one of the 12 manors owned by Glastonbury Abbey which lies just to the northwest. In those days, the lives of the people of the village were completely governed by the monks. The permission of the abbey had to be sought before a daughter could be married, while on a man's death his chattels and beasts became the property of the abbey. **St Dunstan** is said to have been born here between 909 and 925 - the ancient flour mill in the village is thought to have been owned by Dunstan's father. Before entering Glastonbury Abbey, Dunstan found favour at the court of King Athelstan but, once he had given up his worldly possessions, Dunstan

POTTING SHED HOLIDAY COTTAGES

*Harter's Hill Cottage, Pillmoor Lane, Coxley,
nr Wells, Somerset BA5 1RF
Tel: 01749 672857 Fax: 01749 679925
e-mail: info@pottingshedholidays.co.uk
website: www.pottingshedholidays.co.uk*

Chris and John van Bergen have created something very special with their **Potting Shed Holiday Cottages**, six beautifully renovated self-catering properties located in Wells – one of them almost under the cathedral roof – and in Coxley village. Spiders End, dating from about 1670, provides up-to-date comforts in a setting of old world charm that includes original features such as beams, sturdy stone and a section of ancient wattle and daub walls, all carefully restored by local craftsmen using local materials. This cottage has one double and one twin bedrooms, two bathrooms, a fully equipped modern kitchen, dining room and sitting room.

The Potting Shed, originally a farmhand's shed and animal shelter, is now a cosy retreat for two with a luxurious emperor size double bed among its many attractions. Guests at the cottage have the use of a lovingly cared for garden full of interesting botanical specimens and a haven for wildlife. A new addition for 2006 is the quirky Hobbits Den in the garden which has its own garden spa.

ABBEY TEA ROOMS

*16 Magdalene Street, Glastonbury, Somerset BA6 9EH
Tel: 01458 832852*

The popular **Abbey Tea Rooms** is located opposite the historic Glastonbury Abbey. Parts of the building are believed to be 500 years old and the present owner, Mary Parker, has been here for the last 18 of them. There is a traditional atmosphere in the Tea Rooms with waitress service, linen tablecloths and china, and brasses and pictures adorning the walls.

It is open daily offering something to suit everyone including morning coffees, traditional Somerset cream teas, teacakes, crumpets, a range of around 20 speciality teas and an excellent choice of homemade cakes. In addition there is a wide variety of light meals, including jacket potatoes and toasted sandwiches as well as a specials board which changes regularly and offers a choice of delicious homemade meals including casseroles, roasts and pies. Vegetarian options are always available and where possible dishes are made using local produce.

The Abbey Tea Rooms are also well known for their homemade puddings served with clotted cream, custard or locally made ice cream. Sunday lunches based on locally sourced meats are extremely popular with locals and visitors alike and advance bookings are highly recommended.

followed an austere regime. By setting himself apart from the abbey's other novices, Dunstan soon rose through the ranks of the religious house to become abbot, whereupon he enforced the strict Benedictine code. The wealth of Glastonbury grew under Dunstan and he also encouraged pilgrims to make their way here to see the holy relics. As well as being a great cleric and an entrepreneur, Dunstan was also an engineer. He was one of the first people to instigate the draining of the land in this area. From Glastonbury, Dunstan moved to Canterbury, where he was Archbishop until his death.

GLASTONBURY
6 miles SW of Wells on the A39

A Glastonbury Abbey   Lake Village

George & Pilgrim Hotel

Somerset Rural Life Museum

Glastonbury Tor   Glastonbury Festival

King Arthur

Today this ancient town of myths and legends, of tales of King Arthur and the early Christians, is an attractive market town still dominated by the ruins of its abbey, which continues to attract visitors. The dramatic remains of **Glastonbury Abbey** lie in the heart of the old town and, if the legend of Joseph of Arimathea is to be believed, this is the site of the earliest Christian foundation in the British Isles. By the Middle Ages, Glastonbury was second only to Rome as a place of Christian pilgrimage.

Joseph of Arimathea, the wealthy Jerusalem merchant who had provided a tomb for the crucified Jesus, is said to have arrived at Glastonbury in around 60AD. According to legend, while he was walking on the tor, Joseph drove his staff into the ground whereupon it took root and burst into leaf. Taking this as a sign that he should build a church, Joseph erected a simple church on the site now taken by the abbey. His staff is reputed to have grown into the celebrated Christmas-flowering Glastonbury hawthorn.

Today, the picturesque abbey ruins, with their associations with the legend of **King Arthur,** remain a great tourist attraction. It was Henry III who "caused search to be made for King Arthur's tomb" at Glastonbury. His workmen found it with suspiciously little difficulty. After digging down some seven feet, they unearthed a huge stone slab bearing a cross of lead. No body, however. So they continued digging another nine feet and then "found the bones of the great prince". This fortuitous find brought a further influx of sightseers to the town.

During the Middle Ages, Glastonbury Abbey was also an internationally renowned centre of learning, and scholars and pilgrims from all over Christendom made their way here. One of the guest houses built to accommodate them is now the **George and Pilgrim Hotel.** Originally constructed in

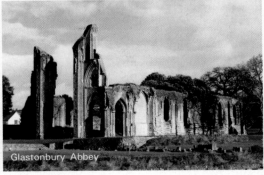

Glastonbury Abbey

THE GAUNTLET

Glastonbury's Premier Shopping Thoroughfare

Glastonbury, Somerset, BA6 9DP
Tel: 01458 832426
website: www.thegauntletshops.co.uk

Situated in the Ancient Isle of Avalon you will find Glastonbury's premier shopping thoroughfare. The Gauntlet is in the heart of the historic town and within walking distance of The Abbey and other attractions. The Gauntlet is steeped in history and is built on a typical

medieval styled burgage plot. When entering the excellent facilities at St Johns car park in the centre of the town you will be welcomed by the quirkiness of The Gauntlet. As you stroll along the intriguing walkway that leads directly to the High Street you will pass the Gauntlet Knight and an assortment of specialist shops with a variety of unusual and interesting quality merchandise to suit everyone and their pockets.

- Right on the entrance to the car park the **COFFEE BEAN** is the ideal starting place for coffees and lunch or to end the day with tea and homemade cakes or a takeaway Somerset cream tea.
- A wide range of handcrafted products from artists locally and around the world are offered at **SERENDIPITY**, where orders can be taken for custom made personalised items for unique and original gifts.
- Life coaching and readings are available at **YVONNE ANNE**, a qualified herbalist. A spiritual shop for enlightenment and development. Tools for healing, focal points for spiritual altars, angels, fairies, tarot cards and CDs for healing and meditation are available.
- Celtic and Norse gifts ranging from glassware and tweed items, Viking drinking / celebration horns, collectable Trolls, Celtic and Norse jewellery, books, t-shirts and lots more can be found in **CEILTEACH**.
- Look inside **THE WARDROBE** for fashion inspiration and find an eclectic mix of colourful, feminine styles handpicked and exclusively designed for you by the proprietor reflecting her East meets West influences.
- Specialising in unique handcrafted magical supplies for the pagan and witchcraft community the **WITCHCRAFT EMPORIUM** is a wonderful treasure trove of the magical arts.
- Step into **ENCHANTED FLORALS**, a magical florist with earthy and rustic designs in hand tied bouquets, plants and floral arrangements. Amongst the flowers you will find many unique enchanted pixie and fairy gifts.
- See handcrafted gifts such as hand painted glass, handbags, costume jewellery, mirrors, candles, incense, burners and oils and a heavenly host of Angels at **WHISPERED WISHES**.
- **READY FOR TAKE OFF!** has everything a girl needs for a night in or out. Handcrafted soaps and bath bombs and gorgeous lingerie.
- For many unusual gift ideas stop at **DEBRAROSE**, from gothic fairies and handmade items to gothic clothing, shoes and accessories, plus a large selection of Nightmare before Christmas merchandise.
- Glastonbury's first 'girly boutique', **CHARM** features selections of handmade items including handbags, cushions, soaps and jewellery. As well as many fairy themed products.
- An abundance of hand chosen, high quality silver jewellery all set with semi precious stones, amber and shell can be found at **ELEMENTS OF DESIRE**, a beautiful shop that is also stockist of the Sajen Goddess range.

You are invited to come and browse the shops where a warm welcome awaits you, whilst soaking up the atmosphere of bygone days and historical architecture.

Open 7 days a week

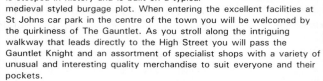

🏛 historic building   🏛 museum and heritage   🏛 historic site   ♨ scenic attraction   🌿 flora and fauna

HEARTFELT TRADING

3 Market Place, Glastonbury,
Somerset BA6 9HD
Tel: 01458 833910
website: www.secretfairygarden.co.uk

Heartfelt Trading has been in the heart of the historic town of Glastonbury since 1994. Heartfelt now offers two completely different shopping experiences in one store. Lesley Wright, who has run this "Fairy Shop" from the beginning, has now been joined by her husband, Chris Wright. Chris is running his own Crystal Room at Heartfelt Trading and the word quickly spread that not only is it the best selection of quality crystals, but also the most reasonably priced in Glastonbury. All the crystals are ethically sourced and hand-picked by the supplier.

The Fairy Room (now on the ground floor) offers unusual gifts which are either Fair Trade or British made where possible, appealing to the child in all of us. The current selection includes anything from fairy tea sets, pixie ears and fairy dust, to exclusive hand-finished bronze and freshwater pearl jewellery inspired by nature.

The shop also stocks cards and prints by collected artists, fairy collectables, books and activity packs for boys and girls. The shop's website is designed to encourage customers to create their own fairy space indoors or outside with the help of Heartfelt Trading.

THE CRYSTALMAN

7 Northload Street, Glastonbury, Somerset BA6 9JJ
Tel: 01458 833522
www.thecrystalman.co.uk

The Crystalman is a shop of beauty and knowledge. It is also home to the world-famous gemstone of Somerset - The Mendip Potato Stone. This gem, found only in Somerset and particularly the Mendip Hills, is unique. The shop stocks it as natural pieces and exclusively as spheres, eggs, hearts and carvings (pictured right). **Mike Jackson**, who owns the Crystalman, offers his lifelong passion and knowledge, guiding and advising you toward the understanding of gems, minerals and fossils. The Crystalman in Glastonbury is a Mecca for all. Full of amazing treasures from the hidden corners of the planet. Wide varieties of stones in their natural state are stocked - carved, cut, shaped,

and polished. Small and large amber nuggets, as well as gold nuggets silver, ruby, sapphire, Bristol Diamonds, copal, aquamarine, jasper, rose quartz and turquoise. There are extensive varieties of minerals, stones, crystals and spheres made from semi-precious stones - from marble size up to a 15kg quartz spheres. Moldavite carvings formed from meteorite remains from millions of years ago are not to be missed. There are spheres to roll you over with pleasure. Rhodonite from Cornwall, eggs of Scottish agate, stone polishers for those pebbles picked up on the beach years ago and treasured. Extensive carvings in Whitby jet, amber, rhodochrosite, turquoise and palm nut have to be seen to be believed. The best way to know what's in store is to visit this emporium of wonder and delight!

📖 stories and anecdotes ⚘ famous people ⚲ art and craft ✐ entertainment and sport ⚶ walks

Glastonbury

Distance: *3.0 miles (4.8 kilometres)*

Typical time: *120 mins*

Height gain: *50 metres*

Map: *Explorer 141*

Walk: *www.walkingworld.com ID:1081*

Contributor: *Tony Brotherton*

Park in Magdalene Street, next to Glastonbury Abbey grounds (current charge £3 all day).

DESCRIPTION:

A short tour of the town, allowing optional visits to the Abbey Ruins and Glastonbury Thorn, the Chalice Well and other points of religious interest, plus the 'obligatory pilgrimage' to Glastonbury Tor and a suggested visit to the Rural Life Museum and its tea room.

ADDITIONAL INFORMATION:

Glastonbury was the first Christian sanctuary in Great Britain and is the legendary burial-place of King Arthur. The legend of the Glastonbury Thorn and Joseph of Arimathea's visit is well-known. Chalice Well is open every day of year, 10am - 6pm or 11am - 5pm or noon - 4pm according to season. Somerset Rural Life Museum is open 10am - 5pm on Tuesday to Friday between April and October and at weekends from 2pm -

6pm; tea shop. The abbey ruins may be visited every day (except Christmas Day). Open 9:30am to 6pm (or dusk if earlier).

FEATURES:

Hills or fells, pub, toilets, museum, National Trust/NTS, wildlife, birds, flowers, great views, Butterflies, food shop, tea shop

WALK DIRECTIONS:

1 | From car park in Magdalene Street may be seen 14th Century Abbot's Kitchen in grounds of Glastonbury Abbey. Turn right along street, passing entrance to Abbey, to reach bottom of High Street. Go right to see on left, historic George & Pilgrims Hotel, founded in 1400s.

2 | Walk up High Street. Tourist Information Office is located on left, in 15th Century Tribunal: here is housed also, Lake Village Museum. Further up on left is St John's Church. This contains stained glass window depicting Joseph of Arimathea. Carry on up

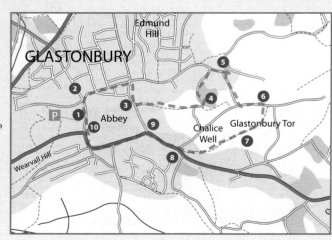

High Street and turn right along Lambrook Street, as far as imposing gateway of Abbey House on right.

3 | Now turn up Dod Lane and take driveway on right signed 'Footpath to Tor', to reach squeeze-stile. Follow path uphill through fields to lane and continue ahead to see tor at bend.

4 | Turn left to follow Bulwarks Lane to end. At road (Wick Hollow) turn uphill to crossroads.

5 | Take lane to right, with tor visible ahead, to reach lane junction. Here turn left as far as footpath to Tor.

6 | Follow path into field, soon to climb past information board and squeeze-gate, through trees and onto stepped path. Path rises steeply around Tor to summit and monument. Here are superb views over surrounding countryside.

7 | Continue walk by descending Glastonbury Tor to metal gate. Take footpath running downhill to reach Well House Lane. Turn left, then right at main road to arrive at Chalice Well. Chalybeate waters of Chalice Well were considered curative.

8 | Turn right along Chilkwell Street to reach, on left at junction with Bere Lane, Somerset Rural Life Museum.

9 | To continue the walk, turn left on Bere Lane and then right downhill at crossroads to return to Magdalene Street, to visit Almshouses Chapel. The tiny chapel and garden of almshouses afford a quiet place for meditation.

10 | To complete the walk, turn left along the street, past a former pumphouse (Glastonbury was once spa-town) to return to start.

1475, this striking building has old timber beams adorned with carved angels and an interior guarded by a series of curious monks' death masks. Close by is another 15th century building, the handsome **Tribunal** that is home to the town's Tourist Information Centre.

Even the town's **Somerset Rural Life Museum,** which explores the life of farmers in this area during the 19th and early 20th centuries, cannot escape from the influence of the abbey. Although the museum is housed in a Victorian farmhouse, there is an impressive 14th century barn here that once belonged to Glastonbury Abbey.

To the east of the town, **Glastonbury Tor** is a dramatic hill that rises high above the surrounding Somerset Levels. The 520-feet tor has been inhabited since prehistoric times and excavations on the site have revealed evidence of Celtic, Roman and pre-Saxon occupation. Because of its unusually regular conical shape the hill has long been associated with myth and legends and, in its time, has been identified as the Land of the Dead, the Celtic Otherworld, a Druid's temple, a magic mountain, an Arthurian hill fort, a ley line intersection and a rendezvous point for passing UFOs. Along with its mystical energy, the tor also offers magnificent panoramic views across Somerset to Wells, the Mendips, the Quantocks and the Bristol Channel. The striking tower at the summit is all that remains of the 15th century **Church of St Michael**, an offshoot of Glastonbury Abbey. Between the tor and the town lies the wooded rise of Chalice Hill, where, it is said, Joseph buried the Holy Grail, the chalice used at the Last Supper.

In recent years, a new band of pilgrims has been making their way to Glastonbury every June. The first **Glastonbury Festival** took place in 1970 and 1500 people came; that figure has now multiplied by 100. Pop idols who have played here include Johnny Cash, David Bowie, Van Morrison, Led Zeppelin and many more. The event is now the largest open air festival in Europe.

To the northwest of the town is the site of a prehistoric **Lake Village** discovered in 1892 when it was noticed that the otherwise level fields were studded with irregular mounds. Thought to date from around 150BC, the dwellings were built on a series of tall platforms that raised them above the surrounding marshland.

STREET
7 miles SW of Wells on the A39

🏛 Friends' Meeting House 🏛 Shoe Museum

The oldest part of this now sprawling town lies around the 14th century parish Church of the Holy Trinity although most of the town itself dates from the 19th century when Street began to expand from a small rural village into the light industrial town of today. Much of this growth was due to one family, the Clarks. In the 1820s, the Quaker brothers, Cyrus and James Clark began to produce sheepskin slippers from the hides of local animals. Many of the town's older buildings owe their existence to the family and, in particular, there is the **Friends' Meeting House** of 1850 and the building that housed the original Millfield School. The oldest part of the Clark's factory has now been converted into a fascinating **Shoe Museum.** Although the company is one of the largest manufacturers of quality footwear in Europe, it continues to keep its headquarters in the town and also operates the Clarks Village Shopping Outlet where 90 leading brands offer discounts of up to 60% every day.

MEARE
6½ miles SW of Wells on the B3151

🏛 Abbot's Fish House

🌱 Shapwick Heath Nature Reserve

Just to the east of this attractive village is an unusual medieval building known as the **Abbot's Fish House**. Before 1700, this isolated building stood on the edge of Meare Pool, once a substantial lake that provided nearby Glastonbury Abbey with a regular supply of freshwater fish. Before the lake was drained, this early-14th century building was used for storing fishing equipment and salting the catches.

To the southwest of Meare, in terrain scarred by years of peat extraction, is the **Shapwick Heath Nature Reserve**, which provides a safe haven for rare plants and wildlife. Parts of the Neolithic 'Sweet Track', the oldest man-made routeway in Britain, still exist beneath the wet peat. This remarkable timber track was constructed around 3800BC to cross a mile or so of reed swamp. Many artefacts have been found beside the trackway including stone axes, pots containing hazelnuts, a child's toy tomahawk and a polished jadeite axe from the Alps.

WESTHAY
8 miles SW of Wells on the B3151

🏛 Peat Moors Visitor Centre

Just outside the village of Westhay is the **Peat Moors Visitor Centre.** The centre offers visitors a fascinating insight into the history and ecology of the Somerset Levels and, through a series of imaginative displays, describes the development of commercial peat digging, the special trades that have grown up in this unique environment and the measures that have been taken to conserve the area's flora and fauna.

WOOKEY
2 miles W of Wells off the A371

🏚 Burcott Mill

A rare and historic working watermill, **Burcott Mill** has its origins in pre-Domesday times. Visitors can see stone-ground flour being hand-made and join a tour led by the miller himself. The site also has an adventure playground, country tearoom, pets and picnic area, and a pottery.

WEDMORE
7½ miles W of Wells on the B3139

🏚 Ashton Windmill

This remote village was the ancient capital of the Somerset marshes. King Alfred is said to have brought the newly baptised Danish King Guthrum to sign the Peace of Wedmore here in 878. This treaty left Wessex in Alfred's hands but gave East Anglia, East Mercia and the Kingdom of York to the Danes. The village's main street, the Borough, is lined with fine stone buildings, including a lovely old coaching inn. The parish church's spectacular Norman south doorway is thought to have been carved by the craftsmen who built Wells Cathedral.

To the northwest of the village, near Chapel Allerton, is **Ashton Windmill**. It was built in the 1700s and is now the only complete windmill left in Somerset. The site provides wonderful views over Cheddar Gorge and the Somerset levels.

WOOKEY HOLE
1½ miles NW of Wells off the A371

💧 Great Cave 💧 Ebbor Gorge

Throughout the centuries, the carboniferous limestone core of the Mendip Hills has been gradually dissolved away by the small amount

THE DINING ROOM
The Borough, Wedmore, Somerset BS28 4EB
Tel: 01934 710080

The Dining Room restaurant in the beautiful Georgian village of Wedmore is a family run restaurant located in a charming Grade II listed building. The restaurant is run by husband and wife team, Martin and Amanda Lucas. They have a full bar and an extensive wine list, which is available for both lunches and evening meals.

They provide a relaxed family environment, beautifully decorated and furnished with traditional furniture to create an English dining room, where you can enjoy the delicious cakes, scones and home cooked menus. There is a patio at the front, which in summer is surrounded with blooms from the hanging baskets. The family piano is located in the restaurant where there is occasional live music during the evening service on Fridays and Saturdays.

They say, "we are keen to support local farmers and trades people who are part of our community so wherever possible we always use locally grown and farmed produce."

The Dining Room is open for morning coffee, lunch and afternoon tea Monday to Saturday, opening at 9.30am (10am on Mondays) and closing at 5pm (4pm on Mondays). It is also open Friday and Saturday evenings from 7pm when they serve the delicious seasonal home cooked menu.

of carbonic acid in rainwater. This erosion has created more than 25 caverns around Wookey Hole, of which only the largest half dozen or so are open to the public. The **Great Cave** contains a rock formation known as the Witch of Wookey that casts a ghostly shadow and is associated with gruesome legends of child-eating. During prehistoric times, lions, bears and woolly mammoths lived in the area. In a recess known as the Hyena's Den, a large cache of bones has been found, many of them showing signs of other animal's tooth marks. The river emerging from Wookey Hole, the River Axe, has been harnessed to provide power since the 15th century and the present building here was originally constructed in the early 17th century as a paper mill.

Just to the northwest runs the dramatic **Ebbor Gorge** now a National Nature Reserve managed by English Nature. There are two walks here, the shorter one suitable for wheelchairs accompanied by a strong pusher. The longer walk involves a certain amount of rock scrambling. However, the hard work is rewarded as there is a wealth of wildlife here, including badger and sparrow hawk in the woodland, lesser horseshoe bats in and around the caves and buzzards flying overhead.

Cheddar Gorge

CHEDDAR
8 miles NW of Wells on the A371

- ⚶ Cheddar Gorge   ⚶ Pavey's Lookout Tower
- 🏛 Cheddar Man Museum

This sprawling village is best known for its dramatic limestone gorge, **Cheddar Gorge** which extends for some two miles and is one of the most famous and most often visited of Britain's many natural attractions. It is characterised by its high vertical cliffs, from which there are outstanding views out over the Somerset Levels, the Quantock Hills and,

on a clear day, across the Bristol Channel to South Wales. The National Trust owns most of the land around this magnificent ravine, which is a Site of Special Scientific Interest. Numerous rare plants grow here and it is also a haven for butterflies. A circular walk through the area takes in plantations, natural woodland and rough downland. This is a place that draws rock climbers, but the less ambitious may like to take the 274 steps of **Jacob's Ladder** that lead from the bottom of the gorge to the top of the cliffs. Here, **Pavey's Lookout Tower** offers yet more spectacular views of the surrounding area.

While the gorge is undoubtedly everyone's idea of Cheddar, the village is also renowned for its caves and, of course, its cheese. Although much embellished by modern tourist paraphernalia, its two main show caves,

Gough's Cave – an underground 'cathedral' – and the brilliantly coloured **Cox's Cave**, are worth seeing for their sheer scale and spectacular calcite formations. In 1903 an almost complete skeleton, named 'Cheddar Man', was discovered in Gough's Cave and this can be seen in the **Cheddar Man Museum,** along with cannibalised human skulls and flint tools. There are demonstrations of Stone Age survival skills and some intriguing cave art.

Back in 1726, Daniel Defoe was already singing the praises of Cheddar's most famous product. "Without all dispute," he wrote, "Cheddar is the best cheese that England affords, if not that the whole world affords." Today, in south Somerset alone, some 50 tonnes of Cheddar cheese is produced each day by nine cheese-makers. The original unpasteurised handmade farmhouse Cheddar is still produced on just two farms: Montgomery's in North Cadbury, and Keen's near Wincanton. Their round half-hundredweight cheeses are wrapped in muslin, kept for more than a year and turned regularly as they mature. The result is Cheddar cheese at its most perfect.

Since the term 'Cheddar Cheese' refers to a recipe and not a place, the cheese can be made anywhere in the world. Somerset itself is dotted with cheese manufacturers of various sizes and a number of these establishments supplement their income by offering guided tours, cheese demonstrations and catering facilities for the many visitors who come to gorge on the local speciality.

CHARTERHOUSE
9 miles NW of Wells off the B3134

Mendips   Black Down

Rising, in some places, to more than 1,000 feet above sea level, the **Mendips** form a landscape that is like no other in the region. Although hard to imagine today, lead and silver were once mined from these picturesque uplands. The Mendip lead-mining activity was centred around the remote village of Charterhouse – the last mine in the district, at Priddy, closed in 1908.

Charterhouse takes its name from a Carthusian monastery, **Witham Priory**, which owned one of the four Mendip mining sectors, or liberties. This area has been known for its mineral deposits since the Iron Age and such was its importance that the Romans declared the mines here state property within just six years of their arrival in Britain. Under their influence, silver and lead ingots, or pigs, were exported to France and to Rome, and the settlement grew into a sizable town with its own fort and amphitheatre, the remains of which can still be seen today. Centuries later, improved technology allowed the original seams to be reworked and the area is now littered with abandoned mine buildings and smelting houses.

Roman Amphitheatre, Charterhouse

stories and anecdotes   famous people   art and craft   entertainment and sport   walks

A footpath from Charterhouse church leads up onto **Black Down** which is, at 1,067ft, the highest point in the Mendips. From here, to the northwest, the land descends down into Burrington Combe, a deep cleft said to have inspired the Reverend Augustus Toplady to write the hymn *Rock of Ages*.

AXBRIDGE
10 miles NW of Wells off the A371

🏛 King John's Hunting Lodge   🦢 Frankie Howerd

A small town with a delightful centre, Axbridge is now a conservation area. In its ancient market square stands an exceptional example of a half-timbered merchant's house dating from around 1500. Three storeys high and known as **King John's Hunting Lodge** (National Trust) the building was extensively restored in the early 1970s and is now home to an excellent **Local History Museum**. Although the Lodge has nothing to do with King John or hunting, its name is a reminder that the Mendip hills were once a royal hunting ground. Elsewhere in the centre of Axbridge

there are many handsome Georgian shops and town houses.

About a mile west of Axbridge, near the village of Cross, is an unusual attraction. The late comedian **Frankie Howerd** lived in a cottage here for many years and his home was opened to the public at Easter 2006. He was a great hoarder so the cottage is full of hundreds of scripts, photographs and props, along with a pair of swords used in the film *Cleopatra,* (a gift from Richard Burton and Elizabeth Taylor), two stone cats from Laurence Olivier, and a fossilised egg presented to Frankie by the Italian government after he starred in the film *Up Pompeii.*

In May 2008, the four-bedroom, pink cottage was put up for sale with an asking price of £800,000. The thousands of items of memorabilia, including Frankie's toupee, were available as optional extras for an additional £600,000.

Bristol

🏛 Bristol Cathedral   🏚 Castle Park

🏚 Floating Harbour   🏛 Clifton Suspension Bridge

🏛 Bristol Industrial Museum   🌿 @t Bristol

🦢 Isambard Kingdom Brunel   🌿 Theatre Royal

🏛 Maritime Heritage Centre   🏞 Redcliffe Caves

🏛 Church of St Mary Radcliffe   🏛 Goldney Grotto

🏛 British Empire & Commonwealth Museum

🏛 John Wesley's Chapel   🐾 Bristol Zoo Gardens

🏛 City Museum & Art Gallery

🐾 Avon Gorge Nature Reserve

Bristol was Sir John Betjeman's favourite English city. It had, he said "the finest architectural heritage of any city outside London". Today it is also one of Britain's most vibrant and stimulating cities and offers

King John's Hunting Lodge, Axbridge

🏛 historic building   🏛 museum and heritage   🏚 historic site   🏞 scenic attraction   🐾 flora and fauna

a fascinating combination of grand buildings, reverberant history and contemporary creativity.

Situated at a strategically important bridging point at the head of the Avon gorge, Bristol was founded in Saxon times and soon became a major port and market centre. By the early 11th century, it had its own mint and was trading with other ports throughout western Europe, Wales and Ireland. The Normans quickly realised the importance of the port and, in 1067, began to build a massive stone keep. Although the castle was all but destroyed at the end of the English Civil War, the site of the fortification remains as **Castle Park**. Situated just to the west of the castle site stands **Bristol Cathedral** founded in around 1140 by Robert Fitzhardinge as the great church of an Augustinian abbey. While the abbey no longer exists, several original Norman features, such as the chapter house, gatehouse and the east side of the abbey cloisters, remain. Following the Dissolution in 1539, Henry VIII took the unusual step of elevating the abbey church to a cathedral and, soon after, the richly-carved choir stalls were added. However, the building was not fully completed until the 19th century, when a new nave was built. Among the cathedral's treasures is a pair of candlesticks donated in 1712 by the rescuers of Alexander Selkirk, the castaway on whom Daniel Defoe based his hero Robinson Crusoe.

During the Middle Ages, Bristol expanded as a trading centre and, at one time, it was second only to London as a seaport. Its trade was built on the export of raw wool and woollen cloth from the Mendip and Cotswold Hills and the import of wines from Spain and southwest France. It was around this time that the city's first major wharf development took place when the River Frome was diverted from its

Christmas Steps, Bristol

original course into a wide artificial channel now known as St Augustine's Reach. A remarkable achievement for its day, the excavation created over 500 yards of new berthing and was crucial in the city's development. Later, in the early 19th century the harbour was further increased when a semi-artificial waterway, the **Floating Harbour**, was created by diverting the course of the River Avon to the south. Another huge feat of engineering, the work took over five years to complete and was largely carried out by Napoleonic prisoners of war using only picks and shovels. Today, the main docks have moved downstream to Avonmouth and the Floating Harbour has become home port to a wide assortment of pleasure and small working craft.

Much of Bristol's waterfront has now been redeveloped for recreation. Down on the harbourside is @t **Bristol** is **Explore** a hands-on centre of science and discovery. Also in the old port area is the **Bristol Industrial Museum** (undergoing an extensive refurbihment at present), which presents a fascinating record of the achievements of the city's industrial and commercial pioneers, including those with household names such as Harvey (wines and sherries), McAdam (road building), Wills (tobacco) and Fry (chocolate). Visitors can also find out about the port's history, view the aircraft and aero engines that have been made here since 1910 and inspect some of the many famous vehicles that have borne the Bristol name since Victorian times.

Another famous name, that of the engineer and inventor **Isambard Kingdom Brunel** is closely associated with the city. His graceful **Clifton Suspension Bridge** soars 200ft above the Avon gorge to the west of the city centre. Opened in 1864, five years after the death of its designer, the bridge continues to be a major route into the city and provides magnificent views over Bristol and the surrounding countryside. Brunel's

mighty *SS Great Britain*, the world's first iron-hulled passenger liner was launched in 1843 and is now berthed in the harbour. Next to it is the **Maritime Heritage Centre,** dedicated to the history of shipbuilding in Bristol. A new exhibition, called 'The Nine Lives of IK Brunel', tells Brunel's compelling and entertaining life story, inlcuding his strengths and achievements, failures and faults. And if you arrive in the city by train from London you will have travelled along the route Brunel engineered for the Great Western Railway. He also designed every one of the bridges and stations along the way, including Bristol's Temple Meads station. Brunel was born in 1806 and to mark his bi-centenary the city has devised a year-long celebration of his life and works, including major exhibitions at the *SS Great Britain,* At Bristol and the City Museum and Art Gallery. The celebrations culminate in September 2006 with a community performance and procession at Swindon Railway Village and Works where the GWR built all its locomotives and rolling stock.

Brunel's original terminus for the GWR at Temple Meads is now home to the **British Empire and Commonwealth Museum** which traces the history of British discovery and colonisation of foreign lands and the rich cultural legacy of the Commonwealth.

In medieval times, the city's prosperous merchants gave liberally for the building of one of the most impressive

SS Great Britain, Bristol

🏛 historic building   🏛 museum and heritage   🏛 historic site   ⌘ scenic attraction   ⸙ flora and fauna

parish churches in the country. **The Church of St Mary Redcliffe** was described by Queen Elizabeth I as "the fairest, goodliest and most famous Parish Church in England". Along with its glorious exterior, the church contains monuments to Admiral Sir William Penn, whose son founded the state of Pennsylvania in the United States, and John Cabot, the maritime pioneer who in 1497 was the first non-Scandinavian European to set foot on Newfoundland. (A replica of the tiny boat, *The Matthew,* in which Cabot made his perilous journey can be seen alongside Brunel's *SS Great Britain*). The sandstone beneath St Mary's church is riddled with underground passages known as the **Redcliffe Caves** and there are occasional guided tours of these unusual natural subterranean caverns.

Another ecclesiastical building of note is **John Wesley's Chapel**, the oldest Methodist building in the world. It was built in 1739 and remains completely unspoilt. Visitors can explore the preacher's rooms above the chapel, stand in Wesley's pulpit and see his preaching gown, riding whip and bed.

Elsewhere in the city are **The Red Lodge,** the only remaining Tudor domestic interior in Bristol which also has a lovely walled garden with a re-created Elizabethan-style knot garden; and the elegant Georgian House in Great George Street which was built in 1791. This is one of the most complete 18th century townhouses to have survived in Britain, its four floors all fully furnished and providing a fascinating insight into life at that time both above and below stairs.

The city is also home to one of the oldest theatres in the country to still be in use. The **Theatre Royal** was built in the 1760s and is the home of the famous Bristol Old Vic

theatre company. Backstage tours are available.

Next to the University, the **City Museum and Art Gallery** occupies a magnificent building which contains no fewer than seven art galleries as well as temporary exhibitions. It also houses important collections of minerals and fossils, eastern art, world wildlife, Egyptology, archaeology and some exceptional Chinese glass.

The land just to the west of the Clifton Suspension Bridge is now the **Avon Gorge Nature Reserve** and there are some delightful walks here through Leigh Woods up to the summit of an Iron Age hill fort. On the eastern side of the gorge an old snuff mill has been converted into an observatory whose attractions include a camera obscura. Once a genteel suburb, Clifton is now an attractive residential area of elegant Georgian terraces. Here, too, is Goldney House, now a university hall, but also the home of the unique subterranean folly, **Goldney Grotto**, which dates from the 1730s. The walls of this fantastic labyrinth, filled with spectacular rock formations, foaming cascades and a marble statue of Neptune, are covered with thousands of seashells and 'Bristol diamonds', fragments of a rare quartz found in the Avon gorge.

Clifton is also home to **Bristol Zoo Gardens** which cares for more than 400 exotic and endangered species. The summer of 2006 saw the opening of its Monkey Jungle which promises an immersive forest experience where monkeys mingle with gorillas, and visitors can enjoy close-up walk-through encounters with lemurs. A new addition for the summer of 2008 is the Butterfly Forest featuring spectacular butterfly and moth species from across the world.

Around Bristol

CHEW MAGNA
6 miles S of Bristol on the B3130

🏠 Church House 🏛 Stanton Drew

🎞 'The Wedding' 🏛 Wansdyke

🌱 Blagdon Lake 🌱 Chew Valley Lake

Situated just to the north of Chew Valley Lake, this former wool village is a pleasant place with some handsome Georgian houses. The nucleus of the village is its three-sided green whose surrounding shops and pubs are linked by an unusual raised stone pavement. At the top of the green is the striking early-16th century **Church House** that was originally intended to be the venue for the annual church sales and for brewing the ale and baking the bread to be sold on these occasions. The funds raised at this event were used to maintain the parish church for the coming year. These church houses, built

Standing Stones, Stanton Drew

in the 15th or early-16th centuries, were mainly confined to the counties of Somerset and Devon. Close by is the impressive parish Church of St Andrew, a testimony to the former prosperity of this village. Inside can be seen the interesting double effigy of Sir John Loe, a 15th century local squire reputed to be seven feet tall. Behind a high wall adjacent to the churchyard stands **Chew Court**, a former summer palace of the bishops of Bath and Wells.

Just to the east of the village is **Stanton Drew**, an ancient settlement that stands beside a prehistoric site of some importance – a series of stone circles over half a mile across that were constructed by the Bronze Age Beaker people between 2000 and 1600BC. This complex of standing stones consists of three circles, a lone stone known as Hauteville's Quoit and a large chambered burial tomb called The Cove. The stones are composed of three different types of rock; limestone, sandstone and conglomerate. They are thought to have been erected for religious, or perhaps astronomical, purposes. In common with many stone circles in western Britain, the origins of this stone circle are steeped in legend. The most widespread tale tells of a foolhardy wedding party who wanted to continue dancing into the Sabbath. At midnight, the piper refused to carry on, prompting the infuriated bride to declare that if she had to, she would get a piper from hell. At that point, another piper stepped forward to volunteer his services and the party resumed its dancing. As the music got louder and louder and the tempo faster and faster, the dancers realised, too late, that the good natured piper was the Devil himself and, when his playing reached its terrifying climax, he turned the whole party to stone. To this day, this curious group of standing stones is still known as **The Wedding.**

🏠 historic building 🏛 museum and heritage 🏛 historic site 🌳 scenic attraction 🌱 flora and fauna

A couple of miles to the north of Stanton Drew, the line of the ancient **Wansdyke** runs in a roughly east-west direction around the southern fringes of Bristol. Built during the Dark Ages as a boundary line and defensive barrier against the Saxons, short sections of this great earthwork bank can still be seen, notably at Maes Knoll and along the ridge adjoining the Iron Age hill fort on Stantonbury Hill.

To the south of Chew Magna are the two reservoirs constructed to supply Bristol with fresh water but which also provide a first class recreational amenity. The smaller **Blagdon Lake** was completed in 1899 and **Chew Valley Lake** in 1956. Together they have around 15 miles of shoreline and attract visitors from a wide area who come to fish, take part in water sports and observe the wide variety of waterfowl and other bird life that is drawn to this appealing habitat.

BARROW GURNEY
5 miles SW of Bristol on the B3130

Before the construction of the reservoirs of Blagdon and Chew Valley, Bristol's fresh water came from the three small reservoirs at Barrow Gurney. The first was opened in 1852 but within two years it developed a leak and had to be drained, causing a serious disruption to the city's water supply. Like many of the villages to the southwest of Bristol, Barrow Gurney has undergone considerable change since World War II and is now becoming a dormitory settlement for the city's commuters.

CONGRESBURY
13 miles SW of Bristol on the A370

🎞 St Congar

This sizeable village, which today appears to be just another commuter town, has a long and

eventful history that goes back to Roman times. Around 2,000 years ago a settlement stood here at the end of a spur of the Somerset marshes. Fragments of Roman and pre-Saxon pottery have been found on the site of the ancient hill that overlooks the present village.

The early Celtic missionary, **St Congar,** is believed to have founded an early wattle chapel at Congresbury in the 6th century. A tree bound by an iron hoop, on the eastern side of the church, is still referred to as 'St Congar's Walking Stick'. This is reputed to have grown from the saint's staff that miraculously sprouted leaves after he had thrust it into the ground outside the chapel.

CLEVEDON
15 miles SW of Bristol on the B3133

🏛 Clevedon Pier ⓓ Poet's Walk

🏛 Clevedon Court

Clevedon was developed in the late 18th and early-19th century as a resort but the lack of a railway prevented the town from expanding further. It was overtaken by Weston-super-Mare as the leading seaside town along this stretch of coast. As a result there are few of the attractions that are normally associated with a holiday resort. A notable exception is **Clevedon Pier**, a remarkably slim and elegant structure that was built in the 1860s from iron rails intended for Brunel's ill-considered South Wales Railway. When part of the pier collapsed in the 1970s, its long term future looked bleak but, following an extensive restoration programme, the pier is now the landing stage, during the summer, for large pleasure steamers such as the *Balmoral* and the *Waverley*, the only surviving sea-going paddle steamers in the world. Unusually for a holiday resort Clevedon has a **Market Hall** that was built in 1869 to provide a place for local

STEAR & BRIGHT JEWELLERY

Studio One, Clevedon Craft Centre, Moor Lane,
Clevedon, Somerset BS21 6TD
Tel: 01275 872149
e-mail: davidstear@f2s.com
website: www.clevedoncraftcentre.co.uk

Stear & Bright have been producing jewellery for the past 38 years. They are located on the Clevedon Craft Centre which David Stear and Jeffrey Bright pioneered when they left university in 1971. There are 11 studio workshops on the Craft Centre, which is situated some 12 miles south west of Bristol on the outskirts of the seaside town of Clevedon.

David and Jeffrey are designer makers of hand-made gold and silver jewellery, and silver wares. They use precious and semi-precious stones in their designs, developing ideas directly from the materials with which they work, to produce their own unique style. Although most of their work is to commission, they do have a full range of designs on display at their workshop, Studio One, on the Clevedon Craft Centre. They are open 9.30am to 5pm, Monday to Saturday; and from 2pm to 5pm on Sundays. Entrance and parking are free, and there is disabled access to most of the site. The studio is easy to find: there are brown and white "Clevedon Craft Centre" signs both from junction 20 of the M5, and off the B3130 Bristol to Clevedon road.

MINI MOI

14 Hill Road, Clevedon, North Somerset BS21 7NZ
Tel: 01275 877735
e-mail: info@minimoiboutique.co.uk   website: www.minimoiboutique.co.uk

Situated in one of the most exclusive areas of Clevedon, **Mini Moi** opened in November 2007 after owner Amanda realised that the area had no outlets for traditional & trendy children's clothing.

The light, airy and stylish interior is now home to a number of the best known and stylish collections of children's wear.

Little boys and girls from ages 0 to 10 can look fantastic in organic cotton hoodies from 'Little Shrimp', vibrantly coloured dresses and tops from 'no added sugar' and shirts and trousers from 'LittleLinins'. Other collections available are from 'Mini a ture', 'Loopy', 'Putumayo', 'Starchild' and 'Avore'. The large range of vintage, funky and traditional clothing ensures that every child can find an outfit for every occasion. There are even some novelty costumes available just for fun!

In addition to the children's clothing, Mini Moi also stocks a number of different gifts, all hand-made in England, candles and organic skincare designed for babies and expectant mothers.

Mini Moi is open Monday to Saturday 9.30am to 5pm. Private shopping is available by appointment only.

ESTUARY

85 Hill Road, Clevedon, Somerset BS21 7PN
Tel: 01275 343030

Estuary is situated on Clevedons popular Hill Road (less than two miles from the M5 junction 20) and just a two-minute walk from the seafront and historic pier. Everyone who visits loves Estuary and its eclectic mix of unusual, quirky gifts ranging from funky melamine tableware covered in strawberries, smarties and marshmallows to beautiful chunky French oak doorstops.

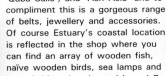

Estuary also stocks an affordable range of ladies casual clothing including 'Joules', 'Quba Sails', and 'Ash Asia' and to compliment this is a gorgeous range of belts, jewellery and accessories. Of course Estuary's coastal location is reflected in the shop where you can find an array of wooden fish, naïve wooden birds, sea lamps and lots of things beachy and boaty! Beautiful Kew Garden pots and vases enhance the rustic interior of Estuary.

For a day out with a difference, combine a visit to Hill Road and the seafront and pier with one of the other local attractions such as the National Trusts recently opened gothic mansion Tyntesfield Estate (just a ten minute drive away) or if you travelling the M5 stop off, refresh and discover Clevedon en route.

market gardeners to sell their produce.

Beginning at Clevedon promenade and leading up to Church and Wain's Hills is the **Poet's Walk**, a flower-lined footpath that is said to have been popular with Victorian poets. On the top of Wain's Hill, are the remains of an Iron Age coastal fort, from which walkers can look out over the town, the Somerset Levels and the Severn Estuary.

However, it is **Clevedon Court** (National Trust), an outstanding 14th century manor house that brings most people to this town. One of the earliest surviving country houses in Britain, this house displays many of its original 14th century features still intact and incorporates a massive 12th century tower and a 13th century great hall. Once partly fortified, this imposing manor house has been the home of the Elton family since 1709. As longstanding patrons of the arts, the family

invited many of the country's finest poets and writers to Clevedon in the early 1800s. These included Coleridge, Tennyson and Thackeray. It was while staying here that Thackeray fell in love with one of his host's daughters, Mrs Brookfield. He was to spend some time here seeing her and writing *Vanity Fair*. Another member of the Elton family was Arthur Hallam, a student friend of Lord Tennyson who showed great promise as a poet but who died very young. Tennyson was devastated by his friend's untimely death and sought to assuage his grief by writing the great elegiac poem *In Memoriam, AHH*, which was published in 1850.

Although the Elton family is closely associated with literature, one member of the family in the Victorian era invented a special technique for making the type of brightly coloured pottery that was to become known as

Eltonware. It was particularly popular in the United States. There are many fine examples on display in the house, along with a collection of rare glass from the works at Nailsea. Clevedon Court is an impressive place housing some fine treasures and is surrounded by beautiful 18th century terraced gardens. A footpath leads through nearby woodland on to a ridge overlooking the low and once marshy Gordano valley.

BANWELL
16 miles SW of Bristol on the A368

🝢 Bone Caves 🏛 Puxton church

This pleasant village was once the site of a Saxon monastery and the parish church here is certainly ancient. Banwell Castle, on the other hand, although it looks like an authentic medieval fortress, is in fact a Victorian mansion house now converted into a hotel. Just to the west of the village, on Banwell Hill, a remarkable discovery was made in 1821. A series of caverns were found containing the remains of prehistoric animals including bison, bear and reindeer. They are now known as the **Bone Caves.**

A couple of miles north of Banwell is the village of **Puxton**, noted for its eccentric church tower that leans at such an angle that it looks as if it might topple at any moment, causing its weathercock to nosedive into the churchyard.

WESTON-SUPER-MARE
22 miles SW of Bristol on the A370

🏛 Grand Pier 🐦 Seaquarium 🝢 Sand Point

🏛 North Somerset Museum 🏛 Woodspring Priory

🝢 Great Weston Train Experience 🏃 Mendip Way

🏛 Helicopter Museum 🏚 Worlebury Camp

This traditional seaside resort, whose greatest asset is undoubtedly its vast expanse of sandy beach, has in recent years also developed as a centre of light industry. As late as 1811, Weston was just a fishing hamlet with just 170 residents. Within 100 years, it had grown to become the second largest town in Somerset and today has a resident population of around 70,000.

The commercial development of Weston began in the 1830s around the Knightstone, an islet joined to the shore at the northern end of the bay, and here were eventually built a large theatre and swimming baths. The arrival of the railway in 1841 stimulated the town's rapid expansion, and in 1867 a pier was built on the headland below Worlebury Camp connecting Birnbeck Island with the mainland. Intended as a berth for steamer traffic, the pier was found to be slightly off the tourist track. Later, a more impressive pier was built nearer the town centre. Prior to serious fires in the 1930s and during World War II, it was approximately twice its current length. The **Grand Pier** now stands at the centre of an area crammed with souvenir shops, ice cream parlours, cafés and assorted attractions that are part and parcel of a British seaside resort. There are also the indoor attractions of the **Winter Gardens**, along the seafront, and the fascinating, family-friendly **North Somerset Museum**.

For anyone wishing to explore Weston on foot, the Museum Trail begins on the seafront and follows a trail of carved stones created by the artist Michael Fairfax. The **Seaquarium** has more than 30 interesting marine displays, along with feeding times and demonstrations, to amuse the whole family. The **Great Weston Train Experience** is one of the country's leading model railway exhibitions with detailed working layouts, exhibits in HO, N, Z and G scales, and further dioramas in the

---

🏛 historic building 🏛 museum and heritage 🏚 historic site 🝢 scenic attraction 🐦 flora and fauna

Model Masters shop as you enter.

An excellent viewpoint to the north of the resort is **Sand Point**, a ridge overlooking a lonely salt marsh that is home to a wide variety of wading birds. Just back from the headland is **Woodspring Priory**, a surprisingly intact medieval monastery founded in the early 13th century by a grandson of one of Thomas à Becket's murderers, William de Courtenay. The priory fell into disrepair following the Dissolution when the buildings were given over to agricultural use but the church, tower, refectory and tithe barn have all survived and the outline of the cloister can also still be made out.

Worlebury Camp, Weston super Mare

At the southern end of Weston Bay, another spectacular view can be found from the clifftop site of the semi-ruined church at Uphill. This village lies at the start of the sometimes demanding **Mendip Way**, a 50-mile footpath that takes in the whole length of the Mendip Hills, including the broad vale of the Western Mendips, the high plateau of the central part and the wooded valleys in the eastern region.

Just to the southeast of the town is Weston Airport, home to the world's largest collection of helicopters and autogyros. The only museum in Britain dedicated to rotary wing aircraft, **The Helicopter Museum** has more than 70 helicopters with exhibits ranging from single-seater autogyros to multi-passenger helicopters. Visitors can see displays on the history and development of these flying machines and a conservation hangar where the aircraft are restored. Grown-ups can take a Helicopter Experience Flight; under-12s can stage a rescue in the Lynx helicopter play area.

The area around Weston has been inhabited since prehistoric times. The wooded promontory at the northern end of Weston Bay was the site of a sizable Iron Age hill settlement known as **Worlebury Camp**. In the 1st century AD this is said to have been captured by the Romans after a bloody battle. Recent excavations, which revealed a number of skeletons showing the effects of sword damage, provided confirmation. A pleasant walk from the town centre now leads up through attractive woodland to this ancient hilltop site from where there are magnificent views out across the mouth of the River Severn to Wales.

WRAXALL
6 miles W of Bristol on the B3128

🏛 Tyntesfield   🐑 Noah's Ark Zoo Farm

One of the National Trust's most fascinating properties, **Tyntesfield** is an extraordinary Victorian Gothic Revival house that was home to four generations of the Gibbs family. The Gibbs' lived on a grand scale and spent lavishly on opulent furnishings for their magnificent mansion, including its stunning private chapel.

When the house was saved for the nation in June 2002, it needed a huge amount of conservation work which still continues with parts of the house still not open to the public. Visitors will see this work in progress but are no longer restricted to guided tours only but can wander at will through the permitted areas. Outside, there are formal gardens, an arboretum, walled garden and a working kitchen garden. Admission to the house is by timed ticket for all visitors. Tickets are issued at visitor reception on arrival and cannot be booked.

Also at Wraxall is **Noah's Ark Zoo Farm,** a hands-on real working farm with a rare collection of more than 60 types of animals including meerkats, camels, rhinos, wallabies, moneys and giraffes. There are also 9 all-weather playgrounds and a huge indoor play barn.

HENBURY
4 miles NW of Bristol off the A38

🏛 Blaise Castle

In her novel *Northanger Abbey*, Jane Austen described **Blaise Castle** at Henbury as "one of the finest places in England". This impressive 18th century house is set in parkland and boasts a large collection of everyday objects from times past including model trains, dolls and toy soldiers. There's also a Victorian schoolroom, picture gallery and period costumes. Within the estate grounds is Blaise Hamlet, an impossibly picturesque group of nine detached and individual stone cottages designed in a romantic rustic style by John Nash in 1809. The cottages are owned by the National Trust but are not open to the public.

Bath

🏛 Great Bath		🏛 Thermae Bath Spa	
🏛 Bath Abbey		⬥ 'Beau' Nash	
🏛 Holburne Museum of Art		🏛 Royal Crescent	
🏛 Pump Room		✐ Theatre Royal	
🏛 Museum of East Asian Art		🏛 Pulteney Bridge	
🏛 Assembly Rooms		🏛 Museum of Bath at Work	
🏛 Bath Postal Museum		⬥ Jane Austen Centre	
⬥ William Herschel Museum		🧍 Bath Skyline Walk	
🌱 Prior Park Landscape Garden			

Designated a World Heritage City, Bath is Britain's finest Georgian city, replete with gracious buildings of which around 5,000 are listed because of their architectural merit. Set in a sheltered valley, it is surrounded like Rome by seven hills which may have been one reason why the Romans took to it with such enthusiasm. Another important reason was, of course, its natural hot springs.

Since time immemorial more than a million gallons of water a day, at a constant temperature of 46°C, have bubbled to the surface at Bath. The ancient Celts believed the mysterious steaming spring was the domain of the goddess Sulis and they were aware of the water's healing powers long before the invasion of the Romans. However, it was the Romans who first enclosed the spring and went on to create a gracious health resort that became known as Aquae Sulis. By the 3rd century, Bath had become so renowned that high ranking soldiers and officials were coming here from all over the Roman Empire. Public buildings and temples were constructed and the whole city was enclosed by a stone wall. By 410AD, the last remaining Roman legions had left and, within a few years, the drainage systems failed and the area returned

SHANNON FURNITURE LTD
SCANDINAVIAN FURNITURE AND FABRICS

S**h**annon

68 Walcot Street, Bath BA1 5BD
Tel: 01225 424222
website: www.shannon-uk.com

Shannon Furniture Ltd. features a wide selection of Scandinavian furniture, lighting, fabric and gifts of timeless design and quality.

The Danish furniture includes several chairs by Hans Wegner such as the classic Wishbone, Arne Jacobsen's famous Egg, Swan and series 7 chairs. The Lamino chair upholstered in sheepskin from Swedese is displayed with beautiful oak and beech wooden furniture with limestone tops from GAD in Sweden's Gotland region.

The lamps and lighting are Danish Louis Poulsen, and Pandul with le Klint lampshades. Gifts and homewares include the glorious colourful designs of Marimekko fabrics and shoulder bags, Vipp bins, Playsam toys, Hoganas ceramics, iittala, Eva Solo, glassware, Klippan throws, Menu products and lots of Moomin products like mugs, duvet covers, lunchboxes and clocks.

The Shop is open 10am – 5.30pm
Monday to Saturday.

to marshland. Ironically, the ancient baths remained hidden throughout the entire period of Bath's 18th century renaissance and were only discovered in the late 19th century. The restored Roman remains can be seen today. They centre around the **Great Bath**, a rectangular lead-lined pool standing at the centre of a complex system of buildings that took over 200 years to complete. It comprised a swimming pool, mineral baths and a series of chambers heated by underfloor air ducts.

One hundred yards from the Great Bath, the **Thermae Bath Spa** opened in the summer of 2006. Visitors can bathe in the natural thermal waters that the Romans enjoyed almost 2,000 years ago. There's a spectacular rooftop pool, an innovative series of steam rooms, and an extensive range of spa treatments are available.

In a city crammed with beautiful buildings, **Bath Abbey** is still outstanding. The present great church was begun in 1499, after its Norman predecessor had been destroyed by fire. Building work was halted at the time of the Dissolution in the 1540s and the church remained without a roof for 75 years. It was not finally completed until 1901. It is now considered to be the ultimate example of English Perpendicular church architecture.

Inside, there is a memorial to **Richard 'Beau' Nash**, one of the people responsible for turning Bath into a fashionable Georgian spa town. Prior to Nash's arrival in the early 18th century, Bath was a squalid place with farm animals roaming the streets within the confines of the old Roman town.

VINTAGE LIVING

13 Broad Street, Bath, BA1 5LJ
Tel: 01225 335068
Also at; 61 High Street, Totnes, Devon TQ9 5PB
Tel: 01803 863999
website: www.vintageliving.co.uk

Specialising in stylish French country interiors, Vintage Living offers a wide selection of painted furniture and decorative accessories to adorn your home. Usually in stock are a selection of rustic country dining tables and dining chairs, together with French buffets. Also, a range of antique and new sofas, armchairs and upholstered furniture. Specially featuring lots of storage ideas for your home with chest of drawers, wardrobes, pigeon hole units and lots more. Customers are welcomed with the sound of old French café music and scented roses wafting through the air. Once inside, there are a feast of delights and customers can imagine that they've just landed in rural France. Diana Warszawski, the owner travels extensively to find her unique mix of vintage and characterful new stock which shows 'years of wear', even if it's new!

Vintage Living is a stockist of Kate Forman lampshades, inspired by 19th century French designs, Lene Bjerre lace curtain panels, and Le Comptoir De Famille home accessories. These two highly individual shops make the people who visit both Totnes and Bath want to spread their discovery to lots of their friends. Many customers now make a weekly visit to not miss out on the ever changing range of one-off pieces and to see the exciting new arrivals.

Notwithstanding, the town had continued to attract small numbers of rich and aristocratic people. Eventually, the town authorities took action to improve sanitation and their initiative was rewarded, in 1702, when Queen Anne paid Bath's spa a visit. The elegant and stylish Beau Nash, who had only come to the town to earn a living as a gambler, became the Master of Ceremonies and, under his leadership, the town became a relaxing place for the elegant and fashionable of the day's high society. Among the entrepreneurs and architects who shared Nash's vision was the architect John Wood who, along with his son, designed many of the city's fine neoclassical squares and terraces. Among these is the **Royal Crescent**, John Wood the Younger's Palladian masterpiece and one of the first terraces in Britain to be built to an elliptical

design. It has now been designated a World Heritage Building. Open to the public, No 1, Royal Crescent has been restored, redecorated and furnished so that it appears as it might have done when it was first built.

Bath's other 18th century founding father was Ralph Allen, an entrepreneur who made his first fortune developing an efficient postal system for the provinces and who went on to make a second as the owner of the local quarries that supplied most of the honey-coloured Bath stone to the city's Georgian building sites.

Famed for its wealth of Georgian architecture, Bath is a delightful city to wander around and marvel at the buildings. Beside the original Roman Baths is the **Pump Room**, which looks much as it did when it was completed in 1796. The **Theatre Royal** is one

🏛 historic building   🏛 museum and heritage   🏛 historic site   🍃 scenic attraction   🌱 flora and fauna

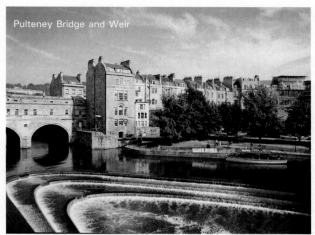

Pulteney Bridge and Weir

together by Sir William Holburne in the 19th century. Landscapes by Turner and Guardi and portraits by Stubbs, Ramsey, Raeburn, Zoffany and Gainborough are among its many treasures. The **Museum of Bath at Work** holds a fascinating collection that chronicles the city's unique architectural evolution; the **Museum of East Asian Art** displays artefacts from China, Japan, Korea and Southeast Asia; and the **Bath Postal Museum** illustrates 4000 years of communication from 'clay-mail to e-mail' and has a reconstruction of a Victorian sorting office.

of Britain's oldest and most beautiful theatres and offers a year-round programme of top quality drama, opera, dance and frequent Sunday concerts. Spanning the River Avon, in the centre of the city, is the magnificent **Pulteney Bridge**, designed by Robert Adam and inspired by Florence's Ponte Vecchio with its built-in shops.

The National Trust-owned **Assembly Rooms**, one of the places where polite 18th century society met to dance, play cards or just be seen, were severely damaged during World War II and not re-opened until 1963. They now incorporate the interesting **Museum of Costume** with a collection of more than 30,000 original items illuminating the vagaries of fashion over the last 400 years.

This is just one of the city's many excellent museums. The **Holburne Museum of Art** is housed in one of the city's finest examples of Georgian architecture and set in beautiful gardens. Originally a spa hotel, it was converted into a museum in the early 20th century and now contains the superb collection of decorative and fine art put

The city is synonymous with Jane Austen and her novels and, at the **Jane Austen Centre**, enthusiasts can learn more about the Bath of her time and the importance of the city to her life and works. Another famous resident is celebrated at the **William Herschel Museum** which occupies the mid-Georgian house where the famous astronomer and musician lived in the late 1700s and where he made his discovery of the planet Uranus.

An ideal way to gather a general impression of this magnificent city is to take the **Bath Skyline Walk**, an eight-mile footpath, through National Trust-owned land, taking in some superb landscaped gardens and woodland to the southeast of the city and from where there are extensive views out over Bath. The most striking feature of the skyline is Beckford's Tower which was built for the eccentric William Beckford in 1827. There are yet more magnificent views of the city from another National Trust property, **Prior Park Landscape Garden** which is just a 10-minute walk or short bus ride from the city centre – there is no parking at the garden itself. Within the beautiful grounds of this intimate 18th century garden are three lakes set in sweeping valleys and a famous Palladian bridge which is one of only four of its kind in the world.

Dyrham Park

Around Bath

DYRHAM
7 miles N of Bath off the A46

🏠 Dyrham Park

Set in an extensive deer park just minutes from the M4, **Dyrham Park** (National Trust) is a spectacular Baroque mansion containing a fabulous collection of 17th century furnishings, textiles, paintings and Delftware reflecting the taste for Dutch fashions at the time it was built. Visitors can wander round the park with its woodlands and formal garden, and discover how Victorian servants worked 'below stairs'.

BATHFORD
3 miles NE of Bath off the A363

🏠 Eagle House   🏠 Brown's Folly

🏛 Bathampton Down

This residential community once belonged to Bath Abbey. Among the many fine 18th century buildings to be seen here is **Eagle House**, a handsome residence that takes its name from the great stone eagle that stands with its wings outstretched on the gabled roof. On the hill above Bathford, there is a tall Italianate tower known as **Brown's Folly** built

following the Napoleonic Wars to provide local craftsmen with work during the economic depression of the 1830s.

To the west lies **Bathampton** whose church is the last resting place of Admiral Arthur Phillip, the first governor of New South Wales, who took the initial shipload of convicts out to the colony and established the settlement of Sydney. He is regarded by some as the founder of modern Australia. A chapel in the south aisle, known as the Australian Chapel, contains memorials to the admiral's family. Above the village lies **Bathampton Down**, which is crowned with an ancient hillfort that, according to some historians, was the site of the 6th century Battle of Badon in which the forces of King Arthur defeated the Saxons.

CLAVERTON
2 miles E of Bath on the A36

🏠 Claverton Manor

🏛 American Museum & Gardens

Just to the west of the village stands the 16th century country mansion, **Claverton Manor**, bought in 1764 by Ralph Allen, the quarry-owning co-founder of 18th century Bath. The mansion that Allen knew has been demolished, leaving only a series of

---

🏠 historic building 🏛 museum and heritage 🏛 historic site 🍃 scenic attraction 🌿 flora and fauna

overgrown terraces, but some of the stone from the old house was used in the construction of the new mansion on the hill above the village. It was here, in 1897, that Sir Winston Churchill is said to have given his first political speech. Claverton Manor is best known as the **American Museum and Gardens**. Founded in 1961, it is the only establishment of its kind outside the United States. The rooms of the house have been furnished to show the gradual changes in American living styles from the arrival of the Pilgrim Fathers in the 17th century to New York of the 19th century. The arboretum contains a collection of native American trees and shrubs.

HINTON PRIORY
3½ miles SE of Bath off the B3110

🏛 Stoney Littleton Long Barrow

All that remains of the early Carthusian monastery founded here by Ela, Countess of Salisbury, are atmospheric ruins. As in other religious houses belonging to this order, the monks occupied their own small dwellings set around the main cloister, often with a small garden attached. These communities were generally known for their reclusiveness. However, one outspoken monk from Hinton Priory, Nicholas Hopkins, achieved notoriety in Tudor times as the confessor and spiritual adviser to the 3rd Duke of Buckingham and his story is recounted by Shakespeare in *Henry VIII*. Several sections of the old priory remain, including the chapter house, parts of the guest quarters and the undercroft of the refectory.

Close by can be found one of the finest examples of a Neolithic monument in the west of England,

Stoney Littleton Long Barrow (English Heritage), built more than 4,000 years ago. This striking multi-chambered tomb has recently been restored following vandalism and the interior can be inspected by obtaining a key from nearby Stoney Littleton Farm.

FARLEIGH HUNGERFORD
5 miles SE of Bath on the A366

🏰 Farleigh Hungerford Castle 🌱 The Peto Garden

This old fortified settlement is still overlooked by the impressive remains of **Farleigh Hungerford Castle** that stands on a rise above the River Frome to the northeast of the village. It was built by Sir Thomas Hungerford, the first Speaker of the House of Commons, on the site of an old manor house that he acquired in the late 14th century. Legend has it that Sir Thomas failed to gain the proper permission from the Crown for his fortification and this oversight led to his downfall. The castle changed hands in the early 18th century and the incoming family saw it as a quarry for building stone rather than as a place to live. Much of the castle was left to go to ruin while the family built a new mansion on the other side of the village. Nevertheless, an impressive shell of towers and perimeter walls has survived intact, along with the castle's Chapel of St Leonard. This

Farleigh Hungerford Castle

contains a striking 15th century mural of St George, some fine stained glass and a number of interesting monuments, including the tomb of Sir Thomas Hungerford himself.

To the north, just inside Wiltshire, is Iford Manor, home to **The Peto Garden**, a Grade I listed Italian style garden famed for its tranquil beauty. A unique hillside garden, it was the creation of architect and landscape gardener Harold Peto, who lived at the manor from 1899 until 1933.

NORTON ST PHILIP
5½ miles S of Bath on the A366

🏠 George Inn   🌿 Norwood Farm

In the 13th century, a group of Carthusian monks were given some land near here where they founded a Priory that was completed in 1232. The monks were also responsible for building the village's most famous landmark, the splendid **George Inn**, originally established as a house of hospitality for those visiting the priory. A wonderful fusion of medieval stonework, oriel windows and timber framing, it is still a hostelry today. The inn's timber framed upper floors were added in the 15th century when the inn doubled as a warehouse for storing the locally produced woollen cloth. In 1668, the diarist Samuel Pepys stayed here while on his way to Bath with his family and noted, "Dined well. 10 shillings." Just a short while later, the inn played host to the Duke of Monmouth, who made the George his headquarters shortly before his defeat at the Battle of Sedgemoor in 1685. According to a local story, 12 men implicated in the uprising were imprisoned

GREYFIELD FARM COTTAGES

Greyfield Farm, High Littleton, Bristol BS39 6YQ
Tel: 01761 471132
e-mail: june@greyfieldfarm.com
website: www.greyfieldfarm.com

Greyfield Farm Cottages nestle in a private and peaceful 3.5 acre setting overlooking the Mendips, an Area of Outstanding Natural Beauty. They provide an ideal base for exploring the South West. There are five attractive stone cottages, each one unique, spacious, double-glazed, centrally heated, comfortably furnished and each equipped with TV, DVD, video and wi-fi internet access. All except Mendip Magic also have log fires. Luxurious feather and down duvets and pillows - synthetic ones are also available if preferred - quality linen and towels are all provided.

Each cottage has its own garden/patio area where guests can enjoy breakfast or a relaxing late afternoon drink. Also on site are a hot tub, sauna, gym and barbecue which guests may use freely. Owner June Merry is happy to accept flexible booking and short breaks are available all year round.

With Greyfield Farm as your base, you are within easy reach of historic sites such as Longleat, Stourhead, Tyntesfield and Cheddar Caves. The local market towns of Frome, Glastonbury and Bradford-upon-Avon, along with Bath, Bristol and Wells, have many small independent shops as well as fairs and markets.

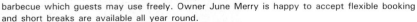

🏠 historic building   🏛 museum and heritage   🏚 historic site   � scenic attraction   🌿 flora and fauna

here after the battle, in what is now the Dungeon Bar. They were later were taken away to be hung, drawn and quartered at the local market place.

To the north of the village, **Norwood Farm** offers an introduction to the objectives and practicalities of organic farming. A Farm Walk takes in a recycling area, explains the use of wind turbines and provides a view of more than 30 rare and beautiful animal

George Inn, Norton St Philip

breeds including Saddleback pigs, Shetland ponies and Wiltshire Horn sheep. A café and farm shop on site make good use of the organic food produced on the farm.

KEYNSHAM
6½ miles NW of Bath on the A4175

🏛 Museum 🐾 Avon Valley Country Park

A former industrial centre, Keynsham is also a dormitory town for Bristol. Despite its modern appearance, it has ancient roots. During the excavations for a chocolate factory, the remains of two Roman villas were discovered. These remains have since been incorporated into an interesting small **Museum** near the factory entrance. In the late 12th century an abbey was founded here, close to the River Chew, but it seems that the medieval monks were not as pious as they should have been. Eventually, they were banned from keeping sporting dogs, going out at night, employing private washerwomen and

entertaining female guests in the monastery. Today, the abbey foundations lie under the bypass but the part-13th century parish church has survived and, along with being a good example of the Somerset Gothic architectural style, it contains some impressive tombs to members of the Bridges family.

Much later, two large brass mills were established at Keynsham during the town's 18th century industrial heyday, one on the River Avon and the other on the River Chew. Though production had ceased at both mills by the late 1920s, they are still impressive industrial remains.

Just to the east of Keynsham, the **Avon Valley Country Park** provides a popular day out for families. There's a large adventure playground, indoor play area, friendly animals and pets corner, falconry displays, boating lake, 1.5 mile nature trail walk, mini-steam train rides, land train rides, quad bikes, picnic and barbecue area, café and gift shop.

TOURIST INFORMATION CENTRES

Cornwall

BODMIN
*Shire Hall, Mount Folly Square, Bodmin,
Cornwall PL31 2DQ
e-mail: bodmintic@visit.org.uk
Tel: 01208 76616*

BUDE
*Bude Visitor Centre, The Crescent, Bude,
Cornwall EX23 8LE
e-mail: budetic@visitbude.info
Tel: 01288 354240*

CAMELFORD
*North Cornwall Museum, The Clease,
Camelford, Cornwall PL32 9PL
e-mail: manager@camelfordtic.eclipse.co.uk
Tel: 01840 212954*

FALMOUTH
*11 Market Strand, Prince of Wales Pier,
Falmouth, Cornwall TR11 3DF
e-mail: falmouthtic@yahoo.co.uk
Tel: 01326 312300*

FOWEY
*5 South Street, Fowey, Cornwall PL23 1AR
e-mail: info@fowey.co.uk
Tel: 01726 833616*

LAUNCESTON
*Market House Arcade, Market Street,
Launceston, Cornwall PL15 8EP
e-mail: launcestontic@btconnect.com
Tel: 01566 772321*

LOOE
*The Guildhall, Fore Street, East Looe,
Cornwall PL13 1AA
e-mail: looetic@btconnect.com
Tel: 01503 262072*

NEWQUAY
*Municipal Offices, Marcus Hill, Newquay,
Cornwall TR7 1BD
e-mail: info@newquay.co.uk
Tel: 01637 854020*

PADSTOW
*Red Brick Building, North Quay, Padstow,
Cornwall PL28 8AF
e-mail: padstowtic@btconnect.com
Tel: 01841 533449*

PENZANCE
*Station Road, Penzance,
Cornwall TR18 2NF
e-mail: pztic@penwith.gov.uk
Tel: 01736 362207*

ST AUSTELL
*Southbourne Road, St Austell,
Cornwall PL25 4RS
e-mail: tic@cornish-riviera.co.uk
Tel: 01726 879 500*

ST IVES
*The Guildhall, Street-an-Pol, St Ives,
Cornwall TR26 2DS
e-mail: ivtic@penwith.gov.uk
Tel: 01736 796297*

TRURO
*Municipal Building, Boscawen Street, Truro,
Cornwall TR1 2NE
e-mail: tic@truro.gov.uk
Tel: 01872 274555*

WADEBRIDGE
*Rotunda Building, Eddystone Road,
Wadebridge, Cornwall PL27 7AL
e-mail: wadebridgetic@btconnect.com
Tel: 0870 1223337*

Devon

AXMINSTER
*The Old Courthouse, Church Street,
Axminster, Devon EX13 5AQ
e-mail: axminstertic@btopenworld.com
Tel: 01297 34386*

BARNSTAPLE
*Museum of North Devon, The Square,
Barnstaple, Devon EX32 8LN
e-mail: info@staynorthdevon.co.uk
Tel: 01271 375000*

BIDEFORD
*Victoria Park, The Quay, Bideford,
Devon EX39 2QQ
e-mail: bidefordtic@visit.org.uk
Tel: 01237 477676*

BRAUNTON
*The Bakehouse Centre, Caen Street, Braunton,
Devon EX33 1AA
e-mail: info@brauntontic.co.uk
Tel: 01271 816400*

BRIXHAM
*The Old Market House, The Quay,
Brixham, Devon TQ5 8TB
e-mail: brixham.tic@torbay.gov.uk
Tel: 01803 211 211*

BUDLEIGH SALTERTON
*Fore Street, Budleigh Salterton,
Devon EX9 6NG
e-mail: budleigh.tic@btconnect.com
Tel: 01395 445275*

COMBE MARTIN
*Seacot Cross Street, Combe Martin,
Devon EX34 0DH
e-mail: mail@visitcombemartin.co.uk
Tel: 01271 883319*

CREDITON
*The Old Town Hall, High Street, Crediton,
Devon EX17 3LF
e-mail: info@devonshireheartland.co.uk
Tel: 01363 772006*

DARTMOUTH
*The Engine House, Mayor's Avenue,
Dartmouth, Devon TQ6 9YY
e-mail: holidays@discoverdartmouth.com
Tel: 01803 834224*

DAWLISH
*The Lawn, Dawlish, Devon EX7 9PW
e-mail: dawtic@Teignbridge.gov.uk
Tel: 01626 215665*

EXETER
*Civic Centre, Dix's Field, Exeter,
Devon EX1 1RQ
e-mail: tic@exeter.gov.uk
Tel: 01392 265700*

EXMOUTH
Alexandra Terrace, Exmouth ,
Devon EX8 1NZ
e-mail: info@exmouthtourism.co.uk
Tel: 01395 222299

HONITON
Lace Walk Car Park, Honiton,
Devon EX14 1LT
e-mail: honitontic@btconnect.com
Tel: 01404 43716

ILFRACOMBE
The Landmark, The Seafront, Ilfracombe,
Devon EX34 9BX
e-mail: info@ilfracombe-tourism.co.uk
Tel: 01271 863001

IVYBRIDGE
Global Travel, 19 Fore Street, Ivybridge,
Devon PL21 9AB
e-mail: bookends.ivybridge@virgin.net
Tel: 01752 897035

KINGSBRIDGE
The Quay, Kingsbridge, Devon TQ7 1HS
e-mail: advice@kingsbridgeinfo.co.uk
Tel: 01548 853195

LYNTON AND LYNMOUTH
Town Hall, Lee Road, Lynton,
Devon EX35 6BT
e-mail: info@lyntourism.co.uk
Tel: 0845 660 3232

MODBURY
5 Modbury Court, Modbury,
Devon PL21 0QR
e-mail: modburytic@lineone.net
Tel: 01548 830159

NEWTON ABBOT
6 Bridge House, Courtenay Street,
Newton Abbot, Devon TQ12 2QS
e-mail: natic@Teignbridge.gov.uk
Tel: 01626 215667

OKEHAMPTON
Museum Courtyard, 3 West Street,
Okehampton, Devon EX20 1HQ
e-mail: okehamptontic@westdevon.gov.uk
Tel: 01837 53020

OTTERY ST MARY
10a Broad Street, Ottery St Mary,
Devon EX11 1BZ
e-mail: tic.osm@cosmic.org.uk
Tel: 01404 813964

PAIGNTON
The Esplanade, Paignton, Devon TQ4 6ED
e-mail: paignton.tic@torbay.gov.uk
Tel: 01803 211 211

PLYMOUTH: PLYMOUTH MAYFLOWER
Plymouth Mayflower Centre, 3-5 The
Barbican, Plymouth, Devon PL1 2LR
e-mail: barbicantic@plymouth.gov.uk
Tel: 01752 306330

SALCOMBE
Market Street, Salcombe, Devon TQ8 8DE
e-mail: info@salcombeinformation.co.uk
Tel: 01548 843927

SEATON
The Underfleet, Seaton, Devon EX12 2TB
e-mail: info@seatontic.freeserve.co.uk
Tel: 01297 21660

SIDMOUTH
Ham Lane, Sidmouth, Devon EX10 8XR
e-mail: sidmouthtic@eclipse.co.uk
Tel: 01395 516441

SOUTH MOLTON
1 East Street, South Molton,
Devon EX36 3BU
e-mail: visitsouthmolton@btconnect.com
Tel: 01769 574122

TAVISTOCK
Town Hall, Bedford Square, Tavistock,
Devon PL19 0AE
e-mail: tavistocktic@westdevon.gov.uk
Tel: 01822 612938

TEIGNMOUTH
The Den Sea Front, Teignmouth,
Devon TQ14 8BE
e-mail: teigntic@teignbridge.gov.uk
Tel: 01626 215666

TIVERTON
Phoenix Lane, Tiverton, Devon EX16 6LU
e-mail: tivertontic@btconnect.com
Tel: 01884 255827

TORQUAY
The Tourist Centre, Vaughan Parade,
Torquay , Devon TQ2 5JG
e-mail: torquay.tic@torbay.gov.uk
Tel: 01803 211 211

TORRINGTON
Castle Hill, South Street, Great Torrington,
Devon EX38 8AA
e-mail: info@great-torrington.com
Tel: 01805 626140

TOTNES
The Town Mill, Coronation Road, Totnes,
Devon TQ9 5DF
e-mail: enquire@totnesinformation.co.uk
Tel: 01803 863168

WOOLACOMBE
The Esplanade, Woolacombe,
Devon EX34 7DL
e-mail: info@woolacombetourism.co.uk
Tel: 01271 870553

Dorset

BLANDFORD FORUM
1 Greyhound Yard, Blandford Forum,
Dorset DT11 7EB
e-mail: blandfordtic@north-dorset.gov.uk
Tel: 01258 454770

BOURNEMOUTH
Westover Road, Bournemouth,
Dorset BH1 2BU
e-mail: info@bournemouth.gov.uk
Tel: 0845 051 1700

BRIDPORT
47 South Street, Bridport,
Dorset DT6 3NY
e-mail: bridport.tic@westdorset-dc.gov.uk
Tel: 01308 424901

TOURIST INFORMATION CENTRES

CHRISTCHURCH
49 High Street, Christchurch,
Dorset BH23 1AS
e-mail: enquiries@christchurchtourism.info
Tel: 01202 471780

DORCHESTER
11 Antelope Walk, Dorchester,
Dorset DT1 1BE
e-mail: dorchester.tic@westdorset-dc.gov.uk
Tel: 01305 267992

LYME REGIS
Guildhall Cottage, Church Street, Lyme Regis,
Dorset DT7 3BS
e-mail: lymeregis.tic@westdorset-dc.gov.uk
Tel: 01297 442138

POOLE
Enefco House, Poole Quay, Poole,
Dorset BH15 1HJ
e-mail: info@poole.gov.uk
Tel: 01202 253253

SHAFTESBURY
8 Bell Street, Shaftesbury, Dorset SP7 8AE
e-mail: tourism@shaftesburydorset.com
Tel: 01747 853514

SHERBORNE
3 Tilton Court, Digby Road, Sherborne,
Dorset DT9 3NL
e-mail: sherborne.tic@westdorset-dc.gov.uk
Tel: 01935 815341

SWANAGE
The White House, Shore Road, Swanage,
Dorset BH19 1LB
e-mail: mail@swanage.gov.uk
Tel: 01929 422885

WAREHAM
Holy Trinity Church, South Street, Wareham,
Dorset BH20 4LU
e-mail: tic@purbeck-dc.gov.uk
Tel: 01929 552740

WEYMOUTH
The King's Statue, The Esplanade, Weymouth,
Dorset DT4 7AN
e-mail: tic@weymouth.gov.uk
Tel: 01305 785747

WIMBORNE MINSTER
29 High Street, Wimborne Minster,
Dorset BH21 1HR
e-mail: wimbornetic@eastdorset.gov.uk
Tel: 01202 886116

Somerset

BATH
Abbey Chambers, Abbey Church Yard,
Bath, Somerset BA1 1LY
e-mail: tourism@bathtourism.co.uk
Tel: 0906 711 2000

BRISTOL: HARBOURSIDE
Wildwalk @Bristol, Harbourside, Bristol,
Somerset BS1 5DB
e-mail: ticharbourside@bristol-city.gov.uk
Tel: 0906 711 2191

BURNHAM-ON-SEA
South Esplanade, Burnham-on-Sea,
Somerset TA8 1BU
e-mail: burnham.tic@sedgemoor.gov.uk
Tel: 01278 787852

CARTGATE
South Somerset TIC, A303/A3088
Cartgate Picnic Site Stoke-sub-Hamdon,
Somerset TA14 6RA
e-mail: cartgate.tic@southsomerset.gov.uk
Tel: 01935 829333

CHEDDAR
The Gorge, Cheddar , Somerset BS27 3QE
e-mail: cheddar.tic@sedgemoor.gov.uk
Tel: 01934 744071

FROME
The Round Tower, Justice Lane, Frome,
Somerset BA11 1BB
e-mail: enquiries@frometouristinfo.co.uk
Tel: 01373 467271

GLASTONBURY
The Tribunal, 9 High Street, Glastonbury,
Somerset BA6 9DP
e-mail: glastonbury.tic@ukonline.co.uk
Tel: 01458 832954

MINEHEAD
17 Friday Street, Minehead,
Somerset TA24 5UB
e-mail: info@mineheadtic.co.uk
Tel: 01643 702624

SHEPTON MALLET
48 High Street, Shepton Mallet,
Somerset BA4 5AS
e-mail: sheptonmallet.tic@ukonline.co.uk
Tel: 01749 345258

SOMERSET VISITOR CENTRE
Road Chef Services, M5 Southbound,
Axbridge, Somerset BS26 2UF
e-mail:
somersetvisitorcentre@somserset.gov.uk
Tel: 01934 750833

TAUNTON
The Library, Paul Street, Taunton ,
Somerset TA1 3XZ
e-mail: tauntontic@tauntondeane.gov.uk
Tel: 01823 336344

WELLINGTON
30 Fore Street, Wellington,
Somerset TA21 8AQ
e-mail: wellingtontic@tauntondeane.gov.uk
Tel: 01823 663379

WELLS
Town Hall, Market Place, Wells,
Somerset BA5 2RB
e-mail: touristinfo@wells.gov.uk
Tel: 01749 672552

WESTON-SUPER-MARE
Beach Lawns, Weston-super-Mare,
Somerset BS23 1AT
e-mail: westontouristinfo@n-somerset.gov.uk
Tel: 01934 888800

YEOVIL
Hendford, Yeovil, Somerset BA20 1UN
e-mail: yeoviltic@southsomerset.gov.uk
Tel: 01935 845946/7

ACCOMMODATION, FOOD AND DRINK

INDEX OF ADVERTISERS

FASHIONS

INDEX OF ADVERTISERS

JEWELLERY

INDEX OF ADVERTISERS

Looking for more walks?

The walks in this book have been gleaned from Britain's largest online walking guide, to be found at *www.walkingworld.com*.

The site contains over 2000 walks from all over England, Scotland and Wales so there are plenty more to choose from in this book's region as well as further afield - ideal if you are taking a short break as you can plan your walks in advance. There are walks of every length and type to suit all tastes.

Want more detail for the walks in this book? Next to every walk in this book you will see a Walk ID. You can enter this ID number on Walkingworld's 'Find a Walk' page and you will be taken straight to the details of that walk.

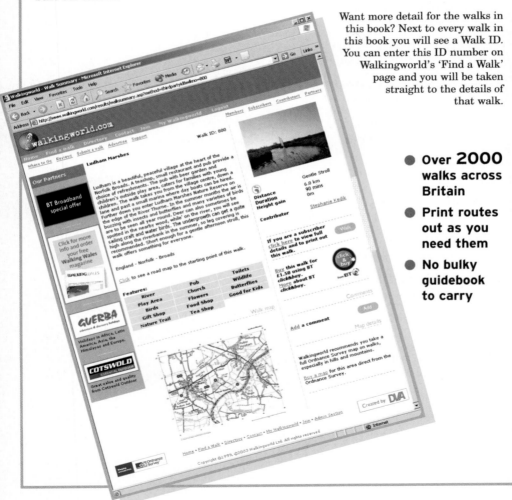

- ● Over **2000** walks across Britain
- ● Print routes out as you need them
- ● No bulky guidebook to carry

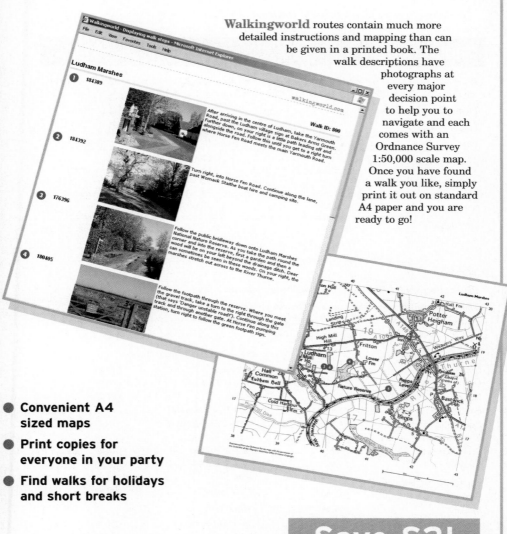

Walkingworld routes contain much more detailed instructions and mapping than can be given in a printed book. The walk descriptions have photographs at every major decision point to help you to navigate and each comes with an Ordnance Survey 1:50,000 scale map. Once you have found a walk you like, simply print it out on standard A4 paper and you are ready to go!

● **Convenient A4 sized maps**

● **Print copies for everyone in your party**

● **Find walks for holidays and short breaks**

A modest annual subscription gives you access to over 2000 walks, all in Walkingworld's easy to follow format. The database of walks is growing all the time and as a subscriber you gain access to new routes as soon as they are published.

Visit the Walkingworld website at *www.walkingworld.com*

ORDER FORM

To order any of our publications just fill in the payment details below and complete the order form. For orders of less than 4 copies please add £1 per book for postage and packing. Orders over 4 copies are P & P free.

Please Complete Either:

I enclose a cheque for £ [   ] made payable to Travel Publishing Ltd

Or:

CARD NO: [   ]   EXPIRY DATE: [   ]

SIGNATURE: [   ]

NAME: [   ]

ADDRESS: [   ]

TEL NO: [   ]

Please either send, telephone, fax or e-mail your order to:

Travel Publishing Ltd, 64-66 Ebrington Street, Plymouth, Devon PL4 9AQ
Tel: 01752 276660   Fax: 01752 276699   e-mail: info@travelpublishing.co.uk

	PRICE	QUANTITY		PRICE	QUANTITY
HIDDEN PLACES REGIONAL TITLES			**COUNTRY LIVING RURAL GUIDES**		
Cornwall	£8.99	....	East Anglia	£10.99	....
Devon	£8.99	....	Heart of England	£10.99	....
Dorset, Hants & Isle of Wight	£8.99	....	Ireland	£11.99	....
East Anglia	£8.99	....	North East of England	£10.99	....
Lake District & Cumbria	£8.99	....	North West of England	£10.99	....
Northumberland & Durham	£8.99	....	Scotland	£11.99	....
Peak District and Derbyshire	£8.99	....	South of England	£10.99	....
Yorkshire	£8.99	....	South East of England	£10.99	....
			Wales	£11.99	....
HIDDEN PLACES NATIONAL TITLES			West Country	£10.99	....
England	£11.99	....			
Ireland	£11.99	....	**OTHER TITLES**		
Scotland	£11.99	....	Off The Motorway	£11.99	....
Wales	£11.99	....	Garden Centres and Nurseries of Britain	£11.99	....
COUNTRY PUBS AND INNS TITLES					
Cornwall	£5.99	....			
Devon	£7.99	....			
Sussex	£5.99	....	**TOTAL QUANTITY**		
Wales	£8.99	....			
Yorkshire	£7.99	....	**TOTAL VALUE**		

READER REACTION FORM

The **Travel Publishing** *research team would like to receive readers' comments on any visitor attractions or places reviewed in the book and also recommendations for suitable entries to be included in the next edition. This will help ensure that the* **Country Living series of Rural Guides** *continues to provide its readers with useful information on the more interesting, unusual or unique features of each attraction or place ensuring that their visit to the local area is an enjoyable and stimulating experience. To provide your comments or recommendations would you please complete the forms below and overleaf as indicated and send to:*

The Research Department, Travel Publishing Ltd, 64-66 Ebrington Street, Plymouth, Devon PL4 9AQ

YOUR NAME:

YOUR ADDRESS:

YOUR TEL NO:

Please tick as appropriate: COMMENTS ☐   RECOMMENDATION ☐

ESTABLISHMENT:

ADDRESS:

TEL NO:

CONTACT NAME:

PLEASE COMPLETE FORM OVERLEAF

READER REACTION FORM

COMMENT OR REASON FOR RECOMMENDATION:

....

....

....

....

....

....

....

....

....

....

....

....

READER REACTION FORM

The **Travel Publishing** *research team would like to receive readers' comments on any visitor attractions or places reviewed in the book and also recommendations for suitable entries to be included in the next edition. This will help ensure that the* **Country Living series of Rural Guides** *continues to provide its readers with useful information on the more interesting, unusual or unique features of each attraction or place ensuring that their visit to the local area is an enjoyable and stimulating experience. To provide your comments or recommendations would you please complete the forms below and overleaf as indicated and send to:*

The Research Department, Travel Publishing Ltd, 64-66 Ebrington Street, Plymouth, Devon PL4 9AQ

YOUR NAME:

YOUR ADDRESS:

YOUR TEL NO:

Please tick as appropriate: COMMENTS   RECOMMENDATION

ESTABLISHMENT:

ADDRESS:

TEL NO:

CONTACT NAME:

PLEASE COMPLETE FORM OVERLEAF

READER REACTION FORM

COMMENT OR REASON FOR RECOMMENDATION:

....

....

....

....

....

....

....

....

....

....

....

TOWNS, VILLAGES AND PLACES OF INTEREST

TOWNS, VILLAGES AND PLACES OF INTEREST

TOWNS, VILLAGES AND PLACES OF INTEREST

TOWNS, VILLAGES AND PLACES OF INTEREST

TOWNS, VILLAGES AND PLACES OF INTEREST

TOWNS, VILLAGES AND PLACES OF INTEREST

TOWNS, VILLAGES AND PLACES OF INTEREST

TOWNS, VILLAGES AND PLACES OF INTEREST

TOWNS, VILLAGES AND PLACES OF INTEREST

TOWNS, VILLAGES AND PLACES OF INTEREST